GREAT WESTERN STEAM RAIL MOTORS

AND THEIR SERVICES

JOHN LEWIS

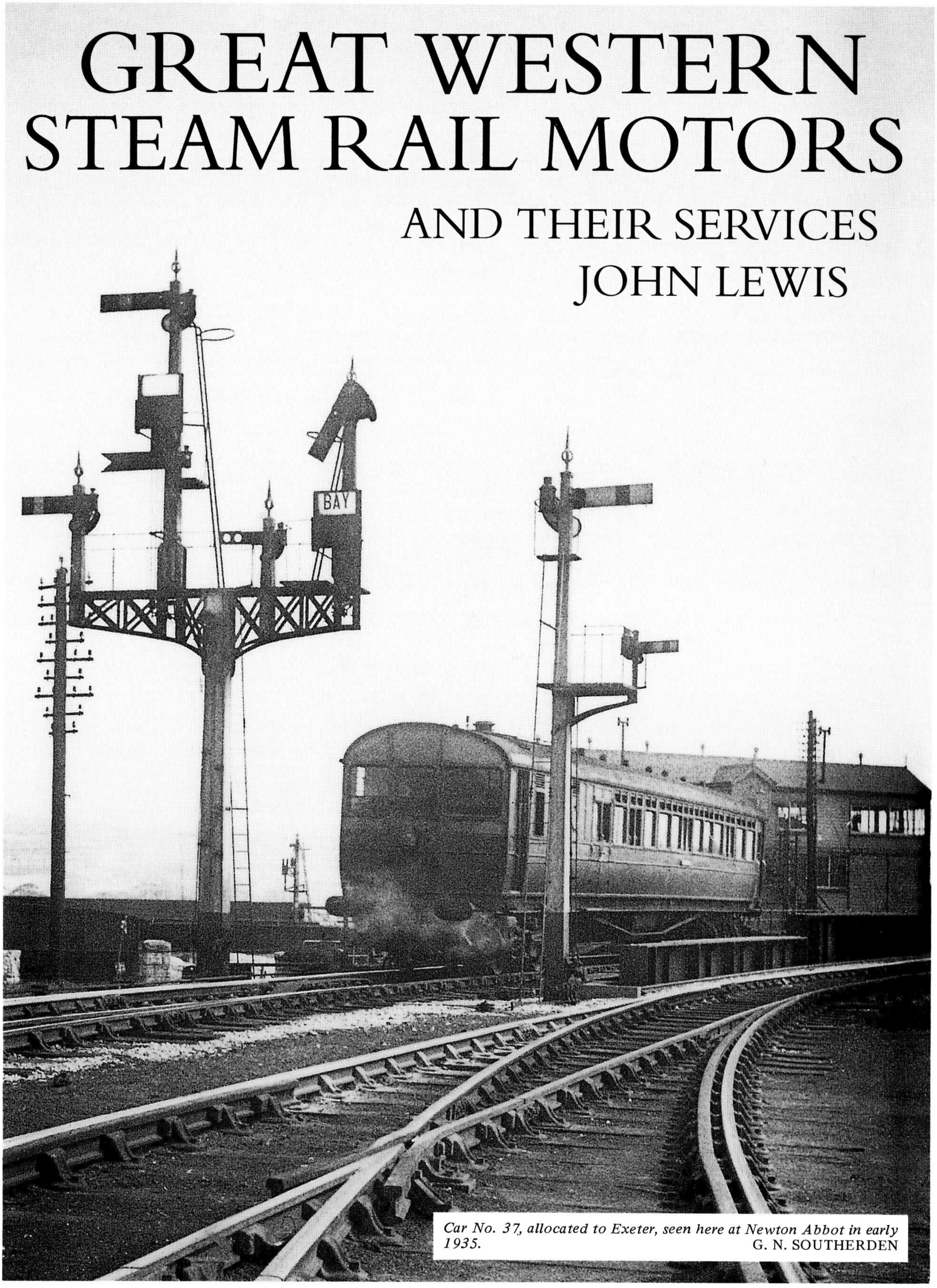

Car No. 37, allocated to Exeter, seen here at Newton Abbot in early 1935. G. N. SOUTHERDEN

WILD SWAN PUBLICATIONS LTD.

ISBN 1 874103 96 8

Designed by Paul Karau
Printed by Amadeus Press, Cleckheaton

Published by
WILD SWAN PUBLICATIONS LTD.
1-3 Hagbourne Road, Didcot, Oxon, OX11 8DP

A Diagram O or R SRM at Wolvercot Platform, probably around 1910, hauling a horse-box. The picture was taken looking northwards with the up loop on the right. Wolvercot Platform was opened in 1908 and closed in 1916.

A Diagram K SRM approaching Penzance across the viaduct. This was probably either No. 38 or No. 40 which were allocated to Penzance at times during 1908. COLLECTION R. M. CASSERLEY

CONTENTS

This view of Westham Halt on the Weymouth–Portland branch shows Car No. 36 of Diagram K hauling a trailer. The date was probably June 1909 as workmen were still putting the finishing touches to the halt which opened on 1st July that year. Car No. 36 arrived at Weymouth during June 1909. COLLECTION PAUL LAMMING

CHAPTER ONE

THE INTRODUCTION OF STEAM RAIL MOTORS ON THE GWR

During the first years of the 20th century, 'rail motors' were seen as a possible solution to a number of problems facing the established railways of the United Kingdom. A 'Rail Motor', as perceived around 1905, may perhaps be defined as 'self-propelled single carriage passenger train which can be driven from either end'. The definition can become a little blurred when electric propulsion was used – the tram is an obvious example – but the power used could equally be a built-in steam engine, or an internal combustion engine, either coupled mechanically to one or more axles, or indirectly via electric transmission. An 'auto train', or an 'auto car', where there was a separate steam engine with one or more trailer coaches arranged so the train could be driven from either end, is obviously a close relation to the rail motor, as is the 'multiple unit' which nowadays usually refers to electric or diesel passenger trains, but in 1905 might have referred to a pair of steam rail motors coupled back to back with a coach or two between them. 'Double unit' was an expression used at that time.

The advantages of rail motors over conventional steam trains were that they could be reversed easily and quickly – it was only necessary for the driver to walk to the other end of the car; and they could be purpose-designed for local trains with frequent stops serving unmanned stations or 'halts'. Other advantages included:

1. Enabling the railway to compete effectively with omnibuses, tramways and light railway schemes (and, preferably, discouraging these modes of transport from being introduced in competition with the railway).
2. Developing local traffic on new lines, or on lines without a passenger service, and in places where housing development might be encouraged.
3. Enabling frequent services on short branch lines to be provided more efficiently.
4. An economical way of providing local trains on lightly-used lines, and on main lines through districts with relatively little local passenger traffic potential.

Because of the high capital costs involved, electrification was seen to be primarily suitable for heavily-used commuter routes in large conurbations like London, where the GWR invested in the electrification of the London & Hammersmith Railway, and the Taff Vale Railway investigated the possibilities of electrifying its line from Cardiff to Penarth.

Battery-powered vehicles were found to be unsuitable and too expensive. Again, the Taff Vale Railway investigated the possibilities of battery-powered electric railcars for one of its lightly-used rural lines.

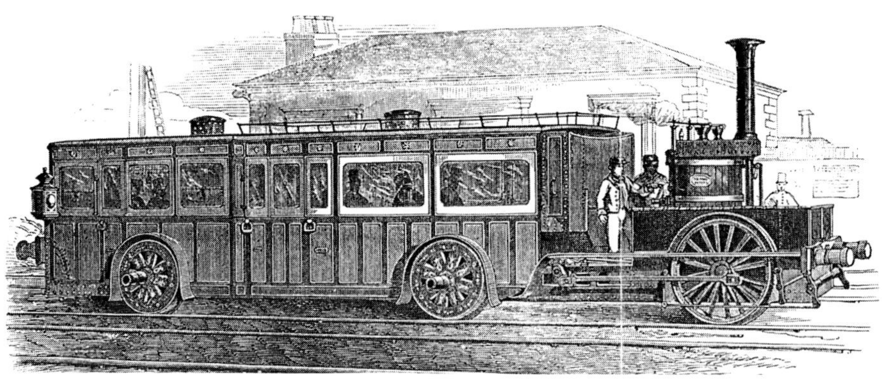

The Fairfield steam rail motor 1848.

At the same time, the Taff Vale also looked at a petrol-electric car for the same route. The GWR drawing office did get as far as officially producing a diagram of a petrol-engined car as early as February 1903, which predated the introduction of the GWR's steam rail motors, and indeed the use of petrol-engined omnibuses by the company. About this time, the North Eastern Railway built three petrol-electric cars, but they were underpowered, and the investment was not repeated.

In 1911, the Great Western actually purchased a petrol-electric car, but it did not have a very long life on the railway, and was sold.

This left steam as the prime mover of most railmotors of the period, and the GWR adopted the concept with some enthusiasm; by early 1908, it had 99 of its own, plus one on the Port Talbot Railway, which was operated by the Great Western.

THE STROUD VALLEY SERVICE

Rail motors were not a new idea – W. Bridges Adams produced four examples, one of which ran on the Bristol & Exeter Railway as early as 1848. However, it seems not to have been a real success, and the concept was quietly forgotten until the early 1900s, when it was revived by several railway companies. The GWR's first foray into steam rail motor services came about as the result of a proposal for a light railway to parallel the Swindon & Gloucester main line through the Stroud valley in Gloucestershire. This proposal was unsuccessful, but it was promptly succeeded by one for an electric tramway instead; the evident dissatisfaction with the local railway service prompted action by the officers of the GWR.

Sir Joseph Wilkinson, the GWR's General Manager, submitted a report to the Traffic Committee of the Board of Directors on 29th April 1903 recommending that two steam rail motors – to a design by the CME, Churchward – should be built at an estimated cost of £2,500 each. The total capital cost of the new service was estimated at £7,000, and the running costs £1,780 per annum. The report, titled 'Steam Motor Car for Local Rly Service in the Stroud Valley' read as follows:

'GENERAL MANAGER'S REPORT
'29 April 1903

'MEMORANDUM
'Attention has for the past two years been directed to various sections of the line where a passenger service by means of Motor Cars might be worked economically and advantageously.

'The Locomotive Engineer has designed and submitted a plan of a steam motor car weighing 34 tons 10 cwt capable of developing a speed of 30 miles per hour fully loaded, affording seating room for 52 passengers. The engine equipment will be contained in a compartment at one end of the car connected with driving and brake gear at the opposite end so that the car may be driven from either end. It is considered that a self-propelled car of this description will be suitable for furnishing local passenger services where the traffic is so light as to preclude the profitable running of trains except at long intervals; and that in instituting services of single cars, which will be run frequently at less cost than existing services of infrequent trains composed of several carriages, the local traffic in country districts and on branch lines will be stimulated and the districts developed, while the frequency of the service will enable the railway Company to resist the encroachments of tramway enterprise.

'Among other sections of the line the Stroud Valley, with a population of some 40,000, offers an attractive field for experiments. Following up on the opening of the South Wales Direct Line for goods traffic in May, and the diversion from the 1st July of certain trains from the Swindon and Gloucester route to the South Wales direct route, it is suggested that a motor car service of the character described herein might be adopted in the Stroud Valley between Chalford and Stonehouse Stations, where there is already a considerable local traffic, a great part of which is conveyed by Omnibuses and other road vehicles, and where it is now sought to establish a tramway service which would be competitive with the railway. It is suggested that, as a commencement, an hourly service should be tried, and when this is found to work satisfactorily more trips might he run as far as practicable in the direction of a half-hourly service. The motor-car service would commence running at 7 o'clock in the morning – or 6 o'clock if an early traffic be developed – and finish at 10 p.m., and it is submitted that a quick, reliable railway service at regular intervals would supply the needs of the district.

'The local railway service at present consists of six trains in one direction and five in the other, i.e.:

Down:
Chalford. to Stonehouse 8.43 a.m., 9.55 a.m., 2.19 p.m., 5.41 p.m., 7.57 p.m., 9.10 p.m.
Up:
Stonehouse to Chalford 9.13 a.m., 12.0 noon, 3.36 p.m., 7.3 p.m., 8.21 p.m.

'Omnibuses run between Chalford and Stroud every hour and between Brimscombe and Stroud every half hour: there is a frequent service also between Stroud and Stonehouse. The services are supplemented on market days and Saturdays by additional vehicles.

'Agitation for Greater Facilities
'The present rail and omnibus services do not satisfy the needs of the inhabitants, who started an agitation for a light railway, which fell through, to be succeeded by a demand for an electric tramway system, and powers are sought this Session to build tram lines paralleling the railway between Chalford and Stonehouse, and lateral lines from Stroud through Painswick to Cheltenham, linking up with a line into Gloucester, and between Stroud and Nailsworth.

'The proposed tram lines paralleling the railway through the Stroud Valley would be on the up side of the railway between Chalford and Stroud, and on the down side between Stroud and Stonehouse, and in few places more than 150 yards from the railway, while for a great part of the way they would be within a few yards of it.

'The fare charged by the railway and omnibus services are as under:

TABLE 1
STROUD VALLEY FARES

Section	*Distances*		*Rail*	*Omnibus*
	m.	*c.*	*d*	*d*
Chalford and Brimscombe	1	24	1½	-
Brimscombe and Stroud	2	71	3	2
Bowbridge and Stroud			-	1
Chalford and Stroud	4	13	4	3
Stroud and Ebley			-	2
Stroud and Stonehouse	2	62	3	3
Chalford and Stonehouse	6	75	7	-

'Low fares are charged by the omnibuses for intermediate journeys.

'The local railway bookings between Chalford, Brimscombe, Stroud, and Stonehouse aggregate 68,000 passengers a year, and it has been stated that the omnibuses carry eight times the number carried by railway, or 540,000 a year.

'It is recommended that, in establishing an improved local service, the railway fares for single journeys should be the same as now charged by the omnibuses, i.e. 3d between Stroud and Chalford (against 4d charged to-day) and 3d between Stroud and Stonehouse, and that really cheap return fares of 4d between Stroud and Chalford, and between Stroud and Stonehouse, be introduced.

'It is recommended that no through tickets be issued either to or from the Car service, but that all passengers pay local fares to the Guard, the Bell punch, or any better system that may be devised, being adopted.

'Auxiliary stopping places
'It is recognized that if an improved railway service is to compete successfully with the existing omnibuses, or the proposed tram services, facilities should be provided for passengers to join and leave the Motor Cars at intermediate points, and taking into account all the local environments, it is suggested that at the outset the Motor Cars should be stopped at four intermediate points, i.e.:

Between Chalford and Brimscombe – at St Mary's Crossing
Between Brimscombe and Stroud – at Ham Mill
Between Stroud and Stonehouse – at Downfield & Ebley Xings.

'At each of these four places there are level crossings with men in charge from 8.0 a.m. to 8.0 p.m., and signals – in some cases both distant and home – and after an interview the Officers have had with an official of the Board of Trade it is not anticipated that the Company will have difficulty in complying with any requirement that the Board of Trade will be likely to impose in regard to the Motor Cars stopping at selected places between stations for passengers.

'Each suggested intermediate stopping place is conveniently contiguous to the main road and centres of population.

'It is not considered that raised platforms are needed at these intermediate stopping places, (the ballast would want raising a little, and covering over with fine toppings which would be all the work required) provided the cars are suitably constructed.

'There is a suitable site at Chalford for stabling Motor Cars on the Up side at the London end of the station, the points leading to which would be within reach of the signal box, and there are sufficient spare levers in the signal box.

'It is not anticipated that it will be necessary to employ any additional men either at the starting or the intermediate stopping places.

'Advantages for running a Single car for Local traffic.

1. Greater acceleration in starting and reaching full speed. In the case of the Stroud Valley a railway Motor Car service should perform the journey in one-third of the time occupied by the omnibuses, and in half the time that would be occupied by electric tram cars on the high road: the outside time between Stroud and Chalford being 20 minutes, and between Stroud and Stonehouse 15 minutes, including intermediate stops. In one direction the times would be less that 20 and 15 minutes respectively.
2. More easily manipulated at terminal stations – no 'running round' or 'turning' necessary: can be shunted clear of running lines more quickly: and will stand where an ordinary train will not stand.
3. A single motor car may take up and set down passengers at selected stopping places between stations, whereas a train composed of several carriages could not conveniently do so without platforms.

'It is recommended that the construction of two Steam Motor Cars of the pattern designed by Mr. Churchward and shewn upon the tracing submitted by him for experimental use, at an estimated cost of £2,500 each, be put in hand at once.

'The approximate cost of a Motor Car service between Chalford and Stonehouse, as outlined, in the foregoing will be as under:

'Capital Costs:

Two motor cars, £2,500 each	£5, 000
Stabling for same at Chalford	£1, 000
Permanent-way work at auxiliary stopping places, signal work, siding connections &c	£1, 000
	£7, 000 total

'Annual Costs:

Capital outlay £7,000 interest at 4%	£280
Wages: Fuel: Stores, and Maintenance.	£1,500
	£1,780 total

'Traffic
'Present day railway traffic worth about £1,000 a year.

'It is estimated that the railway motor service should – if the tramway scheme is not carried out – earn £5,000 a year.

J. L. Wilkinson'

The paper's recommendations were approved, and an order was officially placed on 24th May 1903 for cars Nos. 1 and 2. On this estimate, the service would break even if the takings averaged £5 14s per day, based on a six-day week.

Meanwhile, Dougal Drummond had designed a steam railmotor for the L & SWR & LB & SC Joint Committee which operated the East Southsea branch, near Portsmouth. This car was built by the London & South Western in April 1903, and made some trial trips on the East Southsea branch, followed by a visit to London for inspection and a demonstration run to Woking, which was cut short by the rear bogie overheating. The car had a very small vertical boiler, 7in × 10in cylinders, 0–2–2 wheel arrangement, Walschaerts valve gear, and accommodation that seated 32 third class and 14 first class passengers. Churchward borrowed this car and, commencing on 10th May 1903, it made some trial runs between Stroud and Chalford. As Chalford is approached from the Stroud direction by a rising gradient of 1 in 75, steepening to 1 in 70, it would be interesting to know how the L & SWR-built car actually fared. We do have a clue: the *Railway Engineer*, writing about the GWR's new service in its December 1903 issue commented:

> 'It will be noted that the engine of this [GWR] vehicle is of considerable power, but the reason for this is that the gradients of the line through the Stroud Valley are heavy, so much so that when the LSWR motor was tried over the line it refused to mount them.'

Perhaps both Churchward and Drummond learned some lessons from this episode. Drummond had a larger boiler fitted to the second of his railcars, then under construction, while Churchward's first design also had a much bigger boiler, and a tractive effort over three times greater than the original L & SW design, whilst the wheels of the power bogie were coupled. Incidentally, the GWR car also had the automatic vacuum brake and gas lighting, whereas the L & SWR car was only hand-braked with oil light. Given the difference between the designs, it is not surprising that Churchward's cars actually cost £1,738 12s 0d each, compared with £1,280 for Drummond's.

News of the GWR's proposed motor train service reached the ears of the Stroud Rural District Council, who were duly alarmed, so much so that the Clerk to the Council wrote a letter to the Railway Department of the Board of Trade enclosing a resolution passed by the Council on 25th May 1903:

> 'That the Stroud Rural District Council, having been informed that the Great Western Railway Company have announced their intention of running motor cars in between their ordinary passenger and goods trains on the portion of their line between Chalford and Stonehouse (the greater part of which line is in the Rural district of Stroud), desire to call the attention of the Board of Trade to the following facts:
>
> 1. Between Chalford and Stonehouse there are twelve level crossings on the Great Western Railway.
> 2. It is suggested that at some of these level crossings the motor cars will stop to take up and set down passengers.
>
> 'The Stroud Rural District Council respectfully submit to the Board of Trade that if the Board sanction the running of motor cars as suggested they should insist that at each of the twelve crossings above mentioned there should be either a bridge over the line or an attendant to open and close gates and prevent danger to the public, and they also respectfully suggest that at any crossings where it is proposed motor cars shall stop there should be a small station or other protection to the public to prevent people who are waiting for or alighting from the motor cars being endangered by other trains passing on the line.'

Stroud Valley gradient profile.

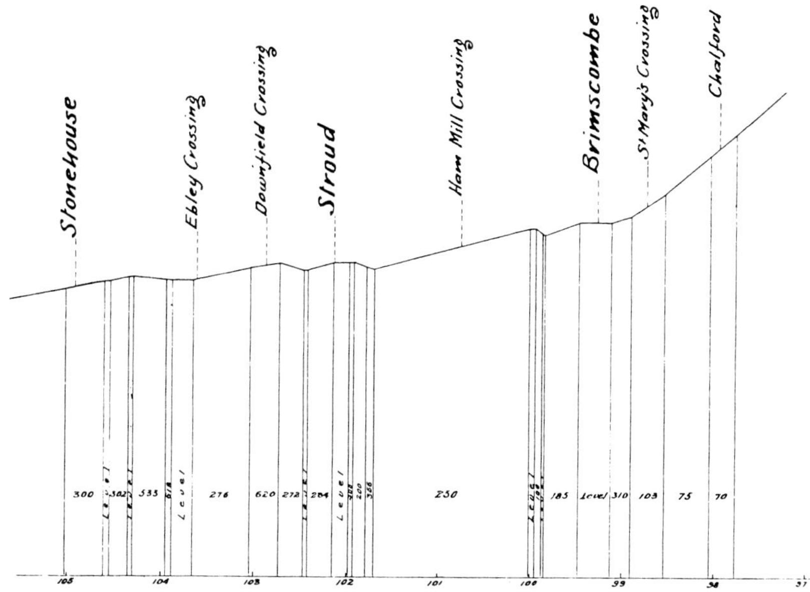

No. 1 of Diagram A1, as built, showing the power end, possibly in Stonehouse station. Note the central droplight in the lowered position, the polished cylinder ends and the power unit number plate on the bogie front stretcher. There is no number visible on the end. Notice the tail lamp on the lower lamp iron. At this time there were no brackets for a destination board above the end windows, which are seen in the original small size, matching the side windows.

COLLECTION R. C. RILEY

This missive was routinely acknowledged, and there was some discussion in the Board of Trade as to what reply should be given. Col. Yorke, of His Majesty's Railways Inspectorate, reported that he had been in informal communication with the GWR, and that the consensus within the Department was that motor car trains were to be encouraged. It was decided that the acknowledgment already sent would suffice, unless the Council pressed the matter. The Council did not.

On 22nd July 1903, James C. Inglis, the new General Manager of the GWR (Sir Joseph Wilkinson had died suddenly in May), wrote to the Assistant Secretary of the Railway Department of the Board of Trade explaining what was proposed concerning the steam rail cars, and how the service was to be operated. He said that intermediate stopping places would be provided at St. Mary's Crossing, Ham Mill Crossing and Cairns Cross, between Stroud and Stonehouse. At the two crossings, passengers for the cars would be looked after by the gatemen already employed there. At Cairns Cross, near the 103¼ milepost, there was an overbridge, and footpaths would be provided from the 'landing places' for passengers so that they would not have to cross over the railway line. He assured the BoT that a locking bar would be provided for the crossover at Stonehouse, in order that loaded cars could leave the down platform in the up direction. He asked that 'exemption from the ordinary requirements of the Board of Trade may be given in respect of:

> 1. Raised platforms at the intermediate stopping places.
> 2. Passengers conveniences and shelters at the intermediate stopping places.
> 3. Signals at the intermediate stopping places.'

and said that 'the early extension of similar Motor Car services to other sections of line is contemplated.'

The exemptions were granted and the GWR went ahead with its plans.

Before the GWR's service started, suitable publicity was effected: on Friday, 9th October 1903, 'No.1 car left Swindon about 11.5 a.m. with Paddington and Swindon Officials and a number of representatives of the Press, made a trip over the section covered by the Motor Cars, and returned to Swindon in the afternoon.' This comes from a Locomotive Department scrapbook-cum-diary now in the Public Record Office (Ref: RAIL 254/9) which includes several items about the new services recounted below.

Rail motor services utilising the two GWR cars were introduced between Stonehouse and Chalford on Monday, 12th October 1903, and included the opening of rail-level platforms (which only the rail motors served) at Ebley Crossing, Downfield Crossing, Ham Mill Crossing, and St. Mary's Crossing. At these places, passengers boarded and alighted from the cars using their built-in steps. These locations were initially called 'Haltes' by the GWR, but this name was criticised in the railway press as being too German or French, and they were later renamed 'Halts'.

The PRO source also reports that the service was provided 'by No.1 Motor Car' on 12th October, 'and on the following day No. 2 Motor Car commenced work.' The publicity seems to have paid off: 'On 12th Oct '03, the number of passengers was 2,500 and the takings £16' (an average fare of just over 1½d per passenger). 'On the following day the passengers numbered 1,700 and this represented £9 10s od.' A 'halte' was not provided at Cairns Cross until 1930, when it opened as Cashes Green Halt.

James Holden, of the Great Eastern Railway, was quick off the mark and 'inspected the Motor Car Service on 15th Oct '03, accompanied by Mr. Churchward.' Mr. Holden was, of course, an ex-GWR man.

The GWR Directors' Traffic Committee met on 19th October 1903 and the General Manager reported on the first week's experience of the new service:

'STEAM MOTOR CAR SERVICE,
CHALFORD AND STONEHOUSE.

'This service commenced on Monday, 12th October, cars running in each direction once in every hour from 8.0 a.m. to 8.0 p.m. On Fridays and Saturdays the cars run up to 11.0 p.m. for the convenience of Market passengers.

'Two cars have been provided and put on the service. Only one car is required to work the scheduled service but it is found that one car cannot work all the day through, and the second is used for relief purposes.

'On Saturday last, owing to the large number of passengers to be conveyed, the two cars ran coupled together after 3.0 pm.

'The cars are constructed to seat 52 passengers, and there is ample standing room for nearly as many as can be seated. The figures given below show that the average number of passengers carried on all the trips run during the first week was 77 per car trip.

'Some 2500 passengers were carried on the opening day, and upwards of 4000 on Saturday. During the first week (of six days) nearly 12, 000 passengers were carried, viz:

No. of Passengers	11,953
Receipts.	£101 18s 7d
No. of single trips run.	154
No. of car miles run.	1,177
No. of passengers per trip	77·61
Receipts per trip.	13s 2·85d
No. of passengers per car mile.	10.15
Receipts per car mile.	1s 8·7d

'Prior to the inauguration of the Motor Car services the normal local traffic between the several stations served by the car service averaged 1300 passengers per week.

'Particulars of the working costs have not yet been obtained.

'After discounting the 'curiosity' traffic attracted by the novelty of the service no doubt is felt that this and similar services elsewhere will prove remunerative.

'The intermediate stopping places at level crossings have, in the case of the Chalford and Stonehouse service, been well patronised and are popular.

'The attitude of the populace served by the motor cars is described as one of great interest and satisfaction.

GREAT WESTERN RAILWAY.

(PRIVATE AND NOT FOR PUBLICATION.)

No. 1,465.

MOTOR CAR SERVICE OF TRAINS BETWEEN CHALFORD AND STONEHOUSE.

1. On October 12th next the service of Motor Car Trains between the above points, as set out in the public notice, will be commenced.

2. The points at which Passengers will be taken up and set down will be Chalford Station, St. Mary's Crossing, Brimscombe Station, Ham Mill Crossing, Stroud Station, Downfield Crossing, Ebley Crossing, and Stonehouse Station.

3. As no separate luggage compartment can be conveniently provided on the Motor Train, Passengers will be limited to carrying with them only such light articles as they can handle themselves, and which will not interfere with the seating accommodation for Passengers.

4. Parcels Traffic will only be carried by the Motor Car between the Chalford, Brimscombe, Stroud, and Stonehouse Stations.

5. The Motor Train will be stabled at Chalford, and the Service will commence and finish at that station.

6. When the Train arrives at Chalford on the up journey Passengers must not be allowed to enter it for the down trip whilst at the Up Platform; they must cross over the bridge and join it at the Down Platform after it has been shunted over the cross-over road.

7. When the Train arrives at Stonehouse on the down journey Passengers for the up journey must take their seats at the Down Platform, and the Train, when ready, must be started away from that Platform over the cross-over road for Chalford and intermediate points.

8. When the Train stops at the Level Crossings the Driver must be careful to see that the steps of the carriage are opposite to the place on the Ballast provided in lieu of a regular platform. The Conductor must use every care to get the Passengers in and out of the car quickly so that there may be no delay. Special care must also be exercised by the Gatemen to see that Passengers are kept clear of Trains on the opposite line.

9. The Motor Trains must be dealt with in all respects as ordinary Passenger Trains, and they will be signalled by special "Is Line Clear" signal, 7 beats given thus:—3-1-3.

10. The Fares to be charged will be as set out in the public notice. The Tickets for Passengers travelling by the Motor Trains will all be issued and cancelled at the time of issue by the Conductor on the Train itself, and need not be collected at the end of the journey. They must be punched (opposite the place to which the Passenger is going) on the down journey on that side of the Ticket marked "Down," and on the up journey on the side marked "Up." The Conductor must in like manner also cancel the Return Tickets at the point where the Passenger joins the Return Motor Train. Local Return Tickets are available on the day of issue only. Tickets will be limited entirely to the district over which the Train travels, and Passengers who desire to travel beyond these points must re-book at Chalford, Brimscombe, Stroud, or Stonehouse Station, from which they will continue their journey by regular Train. Passengers booked through at ordinary fares from stations beyond Chalford or Stonehouse may be allowed to continue their journey to the station (or crossing next in rear of the station) for which the Through Ticket is held by Motor Car if the service is suitable. Such Tickets to be collected by the Conductor and handed over at the proper station. Return halves of Motor Train Tickets are available by ordinary trains to the stations served. Tickets so used to be collected at destination station.

11. The Station Master at Chalford will keep the spare stock of Motor Train Tickets, and must each day (or oftener as necessary) check and collect the receipts from the Conductor after comparing the last numbers issued with the numbers when the previous settlement was made, and keep a record of each transaction

PADDINGTON, SEPTEMBER, 1903. **T. I. ALLEN,** *Superintendent*

'Beyond minor troubles developed on the first day of the service in the mechanism of the new cars, which necessitated their temporary withdrawal and the substitution of a service provided by a small engine and corridor carriage, for a few hours, no troubles or difficulties have been experienced.

'Excellent time has been maintained throughout.

'It is realised that it will be necessary to provide a third car for this service, and it is intended to alter the designs and construction so as to increase the carrying capacity considerably.'

In spite of the word 'Junior' in its title, the Junior Engineering Society of the GWR was quite a prestigious organisation, and they held a meeting at Swindon on Tuesday, 27th October 1903 when Mr. F. W. Marillier read a paper on *Carriage and Wagon Rolling Stock*. Mr. Marillier was a Vice-President of the Society, and the manager of the GWR Carriage & Wagon Works at Swindon.

In the Society's *Transactions*, the content of Mr. Marillier's paper was reported thus:

'The latest device for the benefit of the public was the rail steam motor. Two cars at present were working most successfully on the Gloucester Branch, between Chalford and Stonehouse, a distance of nearly 7 miles, having 8 stopping places, and the journey taking 23 minutes.

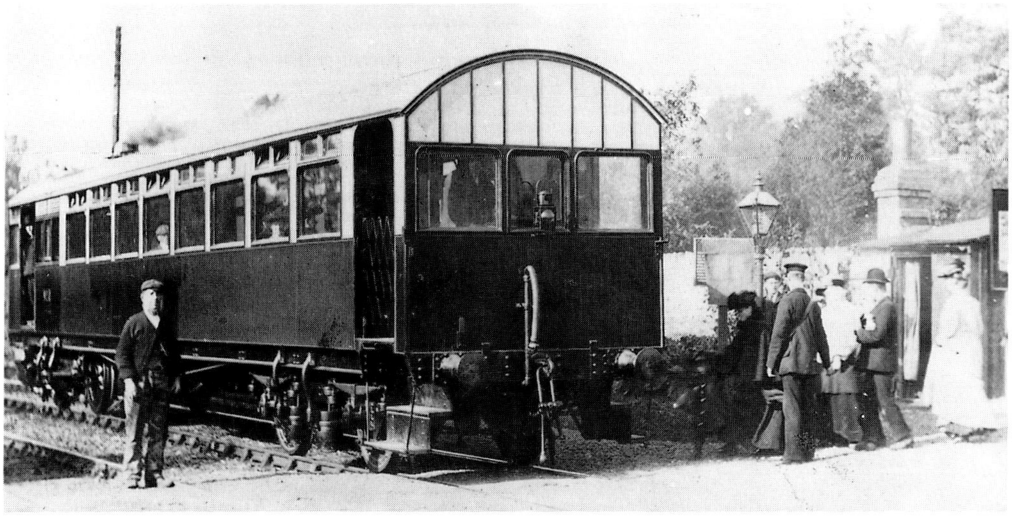

Car No. 2 of Diagram A1, at Downfield Crossing Halt during the early days of the Chalford to Stonehouse service. L&GRP CTY. R. C. RILEY

The interior of one of the first two cars, complete with crew and a notice about the new Chalford–Stonehouse motor service.

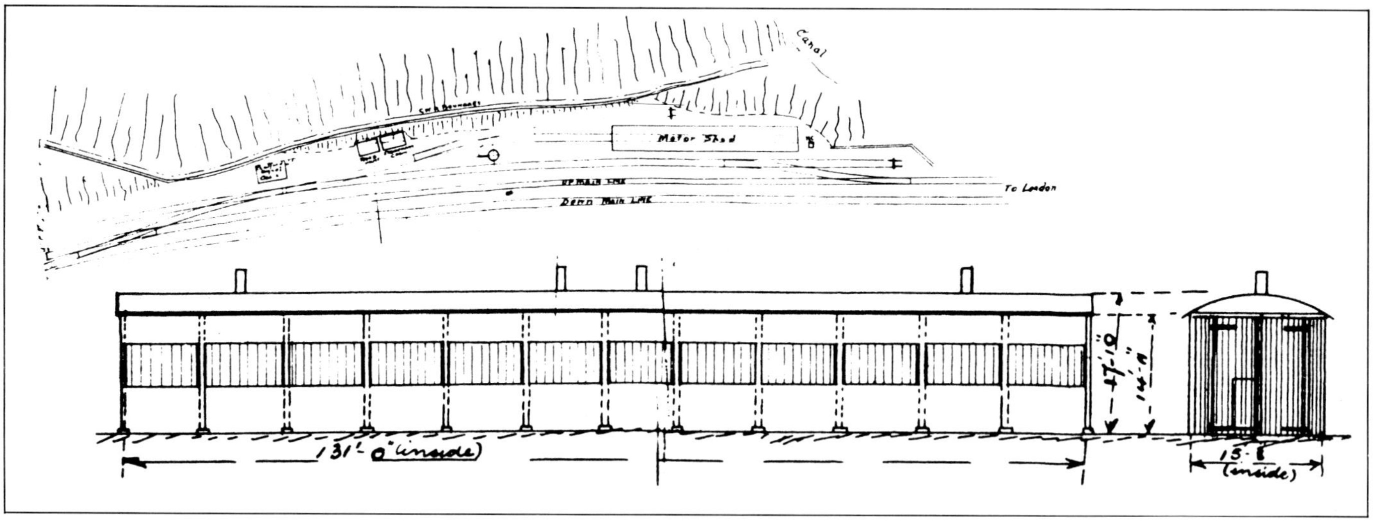

Official sketch plans of Chalford rail motor shed. The track plan is approx. 2 chains to 1 inch, but the elevations are not to scale.

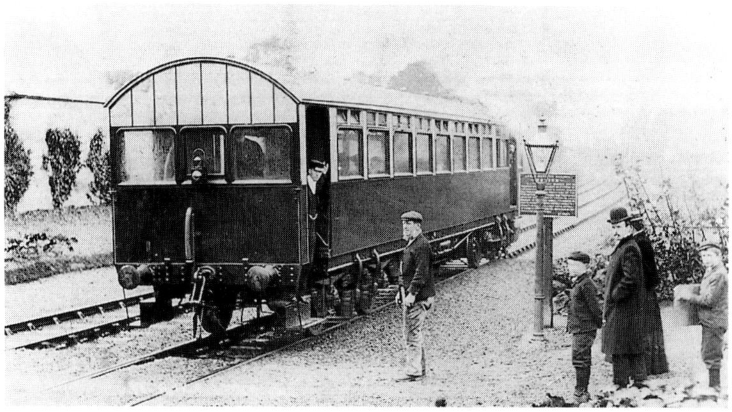

Car No. 2 in as-built condition at one of the crossings, believed to be Downfield, on the Chalford–Stonehouse line. This view shows the steps in use with a railway official standing on the top one. COLLECTION R. C. RILEY

Car No. 2 at Ebley Crossing Halt. Still in brown and cream livery, with unmodified side windows, but altered end windows, and the steps at the trailing end removed. This would seem to date the photograph to between 1905 after it had left the Lambourn Valley Railway and 1908 when it went to store at Swindon, not to reappear until 1910, after which it should have been painted brown. COLLECTION R. C. RILEY

'The cars were 59ft 6¾in long; 8ft 6¾in wide; 8ft 2in floor to roof, and were divided into engine or motor compartment, 14ft 0⅛in long; passenger compartment, 39ft 6in long; vestibule, 4ft 9in long.

'The vestibule, which was at the end of the car, was so arranged to enable passengers to leave and enter the car from level crossings by means of steps; hinged flaps, made to cover these steps, enabled passengers to enter from platform level. Collapsible swing gates were fitted to prevent passengers from entering or leaving the cars whilst in motion. Sliding doors were placed between the vestibule and the passenger compartment, which carried 52 passengers – 36in longitudinal seats at either end, and in 16 cross seats, placed in the centre to stiffen the sides of the car. The seats and seat backs were composed of woven wire covered with rattan cane, made by the Longford Wire Company, Warrington, thus saving the cost of horsehair or other padding, which harboured the moth and dust. The longitudinal seats were divided up by arm rests into sets of three. Each side of the car was fitted with large side lights, with top hinged lights, which opened inwards for ventilating.

'The cars were lighted by gas, and could be driven from either end, electric communication being provided between vestibule and motor end. Hand and vacuum brakes were fitted to each bogie and were worked from either end. The whistle could be blown from the vestibule end by a cord to the boiler, and was carried through the passenger compartment inside a tube, which served as a handrail, to which leather straps were hung for passengers to grasp.

'The total wheel base of this car was 48ft 9in; the bogie under the passenger end was of the standard carriage type, viz.:- Mansell wheels 3ft 7½in diameter, and 8ft 6in wheel base. The motor bogie wheels were 8ft 0in wheel base, 3ft 8in diameter, with cast steel centres, and coupled. The cylinders, which were attached to the bogie side plates, were horizontal, 12in diameter, with 16in stroke. The boiler fixed to centre of bogie was vertical, with 477 tubes 1⅛in diameter; heating surface of tubes, 625·58 sq ft; firebox, 44·34 sq ft: total 669·92 sq ft; grate area 11·48 sq ft; pressure of boiler, 160lbs; tractive force of engine, 8,483lbs. The water tank was attached to underframe of car, and contained 450 gallons.'

A curious thing about this paper, which was given only a little more than a fortnight after the service started between Chalford and Stonehouse, is that although the *description* matches the first cars, Nos. 1 and 2 (as shown in due course on Diagram A1), many of the *dimensions* relate to subsequent cars which had not then been authorised, and which did not appear until 1904. The illustration of an SRM in *Fig 2* of *Transactions* is of that which became Diagram D1, and does not show steps at all! However, the publication date of this volume of *Transactions* was 1905, and the illustrations were provided by drawings published in the *Railway Engineer* in January 1905, so the report of his remarks was presumably altered to agree with the illustrations.

Mr. Fowler 'of the Midland Railway, Derby' was present at the meeting, and the Chairman invited him to contribute to the discussion. *Transactions* reported:

'Mr. Fowler commenced by congratulating the Great Western Railway on the very successful and handsome motor he had seen that day. Considering the circumstances under which the car worked, the banks and curves which had to be negotiated, it was probably the most powerful of the many which he had had the opportunity of seeing lately. He had been nearly all over the Continent recently, and had seen nothing during his extensive tour of the size and carrying capacity of that he had inspected at Chalford that day. The only point which it appeared to him was capable of improvement was, perhaps, the question of having to employ three men. The only saving, he assumed, at present, was the economy in the consumption of coal, but this would not be a very large amount. It seemed to him that if it could be managed to dispense with the fireman, the advantage would be very much greater than it was at present. Another weak point, perhaps, was the step at the back. Of course, as it was imperative to pick up passengers at level crossings, some arrangements of the kind must be provided, but he thought the present one was capable of improvement.'

In reply on this subject, Mr. Marillier is reported as saying:

'Mr. Fowler had mentioned the disadvantage of the steps on the Chalford Motor Car, and explained that to obviate that difficulty the Company was going to provide raised platforms at the level crossings. Another system considered was that of having swing steps from the side of the frame, but there were objections to it. The Taff Vale Railway, however, were about to start a motor with swing steps, the steps being swung out from the side of the solebar. Even that was not so convenient as the raised platforms, which, he believed, was the only practical way of meeting the difficulty.'

It is interesting to note that problems with the steps had evidenced themselves at such an early date, and it had already been decided to provide raised platforms; these were authorised by the GWR Traffic Committee on 11th November 1903 at a total estimated cost of £336, and were constructed shortly afterwards. At the same meeting, a Memorial from inhabitants of the Stroud Valley against the rail motor car service on Sundays was placed before the Committee, and was duly declined.

Next to look at the service was a member of His Majesty's Railways Inspectorate. Mr. Inglis wrote to the Board of Trade on 14th October reporting that the new service had started two days earlier, and this correspondence raised some debate within the Department as to whether formal inspection of the new service was required. It was decided that Col. Yorke should do the honours anyway. The GWR Loco. Department recorded that:

'The Cars and the section of line covered by them were inspected by Col. Yorke on 5th Dec '03, on behalf of the Board of Trade. Col. Yorke travelled by ordinary train from Gloucester to Stonehouse where he was met by Mr. Waister. No. 1 Car left Stonehouse specially at 9.35 a.m., and after running as required by Col. Yorke to Chalford, it ran on to Swindon, arriving at 11.38.'

Col. Yorke's report to the Assistant Secretary of the Railway Department of the Board of Trade, dated 'Decr. 27. 1903' read:

'SIR,

'I have the honour to report for information of the Board of Trade, that in compliance with the instructions contained in your Minute of the 4th Nov. 1903, I have inspected the arrangements in connection with the steam motor car service, which has been established by the Gt. Western Railway Company between Chalford and Stonehouse stations on the Swindon & Gloucester section of their line.

'The motor cars have two four-wheeled bogies, the engine & boiler being at one end and a gangway by which passengers enter & leave the car at the other. The boiler, which is vertical, is carried upon the bogie truck below it, & is not connected in any way with the floor or framework of the car, which is built around it. The engine which is attached to the same bogie has two small horizontal cylinders and the bogie wheels are coupled. The car is 57ft long from end to end (excluding buffers) and the passenger compartment is 38ft 9in long, affording accommodation for 52 passengers. There is only one class, viz 3rd. The wheels are fitted with the automatic vacuum brake and hand brake, and there is a regulator handle and handles for both brakes at each end of the car. The car can therefore be driven in the usual manner from either end, and the driver is invariably placed at the leading end of the car. This is an important detail, as I regard it as essential for the safety both of the passengers in the car, of the public at level crossings, and of the men working upon the line, that the person in charge of the motive machinery should always be stationed at the leading [end of] the car, & should, so long as he is in charge of the machinery, have no other duties to perform. I attach a drawing of the car.

'There are four existing stations on the section served by the motor car, viz Chalford, Brimscombe, Stroud and Stonehouse, and four additional stopping places have been provided at public road level crossings, viz St. Marys Crossing, Ham Mill crossing, Downfield crossing & Ebley crossing, making a total of eight stopping places. The car makes 12 journeys each way daily, with extra trips on Fridays and Saturdays. (Time table attached).

'It was originally proposed that platforms should not be provided at the level crossings, and the Bd. of Trade consented to this arrangement on the condition that the car was fitted with steps to enable passengers to alight on the ground or enter the car with safety. The Company has however found it expeditious to provide platforms 100ft long at each crossing, as the picking up and discharge of passengers is thereby greatly accelerated.

'These platforms are fenced at the back, have each two lamps, and are connected by footpaths with the adjacent road. The gatekeepers in charge of the level crossing look after the platforms.

'I am informed by the officers of the Company that this motor car service has given great local satisfaction, and so far has been highly successful, and I understand that further developments are in contemplation. The experiment is one which may, I submit, be regarded with appreciation.

'I have the honour

&c &c

H A. Yorke.'

Sir Herbert Jekyll of the Board of Trade commented on the file 'This may lead to a considerable development of local traffic upon branch lines which are at present unremunerative', to which Sir J. Hopwood of the Department commented 'Yes, Lord Cawdor gave me some remarkable figures to show development of traffic' (both 31st December 1903). Lord Cawdor was the Chairman of the GWR.

Col. Yorke's comments about the importance of having the driver at the leading end of the car, and that only he should drive, were probably directed at the Taff Vale Railway, who wanted to dispense with the fireman, position the driver permanently at the power unit end of the car, and utilise the conductor to operate the regulator and brake at the opposite end when that end was leading. Raised platforms at the halts had already been provided.

In its early days, the service attracted quite a stream of senior officers from other railways, most of whom were given special rides:

'Mr. Worsdell of the North Eastern Railway inspected the Motor Car Service on 21st Dec '03. No.2 Car came to Swindon and left special at 1.15 for Stonehouse.

'On 4th Jan '04 the General Manager, General and Loco Supts. of the Caledonian Rly left Swindon at 1.15 p.m. in No.1 Car, accompanied by [not recorded] and ran to Chalford.

'Mr. J. G. Robinson, of the Great Central, inspected the service on 15th Jan '04, accompanied by Mr. W. H. Waister. No.1 car ran to Gloucester to fetch Mr. Robinson and left there at 1.22, arriving at Stonehouse 1.40. The same car returned to Gloucester with him reaching there at 3.40 p.m.

'Mr. J. H. Hosgood of the Barry Rly inspected the Cars on 21st Jan '04, accompanied by Mr. J. H. Read.'

In January 1904, a report on the operation of the Chalford & Stroud rail motor service, together with two road motor services, was prepared for the Traffic Committee of the GWR Board. This report pronounced them to be a success, particularly the rail motor service, which had seen off the electric tramway proposal. It was followed by the opening of Brimscombe Bridge Halte in February 1904.

'MEMORANDUM for the TRAFFIC COMMITTEE.
'MOTOR CAR SERVICES.

'Motor Car services are now in operation between:

		Distance
Road. 1.	Helston Station and the Lizard	11 miles
Road. 2.	Penzance station, Newlyn and Marazion	4½ miles
Rail. 3.	Chalford and Stonehouse Stations	7 miles

'The numbers of passengers carried by these services to the 31st December 1903 were:

	Service commenced.	*Total Passengers*
1. Helston	Aug. 17th 1903	7,042
2. Penzance	Oct. 31st 1903	46,091
3. Chalford	Oct. 12th 1903	100,681

'The working results to the end of the year (week ending January 2nd) have been:

TABLE 2

RECEIPTS & EXPENSES - MOTOR WORKING

Service	*Traffic Receipts*	*Working expenses †*	*Car Miles Run*	*Receipts per Car Mile*	*Working Expenses per Car Mile*
1. Helston	£413 13s 6d	£362 10s 11d	7, 960	1s. 0·48d	10·92d
2. Penzance	£198 19s 3d	£205 17s 1d	4, 915	9·71d	10·05d
3. Chalford	£819 9s 4d	£363 8s 7d	14, 011	1s 2·03d	6·22d

NOTE
† The depreciation and interest figures were excluded from these figures

'Note. For depreciation and interest £97.11.1 should be added to Helston expenses, £62.19.0 to Penzance expenses, and £98.0.6 to Chalford expenses.'

The report then went on to provide details of the running of the two road motor services, followed by a similar analysis of the SRM operations:

'3. Chalford and Stonehouse Rail Service.
'The success of the rail motor service in the Stroud valley has exceeded expectations. The carryings by the motor cars and the local passenger trains average 1,354 passengers per day and 474,000 per annum. Prior to the introduction of the cars the carryings were 194 per day and 68,000 per annum. This gives an increase of 597 per cent per annum in the number of passengers carried.

'During the period the service has been in operation the average weekly traffics to the 2nd January 1904 have been:

Passengers	*Receipts*	*Passengers per Car Mile*
6,678	£66. 5. 9.	7·43

'Nearly all the local traffic passing between the villages and towns in the Stroud Valley has now been secured to the railway, and when the additional stopping places at Brimscombe Village, authorised by the Traffic Committee on the 16th December, is ready for use it is expected the last of the omnibuses will disappear from the road between Chalford and Stroud.

'The excellent performance of the steam motor cars ensure a punctual and regular service, and the rapidity with which full speed is attained after starting will enable the additional stop to be made without adding to the time on the journey between Chalford and Stonehouse.

'The intermediate stopping places at the four level crossings between stations are largely used, and are the means of bringing many passengers to the cars who would not otherwise use them. The sleeper platforms at these places, authorised by the Traffic Committee on the 11th November, have been provided, and enable passengers to enter and leave the cars much more expeditiously than formerly, and a general quickening of the service has in consequence been made possible.

'The service was inspected by Colonel Yorke R.E. on behalf of the Board of Trade, on the 5th December, when that officer expressed, in complimentary terms, his approval of the general arrangements connected with the service and intimated that the attitude of the Board of Trade in regard to such facilities as have been provided in the Stroud Valley was a sympathetic one.

'Widespread interest has been aroused by this new departure in railway working. Officials of the principal railways in the United Kingdom have visited the Stroud Valley to see the service in operation, and enquiries respecting it have been received from Railway officials in the United States and many of the Colonies.'

It is interesting to note just how expensive it was to operate a (petrol-engined) road motor service in 1904, and to compare their costs with the railway (steam) motor cars – including depreciation and interest, the road services to Helston and Penzance cost 13·87d and 13·13d per mile respectively, while the railway motor service cost only 7·9 d per mile. With receipts of 12·48 d/mile (Helston) and 9·71 d/mile (Penzance), neither road service covered all its costs, although the Helston car did cover its running expenses. In contrast, the rail motor service receipts of 14·03 d/mile were nearly twice the 'cost per mile' figure.

The final visitors recorded in the PRO document were from Scotland:

'On 6th Feb. '04, Mr. Moffatt, Mr. Pickersgill of the Great North of Scotland, accompanied by Mr. Waister and Mr. Dawson, left Swindon special in No. [Not recorded] Motor Car at 1.10 p.m. for Chalford. The party travelled by ordinary Motor Car over the route and back to Swindon by ordinary train.'

The early success of the Stroud Valley service encouraged the GWR to introduce further rail motor services. In fact, passenger numbers on the Stroud Valley service continued to grow, so much so that, in July 1904, the GWR Board was told that the lighting at Chalford station was to be changed from oil to gas because of the increased number of passengers using the station.

CHAPTER TWO

EARLY DEVELOPMENT OF SERVICES

THIS chapter looks at a selection of the rail motor services introduced in 1904 and 1905.

At the GWR Traffic Committee's meeting on 2nd December 1903 a memorandum was received from the General Manager about rail motor services. In view of the success of the Chalford & Stonehouse service, he considered that similar services might with advantage be established between:

Southall and Brentford
Ycalmpton, Plymouth and Saltash
Teignmouth and Paignton
Worcester Shrub Hill and Malvern Wells

'or other likely places'. With this in view, he recommended the construction of 12 additional cars on the lines of the existing cars, but of lighter build, at an approximate cost of £21,500. The Committee agreed, and recommended that the Board sanction this expenditure. The Board in turn agreed, and cars 3–14 were ordered.

A further twelve steam rail motors were ordered in February 1904, and when built were numbered 17–28. These 24 cars on order were delivered as two types: Nos.3–14 were, like 1 and 2, without a luggage compartment, and became known as 'Suburban' cars, whilst Nos.17–28 did have a luggage compartment and became known as 'Branch' types. The use of the term 'Branch' possibly derived from the 1905 *Instructions for Rail Motor Cars*:

'On Branch and other lines where cars are run in place of ordinary trains, necessary luggage accommodation must be provided.'

Of the first Branch cars, nine (Nos.19–24 and 26–28) had retractable steps, as opposed to built-in (as in Nos.1 and 2), to enable passengers to use low-level stopping places; the remainder of the 24 cars ordered did not have steps for passengers. These 24 cars were not built in numerical order, possibly so that there was a balance in supply of suburban and branch cars. The 14 cars without steps were built first; presumably it had been decided that halts on the first services to be introduced would have platforms.

With the increase in the number of cars running, the Board approved an additional Inspector's post in the 'Motor Car Department' at an annual cost of £83, 'To supervise the running of rail motor cars and incidentally exercise a check on the issue of tickets by conductors.' The Motor Car Department may have been part of the Superintendent of the Line's organization – a significant number of returns were made on motor car usage.

In May 1904, the Traffic Committee recommended the construction of '30 extra cars' at an approximate cost of £50,000, comprising 12 for suburban traffic and 12 branch types, along with '6 trailers for use when traffic is heavy'. In October of that year, the Committee recommended the construction of a further 30 cars and 14 trailers at an estimated cost of £80,250. The Locomotive, Carriage & Stores Committee approved the seeking of offers from outside contractors for their construction, though they were to be built to GWR drawings. It was later decided that they should be built at Swindon, although cars Nos.14 and 15 were built by Kerr, Stuart to a design of their own, which resembled the early Taff Vale SRMs.

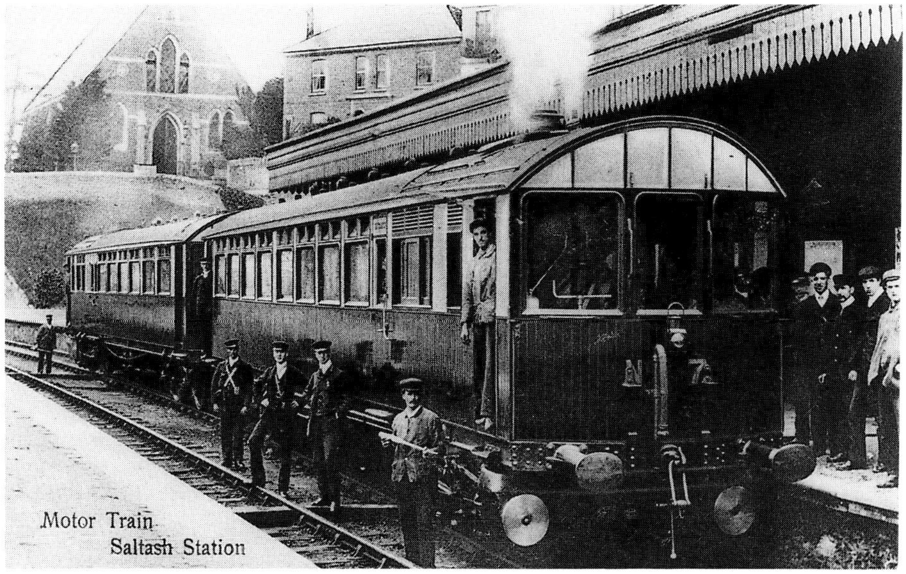

Car No. 7 of Diagram C1 with a Diagram F1 SRM at Saltash. LENS OF SUTTON

THE LONDON DISTRICT

Early in 1904, a paper was put to the GWR Board's Traffic Committee proposing the use of rail motors for services between Westbourne Park and Southall, via the 'New Line' which was then under construction:

'PROPOSED RAIL MOTOR SERVICE – WESTBOURNE PARK AND SOUTHALL VIA GREENFORD

'The section of the Acton and High Wycombe line between the junction with the main line at West London Junction and Greenford East Junction, and the loop linking the main line at Hanwell being available for traffic, steps are being taken to open up the district for residential purposes and, as a commencement, it is proposed to run rail motor cars between Westbourne Park station and Southall via Park Royal, Greenford East Junction and Hanwell with intermediate stopping places, where short temporary platforms – similar to those in the Stroud Valley – will be provided, at

North Acton (for Willesden and Harlesden)
Twyford Abbey (for Alperton)
Perivale (for Horsenden)
Castle Bar Park (for Greenford, the Great Western employees' recreation ground, and

TABLE 3

BUILDING DATES

Car	*Built*	*Luggage Compt.*	*Steps*	*Car*	*Built*	*Luggage Compt.*	*Steps*
3	Apr 04	No	No	12	Jun 04	No	No
4	Apr 04	No	No	13	Jun 04	No	No
5	Apr 04	No	No	21	Jun 04	Yes	Yes
6	Apr 04	No	No	26	Jun 04	Yes	Yes
17	Apr 04	Yes	No	14	Jul 04	No	No
18	Apr 04	Yes	No	19	Jul 04	Yes	Yes
7	May 04	No	No	22	Jul 04	Yes	Yes
8	May 04	No	No	24	Jul 04	Yes	Yes
9	May 04	No	No	20	Aug 04	Yes	Yes
10	May 04	No	No	23	Aug 04	Yes	Yes
25	May 04	Yes	No	27	Aug 04	Yes	Yes
11	Jun 04	No	No	28	Sep 04	Yes	Yes

the building estates in the vicinity of Castle Bar Park).

'The cars will call also at Park Royal and Hanwell stations. At Westbourne Park passengers will be exchanged with the City trains, the main line trains to Paddington, the Kensington (Addison Road) and Hammersmith trains, and at Southall with the main line trains to and from Uxbridge, Slough, Windsor, Maidenhead, Reading &c.

'The service will consist of one car in each direction every hour between the hours of 7.0 a.m. and 11.45 p.m. A schedule of the proposed timetable is appended. The mileage will amount to 339 car miles per day, and authority is asked for this.

'The scale of fares to be charged is governed by the existing fares between the stations on the paralleling main line, and is as follows:-

FARES - LONDON DISTRICT

	Westbourne Park	North Acton	Park Royal	Twyford Abbey	Perivale	Castle Bar Park	Hanwell
	d						
North Acton	3	d					
Park Royal	3	1	d				
Tywford Abbey	4	1	1	d			
Perivale	4	2	2	1	d		
Castle Bar Park	5	3	3	2	1	d	
Hanwell	5	3	3	3	2	1	d
Southall	6	5	5	4	3	2	1

'It is also proposed to issue books of 24 tickets each at a discount of 12½ per cent per ticket.

'It is proposed to carry out the necessary works at the intermediate stopping places on account for the vote for the Acton and Wycombe line.

'Preliminary notices – of which a proof copy is attached – will be sent to Landowners, Builder, Contractors, Householders, Estate Agents, Auctioneers and other interested persons, notifying the opening of the line for passenger traffic by means of a Motor car service.

'Provision is being made by the Locomotive Department for housing three Rail Motors at Southall, for working the service on the new line and the Brentford branch.'

The 'provision' for housing three cars at Southall was a corrugated iron shed, approved by the Locomotive, Carriage & Stores Committee in May 1904 at an estimated cost of £660. This was built alongside the Brentford branch, measured 200 ft in length with a 180 ft pit, and was completed in September 1904.

An associated service on the Brentford branch was also put to the Traffic Committee:

'RAIL MOTOR SERVICES ON BRENTFORD BRANCH

'On and from Monday, May 2nd, it is proposed to substitute a rail motor service for the existing branch train service between Southall and Brentford.

'The existing passenger train service consists of nine trains in each direction daily, the total train mileage being 70¼ miles. It is proposed to run a motor car service at half hourly intervals in each direction from 7.0 a.m. to 10 p.m., the total daily car mileage being 196 miles, and it is hoped that a service of this character will encourage the development of a new local traffic between Southall and Brentford, both of which places are on main routes of the London United Electric Tramway services.

'The London United Electric Tramway Co. will be asked to stop their cars opposite the station approach at Brentford for the convenience of passengers exchanging between the Railway Cars.

'It is proposed that on and from the date of the inauguration of the rail motor service, a 2d single fare between Southall and Brentford be put into operation.

'Authority is asked for the 125¾ car miles additional mileage.

'One engine will be saved.'

It is interesting to note that the Traffic Committee appear not to have been given financial estimates for these services. The object of the service via Park Royal was to develop a completely new traffic, so presumably the Board saw a rail motor service as the most economical way of doing so. The existing Brentford branch train service was described in the *Engineer* as 'a hopeless failure as to passenger traffic during the 44 years it has been operated',

PRIVATE AND NOT FOR PUBLICATION.—(For use of the Company's Servants only.)

GREAT WESTERN RAILWAY.

(Circular No. 1495.)

OFFICE OF SUPERINTENDENT OF THE LINE,
PADDINGTON STATION, APRIL, 1904.

F. 71/78300.

RAIL MOTOR SERVICE

BETWEEN

SOUTHALL & BRENTFORD.

On and from Sunday, May 1st next, the present Passenger Train Service (1st, 2nd, and 3rd class) between **SOUTHALL** and **BRENTFORD** will be superseded by a Rail Motor Service (**one class only**).

A single fare of Twopence will be charged between Brentford and Southall, and revised 1st, 2nd, and 3rd class fares between Brentford and Stations beyond Southall will be put into operation, enabling passengers to travel 1st, 2nd or 3rd class by ordinary Trains to and from Southall.

Parcels, etc., traffic will be conveyed by the Motor Trains, and rates will be the same as heretofore.

RAIL MOTOR SERVICE

BETWEEN

Westbourne Park & Southall

Via PARK ROYAL and HANWELL.

Rail Motor Cars, (one class only,) will run on week days, (commencing May 2nd), between **WESTBOURNE PARK** and **SOUTHALL** via Park Royal and Hanwell.

On Sundays, (commencing May 1st,) the Cars will run between **PADDINGTON** and **SOUTHALL** via Park Royal and Hanwell.

For particulars of the service see May Time Bills.

Advise all concerned, and acknowledge receipt to your Divisional Superintendent by First Train.

J. MORRIS, *Superintendent of the Line.*

*Mr.*____________________

____________________*Station.*

WYMAN & SONS, Ltd., Printers, Fetter Lane, London, E.C. and Reading.—9344a.

so motor trains were probably seen as a way of reducing the losses, with the hope that eventually it might prove profitable.

On 30th April 1904, the Paddington Divisional Superintendent issued instructions that, as from Sunday, 1st May 1904, rail motor cars were to be signalled by 7 beats on the bell, given 3–1–3; from that date the local code operating at signal boxes between Paddington and West London Junction for light engines running to West London Junction was changed to 5 beats, given 1–3–1.

In its issue of 6th May 1904, *Engineer* carried an article entitled

'THE NEW GREAT WESTERN MOTOR COACH SERVICE

'On Sunday, May 1st, the Great Western Railway Company commenced to run a service of motor-coaches between Westbourne Park and Southall, *via* the new Acton and Northolt line. No passenger trains had been run over this since the Royal Agricultural Society's Show was held at Park Royal last June, when there was a very brisk traffic for nearly a week. In view, no doubt, of the considerable time that will yet elapse before the line is opened between Northolt and High Wycombe, no stations had been built on the section nearest London, except at Park Royal itself. Lately, however, a more enterprising policy has prevailed at Paddington. Instead of waiting for the completion of the whole line, it has been determined to see what can be done to get up a traffic meanwhile, on a cheap, yet amply commodious scale. To this end a preliminary notice was issued in March to landowners, builders and others desirous of erecting houses in the district served by the new line, that the service just started would begin on May 2nd, and would be increased as the traffic developed.

'Four intermediate stopping places have been specially provided, and whilst of an extremely sensible and practicable type, are in amusing contrast to the massive solidity which all other structures on the line present. They consist merely of a rough wooden platform on each side, floored with old sleepers, and about 100ft. long by 6ft. wide. As the vehicles are entered only from one end, even shorter platforms would have sufficed, but it is necessary to give people a little space to move about. A ramp, not steps, leads up to each end; there is a lamp against these, useful to show where the platform ends and to guide the drivers in pulling up after dark. There are no other lights. On each platform is a small erection of galvanised iron, 22ft. long by 10ft. wide or thereabouts, with a pointed roof of the same material. Round the interior are fixed wooden seats, except where the folding doors, also of galvanised iron, come in the centre. These doors are locked by the guard of the last train. There is a square window on each side of them, and when painted these quaint little structures will not be so inartistic as the nature of the material might lead one to suppose. Messrs. Samuel Taylor and Co., of Birmingham, supplied them. There are no other buildings of any kind at these "haltes", as the company calls them. If they must go to Germany for a name, they might at least leave out the "e", as quite superfluous in this country.

'The first of these halts is called North Acton, but is really in Willesden-lane, which runs from Acton to Harlesden. It is just 4 miles from Paddington and on the ground level, approached from the top of the road bridge by footpaths with railings. Park Royal Station, 4½ miles, is a permanent structure of considerable size. Twyford Abbey, 5¼ miles, is the next halt, though Hanger Hill, we venture to think, would be a more correct description. This is in a cutting, but reached from a bridge again. Perivale, 6¾ miles, stands on an embankment, about three furlongs from the village in the direction of Harrow. At a junction termed Greenford East Loop the line turns off to the left. Another box has been erected at the south point of the triangle, the large space within which has been filled with spoil level with the running lines and will be laid out with sidings. The last halt, Castle Bar Park, is about 8¼ miles from Paddington across some swampy fields and a by-road leading to the Great Western Railway Athletic Association's grounds. Though not visible from the halt, a great number of houses have been built near quite lately, and this place will probably serve a residential population sooner than any of the others. In half a mile the line divides, the east fork not yet being in use. The motor coaches go round the western side to the main-line, reaching it just before Hanwell station, and going on along the "slow road" to Southall, about 11 miles from London this way and 9¾ direct.

'The scenery from each of the last three halts is exceedingly pretty and extensive, ranging over the valley of the Brent from the Watkin tower at Wembley on the right, with Uxbridge on the left. It will be a revelation, we fancy, to many Londoners that so beautiful a district should be so close at hand.

'The coach running – No.4 – is, we believe, identical in all respects with those put on the Chalford and Stonehouse service last year and described in our columns on October 16th, 1903. It carries 52 persons, 16 of whom have cross seats in the middle of the vehicle. Passengers who get in at the halts receive tramway type tickets from the guard, who carries a bell-punch, but at Hanwell, and of course at the starting points, tickets must be got at the booking office in the usual way. On week-days the motor coach runs to and from Westbourne Park only, No.4 platform, leaving there every 70 minutes, from 7.32 a.m. till 10.42 p.m. The trips take just half an hour. On Sundays, however, it begins and ends at Paddington, three minutes more being allowed, the service averaging about every 90 minutes from 9.50 a.m. till 9.25 p.m. As there is only a single large compartment, passengers are requested to refrain from smoking in it. Only light articles of luggage will be taken. The times at the halts are but approximately given, the company stating that the coaches may start a minute or two earlier, though we fail to see any reason why they should do so.

'On the same day, May 1st, a service of similar nature was put into operation on the Southall – Brentford branch, leaving Southall every half-hour from 7.15 a.m. till 10.15 p.m. On Sundays the service is hourly, beginning an hour later, but ending at 10.15 as usual. Notice is given that both services will be increased before long. It seems hardly likely that more accommodation will be required on the Brentford line, which has been a hopeless failure as to passenger traffic during the 44 years it has been open. However, the fare on it (there are no intermediate stations, or even halts) has been reduced from 3d to 2d and relations are cultivated with the London United Electric Tramways at Brentford, where the cars pass the station door. Southall, too, is now a large place.

'The Great Western Company's bold experiment will be watched with great interest. There are many places in the London district, on other lines, where similar services might, in all probability, be run with advantage.

'The running of these vehicles is admirably smooth when the engine compartment is behind, but when the reverse is the case a slight amount of vibration is noticeable, which might not be pleasant on a long journey. The engines seem to have plenty of power, and as regards acceleration, equal of, but they do not surpass, any electric train or tram-car that we have yet travelled in.'

According to an article by Rev W. J. Scott in the 1908 *Great Western Magazine*, the cars terminated at Westbourne Park on weekdays because of a lack of capacity between there and Paddington. Because Westbourne Park had no bay platform or turnback siding, the new service arrived and departed from the Up Relief platform, with very short turn-round times: the timetable shows that in several cases only two minutes were allowed for this.

Of the second batch of cars, it is recorded that 'No.3 Motor Car ran down [from Swindon] to Chalford on 11th April '04 and took up working of ordinary service alternately with the other car. This car [No.3] left for Paddington on 15th April '04, following 6.35 a.m. from Swindon.' Presumably Nos.1 or 2 (or both) required some attention. After this excursion, motors Nos.3, 4 and 17 were allocated to Southall for the services to Westbourne Park via the Greenford Loop and Park Royal, and from Southall to Brentford. SRM No.17 was a 'branch' type, and was presumably used on the Brentford branch as the instructions for the service include: '3. Passengers' luggage and parcels traffic will be conveyed by the Cars, in the luggage compartment provided for the purpose.'

The service at Perivale seems to have immediately proved popular; the Board were told in June that the platforms at the halt were to be lengthened by 100 ft because of the large numbers of passengers using it. The cost of £110 would be charged to the 'New Line' account.

From 1st July 1904, the Southall, Park Royal & Westbourne Park SRM service was supplemented by another, running between Park Royal and Acton via the Greenford Loop; this, in spite of its nearly circular route, did have the advantage of serving Ealing. Park Royal is only about

RAIL MOTOR CAR SERVICES—WESTBOURNE PARK, GREENFORD, AND WILLESDEN, &c.

WEEK DAYS.

Distance from Greenford. M.	C.	STATIONS.	1	2	3	4	5	6	7	8	9	10	11	12	13	14	15	16	17	18	19	20	21
			A.M.	A.M.	A.M.	A.M.	A.M.	A.M.	A.M.	A.M.	A.M.	P.M.	P.M.	P.M.	P.M.	P.M.	P.M.	P.M.		P.M.		P.M.	
6‡	45	**Westbourne Park** dep.	....	....	....	**8 12**	....	**9 43**	....	**10 50**	**11 52**	....	**12 50**	....	....	**1 50**	....	....	....	**2 52**	....	....	....
4	21	Old Oak Lane* .. ,,	..	..	..	8 18	..	9 48	..	10 56	11 58	..	12 56	..	..	1 56	..	..	..	2 57	..	..	..
3	59	North Acton* .... ,,	....	....	....	8 20	....	9 50	....	10 58	12 0	....	12 58	....	....	1 58	....	....	....	2 59	....	....	....
3	21	Park Royal .. ,,	..	..	..	8 22	..	9 52	..	11 0	12 2	..	1 0	..	..	2 0	..	..	..	3 1	..	..	..
2	37	Twyford Abbey* ,,	....	....	....	8 24	....	9 55	....	11 3	12 4	....	1 3	....	....	2 3	....	....	....	3 3	....	....	....
1	2	Perivale* .. .. ,,	..	..	..	8 28	..	9 59	..	11 7	12 7	..	1 7	..	..	2 7	..	..	..	3 7	..	..	..
6	37	**Willesden Junc.** ,,	....	....	**8 23**	....	**9 25**	....	....	....	....	....	....	....	**1 40**	....	....	....	....	....	....	**3 5**	....
4	75	Acton .. .. ,,	Car **A**	Car **B**	8 28	..	9 30	..	**10 50**	..	..	**12 10**	..	**1 10**	1 46	..	..	Car **C**	..	..	..	3 10	..
3	36	Ealing (Broadway) ,,	begins	begins	8 32	....	9 34	....	10 54	....	....	12 14	....	1 14	1 52	....	....	begins	....	....	....	3 14	....
4	30	**Southall** .. ,,	**7 35**	**7 53**	..	..	..	..	..	..	..	..	..	..	..	..	..	**2 38**	..	..	..	..	..
2	51	Hanwell .... ,,	7 40	7 57	....	....	....	....	....	....	....	....	....	....	....	....	....	2 42	....	....	....	....	....
2	52	West Ealing .. ,,	via Loop	8 0	8 35	..	9 37	..	10 57	..	..	12 16	..	1 16	1 55	..	**2 24**	2 46	..	..	..	3 17	..
2	8	Drayton Green* .... ,,	7 42	....	—	....	—	....	10 59	....	....	12 18	....	1 18	1 57	....	2 26	....	....	....	....	3 19	....
1	50	Castle Bar Park* .. ,,	7 44	..	—	..	—	..	11 1	..	..	12 20	..	1 20	1 59	..	2 28	..	..	..	..	3 21	..
—	—	**Greenford** .... arr.	**7 49**	..	**8 41**	**8 31**	**9 43**	**10 2**	**11 5**	**11 10**	**12 10**	**12 24**	**1 10**	**1 24**	**2 3**	**2 10**	**2 31**	....	....	**3 10**	....	**3 26**	....
Distance from Greenford.		Letters to indicate Car Working.	A	B	B	A	B	A	B	A	A	B	B	A	B	A	A	C		A		C	
M.	C.		A.M.	A.M.	A.M.	A.M.	A.M.	A.M.	A.M.	A.M.	P.M.	P.M.	P.M.	P.M.	P.M.	P.M.	P.M.	P.M.		P.M.		P.M.	
—	—	**Greenford** .. dep.	**7 50**	..	**8 42**	**9 17**	**10 5**	**10 27**	**11 24**	**11 27**	**12 11**	**12 27**	**1 11**	**1 27**	**2 4**	**2 11**	**2 32**	..	..	**3 18**	..	**3 27**	..
1	50	Castle Bar Park* ,,	....	....	—	....	10 9	....	11 28	....	12 15	....	1 15	....	2 8	2 15	....	....	....	3 23	....	....	....
2	8	Drayton Green* ,,	..	..	8 47	..	10 11	..	11 30	..	12 17	..	1 17	..	2 10	2 17	..	..	..	3 25	..	..	..
2	52	West Ealing .... ,,	....	8 0	8 49	....	10 14	....	11 33	....	12 19	....	1 20	....	via Loop.	**2 23**	....	2 46	....	3 27	....	....	....
2	51	Hanwell .. ,,	..	..	..	..	..	..	..	..	..	..	..	..	2 12	..	..	..	..	..	..	..	..
4	30	**Southall** .... ,,	....	....	....	....	....	....	....	....	....	....	....	....	**2 16**	....	....	....	....	....	....	....	....
3	36	Ealing (Broadway) ,,	..	8 3	8 52	..	10 17	..	11 36	..	12 21	..	1 23	..		..	..	2 48	..	3 30	..	..	..
4	75	Acton .... ,,	....	8 7	8 58	....	**10 21**	....	**11 40**	....	**12 25**	....	1 27	....		....	....	2 52	....	**3 34**	....	....	....
6	37	**Willesden Junc** arr.	..	**8 12**	**9 4**	..	..	..	..	..	..	..	**1 32**	..		..	..	**2 57**	..	..	..	..	..
1	2	Perivale* .... dep.	7 53	....	....	9 20	....	10 30	....	11 30	....	12 30	....	1 30	Car [illegible] finishes.	....	2 35	....	....	....	....	3 30	....
2	37	Twyford Abbey* ,,	7 57	..	..	9 24	..	10 34	..	11 34	..	12 34	..	1 34		..	2 38	..	..	..	..	3 34	..
3	21	Park Royal ,,	8 1	....	....	9 29	....	10 39	....	11 39	....	12 39	....	1 39		....	2 42	....	....	....	....	3 39	....
3	59	North Acton* ,,	8 3	..	..	9 31	..	10 41	..	11 41	..	12 41	..	1 41		..	2 44	..	..	..	..	3 41	..
4	21	Old Oak Lane* ,,	8 5	....	....	9 33	....	10 43	....	11 43	....	12 43	....	1 43		....	2 46	....	....	....	....	3 43	....
6‡	45	**Westbourne Park** arr.	**8 11**	..	..	**9 39**	..	**10 49**	..	**11 49**	..	**12 49**	..	**1 49**	..	..	**2 51**	..	..	..	..	**3 49**	..

WEEK DAYS.

STATIONS.	22	23	24	25	26	27	28	29	30	31	32	33	34	35	36	37
	P.M.	P.M.	P.M.	P.M.	P.M.	P.M.	P.M.	P.M.	P.M.		P.M.	P.M.			P.M.	
Westbourne Park dep.	..	**3 50**	..		**5 0**	5†25	..	**6 50**	..	..	**7 50**	..	..	..	**8 50**	..
Old Oak Lane* ,,	....	3 56	....	....	5 6	....	....	6 56	....	....	7 56	....	....	....	8 56	....
North Acton* ,,	..	3 58	..	..	5 8	..	..	6 58	..	..	7 58	..	..	..	8 58	..
Park Royal .... ,,	....	4 0	....	....	5 10	....	....	7 0	....	....	8 0	....	....	....	9 0	....
Twyford Abbey* ,,	..	4 3	..	..	5 13	..	..	7 3	..	..	8 3	..	..	..	9 3	..
Perivale* .... ,,	....	4 7	....	....	5 17	....	....	7 7	....	....	8 7	....	....	....	9 7	....
Willesden Junct. ,,	..	..	**4 35**	..	..	..	**5 57**	..	..	..	..	**7 55**	..	..	..	..
Acton .... ,,	**3 55**	....	4 40	....	....	†	6 7	....	7 11	..	....	8 0	....	....	....	....
Ealing (Broadway) ,,	3 58	..	4 44	..	..	**5 45**	6 11	..	7 15	....	..	8 4	..	..	..	..
Southall .... ,,	....	....	....	....	....	....	....	....	....	..	....	....	....	....	....	....
Hanwell .. ,,	..	..	..	..	..	..	..	..	..	....	..	..	..	..	..	..
West Ealing .... ,,	4 0	....	4 47	....	....	5 48	6 13	....	7 18	....	....	8 7	....	....	....	....
Drayton Green* ,,	4 2	..	4 49	..	..	5 50	6 15	..	7 20	..	..	8 9	..	..	..	..
Castle Bar Park* ,,	4 4	....	4 51	....	....	5 53	6 17	....	7 22	....	....	8 11	....	....	....	....
Greenford .. arr.	**4 7**	**4 10**	**4 56**	..	**5 20**	**5 58**	**6 21**	**7 10**	**7 26**	..	**8 10**	**8 15**	..	..	**9 10**	..
Letters to indicate Car Working.	A	C	C		A	C	A	A	C	A	C	A		A	C	C
	P.M.	P.M.	P.M.		P.M.	P.M.	P.M.	P.M.	P.M.	P.M.	P.M.	P.M.		P.M.	P.M.	P.M.
Greenford .. dep.	**4 8**	**4 11**	**4 57**	..	**5 21**	**6 5**	**6 27**	**7 11**	**7 27**	..	**8 27**	**8 46**	..	..	**9 13**	..
Castle Bar Park* ,,	....	4 15	....	....	5 25	6 9	....	7 15	....	....	....	8 50	....	....	9 18	....
Drayton Green* ,,	..	4 17	..	..	5 27	6 11	..	7 17	..	..	..	8 52	..	..	9 20	..
West Ealing .... ,,	....	4 19	....	....	5 29	6 13	....	**7 19**	....	**7 31**	....	**8 54**	....	**8 56**	**9 23**	**9 26**
Hanwell .. ,,	..	..	..	..	..	..	..	..	..	..	..	..	..	8 59	..	9 29
Southall .... ,,	....	....	....	....	....	....	....	....	....	....	....	....	....	**9 4**	..	**9 34**
Ealing (Broadway) ,,	..	4 22	..	..	5 32	6 16	..	..	..	7 33	..	..	..	..	..	..
Acton .... ,,	....	4 25	....	....	5 37	**6 20**	....	....	....	7 37	....	....	....	....	....	....
Willesden Junc. arr.	..	**4 30**	..	..	**5 43**	..	..	..	..	**7 42**	..	..	..	..	..	..
Perivale* .... dep.	4 11	....	5 0	....	....	....	6 30	....	7 30	....	8 30	....	....	Car **A** finishes.	....	Car **C** finishes.
Twyford Abbey* ,,	4 15	..	5 4	..	..	..	6 34	..	7 34	..	8 34	..	..		..	
Park Royal ,,	4 22	....	5 10	....	....	....	6 39	....	7 39	....	8 39	....	....		....	
North Acton* ,,	4 24	..	5 12	..	..	..	6 41	..	7 41	..	8 41	..	..		..	
Old Oak Lane* ,,	4 26	....	5 17	....	....	....	6 43	....	7 43	....	8 43	....	....	....	....	....
Westbourne Park arr.	**4•33**	**5 24**	**5 24**	..	..	..	**6 49**	..	**7 49**	..	**8 49**	..	..	..	..	..

* These places are Halts.

† To run empty to Ealing, via Goods Line from Old Oak West to Friars Junction and follow 5.32 p.m. Paddington from latter place. If Goods Line is occupied car must run to Acton Middle Box and shunt there.

‡ Via Park Royal—via Ealing 7 m. 74 c. Distance via East Loop at Greenford is 71 chains less than via Greenford Station.

• Car to run to Subway Junction and be shunted there.

Time allowed for running between Westbourne Park and Greenford, including all stops, 17 mins., between Acton and Greenford including all stops, 13 mins. Time in excess of the above is in respect of signal checks, water, extra passengers, &c. When the working time is later than the advertised time, the car may start as soon after the advertised time as practicable.

DAILY CAR MILEAGE:—

Car A 164 m. 18 c.

Car B 75 m. 74 c.

Also works 5.45 & 6.15 a.m. Trips on Brentford Branch.

Car C 94 m. 53 c.

1907 Working Timetable for the rail motor service via Park Royal. Note how the car working letters are shown.

¾ mile from Acton, although in those days it was about 1½ miles by road. Col. Yorke inspected the Westbourne Park & Southall service on 14th July 1904 and reported favourably upon it. Motors Nos. 11, 12 (both in June), 19 (July), 21 (July) and 26 (August) all went new to Southall.

Commencing on Sunday, 7th August 1904, the Park Royal & Acton Sunday service was replaced by one between West Ealing and Addison Road (now Kensington Olympia) via Park Royal. The first two trains of the day ran direct from West Ealing to Uxbridge Road via Ealing, and the last two returned this way also. This service was provided by two SRMs with a saloon coupled between them, and a trial return trip was made at 8 a.m. from Southall via Ealing to Addison Road the day the service started. Someone must have been confident that the arrangements would work! A note added to a surviving notice of commencement of this service indicated that 1,246 people travelled on its first day, receipts were £14, and 497 sixpenny tickets were sold – 6d was the return fare between Addison Road or Uxbridge Road and stops as far as Castle Bar Park.

On the Brentford branch, Trumper's Crossing Halte opened on 1st July 1904, and on 1st August a reduced fare of 1d was announced between Trumpers Crossing and both Southall and Brentford. The Southall to Brentford fare was 2d single, and the public notice announced 'Full Fares charged for each Seat occupied'.

Greenford station, which was to the north-west of the Greenford Loop, was opened on 1st October 1904, and the weekday SRM services commenced to run via that station; this involved a reversal. On the same date, most trains on the Park Royal, Ealing & Acton weekday service were extended from Acton to Willesden Junction – a journey of 32 minutes from Park Royal, costing 5p single.

In February 1905, the Traffic Committee was asked to approve the appointment of a clerk at Southall at an annual cost of £60. It was reported that 'there is a large increase in the passenger and parcels traffic at Southall on which the Rail Motor service has largely contributed, and the additional clerk is required to prevent the long hours which are at present being worked by the authorised staff'. In April, the appointment of an additional four conductors at Southall was approved.

Car No. 62 of Diagram O on a Southall 'C' working, probably in 1908.
COLLECTION R. S. CARPENTER

By July 1905, the services required two cars on weekdays (it appears that the Brentford branch was by this time being operated by a locomotive and auto trailer), and five on Sundays. The summer 1905 public timetable showed the Sunday Kensington service as operating from Clapham Junction, via Addison Road, Park Royal, Greenford, Castle Bar Park, Ealing, Acton and Addison Road back to Clapham Junction. There was a service in the reverse direction, too. The winter 1905 public timetable shows a rather less frequent service, with the first and last trains in each direction terminating at and starting from Victoria SE & C. The first train ran up the GWR main line from Southall to Acton and thence via Kensington to Victoria, whilst the last train ran back along that route, but the other trains are shown as running to or from Park Royal via Greenford, Ealing, Acton and Kensington.

In October 1905, authorisation was sought for an extra service:

> 'It is recommended that, commencing on November 1st, a rail motor car should leave Southall for Paddington at 3.15 a.m. for the conveyance of Post Office officials employed in the London District. Additional daily mileage: Railmotor miles 18.'

By October 1908, London rail motor car workings were identified by letters, and each was displayed on the end of the car using a metal cut-out of the appropriate upper case character. On weekdays, cars on workings 'A', 'B' and 'C' were in use on various 'New Line' services as above, some to and from Uxbridge (High Street) and out as far out as Gerrard's Cross. They operated a modified service on Saturdays, supplemented by a motor on working 'D'. Trailers were attached to cars on 'A' and 'D' for some Saturday journeys. Workings 'A' and 'B' also operated on Sundays, supplemented by a car on 'C' during October only. The Sunday Kensington services were still running to Clapham Junction or Victoria. Motors working 'D' and 'E' were used on the Staines and Uxbridge (Vine Street) branches. On Sundays, all the cars had a trailer attached for some trips. There were comprehensive instructions issued to ensure that the trailers were facing the right way to be attached to the correct ('trailing') end of the cars; if necessary, cars were to be turned on the Greenford triangle.

In 1910, the Brentford branch service was still operated by an 'auto car', which term seems to indicate an auto-fitted engine and trailer. It started from Southall at 3.22 a.m. on weekdays and ran to Paddington, presumably with the Post Office officials. It then shuttled between Westbourne Park and Paddington a couple of times, carried out an early morning trip to Uxbridge (Vine Street), and then spent from 7.15 a.m. until 11.9 p.m. operating the Brentford branch service – a total distance worked of 262 miles 26 chains, approximately the equivalent of Paddington to Liskeard via Bristol, and was perhaps the reason why a locomotive and trailer was used instead of a steam rail motor.

The interest of this photograph is that it shows Car No. 7 with a saloon and another SRM in use on the Plymouth suburban service at Ford Platform. NATIONAL RAILWAY MUSEUM

Ford Halt before any buildings were provided. NATIONAL RAILWAY MUSEUM

THE PLYMOUTH DISTRICT

In Plymouth and Devonport, the GWR's suburban railway service was in competition with local tram operations, and to a certain extent with the London & South Western Railway. At their meeting on 20th January 1904, the GWR Traffic Committee approved the running 'from the 1st Proximo between Plympton, Plymouth and Saltash of trains consisting of a light engine and two coaches' so as to provide a local service at approximately hourly intervals 'pending the introduction of Rail Motor Cars in the Plymouth District'. This involved an extra 95¾ train miles per day.

On 23rd March 1904, the Traffic Committee authorised the construction of new 'Haltes' at Laira, Lipson Vale, Wingfield Villas, Ford and St Budeaux at an estimated cost of £1,232, and approved an extra 99 train miles on the Yealmpton service.

Plymouth suburban motor car services were introduced on 1st June 1904, and included a couple of extra trains in addition to those put on in February. The cars ran between Saltash, Plymouth (Millbay) and Plympton, and between Plymouth and Yealmpton. Cars Nos.7, 8 and 18 were very briefly allocated to Newton Abbot, and were also tried out at Penzance, before being allocated to Plymouth, Laira, by June 1904. No.24 arrived at Laira new in August 1904, and No.28 in October that year. Shortly after the services had started, the GWR Traffic Committee were told that

> 'A communication has been received from the Town Clerk of Saltash, stating that the Council of that Borough, upon the motion of the Mayor, desire to convey their heartiest thanks to the Great Western Railway Company for the excellent services thus afforded.'

More importantly, it was also reported to the Committee that, for the first 12 days of the new services, the Plympton, Plymouth & Saltash passenger numbers were up by 25,339 and receipts by £184 8s 10d (74.49%) while on the Yealmpton service passenger numbers had increased by 1,418 and receipts by £14 8s 4d (9.85%), presumably compared with the previous year.

The Plympton & Saltash motor service was integrated with other stopping trains on the line, which served the stations only, i.e. Plympton, Mutley, North Road, Millbay, Devonport, Keyham, and Saltash, leaving the intermediate halts to be served by the motor trains. In addition to the services over the whole suburban route, there were a number of short workings, starting from or terminating at Millbay. One curious feature was that most Plymouth & Plympton motor trains did not stop at North Road, and there were even one or two each way which ran non-stop between Mutley and Wingfield Villas Halt, thus omitting Millbay as well. It would appear that main line connections were to be made at Millbay or Devonport – neither served by the L & SWR. Along the route, Mutley station was only about ¼ mile from North Road, and Millbay station was more convenient for Plymouth city centre than North Road. However, the Yealmpton service did call at North Road.

On Sundays, the service ran at two-hourly intervals, the down service starting at 10 a.m. from Plympton to Saltash with the last train at 10 p.m. terminating at Millbay. The up service was similar, with the first train at 9.40 a.m. from Millbay to Plympton and thereafter running from Saltash to Plympton every two hours from 11.0 a.m. until 9.0 p.m. All trains called at Millbay, none stopped at North Road.

The Traffic Committee, on 12th August 1904, authorised the provision of shelters at Laira (2), Lipson Vale (2), Wingfield Villas (1), Ford (2) and St. Budeaux (1) at an estimated cost of £40 each – a total of £320.

In April 1905, the Traffic Committee agreed to four additional rail motor conductors being appointed at Plymouth, and a porter at Ford Halt. At the beginning of November 1905, an additional porter was sought for Saltash at a cost of £40 per annum:

> 'The work at Saltash has greatly increased, partly on account of the introduction of rail motors, and the appointment of an additional porter is found to be necessary for the efficient performance of the work at the station. The traffic return for the 12 months ending June 1905 shows an increase of £5,000 per annum over the previous 12 months.'

On 29th November 1905, the Traffic Committee was asked to approve an additional clerk at Plymouth S.O. (station office?) at £80 per annum. 'This additional Clerk is required to deal with the heavy work caused by the inauguration of rail motor services in the West of England.'

Defiance Halt, about ¼ mile west of Saltash, had rather a curious history. It was built by sailors using material supplied by the GWR, and was opened in March 1905. It was principally for the benefit of RN personnel, as the Torpedo Instruction Ship *HMS Defiance* was moored near there, and there was an Admiralty landing place close to the halt. The railway line and the halt itself were crossed by an overbridge carrying the road from St. Stephens, and there was a gate for the public to use as well as a rather steep path with steps for sailors. This halt (referred to as such by the *GWR Magazine*, and not as a 'halte') had a single platform 150ft long and 6ft wide, the main line there being single track at this time.

The original Defiance Halt must have been one of the shortest-lived of any GWR halt. The company was constructing a deviation line from Saltash to St. Germans, and Defiance had to be rebuilt on the new section of the route, which was situated a few yards inland of the original at this point. The letter from the GWR to the Board of Trade notifying them of the

Steer Point station on the Plymouth–Yealmpton line.

No. 7 again, at Plympton, coupled to a saloon and another SRM. It now had an end destination board in use and the end steps fitted very closely to the number. AUTHOR'S COLLECTION

VIII.

PLYMOUTH, PLYMPTON &

Week Days.

		L	M	M				M			M	M	M				M					M			M
	a.m.	a.m.	a.m.	a.m.		a.m.	a.m.	a.m.		a.m.	a.m.	a.m.	a.m.	a.m.	a.m.	a.m.	a.m.	a.m.	a.m.	a.m.	a.m.	a.m.		a.m.	a.m.
Plympton dep.	.	5 40	6 10	.	.	.	.	7 50	.	.	.	.	.	8 41	.	.	.	9 20	.	.	.	10 0	.	.	.
Marsh Mills ,,	...	...	...	...	...	...	...	...	...	8 10	...	...	...	...	8 55	...	...	...	...	...	...	...	...	10 16	...
*Laira ,,	.	.	6 15	.	.	.	.	7 55	.	.	8 18	.	.	.	.	.	9 10	.	.	.	.	10 5	.	.	.
*Lipson Vale ,,	...	...	6 18	...	...	...	...	7 58	...	...	8 21	...	8 40	...	...	...	9 13	...	...	...	...	10 8	...	...	10 26
Mutley ,,	.	5 48	6 20	.	.	6 50	.	8 0	.	8 16	8 23	.	8 42	8 48	9 0	.	9 15	9 27	.	.	.	10 10	.	10 22	10 29
North Road ,,	4 50	5 50	...	...	...	6 52	...	...	...	8 18	.	...	8 46	8 50	9 2	...	...	9 30	...	10 0	10 4	...	...	10 25	10 32
Millbay arr.	4 53	.	.	.	.	7 0	.	8 4	.	8 25	8 27	.	8 51	8 56	9 8	.	9 19	9 37	.	.	10 7	10 14	.	10 32	10 36
Millbay dep.		...	...	6 45	...		7 15	8 10	...		8 33	8 50				9 20	9 35		9 50	...		10 20	.		
*Wingfield Villas ,,	.	.	6 24	6 49	.		.	8 13	.	.	8 38	8 53	.	.	.	.	9 38	.	.	.	.	10 23	.	.	.
Devonport ,,	...	5 57	6 26	6 51	...	Mondays excepted.	7 22	8 15	...	...	8 40	8 55	...	...	...	9 27	9 40	...	9 55	10 4	...	10 25	...	...	...
*Dockyard ,,	.	.	6 27	6 52	.		.	8 16	.	.		8 56	.	.	.	.	9 41	.			.	10 26	.	.	.
*Ford ,,	...	...	6 30	6 54	...		...	8 18	...	...	...	8 58	...	...	...	...	9 43	...	...	...	...	10 28	...	...	...
Keyham ,,	.	6 0	6 32	6 56	.		7 27	8 20	.	.	.	9 0	.	.	.	9 31	9 45	.	.	.	.	10 30	.	.	.
*St. Budeaux ,,	...	.		6 59	...		...	8 22	...	...	...	9 2	...	...	...	...	9 48	...	...	...	...	10 32	...	...	...
Saltash ,,	.	6 5	.	7 3	.		7 33	8 26	.	.	.	9 6	.	.	.	9 35		.	.	.	.	10 36	.	.	.
*Defiance arr.	...		..	7 5	...					...	...	9 8	...	...	...	...	...	...	...	...	...	...	...	...	...

	M	M			M			M	M	M					M		M	M			M			M
	a.m.	a.m.	a.m.	a.m.	a.m.		p.m.	p.m.	p.m.	p.m.	p.m.	p.m.	p.m.	p.m.	p.m.	p.m.	p.m.	p.m.	p.m.	p.m.	p.m.	p.m.		p.m.	p.m.
Plympton dep.	10 35	.	10 47	.	11 30	.	.	.	.	1 0	1 5	.	.	1 30	1 50	.	.	.	.	.	3 4	.	.	.	3 50
Marsh Mills ,,	...	...	...	11 14	...	...	...	12 30	...	...	...	...	1 20	...	.	...	...	...	...	2 52	...	...	...	...	...
*Laira ,,	10 40	.	.	.	11 35	.	.	12 35	.	1 6	.	.	.	.	1 55	.	.	.	.	.	.		.	.	3 56
*Lipson Vale ,,	10 43	...	...	...	11 38	..	...	12 38	1 4	1 9	...	...	...	...	1 58	...	2 27	...	...	...	...	...	...	...	3 59
Mutley ,,	10 45	.	.	11 21	11 40	.	.	12 40	1 6	1 12	1 15	.	1 32	1 38	2 0	2 12	2 29	.	.	2 50	3 11	.	.	.	4 1
North Road ,,	...	...	10 54	11 24	...	...	12 1	12 42	1 8	...	1 18	...	1 34	1 40	...	2 14	2 31	...	...	3 4	3 13	...	...	3 58	...
Millbay arr.	10 50	.	11 2	11 30	11 45	.	12 7	12 45	1 11	1 16	1 24	.	1 40	1 46	2 4	2 20	2 34	.	.	3 10	3 20	.	.	.	4 5
Millbay dep.		10 55	11 10		12 0	...	12 20	1 0				1 35			2 7			2 50	3 0			3 40	...	...	
*Wingfield Villas ,,	.	10 58	.	.	12 3	.	.	1 3	.	.	.	.	.	.	2 9	.	.	2 53	.	.	.	3 43	.	.	.
Devonport ,,	...	11 0	11 16	...	12 5	...	12 26	1 5	...	...	...	1 40	...	...	2 11	...	...	2 55	3 7	...	...	3 45	...	4 2	...
*Dockyard ,,	.	11 1	.	.	12 6	.	.	1 6	.	.	.	.	.	.	2 13	.	.	2 56	.	.	.	3 46	.		.
*Ford ,,	...	11 3	...	...	12 8	...	...	1 8	...	...	...	...	...	...	2 15	...	...	2 58	...	...	...	3 48	...	...	...
Keyham ,,	.	11 5	11 21	.	12 10	.	.	1 10	.	.	.	1 45	.	.	2 17	.	.	3 0	3 12	.	.	3 50	.	.	.
*St. Budeaux ,,	...	11 8	...	...	12 13	...	...	1 13	...	...	...	...	...	...	2 20	...	...	3 3	...	...	...	3 53	...	...	...
Saltash ,,	.	11 15	11 26	.	12 16	.	12 34	1 16	.	.	.	1 50	.	.	2 24	.	.	3 7	3 18	.	.	3 56	.	.	.
*Defiance arr.	...	11 18		...	12 20	...			...	...	...	...	...	...	2 27	...	...			...	...	3 59	...	...	...

	M	M				M	M			M		M			M			M	M		M			M	
	p.m.	p.m.		p.m.	p.m.	p.m.	p.m.		p.m.	p.m.	p.m.	p.m.	p.m.	p.m.	p.m.	p.m.	p.m.	p.m.	p.m.	p.m.	p.m.	p.m.	p.m.	p.m.	p.m.
Plympton dep.	.	.	.	4 26	.	.	.	..	.	.	5 40	.	.	.	6 17	.	6 50	.	.	.	7 5	.	.	.	.
Marsh Mills ,,	...	...	..	..	...	...	5 5	...	..	.	...	...	...	6 8	...	...	...	...	...	7 4	...	...	...	..	7 44
*Lair[illegible]																									

M—Rail Motor Car. One class only. * These places are Halts.

The times for the Rail Motor Cars are subject to alteration.

Summer 1905

proposed new halt for motor car traffic was dated 19th July 1905 – just over a month after Col. Yorke had inspected the original! The new halt was on a double line, and thus had two platforms 250ft long by 7ft wide, each with lamps, a small shelter and access via steps to either side of another overbridge carrying the St. Stephens road. It was opened in May 1906, and was referred to in the service timetable as 'Defiance Platform'. About half of the motor trains serving Saltash were extended to Defiance Halt, and reversed from there for the return, but when the new Defiance Platform came into use, the timetable shows some of the trains being extended to Wearde Siding, which was about ¼ mile west of Defiance, although it did not have a platform. At this time, Wearde was the end of the new double-track line from Saltash.

An additional halt at Dockyard was authorised in March 1905 at an estimated cost of £557, and was opened in June 1905. It was situated between Ford and Devonport. Ford had became known as 'Ford Platform' by the middle of 1906, if not before.

In June 1906, approval was given to the estimated expenditure shown for the extension of platforms and improved waiting accommodation at Ford (£594), St. Budeaux (£445) and Defiance (£263). Attributing this need to the 'success of the rail motor service' the *GWR Magazine* went on to report that the additional facilities had the effect of 'practically converting these halts to small roadside stations'.

The Plymouth suburban service continued to prove very popular, and the numbers travelling rapidly outgrew the capacity of single motor units; pairs of cars, sometimes with a saloon coupled between them, had therefore to be used. The economics of such usage were raised, and before long, locomotives with auto trailers were appearing on the services: by mid-1906, some of the suburban trains appear in the service timetable as 'Auto' instead of 'Motor'. Eventually, locomotives with up to four auto trailers were utilised on the services, and the steam rail motors were redeployed elsewhere. Laira had none by mid-1914, although they were occasionally allocated there later.

THE EXETER AND NEWTON ABBOT AREAS

The GWR Board was given a situation report on the introduction of rail motor services in June 1904 which incorporated a list of services to commence on 1st July, including the Exeter Railway (Exeter & Christow), which the GWR operated. However, the Board of the Exeter Railway, who still had a degree of control, wanted an increased service of 'proper' trains, and so additional Exeter & Christow trains were introduced, but formed of a small tank engine plus a single coach.

The ordinary train service on the Totnes & Ashburton branch was replaced by rail motors from Saturday 1st October 1904. Cars Nos.7 and 10 were allocated to Newton Abbot and Ashburton at this period.

NORTH WALES

Rail motors were introduced on local services between Ruabon and Dolgelly from 1st July 1904. Croes Newydd (Wrexham) received cars Nos.9 and 10 in June, No.13 in July and No.22 in September.

With effect from Saturday 1st October 1904, the existing conventional services on the Wrexham & Rhos and Wrexham & Coed Poeth lines were withdrawn, and replaced by one class rail motor services.

On 14th December 1904, the Traffic Committee approved the expenditure of £8,842 'to adapt other branches in the Wrexham area for rail motor services', including the provision of new halts:

Legacy Branch: at Cutter Hill, Aberderfyn and Fennant Road (£2,593).
Moss Valley branch: at Gatewen, Pentre & Broughton and Moss level crossing (£2,295).
Rhos branch: at Brook Street level crossing, Pant siding and Wynn Hall (£2,414).
Minera and Brymbo line: at Vicarage Siding, Berwig crossing, Pentre Saeson and Brymbo West crossing (£1,541).

Pentre Saeson and Brymbo West Crossing halts were on the Wrexham & Coed Poeth line, on which a motor service was by now operating, and these were opened for traffic in March 1905. The other halts were on mineral lines which had to be made suitable for passenger traffic, hence the relatively high costs.

On 12th April 1905, the GWR Traffic Committee formally 'agreed to recommend that the following lines be opened to passenger traffic when they are ready: Legacy and Cutter Hill; Rhos and Wynn Hall; Coed Poeth and Berwig; and the Moss Valley Branch.' These opened between May and July 1905. Cutter Hill, on the Legacy branch, seems to have been replaced by (or renamed) Ponkey Crossing Halt.

At a meeting on 29th November 1905, the Traffic Committee was asked to approve the expenditure of £90 for the provision of shelters at Berwig and Vicarage Halts.

In December 1905, the Traffic Committee was asked to approve the following additional staff required as a result of the introduction of rail motor services in the Wrexham area, and between Ruabon and Llangollen, at an annual cost of £630:

Aberderfyn Road:	1 Crossing Keeper
Berwig Halt:	1 Signalman/Porter
Brook Street Halt:	1 Signalman/Porter
Brymbo Halt:	1 Signalman/Porter
Legacy:	2 Signalmen
Moss Halt:	1 Signalman/Porter
Ponkey Halt:	1 Signalman/Porter
Rhos:	1 Lad Porter
Ruabon:	1 Conductor
Talwyn:	1 Crossing Keeper
Tennant Road:	1 Crossing Keeper
Wrexham:	4 Conductors
Wynne Hall Halt:	1 Signalman/Porter

Approval to an extension of the platforms at Brymbo West Crossing Halt at an estimated cost of £193 was given in June 1906.

SOUTH WARWICKSHIRE & GLOUCESTERSHIRE

On 10th August 1904, the Traffic Committee had authorised the construction of Halts on the existing line between Honeybourne and Stratford-upon-Avon at Broad Marston (at an estimated cost of £28), Chambers Crossing (£46), and Evesham Road (£58). The Birmingham & Bristol direct line was then under construction, and was opened for local traffic in stages, using steam rail motors; the full service of railmotors commenced thus:

Honeybourne & Stratford and Broadway: 24th October 1904
Broadway & Toddington: 1st December 1904
Toddington & Winchcombe: 1st February 1905
Winchcombe & Bishop's Cleeve: 1st June 1906
Bishop's Cleeve & Cheltenham: 1st August 1906.

The service between Honeybourne and Cheltenham was thereafter operated entirely by rail motors. Through GWR trains between Birmingham and Bristol did not start running

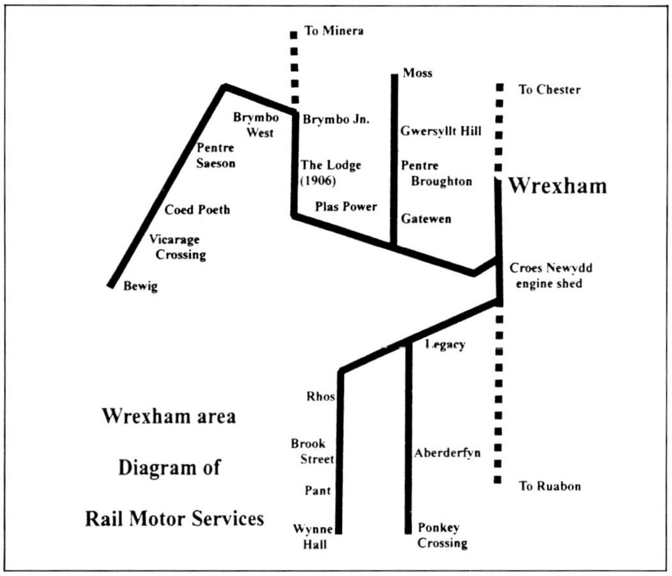

Wrexham area Diagram of Rail Motor Services

Private and not for Publication.

GREAT WESTERN RAILWAY.

(Circular No. 1532.)
OFFICE OF SUPERINTENDENT OF THE LINE.
F. 68/78777
PADDINGTON STATION,
September 23rd, 1904.

RAIL MOTOR SERVICES,
(ONE CLASS ONLY,)
BETWEEN
Totnes and Ashburton,
Wrexham and Rhos,
Wrexham and Coed Poeth.

On and from Saturday, October 1st next, the present Passenger Train Services (1st, 2nd, and 3rd Class) on the above Branches, will be superseded by Rail Motor Services (one class only).

Revised 1st, 2nd, and 3rd Class Fares between Stations on the Branches named and Stations beyond the Junctions with the Main Line will be put into operation, enabling passengers to travel 1st, 2nd or 3rd Class by ordinary Trains on the Main Line to and from the Junction Stations.

Parcels, etc., traffic will be conveyed by the Motor Trains, and the rates will be the same as heretofore.

For particulars of the service see October Time Bills.

ADVISE ALL CONCERNED, AND ACKNOWLEDGE RECEIPT TO YOUR DIVISIONAL SUPERINTENDENT BY FIRST TRAIN.

J. MORRIS,
Superintendent of the Line.

Mr.

Station.

Printed at the Company's Office, 150, Westbourne Terrace, Paddington, W.

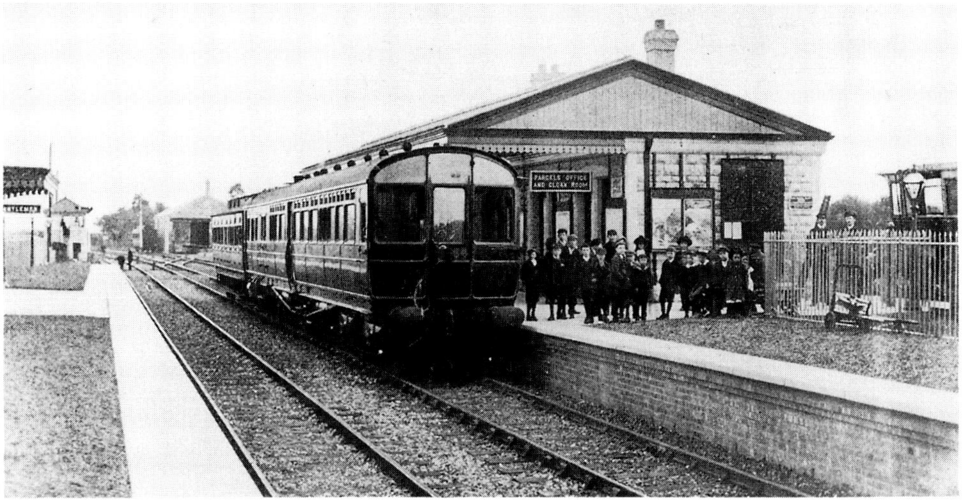

Car No. 64 of Diagram O seen as built at Bishop's Cleeve on the section of the Cheltenham–Honeybourne line on 1st June 1906. CTY. M. P. BARNSLEY

REAT WESTERN RAILWAY.

UGMENTED SERVICE BY RAIL MOTOR CAR

BETWEEN

KIDDERMINSTER, BEWDLEY, STOURPORT & HARTLEBURY.

Commencing January 2nd, 1905.

WEEK DAYS.

	a.m.		a.m.	a.m.	a.m.	a.m.	a.m.	a.m.	a.m.			p.m.	p.m.		p.m.	p.m.	p.m.		p.m.	p.m.	p.m.		p.m.	p.m.	p.m.	p.m.	
WORCESTER Foregate St. dep.	....	....	....	....	8 53	....	....	10 26	....	....	....	12 19	....	....	....	....	....	....	4 30	5 10	....	....	5F47	....	7 5	....	....
WORCESTER Shrub Hill „	..	..	..	..	..	..	9 55	..	..	..	..	..	12 57	..	..	2 28	4 5	..	..	..	..	..	..	6 20	..	7 44	..
WOLVERHAMPTON .... dep.	5 52	....	7 20	8B0	8 30	....	9 10	10 5	10 25	....	....	12 5	....	....	1 12	2 25	3 48	....	4 0	....	4 50	....	5 35	5 48	6 38	7 35	....
BIRMINGHAM .. .. „	..	..	7 10	8B5	8 10	9 0	9 35	10 15	10 30	..	..	11 45	12 35	..	..	2 35	3 55	..	..	4 25	..	..	5 50	5 58	7 5	7 10	..
	a.m.	a.m.	a.m.	a.m.	a.m.	a.m.	a.m.	a.m.	a.m.	p.m.	p.m.	p.m.	p.m.	p.m.	p.m.	p.m.	p.m.	p.m.	p.m.	p.m.	p.m.	p.m.	p.m.	p.m.	p.m.	p.m.	p.m.
	M				M		M		M			M			M	M	M		M		M		M		M		
KIDDERMINSTER .... dep.	7 15	....	8 40	9 5	9 27	10 15	10 45	11 15	11 50	....	....	1 25	1 45	....	2 30	3 38	4 46	....	5 15	5 39	6 5	....	6 40	7 11	8 0	8 38	....
FOLEY PARK HALTE .. „	7 19	..	..	..	9 31	..	10 49	..	11 54	..	..	1 29	..	..	2 34	3 42	4 50	..	5 19	..	6 9	..	6 44	..	8 4	8 42	..
BEWDLEY .. .. arr.	7 25	....	8 48	9 14	9 37	10 23	10 55	11 23	12 0	....	....	1 35	1 53	....	2 40	3 48	4 56	....	5 27	5 47	6 15	....	6 50	7 19	8 10	8 46	....
BEWDLEY dep.	7 28	8 10		9 24	9 40		10 58		12 3	12 41	1 3	1 38		2 20	2 43	3 51		5 25				6 30					8 51
STOURPORT .... „	7 35	8 18	....	9 32	9 49	....	11 8	....	12 16	12 49	1 11	1 45	....	2 29	2 50	3 59	....	5 34	....	....	....	6 39	....	....	....	....	8 58
HARTLEBURY .. .. arr.		8 24	..	9 39	9 56	..	11 15	..	12 23	12 55	1 17		..	2 36			..	5 42	..	..	..	6 49	..	..	..	..	9 5
HARTLEBURY A .... dep.	....	9 25	....	....	9 59	....	11 19	....	12 27	....	1 24	....	....	2 59	....	....	....	....	....	....	....	7 43	....	....	....	....	....
KIDDERMINSTER A .. arr.	..	9 33	..	..	10 8	..	11 28	..	12 36	..	1 33	..	..	3 8	..	..	..	..	..	..	..	7 54	..	..	..	..	..
BIRMINGHAM............ arr.	....	10 51	....	....	11 15	....	12 43	....	1 27	....	3 15	....	....	4 20	....	....	....	....	....	....	....	9 9	....	....	....	....	....
WOLVERHAMPTON .. „	..	10 53	..	..	11 5	..	1 0	..	1 51	..	2 53	..	..	4 20	..	..	..	..	..	..	..	9 13	..	..	..	..	..
WORCESTER (Shrub Hill).. arr.	....	8 52	....	10 5	11 12	....	....	....	....	1 30	2 0	....	....	3 25	....	....	....	6!17	....	....	....	9 5	....	....	....	....	9 46

		a.m.	a.m.			a.m.		a.m.			p.m.			p.m.				p.m.	p.m.		p.m.		p.m.				
WORCESTER (Shrub Hill).. dep.	....	7 20	....	Tues. Jan. 3rd, 17th, 31st, Feb. 14th, 28th, March 14th, 28th, April 11th, and 25th, excepted.	....	9 45	Tues. Jan. 3rd, 17th, 31st, Feb. 14th, 28th, March 14th, 28th, April 11th, and 25th only.	10 40	....	....	12 57	....	....	2 28	....	....	....	4 48	....	....	6 20	....	....	....	....	....	....
WOLVERHAMPTON .. ..dep.	..	..	5 52		..	8 30		9 10	..	..	12 5	..	..	1 33	..	..	..	4 0	..	..	4 50	..	7 55	..	..	..	..
BIRMINGHAM .... „	....	....	....		....	8 10		9 35	....	....	11 45	....	....	1$10	....	....	....	3 55	4 25	....	....	....	8 0	....	....	....	....
			M																				M				
KIDDERMINSTER A .. ..dep.	..	..	8 10		..	9 24		10 37	..	..	1 18	..	..	2.48	..	..	..	5 7	5 29	..	6 2	..	9 12	..	..	..	..
HARTLEBURY A .... arr.	....	....	8 16		....	9 29		10 44	....	....	1 24	....	....	2 55	....	....	....	5 14	5 35	....	6 9	....	9 19	....	....	....	....
	a.m.	a.m.	a.m.	a.m.	a.m.	a.m.	a.m.	a.m.	a.m.	p.m.	p.m.	p.m.	p.m.	p.m.	p.m.	p.m.	p.m.	p.m.	p.m.	p.m.	p.m.	p.m.	p.m.	p.m.			
HARTLEBURY.. .. .. ..dep.	M	7 47	8 30	..	..	10 11	..	11 3	..	..	1 45	M	M	3 10	M	..	..	5 23	5 55	..	7 2	..	9 23	..	..	..	..
STOURPORT .... „	7 40	7 53	8 38	....	....	10 19	....	11 9	....	....	1 52	2 0	3 5	3 16	4 5	M	M	5 35	6 4	....	7 13	M	9 31	....	....	....	....
BEWDLEY .. .. arr.	7 49	7 59	8 45	..	..	10 25	..	11 15	..	..	1 59	2 7	3 12	3 22	4 12			5 42	6 10	..	7 20		9 38	..	..	..	..
BEWDLEY dep.	7 53	8 15	8 50	9 52	10 4	—	10 35	11 25	11 35	[illegible]		2 10	3 15		4 15	5 0	5 28	5 48	6M20	7 4	7M35	8 55	9 40	10 5	....	....	....
FOLEY PARK HALTE .... „	7 58	..	8 55	..	..	..	..	..	..	..	..	2 16	3 21	..	4 21	5 6	5 35	..	6M26	..	7M39	9 1	9 46	—	..	..	..
KIDDERMINSTER.. .. ..arr.	8 1	8 24	8 58	10 0	10 12	....	10 43	11 33	11 43	1 14	....	2 20	3 25	....	4 25	5 10	5 39	5 56	6M30	7 12	7M45	9 5	9 50	10 13	....	....	....
BIRMINGHAM .. .. arr.	9 11	9 40	10 0	....	11 15	..	11 25	12 43	1 27	2 30	..	3 35	4 20	..	5 56	6 15	..	7V13	7 27	8 10	9 9	..	11 24	11 24	..	..	..
WOLVERHAMPTON .. .. „	8 50	9 52	10 53	..	11 5	....	12 10	1 0	1 0	2 53	....	4 20	4 38	....	5 36	6 45	....	7 18	7 43	8 40	9 13	....	11 40	11 40	....	....	....
WORCESTER Foregate St... arr.	..	..	..	..	10 50	..	11 22	..	12 44	..	..	..	..	..	5 5	..	..	..	7 0	..	8 6	..	..	..	..	..	..
WORCESTER Shrub Hill .. „	....	....	9 58	....	....	....	....	....	....	2 0	....	3 25	....	....	....	6 0	....	6 31	....	....	....	9 46	....	....	....	....	....

A For complete Service of Trains between Kidderminster and Hartlebury see Public Time Tables. B Mondays only. F Fridays only. M Rail Motor Car, one class only. $ On Saturdays leave Birmingham at 1.23 p.m. V On Fridays Birmingham arrive 6.50 p.m.

TICKETS.—Passengers desiring to travel by the Motor Cars from the Stations must get their tickets at the Station Booking Offices, and must produce them on entering the Cars. Passengers joining the Cars at the "Haltes" will receive their tickets from the Conductor on the Car.

PARCELS.—Parcels will be conveyed between the Stations only, and not from the "Haltes."

SMOKING.—Passengers are respectfully requested to refrain from Smoking and Spitting in the Motor Cars.

PUNCTUALITY.—The Company have the greatest desire to make the Motor Car Service punctual, and the public can very materially assist in that direction if they will be alert in getting in and out of the Cars.

NOTICE.—Public Notice is hereby given that the times fixed for the Motor Cars leaving the "Haltes" are only approximate. The Cars may start a minute or two earlier, and intending Passengers are desired to time their arrival accordingly.

Paddington, December, 1904. **JAMES C. INGLIS, General Manager.**

WYMAN & SONS, LTD., Printers, Fetter Lane, London, E.C., and Reading.—12433a.

until July 1908, by which time the North Warwickshire line had been opened.

Commencing on Monday, 2nd January 1905, a steam rail motor service was introduced between Kidderminster and Hartlebury, which involved the opening of Foley Park Halte. On this service, the rail motors were used to supplement the ordinary train service, which did not call at Foley Park. Parcels were conveyed by the cars, but only between stations, not to or from the 'haltes'. Passengers were 'respectfully requested to refrain from Smoking and Spitting in the Motor Cars'. They were also enjoined to be 'alert' in getting in and out of the cars, and were warned that the times fixed for the cars leaving the haltes were only approximate: 'The Cars may start a minute or two earlier, and intending Passengers are desired to time their arrival accordingly.' In April 1905, the Traffic Committee approved the appointment of two additional conductors and a porter in connection with these rail motor car services.

Car No. 41 of Diagram L1 at Winchcombe, probably on 1st February 1906. HAWLEY

GENERAL PROGRESS

During the first few months of 1905, the GWR Superintendent's meetings started to receive financial returns relating to the new rail motor car services. The first summarised the position from the commencement of each service to 31st December 1904, and showed the following criteria:

Passenger Bookings: 1·7 million
Receipts: nearly £17,000
Mileage: over 412,000
Receipts per Car Mile, average: 9·86d
Receipts per passenger, average: 2·38d.

These averages concealed quite a wide range of results. The best performing service was the Sunday Plymouth & Tavistock, which produced receipts of 1s 7·61d per mile, with the average passenger paying just over 8d, followed by the Wrexham, Llangollen & Llanuwchllyn, a relatively long-distance service (37 miles) where the figures were 1s 5·84d per mile and receipts per passenger averaged 7·87d. The worst performing service was shown as the Park Royal & Willesden, which was said to have produced receipts of only 1·04d per car mile and 0·65d per passenger: I am not sure how this was calculated, as I believe the lowest fare was 1d! However, in subsequent returns it was stated that receipts from season and through ticket holders were not included, and that is presumably the case here, resulting in an appreciable distortion of the figures. Over 39,000 passengers used the service. The same applied to the Southall & Westbourne Park service, which was used by over 77,000 passengers, while receipts are shown to be only 2·27d per car mile and 1·69d per passenger.

The final return produced was for the four weeks ended 30th April 1905, and is reproduced herewith. It appears that the Southall & Westbourne Park service carried nearly as many season and through ticket holders as people who held car tickets, while the Southall & Willesden Junction service had about three times as many season and through ticket holders as people who purchased car tickets. Incidentally, there are mistakes in the Stourbridge Town & Stourbridge Jct. service; based on the previous four weeks, the receipts should read £58 6s 7d and the receipts per passenger, 1·156d.

RAIL MOTOR-CAR RECEIPTS FOR 4 WEEKS ENDED 30TH APRIL, 1905.

Date Service commenced.	Motor-Car Centre.	Between	Distance. M.	No. of Passrs. Holding Car Tickets.	No. of Passrs. Seasons, Thro' booked Passrs., &c. (Receipts *not* included).	Receipts from Passengers holding Car Tickets. £ s. d.	Mileage	Receipts per Car Mile.	Receipts per Passenger.	Corresponding 4 Weeks (previous Year). £ s. d.	Increase. £ s. d.	Receipts from Ordinary Train Bookings (previous Year). £ s. d.	Receipts from Ordinary Trains and Rail Motors this year. £ s. d.	Increase. £ s. d.	Decrease. £ s. d.	Remarks.
1903																
12th Oct. ...	Chalford ...	Chalford and Stonehouse...	7	50,743	5,219	346 10 1	5,046	1s. 4·48d.	1·64d.	295 4 11	51 5 2	*330 2 10	386 14 2	56 11 4	...	Supplementing ordinary Train Service.
1904																
1st May ...	Southall ...	Southall and Westbourne Park	10	3,808	3,356	46 14 6	5,398	2·08d.	2·94d.	...	...	47 0 11	107 13 8	60 12 9	...	New Line Service.
1st Oct. ...	Southall ...	Park Royal and Willesden	6¼	2,299	6,561	21 6 11	3,806	1·35d.	2·22d.	...	...	...	...	...	...	
1st May ...	Southall ...	Southall and Brentford ...	3½	26,064	...	190 13 1	6,452	7·09d.	1·76d.	...	...	76 15 1	190 13 1	113 18 0	...	Replaced ordinary Train Service.
1st June ...	Plymouth ...	Plympton and Saltash ..	9½	88,063	14,401	726 14 7	12,111	1s. 2·4d.	1·98d.	...	...	676 9 3	1,269 13 9	593 4 6	...	Supplementing ordinary Train Services.
1st June ...	Plymouth ...	Plymouth and Yealmpton	10¼	9,798	1,316	204 10 4	3,698	1s. 1·27d.	5·01d	...	...	280 3 0	372 11 4	92 8 4	...	
19th June	Plymouth ...	Plymouth and Tavistock (Sundays)	16½	670	28	20 9 1	198	2s. 0·79d.	7·33d.	...	...	...	...	...	...	
1st July ...	Croes Newydd	Wrexham, Gobowen, Llangollen and Llanuwchllyn	37	7,063	...	223 13 9	3,690	1s. 2·55d.	7·6d.	...	...	1,096 1 5	1,332 19 10	236 18 5	...	
1st Oct. ...	Croes Newydd	Wrexham and Coed Poeth	6	16,171	...	302 7 3	2,857	2s. 1·36d.	4·49d.	...	...	191 3 3	554 9 8	363 6 5	...	Replaced ordinary Train Services.
1st Oct. ...	Croes Newydd	Wrexham and Rhos ...	4¼	9,325	...	186 17 3	2,658	1s. 4·87d.	4·81d.	...	...	97 19 1	308 17 2	210 18 1	...	
1st Oct. ...	Ashburton ...	Ashburton and Totnes ...	9¼	7,628	2,901	172 6 8	3,785	10·93d.	5·42d.	...	...	106 11 8	293 14 11	187 3 3	...	
1st Oct. ...	Penzance ...	Penzance and Truro ...	26	3,824	283	110 1 11	2,333	11·33d.	6·91d.	...	...	1,585 18 5	1,570 4 1	...	15 14 4	Supplementing ordinary Train service.
1st Oct. ...	Honeybourne	Honeybourne, Broadway and Winchcombe	12¼	8,203	452	223 5 5	8,472	6·32d.	6·53d.	...	...	...	...	...	...	New Line Service.
1905																
1st Jan. ...	Kidderminster	Kidderminster, Bewdley and Stourport	8¾	10,912	391	125 3 3	2,971	10·11d.	2·75d.	...	...	84 19 8	186 19 6	101 19 10	...	Supplementing ordinary Train Service.
1st Jan. ...	Stourbridge	Stourbridge and Stourbridge Junction	¾	14,182	3,504	68 6 7	1,715	9·56d.	11·56d.	...	...	51 15 6	68 6 7	16 11 1	...	Supplementing ordinary Train Service.
1st Feb. ...	Chippenham	Chippenham and Calne ...	5½	5,860	209	167 7 3	3,063	1s. 1·11d.	6·8d.	...	...	81 0 4	167 7 3	86 6 11	...	Replaced ordinary Train Service.
1st Feb. ...	Truro ...	Truro and Newquay ...	18½	7,526	574	273 9 4	6,265	10·48d.	8·72d.	...	...	...	...	...	...	New Line Service.
1st Mar. ...	Stourbdg. Jn.	Old Hill and Halesowen ...	1½	6,180	2,600	41 13 3	1,361	7·34d.	1·62d.	...	...	33 16 7	41 13 3	7 16 8	...	Supplementing ordinary Train Services.
1st Mar. ...	Stourbdg. Jn.	Langley Green and Oldbury	¾	5,051	2,000	21 16 11	984	5·33d.	1·04d.	...	...	13 10 8	21 16 11	8 6 3	...	
1st Mar. ...	Brynamman	Brynamman and Llandilo	14¼	11,751	...	160 16 2	2,169	1s. 5·79d.	3·28d.	...	...	182 16 1	236 12 8	53 16 7	...	
2nd Apl. ..	Stourbdg. Jn.	Stourbridge Junction and Stourport (Sundays)	13	2,707	...	44 5 8	984	10·8d.	3·92d.	...	...	...	...	...	...	
3rd Apl. ...	Swansea ...	Swansea E. Dk. and Glyn Neath	15½	12,558	...	204 7 6	4,328	11·33d.	3·91d.	...	...	55 5 1	216 0 6	160 15 5	...	New Line Service.
16th Apl. ...	Southall ...	Clapham Jcn. and West Ealing (Sundays)	14	1,698	2,799	27 13 0	1,689	3·92d.	3·91d.	...	...	...	...	...	...	...
		Total ...		312,084	46,594	3,910 9 9	86,033	10·91d.	3·07d.	295 4 11	51 5 2	4,991 8 10	7,320 8 4	2,350 13 10	15 14 4	
				358,678												

* Ordinary Trains and Rail Motors.

Power unit of Cars 1 and 2 with 3ft 8in wheels.

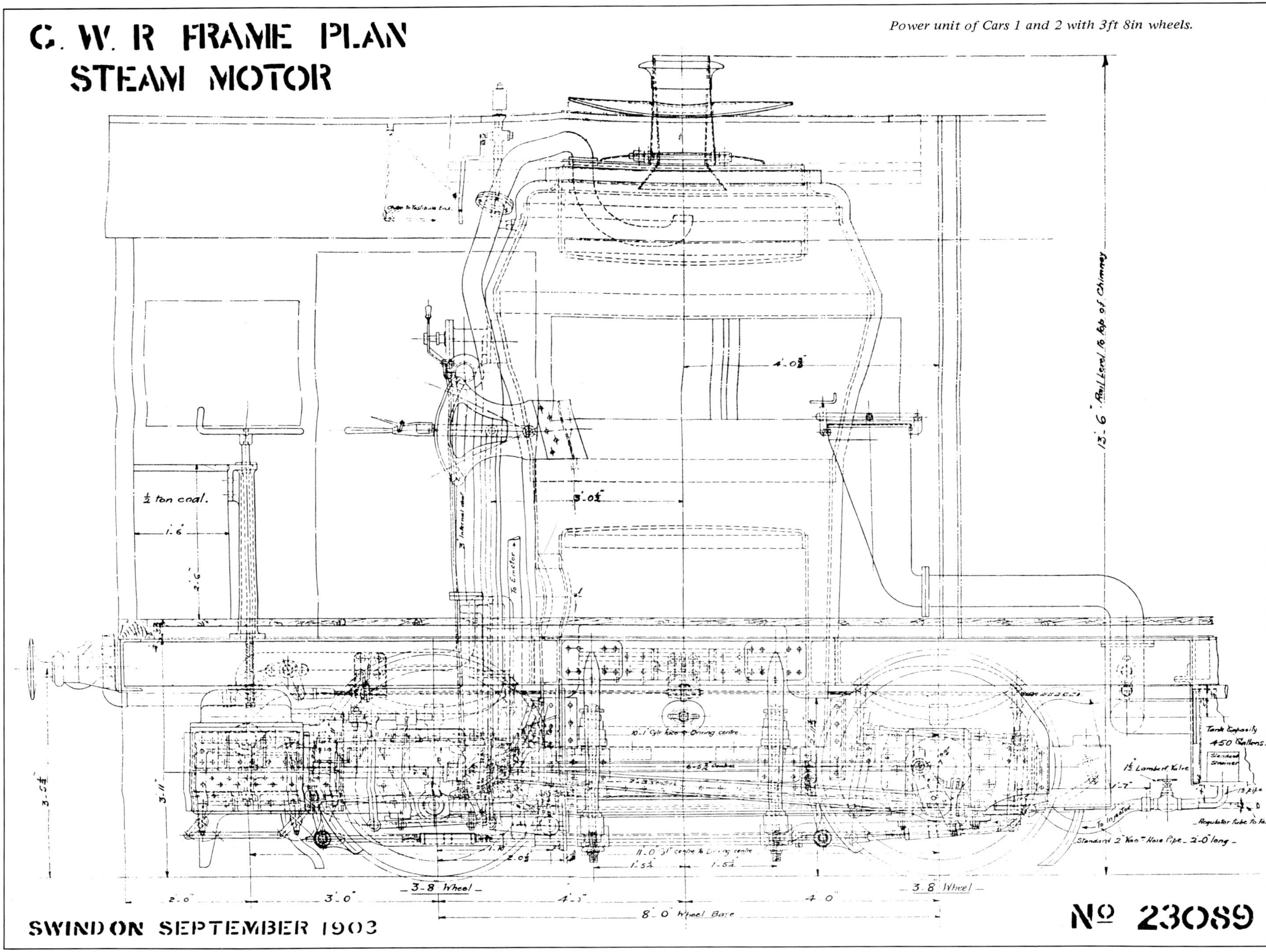

CHAPTER THREE

THE STEAM RAIL MOTOR POWER UNITS

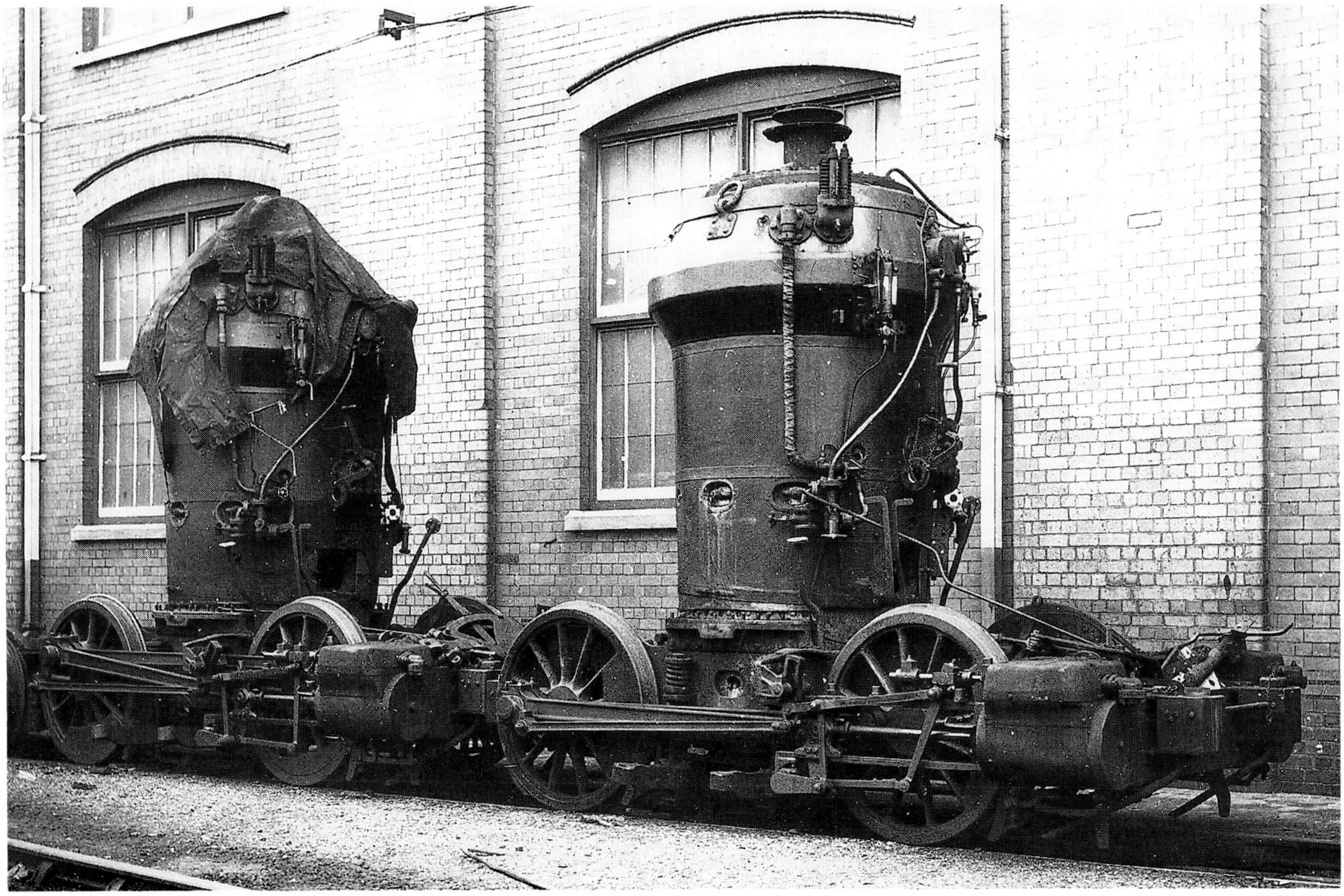

Two power units with boilers in a partly dismantled state at Swindon. H. F. WHEELLER, CTY. R. C. RILEY

THIS chapter deals with the standard SRM power units: the engine (i.e. the power bogie, less the boiler) and the boiler itself. The non-standard power units of SRMs 15 and 16 are dealt with in the chapter on those cars.

NUMBERING

A GWR Steam Rail Motor consisted of three basic parts. With few exceptions, these three main components were apparently interchangeable, and each were numbered in a separate series:

The Carriage: this included the underframe, the coach body and the trailing bogie. These were numbered from 1 to 99 in a 'Rail Motor' series, and the whole vehicle was usually known by this number.

The 'Engine': or 'power bogie' – this consisted of the power unit less the boiler: i.e. the cylinders, motion, driving wheels and bogie frame and associated pipework. The engines were given numbers in an 08xx and 09xx series, and were displayed together with the building date on a small brass plate on the power bogie front stretcher, and so are often visible (but not legible) in photographs. In some official documents, these numbers are typewritten "O.8xx".

The Boiler: these were mostly given numbers in a series starting at 1000, the exceptions being those built for SRMs 1 and 2 which were numbered 111 and 112, and those for Nos.15 and 16 which were 894 and 895.

The GWR tended to call the power bogie (complete with its boiler) the 'motor', although they sometimes referred to complete SRMs as 'motors'. This is presumably the derivation of the expression 'motor train' for an auto train, eventually regardless of whether it comprised a locomotive and trailers, or an SRM.

DIAGRAMS

The GWR produced slightly simplified drawings of their rail motors which showed the side and end elevations, plus a seating plan. These were grouped together in a *Diagram Book* about 1907, and each page was given an index code which eventually ran from A to U.

By the time the *Diagram Book* was compiled, many early cars had been modified: for example, droplights had been substituted for some of the original large fixed windows, and the passenger compartment divided into smoking and non-smoking saloons. These *modified* cars were shown on Diagrams with simple index letter codes: 'A', 'B', etc.

The early cars had of course been built without the droplights, and with a single passenger compartment, and contrary to usual practice, the diagrams showing the *unmodified* cars in their original state were given '1' suffixes ('A1', 'B1', etc). However, there was one exception to this process: diagrams Q and Q1 differed only in their doors, and Dia. Q cars were *not* rebuilt from Dia. Q1 cars.

Presumably because SRMs were hybrids, there were two different sets of diagrams. One gave details of the boiler, as built, the capacity of the water tank and coal bunker, the size of the cylinders, the wheel diameters and the car's 'tractive force'. These diagrams also showed the weight distribution of the cars, usually both full and empty, and are believed to be for the benefit of the Locomotive Department, and will be referred to as such. The other set of diagrams, presumably for more general use, omitted all the specialist power unit informa-

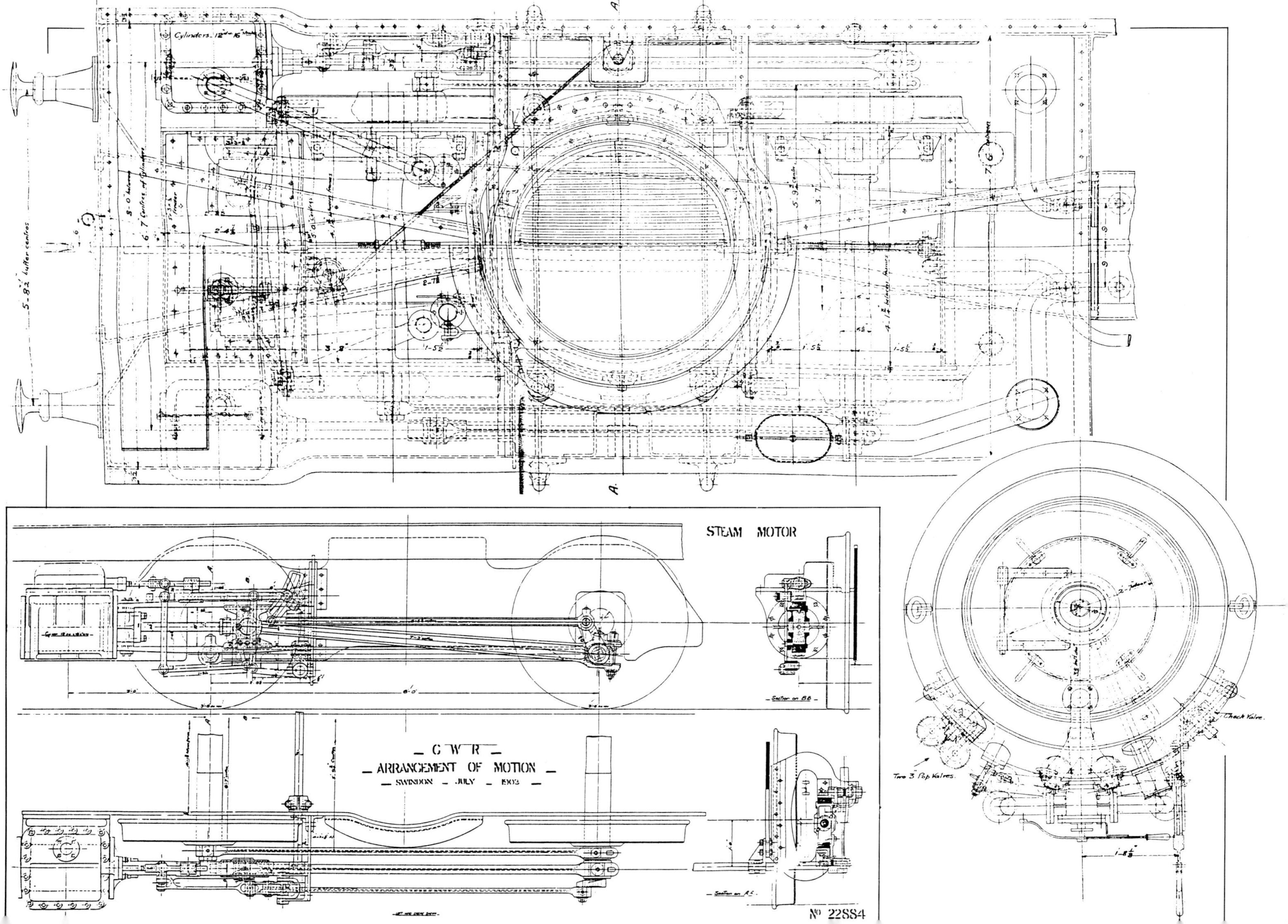
STEAM MOTOR
— G W R —
— ARRANGEMENT OF MOTION —
— SWINDON — JULY — 1903 —
No 22SS4
Cylinders 12" dia 16" stroke
5-8½ buffer centres
8-0 between
6-7 Centres of Cylinders
Check Valve.
Two 3" Pop Valves.
Section on B.B.
Section on A.C.
7-6
3-7
5-9½ centres
2-7½
3-8
1-8½

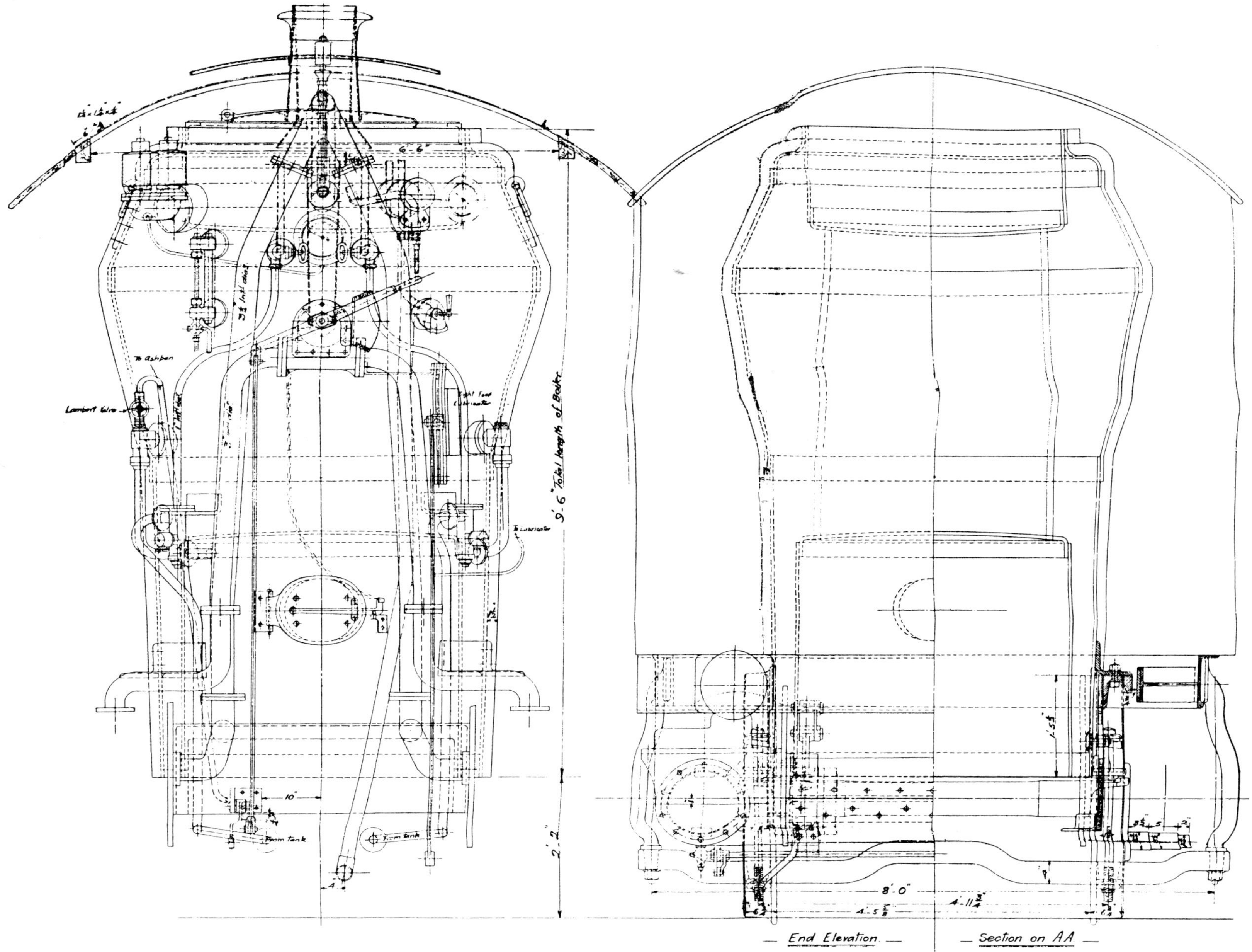

Power units of Cars 1 and 2.

Power unit with 3ft 6½in wheels.

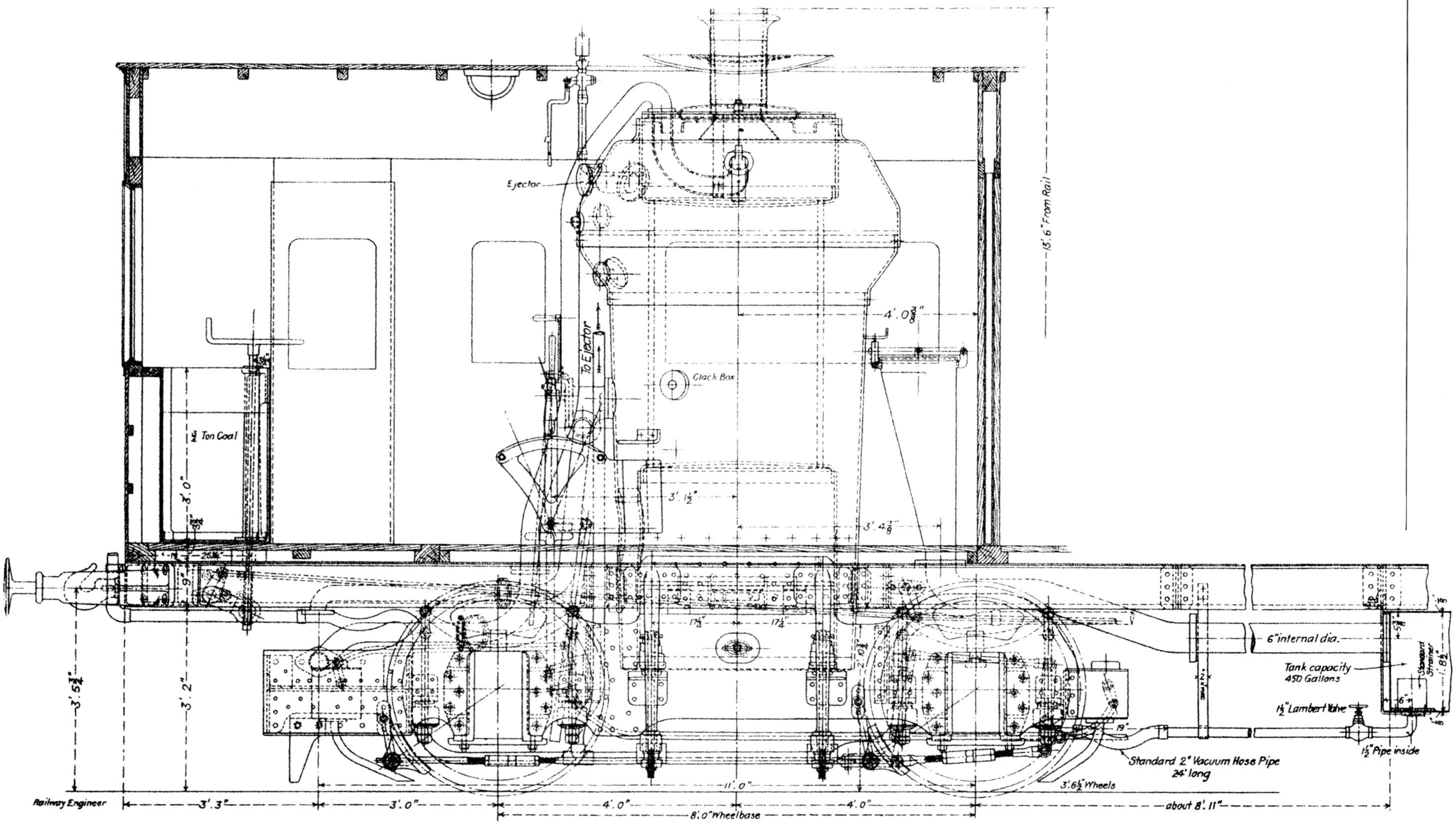

Arrangement of Steam Motor—Sectional Elevation.

tion. The same diagram index codes were used with both sets.

ENGINES

The GWR eventually owned 99 SRM carriages, built by or for it. To power these there were 112 engines of four types, the second and third of which may be regarded as standard types:

1. Nos.0801 and 0802, which worked under cars 1 and 2 respectively, had 3ft 8in diameter wheels.
2. Nos.0803–0836 had 3ft 6½in wheels.
3. Nos.0837–0863 and 0866–0912 had 4ft 0in diameter wheels.
4. Nos.0864 and 0865, which were completely non-standard, had 3ft 5in diameter wheels and were part of cars 15 and 16 respectively. They were of the 2–2–0 wheel arrangement, whilst all others were 0–4–0s. *The comments which follow do not apply to these two engines, their boilers, or to their cars, 15 and 16.*

All engines had 12in diameter × 16in stroke outside cylinders driving on the rear wheels of the bogie. The frames were of ⅞in steel plate set 4ft 1¾in apart, and the four coupled wheels were at 8ft 0in wheelbase. Outside Walschaerts valve gear was employed. Balanced overhead 'D' type slide valves were used, and were set up to have 1⅞in steam lap, 1/16in positive exhaust lap and 4½in maximum travel with a constant lead of ⅛in. This meant the valves had quite long travel in relation to the 16in stroke. The cylinders were bolted to the main bogie frames with centres 1in below the driving wheel centre. The crossheads were made of cast steel with ⅛in white metal bearing surfaces. The connecting and coupled roads were of forged steel of 'I' section and were provided with adjustable bronze bearings.

The coach portion of the SRM was suspended from the engine by a swing link suspension, developed from the Dean carriage bogies. This employed two large scroll irons riveted to the solebars on each side of the coach, attached at their lower ends to a pair of beams extending across the car, passing underneath the engine main frames. Swing links were attached to these beams and to the outside of the main frames just above axle height using ball-and-cup joints, the lower ones of which incorporated a coil spring round a suspension bolt. This arrangement allowed the bogie to turn about 5 degrees relative to the coach portion – equivalent to a displacement of about 8 inches in either direction at the cylinders. A lateral movement of ¾in was also allowed in either direction. The primary suspension was provided by leaf springs acting on the coupled wheel axleboxes. These springs were positioned behind the frames.

On all engines, the scroll irons and swing links were positioned symmetrically about the boiler centre line. On engines with 3ft 8in or 3ft 6½in diameter driving wheels, the scroll irons and swing links were positioned 2ft

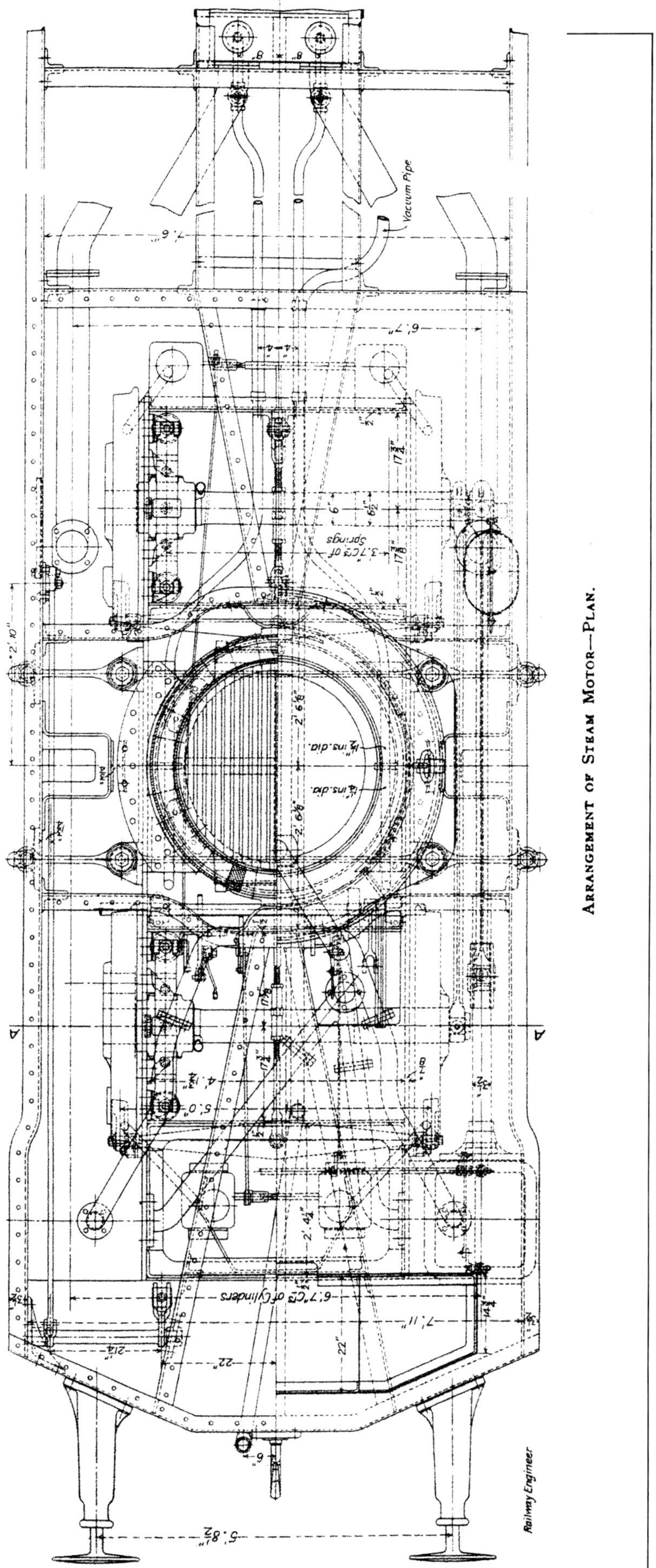

Power unit with 3ft 6½in wheels.

10½in apart, and the vertical centre line of the boiler was at the mid-point of the wheelbase. However, on the frame plan for cars with 4ft diameter drivers, the scroll irons and swing links were only 2ft 4in apart, and the boiler centre line is shown as displaced 2 inches to the rear in relation to the wheelbase – i.e. the distance from the leading axle to the boiler centre line was 4ft 2in, and the distance to the rear driving axle was 3ft 10in. On the cars with 3ft 6½in drivers, the distance from the centre of the cylinders to the driving axle centre was 11ft 0in, while on the engines with 4ft diameter wheels this distance was 11ft 2in.

Between the attachment points for the swing links, the engine frames were extended upwards and bowed outwards to clear the lower part of the boiler casing. Around the top of the frame here was attached a heavy cast bracket on which a similar bracket attached to the boiler casing rested, the boiler being attached to the engine's frames by 12 bolts through each of these brackets. The boiler, therefore, was carried entirely by the engine frames and not by the carriage portion's underframe.

Rear sandboxes were attached to the rear of the rear engine frame stretcher, whilst the front boxes were originally inside the frames, behind the cylinders and attached to a the front of a cross member positioned at the rear of the cylinders, and this is the arrangement shown on the frame plans. Dry sand was used. However, later photographs show the front sandboxes to have been repositioned so that they were attached to the front of the front bogie stretcher; this change may have been recorded as the fitting of dry sand boxes to the cars.

The 450-gallon water tank was carried on the carriage portion's underframe. Water for the boiler was taken via a strainer inside the tank and a 1½in internal diameter pipe having a 'Lambert' valve (i.e. one with a hand wheel). The flexible connection to the pipework leading to the injector was provided by a 2ft length of standard 2in vacuum hose pipe.

Engines with 4ft diameter wheels were introduced early in 1905 on the diagram K1 70ft cars, and were intended to reduce wear on the moving parts – particularly at speeds above 30 mph. At the same time this reduced the tractive efficiency slightly, and presumably lowered the acceleration rates that could be expected, although it is questionable to what extent this would have been noticeable in practice.

TRACTIVE EFFORT

The tractive effort (T.E.) in lbs developed by a two-cylinder locomotive is usually calculated by the formula:

$$\frac{(\text{cylinder diameter})^2 \times \text{cylinder stroke} \times \text{boiler pressure} \times E\%}{\text{driving wheel diameter}}$$

Nominal efficiency (E% above) is usually taken as about 80%. The GWR Locomotive Department's copies of the SRM Diagrams have the T.E. (shown as 'Tractive Force') marked on them, but there are a few points worth noting:

1. The nominal efficiency used was 90% in most cases.
2. According to various sources, boiler 111, fitted to car No.1 (Diagrams A1 and A) worked at 180 lbs/sq in, giving 8,483 lbs tractive force or 140 lbs/sq in, giving 6,598 lbs tractive force. Boiler 112 used on car No.2, according to the diagrams, worked at 140 lbs/sq in.
3. All other standard GWR SRM boilers worked at 160 lbs/sq in.
4. The tractive force for those engines fitted with 3ft 6½in driving wheels was 7,806 lbs (at 90% efficiency).
5. The tractive force for those engines fitted with 4ft driving wheels was 6,912 lbs (at 90%).

Diagram B1 shows a smaller than usual boiler, and an engine with 3ft 6½in wheels working at the standard 160 lbs/sq in. This diagram shows the tractive force as only 6,702 lbs, but it should have been 7,806 lbs at the standard 90% – a boiler's size does not affect the engine's nominal tractive effort. Diagram F1, for some reason, also shows a tractive force of 6,702 lbs.

The Port Talbot Railway car, illustrated by GWR diagram S, is shown as developing 9,792 lbs T.E., whereas it should have been 9,216 lbs at 90%. Its boiler pressure was 170 lbs/sq in.

OTHER RECORDS

In the Public Record Office, Kew, there are a number of different records relating to the GWR's steam rail motors. These include:

Engine History Cards: these are small, buff-coloured cards, about postcard size, showing which car the

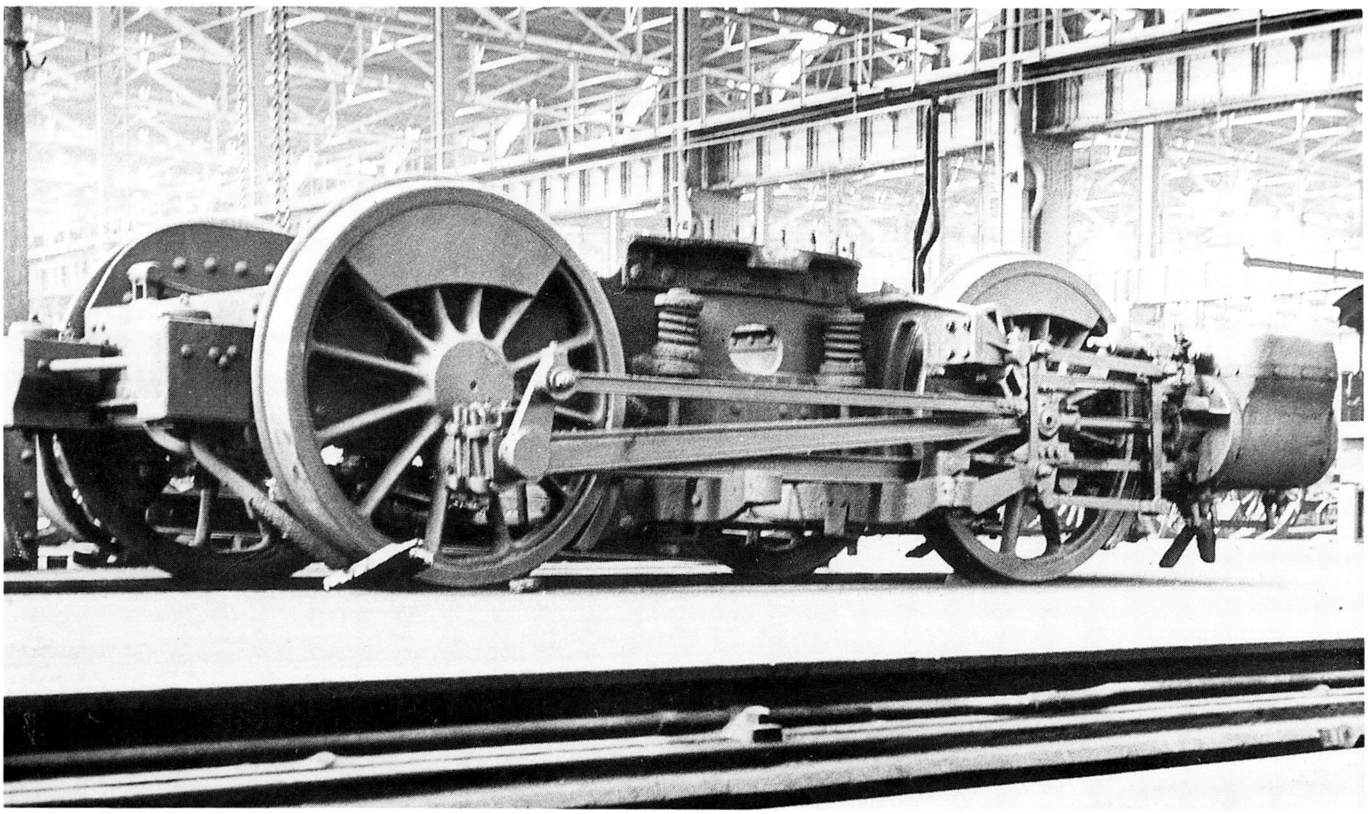

A steam rail motor engine without a boiler in Swindon Works. COLLECTION R. C. RILEY

The arrangement of valve gear on power units with 3ft 6½in wheels.

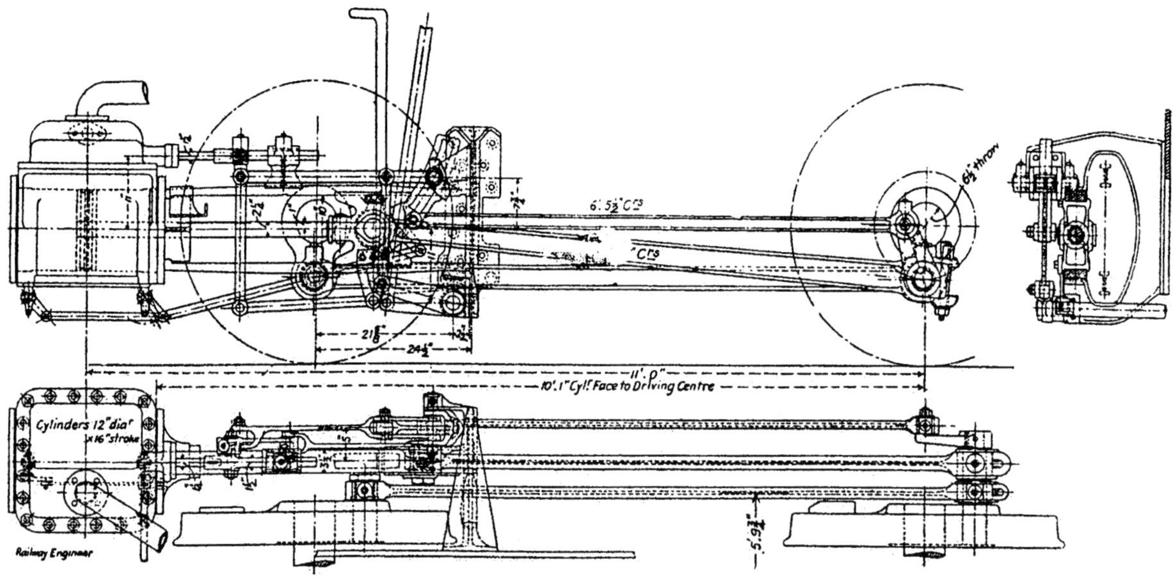

ARRANGEMENT OF VALVE GEAR.

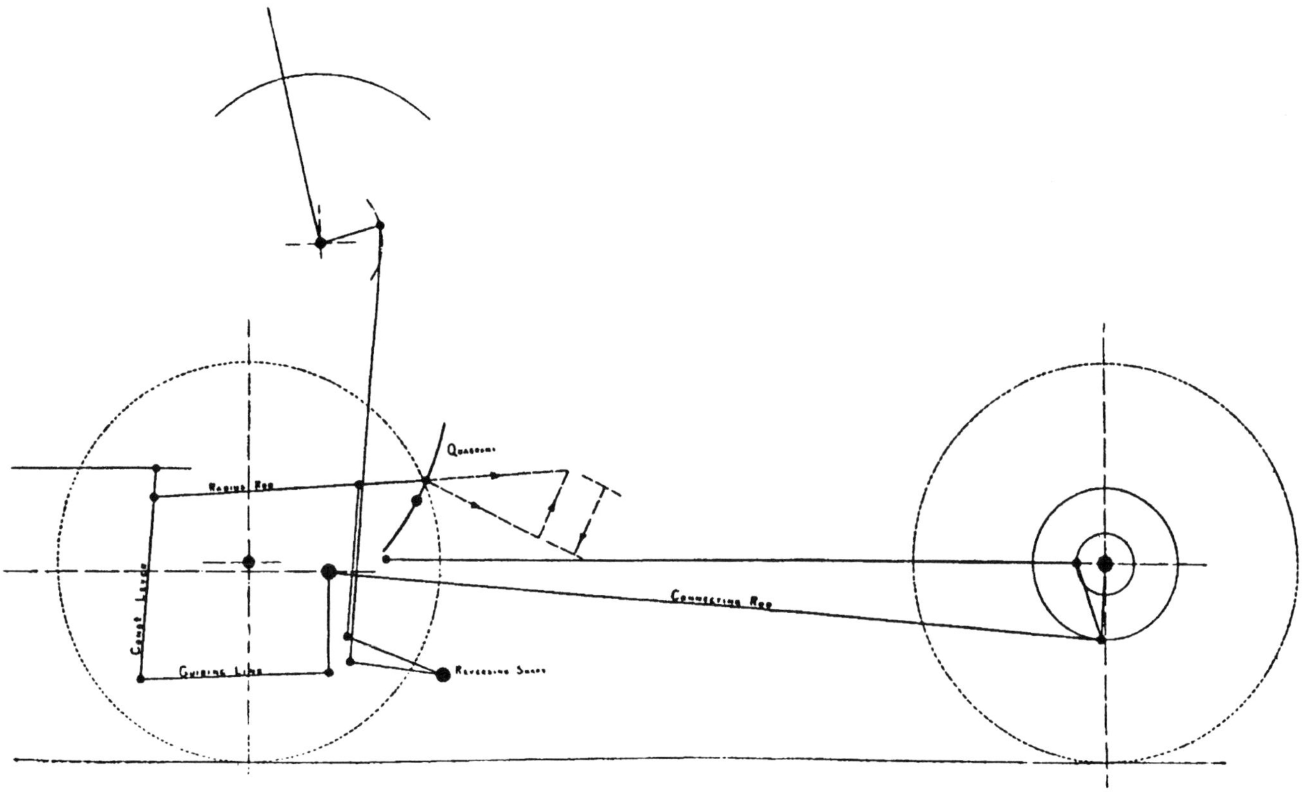

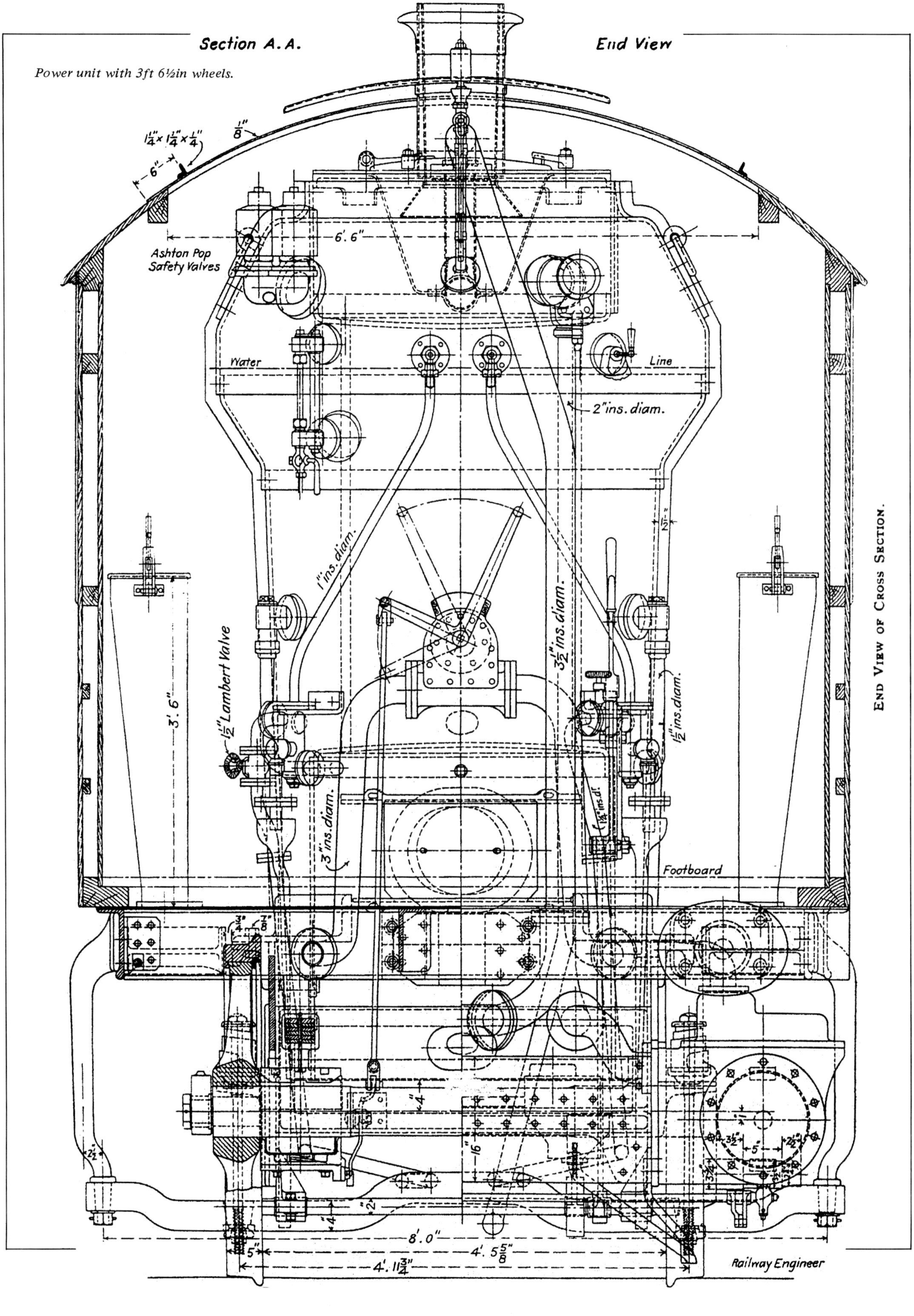

Power unit with 3ft 6½in wheels.

A 4ft diameter wheeled power unit complete with boiler at Swindon, showing the regulator handle, the cut-off lever with its quadrant, the safety valve and the boiler lifting ring. The chimney had been removed.

engine was fitted to, and when; they are attached to a much larger card which has similar information, and sometimes shows the cost of some repairs, and which boiler was fitted. The cards show on which order they were built, and usually where, but unfortunately the space for the number of the drawing to which they relate was not filled in – sometimes they show simply '70ft car'.

Boiler History Cards: a similar set of cards, but only normally showing the car in which they were fitted.

Car History Cards: another similar set, which usually give the boiler fitted.

Unfortunately, these history card records are incomplete. It would appear that a new system was started c.1912–14, and only a few cards covering histories before then survive. However, there is also an *SRM Register* started in 1904 which lists when each car was stopped for maintenance, where, for how long, and the category of repairs. It lists car mileages and boiler changes, but not engine data. Some of the information has been lost because of repairs to the book.

It was replaced by a further system of 'Engine History Cards' – which were identified by *car* – from about 1928, showing the engine fitted as well as the other stoppage information. These cards were large, nearly A3 in size. With such a number of different records covering steam rail motors, their components and their conversion to auto trailers, it is not surprising that there are occasional discrepancies.

BOILERS

CONSTRUCTION

The boilers were attached to the tops of the frames via curved angle irons bolted to the boiler shell each side. The boilers themselves were vertical multitubular types, 9ft 6in or 9ft 8in high and tapered gently outwards from the base to just below the normal water level where they widened sharply to a ring, and then tapered inwards towards the top.

A central chimney, which projected through the car's roof, was provided for the boiler's exhaust. Around the chimney, a plate protected

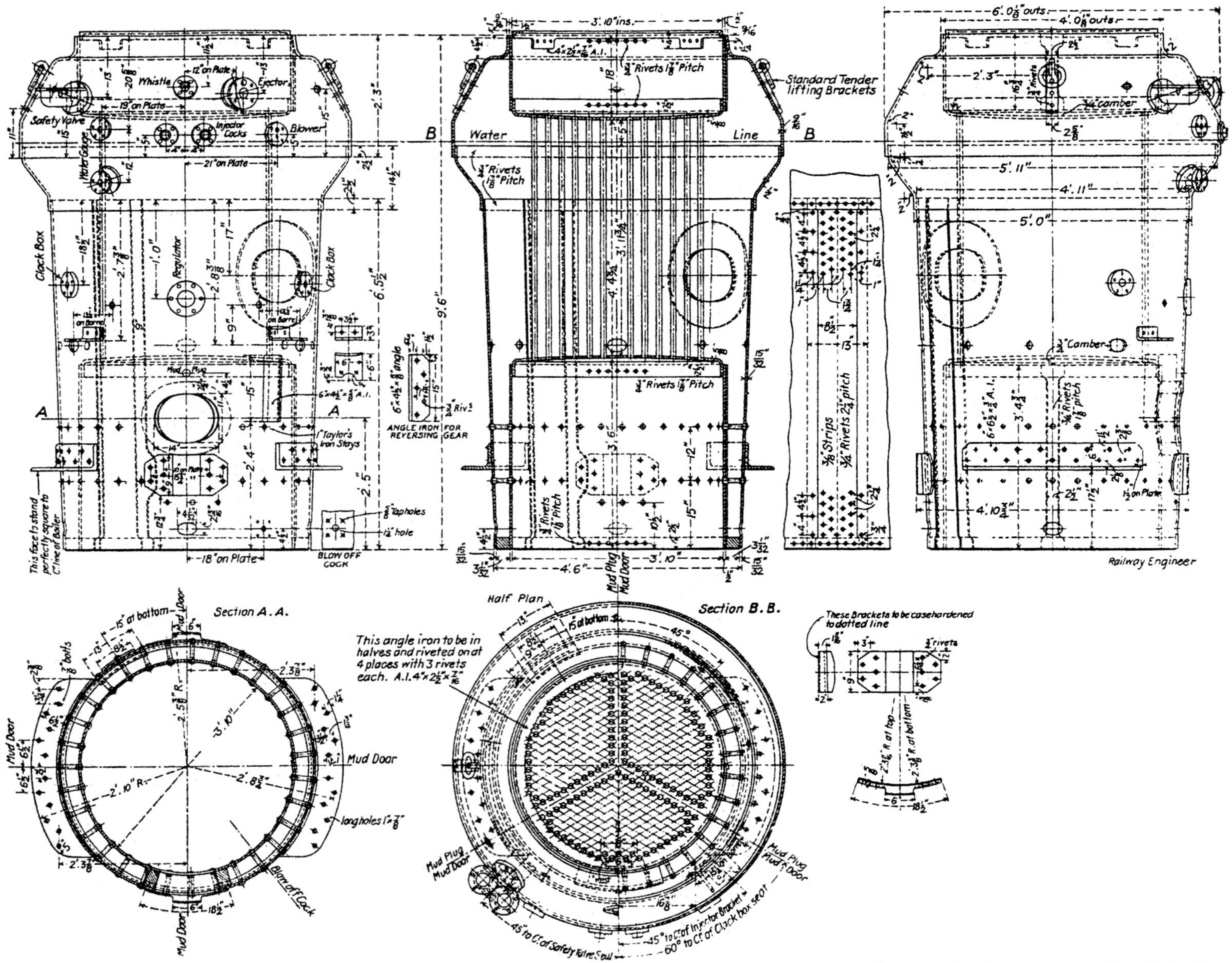

BOILER.

Example of boiler for power unit with 3ft 6½in wheels.

the roof; this plate appeared to be attached to the chimney, and followed the roof profile, although it was clear of the roof. Ashton 'pop' safety valves were fitted to the boiler a little to one side of the centre line, and they exhausted through a hole in the roof and the protective plate. A whistle was mounted on the centre line in front of the chimney.

The boiler was of such height that, with the firebox, it extended well below the carriage underframe level, which meant that the power bogie could not have a conventional centre pin. The swing link suspension was only designed to control the bogie rotary motion relative to the car body, and it was not intended to be able to transmit the propulsion and braking forces generated between the bogie and the coach underframe. The GWR's solution to this problem was to make the boiler itself transmit the propulsion and braking forces through sprung buffers fore and aft of the boiler. These buffers were attached to the coach underframe, and bore onto a rubbing plate attached to the boiler, one just below the firebox door, and the other at the opposite side of the boiler. The buffer heads and the rubbing strips were case-hardened.

In total, the GWR had 120 boilers for its 99 cars.

The surviving boiler history cards show their drawing numbers as follows:

Boilers	*Drawing No.*
111 and 112	Not shown (cars 1 and 2)
894 and 895	29171.(cars 15 and 16)
1001–3	Cards missing
1004–12, 1019–30, 1036–1074	24021
1075–1127	28051

Boilers 1013–18 and 1031–35, assuming they existed, were not used on steam rail motors.

The following grouping of boilers is unofficial, and mostly comes from the diagrams. It is possible that the boilers were (or became) standardised as indicated in the history cards. Most boilers were interchangeable, and apart from 111, 112, 894, 895, and possibly 1001–3, were regularly moved between engines and between cars, so it is difficult to be certain which boiler fell into which group.

TYPE I BOILERS

Boilers 111 and 112, as shown on diagrams A1 and A, were 9ft 6in high and had a minimum diameter of 4ft, a maximum of 6ft and were fitted with 477 tubes 1⅛in diameter, 4ft 4¾in long. The firebox was 3ft 6in high and 3ft 9⅞in diameter. The grate area was 11·46 sq ft and the total heating surface is given as 669·92 sq ft. As far as is known, these boilers were only used on cars 1 and 2, in conjunction with engines 0801 and 0802 respectively. Boiler 111 was removed from car No.1 by October 1913 and was condemned in February 1914; 112 was removed from car No.2 by January 1915. The A1 and A diagrams and the frame plan show that cars 1 and 2 had fairly short chimneys with a lip. Photographs, however, show them to have been fitted with an extension like a short stovepipe.

TYPE II BOILERS

Loco. Dept. diagram B1 shows cars Nos.3–5, which were originally fitted with boilers 1001–03. This diagram illustrates boilers which were rather smaller than usual, 9ft 6in high with a minimum diameter of 3ft 11in and a maximum of 5ft 5⅛in They were fitted with only 333 tubes of 1⅛in diameter and 4ft 4¾in long; a grate with an area of only 8·4 sq ft and a total heating surface of 475·54 sq ft – a reduction of 29% over the first two boilers. 1001 was removed from car 3 by January 1906, but no records seem to survive of its subsequent allocations. 1002 was in car 2 until September 1905, and then was reported to have been with car 6 from January to April 1909, and car 76 from March until September 1909. Boiler 1003 was removed from car 5 in May 1905, and was put in car 4 from October 1905 until August 1906, which seems to be its last recorded use. It may be significant that the boiler history cards for 1001–3 seem not to have survived.

SUBSEQUENT STANDARD DIMENSIONS

After boiler 1003, future examples were all 9ft 8in high with a minimum diameter of 4ft 6in and a maximum one of 6ft 0⅛in The firebox was 3ft 10in diameter and, except as noted below, 3ft 6in high with a heating surface of 46·75 sq. ft. The firegrate had an area of 11·54 sq. ft. Most of the subsequent differences between the different types of boiler relate to the boiler tubes.

TYPE III BOILERS

There are two versions of the Locomotive Department's copy of diagram D1. One version (cars 10 and 14) shows the same boiler as on diagrams C, F1, F, G1, G and J (but not the earlier diagram J1), and seems to have been a standard boiler having 477 tubes 1⅛in diameter, 4ft 4¾in long. The total heating area is shown as 672·33 sq ft. Diagram C is marked as applying to cars 3–8, which includes those shown on the earlier diagram B1 and on diagram B. As noted above, the tractive force shown on diagram F1 was only 6,702 lbs.

TYPE IV BOILERS

The other version of the Locomotive Department's copy of diagram D1 shows cars 10 (deleted) and 14 fitted with a boiler having 317 tubes 1¾in diameter, 4ft 5½in long. The total heating surface is given as 647·36 sq ft. The original boilers in these cars were 1010 and 1022, of which the latter is known to have survived until August 1925, but it is not known if it was retubed.

TYPE V BOILERS

The boilers shown on diagrams H, K1, K, J1, M1, M and N differ from the Type III design by having 462 tubes 1⅛in diameter and 4ft 5½in long, giving a total heating surface of 652·65 sq ft. This seems to have been a second standard boiler.

TYPE VI BOILERS

Diagrams O, P, Q and Q1 show a third standard boiler with 420 × 1¼in tubes, 4ft 5½in long and the firebox as being 3ft 5⅞in high and 3ft 10in diameter, giving a total heating area of 659·24 sq. ft.

TYPE VII BOILERS

Diagrams P and T show cars 59 and 60 to have been fitted with boilers differing from the Type VI design only in having one boiler tube less – 419 tubes – so the heating surface was correspondingly reduced to 657·78 sq ft. When new, these cars were fitted with boilers 1095 and 1093 respectively, although both boilers went to other cars in the autumn of 1906.

TYPE VIII BOILERS

Not shown on any of the diagrams, but some boiler history cards record that they were retubed with 317 second-hand tubes of 1⅝ inches diameter. For example, boiler 1072 was so altered in July 1927, 1069 in June 1928 and 1075 in March 1929. Boiler 1062 seems to have 317 tubes fitted in February 1914 and again in April 1926.

INTERCHANGE

Because the surviving records are incomplete, we do not know all car + engine + boiler combinations, but the following would appear to be the case (ignoring cars 15 and 16):

Boiler 111 was always fitted on engine 0801 in car 1. 0801 only ran under car 1.

Boiler 112 was always fitted on engine 0802 in car 2. 0802 only ran under car 2.

Both 0801 and 0802 were eventually fitted with different boilers, and finally cars 1 and 2 were fitted with different engines; 0801 and 0802 were condemned in November 1914 and scrapped.

Boilers with numbers 1001 and above would appear to have been interchangeable, although there seems to be only one surviving recorded use of boilers 1001–3 other than in cars 3–6.

Engines 0803 – 0836 had 3ft 6½in driving wheels, and seem to have only been interchanged between cars that were originally fitted with engines in this group, plus cars 1 and 2. Cars to diagrams B1–D1, F1–H1, J1 and L1 were originally fitted with these engines.

Engines 0837–63, 0866–0900, 0904–12 had 4ft driving wheels, and seem to have been regularly interchanged between those cars that were originally fitted with engines in this group. However, a limited number were eventually fitted to cars originally paired with engines having 3ft 6½in or 3ft 8in drivers, and car 30 outlived all engines with the small drivers. Examples are shown in Table 4.

Two apparently recently repaired power units at Swindon, said to be in 1932. The number on the boiler of the nearer one appears to read 1084, in which case the photo was probably taken in 1931. In November that year it was mounted on engine O861 and the power unit was fitted to Car No. 58. Again the chimneys were absent. T. E. LAYNE

It would appear that only seven engines with 4ft drivers were fitted to cars built for 3ft 6½in drivers, so it is possible that they had to be modified for this work. The engines involved were 0851, 0852, 0886, 0887 and 0891–93.

Although carriage portions, engines and boilers were normally ordered together, new cars were not necessarily put into service with the boiler and/or engine unit that was ordered with it. Engines 0851/52/54/58/63, 0886–88 and 0891–96 were apparently originally spares, as were boilers 1036/37/41, 1061–69, 1094, 1096–1108 and 1125–27. The Minutes of the Locomotive, Carriage & Stores Committee meeting on 31st October 1908 record:

> 'The Locomotive Superintendent reports that in cases of extensive repairs to motor cars the time these vehicles are out of traffic would be considerably lessened if spare engines and boilers were available to enable those requiring a thorough overhaul to be changed and he therefore recommended the construction of six spare motor car engines and boilers at a cost of £6,900. It was agreed to recommend the expenditure to the Board.'

However, this proposal seems not to have been put to the Board, and the additional engines were not built.

TABLE 4

SRMs - ENGINES (3 ft 6 in Drivers) REPLACED BY ENGINES (4 ft Drivers)

Car	*Engine*	*Boiler*	*From*	*To*	*Comments*
1	891	1124	Mar 15	Jun 17	Car to Trailer
3	851	1007	Sep 13	Jan 15	Car to Trailer.
5	891	1101	Jul 12	Nov 13	
14	893	1113	Nov 11	Nov 13	
17	893	1120	Jan 15	Apr 18	Car to trailer, boiler cond Apr 18.
18	892	1116	Dec 13	Aug 14	Engine then spare until Dec 23
19	892	1126	Jan 10	Apr 11	
19	851	1065	Jun 15	Aug 18	Car to Trailer.
22	852	1078	Nov 14	Sep 19	Car to Trailer
26	851	1094	Feb 12	May 13	
26	887	1056	Oct 14	Jul 16	Car to Trailer
28	892	1105	Feb 12	Apr 13	
28	887	1074	Apr 13	Jan 14	
29	886	1095	Apr 14	Aug 16	Car reverted to 3 ft. 6½ in. drivers
30	892	1045	Dec 23	Mar 24	Engine then spare until Aug 24.
30	892	1058	Aug 24	May 26	
30	891	1086	May 26	Sep 29	Engine cond 23 Aug 30.
30	892	1040	Sep 29	Oct 35	Cond. with car 30: Apr 35.
33	886	1079	Mar 17	Dec 19	Car to Trailer
33	886	1079	Jun 17	Dec 19	Car to Trailer
34	892	1042	Jan 09	Sep 09	
34	891	1074	Jul 18	Nov 22	Car to Trailer
36	886	1050	Oct 12	Nov 13	
41	892	?	May 07	Oct 08	Car reverted to 3 ft. 6½ in. drivers

THE POWER UNITS IN SERVICE

There were, inevitably, a number of problems with the power units, some of which were inherent in the general design adopted. These were considered by the Swindon Engineering Society at a meeting chaired by Mr G. H. Burrows on Tuesday, 12th March 1906 at the GWR Mechanics Institution. At this meeting, a paper was read by Mr A. H. Nash on 'The Construction of Steam Rail Motors' which was followed by a discussion. Unfortunately, this is too long to quote in its entirety, but what follows is partly based on the report of this meeting (*Transactions* 1906–7, Pages 241–254, with drawings).

As indicated above, removal of the boiler (which had to be done before the power unit could be removed from the car) was awkward, and, no doubt, quite time consuming. The main problem was that the boiler had to be lifted through the roof of the car, and this in turn required a 23ft lift from rail level. Consequently, this could only be done at the main works and at sheds which had the use of a breakdown crane, or could borrow one. Mr H. Holcroft said at the 1906 meeting that 'this brought about a good deal of empty running as the boilers were often coming out for attention'.

To start with, the cars suffered particularly from hard water, causing problems with the tubes, and problems with scale being deposited round the feed pipe inlet. This was overcome, partly by a deflector pipe fitted in the boiler, and generally as water-softening plants were installed round the system.

Although the power unit frames were well braced, there were initially problems with the cylinders: due to the inevitable racking strains, the cylinders tended to work loose on the frames. The cure was found to be additional bolts attaching the cylinders to the frames. The earlier cars in particular were found to suffer generally from this racking action, and stiffer angle irons and plates had to be used. Care was also necessary to ensure that all the rivets of the frames were properly closed-up tightly.

A major source of trouble proved to be the high centre of gravity of the boiler, and the way it was only supported on each side by angle irons bolted to the bogie and to the boiler shell. These angle irons covered a total of 74 degrees on each side of the boiler, leaving 106 degrees at both front and rear of the boiler unsupported, because of the fire hole and other fittings. The centre of gravity was about 4ft above the level of the angle brackets, and as this part of the boiler was full of water, there were considerable fore and aft forces acting on the bogie, which in turn caused problems with the ride of the car. There was not a lot that could be done about this particular problem, apart from ensuring that all bolts and rivets were tight, although an apparently serious suggestion was made at the 1906 meeting that the boiler should be held in place by guy rods or wires, which would have their lower ends fastened to the car underframe. This was considered not to be really practicable as the forward tie rod would get in the way of the fireman, and the rear one would have intruded into the passenger or luggage accommodation.

The relatively short wheelbase of the power unit, combined with the outside cylinders, the leaf springs of the primary suspension, and the influence of the boiler could set up a vertical vibration which was transmitted to the coach portion through the scroll irons as a cyclic up-and-down motion that increased to a maximum, then decreased to a minimum, or zero, and then started up again. This was the result of vibrations of two different periods being superimposed.

The buffers used to transmit the traction and braking forces to the underframe via the boiler were initially provided with different springing arrangements, one having a coil spring that was adjustable by means of a nut, and the other having a laminated spring. This arrangement was presumably to provide a degree of simple adjustment, and to prevent the buffers setting up their own sympathetic vibrations, which could have occurred if springs with similar characteristics were used in both. However, in practice it was found that the adjusting nut on the plunger of the coil spring could work loose, and if this happened 'the underframe receives a severe blow in alternate directions twice every revolution' of the driving wheels, 'which soon reveals any defects in the woodwork of the body. A ride in a car with a slack buffing spring is not easily forgotten' (*Transactions*). This problem was overcome by replacing the coil springs by laminated.

Habitually running the cars above their design speed of 30 mph led to increased wear of the motion and bearings, though this was partly reduced by the introduction of units with 4ft wheels. In this context, the '50 mph on the level', which SRMs were said to achieve,

80
16

This picture, taken at Swindon to show work on the extension to 'A' Shop, shows from the left: Car No. 80 of Diagram Q, No. 16 of Diagram E, No. 77 also of Diagram Q and SRM boiler 1036 which was built in November 1904 and lasted until February 1928. All three SRMs are seen in the lined lake livery. The date was probably May-July 1915. NATIONAL RAILWAY MUSEUM

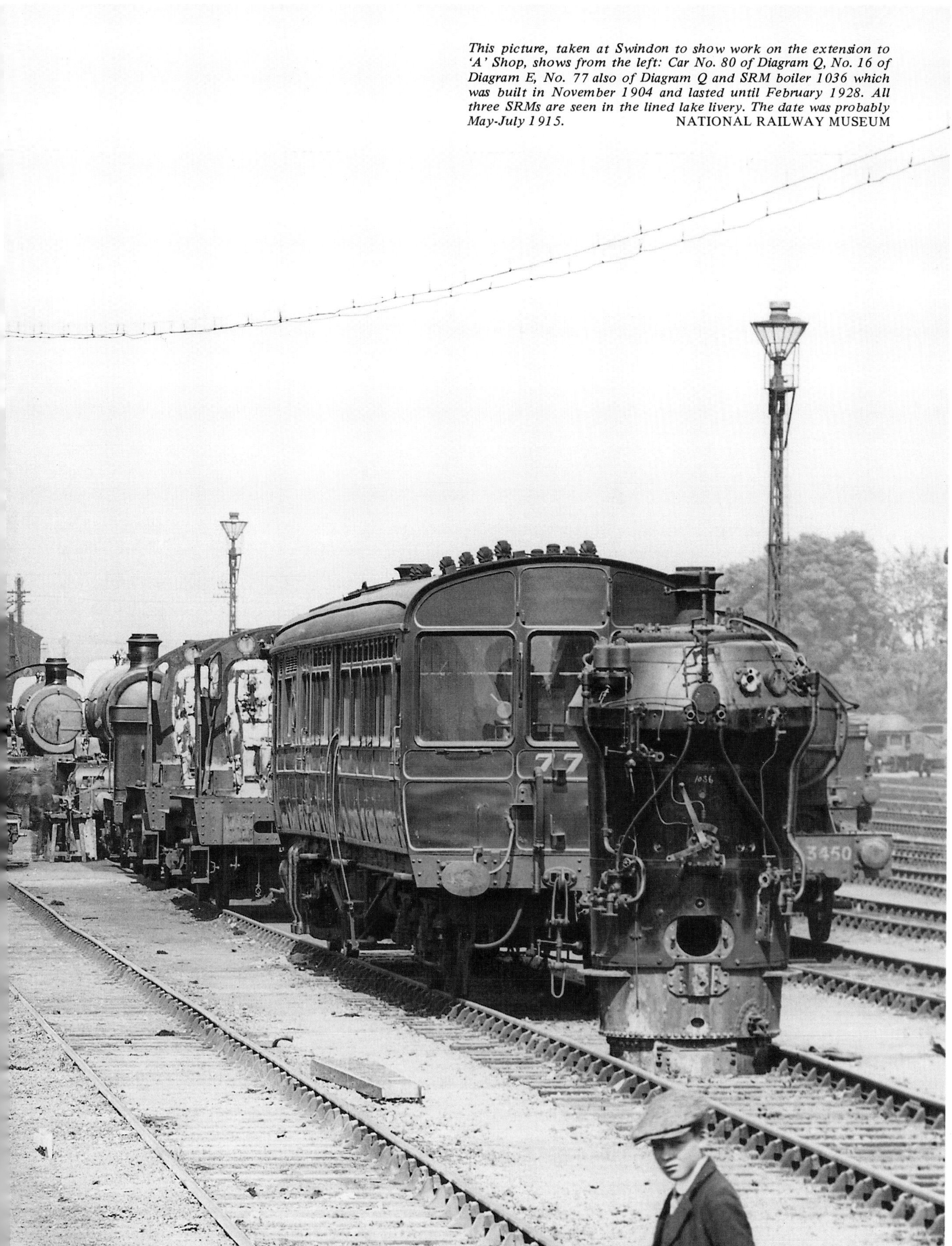

Power unit with 4ft wheels.

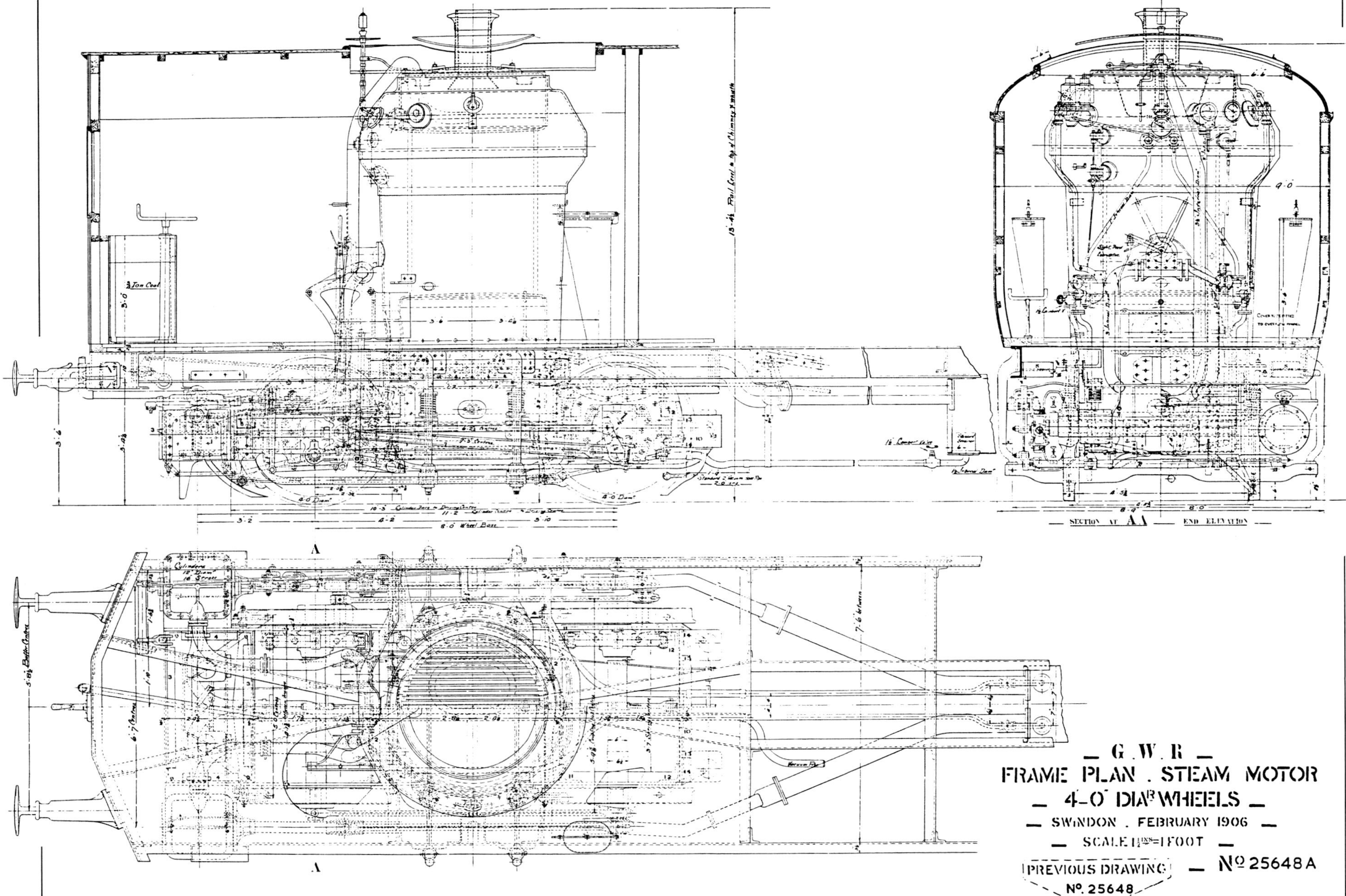

meant that the driving wheels were rotating at 350 rpm (4ft diameter), whilst to reach this speed with 3ft 6½in wheels, 395 rpm had to be made. By way of comparison, *City of Truro* (with 6ft 8in driving wheels) on her 102 mph descent of Wellington bank developed 426 rpm, whilst 80 mph with the same locomotive required only 336 rpm by the driving wheels.

At an early stage, the GWR considered the number of rail motor failures to be unacceptably high, and they were commented upon separately from locomotive failures at the Locomotive & Carriage Department Superintendents' meetings. Minute 179 recorded:

'The record for four weeks ended 7th December, 1905, shews great improvement on the previous month, and by constantly closely following up each failure, it is hoped that a steady decrease in the number of failures will continue, as experience gained up to now has enabled us to improve upon a number of fittings which formerly were frequently giving way and causing failures.'

From September 1906 until December 1907, Superintendents' meetings were provided with a list, a compilation of which is reproduced below, showing each failure and its cause. The most common problem was leaking tubes, which accounted for a third of all failures, whilst faults with the engine and valve gear were next with 27%. Then came faults with the suspension (12%), firebars and injectors (7% each), brakes (6%), buffers and drawgear (3%), leaving 5% of miscellaneous faults. These reports show a general downwards trend, but from a relatively high-level start. In October 1905, for example, there were no less than 31 rail motor car failures – the equivalent of about one half of the SRM fleet broke down during that month. In January 1906 the number had dropped to 10, but in May 1906 there were 27. In August of that year there were again only 10, but 21 in September, 15 in October and 20 in November. After January 1907, the failure rate was kept below 11 per month, and by 1909 was usually about 1 per week.

TABLE 5

SRM FAILURES - September 1906 to December 1907

Date	*Service*	*Car No.*	*At/Between*	*Mins. delay*	*Cause of failure*	*Month Total*
1 Sep 06	Truro - Camborne	30	Truro	0	Wear & tear	
3 Sep 06	Kidderminster District	54	Kidderminster	0	Leaking tubes	
4 Sep 06	Wellington & Craven Arms	76	Wellington	0	Leaking tubes	
5 Sep 06	Penzance & Redruth	63	Camborne	3	Broken suspension bolt	
5 Sep 06	Wellington & Craven Arms	26	Buildwas	0	Broken brake pull rod	
6 Sep 06	Trowbridge District	66	Trowbridge	0	Firebars falling out	
6 Sep 06	Stonehouse & Chalford	52	Chalford	17	Spring fracture	
6 Sep 06	Newquay & Chacewater	33	Shepherds	58	Leaking tubes	
7 Sep 06	Stonehouse & Chalford	51	Chalford	0	Replacing brake blocks	
10 Sep 06	Truro & Camborne	33	Truro	0	Leaking tubes	
10 Sep 06	Trowbridge District	70	Chipping Sodbury	10	Unable to make steam	
13 Sep 06	Swansea E Dock & British Rhondda	8	Resolven & Glyn Neath	75	Steam pipe burst	
14 Sep 06	Trowbridge District	80	Chippenham	0	Leaking tubes	
21 Sep 06	Trowbridge District	70	Trowbridge	0	Broken spring	
22 Sep 06	Wellington & Craven Arms	26	Longville	65	Bad leakage in firebox	
24 Sep 06	Plymouth District	44	Plymouth	0	Broken spring	
25 Sep 06	Trowbridge District	70	Portishead	0	Broken buffer	
25 Sep 06	Wellington & Craven Arms	26	Lightmoor	27	Piston gland packing blown out	
26 Sep 06	Wellington & Craven Arms	76	Shifnal	15	Two firebars burnt	
26 Sep 06	Trowbridge District	70	Trowbridge	0	Damaged buffer guide	
28 Sep 06	Plymouth District	44	Plympton	0	Broken spring hanger	21
03 Oct 06	Wellington & Much Wenlock	74	Buildwas	68	Driving gear breaking	
03 Oct 06	Wellington & Craven Arms	76	Much Wenlock	0	Broken flange on exhaust steam pipe	
05 Oct 06	Bath & Bristol District	70	Bristol	0	Faulty steam pipe	
08 Oct 06	Wellington & Craven Arms	77	Much Wenlock	0	Leaky tubes	
10 Oct 06	Taunton & Castle Cary	71	Taunton	0	Bupping arrangement broken	
11 Oct 06	Taunton & Castle Cary	72	Taunton	0	Window glass broken	
12 Oct 06	Wellington & Craven Arms	23	Wellington	0	Displaced fire bars	
12 Oct 06	Wellington & Craven Arms	76	Lawley Bank	0	Valve spindle broken	
16 Oct 06	Taunton & Castle Cary	71	Taunton	0	Fire bar bracket broken off	
17 Oct 06	Weymouth & Dorchester	10	Weymouth	0	Valve spindle broken	
18 Oct 06	Wellington & Much Wenlock	77	Ketley	25	Manhole door joint blown out	
21 Oct 07	Victoria & Greenford	41	West Ealing	86	Leaky tubes	
23 Oct 06	Swansea & British Rhondda	47	Resolven & Glyn Neath	111	Broken steam pipe	
27 Oct 06	Trowbridge District	53	Trowbridge	0	Leaky tubes	
31 Oct 06	Wellington & Craven Arms	77	Harton Rd. & Rushbury	42	Valve spindle broken	15
01 Nov 06	Yealmpton	39	Yealmpton	6	Brass & pin missing	
02 Nov 06	Trowbridge District	55	Trowbridge	0	Tubes leaking	
02 Nov 06	Trowbridge District	56	Trowbridge	0	Tubes leaking	

06 Nov 06	Wellington & Craven Arms	26	Much Wenlock	27	Valve gear out of order	
09 Nov 06	Wellington & Craven Arms	74	Much Wenlock	12	Set pin worked out	
10 Nov 06	Wellington & Craven Arms	73	Much Wenlock	27	Valve blown out	
12 Nov 06	Wellington & Craven Arms	77	Wellington	15	Tubes leaking	
12 Nov 06	Kidderminster District	54	Worcester	0	Valve blown out	
12 Nov 06	Trowbridge District	70	Trowbridge	0	RH exhaust steam pipe broke	
12 Nov 06	Trowbridge District	56	Trowbridge	0	Tubes leaking	
13 Nov 06	Frome, Castle Cary & Taunton	18	Frome	25	Injector failed	
14 Nov 06	Wellington & Craven Arms	77	Wellington	18	Tubes leaking	
15 Nov 06	Trowbridge District	56	Trowbridge shed	0	Tubes leaking	
17 Nov 06	Trowbridge District	56	Frome	0	Tubes leaking	
17 Nov 06	Trowbridge District	55	Westbury	0	Tubes leaking	
22 Nov 06	Wellington & Craven Arms	77	Shifnal	0	Tubes leaking	
23 Nov 06	Chalford & Stonehouse	48	Chalford	24	Tubes leaking	
24 Nov 06	Trowbridge District	70	Winterbourne	0	Faulty exhaust steam pipe	
30 Nov 06	Taunton & Castle Cary	72	Castle Cary & Taunton	0	Steam pipe broken	
30 Nov 06	Wellington & Craven Arms	80	Lightmoor	36	End of blower pipe blown out	20
02 Dec 06	Kidderminster District	37	Kidderminster & Churchill	11	Brake pull rod uncoupled	
03 Dec 06	Truro & Newquay	63	Newquay & Shepherds	11	Suspension bolt broken	
03 Dec 06	Trowbridge District	70	Bristol	0	LH exhaust pipe broken	
07 Dec 06	Taunton & Castle Cary	72	Castle Cary & Keinton	30	Broken steam pipe	
08 Dec 06	Swansea District	50	Glyn Neath	23	RH quadrant block pin worked out	
10 Dec 06	Truro - Camborne	30	Truro	0	Foregn matter on face of safety valve	
12 Dec 06	Truro - Camborne	63	Chacewater	0	Lubricator steam pipe broken	
15 Dec 06	Trowbridge District	56	Westbury	0	Mud hole door blown out	
24 Dec 06	Trowbridge District	62	Corsham	85	Frozen injectors	
26 Dec 06	Truro - Camborne	30	Truro	0	Fire bars dropped	
27 Dec 06	Truro - Camborne	30	Truro	0	Fire bars dropped	
31 Dec 06	Trowbridge District	75	Melksham	18	Mud hole door blown out	12
01 Jan 07	Kensington & Westbourne Pk (spl)	41	Acton	0	Leaky tubes	
07 Jan 07	Chester & Llanuwchllyn	21	Wrexham	17	Side-bar bolts broken	
09 Jan 07	Kidderminster District	64	Kidderminster	0	Steam pipe broken	
12 Jan 07	Kidderminster District	54	Worcester	0	Boiler buffing spring broken	
18 Jan 07	Oswestry & Corwen	66	Wrexham	5	Mud hole joint blown out	
19 Jan 07	Oswestry & Corwen	66	Wrexham	6	Spring pin broke	
23 Jan 07	Trowbridge District	75	Trowbridge	21	Injector out of order	
24 Jan 07	Trowbridge District	61	Keynsham	53	Vacuum cylinder failed	
25 Jan 07	Truro & Camborne	38	Truro	0	Broken spring hanger	
29 Jan 07	Evesham & Cheltenham	78	Evesham	35	Blower ring broken & tubes leaking	10
04 Feb 07	Trowbridge District	62	Freshford	0	Steps broken	
04 Feb 07	Cheltenham & Honeybourne	68	Gloucester	0	Feed pipes broken	
06 Feb 07	Rhos	15	Rhostyllen & Legacy	53	Short of steam	
07 Feb 07	Truro & Camborne	30	Truro	0	Fire door leaking	
13 Feb 07	Kidderminster District	54	Bewdley	81	Short of steam	
19 Feb 07	Plymouth District	59	Plymouth	4	LH steam pipe blowout	6
01 Mar 07	Newquay & Chacewater	79	Newquay	3	Back cylinder cock broken	
02 Mar 07	Cheltenham & Honeybourne	17	Cheltenham	4	Mud hole joint blown out	
06 Mar 07	Cheltenham & Honeybourne	37	Near Bishop's Cleeve	11	Valve gear failed	
30 Mar 07	Frome & Bridgwater	18	Castle Cary	0	Leaky tubes	4
02 Apr 07	Frome	18	Castle Cary	30	Leaky tubes	
03 Apr 07	Chipenham & Bristol	32	Box	5	Leaky tubes	
05 Apr 07	Newquay	78	Goonbell	2	Leaky tubes	
06 Apr 07	Swansea	3	Cardonnel	8	Defective cylinder	
07 Apr 07	Chalford & Stonehouse	51	Stroud	30	Broken blower in smoke box	
19 Apr 07	Bath, Trowbridge & Bristol	61	Coalpit Heath	0	Leaky tubes	6

14 May 07	1.40 pm Bath	62	Bristol	0	Missing brake block	
20 May 07	2.20 pm Plymouth	60	Devonport	0	Safety valve sticking	
21 May 07	10.56 pm Yealmpton	77	Steer Point	38	Injector failed	
23 May 07	2.33 pm Ruabon	22	On journey	0	Tubes leaking	
23 May 07	7.0 am Bristol	61	Near Filton	12	Cylinder defective	
23 May 07	4.10 Newquay	79	Near Perranporth	13	Eccentrics defective	
24 May 07	6.27 pm Greenford	11	Late start	20	Safety valve sticking	
24 May 07	6.30 pm Chippenham	83	Late start	20	Regulator valve defective	8
07 Jun 07	6.30 pm Newport	70	Llancaiach	5	Sand pipe falling	
20 Jun 07	5.45 am Stourbridge	27	Netherton	8	Tubes leaking	
22 Jun 07	4.0 pm Merthyr	70	Quaker's Yard	34	Injectors failed	
27 Jun 07	8.12 pm Bath	83	Chippenham	15	Pin of side rod broken	4
01 Jul 07	10.42 am Kidderminster	73	Kidderminster	0	Tubes leaking	
05 Jul 07	6.15 pm Honeybourne	40	Broadway	3	Pin of quadrant bolt broken	
11 Jul 07	8.30 am Wrexham	23	Brymbo	22	Tubes leaking	
13 Jul 07	3.55 pm Merthyr	70	Llancaiach	3	Buffer broken	
15 Jul 07	6.40 am Frome	55	Trowbridge	3	Firebars dropping	
15 Jul 07	1.23 pm Kidderminster	71	Kidderminster	0	Injectors failed	
20 Jul 07	8.3 am Bristol	55	On journey	3	Tubes leaking	
24 Jul 07	3.45 pm Kidderminster	29	Easton Court	5	Brake rod broken	8
12 Aug 07	4.29 pm Plymouth	60	On journey	3	Suspension bolt broken	
17 Aug 07	2.40 pm Plymouth	46	Plymouth & Saltash	7	Mud hole door blowing	
02 Sep 07	7.50 am Newquay	46	Newlyn	15	Both injectors failed	
04 Sep 07	12.38 pm Cheltenham	40	Laverton Halt	50	Quadrant block pin failed	
09 Sep 07	8.22 pmPlymouth	47	Yealmpton	92	RH crank shaft pin broken	
11 Sep 07	4.25 pm Evesham	34	Honeybourne	13	Blower plug worked out	
13 Sep 07	7.11 pm Wearde	30	Near Wearde	20	LHL suspension bolt broken	5
02 Oct 07	7.47 am Frome	18	Castle Cary & Durston	15	Tubes leaking	
04 Oct 07	2.0 pm Yealmpton	76	Brixton Road	18	Blower defective	
05 Oct 07	5.55 pm Helston	46	Redruth	22	Steam chest defective	
08 Oct 07	4.10 pm Ruabon	26	Corwen	32	Valve spindle broke	
08 Oct 07	4.10 pm Ruabon	26	Llangollen	23	Valve spindle broke	
21 Oct 07	7.15 am Wrexham	26	Ruabon	3	Blower pipe split	
28 Oct 07	3.55 pm Merthyr	70	Merthyr	26	Regulator rod defective	7
22 Nov 07	6.30 am Chippenham	83	Box	21	Tubes leaking	
23 Nov 07	9.2 pm Old Hill	21	Lye	21	Blower defective	
24 Nov 07	5.42 pm Stourbridge Junction	35	Near Cradley	33	Steam chest defective	
25 Nov 07	2.25 pm Newport	70	Newport	28	Valve spindle broken	
30 Nov 07	3.15 pm Penzance	46	Near St Erth	15	Valve spindle broken	5
14 Dec 07	8.20 am Penzance	46	Marazion	15	Reversing lever broken	
16 Dec 07	3.10 pm Bristol	69	Holt Junction	10	Tubes leaking	
25 Dec 07	3.35 pm Frome	17	Durston	55	Valve spindle guide broken	
26 Dec 07	8.12 pm Bath	83	Near Bath	40	Snifting valve broken	
31 Dec 07	7.6 pm Bath	83	Bathampton	3	Regulator rod broken	5

A report of 23rd July 1906 referred to two SRM acceleration trials, one carried out in September 1904 using Car No.27 which was a matchboarded example and brand new, and one, presumably in 1906, using SRM No.50 and the dynamometer car. No.50 was a 70ft car to Diagram N, and had been built in March 1905. The best performance from No.27 solo was at 70% cut-off, although the regulator position was not stated, but was probably fully open. This car accelerated from 4 mph to 34 mph in only 21 seconds whilst covering 225 yards. The 27-ton trailing load of No.50 slowed it down appreciably, but this latter test started from rest, so it is difficult to compare the two.

The SRMs seem to have been generally successful in the mechanical sphere once the early problems had been ironed out. The boilers were said to steam very well (at least when the tubes were clean, and did not leak), but the steam capacity seems to have been really rather too limited, particularly if a trailing load was being hauled. According to Holcroft, the fireman would put the SRM's engine into full gear (75%) as a stop was approached, and the cut-off lever was left in that position until the car was well under way again, when it would be reduced by one notch and left there. This driving technique would have enabled the cars to produce the rapid acceleration required, but cannot have done anything for maintenance. In addition, it produced such a sharp exhaust blast that it was accepted practice for all the firing to take place during station stops, contrary to general locomotive firing practice and official instructions.

TABLE 6

Report - 23rd July 1906

SRM ACCELERATION TRIALS

Motor No.27

Tested: 21st September 1904.

Diameter of Driving Wheels: 3 ft 6½ in

Load: Nil

Initial Speed: 4 m.p.h.

Distance Run: 225 yards.

Notch from Centre	*Cut-off (%)*	*Velocity Attained m.p.h.*	*Time Taken (secs.)*	*Average Acceleratio per sec. per*
1		23	25¼	1.10
2	25%	25½	24	1.31
3	35%	25½	23	1.37
4	50%	25½	21	1.50
5	60%	25½	21½	1.47
6	70%	34	21	2.09
7	75%	25½	22½	1.40

Motor No. 50

Diameter of Driving Wheels: 4 ft 0 in.

Load: Dynamometer Car - 27 tons.

Initial Speed: Nil.

Distance Run: 440 yards.

Velocity	*Time*	*Average*
26	50½	0.75

An SRM engine works plate. It is rather battered because, being positioned on the centre of the front stretcher, it was liable to be hit by a swinging screw coupling. The original size is 5½ inches wide x 4 inches high. Engine 0837 was the first one with 4ft diameter wheels. It was first fitted with boiler 1050 and in February 1905 was placed in Car No. 43 of Diagram K1, the first 70ft SRM. It is known to have been fitted to Cars 72 (October 1911), 59 (April 1915), 83 (June 1921), 80 (March 1925), 93 (February 1929) and 97 (October 1931). Together with boiler 1084 it was fitted to Car No. 88 in April 1934. In May 1935 it was removed and condemned. CTY. BRIAN ARMAN

CHAPTER FOUR

SRM COACH BODIES

Car No. 7 of Diagram C at Resolven, probably in 1908 when it was allocated to Neath. It had been fitted with end steps and handles, destination board brackets, a hole for a whistle cord and a bell cable for connecting to a trailer. It is just possible to see that the open door at the far end was lettered 'ENTRANCE'.
J. T. DAVIES, CTY. R. C. RILEY

THIS chapter considers in some detail the development and features of the SRM's coach portion, excluding the underframe, but including the liveries applied to the cars.

For ease of reference, the 'front' of an SRM will be taken to mean the end with the power unit, and the 'rear' or 'trailing' end will be the non-powered. In GWR terminology, the compartment at the power end containing the boiler, coal bunker, driving position, etc. was known as the 'motor compartment' and the trailing end compartment (without side doors on some designs) was called the 'driver's vestibule'.

The comments in this chapter principally apply to the GWR mainstream designs of SRM, and not to Nos.15 and 16, which were based on a Taff Vale Railway design and built by contractors for the GWR.

As well as being a new type of vehicle for the GWR at that period, the steam rail motor carriage portions exhibited a number of novel features, when compared with most contemporary coaches on that railway:

1. They had tall, elliptical profile roofs, which, although not much different in overall height from contemporary clerestory roofed stock, made them completely different in appearance. They first appeared 10 months before the first of the 'Dreadnought' coaches.
2. The first two cars had flat sides and ends, whilst standard passenger stock had been given turnunder ends since 1874, and turnunder sides for even longer. Bow ends on rail motors were introduced after the first two had been built.
3. On the first 26 GWR-built cars, vertical 'matchboarding' was used below the waist instead of panelling with raised wooden mouldings. From car No.29 onwards, turnunder sides with traditional wood panelling was used, but with wider-than-normal waist panels. These cars also had bow ends with wood panelling.
4. The passenger accommodation was in open saloons, which had large fixed windows with twin hinged toplights above each. Contemporary passenger coaches usually had traditional compartments with relatively small quarterlights either side of a door, which had a droplight and a ventilator over it.
5. 'Smoking' accommodation in corridor coaches was often in open saloons, but with compartment layout windows.
6. The first two SRMs had one-end access only, instead of a large number of side doors, and all subsequent cars had a limited number of doors. This was to help a conductor-guard to issue tickets to passengers boarding at halts.

BODY STYLES

As indicated, there were two standard Great Western SRM body styles: 'matchboarded' and 'wood panelled'. Both came in what was basically a 57ft length over corner pillars, and which on all but the first two cars was extended overall to approximately 59ft 6in by the car's bow ends. In addition, the wood panelled variety appeared in a 70ft length, including the standard bow ends.

In both styles, the glass of the original fixed windows (lights) were held in position by external bolection ('stepped') mouldings, but subsequent additional or modified windows, usually droplights, did not have these mouldings. Thus, later modifications to the windows can often be identified, given a clear photograph. In the case of SRMs, alterations to windows were normally the substitution of pairs of droplights for single, larger fixed lights, or in a few cases the substitution of a single droplight and small fixed windows either side (rather like quarterlights) for a single, large fixed light.

MATCHBOARDED STYLE

The matchboarded style of body had vertical 3-inch matchboarding (planking) below the waist line, and square-cornered wooden panelling, with mouldings, above. The windows had quadrant corners at the top, but were square at the bottom.

In 1904, there was a change of policy relating to coach dimensions. Hitherto – for many years – the GWR had usually built its standard coach bodies to an exact number of inches in length and width, to which would be added ⅜in at each side or end for the mouldings, so that these dimensions normally finished with ¾in. This policy change came in the middle of the matchboarded period as far as SRMs were concerned, so that cars 1 and 2 were 57ft 0¾in long by 8ft 6¾in wide; cars 3–8 were 59ft 6¾in long and 8ft 6¾in wide, but subsequent matchboarded SRMs were 59ft 6in long and 8ft 6in wide.

They were 12ft 6in from rail to roof, or 13ft 4½in to the chimney top, although an early frame plan (for cars of Diagrams B1 or C1) shows 13ft 6in. They had an elliptical roof of almost circular profile, though in this style it appeared to have a minor radius through the centre line of the roof, with the profile flattened out slightly towards the eaves.

WOOD PANELLED STYLE

These cars had wood panelled sides and ends with wooden mouldings having quadrant corners throughout. They had turnunder sides, and inward-opening doors that were usually flat, and slightly recessed. They were either 70ft or 59ft 6in long, 9ft 0in wide, 12ft 2¾in – 12ft 6in high from rail to roof, and 13ft 4½in from rail to chimney top. They also had an elliptical profile roof, but in this case the profile seems flatter at the top and tighter near the eaves compared with the earlier cars. This appears to be the standard GWR roof profile for coaches of the 'Dreadnought' era onwards.

Some other standard dimensions for wood panelled cars were:

Horizontal mouldings :	1½in wide
Panels above door windows:	7in deep
Window height panels:	2ft 6in deep.
Front waist panel of motor compartment:	1ft 6½in deep
Other waist panels:	9⅛in deep
Body panel below waist:	1ft10¼in deep
Motor compartment door:	2ft 0in wide opening
Driver's vestibule doorway:	2ft 0in wide opening.

Passenger vestibule doorway: 2ft 10½in wide opening
Luggage compartment doorway: 4ft wide opening.

Motor compartment door ventilators had 5 louvres ½in thick, projecting ¼in, with rounded ends.

DEVELOPMENTS

There were a number of modifications made to many SRMs during their existence, depending on their building and scrapping dates. Usually these modifications were not recorded in the register, and often not on the diagrams either, so photographs and drawings have to be relied on.

EXTERNAL DETAILS

END WINDOWS – MOTOR COMPARTMENT

All SRMs had three windows at each end. Nos.1 and 2 had short end windows 2ft 1in high – the same height as the side windows; these were positioned at the same height as the side windows, and were quickly modified to improve the driver's view. Subsequent SRMs all had end windows where the top was approximately at eaves level.

The other matchboarded SRMs had 3ft 1½in-tall end windows, which extended down to the same level as the bottom of the side windows at both ends. However, it appears that those in the motor compartment were liable to be broken by coal, as this was stored in the bunker just below the end windows. Coal was said to have been loaded into SRMs using sacks, but photographs of cars at Exeter shed show them next to a loco coal wagon with the side door open. So some, if not all, matchboarded cars had the lower edge of the end windows in the power compartment raised by perhaps 9 inches. In some cases this was done 'properly' to produce a panel below each window, while car 11 was given what appeared to be a metal-sheathed end below the windows, with the smaller windows above. These changes are not recorded in the *SRM Register*, and mostly appear in photographs of cars in brown or lake livery, but there is a photograph in the January 1906 issue of the *Railway Magazine* of car 5 at Kensington (Addison Road) station with this modification to the motor compartment end windows, so the process probably started during 1905.

Wood panelled SRMs all had a wider waist panel below the motor compartment end windows from new, with correspondingly shorter end windows; the waist panel here was 1ft 6½in deep.

Car No. 1 of Diagram A1, as built, with round-headed buffers, collapsible metal gate to the vestibule and fixed steps. NATIONAL RAILWAY MUSEUM

The *SRM Register* contains references, dated 1912–16, to some cars being fitted with protection bars to the motor compartment droplight, but photographs indicate that this must refer to protection bars being fitted to the end windows in the motor compartment. Again, this would have been an attempt to stop the glass being broken by coal. It was probably done to all, with the possible exception of some early conversions to trailers.

Some photographs show SRMs with wood pieces placed inside the front window glass to protect it, possibly as an extension to the bunker. These pieces of wood were sometimes painted cream, and could be visible from the outside of the car. They seem to have extended nearly half-way up the window, which implies that a lot of coal was packed into the bunkers of these cars. I understand that a drawing showing this existed: it shows three planks, totalling 10 inches in height, the planks being 1¼in thick. According to this drawing, the inside of the glass was to be painted cream; however, photographs show that, in practice, some had the glass or the bunker extensions painted in a dark colour, probably black.

END WINDOWS – DRIVER'S VESTIBULE

At the trailing end, all (except cars 1 and 2) had tall end windows that extended from the normal waist height to about the eaves level. Nos. 1 and 2 had shorter end windows that were modified in the same way as the power compartment end windows.

Sometimes, and particularly in later years, horizontal white lines were painted across the driver's vestibule end windows of SRMs, which were apparently supposed to remind staff coaling locomotives of the presence of the glass, and thus reduce breakages. Sometimes, the lines were even painted on the droplights in this vestibule. The earliest examples of this date from about 1911–13.

WINDSCREEN WIPERS

These are believed to have been introduced in the 1920s, and were, like automobile types, hand operated. Two designs existed: one had its spindle actually passing through the glass of the window to which it was fitted, whilst the other, later style had the spindle passing through the window frame. Windscreen wipers had been fitted to all surviving SRMs by 1926, according to a GWR internal report following a comment made by the Railway Inspectorate in a report on an accident that year in driving rain at Clevedon.

On 11th October 1929, a GWR circular signed by Mr Collett instructed that the later pattern of wiper was to be fitted in future:

> 'Certain of our rail motor cars and trailers are fitted with windscreen wipers in which the spindle is passed through a hole in the glass. We have had a large number of window breakages due to this and the wiper has been re-designed –

Car No. 92 of Diagram R in the 1930 livery with two gold and black lines at the waist. The protection bars for the end windows and the coal bunker extension are visible and notice that part of the centre end window had been painted over.

An extract from another Swindon photo taken during the construction of the foundations for the extension to 'A' Shop, showing on the left Car No. 85 of Diagram R, and to the right Car No. 10 of Diagram D. Both are seen in the 1912 lined lake livery. No. 10 had modified side windows and No. 85 had received a white line across the end windows. The date was probably the second half of 1916. NATIONAL RAILWAY MUSEUM

see Print 81514 attached – the spindle now passing through the body frame.

'If you have any motors or trailers in your Division fitted with the old pattern wiper, they may be allowed to run until the windows require renewal, when they should be fitted with the new pattern, and the wiper and gear should be ordered from Mr G. C. Dickson, C & W Storekeeper, Swindon.'

Unfortunately, Print 81514 was not attached to the copy of the circular seen.

A subsequent circular of 18th October 1929 asked for the old wipers to be sent back to Swindon, as they could be converted to the new pattern.

END DESTINATION BOARD HOLDERS, ETC.

End destination board holders, which were two small brackets fitted on the panel above the central end window, came into use during 1904 (the drawing, illustrating a matchboarded trailer, is dated 30th June 1904). In order that staff could reach the boards, two steps were provided on the car ends, below the windows, and positioned so that they were very close to the 'N°' on one side and the actual running number on the other; sometimes, they actually interfered with these numbers. The steps were accompanied by a horizontal commode handle beneath each of the outer end windows, and vertical commode handles between the central and outer windows.

Later, some SRMs ran with brackets that were fitted to the vertical mouldings above the central end window, thus requiring a wider destination board (e.g. No.11, photographed about October 1915, and No.78). Some cars had both the original and the wider fittings, with the new pattern higher up the ends than the older ones (e.g. No.50, photographed about 1913–15, and No.74, also in lake livery), whilst some had the wider arrangement at the junction of the horizontal and vertical mouldings above the central window. Examples having this arrangement were Nos.32, 40 and 93.

As far as can be ascertained from photographs, end destination boards went out of use during the Great War, but the brackets and steps, etc. were not usually removed; indeed, when surviving SRMs were fitted with passenger alarm equipment in the late 1920s, the destination board brackets were fitted onto the ends of 'U'- shaped brackets so as to keep any destination board clear of the alarm pipework, etc. Examples of cars fitted with this arrangement included Nos.74, 88 and 92.

SIDE DESTINATION BOARD HOLDERS

Unfortunately, there seems to be no great consistency with their positioning, and photographs need to be consulted for individual examples. The dates of fitting are also unknown, but a photograph of No.38 said to be taken in 'about 1908' at Dawlish shows these brackets fitted and in use. There are several photographs of cars in monochrome livery with side destination board holders, and several without them!

LAMP BRACKETS

SRMs ran as class 'B' trains, and a single, central headlamp bracket was fitted below the central end windows. The official photographs of No.1 as built do not show this lamp bracket, but it seems to have been fitted by the time the car went into service. On Nos.1 and 2, the headlamp bracket was initially fitted so that the lamp was above the bottom of the window, but the bracket was soon lowered.

On each side of the end, just below the windows, a tail lamp bracket was fitted for use with side lamps that faced forwards along the train, as well as backwards. Although fitting these lamps to SRMs seems to have gone out of practice by about 1908, the brackets were not removed unless major work was done to the car end, and some survived well into the 1920s, if not until the 1930s. Officially, passenger trains were supposed to have these tail lamps until 1934.

In addition, on Nos. 1 and 2, a lower tail lamp bracket was provided from new, positioned above the left-hand buffer, as you looked at the end of the car. On other SRMs, additional tail lamp brackets do not seem to have been provided until after lake livery was adopted in 1912, and some cars were never fitted with them. Where fitted, they were placed immediately to the right of the vacuum pipe, a little way above the bottom of the body.

COMMUNICATION AND ALARM SYSTEMS

BELL CIRCUITS

To enable the driver to communicate with the guard and the fireman, a bell circuit was provided with push buttons and bells in the driver's vestibule, the guard's vestibule or the luggage compartment, and the motor compartment. A connecting cable for trailers was fitted to the trailing end only of SRMs; this looked like a length of armoured cable with a connector on the end. The cable first appeared about 1906, and either emerged at the angle of the bow end, or about the middle of the area below the left-hand window.

The trailing end of Car No. 88, taken at Brentford on 22nd June 1932, showing the warning gong and communication apparatus together with the numerals '45' above the window recording the car's weight. The car had the double waist lines, but the end windows did not have the painted horizontal white lines.
F. M. GATES
CTY. R. C. RILEY

The trailing end of Car No. 74 of Diagram Q, showing the gong and the passenger alarm apparatus.

WHISTLE CORDS

Drivers of SRMs could operate the whistle from either of their positions by means of a cord which ran the length of the car internally.

With the introduction of trailers in late 1904, it also became necessary to be able to operate the SRM's whistle from the driver's vestibule of a trailer which was being propelled by the car. This was accomplished by a similar whistle cord in the trailer driver's vestibule, which extended to the other end of the trailer and was then connected across to the SRM's whistle cord. These cords, which became common from about 1906, emerged from the SRM above the end windows through a chamfered or trumpet-shaped small hole, which looked rather like a washer, on a moulding above the right-hand end window of the car. Because trailers could not be coupled to the front of an SRM and have the through regulator gear operative, the whistle cord mouth was only to be found on the trailing ends of cars.

REGULATOR GEAR

All SRMs had the regulator in the driver's vestibule attached by various linkages to the regulator in the motor compartment. With the advent of trailers, a means had to be achieved of extending the regulator control system to the driving vestibule of the trailer; this was done by means of a telescopic linkage on the trailer that was attached to the regulator control rod on the SRM via an 'eye' coupling, through which a pin was passed. Auto-fitted locomotives had the same fitting at both ends, but SRMs only had one at the trailing end, where it emerged just below the buffer beam, so an SRM could not be controlled from a trailer coupled at the motor end. Because all SRMs had the same 'eye' coupling at the trailing end, it was not possible to couple two cars together and operate the regulator of the rear car from the front one. If two were operated together like this, the fireman on the rear car had to operate its regulator in accordance with signals given by the driver of the front car.

GONGS

SRM whistles were eventually judged to be inadequate when the car was travelling with the driver's vestibule leading, so, like auto trailers and slip coaches, a warning gong was fitted to the trailing end of the surviving cars from the mid-1920s onwards. This was placed above the left-hand end window, viewed externally. The gong was operated by a foot pedal in the driver's vestibule.

PASSENGER ALARMS

In the late 1920s, surviving cars were fitted with passenger alarm apparatus, officially 'communication chains', which partially applied the brakes when pulled by a passenger. The external parts of the alarm apparatus, including the tell-tales, were fitted to the trailing end of SRMs above the end windows. The dates recorded for the fitting of communication chains in the *Register* are somewhat doubtful, as photographs show a significant number of cars fitted with them at earlier dates than recorded in that document. The number of alarms recorded as fitted in February 1933 seem to indicate that a survey was carried out at that time, and the *Register* dates may well be those when note was made, and not the fitting dates.

ROOF DETAILS

VENTILATORS

Ventilators were not original equipment on the earlier matchboarded trailers, but were soon fitted above the passenger accommodation. These probably date from about mid-1904 (No.7 did not have them when new in May of that year, but No.11, built in June, did have them). On matchboarded cars, ventilators were arranged in a single line centrally, between the gas lamps. The number of ventilators fitted did vary: Nos.5 and 7 had five, diagrams D, F and G cars seem to have had four, and whilst shell ventilators seem to have been standard, car 7 appears to have had a small torpedo type with rounded ends. Wood panelled cars had roof ventilators in pairs. Ventilators were not shown on diagrams.

RAIN STRIPS

SRMs initially had one rain strip on each side of the roof, running from the trailing end to the power unit roof cover. In practice, most were fitted with a second rain strip at a reasonably early date. Photographs should be consulted as to the positioning of these strips on individual cars.

GAS LIGHTING

All GWR SRMs were fitted with gas lighting. The earliest cars were fitted with the GWR's standard flat flame burners, but from about mid-1905 (No.53 onwards), lamps with incandescent burners became standard. Nos.39 and 50 also seem to have been fitted with these lamps from new (April and March 1905), and whilst Nos.15 and 16 were initially supplied with electric lighting, they were fitted with incandescent gas lighting before they entered service. Cars fitted with flat flame burners had them replaced between 1910 and 1914, and this was often accompanied by a reduction in the number of lamps by one.

The lamps with flat flame burners were fed by a single pipe running along the roof, but those with incandescent lamps (which were much more efficient) had two pipes on the roof, each with feeders to each lamp. One pipe was the main gas supply, the other, narrower, pipe fed a pilot light.

Gas lights in driving vestibules often had the half of the lamp glass globe facing the windows painted black, to minimise reflection. A circular of 14th September 1921 asked for this to be done in all cases.

This view of the roof of Car No. 96 of Diagram R with a small saloon was taken at Trusham on the Teign Valley line on 12th May 1934. It shows the twin gas pipes and the way the ventilators were positioned outboard of these pipes. The plate round the chimney seems askew.

G. N. SOUTHERDEN

OTHER DETAILS

MOTOR COMPARTMENT

In bow-ended SRMs, the motor compartment had external sliding doors each side giving access to the driving and firing positions, a droplight in the side behind the door, and sliding windows. Nos.1 and 2 were slightly different, and had a fixed window forward of the side doors.

The matchboarded cars originally had three horizontally-sliding windows with louvre ventilators above them, located in the sides towards the rear of the motor compartment. The outer two frames could both slide behind the central one, the rearmost giving access to the water filler pipes, which were situated just behind it. These windows are incorrectly shown on the diagrams (and GA drawings) as twin. In due course the rearmost window was removed, and a fixed panel containing a water filler with a hinged cover was substituted. There were twin louvres above the sliding windows of Nos.1 and 2, and triple louvres in other instances. The louvres were not modified when a fixed panel replaced the rearmost window.

Wood panelled SRMs had twin sliding windows to the motor compartment, as shown in the diagrams, again with three louvre ventilators above them, and not twin as shown on the diagrams. In due course, these cars had the width of their two sliding windows reduced, and a panel incorporating a water filler was fitted at their trailing end.

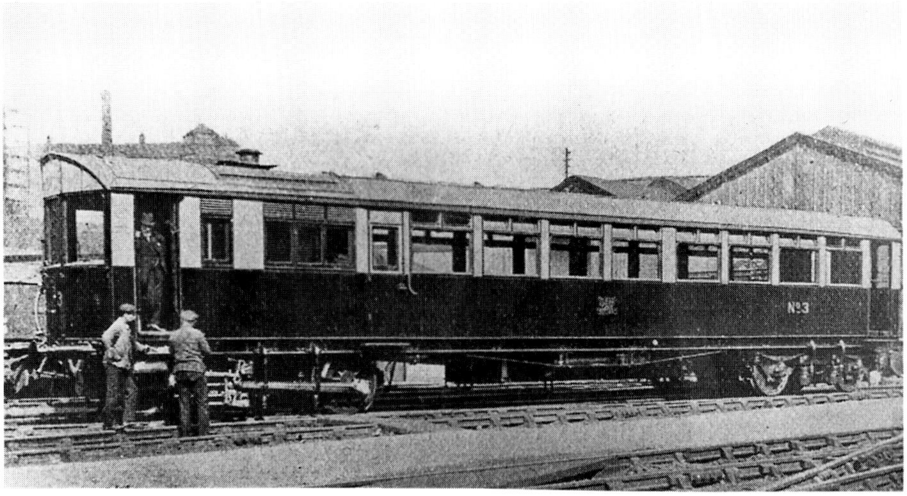

Car No. 3 of Diagram B1 in as-built condition with the original configuration of sliding windows to the motor compartment, and its number once on its side, near the trailing end, and centrally on the end close to the vacuum pipe. It had no steps for passengers. COLLECTION R. C. RILEY

WATER FILLER COVERS

Originally, the water filler pipes had a flat cover fastened by a screw fitting just inboard of the rear sliding window. When this arrangement was replaced by external access, there were two types of water filler cover used; both were oval, hinged at the bottom with two hinges, and had a catch at the top to keep them closed. On one design there was a reinforcing cross shape, which was omitted from the other. It is known that No.70 was fitted with external water filler covers in March 1907, so it is possible that the last cars built, Nos 81–99, had modified windows and external water filler covers from new, but photographic evidence is lacking.

Car No. 64 of Diagram O in lake livery, possibly at Reading, and showing the door to the power compartment slid partly open, the driving windows fitted with potection bars and a plain water filler lid. COLLECTION R. C. RILEY

SRM 98 of Diagram R, at Southall in 1927/8 with modified side windows to the engine compartment and a plain water filler cover. This is also a useful view of the roof.
LENS OF SUTTON

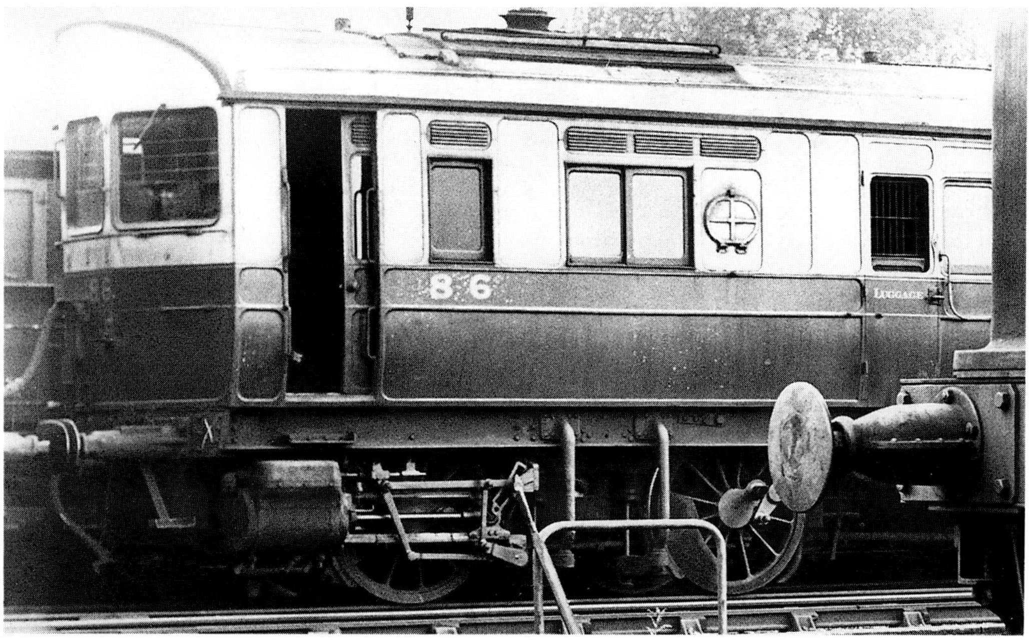

This view of Car No. 86 at Swindon in February 1933 with coupling rods removed shows the water filler lid with a reinforcing cross.
W. LESLIE GOOD

SRM No. 70 with power unit removed, photographed at Swindon in March 1907 to show defective paintwork. It was at Swindon from December 1906 until 14th March 1907. These pictures show a 'supporter', thus confirming that the garter device was in use.
NATIONAL RAILWAY MUSEUM

Interior of a 70ft car, showing the fixed longitudinal seats nearest the camera and the walkover seats beyond.
NATIONAL RAILWAY MUSEUM

Below: *Interior of Car No. 75 in 1906, with walkover-type seats in the foreground.*
COLLECTION ALAN HALL

PASSENGER ACCOMMODATION

WINDOWS

SRMs originally had large, fixed windows with two hinged toplights above each for ventilation. Depending on the individual SRM design, these fixed windows came in more than one size, the smallest types being almost square. Some of the large, fixed lights were subsequently replaced by pairs of droplights, whilst later SRMs had these features from new. Passenger compartment droplights had a single horizontal bar across them, fixed inside the car; these do not seem to have been provided immediately on most cars built with droplights – for example, Nos.61 and 67 did not have them when new – but No.70 had them fitted by March 1907. It is possible that Nos.81–99 did have them from new.

SEATING

The passenger seating was of four types.

Longitudinal bench seating

This was placed along the sides of the SRM, usually at each end of the saloon, with cross seating between.

Seating bays

These comprised seats with fixed backs arranged transversely either side of the gangway across the coach, in pairs facing each other. Each seat accommodated two passengers.

'Walkover' (reversible) seats

These were also placed transversely across the passenger saloon on either side of the gangway. They differed from seating bays in that the seat backs were movable, so that passengers could face forwards or backwards as desired. They were quite popular in trams, and got their name in being easily changed by someone walking past. The end units of these seats had their backs against either a partition or longitudinal seats, so their backs were fixed.

'Drop down' seats

Because of the presence of the motor compartment and the open arrangement of the passenger accommodation, the seating capacity of SRMs was relatively limited. This was made worse in those with luggage compartments, and even more so in the case of the later ones with a passenger vestibule as well. To maximise the number of seats, those with luggage compartments were fitted with drop down seats across the luggage partition common with the motor compartment.

SMOKING AND NON-SMOKING COMPARTMENTS

Those SRMs built with a single passenger saloon were soon divided by a partition to give a small smoking compartment and a large non-smoking one. The few recorded dates for this work were during 1905. The SRMs that sur-

Another view of the interior of Car No. 16 of Diagram E.
NATIONAL RAILWAY MUSEUM

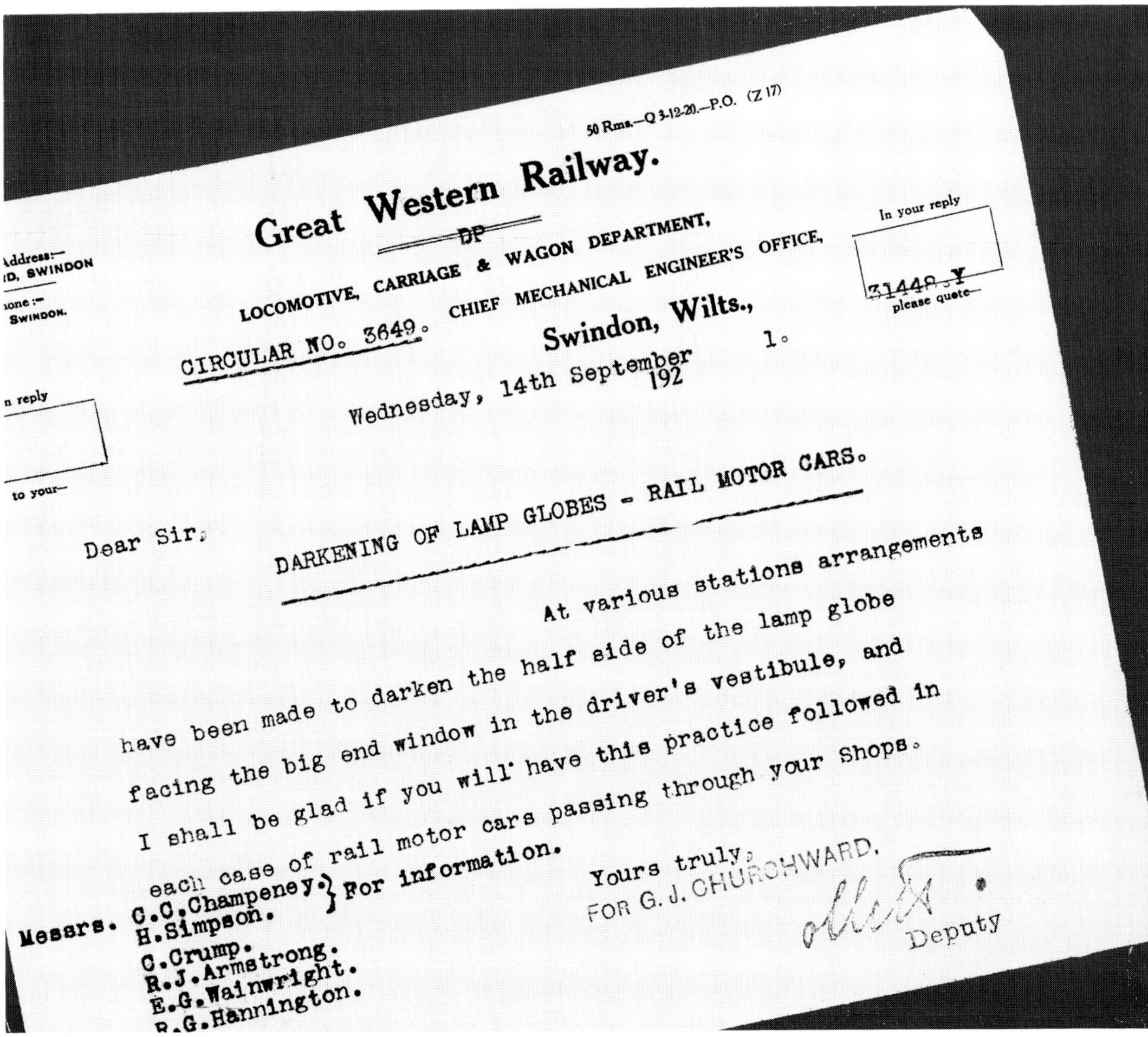

50 Rms.—Q 3-12-20.—P.O. (Z 17)

Great Western Railway.

DP

LOCOMOTIVE, CARRIAGE & WAGON DEPARTMENT,
CHIEF MECHANICAL ENGINEER'S OFFICE,

Swindon, Wilts.,

ddress:—
D, SWINDON
one:—
SWINDON.

In your reply
31448 Y
please quote—

n reply
to your—

CIRCULAR NO. 3649.

Wednesday, 14th September 1921.

DARKENING OF LAMP GLOBES - RAIL MOTOR CARS.

Dear Sir,

At various stations arrangements have been made to darken the half side of the lamp globe facing the big end window in the driver's vestibule, and I shall be glad if you will have this practice followed in each case of rail motor cars passing through your Shops.

Yours truly,
FOR G. J. CHURCHWARD.
Deputy

Messrs. C.C.Champeney. } For information.
H.Simpson.
C.Crump.
R.J.Armstrong.
E.G.Wainwright.
R.G.Hannington.

vived longest had their accommodation redesignated to give the larger compartment to smokers, this taking place from 1928 onwards.

LUGGAGE COMPARTMENT

A luggage compartment, where provided, was situated next to the motor compartment. There was a central sliding door to the motor compartment, which seems to have been provided for emergency use as the drop down seats were normally provided here. A sliding door to the passenger saloons was provided, and access to the outside was by double doors each side.

DRIVER'S VESTIBULE DOORS

Matchboarded SRMs originally had no external doors to the driver's vestibule, only open doorways protected by a 'lazy tongs' type of gate in the case of Nos. 1 and 2, and horizontal bars across the doorway on the others. However, inward-opening doors were fairly quickly provided, but no dates of fitting are known.

The wood panelled SRMs had vestibule doors provided from the beginning, with inward-opening leaves hinged on the corner pillar.

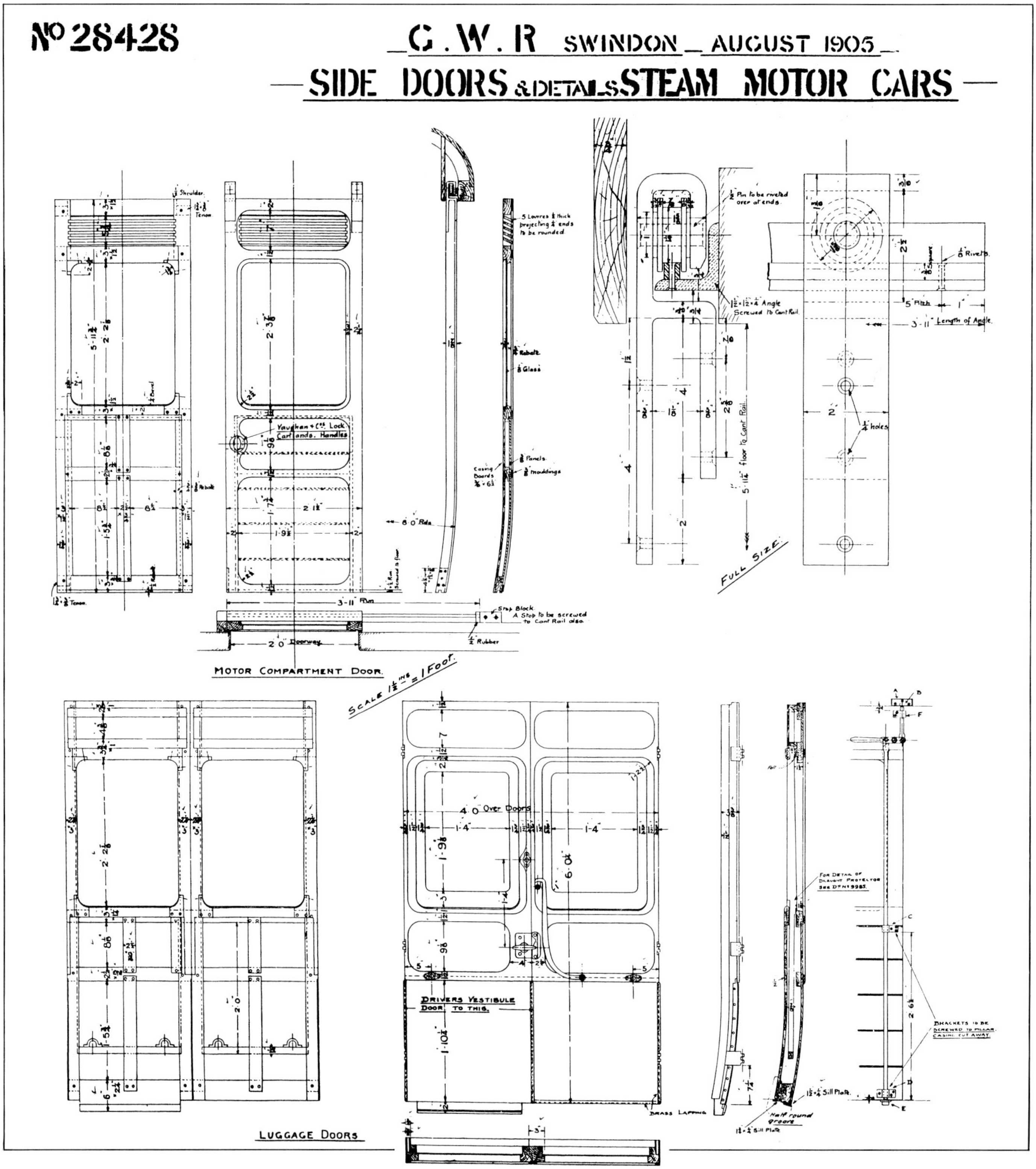

LIVERIES

The two styles of steam rail motor had very similar liveries. The lining-out on the matchboarded cars tended to be simpler than on the wood panelled ones, and there was no attempt to line out non-existent mouldings as happened on steel panelled stock in the 1920s. Matchboarded cars had beading round the edge of the matchboarding, and this was evidently lined on the matchboarding side only.

There are no records of how individual SRMs were painted, apart from photographs and occasional remarks in the *Register* in the 1930s that cream and brown with gold lines had been applied. It is not possible, therefore, to be definitive about the actual style of any particular SRM unless an adequate photograph is found. For example, No.1 had a non-standard livery when built in 1903, but it is not known if the car was repainted into a standard variant before the 1908 brown livery was applied.

As far as can be ascertained, the dates quoted below are those when the change took place for stock that was being built, or that was routinely going through the paint shops. It would appear that, normally, there was no programme of premature repainting of rolling stock following livery changes, except in 1922 when it was intended to complete the change from lake to lined brown and cream within three years. If necessary, coaches could be repainted at intervals of 2 years, although about 3–5 years was probably more common; however, it is possible that the additional handling of SRMs when the power units were removed for maintenance, together with the close proximity of that power

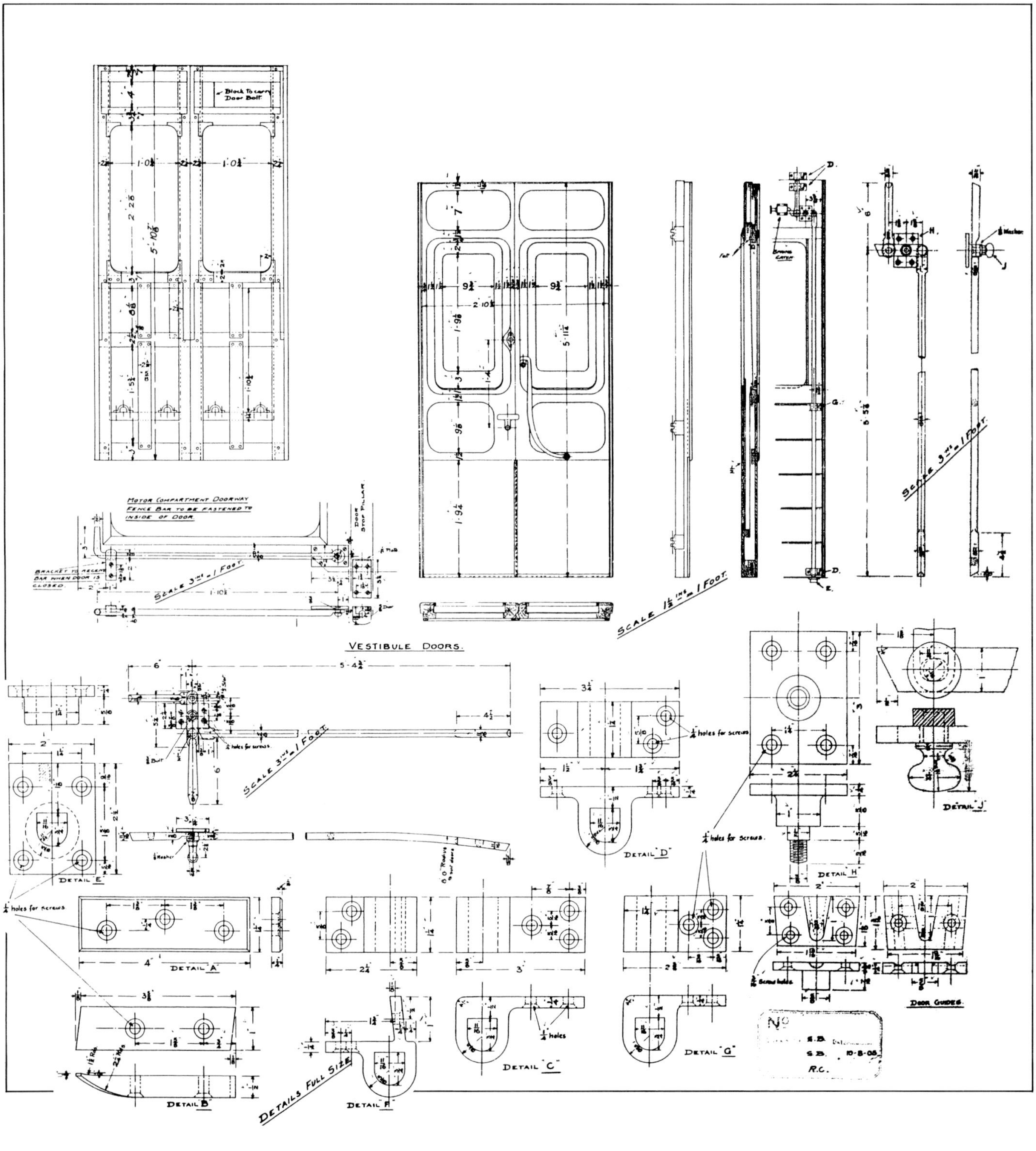

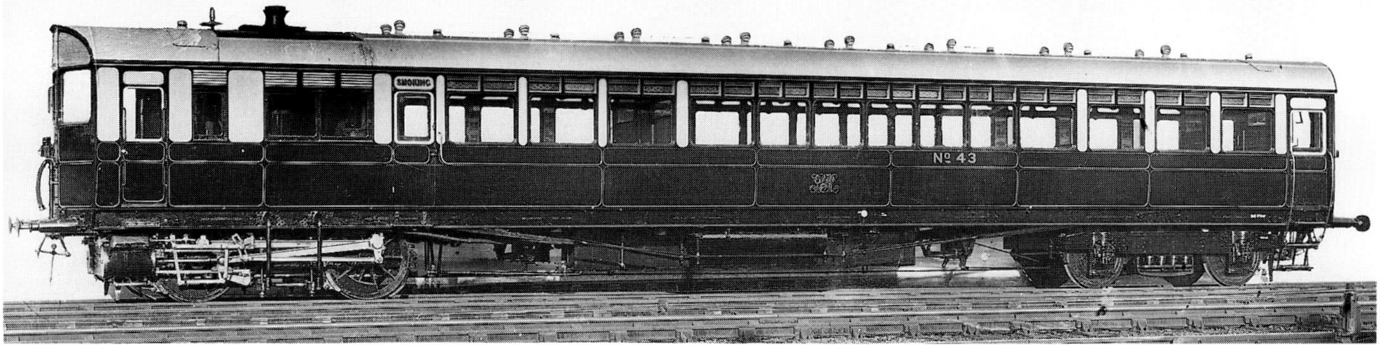

This official photograph of Car No. 43 of Diagram M1 as built in early 1905 shows the full lined brown and cream livery with the entwined monogram. These cars were built with a small smoking compartment at the end nearest the power unit, the external door to which had the word 'SMOKING' over the droplight. The partition between the two passenger compartments is visible through the windows. Car No. 43, which was fitted with 9ft volute spring bogies, was at Laira for most of 1905. NATIONAL RAILWAY MUSEUM

source in service, would lead to earlier painting than was normal for many other coaches.

1903–1908: THE 'FULLY LINED' BROWN AND CREAM LIVERY

The principal sources of our knowledge of the livery of SRMs up to 1908 are photographs and a drawing produced at Swindon in 1952, for filming purposes, showing the livery of clerestory coaches at the turn of the century. This shows the lining of the waist panels as 'black – gold – black – gold – black', where the black lines were ¼in wide and the gold lines ⅜in wide. Where a cream panel was involved, the drawing shows an additional brown line and a cream line, both ⅛in wide. However, official photographs of new SRMs do not seem to show this multiplicity of lines – they only seem to have lines in gold on the edge of the mouldings, which would be ⅜in deep, and there is no sign of a black line either side – which may be due to the limitations of monochrome film. What is visible in some pictures is that the cream panels have a fine dark line, probably brown, around the panel, about an inch or so from the edge. This line usually had quadrant corners, sometimes even where the panel had angled corners, such as above the window of the power compartment doors of matchboarded cars.

One specification for painting the body of an SRM has survived. This is in the contract for the 70ft cars ordered from Kerr Stuart & Co. on Lot 1100 in June 1905. The relevant part reads:

> 'The roof boards, after joints have been levelled, must be well puttied, painted and given a coat of thick white lead paint. Stout canvas of good quality must then be strained over and held in position by a suitable cornice screwed to the cant rails. The canvas must then be given four coats of thick white lead paint.
>
> 'The sides and ends of car must be properly cleaned off and given two coats of lead colour, four coats of filling, then to be rubbed down, one coat of lead colour and faced, one coat of lead colour, one coat of chocolate brown and a second coat of half varnish half colour below the light rails, and four coats of white above the rails. The mouldings are then to have two coats of brown, and the whole given one coat of varnish; the round of mouldings is then to have two coats of gold colour finished with three coats of varnish flattened down after the first coat.'

Thus it would seem that the famous GWR 'cream' at this period was produced by painting the upper parts of the car sides white and then applying varnish, and the mouldings were not edged in black either side of the gold line. These cars evidently did not get the fine brown line round the cream panels, let alone the double gold lines. In the case of the Dia. E cars, Nos.15 and 16 – also ordered from Kerr, Stuart – the GWR supplied the firm with a panel showing the lining to be applied, and these cars did get the fine brown line on the cream panels.

Droplight frames and bolection mouldings were varnished mahogany, although the Swindon drawing mentioned earlier shows them as 'Venetian red'.

Needless to say, the white lead roof colour quickly weathered to a dark grey.

The underframes etc. were black, and the motion and cylinder covers left bright. The Kerr, Stuart contract spelt it out thus:

> 'Before any paint is applied the surfaces must be cleaned and free from all scale and rust. The boiler is to receive one coat of red lead whilst warm. The outside of cleating, plates, wheels, frames, chimney, brake work and springs must have one coat of lead colour, one coat japan black and one coat best engine varnish.'

During this period, roof destination boards on ordinary coaches were red with gold lettering. Photographs of SRMs showing the small boards on the end or sides indicate that, during this period, they had white, or possibly, cream lettering.

Insignia and lettering, 1903–1906: The 'entwined monogram'

In this period, the company's ownership of its SRMs was indicated by the use of the rather florid 'entwined monogram' in gold, shaded black, which incorporated the letters 'GWR'. The positioning of this varied. The car's number was in 6-inch gold lettering, whilst auxiliary lettering like 'ENTRANCE' was in gold, shaded black.

On car No.1 there were eight windows to the passenger saloon. A monogram was placed under the second window from the power end, 'N° 1' under the fourth window, and another monogram under the sixth window. It did not carry its number on either end.

No.2 similarly had its number in the form 'N° 2', centrally under the sliding windows of the motor compartment. There is no clear photographic evidence that the car carried the monogram. Initially it had no number on its ends, but in due course 'N° 2' was placed below the left-hand end window.

Cars Nos.3–14 as built also had eight large windows in the saloon, but they had a passenger vestibule between the saloon and the power compartment. The monogram was positioned beneath the pillar between the third and fourth windows, and the number, again in the form 'N° 7', beneath the seventh window. The number also appeared centrally on the ends in the same style, with 'N°' to the left of the vacuum pipe, and the numeral(s) to the right. These cars had their numbers written in 9-inch letters and figures. This arrangement on the ends became the standard. 'ENTRANCE' was written in the panel above the droplight of the passenger vestibule door.

Nos.17–28 had a luggage compartment with double doors, and only six windows to the saloon. The luggage compartment doors did not carry any wording, and the monogram was placed below the pillar between the second and third windows from the luggage compartment, and (e.g.) 'N° 17' below the fifth window. Some photographs of these cars in service do not show a monogram at all. The number was placed on the end, as with cars 3–14.

The wood panelled cars, including the coach portions of Nos.15 and 16, had the car number (in the familiar format 'N° 43') once in the waist panel to the right of centre in 6-inch figures, and

This official photograph of Car No. 67 of Diagram O shows the car as built with the 'prize monogram'. NATIONAL RAILWAY MUSEUM

Car No. 62 of Diagram O, as new at Swindon in 1906, showing the trailing end. It looks as if the tare weight had only just been painted on the solebar as guide lines are apparent. This view also shows the whistle cord mouth on the right-hand moulding above the end windows and the end of the through regulator gear.

the entwined monogram once below the waist to the left of centre. Where there was a passenger vestibule next to the power compartment and a single passenger saloon, the vestibule door carried 'ENTRANCE' in the eaves panel. Dia. L cars – at least – had the word 'EXIT' in the eaves panel of the trailing vestibule doors. Cars with this arrangement of doors, and where the passenger saloon was divided into smoking and non-smoking areas, the passenger vestibule door carried the word 'SMOKING' (e.g. car No.43), with nothing on the trailing vestibule door. Cars with luggage compartments did not carry any wording in the doors' eaves panels. Cars Nos.15 and 16 had 'LUGGAGE' and 'COMP^T^' in the left and right-hand waist panels of the luggage compartment doors, but it is not known if any other cars had this. The wood panelled cars also had their number painted on the ends in the waist panel above the vacuum pipe in 6-inch figures. This was positioned with 'N^o^' to the left of the headlamp bracket with the numerals to the right, so that the number tended to be partially obscured by the headlamp. The arrangement on the ends of cars 15 and 16 is not known. These two non-standard cars had their locomotive portion painted chocolate brown, lined out with a single yellow line, and the numbers on the front of the locomotive portion were 9 inches in height. Their underframes etc. were to be black and the motion bright, as usual.

Car No. 89 of Diagram R arriving at Paddington on the 5.5 p.m. from Greenford on 21st August 1910. This was part of Southall's 'D' working. KEN NUNN COLLECTION

1905: No monogram

No.43 was built with the standard livery as described above. However, from a photograph, car No.47, built in February 1905 of the same design and Lot as No.43, carried no monogram or 'GWR' lettering when new. Its running number was placed once in the waist panel in the usual form 'N° 47', approximately centrally, above the place where a monogram might have been expected. No.29, when fitted with droplights, was photographed in the same livery, as was No.46 in about 1908 (or possibly later, as it had droplights and external water filler lids fitted).

No.59, built in November 1905, also carried no monogram, but had the running number as 'N^o^59' twice in the waist panel, once more or less centrally, and again towards the trailing end of the car.

It is not known if these cars received company identification while they were still in the pre-1908 two-colour livery.

1906 GW Prize monogram

In early 1905, the *Great Western Railway Magazine* ran a competition in conjunction with *The Studio* magazine for a monogram incorporating the letters 'G' and 'W' for use on the company's coaches, in which a prize of 2 guineas was offered for the winning entrant. In the August 1905 issue, the *Great Western Magazine* published the winning design, but, curiously, not the name of the winning artist, possibly because most entrants used a 'nom-de-plume'. However, *The Studio* later revealed him to be Charles Doust of 24, St. Adians Road, East Dulwich, London, SE. As published in the magazine, the winning monogram was dark in colour with a light-coloured outline, although it actually appeared on coaches in solid gold, with 'shading' only where one letter crossed over the other, whilst the proposed – rather fancy – serifs were simplified.

The earliest confirmed use of the prize monogram seems to have been on Trailer No.13, which was photographed when built in December 1905. As far as SRMs were concerned, the earliest that can be dated was on car No.61, built in March 1906, and its use seems to have been confined to some cars of Lots 1100 (Nos.61–72, built from March to June) and 1101 (Nos.73–80 built between April and June 1906). The latest painting date confirmed was on No.69, built in June 1906, while an official photograph of No.70 taken in March 1907 (see below) shows it with the garter emblem and supporters. It is possible that some other cars carried the prize monogram following a repaint during this period, but no evidence is available.

1906–8 Garter and supporters

As we have seen, the prize monogram was applied to stock for a very short period. The GWR then reverted to the insignia previously applied to coaches with first class accommodation, but now used on all coaches, evidently including SRMs. Unfortunately, there is a lack of clear pictures of SRMs showing this livery, so what follows is partially by deduction, based in part on a photograph of No.70 under repair in March 1907.

It would appear that the car's number was probably placed twice in the waist panel (in the usual form, 'N° 70') at either end of the passenger accommodation. In the case of car 70, one was placed below the end window framing, next to the luggage compartment. The crest would have been placed as centrally as possible in relation to the passenger accommodation – avoiding any doors – in a panel below the waist. The supporters would have been placed in a panel below the waist, and in the case of No.70 this was below the number. The car number was also placed at the ends of the car, as before.

No.70 was one of the first, if not the first, SRM to carry this livery in June 1906, and presumably all cars built after this date would have been similarly treated, as would those cars repainted from, say, mid-June 1906 until the introduction of the brown livery in 1908.

1908–1912: LINED BROWN

The cleanliness of coaches was a matter of particular concern in the 1900s, and was a regular item on the agendas of senior officials' meetings. In 1903, a rake of GWR coaches was painted brown as an experiment, and in May 1905 the *Great Western Railway Magazine* carried – without comment – a photograph of 'Ocean Mails' van No.822 (Dia. M10, built in August 1904) painted in an all-brown, lined livery. The vehicle did not carry 'GWR', and the running number was in the eaves panels. The *Railway Magazine* reported numbers of Great Western coaches being painted in brown, to its intense annoyance. However, I am not aware of an SRM being painted in brown before the general adoption of the lined brown livery in mid-1908.

In September 1908, the introduction of this standard all-chocolate-brown lined livery was announced in the *Great Western Railway Magazine*:

This picture of No. 9 of Diagram D in the Wrexham area between 1910 and 1912, shows the 1908 brown livery. This car had droplights substituted for some fixed lights in the saloon, modified sliding windows to the engine compartment and a water filler added. Notice also that the bottom edge of the end windows had been raised, retaining the original end matchboarding – compare with No. 11 on page 120.
KIDDERMINSTER RAILWAY MUSEUM

Car No. 45 of Diagram M in post-1908 lined brown livery. No. 45 was allocated to Chester from the end of May 1911 until December 1912 and is seen here with modified sliding windows to the power compartment and a water filler lid with a cross. I think the door to the smoking compartment still had the word 'SMOKING' above the window, although it is not very clear.
COLLECTION J. N. SLINN

'The familiar cream panelling in the upper portions of the Company's coaching stock will, as the vehicles pass through the shops, become a thing of the past, it having been decided, after careful observation, to paint the stock wholly brown, or to be more correct chocolate-brown. The new colour gives a pleasing and comfortable appearance to the stock. It will not be difficult to understand that, handsome as the cream panelling undoubtedly is, it gets dirty very quickly, and entails extended cleaning operations. A brown-painted coach is not so expensive to keep clean; therefore, considerable economy should result from the change. The company's carriage cleaning bill runs to many thousands of pounds per annum, so that the alteration is calculated to fully justify itself in results.'

So, the exact date of the introduction of the brown livery is a little uncertain, but it was before September 1908 – possibly in July or August. I think that it is probable that no SRMs carried this livery from new, because the last entered traffic in February 1908.

In this livery, the whole of the car body above the underframe and below the roof was painted brown, which was lined out as before, with matchboarded cars having the slightly simplified lining with no waist panel picked out. As in the final variation of the brown and cream livery, the garter crest and supporters was used.

Changes in lettering were also instigated: the 'N$^{\underline{o}}$' no longer preceded the car number on the sides or the ends, whilst all lettering and numbering characters were now shaded, as on ordinary coaching stock, with 6-inch numbers being used on the ends of all cars in the waist panels. On the sides, the car number appeared twice, close to both the end doors in the waist panel, with 'GWR' also in the waist panel inboard of the car number. The 'GWR' was in a distinctly smaller size than the numbers – presumably standard carriage transfers were used (hauled stock had 5-inch-deep waist panels). Matchboarded cars had a similar positioning of insignia with standard 6 inch numbers on the ends. However, there is a photograph of No.17 in which 'GWR' and the number were placed rather lower on the sides, at about the height of the number in the brown and cream livery.

'LUGGAGE' appeared in the waist panel of the left-hand leaf of cars with double doors to the luggage compartment, and this arrangement continued in subsequent liveries. Standard size, shaded lettering was again used. There is evidence that cars with an end passenger vestibule instead of a luggage compartment had 'SMOKING' in the door's eaves panel as earlier.

Roofs continued to be painted white, underframes black, and the motion and cylinder covers were bright.

All SRMs may well have been repainted into this livery.

On 29th June 1910, a circular was issued in the Bristol Division concerning small destination boards:

'*Colour of small label boards*
In future the small label boards will be written in gold letters with black and red shading on white ground. All to note new boards must only be used on brown coaches, the present boards being kept for the old colour stock.'

This was repeated in the July and September 1910 issues of the operating circulars, although in September 'old colour stock' became 'cream coloured stock'. On SRMs and trailers, the destination boards on the sides were positioned in the waist panels, and were on brown anyway. A couple of photographs probably showing this style of destination board do exist, but there seem to be more photographs of brown- and lake-liveried cars carrying old style destination boards.

1912–1922: LINED LAKE

The year 1912 marked the introduction of a (crimson) lake, lined livery, although its introduction passed unannounced; it was very similar – except for the base colour – to the 1908 brown. With the possible exception of some of the early conversions to trailers, most SRMs would have been repainted in this livery in due course.

There were no significant changes to the lining, although bolection mouldings and droplight frames were now painted crimson lake.

Roofs were again white, the underframes black, and the cylinder covers and motion bright.

On SRMs, the running numbers continued to be painted in the same style and positions as in the lined brown livery, although 'GWR' was now placed, once only, in the waist panel above the garter device, and it was in a larger size to match the car numbers; this change is the simplest way to distinguish between the brown and lake liveries in photographs. 'Luggage' continued in the smaller, standard size, as before.

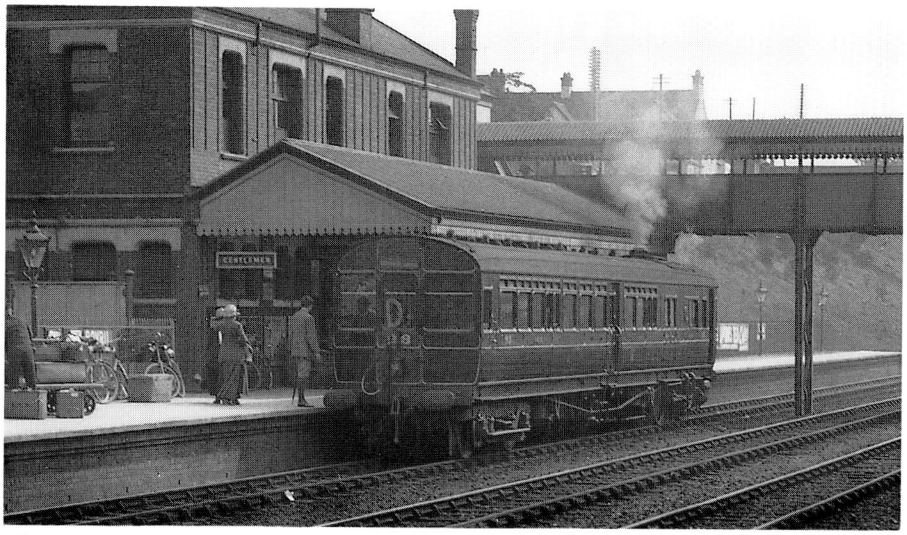

Car No. 98 in the 1908 brown livery at Gerrards Cross in 1912/13. The metal letter 'D' indicated that it was on a Southall car Westbourne Park working. No. 98 was at Southall between April 1912 and April 1913. NATIONAL RAILWAY MUSEUM

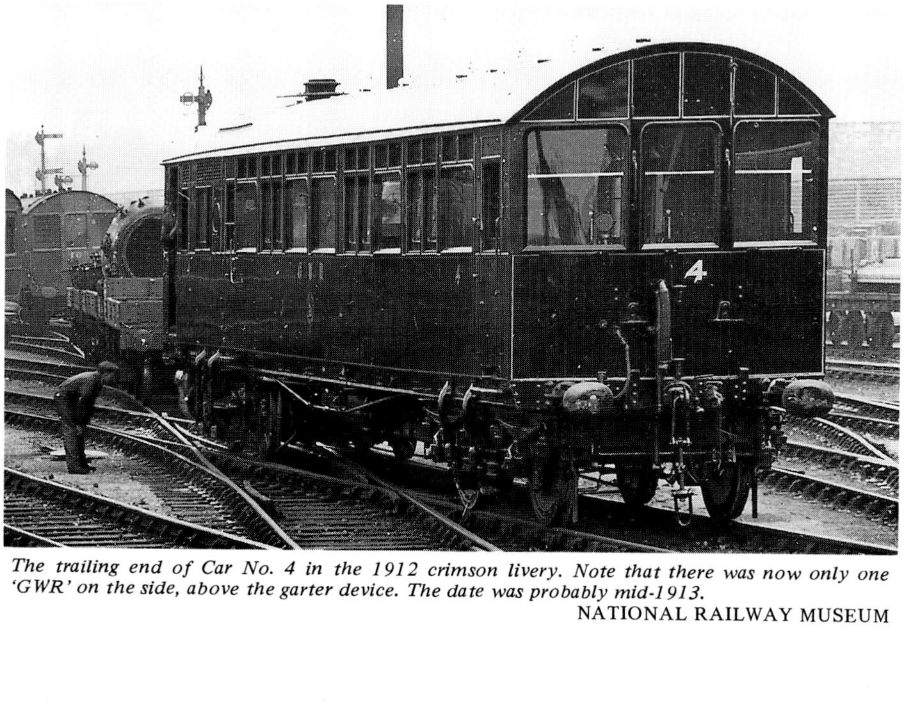

The trailing end of Car No. 4 in the 1912 crimson livery. Note that there was now only one 'GWR' on the side, above the garter device. The date was probably mid-1913. NATIONAL RAILWAY MUSEUM

Car No. 68 of Diagram O in the lined lake livery of 1912.

COLLECTION ALAN HALL

Car No. 61 of Diagram O in the lined lake livery hauling a Diagram T 70ft trailer. This car had been fitted with protection bars to the front windows, a water filler lid with a cross, and additional end steps, one of which can be seen in front of the cylinder. This picture may have been taken at Gloucester Central, in which case it would date from the first half of 1922.

COLLECTION R. C. RILEY

During the Great War, some coaches were said to have been repainted in khaki, and even black, but it is not known if any SRMs suffered this fate. During this period, all the match-boarded SRMs were converted to trailers.

THE 1922 LINED BROWN & CREAM LIVERY

In mid-1922, the GWR built some new 70ft coaches for the 'Cornish Riviera' and other principal trains, and once again, commencing with these vehicles, passenger coaching stock appeared in lined brown and cream. The Minutes of the meeting of the Locomotive, Carriage & Stores Committee held on 9th March 1922 record:

> 'The Chief Mechanical Engineer reported the circumstances under which – in connection with the repainting of the carriage stock – it is proposed to revert to the former Great Western colours of chocolate brown for the lower part of the bodies and cream for the upper panels, and to change the practice in regard to painting and cleaning the vehicles by reducing the number of coats of paint and cheapening the method of painting, at the same time carrying out the work more frequently. He recommended that the whole of the 8-wheeled stock be dealt with during the next three years, the additional cost of doing so being estimated at £39,000, or £13,000 per annum. The proposals were approved and it was agreed to recommend the Board to sanction the expenditure.'

This style was based on the 1906–08 livery, with the garter device and its supporters. Photographs of steam rail motors painted into this livery in 1922–24 have not come to light, but it is probable that 'Nº' no longer preceded the car number on the sides or the ends, and that 'GWR' would be in 6 inch letters to match the car number. Both 'GWR' and the car number appear to have been in shaded characters, because in the photographs referred to below these appear to be applied slightly higher than centrally in the waist panels. 'LUGGAGE', on the other hand, has been applied centrally, so may still not have been shaded. The fine line formerly inside the cream panels was omitted, and bolection mouldings, droplights and other window frames were now painted a mahogany colour. In addition, the general painting specification stated that mouldings were to be painted black with gold lining.

From 1924/5, the livery was altered by increasing the amount of cream paint above the waist. There is an official photograph of No.75 taken in March 1925 which shows the additional cream (in place of brown) applied between the bolection mouldings of those windows which did not have panels between them before. These new cream panels were not obviously lined out. In addition, the toplight frames appear to have been painted cream; they were mahogany before.

Because the photograph is a broadside view it is hard to be certain, but the waist panels below the end windows (at both ends) appear

This official photograph of Car No. 75 of Diagram Q, taken in March 1925, shows the fully-lined livery of 1922 as modified from about 1924. Additional cream had been applied between the bolection mouldings of those windows which did not have panels between them before. This photograph is discussed in detail in the text. As far as the appearance of the car is concerned, it had been fitted with protection bars at the power unit end windows and a plain water filler lid but there was no alarm apparatus. NATIONAL RAILWAY MUSEUM

Car No. 80 of Diagram Q in what appears to have been a modified version of the 1922 fully-lined livery. Compared with No. 75, the boundary between brown and cream was now the same height as on the sides (compare the small photograph above) and there was a dark line above the end windows. COLLECTION R. C. RILEY

to be brown, and there appears to be a narrow cream area between the corner moulding and the front window bolection moulding. It is not known if the vertical mouldings above the end windows were painted black and lined (probably), but the moulding immediately under the roof was painted like this.

For some reason, an eaves panel has appeared in the panel forward of the power unit door; this was not originally present. In it is painted, in shaded characters, '3' over '46', rather like a fraction – presumably 46 seats and 3 compartments – the 46 includes the emergency seats in the luggage compartment.

This picture of car 75 is a bit of a mystery. The area round the chimney is dirty, and on an original print, the new cream areas appear appreciably lighter than the others; it may be that the photograph was taken to record the livery revisions, and that the car was not wholly repainted for the occasion.

There is also a photograph of No.80 in this livery – a three-quarter view, showing the power end – but perhaps carried out at a later date. The principal differences compared to No.75 are that the division between the brown and cream on this end is the same as on the sides, so the colour change divides the wide waist panel, with the car number on the brown. In fact, No.80 seems to have a steel-sheeted end below the windows, so there was no waist panel to line out. The vertical mouldings above the end windows are painted plain cream; this arrangement became standard in future. Although the mouldings appear to be in a darker colour than the brown panelling on No.75, in the case of 80 they seem to be the same, so are perhaps painted brown and lined in gold on their edges. No.80 did not have the extra eaves panel exhibited by 75.

The cylinder covers on No.80 were painted black.

From 1922, the roof destination boards of main-line coaches were painted with unshaded black lettering on a white ground. There is photographic evidence that this was applied to the small, side destination boards on SRMs too, and that the colour scheme was continued on the small boards, although, starting in 1925, roof boards were painted with brown lettering on a cream ground.

1927–1935: 'SIMPLE' LIVERY

A simplified livery was introduced in 1927, and continued with variations until nationalization in 1948. It was subject to a steady evolution, and the relevant changes and dates are indicated below.

Spring 1927

In April 1927 (the date on a drawing), the GWR abandoned the fully-lined-out, two-colour livery for a plain two-colour livery, with brown below the waist and cream above, separated by a 9/16in black line along the top of the waist panel, just below the windows. However,

The power end of Car No. 76 (Diagram Q) in one of the 1927 'simple' brown and cream liveries. G. N. SOUTHERDEN

Car No. 95 of Diagram R at Himley, on the Kingswinford branch in the West Midlands, a line which bypassed Dudley and Wolverhampton. This picture shows a version of the 1924-27 fully-lined brown and cream livery with only the corner mouldings and the ones below the roof and above the windows lined out. The broad waist panel was divided by the brown/cream boundary; however, the mouldings on the side appear to have been lined, and those above the waist appear to have been in black as they look darker than the brown of the lower car side. Notice that weight figures had not yet been introduced at this time. Protection bars can be seen behind the end windows, but there was no extension to the coal bunker. Car No. 95 was allocated to Stourbridge between 30th July 1925 and September 1926, apart from a month in Wolverhampton Works. AUTHOR'S COLLECTION

Car No. 55 of Diagram O at Swindon stock shed with No. 86 on the adjacent line. No. 55 was in the 1930 livery with two gold/black lines at the waist. The window protection bars are visible and the extension to the bunker appears as a black band inside the front windows. The trailing bogie had blue painted axleboxes. No. 55 was at Swindon stock shed from August 1931 until February 1932 and No. 86 was there from April to October 1931. This picture was therefore taken between August and October 1931.

T. E. LAYNE
COLLECTION J. N. SLINN

Car No. 86 of Diagram R at Swindon stock shed in 1931.

H. J. STRETTON WARD

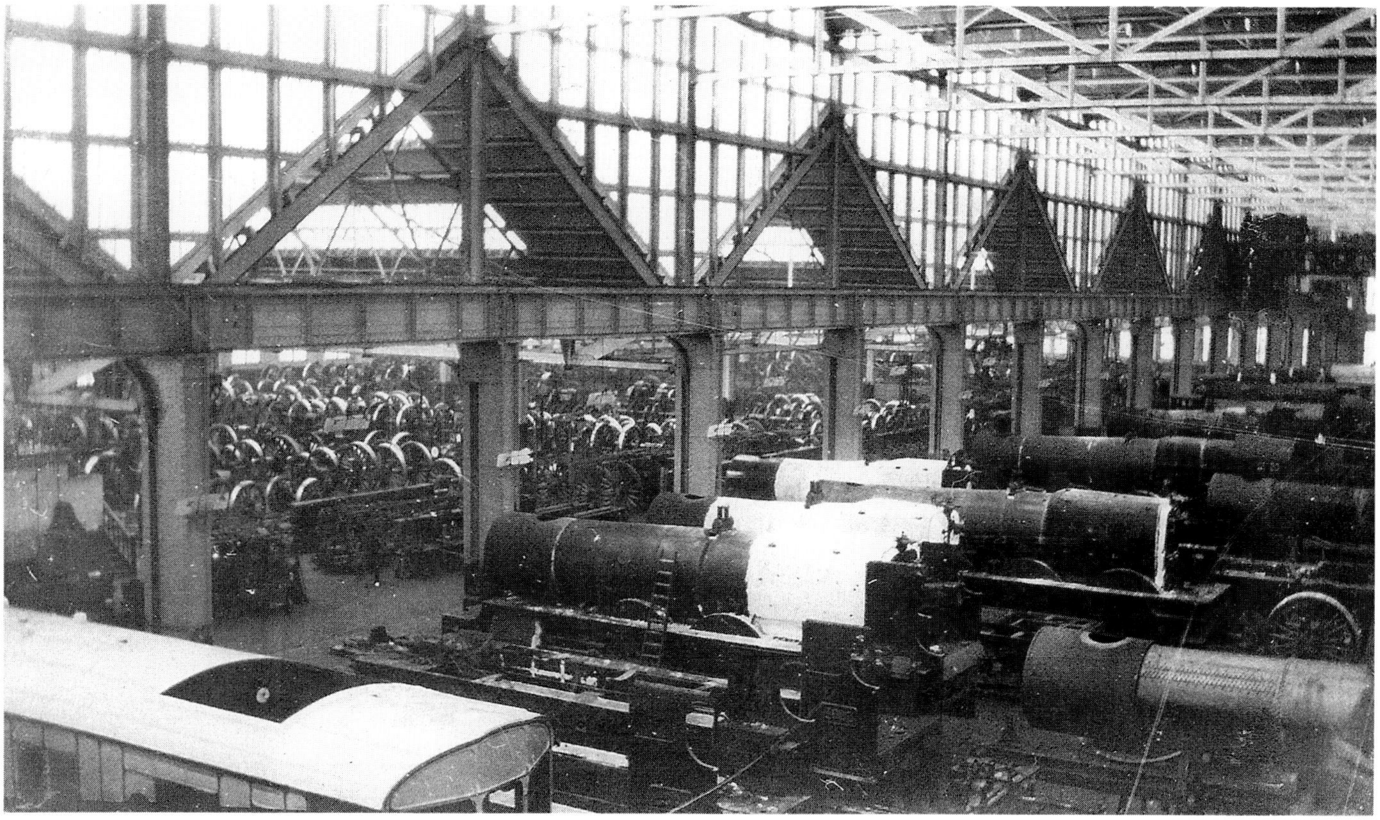

A steam rail motor under repair at Swindon some time between 1922 and 1927.

it is possible that a few vehicles were outshopped without this black line. The ends of SRMs continued to be painted the same as the sides, whilst the style of lettering and numbering on the sides and driving ends was unchanged.

The roofs were still painted white, and although they should have had a black line painted across the roof at the ends, this is not apparent on the SRMs (and not always to hauled stock, either). The gutters were painted brown, instead of white. Window frames and bolection mouldings remained a mahogany colour, and underframes, etc., were black.

July 1927

In about July 1927, the garter crest and its supporters was replaced by a coat of arms device combining the arms of the cities of London and Bristol. This can be dated reasonably closely as composite No.6237 of Lot 1376 (built June 1927) had the garter crest, whilst No.6345 of the same Lot (built July 1927) had the new coat of arms. Curiously, the April 1927 drawing referred to above showed the coat of arms and not the garter device; presumably the supply of the old transfers was to be used up first.

There was also supposed to be a vertical black line along the ends of coach sides, but photographs seem to indicate that this line was not applied to SRMs, presumably because their ends were not painted black, like ordinary coaches. From this period, axle boxes were painted blue.

October 1929

In October 1929 it was decided to revise the livery again, and a ⅜in gold line was painted below the black line along the waist of SRMs. Circular No.4974 was issued by Mr Collett on 29th November 1929, and read:

'It has been decided to make the following modifications in the exterior painting of 8-wheeled coaches as the vehicles are repainted, and I will be glad if you will arrange accordingly.

'All Corridor Bogie Coaches for Main Line working, including Restaurant Cars, Sleeping Cars, Slip Coaches and Mail Vans to have:

(1) A BLACK LINE under cornice at top of cream panel.
(2) Waist panelled out with one Black and Gold line ⅜" wide.
(3) Present standard size "FIRST" and "THIRD" on doors.
(4) Black line on vertical beading on ends of coach.

'Other 8-wheeled coaches to have:

(1) One Black and Gold line separating the cream and brown.
(2) One black line along the top of the coach.
(3) Black line on vertical beading on ends of coach.

'ROOF DESTINATION BOARDS

To have black border and gold line with plain Black letters.

'I am sending you specimen panels and gauges. If you have not already a gilding machine this should be ordered from Mr G.C. Dickens, Carriage & Wagon Storekeeper, Swindon.'

Again, the black line on the ends of the sides does not seem to have been applied.

March 1930

On 10th March 1930, a further circular on the painting of coaching stock was issued (Circular 4974A). This read:

'In my circular 4974 of the 29th November last it is stated "All Corridor Bogie Coaches for Main Line working ...

'Will you kindly note that all bogie coaches should be dealt with as main line vehicles.'

The effect of this circular on SRMs was to add a second gold and black line to effect a waist panel along the car. This was only applied to cars that were repainted, but a few received it. The black lines on the ends of the sides were again omitted.

1934

In 1934, the GWR coat of arms was replaced by the 'shirtbutton' monogram on all new and repainted carriage stock. On photographic evidence, this seems to have been introduced by September that year, so it is *just possible, but not confirmed* that car No.65 received this livery as it emerged from a general overhaul at the end of October 1934, and No.92, which had a general overhaul completed on 13th November. Several other cars had lesser repairs after September 1934, but it is thought doubtful that they received the new monogram.

Dean 8ft 6in bogie, standard for all matchboarded SRMs.

9ft elliptical spring bogie.

9ft coil spring bogie.

9ft 'fishbelly' type bogie used on Kerr, Stuart-built 70ft cars.

8ft 'fishbelly' type bogie used on Gloucester-built 59½ft cars.

9ft 'American' bogie used on Diagram R cars.

Non-standard bogie used on Nos. 15 and 16.

CHAPTER FIVE

BELOW THE BODY

THIS chapter is concerned with the development of the underframes of the GWR-design steam rail motors, what was suspended from them, and details of the trailing bogies. As usual, the power unit end of the car will normally be referred to as the leading end, and the other as the trailing end. The power units, consisting of the boiler plus the engine (the cylinders, wheels and motion), are dealt with in a separate chapter. References to 'short' cars applies to those less than 70ft long.

UNDERFRAMES

SRMS NOS.1 AND 2

Nos.1 and 2 had an underframe design that was not repeated: they had inset, fixed steps, and this prevented the solebars from extending the whole length of the vehicle, which must have weakened the underframe when it came to coping with trailing end buffing loads. However, the design did introduce some features that were included on subsequent versions.

The main underframe was 53ft 3½in long with a 3ft 6½in extension to carry the steps and trailing vestibule. The main solebars were of 9 × 3½ × ⅝in channel set 7ft 6in apart, except that they were bowed out to 7ft 11in for a distance of 3ft from the leading headstock, a feature which was adopted on subsequent short designs. They were strengthened by queen post trusses. The queen posts were castings set at 4ft centres, and the round section truss rods were 10in below the solebars. There was a turnbuckle at the centre of the truss rods so their tension could be adjusted. The truss rods were flattened at the leading end to pass over the transoms either side of the boiler, then bolted to brackets attached to the inside of the solebars, 4ft 11in from the centre line of the boiler. At the trailing end, they were flattened where they passed over a cross member that was positioned across the centre of the trailing bogie, and were fastened to brackets attached to the solebars just in front of the intermediate headstock. The scroll irons for the engine were bolted to the solebars at 2ft 10½in centres, and for the trailing bogie at 3ft 1in centres. The trailing bogie was a standard Dean 8ft 6in wheelbase carriage unit.

Headstocks were of 10 × 4 × ½in channel, 8ft 6in long. The buffers and draw hook were bolted to the leading one, which had square ends chamfered at the bottom corner. The surviving underframe drawing shows buffers with oval heads; as built, these cars had buffers with round heads, but they were changed at an early date.

The boiler was centred 9ft behind the front of the headstocks. There was a cross bearer (or 'transome' as the drawing also has it) of 9 × 3½ × ⅝in channel in front of the boiler, and one behind it, 3ft 11in apart. The leading one (transom 'A') had a small bite 1ft 4½in wide by 3½in deep removed from the bottom on both sides, starting 2in from the ends. These transoms were bowed out to 4ft 10in apart to clear the boiler; however, this dimension has been altered to 5ft 4⅜in on the drawing. There was a pair of diagonal members running from the leading headstock, just inboard of the buffers, to transom 'A', and a similar pair of diagonals from transom 'B' to another cross member. From this cross member, a pair of longitudinals ran along the car 2ft 8in apart, from which the water tank was suspended. At the trailing end of the car, these longitudinals were bowed inwards to the centre pin casting of the trailing bogie, and then outwards again to meet the trailing headstock.

The 'underframe extension' – for want of a better term – had six longitudinals between the intermediate and trailing headstocks, positioned to clear the steps. The buffers were bolted to the trailing headstock, as usual, but the draw bar was a long one, and passed through the trailing headstock, being bolted to the intermediate member. There were small triangular stiffening plates fitted between the headstocks and four of the longitudinals to help carry buffing loads, as there were no solebars outboard of the buffers in the usual manner. The trailing headstock had ends angled inwards. The steps were suspended from brackets and a pair of rods, though all were eventually removed.

Two cylindrical gas tanks, each measuring 7ft by 1ft 6in diameter, were slung from cross members, centrally on either side of the water tank. A single Armstrong-type vacuum cylinder on the off side was suspended from brackets between the solebar and the adjacent longitudinal, whilst the 'V' hangers were fastened to the solebar and the further longitudinal.

The underframe drawing for SRMs 1 and 2 is No.22983 of July 1903 and carries a note about alterations shown on 'drawing 54053 dated 1–3–11'. Unfortunately, this later drawing has not come to light, but one of the diagrams for these cars has a note to the effect that No.2 was fitted with retractable steps. If so, it *may* mean that No.2 (at least) had its solebars extended to the trailing headstock. This date does not fit in with the recorded changes of engine to either car.

OTHER MATCHBOARDED SRMS

Apart from Nos.1 and 2, GWR-designed steam railmotors had bow ends and, as there were no fixed internal steps, the solebars extended the full length of the side of the car – in this case 57ft 0¼in. They were still bowed-out towards the leading end of the SRM, and were made of 9 × 3½in × ⅝in channel as before. In these cars, the headstocks seem to have been made of the same material, but were bowed like the body, so that the cars were 59ft 6in over headstocks. This, in turn, meant that special buffers with angled bases and long guides had to be used. At the leading end there was a short cross member lying between and fastened to the diagonals coming from the headstock; the drawbar was extended through the headstock and was bolted to this. At the trailing end, there was a full width cross member 2ft 3in behind the headstock, to which the trailing drawbar was bolted, and the hand brake column was arranged immediately to one side of this.

The solebars were braced by queen post trusses as on Nos.1 and 2, but the various dimensions varied to take into account the bowed headstocks (on all except 1 and 2), and the retractable steps on Diagram G cars.

TABLE 7

UNDERFRAME DIMENSIONS

Diagrams	*H'stock - Boiler C/L*	*Boiler C/L - Turnbuckle*	*Turnbuckle - Bogie centre*	*Bogie centre - headstock*	*Queenpost spacing*
A	9 ft 0 in	18 ft 7½ in	18 ft 7½ in	10 ft 9 in	4 ft 0 in
B, C, D, F	10 ft 3 in	20 ft 3 in	20 ft 3 in	8 ft 9 in	3 ft 6 in
G	10 ft 2⅝ in	18 ft 9 in	18 ft 8 in	11 ft 8⅝ in	2 ft 6 in

Water tank, gas cylinders and brake gear were suspended from the longitudinals and solebars in a similar fashion to SRMs 1 and 2. At the trailing end, the diagonals were fastened to the headstock.

An important change at the leading end of the underframe on the bow-ended cars was the introduction of a metal plate for stiffening, which extended from the leading headstock back to the first straight cross member behind the boiler. This plate had a large hole in it for the boiler, and smaller ones for pipework etc. In addition, the truss rods had a similar arrangement to that on the first two cars, so they came up through the plate to pass over the two transoms and then descended again to the brackets by which they were fastened to the solebar. At the trailing end the arrangement was similar to the first two SRMs, but in these later cars the truss rods were not flattened where they passed over the transoms.

59FT 6IN WOOD PANELLED SRMS

The underframes for these vehicles were very similar to those of the standard matchboarded cars. Curiously, the underframe was 57ft 0¼in

Underframe for Diagrams Q1 and Q.

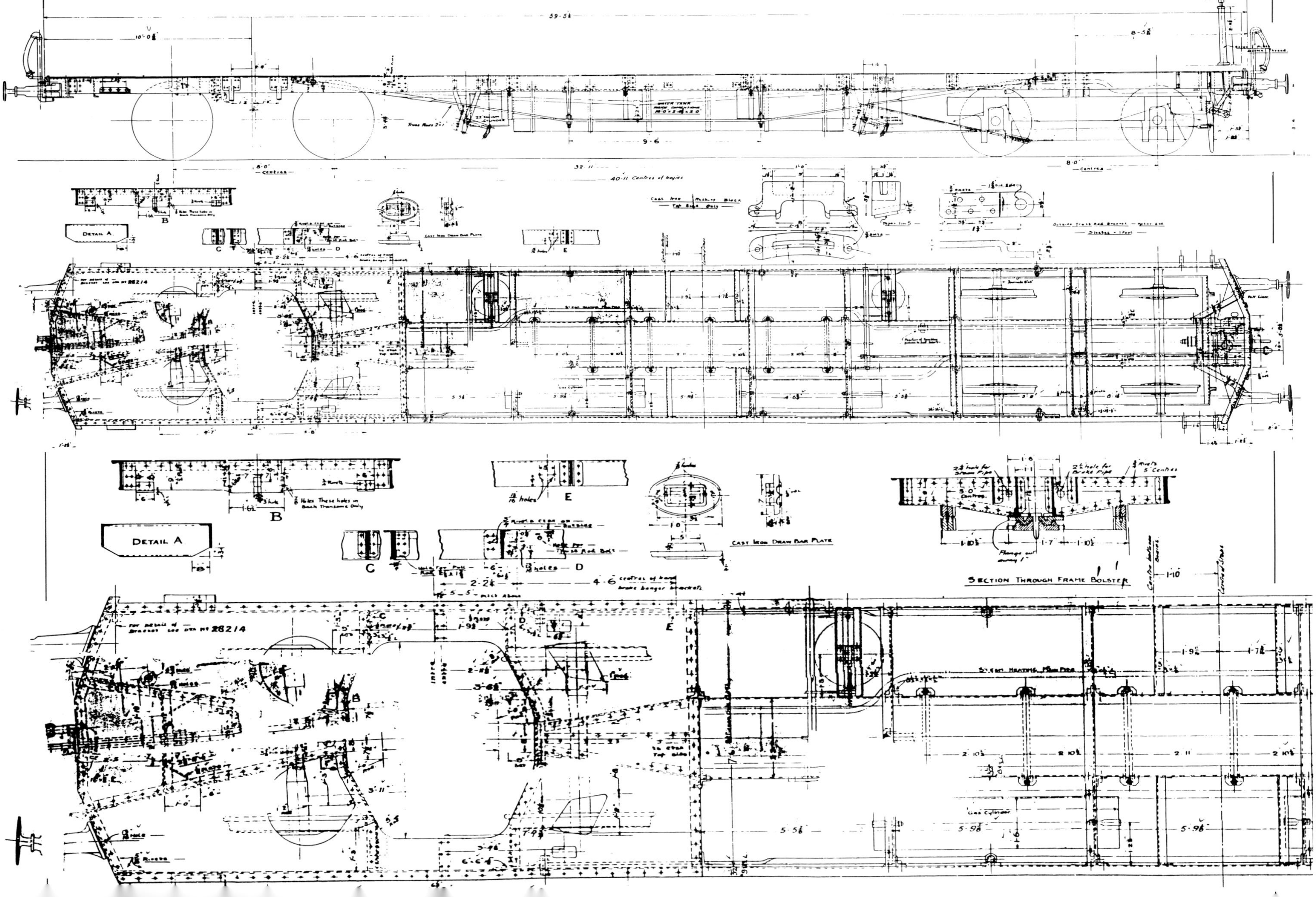

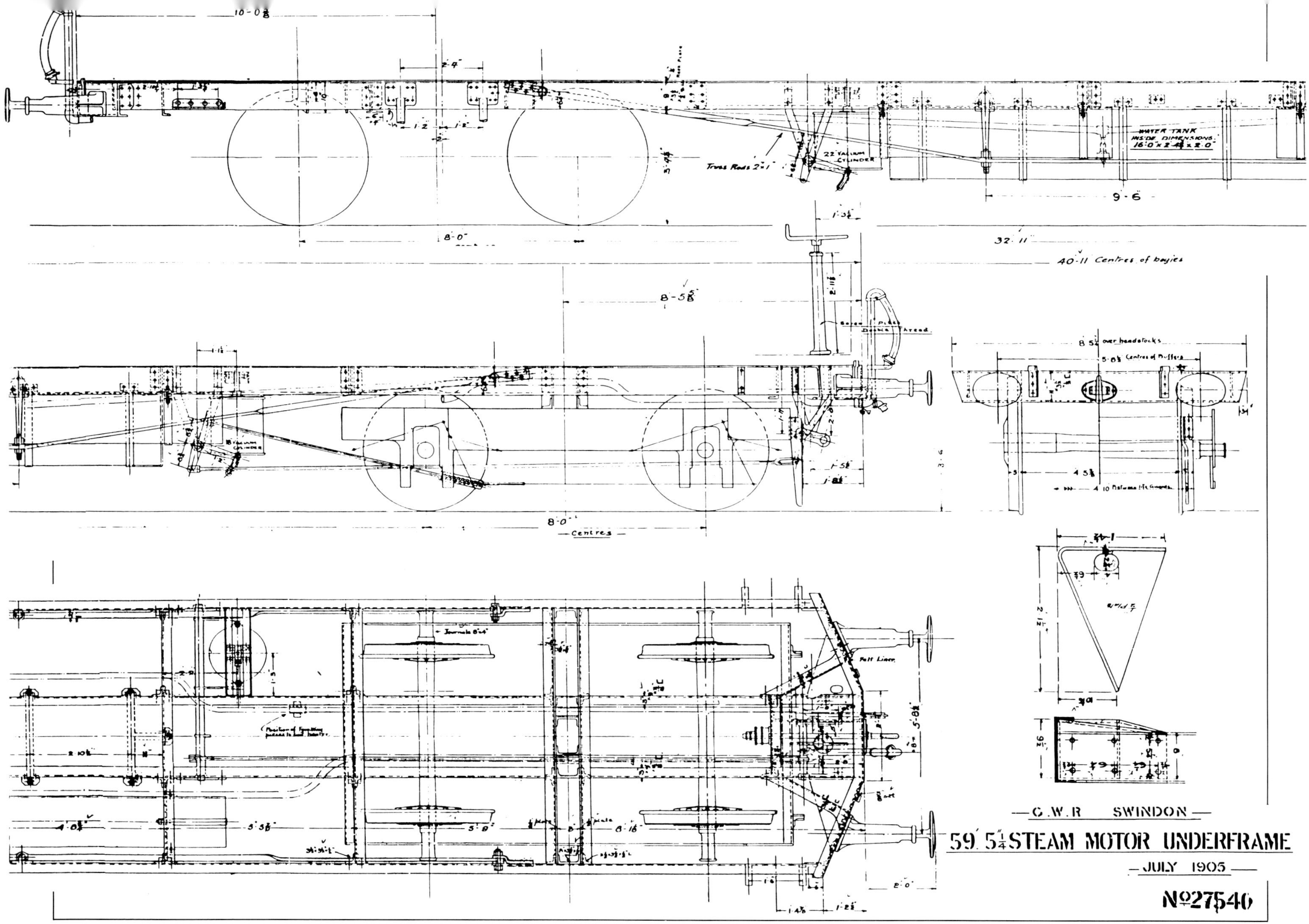

WATER TANK INSIDE DIMENSIONS 16'0" x 2'4" x 2'0"
22" VACUUM CYLINDER
Truss Rods 2¼"
9'-6
32'-11"
40'-11 Centres of bogies
8'-0"
10'-0⅝
2'-4"
8'-5⅝"
8'-0" Centres
8'-5¼" over headstocks
5'-8⅝ Centres of Buffers
4'-10 Between the Guards
Felt Liner
Journals 8"x4"
Position of Bogie Frame
5'-8⅜
2'-1½"
9½"
G.W.R SWINDON
59' 5¼" STEAM MOTOR UNDERFRAME
JULY 1905
No 27540

Underframe for Diagram G1 and G cars. The trailing bogie had been moved away from the end to allow for steps to be fitted.

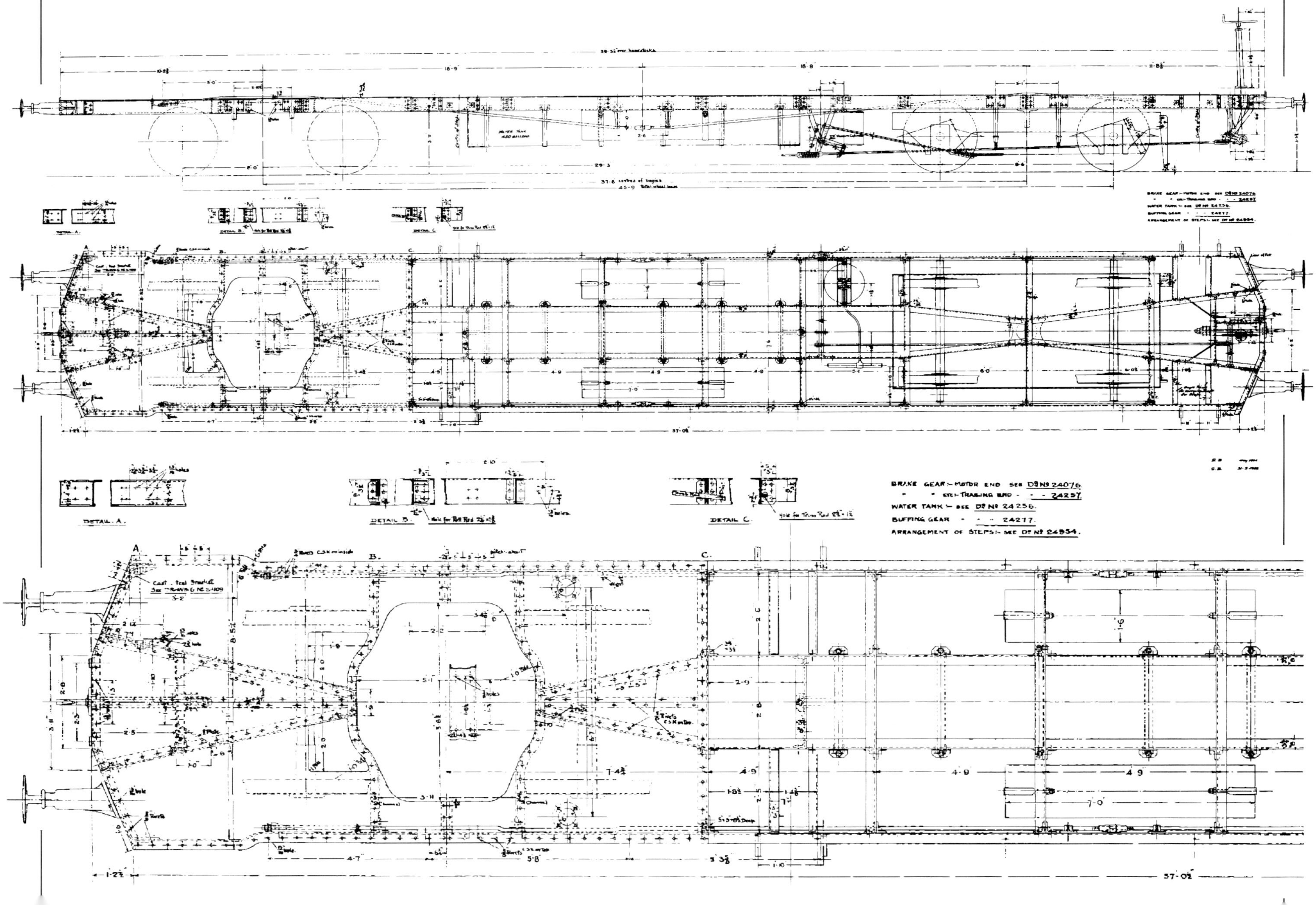

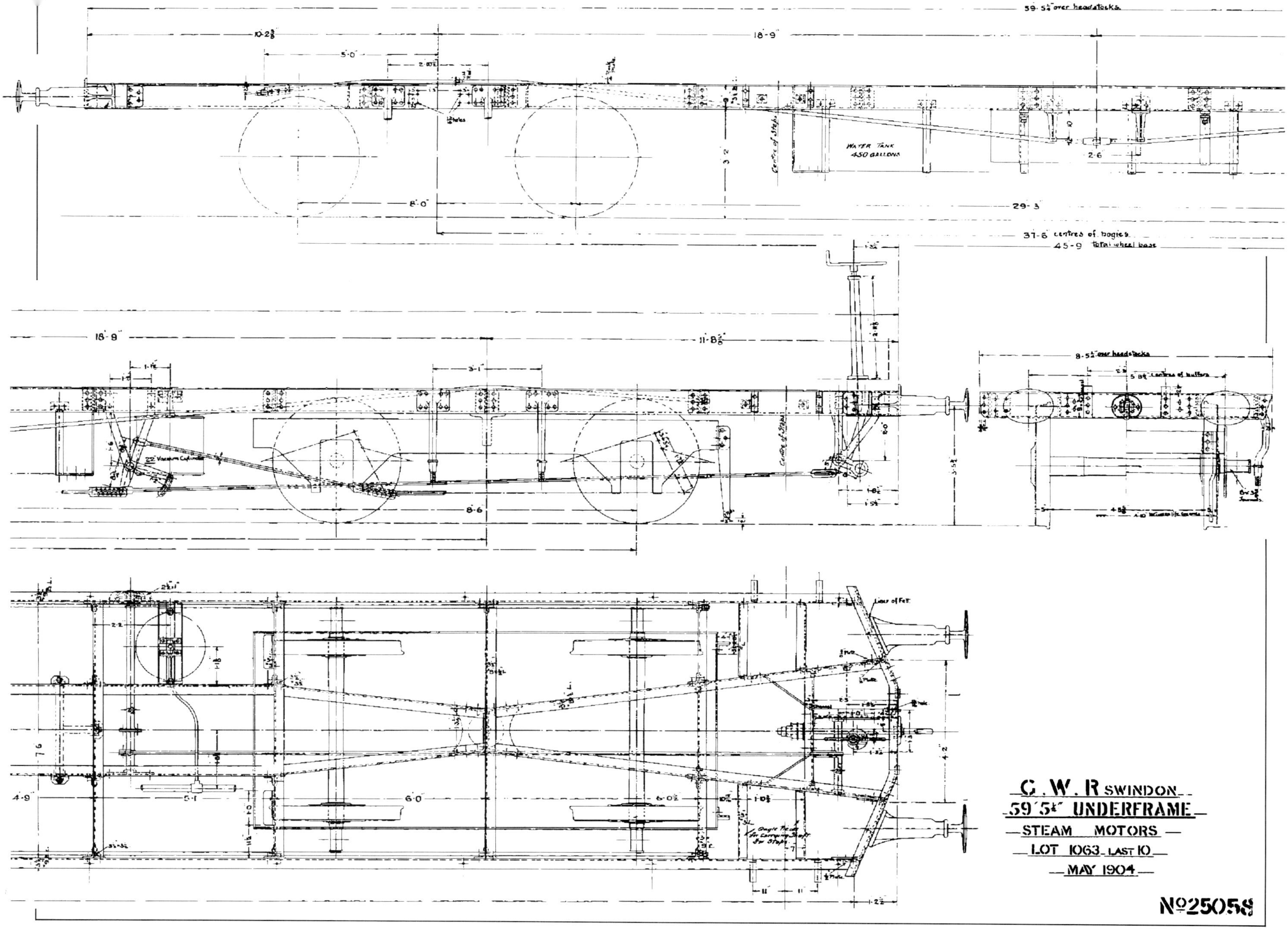
G. W. R SWINDON
59' 5¼" UNDERFRAME
STEAM MOTORS
LOT 1063 LAST 10
MAY 1904
No 25058
59-5¼ over headstocks
37-6 centres of bogies
45-9 total wheel base
WATER TANK 450 GALLONS
Centre of Steps
22" Vacuum Cylinder
8-5¼ over headstocks
5-8½ centres of buffers
Line of Felt

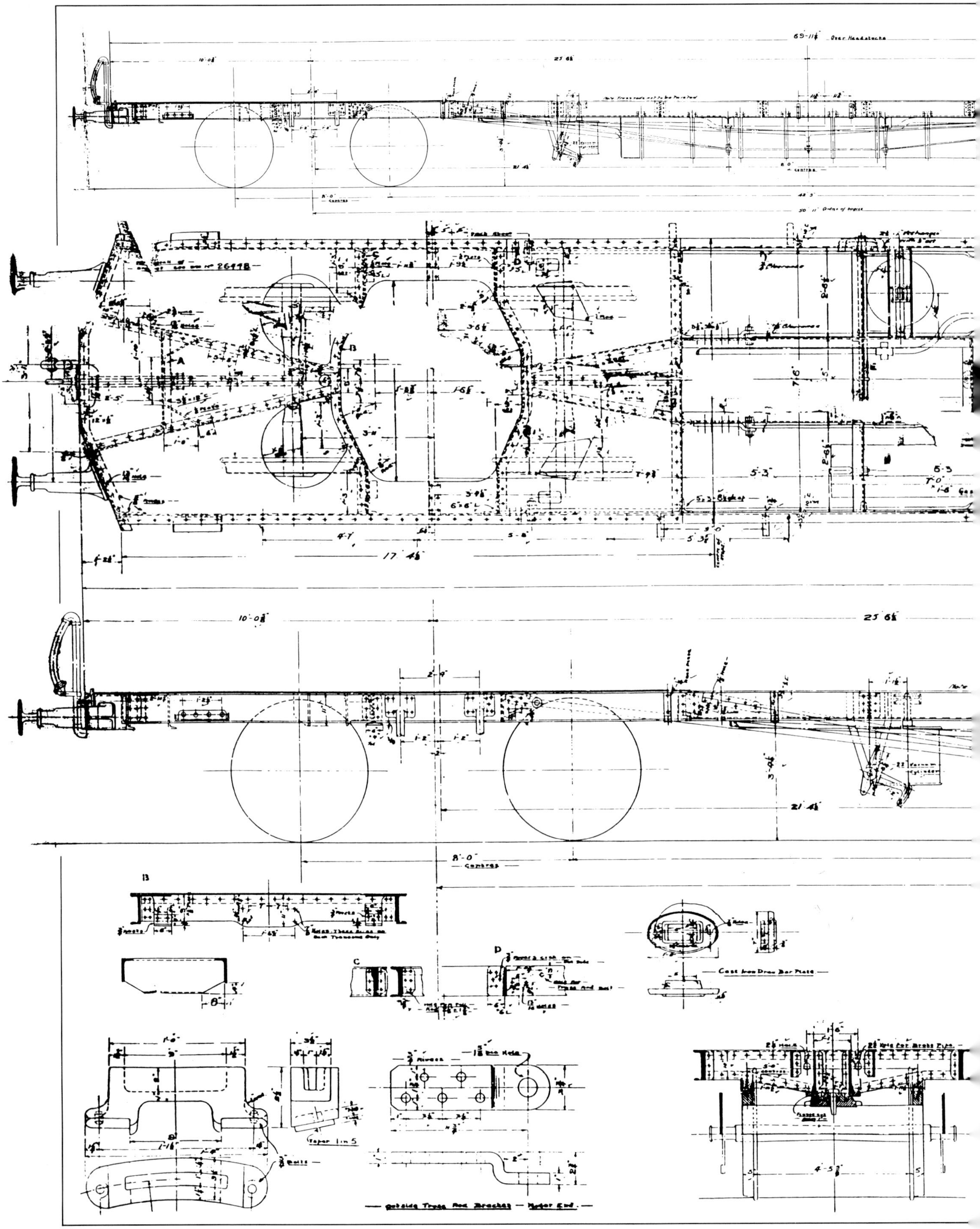
Over Headstocks
Centres
B
C
D
Cast Iron Draw Bar Plate
Taper 1 in 5
Outside Truss Rod Brackets – Motor End

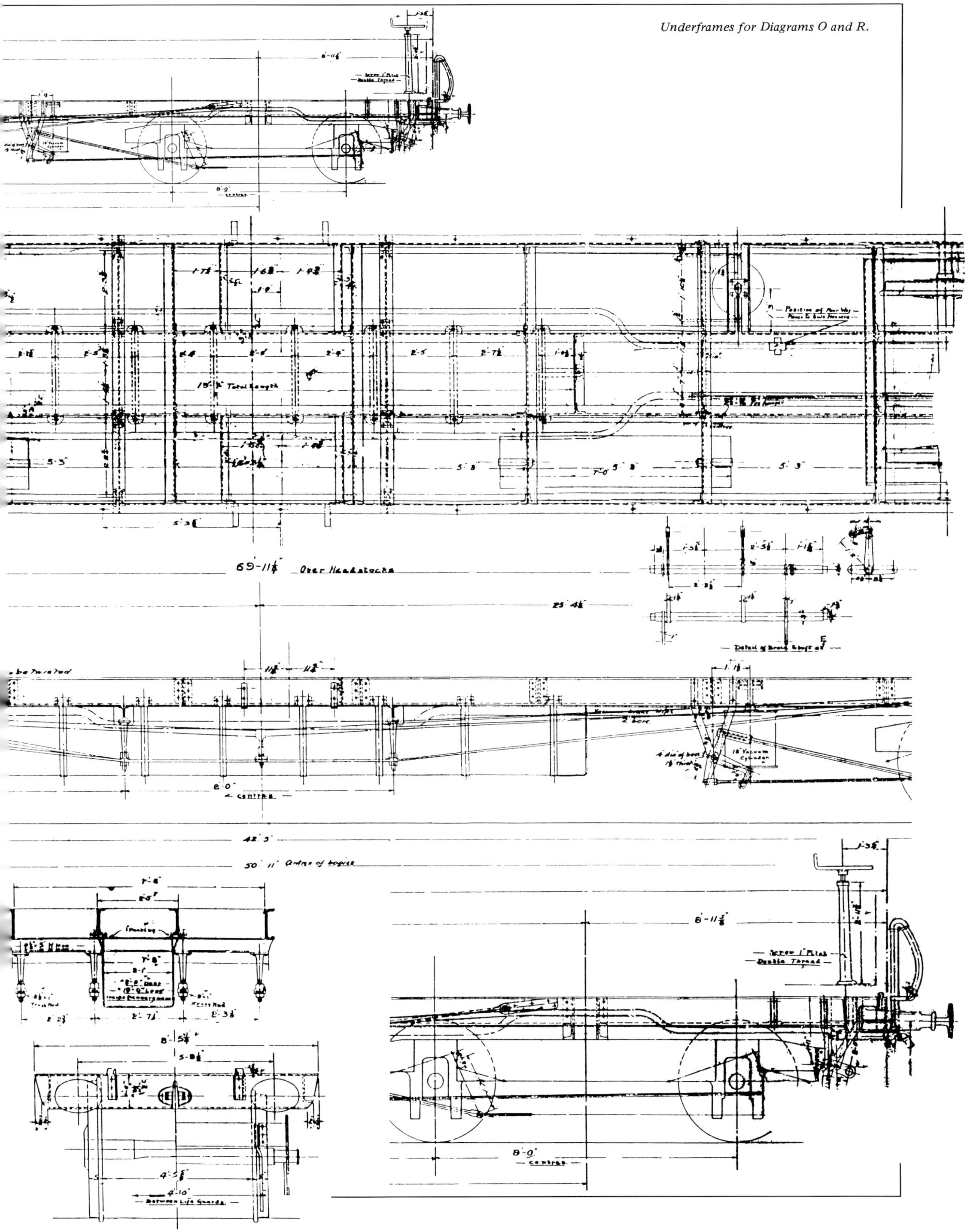

Underframes for Diagrams O and R.

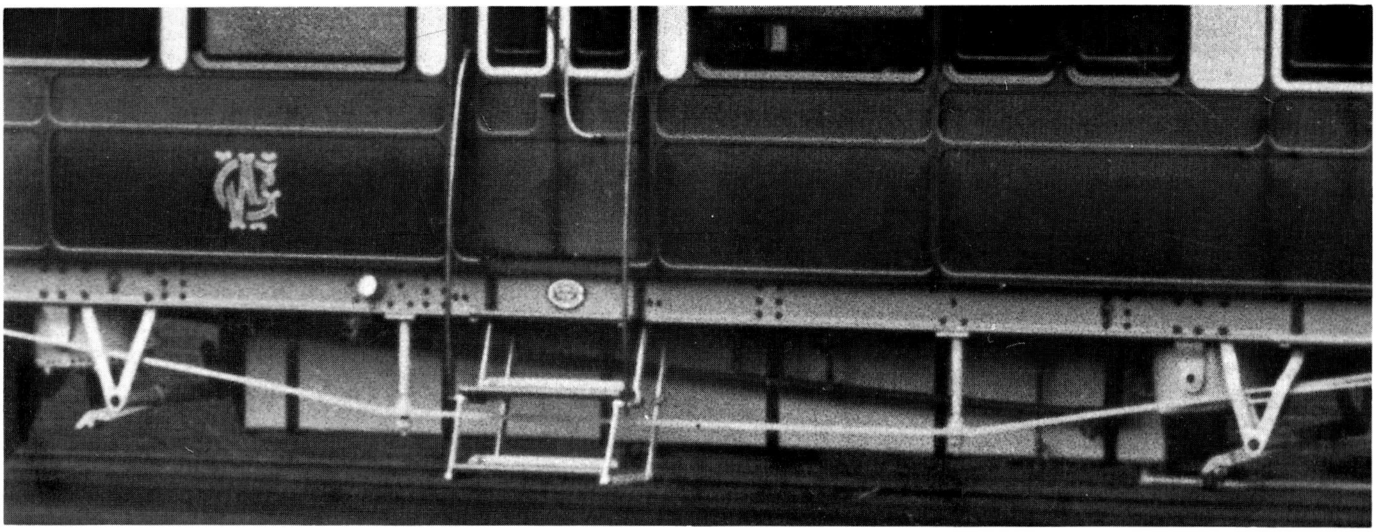

The photographic grey applied for this builders photograph of Car No. 75 of Diagram Q at the Gloucester RC&W Co's works provides a chance to see some of the detail normally lost in the shadows of the underframe. The steps show particularly well here, as does the water tank. HMRS

long over corners (½in shorter than before) and 59ft 5¼in over headstocks (¾in shorter than before). Significant differences between the two designs included:

1. The wood panelled cars had additional holes to the rear of the boiler in the metal plate at the leading end of the underframe, and the existing holes in front of the boiler hole were a different shape. This may have been to provide access to the power unit's axleboxes.
2. The boiler hole in the metal plate was a slightly simpler shape than before.
3. The water tank was positioned a little further forward.

The spacing of the cross members was also slightly different, and at the trailing bogie centre there were two cross members close together (the bogie outlined on this drawing was an 8ft type, and the centre pin casting is shown as being different). These cross members were built up, and were significantly deeper in the centre than at the ends.

Like the Dia. G cars, the queen post spacing was now only 2ft 6in. However, the distance from the boiler centre line to the turnbuckle was now 19ft 3in instead of 20ft 3in.

SRM DIAGRAMS Q AND Q1

These short, wood panelled cars were the last built and, like the 70ft cars, were given underframe trussing with flat bar truss rods and adjustable queen posts. The queen posts were attached to the solebars, and their lower ends had screw threads and a pair of nuts. The truss rod passed between these nuts, and by altering the position of the nuts, the tension in the truss rods could be varied. The queen posts were 9ft 6in apart, and the horizontal portion of the truss was about 1ft 6in below the solebars. Truss rods were of 2in × 1in bar, twisted through 90° near the brake cylinders so they could be fastened to the inside of the solebars. The Q and Q1 diagrams show 'H' section cross members below the solebars with short queenposts, as on the 70ft cars, though in practice the Dia. Q and Q1 cars did not have this 'H' section beam, and the rather longer queenposts were attached directly to the solebars. Thus, the water tanks did not have to be shaped to accommodate the cross beams.

70FT WOOD PANELLED SRMS

The 70ft cars' underframes were similar in principle to those of the short, wood panelled cars, but there were significant differences. The solebars were of 10 × 4 × ½in channel, while the headstocks were of 12 × 4 × ½in material. The inner longitudinals were of 9 × 3 × ⅜in channel, and were straight from the trailing headstock as far as the plate towards the leading end of the car. The underframes were 69ft 11¼in over headstocks, and 2ft 5in less over corners – i.e. the headstocks were each bowed out by 1ft 2½in.

Due to their length, there were four queen post trusses on these cars. The truss rods were of 2in × 1in flat bars which were attached to the solebars and the inner longitudinals 2ft 5in ahead of the trailing bogie centre line, while at the motor end, the inner pair were fastened to the longitudinals just within the motor bogie wheelbase, while the outer pair were fastened to the solebars some way further back. Thus, the truss rods ascended at differing angles at the motor end. They were arranged with their wider faces vertical at their ends, and were twisted so that these faces were horizontal inboard of the 'V' hangers. The queen posts were of the type with screw threads on the lower ends, and passed through the truss rods; tension in the truss rods could be adjusted by means of nuts on the ends of the queen posts. The upper ends of the queen posts were mounted on cross members of 4½in × 5in 'H' section. These were continuous across the underframe, which required the top of the water tank to be shaped to accommodate them.

There were two 7ft × 1ft 6in gas cylinders slung longitudinally from the underframe on the left- hand side of the water tank, looking forward, with two vacuum cylinders on the other side.

WATER TANKS

All GWR-design SRMs had water tanks holding 450 gallons slung centrally from longitudinal members of the underframe. The water tank dimensions are marked on a drawing of the 70ft underframe as 2ft 1in wide, 2ft deep and 19ft long, whilst on a drawing of Dia. Q and Q1 short cars the tanks are shown as 16ft 0in × 2ft 4¾in × 2ft 0in – these are inside dimensions.

The underframe drawings for the matchboarded and earlier short, wood panelled cars do not give dimensions for the water tanks, but they appear to scale at about 17ft 6in long (Nos. 1 and 2), and otherwise about 16ft 6in long (59½ft cars). They seem to have been about 2ft 6in wide (they did not have to clear central truss rods as on the 70ft cars) and 1ft 9in deep.

END STEPS

Photographs show that additional end steps were eventually provided to make it easier for staff to climb onto the end of the car from rail level. These seem to have been below, and possibly slightly outboard of, the buffers, and suspended from a long diagonal bracket that appears to emerge from behind the headstock. They were provided at each corner of the car, and seem to have been accompanied by an additional horizontal handrail, like those under the cars' end windows, but positioned on the lower waist moulding. These are not recorded in the *Registers*, but seem to have been fitted towards the end of the single-colour livery period, perhaps around 1920.

TRAILING BOGIES

At the trailing end, the matchboarded SRMs were carried on a standard Dean 8ft 6in coach bogie, with the suspension units attached to the solebars. 8ft volute spring bogies were fitted to short, wood panelled cars Dias. H, J and L, whilst 9ft volute spring bogies were provided on the 70ft wood panelled cars of Dia. K, and on some of Dias. M, N and O vehicles. These volute spring bogies were subsequently found to be unsuitable, and were replaced by the very similar-looking units of the same wheelbases with coil springs over the axleboxes.

Some of the longer-lived cars with 8ft coil spring bogies eventually had them replaced with Collett 7ft bogies.

The short cars shown on diagram Q, built by the Gloucester Carriage & Wagon Co., had 8ft bogies with leaf bearing springs, whilst the Swindon-built equivalents (Dia. Q1) had 8ft 'American' bogies.

Most of the longer-lasting 70ft cars running with 9ft coil spring bogie were eventually refitted with either the 9ft 'American' type, or with Collett's 7ft-wheelbase bogies.

Car No. 88 of Diagram R showing the additional end steps. This was one of the last cars to remain at work.

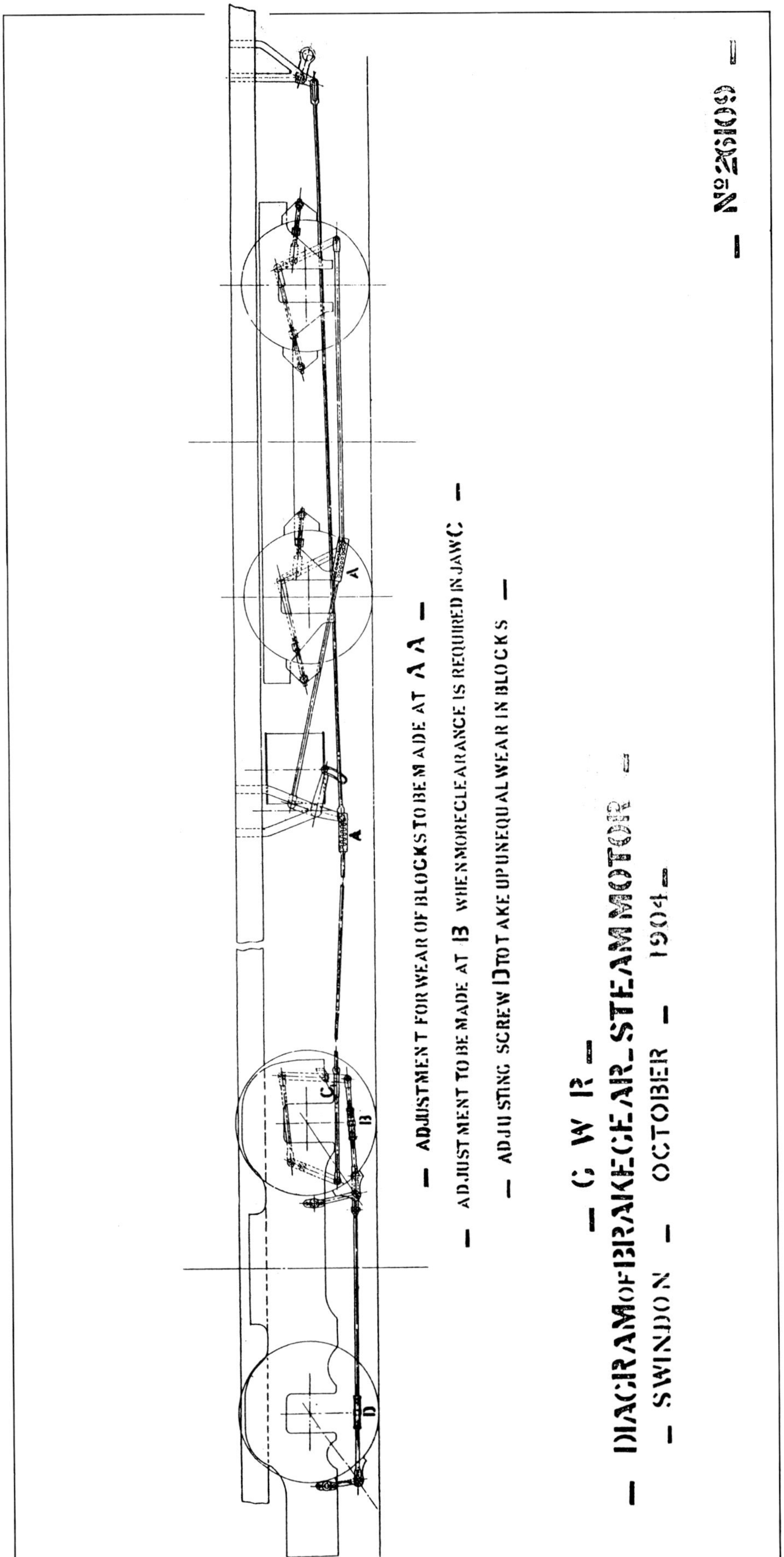

ADJUSTMENT FOR WEAR OF BLOCKS TO BE MADE AT A A
ADJUSTMENT TO BE MADE AT B WHEN MORE CLEARANCE IS REQUIRED IN JAW C
ADJUSTING SCREW D TO TAKE UP UNEQUAL WEAR IN BLOCKS
G W R
DIAGRAM OF BRAKE GEAR STEAM MOTOR
SWINDON
OCTOBER
1904
A
A
B
C
D

BRAKES

Matchboarded SRMs had one vacuum cylinder (Armstrong's moving cylinder type) on each car, suspended from underframe cross members at one side between the water tank and the trailing bogie. On earlier matchboarded cars, the linkage between the vacuum cylinder and the power bogie ran a little off-centre below the water tank. There was a pedestal-type screw handbrake at the driving position at each end.

On Nos.1 and 2, the linkage between the front handbrake and the main cross shaft was by means of a cable; this is clearly shown on the frame plan for the motor bogie, but unfortunately not on the underframe drawing. However, it is just visible in a couple of photographs, and was attached to a crank lever on the main brake shaft just inboard of the outside 'V' hanger; the object of this exercise was to obtain a path round the boiler. The trailing end handbrake was linked via a long rod, just off centre, to another lever on the main cross shaft. The 'V' hangers, brake cylinder, etc. were visible in a view where an SRM had the power unit to the right, and this remained the case for subsequent cars.

Other matchboarded cars (excepting 1 and 2) had the linkage from the motor-end handbrake running by means of a conventional system of rods from the front, initially at solebar level, sloping slightly downwards to the main cross shaft towards the rear. At the cross shaft, the 'V' hanger attached to the solebar was bent outwards to clear a crank on the cross shaft, to which the long rod was attached. The long rod seems to have been pivoted to the rear of the power bogie, and then supported by a series of hook-shaped brackets suspended from the solebar.

The earlier, short SRMs (Dias. H and J, at least) had the same arrangement of brakes as on the later matchboarded cars, but Dia. Q and Q1 cars had two fixed brake cylinders, both on the same side of the car, one between the power unit and the water tank, the other between the water tank and the trailing bogie. On these, the front and rear brakes appear not to have been connected. The motor-end handbrake linkage was attached to the front brake cross shaft by the 'V' hanger, which was cranked outwards to clear.

70ft SRMs were built with two 'V' hangers and had a similar arrangement to the last of the short cars. The earlier 70ft cars had Armstrong type vacuum cylinders, but the later ones (Dias O and R) seem to have had the fixed (Churchward) type, but photographs should be consulted. The cars built by Hurst Nelson (Nos.61–72) had 'V' hangers that were not cranked out from the solebar.

STEAM HEATING HOSES

On photographic evidence, steam heating connections were fitted to SRMs from about 190[illegible] presumably so as to heat trailers or any othe

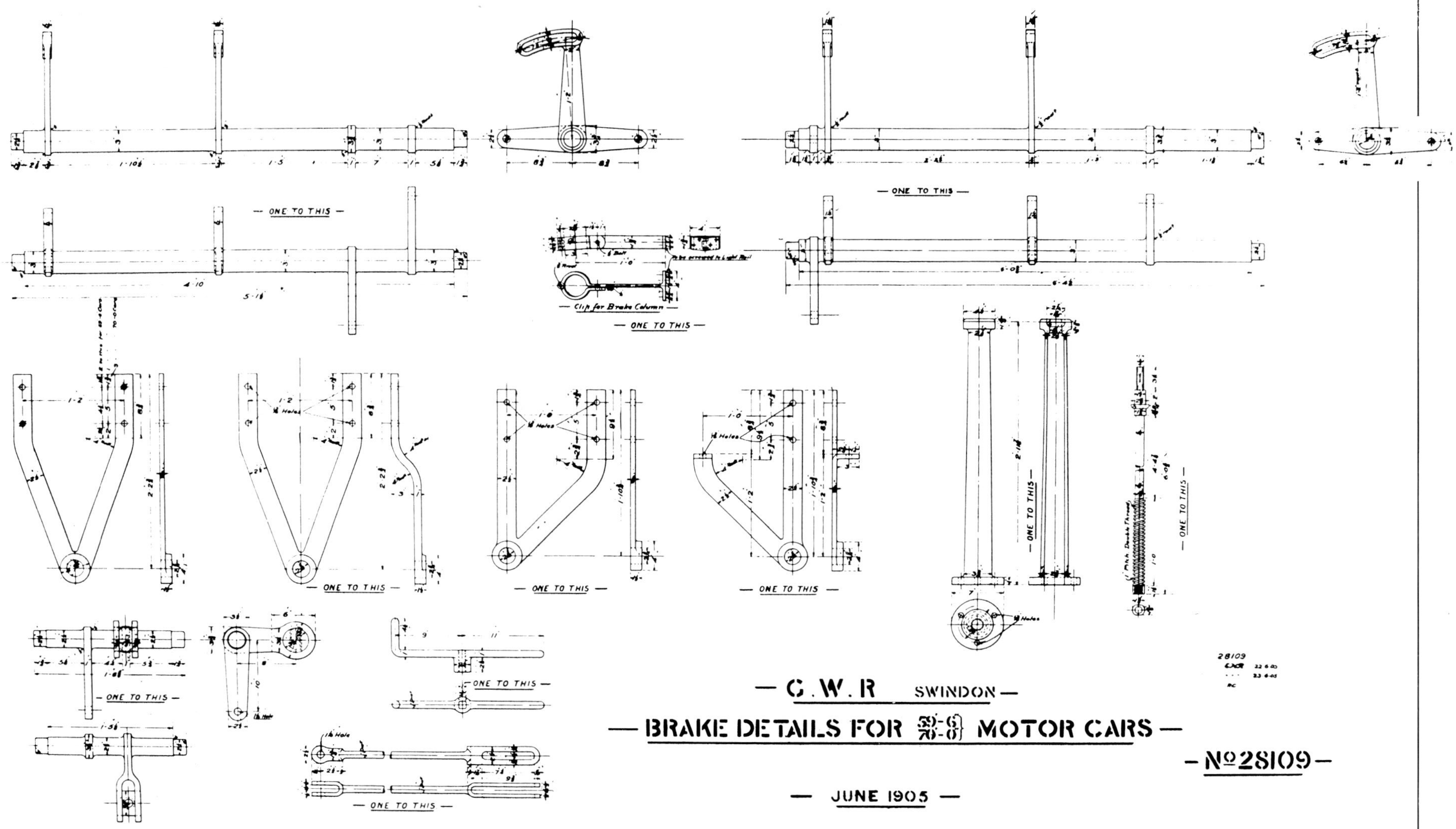

ONE TO THIS
Clip for Brake Column
ONE TO THIS
ONE TO THIS
ONE TO THIS
ONE TO THIS
ONE TO THIS
ONE TO THIS
ONE TO THIS
ONE TO THIS
ONE TO THIS
ONE TO THIS
28109
— G.W.R SWINDON —
— BRAKE DETAILS FOR 59-69 / 70-80 MOTOR CARS —
— №28109 —
— JUNE 1905 —

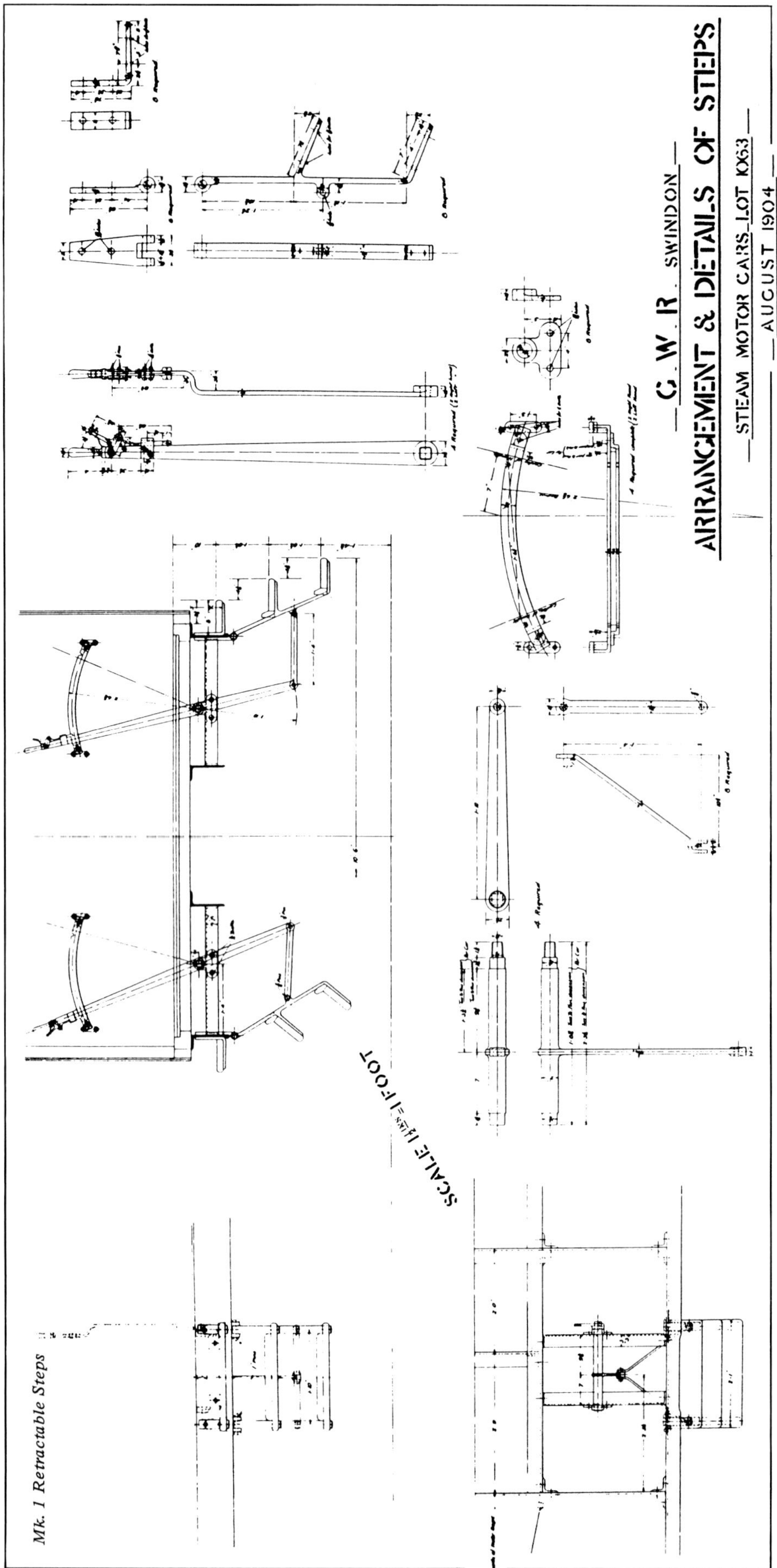

Mk. 1 Retractable Steps

accompanying coach. Hoses were usually taken off during the summer months, but the heating pipe with a tap can be seen just below the headstocks. Connections for hoses seem to have been fitted at both ends of the cars.

PASSENGER STEPS

Most SRMs were fitted with steps to enable passengers to board or alight at 'Haltes' where no raised platform was provided. There were three arrangements of steps to be found on SRMs.

FIXED STEPS

SRMs Nos.1 and 2 were provided with fixed steps for passengers, positioned in the floor of the driver's vestibule, which could be covered by a hinged flap when not in use. These quickly proved to be unsatisfactory in operation, and subsequent cars were not fitted with passenger steps until the Dia. G1 cars were built in 1904. The first rail-level halts on the Stroud Valley line were promptly given full-height platforms, and Nos.1 and 2 were hired to the Lambourn Valley Railway, where there were still low platforms. These steps were removed from Nos.1 and 2, and it is said that retractable steps were fitted, but no photograph showing any modification has been found.

The fixed steps on Cars 1 and 2, with the hinged flap down, providing a floor.

MK. I RETRACTABLE STEPS

[Mk. I and Mk. II are unofficial terms to differentiate between the different patterns of retractable steps.]

The first retractable steps were fitted to SRMs shown on diagram G1; this type can readily be identified because the unit moved as a whole, so that when the steps were retracted their treads were inclined sharply downwards.

These steps were only fitted to the Dia. G1 and G cars, and, incidentally, also to trailer No.1. Diagrams G1 and G show these steps below the driver's vestibule doors, and, unusually, also below one leaf of the luggage compartment doors. Those under the luggage door seem to have been a little narrower than the end ones.

The treads of the two lower steps were both rigidly attached to two vertical arms (one either side) that were pivoted from the solebars. In operation, the guard pulled a lever inside the car which swung the steps outwards, so that the arms were perhaps 30° to the vertical, and the step treads were horizontal. There was also a top step fixed to the solebar that did not move. Passengers would face the car to ascend or descend the steps, using the hand rails fixed to the car's sides on either side of the doors to assist them. Before the car moved off, the guard would reverse the operating lever and the arms with the steps attached would be moved underneath the car so as to be within the loading gauge.

MK. II RETRACTABLE STEPS

These steps can be distinguished from the earlier variety as they were constructed in such a way that the treads were always horizontal, whether the steps were extended or retracted. From Dia. H cars onwards, all had these steps below the driver's vestibule doors, unless the car had a central passenger vestibule, in which case the steps were placed below the passenger vestibule doors. Those beneath the passenger vestibule doors were wider than the others, because these doorways were wider.

These steps were operated and used in a similar fashion to the 'Mk I' variety. There was one particular difference to the earlier type from a passenger's point of view: the handrails were attached to the coach side at the top ends only, while the bottom ends were attached to the upper movable step, and moved out from the coach side as the steps were extended. This type of hand rail must have made it much easier to join or leave the coach.

ATC

No SRMs were fitted with Automatic Train Control.

Mk. 2 Retractable Steps

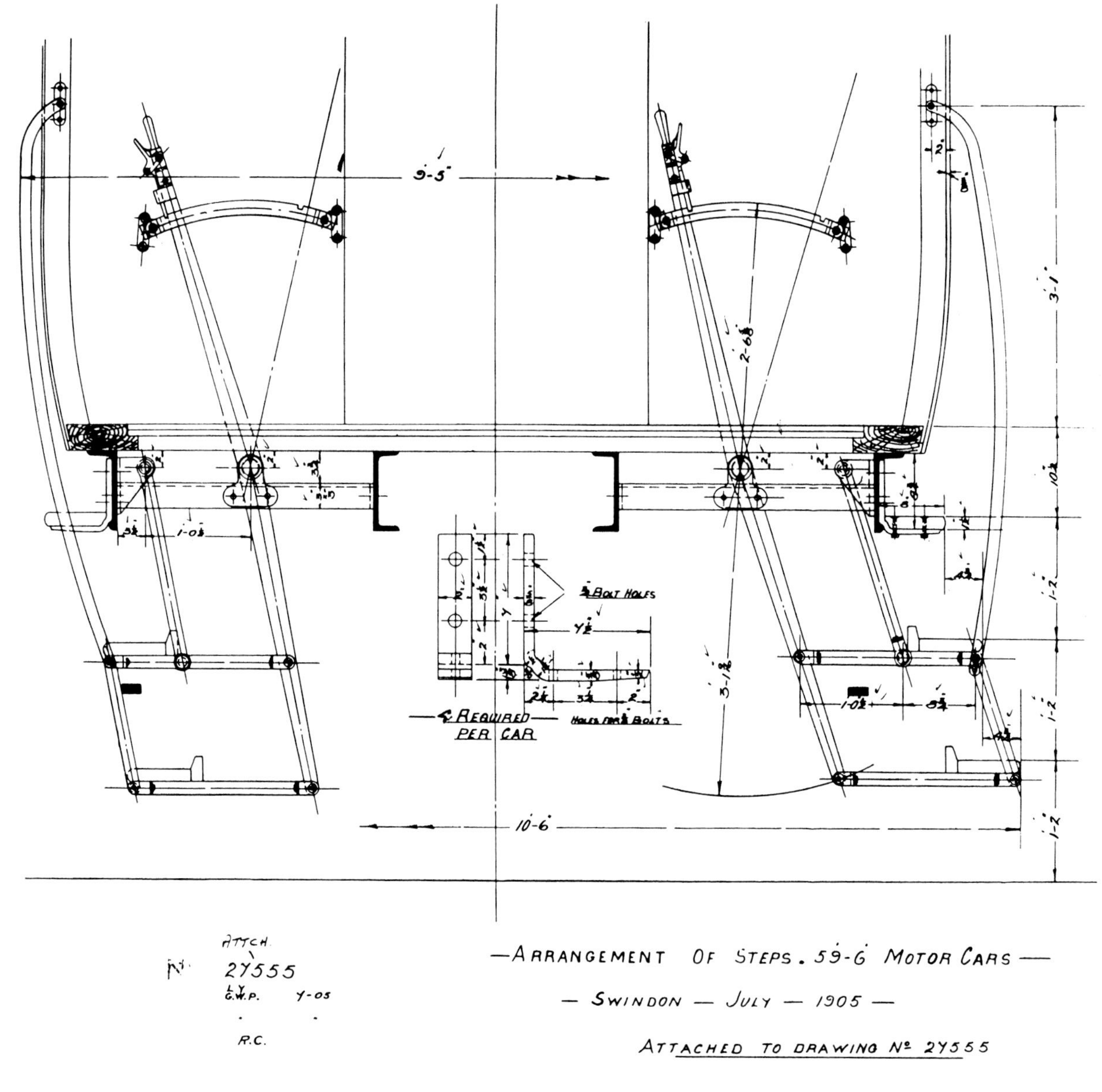

PRIVATE AND NOT FOR PUBLICATION.

GREAT WESTERN RAILWAY.

General Instructions to be observed in connection with Rail Motor Cars.

Motor Cars to be dealt with as Trains.

1. The Cars must be dealt with in all respects as Ordinary Passenger Trains, except as herein otherwise ordered.

Passengers' Luggage.

2. Where a luggage compartment is provided Passengers' luggage will be carried, but where the Cars are not provided with accommodation for luggage Passengers will be limited to carrying with them only such light articles as they can handle themselves, and which will not interfere with the seating accommodation. On Branch and other Lines where Cars are run in place of ordinary trains, necessary luggage accommodation must be provided.

Cars in charge of Conductor.

Hand Signals for Conductors and Enginemen.

3. Conductors of Motor Cars will act as Guards and carry with them a set of flags, hand lamp and detonators in order that they may obey the Standard Regulations in the event of the Car being stopped out of course, or through accidents, etc. A set of flags, hand lamp and detonators must also be carried by Motor Enginemen for use in case of need.

Passengers alighting from and entering Car.

Fastening Doors and Gates.

Passengers not to ride on Car Platforms.

4. The Conductors must use every care in getting Passengers into and out of the Car quickly and safely. Where it is necessary for Passengers to enter Cars at Halts provided with raised Platforms by the door at the Engine end, the Fireman will assist by opening and closing the door. It will be arranged for Passengers to enter and leave the Cars by separate doors where the traffic is heavy and circumstances admit of this being done. Before giving the signal to start Conductors must see that the doors are properly shut and fastened. Where necessary the Fireman of the leading Car must attend to the door at the Engine end. Passengers must not be allowed to travel on the Platforms at the ends of the Cars.

When stopped at Signals.

5. The Conductor will always be held responsible for carrying out the provisions of Rule 55 of the Book of Rules and Regulations in regard to reminding the Signalman of the presence of the Car when it is stopped at signals. When a car is run light and there is no Conductor with it the Fireman must perform this duty.

At those places where difficulty is likely to arise if the Motor Car is allowed to draw up to Advanced Starting Signals or Starting Signals in advanced positions in consequence of the distance which the Conductor would have to walk in going to and from the Signal Box, the Motor Car must be brought to a stand opposite the Signal Box, and kept there until permission is received from the Box in advance to allow it to proceed.

Two Motor Cars coupled.

6. As a rule a Conductor must be provided for each Car, but when necessary two Motor Cars may be coupled and worked together in charge of one Conductor, if there are no Halts on the route, or if men are employed at the Halts. When two Cars are run coupled together there need only be a Fireman on the second Car, who must be in the engine compartment. This Fireman will not be responsible for opening and closing doors.

When ready to start with the coupled Motor Cars the Conductor on the

CHAPTER SIX
THE RAIL MOTORS IN SERVICE

OPERATION

Walter Cotham, who fired steam railmotors in the latter 1920s or early 1930s on the short-lived Stourbridge Jct. & Wolverhampton service via the Kingswinford branch, talked to Mike Lewis, a fireman at Wolverhampton, about his experiences. He said that it was normal for the cars to be coaled on Stourbridge shed from a wheelbarrow, and was rather scathing about the capacity of the coal bunker, which he said was about as much use as a shelf!

In photographs of SRMs at Exeter shed, it appears that there they were placed in a siding with a small loco coal wagon alongside. I have seen no photographs showing coaling, but it is possible that coal was shovelled out of the wagon onto the floor of the power compartment of the SRM, and then shovelled again into the coal bunker. Other sources indicate that coal in sacks was used.

Mr. Cotham was also unimpressed by the small water capacity of the cars, and said that they used to fill up the tank not only at Wolverhampton and Stourbridge Jct. (a 16¼ mile-journey), but also at the intermediate station of Wombourn in each direction.

During November 1917, in connection with the loan of SRM No.45 to the Highland Railway, it was noted that 'On fairly level roads these cars can run 25 miles before taking water, and about 140 miles before being re-coaled. On heavy roads with gradients varying from 1 in 50 to 1 in 100, water would be required after 15 to 20 miles, and coal after running about 100 miles'. Some cars must therefore have required re-coaling during an ordinary day's work; in July 1911, for example, Southall car working 'D' covered 246¾ miles on Saturdays, whilst some others were not much less. Car 'D', incidentally, was not booked to return to Southall for coal during her day's work, but did make lengthy calls at other stations, where, perhaps, a supply was made available.

The rule of good firing on ordinary locomotives was only to feed coal into the firebox when the regulator was open, to avoid producing smoke. However, Mr Cotham recalled that, on an SRM, it was absolutely fatal to steam production to open the firehole door while the regulator was open. Consequently, every station stop brought frantic activity on the part of the fireman to recharge the firebox before the car lurched off on the next stage of its trip. This confirms what Harold Holcroft said about firing practice some twenty years before (see the end of Chapter 3). Some of the longer, uphill runs between stations must have been interesting, to say the least. Mike Lewis said that this problem with firing occurred because the car's firebox had the firehole door immediately below the boiler tubeplate, so that opening the door would immediately send cold secondary air straight across the tubeplate and up the vertical tubes. Apparently, some firemen had their own pet theories as to the best way to fire an SRM, and one driver, Bert Attew, told Mike of a fireman who maintained that the secret was to build the fire up into a cone shape, crowned with a lump of coal wobbling on the top! I wonder how long it stayed there.

It would appear that the driver and fireman of a car were expected to be able to deal with a range of problems that might arise while the car was in service. In a file now held in the Public Record Office there is a list of tools for a steam rail motor. It is stamped 'LOCO. & CARR. DEPT. 7 FEB 1905':

TABLE 8

STEAM MOTOR CAR TOOL SETS

Qty	*Article*	*Qty*	*Article*	*Qty*	*Article*
1	Rake	1	Spring Oil Feeder	1	Packing Drawer
1	Clinker Shovel	12	Detonators in Tin Case	1	Small Monkey Spanner
1	Tommy Bar	1	Spanner ½ x ⅝"	1	Iron Bucket
1	Piece of chain 3' 0"	1	Spanner ⅞ x 1"	1	Pipe for watering coal
1	Hand Hammer	2	Piston Gland Spanners	2	Flat Chisels
1	Coal Pick	1	Ejector Pipe rack spanner	1	Gauge Lamp and Socket
3	Pin Punches ⅛", 3/16", ¼"	1	Spring Spanner 1½"	1	1 Gallon Oil Bottle
1	Grease Pricker	1	Water Gauge Spanner	1	Tallow Can
1	Large Monkey Spanner	1	Pricker	1	Oval Oil Feeder
2	Red Flags	1	Pinch Bar	1	Spanner ⅜" x ½"
1	Fire Shovel	1	Box Spanner	1	Spanner ¾" x ⅞"
1	Hand Brush	1	Padlock	1	Spanner 1" x 1⅛"
2	Centre Lamps	1	Large Hammer	2	Spindle Gland Spanners
1	Flare lamp	1	Large Punch	1	Ejector Gland Spanner

If these seem to be a surprisingly comprehensive collection, it must be remembered that, in the early years of the 20th century, few telephones or other means of communication were available for a train crew to contact signalmen. If a car broke down out on the line, the conductor could be faced with a really long walk to the signal box in the rear to summon help, so any action the driver and fireman could take to either get the car moving again, or at least make it mobile for when help arrived, would minimize delays. Most of the tools are recognizable, but a 'packing drawer' was a tool used for extracting gland packing. I understand this could take several forms, but typically it would be either a length of rod with a shaped hook or barb on the end to get the packing out – this would suit many sizes of gland – or it might resemble a crow's foot spanner armed with several hooks shaped like saw teeth.

Also in February 1905, Mr J. Morris, of the Office of the Superintendent of the Line, wrote to Mr. Waister at Swindon on the subject of 'Rail Motor Cars stopped at Home, Starting and Advanced Starting Signals. Rule 55 Clause (c) paragraph 1'. This rule required that, where a train was detained at a signal on a running line, the guard, shunter or fireman was to proceed immediately to the signal box to remind the signalman of the position of the train. Mr Morris wrote that '... the General Manager has agreed to an instruction being given to the effect that the Conductors are in all cases to go to the Signal Box' to carry out the provisions of this rule. By the time the 1933 *Rule Book* was issued, this had been amended to read:

> 'In the case of rail motors and motor trains, the duty of going to the signal box must be performed by the Guard or Shunter; when, however, there is not a Guard or Shunter the duty must be performed by the Driver if he is at the opposite end of the train to the engine, and by the Fireman if both men are on the engine.'

When rail motor services were first introduced, instructions for operating the cars on each individual service were issued. By April 1905 enough experience with their use had been gained and General Instructions were issued

HIRE OF RAIL CARS

In 1905, a minute of the Superintendent's meeting recorded:

> 'In consequence of some doubt as to the proper charge for running a Rail or Road Motor Car for a private special party, this question was raised, and after full discussion it was decided to Minute the following for the future guidance of all concerned:
>
> SPECIAL RAIL MOTOR CARS –
> 2s 6d per Car mile for all loaded mileage.
> 1s 6d per Car mile for all empty mileage.
> Minimum charge £2.
>
> 'NOTE – All applications for special trips which, for policy or other reason, it is considered should

rear Car must ring the Bell; the Fireman on that Car will then open the engine whistle, and the Driver in front must acknowledge this by sounding his whistle, when both Cars will start and commence working together.

Trailer Cars.

7. When a Trailer Car is attached to a Motor Car a second conductor may be provided if necessary.

Trailer Coach.

8. Where a special Trailer Car is not provided, one Third Class Coach, may, when necessary, be run, in rear of the Motor Car. In such cases the Conductor must ride on the Motor Car.

When an ordinary Coach is attached to a Motor Car, Passengers without Tickets joining at Halts must not be allowed to travel in the Coach, provided there is room for such Passengers to ride in the Motor Car, the object being to enable the Conductor to issue Tickets en route.

Cars run light.

9. When Cars are not being run as Passenger Trains, it will not be necessary to provide a Conductor, but they will be treated as light engines.

Tickets.

10. Passengers without Tickets joining the Car at Halts will be booked by the Conductor after entering the Car. Each Ticket issued by the Conductor must, before being handed to the Passenger, be punched by a special punch opposite the name of the Station (on the Up or Down side of the Ticket, as the case may be) to which it is available. Special care must be exercised to correctly punch the Tickets so that they may not be made use of beyond the proper Station or Halt.

Examination of Tickets by Conductor.

All Tickets must be examined by the Conductor as the Passengers enter his Car or on the journey. Tickets for the stations must be collected from the Passengers by the ticket collecting staff at the stations in the usual way, (unless otherwise specified) but tickets issued for the Halts must be collected by each Conductor when the Passengers leave his Car.

Collected Tickets.

Tickets collected by Conductors must be placed in a box provided on the Car, and this box must be cleared after each journey by men appointed for the purpose at convenient stations to be named by the Divisional Superintendents.

Stock Tickets.

11. Stock Tickets for the use of Conductors and men in charge of Halts will be ordered and kept by Station Masters as instructed by the Divisional Superintendents. Application must be made to such Station Masters for a fresh supply in good time. Car Tickets must be kept apart and recorded separately in the Station Stock Ticket Register.

Ordering Tickets.

The Conductors and men in charge of Halts must keep a record of all Tickets supplied to them. They must be careful to see that they have a sufficient number of Tickets of each series ready for use, and will only issue Tickets to places at which the Car is booked to stop.

Availability of Tickets.

12. Season Tickets of all descriptions and Ordinary and Privilege Tickets, also Free Tickets and Passes, covering the section of the Line used, will be available by the Cars.

Fares and Fare Lists.

13. The Fares to be charged are as announced in the Public Bills. A list of such Fares must be exhibited in the Cars wherever Tickets are issued on the Cars.

At Halts where men are employed, **Fare Lists must be exhibited.**

Cash collected by Conductors.

14. Cash collected by the Conductors must be paid in at the Stations as directed by the Divisional Superintendents. Cash so paid in must be passed through the Station Train Book and remitted with the Station cash. Each Conductor will hand in a slip with his cash, on which the amount will be inserted and initialled by the person to whom it is paid. The Cash collected by men in charge of Halts must be paid in as directed by the Divisional Superintendents.

Announcing Names of Stations and Halts.

15. Conductors in charge of single Cars must announce the names of Stations and Halts to the Passengers in the Cars in a CLEAR AND DISTINCT VOICE, just before reaching the Stations or Halts.

When a Motor Car and Trailer Car or Trailer Coach, not connected by vestibuled gangways, are coupled together, and run in charge of one Conductor, he will ride on the Motor Car. The Conductor must when the Cars stop at a Station or Halt announce the name of the stopping place from the platform.

The Conductor in charge of a Motor Car and Trailer Car connected by vestibuled gangways, must announce the names of Stations and Halts to the passengers in both Cars in a CLEAR AND DISTINCT VOICE just before reaching the Station or Halt.

When Motor Cars or Trailers with separate compartments for smokers are worked, Conductors must announce the names of stopping places in both smoking and non-smoking compartments.

Courtesy to Public and Passengers.

16. In dealing with Passengers, and in general intercourse with the public, employees must be uniformly polite and courteous. It is particularly required that special care and consideration shall be shown to children and elderly or infirm persons using the Cars. While the service must be prompt and quick, yet a constant watch must be kept for the safety and comfort of all passengers.

Level Crossings.

17. Drivers must approach and pass Level Crossings with great care.

Smoking.

18. Except where accommodation for smokers is provided, smoking is prohibited, and the usual Notices must be exhibited accordingly.

No Staff at Halts.

19. When men are not employed at Halts, the Conductors will be held responsible for dealing with the Passengers at those places.

Lighting and Extinguishing Lamps at Halts.

20. The Divisional Superintendents to make the necessary arrangements for lighting and extinguishing the lamps at Halts.

Edges of Platforms at Halts to be Whitewashed.

21. The District Inspectors will see that the edges of the platforms at the Halts are kept whitewashed by the Permanent Way Staff to the width of one foot from the edge, also that the platforms at the Halts are kept clean. The Conductors must report on their Journals any omission in these respects.

Moveable Steps at Halts not provided with raised platforms.

22. The Moveable Steps on Cars are only to be used at Halts not provided with raised platforms.

The Steps at the Engine end must not be used, neither must the doors at this end be used for the purpose of allowing Passengers to enter or leave the Cars. Care must be taken to see that these doors are kept locked.

After the Car has stopped at a Halt not provided with a raised platform the step lever must be released, the Steps put in position, and securely fastened by key pin or spring catch (whichever is provided) and the door then opened. The door must never be opened first.

Before giving the signal to the Driver to start, the Conductor must close the door and then withdraw the Steps, and be careful to see they are securely fastened in running position.

Cars Passing round Curves.

23. The 70 feet Motor Cars with Trailer attached will take any curves on the Main Lines, but in Sidings they should not be put round anything under a six chain curve without slacking the couplings between the two Cars. When the couplings are well slacked out, the Cars will pass round curves down to three chains radius

Lighting of Cars.

24. The Carriage Department will provide for the lighting of the Cars. Conductors must see that the Cars are lighted as, and when, required.

be run at a lower fare than the above should be referred to the Superintendent of the Line.'

In comparison, 'Special Road Motor Cars' were normally to be charged at 2s. per car mile, empty or loaded, while special cases (e.g. the use of a double-decked car) had to be referred to the Superintendent of the Line.

CONDUCTORS

The requirements for rail motor car conductors were discussed at the regular Superintendents' meetings, and in 1905 it was decided that they should form a junior grade to Passenger Guards of ordinary trains:

> 'The conditions of service of these men were again discussed, and a decision arrived at to confirm Minute 6,159 with clause 4 amplified as shewn below:
>
> 1. SCALE OF PAY. To be 20s to 23s, the minimum rate of a Passenger Guard being 23s.
> 2. TRANSFER FROM CARS TO TRAINS. To be eligible for transfer from the Motor-cars to local Trains, as vacancies arise for Local Guards in the country.
> 3. MINIMUM HEIGHT. 5ft 8in. To be adhered to in view of preceding clause.
> 4. PASSENGER GUARDS' EXAMINATION. To be passed by Local Superintendent before going on Cars, and in London before going on Trains.'

COUPLING SRMS AND TRAILERS

It was not until the beginning of 1912 that standard instructions were issued concerning who was to be responsible for coupling rail motors and trailers. At the January 1912 Superintendents' meeting it was minuted:

> 'There is a lack of uniform practice in the various Divisions, and after going thoroughly into the matter, Mr Churchward decided that at the commencement and completion of the day's work the fireman should couple up rail motor cars and trailers, also the vacuum brake, steam, electric bell, and chain communication, when ever such operations are for the convenience of the Locomotive Department. On other occasions the work should be done by the Traffic Department Staff.'

However, it was quickly realised that this gave scope for confusion, and the instructions were amended:

> 'During the time a car is in service, if the regulator, screw connection, whistle, vacuum brake steam heating, electric bell and chain communications have to be disconnected, the work of uncoupling and coupling must be done by the fireman.'

Quite what is meant by the reference to coupling the 'chain communication' is not certain. On photographic evidence, passenger alarm chain communication was not fitted to SRMs and trailers until the later 1920s, and in any event it was not coupled between coaches in such a train. SRM No.65 and trailer 62 (only) are both specifically referred to as 'chain fitted' in the 1930/1 Bristol area *Local Coach Working Programme* book, but no further explanation seems forthcoming.

CAPACITY

Very soon after their introduction, rail motors began to show the limitations of fixed formation, low-capacity trains. The obvious way to overcome this problem was to attach an ordinary hauled coach to the SRM, but this was not usually very satisfactory as it had to be at the rear of the SRM on all stages of the working; thus, the car had to run round the coach at the end of each journey, and sometimes at intermediate terminal stations. In addition, unless a saloon or corridor coach was used, there could be problems with issuing tickets to passengers in the extra coach, particularly where halts were involved. The 1905 instructions indicated that, in this event, passengers from halts were not to be allowed into the coach if there was room for them in the car, unless the halts were manned.

Other solutions were tried.

TWO SRMS (COUPLED TOGETHER, BACK-TO-BACK)

This saved running round, but, with the standard GWR through regulator gear, there was no way in which the trailing SRM could be controlled directly from the leading vehicle. The practice was therefore to have a driver and fireman in the front SRM, and a fireman only in the rear car to tend the boiler and to drive. Although provisions were made in the instructions relating to loads for the front car to haul the rear one, it would appear from the 1905 operating instructions that the cars were to be worked together. To start, the conductor in the rear car gave a signal to the fireman in that car using the electric bell. The fireman then sounded his car's whistle which was acknowledged in a similar fashion by the driver in the front car. At this, the cars were to commence working. The second car required its own conductor to sell tickets, unless all the stations and halts en route were staffed.

4

Destination or Route Boards. 25. Destination or Route Boards to be provided for all Cars. Conductors will be responsible for seeing these Boards are exhibited.

Extra Traffic. 26. When it is known beforehand that more Passengers are likely to use the Motor Service than it will accommodate, a telegraphic or written communication must be sent to the Divisional Superintendent concerned so that an ordinary Train or extra trips, may be run.

Conductors must watch the loading of the Cars, &c., and make any necessary recommendations in regard to increasing or decreasing the accommodation to meet fluctuations of traffic.

If there is not sufficient time to obtain the instructions of the Divisional Superintendent, Station Masters should make such arrangements as they consider advisable to cope with any sudden increase in traffic.

Horse, Carriage, and other Traffic conveyed in vacuum fitted vehicles. 27. The Divisional Superintendents will arrange with the Locomotive Department the number of vacuum fitted vehicles such as Horse Boxes Cattle Trucks, &c., which may be conveyed by the Motor Car.

Cleaning Cars. 28. The Cars must be well cleaned daily; this will be done by the Locomotive Department Staff wherever possible, but the Station Masters at the terminal Stations must arrange for the Cars to be swept out and kept thoroughly clean during the day.

Reports. 29. Records of the working and the traffic dealt with must be punctually rendered on the forms supplied, so as to reach the Divisional Superintendent concerned not later than 9.0 a.m. each day in respect of the previous day.

Special Examination of Tickets. 30. Whenever possible the Special Ticket Examiners must examine the Tickets of the Passengers in the Motor Cars.

Motor Car Inspectors. 31. Motor Car Inspectors attached to the Office of the Superintendent of the Line have been appointed to watch the working of the Motor Car Services on the various parts of the Line where such services exist.

Advertising Arrangements in Cars. 32. A copy of the current Time Book in the Standard Cover must be hung in a conspicuous position in each Motor Car and Trailer. Receptacles for the Company's small Publications should be fixed in each Car. Conductors must see that these receptacles are kept well supplied with small Publications.

J. MORRIS,
Superintendent of Line.

G. J. CHURCHWARD,
Chief Locomotive and Carriage Superintendent

April 1905.

WYMAN & SONS, LTD., Printers, Fetter Lane, London E.C., and Reading.—11799a

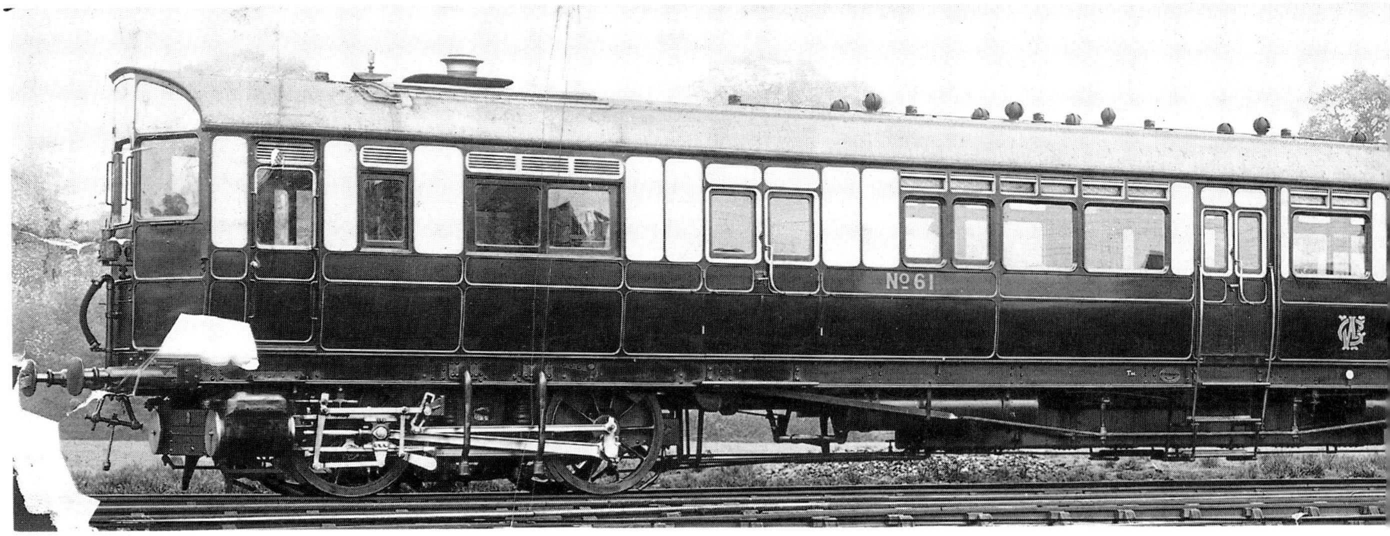

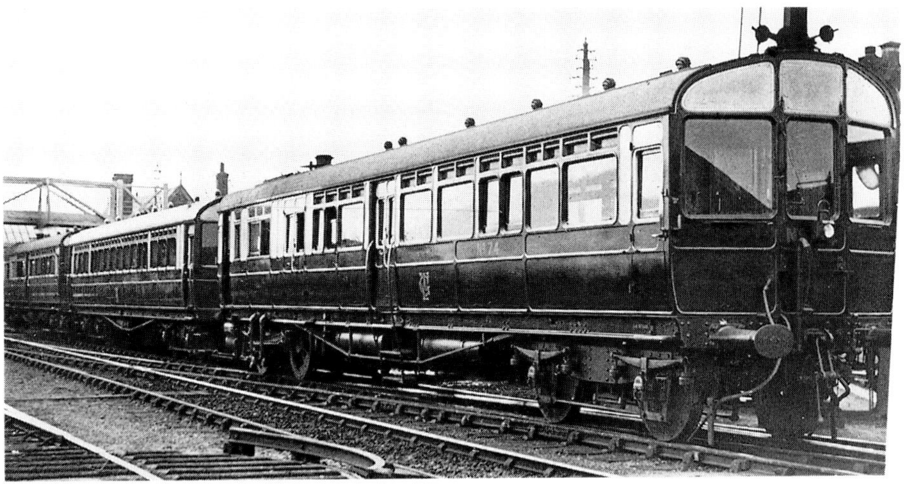

Car No. 74 of Diagram Q at Craven Arms forming a motor train for Wenlock on August Bank Holiday 1906. The formation was two rail motors with a trailer in between. No. 74 carried a headlamp, and the rear SRM had side tail lamps. G. M. PERKINS

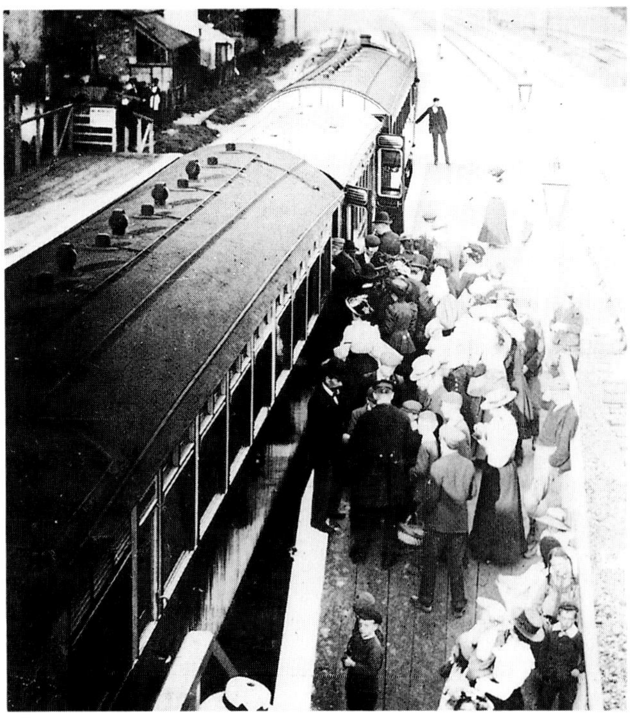

Laira Halt with a train consisting of two SRMs sandwiching a saloon. COLLECTION R. C. RILEY

TWO SRMS (WITH A COACH COUPLED BETWEEN)

The driving arrangements would have been the same as with the two cars, and although the additional coach increased the passenger capacity, it probably required a third conductor on the train.

Photographs show a short saloon coach as the middle vehicle (a compartment coach would have required tickets to be issued at the stations and halts). This arrangement was used on the Sundays Southall & Addison Road cars from 7th August 1904, and was also seen on the Plympton & Saltash service.

SRM & DRIVING TRAILER

In October 1904, trailer No.53 (later No.1) arrived at Laira. This was a 59½ft coach that matched the early SRMs in style, and had a driving compartment at one end with regulator gear and electrical bell circuits arranged so that an SRM propelling it could be controlled from the trailer. It could therefore accompany an SRM without the need for a run-round at each reversal. Trailer No.53 was at Laira for only three months, but 70ft trailers Nos.54 (later 3), 55 (later 4), and 5 arrived there in December 1904, February and April 1905 respectively.

LARGER SRMS

The first 70ft SRM (No.37) appeared in February 1905. This had 63 seats, as opposed to between 52 and 48 of the 57ft and the earlier 59½ft cars.

SRM + DRIVING TRAILER + DRIVING TRAILER + SRM

In December 1905, a 'double unit train' was built for Plymouth. This comprised two pairs of 70ft SRMs and trailers which could run either as two trains, each formed Trailer & SRM close coupled together, or could be combined into one train, formed SRM + Trailer + Trailer + SRM. Doorways were provided between the

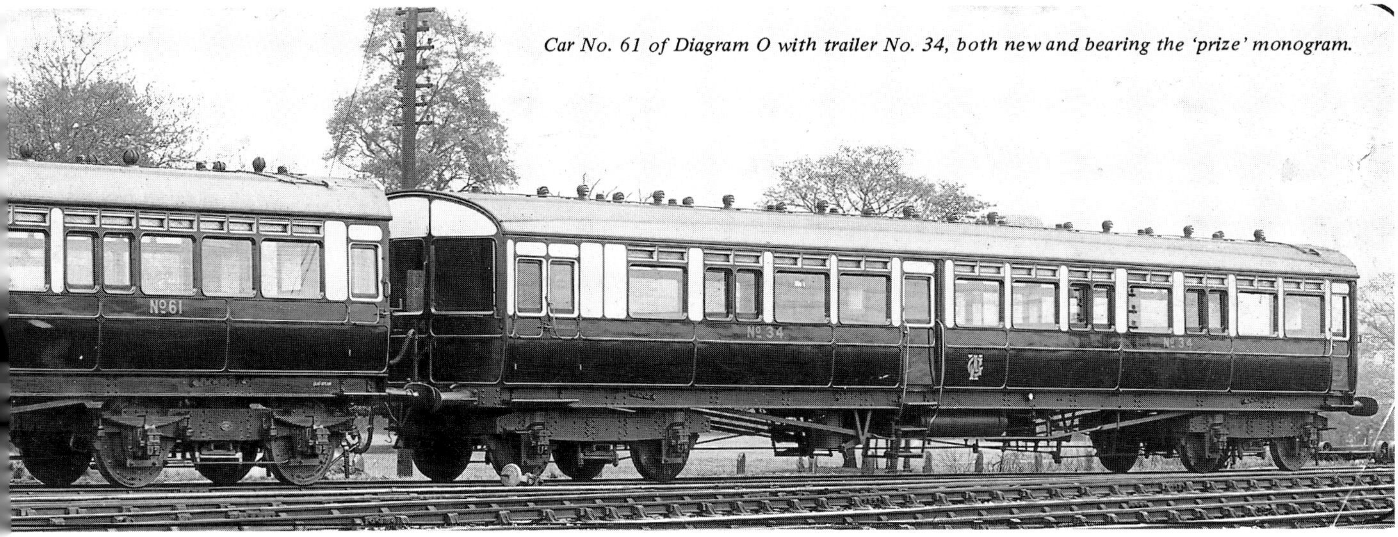

Car No. 61 of Diagram O with trailer No. 34, both new and bearing the 'prize' monogram.

SRMs and the adjacent trailer (and gangways later) so that only one conductor/guard was required for the two vehicles. The SRMs were Nos.59 and 60, and the trailers Nos.9 and 10. 'Double unit' was an interesting expression, echoing the modern 'multiple unit'.

AUTO-FITTED LOCOMOTIVE & TRAILER(S)

The use of an auto-fitted engine with one or more trailers was found to meet the needs for flexibility in passenger accommodation, while still having a train that could reverse quickly without the requirement for running round. The ultimate auto train solution was to use an auto engine with up to four 70ft trailers in pairs, preferably gangwayed together, with one pair ahead of and the other behind the locomotive. This had the advantages of increased capacity (seating for over 300 passengers), with only two conductors, one driver and one fireman required to staff the train. This arrangement was used on the Plymouth local services until the end of steam.

In spite of the relatively inflexible nature of SRMs, evidently there were many services for which they were considered particularly suitable. The GWR rapidly expanded their fleet until, by early 1908, there were 99 in service, joined by the Port Talbot car when the GWR took over the stock of that railway company later in the year.

PERFORMANCE

In September 1905, a memorandum was produced summarising the general situation with regards to Steam Rail Motors. It read as follows:

'Swindon
20/9/05

'GREAT WESTERN RAILWAY RAIL MOTOR CARS

'Cost of engine £850; of 59ft 6in body £884, and of 70ft body £1,010; or a total of £1,734 and £1,860 respectively for 59½ft & 70ft cars.

'The complete cars are built at the Company's Swindon Works, but some have been bought from outside firms.

'Power is not transmitted by spur wheels and a speed change gear is not fitted.

'There is space on the engine for 15 to18 cwt of coal and 450 gallons of water.

'The main line is laid with rails of 97 lbs. per yard, and the branches with rails of not less than 75 lbs. per yard.

'Trailers are attached to the cars when necessary, the cars being capable of hauling one trailer up a gradient of 1 in 40 and one trailer and four horseboxes or milk trucks up a gradient of 1 in 100.

'59ft 6in trailers cost £856 and 70ft trailers £1186. [The original referred to 55ft trailers instead of 59ft 6in]

'Two men are employed to operate the engine, a driver and a fireman. One man is employed to attend to passengers, both when the car runs alone and with a trailer attached.

'Enginemen are paid 5s 6d per day when running on branches, with 6d extra for main line

An early photograph of an auto-train at Trumpers Crossing Halte on the Brentford branch, with 517 class 0–4–2T and trailer 4. The diagram involving the Brentford branch train was a particularly long one and was an early candidate for locomotive + trailer operation.

work. Firemen receive 3s and 3s 6d respectively. A car is not turned for the return journey. When a trailer is attached, this is pushed.

'The maximum grade over which the cars run is 1 in 40, extending for 2¼ miles.

'The Maximum load hauled is 1 trailer up 1 in 40 and 12 horse boxes on the level.

'12 m.p.h. is developed up 1 in 40; 50 m.p.h. on the level. The average speed is 35 m.p.h.

'The mileage of the cars per day varies from 100 to 200 miles and the mileage per stop from ¾ to 4½ miles.

'The coal consumption is 18.45 lbs. per mile.'

On 22nd May 1906, the Locomotive & Carriage Running Department at Swindon produced a more detailed document showing the loads that could be pulled by an SRM up various gradients:

'LOAD for STEAM MOTOR CARS on different gradients
(To be taken in addition to Car).

Gradients	*No. of Wheels*	*Remarks*
1 in 35 to 1 in 39	8*	* Load for car with 3ft 6in wheels
1 in 35 to 1 in 39	6*	* Load for car with 4ft 0in wheels
1 in 40 to 1 in 49	10	
1 in 50 to 1 in 59	12	
1 in 60 to 1 in 69	14	
1 in 70 to 1 in 79	16	
1 in 80 to 1 in 89	18	
1 in 90 to 1 in 99	20	
1 in 100 to1 in 150	24	Maximum for any easier gradient or where line is level

'One converted coach to count as 8 wheels
'One 59ft 6in trailer to count as 10 wheels
'One 70ft 0in trailer to count as 12 wheels.'

In May 1906, there were two types of 'converted coach' altered to trailers: two low-roof 4-wheel coaches and six 8-wheel clerestory coaches.

These figures may be compared with the equivalents for trailing loads that could be hauled by a 'small tank' (0–4–2T '517' class auto engine). Two sets of figures were produced by Mr W. H. Waister of the Locomotive Department, the first in August 1905, and the second, rather more conservative set, later in that year:

'Up a gradient not steeper than:	*(1)*	*(2)*
1 in 40	32 wheels	24 wheels
1 in 50	40 wheels	32 wheels
1 in 60	48 wheels	40 wheels
1 in 80	58 wheels	48 wheels
1 in 100	70 wheels	56 wheels'

One trailer ('Auto-Car'), irrespective of its length, was to be considered equal to 12 wheels, or three 4- wheeled vehicles.

The GWR also produced statements for services, and the contents of one I have seen are reproduced here. Unfortunately, the original had part of the 'Remarks' column missing, so it was not possible to reproduce this in full. This statement is an analysis of the 9.25 a.m. Shifnal to Lightmoor Junction and the 12.23 p.m. from Wellington to Craven Arms. It was produced by the Locomotive & Carriage Running Department at Swindon on 21st November 1906, and shows how fast the car was required to go to keep time between stops, together with the ruling gradients. There is a column showing the load that could be hauled, measured by the number of wheels. In many cases these are significantly less than the loads permitted in the table quoted above, and perhaps take into account the scheduled speeds rather than the gradient. Interestingly, there is a photograph of a train in August 1906 on this service, described as a 'Craven Arms to Much Wenlock train'. The date was the August Bank Holiday, and the train consists of two SRMs with a 59ft 6in trailer coupled between them. Assuming the trailer counts as 10 wheels, in accordance with the formula for steam motor cars above, this combination averages 5 wheels per car, and so falls within the load allowed.

This service commenced on 1st May 1906, but it is believed that steam rail motors were taken off it, probably some time in 1907. If the traffic required two cars plus a trailer, then economies could have been achieved by the use of auto-trailers and an engine. SRMs on this service feature disproportionately in the list of SRM faults from September 1906 in Chapter 3 – no doubt the steep gradients on the route did not help matters.

In July 1905, the Locomotive Department produced a report which showed the 'Allotment of Rail Motor Cars'. This table, the contents of which are reproduced here, listed each working for SRMs by Division, and I have added to this the running numbers of the cars which were available for each service, taken from the 1905 locomotive allocations book.

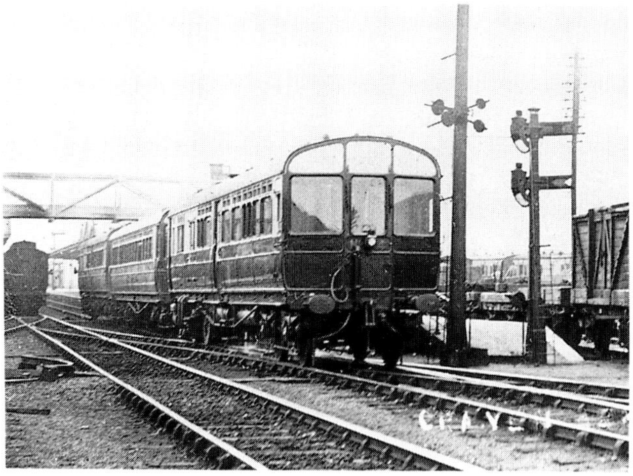

Another view of Car No. 74 of Diagram Q, a Diagram J trailer and another rail motor at Craven Arms, forming a motor train for Wenlock on August Bank Holiday 1906.
G. M. PERKINS
CTY. HMRS

TABLE 9

Wednesday, 21st November 1906

RAIL MOTOR CAR SERVICE - WELLINGTON & CRAVEN ARMS

STATEMENT SHEWING TIMES, SPEED, GRADIENT AND LOADS ETC.

Stations	*Times p.m.*		*Mins*	*Distances*		*Speeds*	*Gradients*		*Load: Wheels*	*Remarks*
	arr	*dep*	*Pt-Pt*	*M*	*Ch*	*m.p.h.*	*Rise*	*Fall*		
Wellington	-	12.23								
Ketley Jct	12x25		2	1	7	32·6	132		6	Reduce speed - staf
Ketley	12.26	12.27	1	0	40	30·0	50		6	
Lawley Bank	12.30	12.31	3	1	36	29·0	46		6	
Horsehay (Dawley)	12.33	12.34	2	0	74	27·8	46	51	6	
Lightmoor Jct	12x38		4	1	51	24·6		39/60/50	6	
Coalbrookdale	12.41	12.42	3	1	34	28·5		50	6	
Buildwas	12.45	12.48	3	1	12	23·0		50	6	
Much Wenlock	12.58	12.59	10	3	20	19·5	40/45/48		6	
Presthope	1.06	1.07	7	2	75	25·2	45/48		6	
Longville	1.14	1.15	7	3	59	32·0		100	8	
Rushbury	1.20	1.21	5	2	17	26·6		100/114	8	
Harton Road	1.25	1.26	4	2	35	36·6	137	100	8	
Marsh Farm Jct	1x31		5	2	52	31·8	142		8	Reduce speed - sta
Craven Arms	1.38	-	7	3	13	27·1		109	8	
Totals			63	28	45	27·2				

	arr	*dep*	*Mins*	*M*	*Ch*	*Speeds*	*Rise*	*Fall*	*Load*
Shifnal	-	9.25							
Madeley Jct	9x30		5	1	75	23·3			
Madeley	9.35	9.36	5	2	70	34·5	92	92	8
Lightmoor Jct	9.38	-	2	1	6	32·3		130	8
Totals			12	5	71	29·4			

NOTE
Gradients easier than 150 not taken into account

TABLE 10

ALLOTMENT OF RAIL MOTOR CARS - July 1905

No of Services	*Cars*	*Spare Cars*	*Service Ref No.*	*Starting times Week days*	*Starting times Sundays*	*From*	*To*	*Average finish Week days*	*Average finish Sundays*	*Cars Allocated*
Paddington Division										
5	5	0	1	5.30	-	Southall	Westbourne Pk.	9/30	-	5, 21, 26, 41, 45
			2	7.25	-	Southall	Willesden	9/3	-	Ditto
			3	2/30 SO	-	Southall	Westbourne Pk.	4/0	-	Ditto
			1A	8.54	-	Southall	Paddington	-	9/7	Ditto
			2A	9.15	-	Southall	Clapham Jn.	-	9/55	Ditto
			3A	9.15	-	Southall	Clapham Jn.	-	9/55	Ditto
			4	-	10.5	Southall	Clapham Jn.	-	8/11	Ditto
			5	-	10.5	Southall	Clapham Jn.	-	8/11	Ditto
Swindon Division										
7	9	2	1	7.45	10.0	Lambourn	Newbury	7/52	2/0	1, 2
			2	12/40 ThSO	-	Lambourn	Newbury	5/11	-	Ditto
			3	7.11	-	Chippenham	Calne &c.	10/40	-	19
			4	6.10	1/37	Trowbridge	Warminster	10/25	8/55	4, 38
			5	8.36	-	Trowbridge	Bath &c	8/34	-	Ditto
			6	7.4	2/40	Weymouth	Dorchester	11/20	9/40	3, 51
			7	8.0	2/40	Chalford	Stonehouse	10/0	10/0	50, 52
South Devon &c										
7	11	4	1	7.35	-	Exeter	Teignmouth	10/38	-	8, 18
			2	7.22	9.45	Plymouth	Yealmpton	11/22	9/45	24, 30, 39, 43
			3	6.0	9.8	Plymouth Suburban		Mdnt	10/20	Ditto
			4	8.16	-	Plymouth Suburban		11/13	-	Ditto
			5	7.50	-	Newquay	Chacewater	9/10	-	7, 25, 34
			6	7.45	-	Truro	Newquay	9/10	-	Ditto
			7	8.35	3/0	Penzance	Helston	7/30	9/15	49
Neath Division										
2	4	2	1	8.36	-	Neath Jn.	Glyn Neath	8/37	-	47, 48
			2	7.45	-	Whitland	Pembroke Dock	8/5	-	31, 42 (Tenby)
Worcester Division										
2	3	1	1	6.30	-	Evesham	Winchcombe	9/31	-	23, 27, 46
			2	7.15	-	Evesham	Stratford	6/12	-	Ditto
Wolverhampton Division										
12	16	4	1	6.15	-	Kidderminster local		10/6	-	35
			2	6.52	8.5	Stourbridge Jct.	Stourbridge Town	11/6	9/30	24, 32, 36, 37
			3	5.32	10.27	Stourbridge Jct.	Halesowen	11/2	10/30	Ditto
			4	5.30	-	Stourbridge Jct.	Oldbury	10/23	10/55	Ditto
			5	7.15	-	Wrexham	Oswestry	4/0	-	6, 9, 11-14, 20, 22, 28, 40
			6	7.35	-	Wrexham	Berwig	9/50	-	Ditto
			7	7.45	-	Wrexham	Wynne Hall	9/30	-	Ditto
			8	7.50	-	Wrexham	Coed Poeth	10/22	-	Ditto
			9	8.0	-	Wrexham	Ponkey	10/30	-	Ditto
			10	8.5	-	Wrexham	Moss	10/20	-	Ditto
			11	1/45 MThSO	-	Wrexham	Berwig	6/45	-	Ditto
			12	1/40	9.30	Corwen	Ruabon	11/30	6/0	17
Swindon Factory										
-	-	2								10, 33
Totals										
35	50	15								

NOTE

Times: 0.0 a.m.; 0/0 p.m.

In this report, the Paddington Division is shown as requiring five SRMs to cover its workings, and five were allocated; thus, none are shown as spare. However, in practice there were only two circuits for SRMs on Mondays to Fridays: one, starting with the 5.30 a.m. from Southall to Westbourne Park, and the other starting with the 7.25 a.m. from Southall to Willesden Junction. The car shown allocated to the Southall & Willesden service spent most of the day running between Park Royal and Willesden via Ealing. Only on Sundays were the five SRMs actually required for services in the Paddington Division, so presumably if a car was not available, it would be relatively easy to provide a conventional locomotive-hauled train in its place. The car on Sunday service 2A spent the day coupled to the one on 3A, and 4 was coupled to 5.

All other Divisions had one or more spare cars, and there were two (Nos. 10 and 33) under repair at Swindon.

The average starting and finishing times on weekdays and Sundays are shown, and it is noteworthy just what a long day many of them had. This is emphasised in Page 2 of the report, entitled *'Details of each Rail Motor Car service in respect to:- hours, miles, stops, speed, gradients, loads & roads.'* where columns 2 and 3 give the numbers of

TABLE 11

RAIL MOTOR CAR SERVICES:

Hours, Miles, Stops, Speeds, Gradients & Loads: July 1905

Service Ref No.	*No. of Hours Out Week days*	*Sundays*	*Average No. of Miles per: Day*	*Hour*	*Stop*	*Speeds (mph) (1 trip taken as typical) Highest*	*Lowest*	*Average*	*Steepest Gradient 1 in*	*Max. Load in addition to Car (Wheels)*
Paddington Division										
1	16	-	220	13·75	1·21	30·0	19·0	22·2	-	28
2	13¾	-	179	13·04	1·08	35·7	18·3	22·0	-	28
3	1¾	-	22	17·60	1·21	30·0	13·7	20·8	-	28
1A	-	12¾	172	14·08	1·22	30·6	14·2	23·2	-	28
2A	-	12¾	201	15·75	1·00	28·7	14·1	22·0	60	-
3A	-	12¾	201	15·75	1·00	28·7	14·1	22·0	60	-
4	-	10	158	15·82	1·02	25·5	14·1	20·9	60	-
5	-	10	158	15·82	1·02	25·5	14·1	20·9	60	-
Swindon Division										
1	12	4	125	10·41	1·55	23·1	15·2	22·2	60	28
2	4½	-	52	11·55	1·55	23·1	15·2	22·2	60	28
3	15½	-	152	9·83	2·75	30·5	21·6	23·0	60	18
4	16¼	7½	187	11·51	4·4	31·0	16·0	29·2	52	16
5	10	-	134	13·4	3·71	31·0	16·0	29·0	52	16
6	15¾	7	152	9·65	1·31	36·2	10·8	23·2	44	8
7	14	8	191	13·63	0·77	37·5	18·5	23·1	70	12
South Devon &c										
1	15¼	-	209	13·73	2·82	30·9	22·1	26·4	50	8
2	16	12	197	12·34	1·12	31·6	13·5	23·7	60	18
3	18	13¼	210	11·66	0·85	30·8	10·5	20·8	60	18
4	15	-	152	10·13	0·85	33·0	6·9	20·4	42	12
5	13¾	-	206	14·98	4·56	28·3	21·0	25·0	45	8
6	13½	-	184	13·66	2·53	28·5	15·6	23·4	45	8
7	10¼	6¼	142	13·25	2·17	31·9	15·6	22·9	60	8
Neath Division										
1	12	-	181	15·05	1·75	27·5	17·5	24·2	80	20
2	12.25	-	155	11·83	1·97	28·7	15·7	25·2	46	14
Worcester Division										
1	15	-	183	12·23	2·48	30·2	20·4	22·0	96	12
2	11	-	140	12·77	3·33	25·4	21·9	24·0	100	14
Wolverhampton Division										
1	16	-	142	8·87	1·56	25·7	16·7	20·8	100	8
2	16¼	13¼	75	4·61	0·73	14·7	14·7	14·7	67	6
3	17½	12¼	118	6·77	1·02	30·7	20·7	23·8	50	12
4	17	13	100	5·88	0·82	24·7	16·5	21·8	40	-
5	8¾	-	148	16·91	2·81	30·0	22·6	27·9	50	6
6	14¼	-	135	9·45	0·98	21·0	8·6	16·1	35	12
7	13¾	-	104	7·60	0·92	49·0	6·7	19·0	50	10
8	14½	-	164	11·31	2·07	29·5	16·3	23·5	35	12
9	14½	-	99	5·83	0·85	49·0	12·8	18·8	40	-
10	14¼	-	101	7·12	0·87	20·1	8·4	13·1	50	10
11	5	-	31	6·30	0·98	21·0	8·6	16·1	35	8
12	9¾	8½	134	13·76	2·03	33·3	16·2	24·1	75	6

hours in service for weekdays and Sundays. The reference numbers in the column 1 of page 2 are the same as in column 4 of page 1.

The average miles per hour column is simply the miles per day divided by the number of hours out (i.e. in service). It includes all layovers at the end of journeys and pauses en route, so is quite a good productivity measure.

There are three columns showing the highest, lowest and average speeds between stops on a typical trip. The speeds quoted reflect the vagaries that are bound to occur when timing trains to the nearest minute over short distances; thus, I do not suppose the 49 mph timing of two of the Wrexham services was ever kept. Nevertheless, the average speed for the journey gives a good idea of what could be achieved by SRMs, with their rapid acceleration. Some of the journey speeds demanded were relatively high: six were 25 mph or faster.

A report to the GWR Board on the abolition of second class in 1909 listed the following services as 'worked by Auto or Rail Motor Car, one class only':

Forest of Dean
Merthyr & Newport
Garnant & Gwaun-cae-Gurwen
Black Lion Crossing & Cwmaman
Banbury & Chipping Norton Jct.
Stourbridge Branch
Rhos Branch
Moss Branch
Coed Poeth Branch
Ponkey Branch
Brentford Branch
Calne Branch
Chacewater & Newquay via St. Agnes
Honeybourne & Cheltenham
Acton, Park Royal, Greenford, Denham & Uxbridge
Lambourn Valley
Acton & Willesden (Southall & Willesden service)
Watlington Branch
Abbotsbury Branch
Yealmpton Branch
Birmingham, Tyseley & Stratford-on-Avon
Oldbury
Dudley, Old Hill & Halesowen
Henley-in-Arden & Lapworth
Swansea (East Dock) & British Rhondda.

This list excludes lines where the motor trains *supplemented* the regular train service, such as the Stroud Valley service, where second class was still available on the ordinary trains.

A Diagram O or R SRM hauling a clerestory coach at Ashton Gate Platform on the Portishead branch, probably 1908-10. The Wapping Wharf branch diverged to the right. The destination board reads 'BATH'. COLLECTION R. C. RILEY

Two rail motors crossing at Perranporth station on the Truro–Newquay line, probably pre-1910. COLLECTION R. C. RILEY

Car No. 72 of Diagram O, when new at Dawlish Warren, bound for Teignmouth with a clerestory coach in tow. COLLECTION J. N. SLINN

ALLOCATIONS

To give an idea of how allocations to locomotive depots changed over the years, two tables show the summer and winter allocations at five yearly intervals from August 1904 until December 1934, divided before and after the Great War. The actual dates quoted are those in the *Locomotive Allocation Registers*. These are necessarily a series of 'snapshots' and a few places which had cars allocated to them briefly do not appear. For example, SRMs Nos.31 and 42 were at Brynamman for a couple of months in 1905; Nos.24 and 27 were at Llanelly in 1908; various cars were sent to Duffryn at times when the Port Talbot Railway's car was at Swindon; No.22 was at Rogerstone twice in 1914 and No.40 was allocated to 'Cambrian lines' and Dolgelly in 1922.

Other noteworthy matters in the allocations registers are:

1. SRMs allocated to Bristol, Bath and Yatton seem to have interchanged depot frequently.
2. SRMs sent to Swindon Works were usually recorded as 'allocated' there, but those known to have been sent to the Wolverhampton Factory were not usually shown as being sent there. Two cars awaiting attention at Swindon Works were allocated to Swindon shed in 1919, presumably to get them out of the way.
3. SRMs awaiting conversion to trailers have been shown as allocated to Swindon Works if the allocation register still shows them as extant there, even if condemned.
4. Car No.45 was loaned to the Highland Railway between 1918 and 1920, so its allocation to Invergordon appears in the second table.
5. Car No.80 was allocated to Monmouth for three months in 1914, although there was no engine shed there.

There is a full history of the known allocations and stoppages of each car in Appendix D.

TABLE 12

SRM ALLOCATIONS: Pre-Great War

Allocation at 4 weeks ending:

	20 Aug 1904	*10 Dec 1904*	*14 Aug 1909*	*04 Dec 1909*	*08 Aug 1914*	*26 Dec 1914*
Aberdare			9, 11	9, 11	5, 11	1, 3, 11
Aberystwyth			42, 43		77, 85	
Ashburton	7, 8	18				
Basingstoke					71	
Bath			82	82	41, 46	26, 41
Bristol			76	41	7, 13, 17, 43, 49, 62, 87	9, 43, 45, 46, 47, 49
Chalford	4, 5	1, 4, 5	50	49	44, 52	44, 52
Cheltenham			89	89	96	96
Chester					50, 98	50
Chippenham			97	45		
Corwen					34	40
Croes Newydd	9, 10, 13	9, 11, 13, 20, 22	5, 8, 10, 12, 20, 22, 23, 37, 70	5, 8, 10, 12, 20, 21, 23, 37, 62, 68	20, 24, 29, 30, 40, 78, 88	24, 29, 30, 31, 34, 88, 97
Didcot					91	91
Evesham		23, 27	18, 99	40, 99		
Exeter			94	94		
Frome			17, 74, 80	17, 74, 80	25, 32	21, 32
Garnant			27	27		
Gloucester			48	50		
Goodwick			79, 81	79, 81	73, 83	76, 77
Gwaun-Cae-Gurwen			26	26	19, 75	19, 75
Helston	25		96			
Kiderminster			24, 53	53, 54	51, 92	22, 57
Laira	7, 18	7, 8, 28	3, 38, 39, 52	3, 39, 52, 59, 60, 66		
Lambourn Valley	1,2	19, 21				
Merthyr			56, 91	71, 91	84, 86	84, 86
Monmouth					80	
Neath			6, 47	42, 43	1, 76	42, 51
Newquay			66, 90	72		
Newton Abbot		10, 24		90	58, 61	58
Oxford			55, 58, 83	55, 58, 83	54, 74, 82	27, 54, 82
Penzance		25		61	63, 72	63, 72
Pontypool Road					53, 59, 89, 93	38, 53, 56, 80
Radstock					81	89
Reading					22	
Slough					16, 100	16
Southall	6, 11, 12, 14, 17, 19, 21, 26	14, 17, 26	35, 51, 65, 73, 84, 92, 93	35, 51, 56, 73, 84, 92	2, 8, 10, 14, 28, 39, 48, 64	10, 14, 28, 39, 64, 71, 73
Stourbridge			15, 16, 25, 28, 29, 30, 31, 64, 75	15, 16, 21, 25, 28, 64, 69, 93	15, 18, 55, 67, 68, 70, 79, 95	15, 18, 68, 70, 79, 93, 95
Stratford-upon-Avon			13, 63	13, 98	60, 98	60, 98
Swindon Stock			1, 2, 7, 33, 41, 49, 98	1, 2, 7, 14, 46, 48	57	12, 13, 20, 25, 48, 74
Swindon Works	3	2, 3, 6	40, 45, 46, 54, 57, 59, 60, 69, 71, 78	6, 18, 19, 22, 29, 30, 32, 36, 38, 47, 57, 63, 65, 70, 75,	3, 4, 6, 9, 12, 21, 31, 45, 56, 65, 94	2, 17, 33, 36, 55, 61, 62, 65, 67, 69, 78, 83, 90, 100
Taunton			19, 67	34, 67	69, 90	85, 99
Tenby			14, 95			
Trowbridge			32, 34	78, 97	23, 36	23, 81
Truro			61, 72, 77	96		
Tyseley			62, 85, 87, 88	85, 86, 87, 88, 95		
Weymouth			4, 36, 44	4, 33, 44	35, 37, 99	35, 37, 59
Whitland			68		27, 38, 42	
Wolverhampton		12	86	31	66	66
Worcester			21	24	33	92
Yatton				76	26, 47	87, 94

TABLE 13

SRM ALLOCATIONS: Post-Great War

Allocation at 4 weeks ending:

	30 Aug 1919	*20 Dec 1919*	*16 Jul 1922*	*10 Aug 1924*	*28 Dec 1924*	*04 Aug 1929*	*22 Dec 1929*	*25 Aug 1934*	*15 Dec 1934*
Aberdare	39, 50, 51	39, 50, 51	38, 50	54, 67	65				
Bath	31	86		40, 70	90	92			
Birkenhead				45	45, 78				
Bristol (SPM)	25, 30, 33, 36, 47, 49, 59, 64, 67, 74, 77, 79, 86, 89, 92	30, 31, 33, 37, 47, 49, 52, 62, 67, 74, 89	53, 54, 67, 69, 90, 91	65, 88, 95, 96	40, 70, 73, 88, 91				
Chalford			52	56	56				
Chester	40, 66	40, 91		74					
Chippenham		65	63						
Croes Newydd	21, 46, 55, 73, 95 97	41, 46, 55, 78, 97	30, 78, 80, 93	97	97	81, 82	69, 98		
Exeter	58		72, 86	81, 86	81, 86	58, 62	72	71	37
Frome	69, 85	69, 85		69	82				
Garnant			76, 83	53, 55	55, 83				
Gloucester		70	43, 45, 87	39, 84, 93	39, 84, 93				
Invergordon (HR)	45	45							
Laira						72, 75			
Malvern Wells	71	71							
Machynlleth			39, 40, 58,	78	76				
Neath			37, 99	94, 99	53, 94	37, 73, 80	30, 37, 73, 83, 91	70	
Newport	43, 44, 53	43, 44, 53							
Oswestry			74, 84, 85	66, 73	66				
Penmaenpool					30				
Penzance			61						
Pontypool Road				90	54	76, 77, 83	76, 77		
Reading	27, 28, 76		62, 64, 98	72, 85, 87	72, 85, 87	94		37	
St Philip Marsh						39, 71, 78, 93	39, 65, 71, 78, 92, 93	76, 77, 81	92
Slough	16					64	55, 64		
Southall	24, 68	68	88, 96	61, 92	41, 61	74, 84, 96	74, 96	30, 91, 97, 98	30, 91, 97, 98
Stourbridge	61, 96	61, 96	70, 92	89	89	40, 53, 66	40, 53, 66	55, 88	55, 88
Swindon Loco	35, 42								
Swindon Stock		15		16	16, 92			72	
Swindon Works	15, 26, 29, 32, 37, 38, 41, 60, 63, 65, 70, 72, 75, 78, 80, 81, 82, 87, 91, 94	16, 21, 35, 36, 42, 56, 57, 58, 60, 63, 64, 66, 72, 73, 75, 76, 77, 79, 80, 81, 82, 84, 87, 92, 94, 95, 98	16, 31, 33, 34, 35, 36, 41, 46, 47, 51, 65, 66, 73, 75, 77, 81, 82, 95	30, 38, 41, 57, 62, 63, 64, 75, 76, 80, 83, 98	38, 57, 58, 62, 63, 64, 65, 69, 74, 75, 80, 95, 99	30, 54, 55, 56, 69, 70, 79, 86, 88, 91, 95, 97	58, 70, 75, 79, 80, 81, 82, 88	64, 65, 66, 80, 92, 93, 96	70, 71, 72, 76, 77, 80
Taunton	57, 84, 88, 90, 98	88, 90	71, 97	71, 77	71, 77				
Tenby	22, 83	83							
Trowbridge	34	34	94						
Truro	52	38							
Westbury			56, 57	58, 82	98				
Wolverhampton	23, 54, 100	54		37	37	98			
Worcester			44, 79	68, 79	68, 79				
Yatton	62, 93	93	55	91	96	65	86		
Yeovil			89						

50'Rms.—Q3-12-20—P.O. (Z 17)

Telegraphic Address:— CHURCHWARD, SWINDON
Telephone:— No. 185 SWINDON.

Great Western Railway.

LOCOMOTIVE, CARRIAGE & WAGON DEPARTMENT Circular No. 3613.

CHIEF MECHANICAL ENGINEER'S OFFICE,

Swindon, Wilts.,

In reply to your—

In your reply please quote— 6400.

NB

22nd July 1921

Dear Sir,

Injectors on Motor Cars and R.O.D. Engines.

Several failures have recently occurred in connection with the injectors of R.O.D. engines and motor cars the trouble no doubt being caused by their being allowed to get too hot through the steam valves being opened too quickly when starting to work injectors.

I shall therefore be glad if you will arrange for the enginemen, and particularly the young firemen, to be instructed that when working cars and R.O.D. engines (on which water has to be lifted) it is necessary to open the steam valves slowly to work the injectors, and thus avoid trouble in the direction indicated.

Yours truly,
For G.J. CHURCHWARD.

All Loco Supt's

C. B. COLLETT, Chief Mechanical Engineer.

GREAT WESTERN RAILWAY

LOCO. SWINDON.

Telephone: SWINDON 711; Ext. 78

CIRCULAR NO. 5433.

Chief Mechanical Engineer's Department,

SWINDON, WILTS.

Your reference :—

Saturday, 28th. January, 1933

Please quote this reference :— 2096 / 33/1

Dear Sir,

Heating and ventilation of Rail Motor Cars.

The Traffic Department have received complaints this Winter of the overheating and lack of ventilation in our Rail Motor Car Services.

As you are aware, vehicles working in these services are not fitted with the passenger control, and the heating is regulated by the Guard requesting the Driver to reduce (or increase) the steam pressure according to the climatic conditions prevailing.

The Traffic staff have been instructed by the Superintendent of the Line to pay special attention to the heating and ventilation of these vehicles and to collaborate with the Drivers to ensure that the heat is so regulated as circumstances demand.

Will you kindly instruct all your Drivers concerned to do everything possible to prevent the vehicles being overheated.

Please acknowledge receipt.

Yours truly,
For C.B.Collett

.N.P.	Insp. Hand
.T.H.R.	" Berry
.R.	" Pyper
E.B.	" Sheldon
W.H.C.	" Parnell
W.A.K.	" Davies
W.H.	" Lovesey
H.G.	" Thomas
J.A.	Mr.Dyer (2)

ACCIDENTS

The GWR's steam rail motors were involved in a few accidents, or 'incidents' as they would be called nowadays, although there seems to be nothing to suggest that, in terms of safety, they were any different from hauled trains. Examples can be found in the Traffic Committee's minutes where claims against the company and subsequent settlements were recorded, whilst the more serious incidents were detailed. For example, A. J. Swanford was 'caught by Motor whilst crossing line' at Ham Hill Crossing on 11th December 1904; his right arm had to be amputated, and he was awarded £10. A Mrs. Butler was alighting from a motor car at Trumper's Crossing on 24th April 1905 when it moved, causing her to fall; she was much shaken, and her infant's foot was injured. She was awarded £12. There were two similar incidents of cars moving when passengers were alighting at St. Budeaux in September and December 1905, following which a Mr. Stephenson was awarded £16 and a Dr. and Mrs Guard £50.

An accident reported in some detail to the Traffic Committee was:

> 'The 11.5 p.m. Motor Car, with trailer attached, from Plymouth (Millbay) to Saltash, was about to start from No.1 bay line on the 4th instant [4th June 1906], when the driver stated that he should require to take water before leaving. Permission was given the driver to back down to the water crane, and the backing out signal was lowered. After water had been taken the driver sounded his whistle for the starting signal to be lowered, but this whistle the signalman took as an indication that the motor train had been drawn back into the platform clear of No.2 road (which the trailer was fouling while standing at the water crane), and lowered the home signal to admit the 8.55 p.m. excursion train from Exeter, with the result that it struck the trailer with some little force.
>
> 'Seventeen passengers have complained of injuries, mostly of a slight character. The motor, trailer, and engine and four coaches on the passenger train were damaged. No vehicle left the rails.
>
> 'The Signalman has been suspended with loss of pay, will lose his bonus and be removed to a less important post.'

After 1905, it is often difficult to be sure that steam rail motors were involved because reports tend not to differentiate between them and auto trains (locomotive and trailer) e.g.:

> 'On June 29th, as the 4.50 p.m. Motor train from Oxford to Princes Risborough with coach attached was leaving the up main line platform at Oxford, the Conductor observing a passenger running towards it, stopped the train after it had run about 50 yards, by means of a bell signal to the Driver. A Pilot engine which was behind the train started forward after the train had run about 40 yards, and the Driver, although several of the platform staff attempted to warn him by shouting, failed to observe that the train had stopped, with the result that the engine came into contact with the coach and 11 passengers sustained slight injuries. No damage was occasioned.
>
> 'The accident was due to the failure of the Enginemen to carry out the instructions with regard to the working of light engines following loaded passenger trains, and they have been cautioned.
>
> 'The conductor is also to blame for stopping to allow a passenger to join and he has been admonished.
>
> 'Several claims have been received and are receiving consideration.'

Two accidents, both involving low-speed buffer stop collisions at Clevedon in the 1920s, resulted in reports by the Railways Inspectorate. The first, involving SRM No.81 hauling trailer No.85 on 27th August 1920, was the result of the handbrake malfunction, and the subsequent failure of the driver to apply the vacuum brake quickly enough. The Inspector commented on the general practice of operating SRMs with empty sandboxes and, on this branch, of running trains without a guard. As a result, instructions were issued that the sandboxes were to be kept full.

The second occurred on 23rd January 1926, when SRM No.75 was hauling trailer No.85 in a heavy rain storm. Again, the car was running with empty sandboxes, and the Inspector thought that the driver had been unable to recognise where he was in the downpour; he suggested that the GWR consider the fitting of road vehicle type windscreen wipers to see if they could improve drivers' sighting in conditions of heavy rain, etc. He also recommended that sandboxes should be modified to make them easier to fill.

Following the Inspector's report, Mr Collett informed the General Manager that the sandboxes on SRMs had been modified – this may refer to the leading sandboxes being moved to the front of the engine's front stretcher. He also said that the instructions on keeping them filled had been reissued, and that the cars (and trailers) had been fitted with windscreen wipers, but there were problems with getting them to work satisfactorily, as they had to be kept clean, and the windows free of grease.

THE END OF THE GWR STEAM RAIL MOTOR

As has been noted above, there were problems with the inherent inflexibility of steam rail motors as far as passenger capacity was concerned. Other disadvantages, when compared with locomotive-operated auto trains, were that servicing of the power unit necessarily took place in engine sheds, which gave rise to problems in keeping the passenger accommodation clean. Because the power unit was built-in, any maintenance on it meant the whole car was out of use. Further, due to the design of the car, with the vertical boiler encased within the bodywork, relatively little serious work could be done on the boiler or engine without first removing the boiler from the car. In addition, a steam rail motor had poor haulage capacity when compared with a locomotive.

Around the time when steam rail motors were being introduced, the GWR had a surplus of small tank locomotives; these had been written off from an accounting point of view, but were suitable for further service on auto trains, so locomotive operated auto-trains could be provided relatively cheaply. A power unit for an SRM could cost over £1,000.

In view of the advantages of locomotive-operated auto trains, it is not surprising that the GWR had as many auto trailers as SRMs by 1912, and it is also not surprising that in 1912, a Superintendents Meeting Minute read:

> '*Conversion of old rail motor cars to trailers.*
> It was considered that a number of old rail motor cars might, with advantage, be converted into trailers, and Mr Churchward will deal with the subject.'

This policy was put into effect in mid-1914 and the Dia. C matchboarded cars Nos.3–8 were withdrawn for conversion between July 1914 and January 1915. The remaining matchboarded cars were withdrawn for conversion between September 1915 and April 1920.

The conversion process involved the removal of the power unit, the rebuilding of the body and some of the underframe from the front of the car as far back as the end of the passenger saloon nearest the power unit. A new bogie in place of the power unit had to be provided, and in some cases the trailing bogie was also replaced. The existing end windows were kept, including the unusual arrangement in the ends of Nos.1 and 2, and the extra deep waist panels of the wood panelled cars. However, those matchboarded cars which had panelling inserted at the bottom of the windows at the motor end reverted to the original full-size end

TRAIN STAFF EXPERIMENTS

In 1931, single-line staff apparatus was erected near the Rodbourne Lane bridge at Swindon on a straight length of line with no super-elevation, apparently in connection with problems experienced at Tolcarn Junction and St. Blazey Bridge. On 1st October 1931, tests were carried out using engine No.5527 coupled to SRM No.77, and engine No.1498 running separately. The apparatus was first tried using the standard position of the hoop at 7ft 11in from rail level and 3ft 7in from the running face of the rail, measurements taken from the centre of the hoop. This gave a distance from the hoop to the body of the car of 1ft 7¼in. Satisfactory results were obtained when picking up from the footplate of the engines and the car at an estimated 15 mph.

The staff position was then altered so that the hoop was 5in further from the rail, but at the same height as before. It was found that the staff was picked up from No.1498 at 15 mph, but this position was rather awkward for the fireman. Picking up from the SRM was also tried, and although no difficulty was experienced, this position was not so good as the standard.

The conclusions were that the standard position was satisfactory when picking up the staff from engines or rail cars on a straight section of line, but it was not possible to replicate the conditions at Tolcarn Junction and St. Blazey Bridge, so trials should be carried out there to obtain reliable results.

One of the problems with SRMs was keeping the passenger accommodation clean at locomotive sheds. This view shows a car just outside the shed at Southall on 22nd June 1932. The Brentford branch can be seen to the right side of the photograph. H. F. WHEELLER

windows. When altered to auto trailers, what had been the driving compartment at the trailing end of the SRM was retained as the driving compartment of the new auto trailer, whilst the former motor end of the car became the 'conventional' end of the trailer, nearest the engine. For further details, the reader is referred to *Great Western Auto Trailers* Part 1 (John Lewis, Wild Swan Publications).

In 1920, the non-standard cars Nos.15 and 16 were sold, but the sale of 16 was not completed and it was put back into stock, to be eventually condemned and broken up in 1927, having travelled just 8 miles since returning to service. Also in 1920, two of the wood panelled cars, Nos.42 and 49, plus the Port Talbot Railway car were sold to the Port of London Authority.

Apart from No.48, which was destroyed by fire in 1916, and the two cars which were sold, the wood panelled cars were withdrawn between July 1919 and October 1935, and most were converted to trailers. None were withdrawn between 1922 and 1926 or in the 1929–31 period.

Presumably due to varying accountancy practices over the years, some cars were simply recorded as converted to a trailer, whilst others were formally condemned first. However, those condemned in July 1933 were recorded as 'Condemned. Recovered parts used in Trailer No. ..', the 'recovered parts' being over 50% of the body, most of the underframe, and the trailing bogie. Dates that may be recorded include 'Stopped work'; 'To Swindon Factory'; 'Condemned'; 'Out of Stock'; and 'Converted to trailer'.

In some cases, the whole process was apparently very quick, whilst in others there was considerable delay: for example, SRM No.26 stopped work on 10th July 1916, but did not appear as trailer No.122 until 8th February 1920. There are also some discrepancies between the various dates recorded for the entry of trailers into service, and in the case of SRM No.41, it is recorded that it was 'stopped' as an SRM at Swindon Factory on 5th January 1928, and was 'Converted to a trailer December 1927' – on the same sheet!

SRM Nos.30, 65, 70, 71 and 77 were condemned and replaced by three diesel railcars. Other cars that were simply condemned and not used for a trailer, or replaced by something else, were: Nos.37, 48, 55, 80, 88, 92, and 97.

The final allocations of steam rail motors were:

TABLE 14

FINAL SRM ALLOCATIONS: 1934/5

Last Allocated Shed	*Car*	*Out of use*	*To Swindon Factory Pool*	*To Swindon Factory*	*Condemned*	*Notes*
Exeter	37	28 May 35	4 Jun 35	-	19 Oct 35	
	71	28 May 35	12 Jun 35	19 Jun 35	19 Oct 35	
Neath	65	16 Oct 35	16 Oct 35	-	19 Oct 35	
	70	22 Sep 34	23 Jan 35	25 Jan 35	19 Oct 35	
St. Philip Marsh	76	12 Oct 34	9 Jan 35	11 Jan 35	-	Converted to trailer: Jan 35
	92	31 Jul 35	15 Oct 35	-	19 Oct 35	
Southall	30	19 Feb 35	18 Mar 35	-	19 Oct 35	
	72	8 Dec 34	8 Dec 34	13 Dec 34	-	Converted to trailer: Jan 35
	77	8 Oct 34	21 Dec 34	2 Jan 35	19 Oct 35	
	91	3 Jan 35	-	1 Jan 35	-	Converted to trailer: Jan 35
	97	27 Mar 35	-	16 Apr 35	25 Apr 35	
	98	18 Apr 35	8 May 35	1 May 35	-	Converted to trailer: May 35
Stourbridge Jct.	55	1 Apr 35	16 Apr 35	23 Apr 35	19 Oct 35	
	88	16 Oct 35	16 Oct 35	-	19 Oct 35	
Swindon Stock	80	29 Jan 34	15 Dec 34	21 Dec 34	19 Oct 35	Stopped at Exeter To Swindon Stock Shed 8 Mar 34.

The final days of the cars were noted in a file at the National Archives, Kew [RAIL 254/9]:

> 'RAIL MOTOR CARS
> 'The last Rail Motors were withdrawn from Service and sent to Swindon during W.E. Oct 19th, 1935, for condemnation.'

The *Great Western Railway Magazine* recorded:

> 'RAIL MOTOR CARS
> 'The last of the Company's steam rail motor car services was discontinued on September 16. The cars were withdrawn and brought to Swindon for condemnation or conversion to trailers. The first service to be run by these vehicles was between Chalford and Stroud on October 12, 1903, and the last service to be regularly worked by them was between Neath (Canal Side) and Court Sart.'

An era had passed.

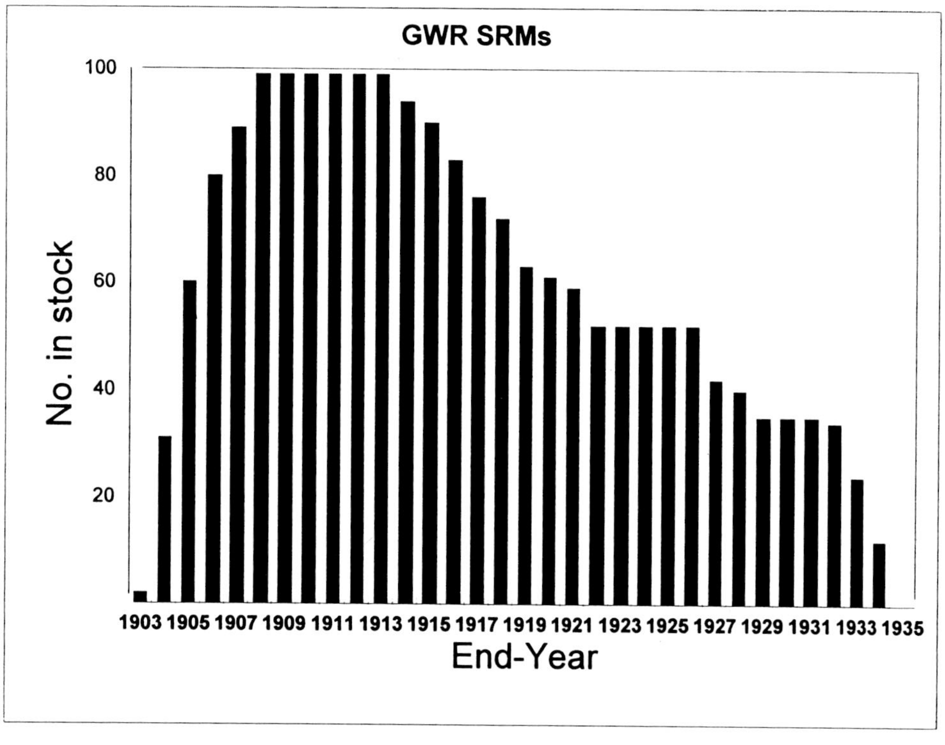

Car No. 1 of Diagram A1, as built. NATIONAL RAILWAY MUSEUM

Car No. 1 as built, showing power end, at Stonehouse station. Note the polished cylinder ends. There are no brackets for a destination board above the end windows, which are seen here in the original small size, matching the side windows. COLLECTION R. C. RILEY

CHAPTER SEVEN

THE MATCHBOARDED SRMS

Diagrams A1, A: Nos.1 and 2

The first two steam rail motors were built to Churchward's design on Lot 1037 (Carriage Department) and Lot F23 (Locomotive Department) at an average cost of £1,738 12s 0d each, divided as £727 17s 10d for the carriage and £1,010 14s 2d for the power unit. They were ordered on 18th May 1903, and entered public service on Monday, 12th October that year. The cars are illustrated by various versions of diagrams A1 in an early condition, and 'A', which shows No.1 with a modified window layout and the passenger saloon divided in two.

DESIGN

SRMs Nos.1 and 2 were 57ft 0¾in long, 8ft 6¾in wide, and 12ft 6in high from rail to roof line. The frame plan and early copies of diagram A1 show them as 13ft 6in high from rail to chimney top, whilst later diagrams show this dimension as 13ft 4½in. In practice, both Nos.1 and 2 seem to have been fitted with a short, lipped chimney to which a short, plain extension had been added before the cars entered service.

The power unit was in its own compartment, 12ft 9⅛in long. This compartment contained the boiler, the driving controls, handbrake, and a coal bunker which held 10 cwt only. In the rear corners were the water tank filler pipes, access to which was via a sliding window in the sides. According to the *SRM Register* at York, the boiler on No.1 (boiler No.111) was pressed to 180 lbs sq in, which gave a tractive effort of 8,483 lbs. This TE was also quoted in Marillier's October 1903 paper. Boiler No.112, fitted to No.2, was recorded in the register as being pressed to 160 lbs sq in, which gave a TE of 7,540 lbs. Just to complicate things further, both Locomotive Dept. diagrams A1 and A in their surviving forms indicate that Nos.1 and 2 had boilers with a working pressure of 140lbs sq in only, and the TE correspondingly reduced to 6,598 lbs. The standard working pressure for SRM boilers was otherwise 160 lbs sq in. SRM 1 seems to have kept its original boiler until October 1913, while boiler 112 seems to have remained fitted to No.2 until it was replaced during repairs to the car in January 1915.

Engines Nos.0801 and 0802 (fitted to cars No.1 and No.2 respectively) had non-standard 3ft 8in diameter driving wheels. No.0801 was fitted with boiler 111, but this was replaced by 1107 in August–October 1913. Engine 0801 remained with SRM No.1 until October/November 1914 when it was replaced by 0807, which had the 3ft 6in drivers, and to which boiler 1107 was fitted. Finally, in 1915, No.1 was given boiler 1124 and engine 0891, which was one with 4ft driving wheels. SRM No.2 seems to have kept boiler 112 and engine 0802 until they were both removed during repairs between October 1914 and January 1915, when it was fitted with boiler 1040 and 3ft 6½in-wheeled engine 0816.

The body of the cars was of wood: the structural framing was of Baltic and Canadian oak, the upper part of the outside being panelled with Honduras mahogany, and the lower part cased in 3in-wide matchboarding.

Each end of the SRM had three windows, the central one of which was rather narrower than the other two, and was a droplight; this gave easy access to the lamp bracket in front of it, and it could be opened in fog or other conditions of poor visibility to give the driver the best chance of seeing ahead.

Inboard of the motor compartment door were three sliding windows to that compartment, with a pair of louvre ventilators above. The water filler pipes were just inside the rearmost one of these windows on each side.

Lighting was by gas, using flat flame burners with a single supply pipe. The power compartment had two lamps in line with the leading ends of the doors, the passenger compartment six, and the trailing vestibule one. Lamps in the passenger compartment were described as 'dual-burner', of 14 candlepower each. The pipe feeding the lamps from the gas cylinder seems to have been attached to the partition between the passenger saloon and the trailing vestibule, and then came up through the roof, as opposed to previous practice where, on non-gangwayed coaches, the feed pipe rose externally on the end of the coach.

The passenger accommodation was in a single, large, open saloon, with access only via

Car No. 1, as built, at Stonehouse station.
COLLECTION R. C. RILEY

the driving vestibule at the trailing end. There was a 14ft 3in length of longitudinal bench seating at each end, and two seating bays 5ft 1⅛in between seat backs in the middle. This gave seating for 52 passengers. According to Marillier's October 1903 paper,

> 'The seats and seat backs were composed of woven wire covered with rattan cane, made by the Longford Wire Company, Warrington, thus saving the cost of horsehair or other padding, which harboured the moth and dust. The longitudinal seats were divided by armrests into sets of three.'

Although there was an internal sliding door to the motor compartment, the only passenger access was via the driving vestibule, also by means a sliding door. Inside the car, the ceiling was painted white 'relieved with blue lining', and the woodwork was of polished oak.

The driving vestibule, as built, did not have external side doors, and was simply supplied with a 'lazy tongs' type of expanding metal door each side; this contrasted with the motor end, which could be entirely closed up. The vestibule was just 4ft between partition and the car end, and contained a screw handbrake, vacuum brake control and a regulator handle. There was also 'electrical communication' (using bells) for the crew between the motor compartment and the driving vestibule. The whistle could be operated from the driving

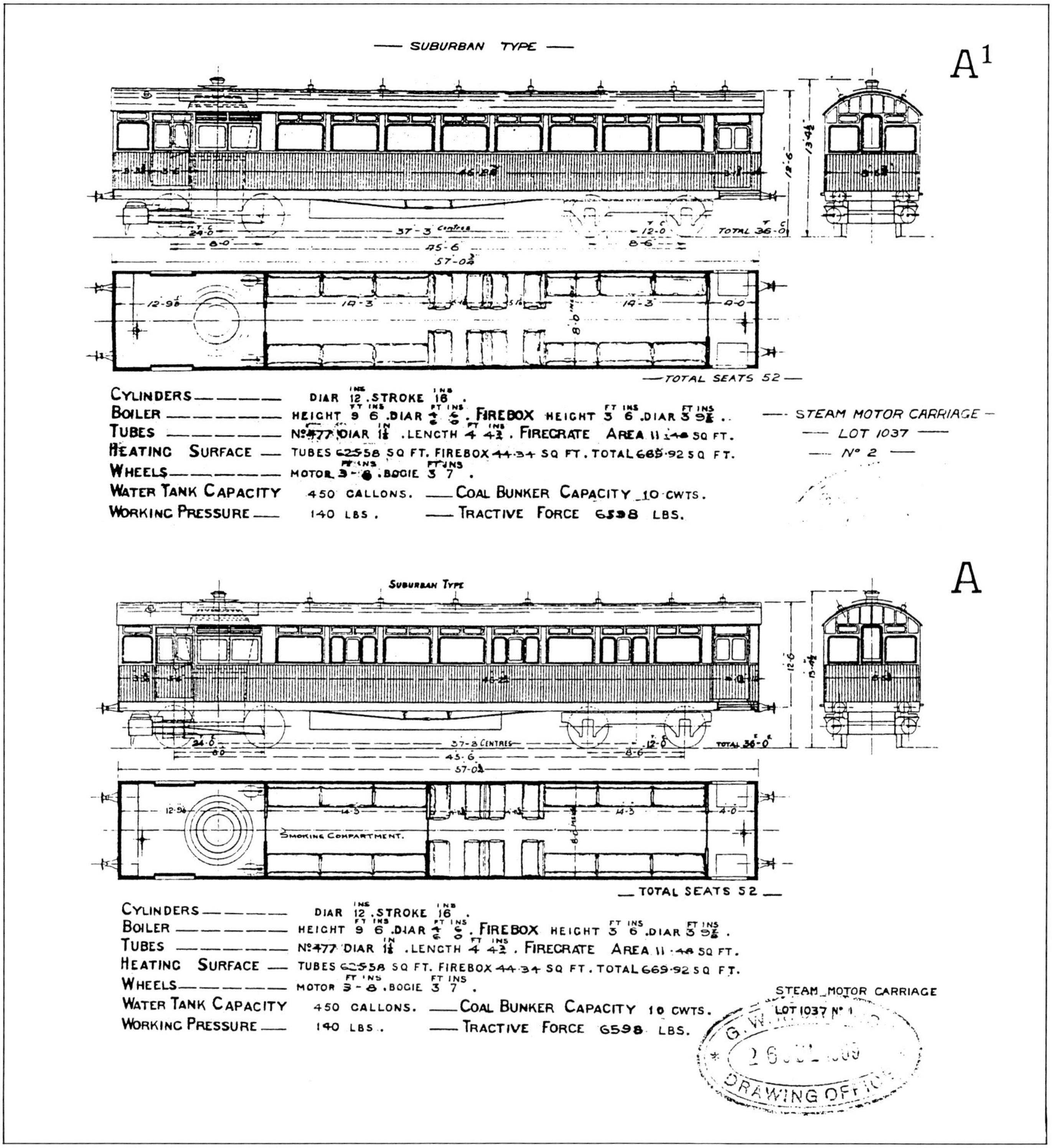

vestibule by means of a cord, which was carried through the passenger compartment inside a tube; this tube supported leather strap handles for standing passengers to grasp.

In Chapter 5 we studied the underframe in some detail. An important feature worthy of repeat is that, as built, they were provided with fixed steps descending from the driving vestibule floor, which could be covered over by a flap; this then acted as the floor of the vestibule, giving safe access at stations with normal-height platforms.

The leading wheel of the power unit was 5ft behind the front headstock, the engine having a wheelbase of 8ft, whilst the trailing bogie was an ordinary Dean 8ft 6in-wheelbase coach type, fitted with lifeguards at the outer end. Bogies were positioned at 37ft 3in centres, giving a total wheelbase of 45ft 6in.

A standard Great Western Armstrong moving cylinder-type brake was positioned at the trailing end of the water tank, to one side of the SRM longitudinal centre line. One of the brake 'V' hangers was positioned outboard of the adjacent truss rod.

The water tank held 450 gallons, and was located towards the motor end of the SRM.

Diagrams A1 and A record the total weight of each car as 36 tons, with 24 tons on the power bogie and 12 tons on the trailing. The *Lot Book* gives the average tare weight as 33 tons 13 cwt, and the gross weight as 34 tons 12 cwt 2 qtrs. The *SRM Register* gives the weight of No.1 as 38 tons 16 cwt, and No.2 as 38 tons 11 cwt.

MODIFICATIONS & DISPOSAL

These pioneer examples of steam rail motors went through several modifications in the course of their lives, as is only to be expected of a completely new design. Unfortunately, the changes are largely undocumented and undated, and can only be deduced from the evidence of photographs and, sometimes, from the diagrams.

Very early modifications were made to the end windows. The top edges of the original end windows were probably too low for a tall, standing driver to be able to obtain a clear view ahead, so on No.2, at the motor end, three top-lights were inserted above the original end windows, their tops approximately level with the roof eaves at the sides of the cars. These outer toplights were not as wide as the windows below them, and are clearly shown in two photographs taken on the Stroud Valley service. It is not known if the trailing end was also modified in this way (although it seems probable), nor is there evidence that No.1 was similarly altered at the time.

However, No.1 had its central end droplights replaced by taller ones, and two toplights were fitted either side above the fixed windows; again, the toplights were narrower than the windows below them. The height of the new, taller droplight matched the toplights. A copy of what became diagram A1 exists, date stamped 17th December 1903, showing this

Official photograph of the interior of Car No. 1, as built. 18th October 1903. NATIONAL RAILWAY MUSEUM

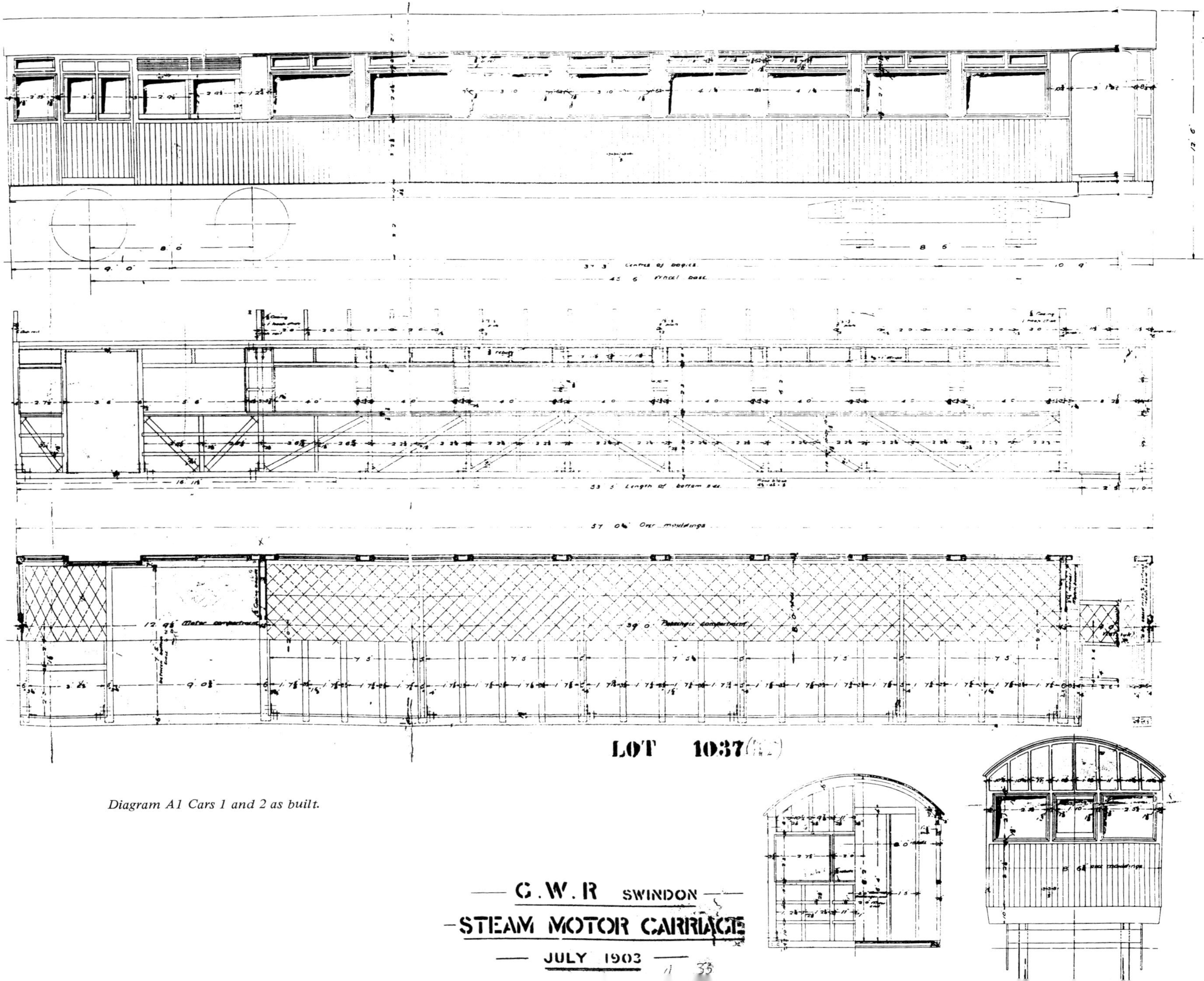

Diagram A1 Cars 1 and 2 as built.

G.W.R SWINDON

STEAM MOTOR CARRIAGE

JULY 1903

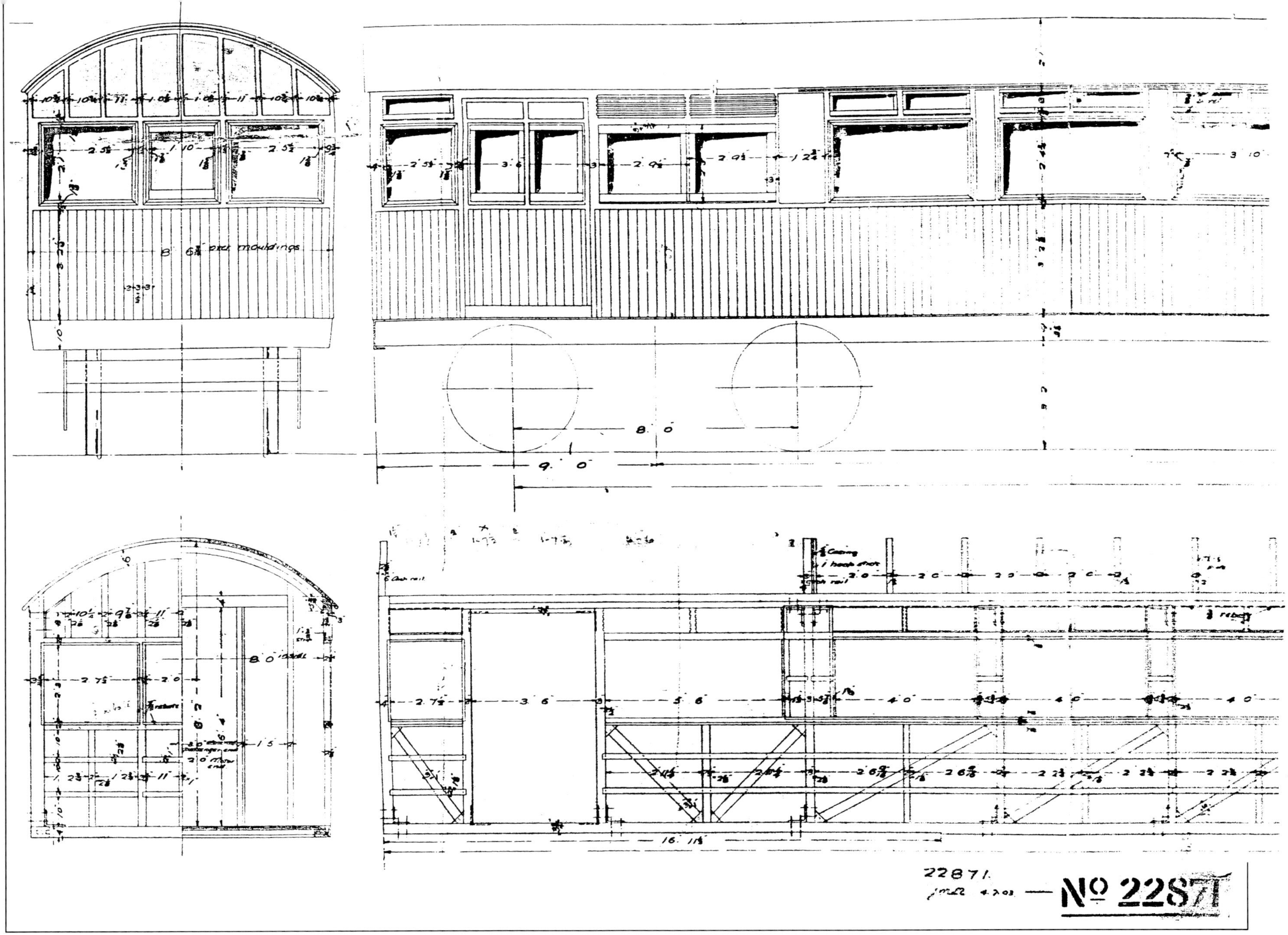

8' 6¾" over mouldings
8' 0"
9' 0"
16' 1½"
22871.
No 22871

Underframe for Cars 1 and 2 as built. Note the fixed steps at the trailing end.

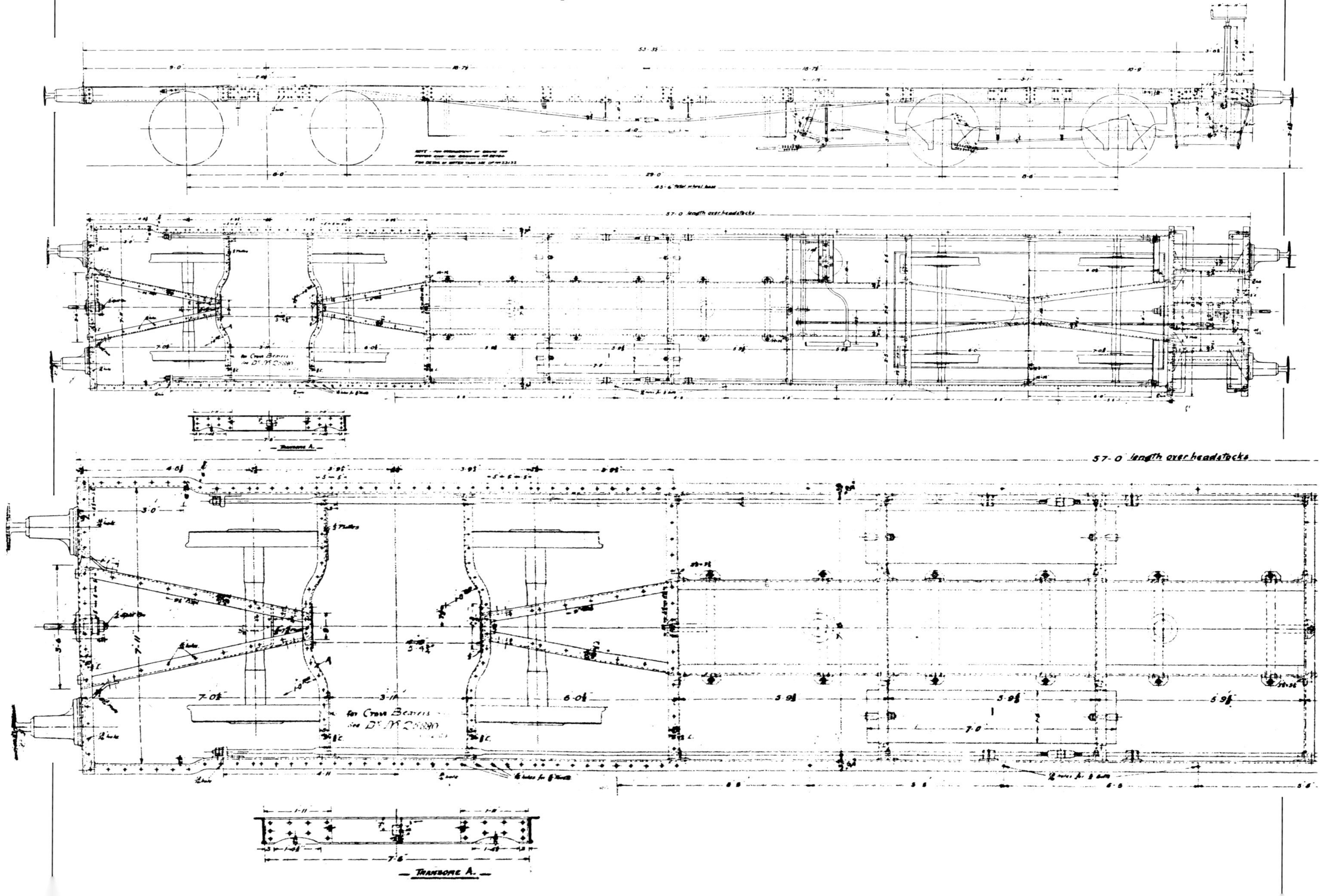

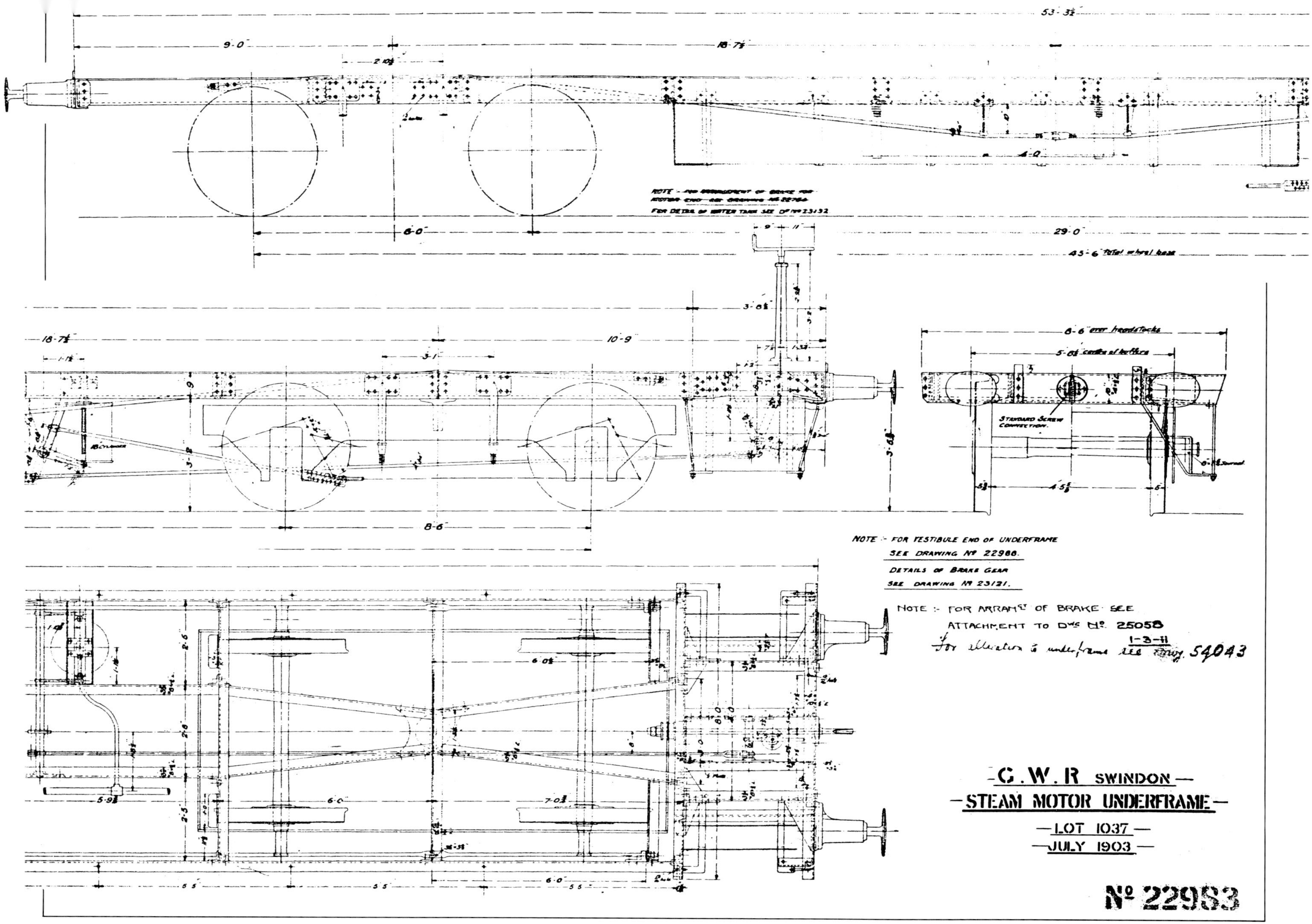

NOTE :- FOR VESTIBULE END OF UNDERFRAME SEE DRAWING Nº 22988.
DETAILS OF BRAKE GEAR SEE DRAWING Nº 23121.
NOTE :- FOR ARRAMT OF BRAKE SEE ATTACHMENT TO DWG Nº 25058
STANDARD SCREW CONNECTION.
FOR DETAIL OF WATER TANK SEE Dg Nº 23132
G.W.R SWINDON
STEAM MOTOR UNDERFRAME
LOT 1037
JULY 1903
Nº 22983

modification at both ends of the car. The end windows of No.2 were also similarly modified. This arrangement of the end windows was retained when the cars were eventually altered to trailers Nos.105 and 106.

The A1 diagram shows only two sliding windows to the power compartment, instead of the three each side with which they were initially fitted. This is an error on the diagram, inherited from the 'General Arrangement' drawing and, incidentally, perpetrated on the diagrams of all other matchboarded SRMs as well. Presumably, there was an even earlier version of diagram A1 with the original end windows, and possibly others showing the initial modifications to No.2, but copies seem not to have survived. Often, modified SRM diagrams appear to have been produced by altering the original, and not by redrawing.

As built, Nos.1 and 2 were equipped with round-headed buffers, their length about 18in from the headstock to the buffer face; this dimension is scaled, and is not recorded on the diagrams or other drawings of these cars. At an early date, these were changed to oval-head buffers, and it seems from photographs that these may well have been longer, whilst the buffer guides had two strengthening ribs on the side nearest the coupling hook only. This alteration is not reflected in any of the diagrams.

No.1 was fitted with steam heating in February 1904, and No.2 in January 1905.

The next modification would appear to have been the fitting of external doors to the driving vestibule. These were 3ft 1¼in wide, and seem to contain a pair of droplights, like the doors to the motor compartment. They may well have opened inwards, and were hinged at the outer end of the car – a feature that survived when

One of the first two cars, believed to have been No. 1, at Chalford station. The modified trailing end is shown and the built-in steps are clearly visible. The guard and another member of staff were standing on the cover over the steps. This had to be raised when the car was at a stopping place without a platform.

COLLECTION R. C. RILEY

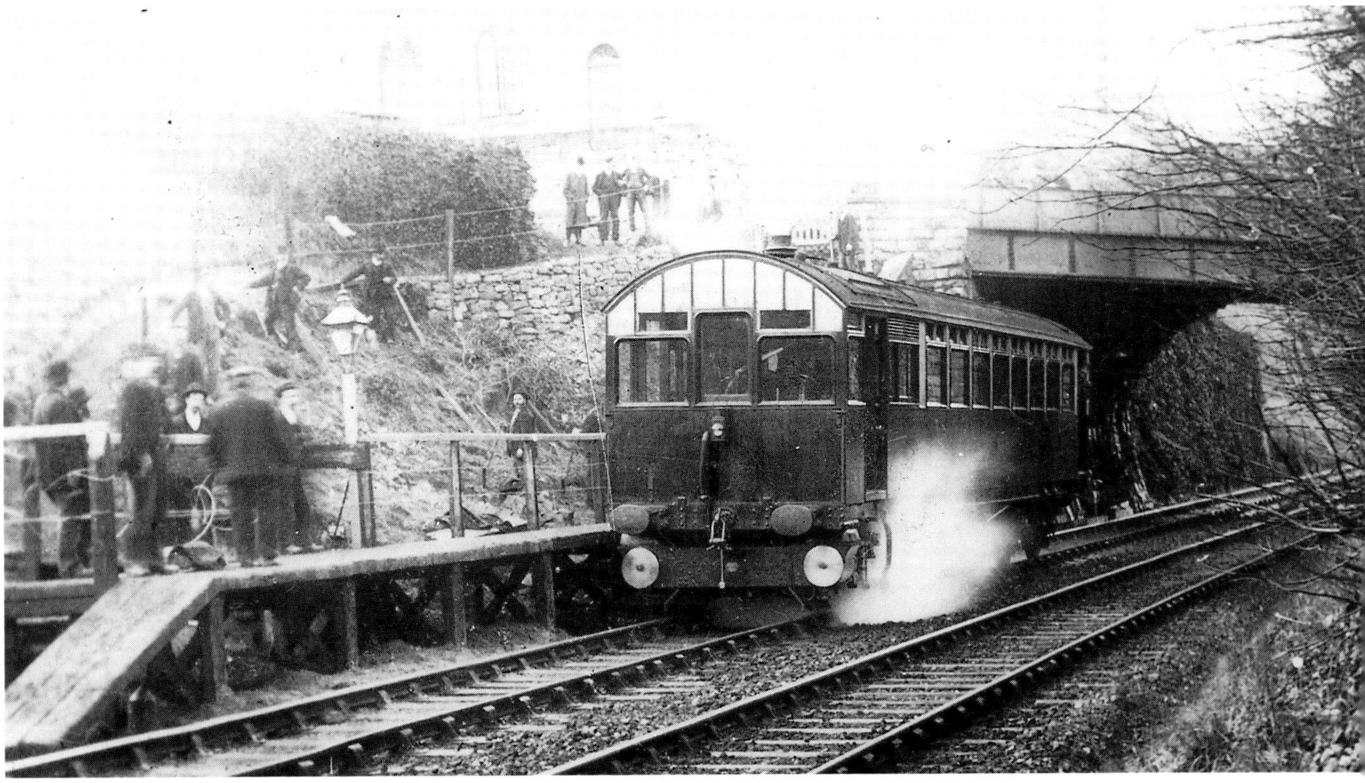

Car No. 1, at Brimscombe Bridge Halt on the Stroud Valley line, after the steps had been removed from the trailing (far) end, but the side windows remained unmodified. Water pipe covers had not been fitted, but a second rain strip seems to have been present on the roof. This photograph is a bit of a mystery. It appears to have been taken about 1906 but No. 1 was not officially allocated to Chalford at that time, so perhaps it had been briefly loaned to Chalford before going to Trowbridge or Aberdare. There appear to be a couple of roof ventilators at the further end.

COLLECTION R. C. RILEY

they were altered to trailers. Unfortunately, all the photographs of this period show these SRMs with the doors open, and usually with someone looking out of the doorway at the camera, so it is very difficult to judge what the exact arrangements were.

Not shown on the diagrams was a second, high-level rain strip, fitted to both cars; this ran from the gas pipe around the engine access hole in the roof at the motor end to the gas pipe at the other end, i.e. the length of the passenger compartment.

In May 1904, both were checked over at Swindon works before being hired out to the Lambourn Valley Railway at a cost of £420 per annum for the pair, plus the costs of any necessary repairs. The LVR line ran from the Great Western's station at Newbury to Lambourn, and was one which the GWR were interested in taking over, although its financial status was doubtful to say the least. This was a light railway – in practice, if not in law – having rails of only 50 lbs per yard, and platforms 9in high, so carriages with steps had to be used. Col. Yorke reported to the Board of Trade on the line's opening in 1898 that 'The girders of the underbridges are designed for a maximum load of 8 tons on one axle.' He recommended that an undertaking should be given that the maximum axle load would therefore be 8 tons. As the 24 tons weight (at least) on the power bogies of Nos.1 and 2 was 50% (or more) in excess of the line's design capacity, Col Yorke was required to re-inspect the line before the railmotors were introduced. He measured the deflection of the line's underbridges when the two cars passed over them, coupled engine to engine, and was satisfied with the results; approval was thus given for use of the cars, subject to repairs to the brickwork of some of the bridges.

On the LVR, the cars showed limitations, suffering from the hard water of the district, and from limited passenger accommodation. Their power reserves, too, were occasionally inadequate for a line where tail traffic was common, and which had a 1 in 60 ruling gradient.

The Lambourn water quality problems were overcome, although the cars had to visit Swindon for attention between November 1904 and February 1905 (No.1), and from October 1904 to January 1905 (No.2). Whilst they were at Swindon, they were replaced at Lambourn by SRMs Nos.19 and 21. The Great Western took over the LVR with effect from 1st July 1905, and Nos.1 and 2 remained there until August/September that year when they were replaced by conventional locomotives hauling special trailers Nos.7 and 8, which at that time were not fitted with through regulator gear.

The initial design of fixed steps for low-level platforms was soon reported as being less than ideal (Marillier's paper), and the halts on the Stroud Valley line were given full-height platforms, as previously discussed. One version of diagram A1 shows the initial design of low level steps, while others omit them from the side view, as does diagram A, and photographs indicate that they were removed. One version of both diagrams A1 and A indicate by a note that these cars were fitted with retractable steps, but this was not recorded in the *Register*, and has not been confirmed photographically. If the notes are correct, this may mean that the solebars were extended to the headstocks at the trailing end, because retractable steps were normally hung from the solebars.

Diagram A shows a partition inserted between the seating bays and the longitudinal bench seats at the motor end; this gave a small 'smoking' compartment at the motor end of the passenger accommodation. The seating capacity remained unchanged at 52. This diagram also shows ventilation increased by the insertion of quarterlight + droplight + quarterlight units in place of each of three of the

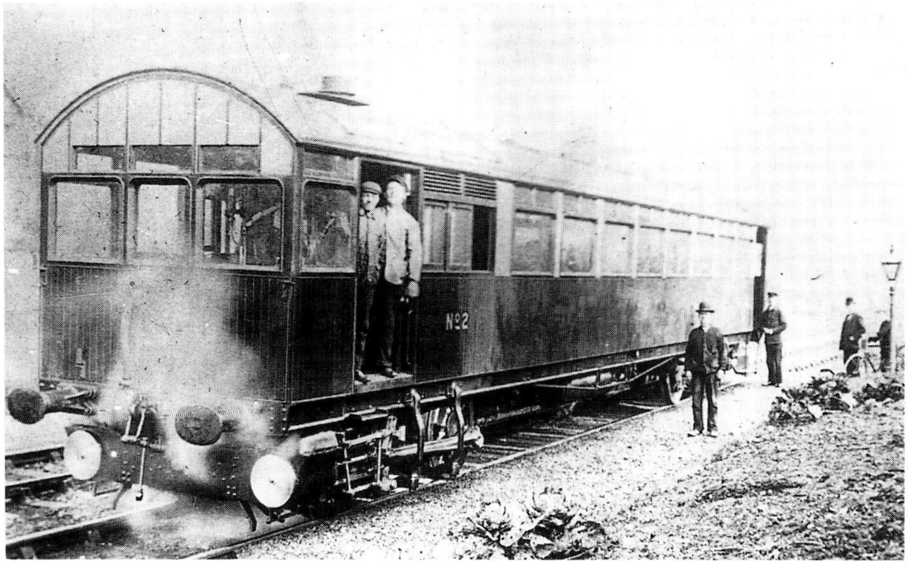

Car No. 2 of Diagram A1 with modified end windows – note the toplight above the central droplight. It had already been fitted with oval buffers and had been lettered 'No. 2' near the driving cab door. This photograph was probably taken in late 1903 or early 1904 before platforms were built at the stopping place. AUTHOR'S COLLECTION

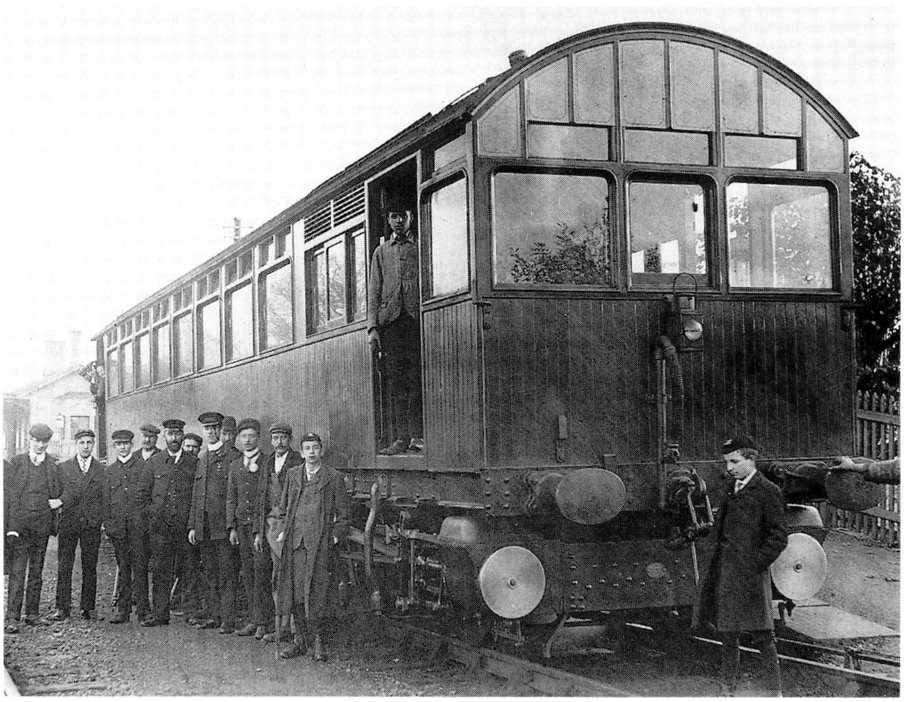

Car No. 2, probably at Stonehouse, showing the modified power end and oval buffers. The arrangement of the sliding windows to the rear of the driver's door shows well.
COLLECTION R. C. RILEY

large fixed windows, so that the window arrangement was:

Fxd qdq Fxd Fxd qdq Fxd, qdq Fxd

where 'Fxd' indicates a large, fixed window and 'qdq' the quarter and droplight units.

Although pairs of toplights are shown as remaining in place above the 'qdq' units, this diagram should be treated with a great deal of caution. No photographs have come to light showing this window arrangement, and trailers Nos.106 and 107, which were produced from SRMs 1 and 2, show pairs of droplights ('dd') instead of 'qdq units', so the arrangement probably was:

Fxd dd Fxd Fxd dd Fxd dd Fxd

The diagram showing these alterations was produced by July 1909, and refers to No.1. I think it possible that both cars were modified in this fashion, but, as usual, there is no record of either being modified in the *Register*.

Other SRMs were given roof ventilators, and it is likely that Nos.1 and 2 acquired them as well, probably having five over the passenger saloon, as on Dia. B and C cars. Other matchboarded cars had the rear sliding window in the power compartment replaced by a fixed panel containing a hinged water filler pipe lid, with the water filler pipe attached to the inside. It is probable that Nos.1 and 2 received this modification as well, probably around 1907, but this is not recorded in the *Register*, and no photographs showing either car with this modification have been seen.

Additional, possible modifications include the raising of the lower edge of the end windows in the motor compartment, and the provision of internal protection bars to these windows to reduce the chances of breakage by coal. No suitable photographs are available to confirm either modification, though dates would have been post-1906 and post-1912 respectively.

It is recorded that both Nos.1 and 2 received incandescent burner gas lighting, in March and November 1912 respectively.

After its Lambourn Valley allocation, No.1 was transferred to Trowbridge for three weeks, and then spent most of its life in South Wales, with relatively brief periods at Weymouth, Southall, St. Blazey, Bristol and Chalford. Possibly because it was non-standard, No.1 spent significant periods out of use: these included 131 days undergoing a general overhaul at Swindon from September 1905; 78 days from November 1906; and 119 days from October 1908, followed by 384 days before it was put back to work. It was then used for a month or so, and then spent about a further 389 days out of use. Following this, No.1 was at Gloucester for a month, and was then under repair and awaiting allocation to a shed for nearly another year. It spent another 6 months out of use from December 1912, and again from February 1915. No.1 was stopped in January 1917, and, altered to trailer No.105, added to stock in June 1917.

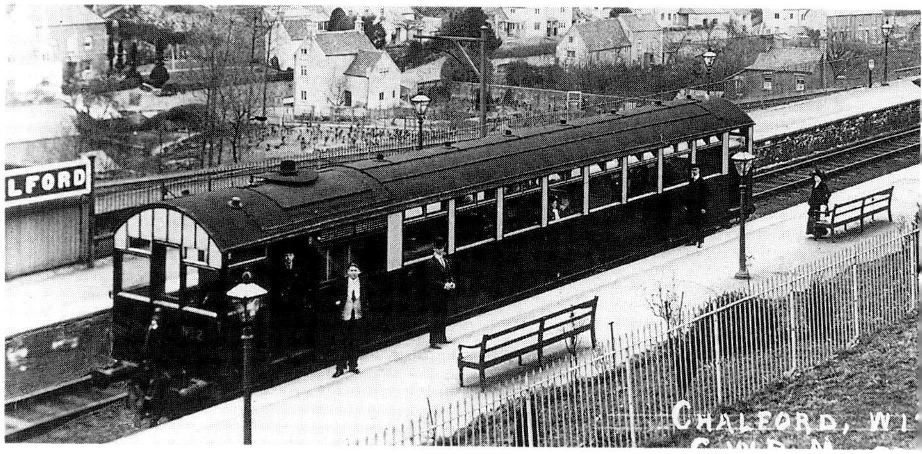

Car No. 2 at Chalford after the centre window in the end had been made taller to take in the toplight, and with 'No. 2' now painted on the end, beneath the right-hand window. This photograph was probably taken in early 1904 before the car was loaned to the Lambourn Valley Railway.
COLLECTION R. C. RILEY

No.2 was also used in South Wales after its work on the Stroud Valley line and the LVR. It was at Aberdare for a couple of years, but was also stationed at Croes Newydd (Wrexham), Gloucester, the Bristol area, and Southall. No.2 also spent significant periods under repair and awaiting allocation, including one from May 1908 to February 1910. In April 1915, it was allocated to Swindon Stock and never worked again. No.2 was officially stopped in January 1917 (with a mileage of 112,321) for conversion to trailer No.106. The conversion is dated February 1917 in the *SRM Stoppages Register* (RAIL 254/210), although trailer 106 was said to have been added to stock in January 1917. Nos.105 and 106 were shown on trailer diagram A6.

DRAWINGS

To summarise, the surviving drawings and diagrams illustrating the bodies of SRMs Nos.1 and 2 are not all as helpful as they might be:

1. *General Arrangement drawing No.22871* dated July 1903, showing the cars as they were to be built, but with the sliding windows to the power compartment shown as two panes instead of three, an error repeated in all the diagrams of matchboarded cars.
2. What became *diagram A1*, showing the final modifications to the end windows, but the cars otherwise as built with large windows only to the single passenger saloon, and with expanding metal external 'doors' to the driver's vestibule. One version of this was produced by mid-December 1903. A second version, with Locomotive Department information, was also produced (undated), and this one shows the fixed passenger steps on the side elevation; it is the only one that does.
3. *Diagram A1*, basically as the previous version, but now showing doors to the driver's vestibule. There are two versions – the Locomotive Department copy, and a general purpose version without the power unit details – and both had 'No.2' written on them. The copy of the former in the Public Record Office is hand stamped '26 Jul 1909'.
4. *Diagram A1*, the general purpose version applying to No.2, now with 'Fixed Steps Removed & Turnunder Steps Substituted', and drawing number 24913A written on it.
5. *Diagram A*, a Loco. Dept. version, shows the doors to the driver's vestibule, the modified end windows, the passenger saloon divided into smoking and non-smoking compartments and windows to the passenger compartments (probably) incorrectly modified. The cover to the steps is shown in position on the plan view, but the steps are omitted from the side and end elevations. Round-headed buffers are shown, but oval would have been correct. The sliding windows in the power compartment sides are still shown as two long ones (as before), and there is no panel with a water filler lid. This diagram is shown as applying to 'Lot 1037, No.1'. The PRO copy is again hand stamped '26 Jul 1909'.
6. *Diagram A*, the general purpose version applying to No.1 as above, but now having written on it 'Fixed Steps Removed & Turnunder Steps Substituted'. This copy has drawing number 24913 appended.

The absence of a diagram A relating to No.2 does raise the possibility that it did not have its saloon side windows modified, or the saloon divided, but it is perhaps more likely that these modifications were carried out, but No.1 was done first and the diagram, having been produced, was simply not updated. Photographs of trailer No.106 do show modified side windows with additional droplights.

TABLE 15

SUMMARY - Diagrams A1, A (Built on Lot 1037)

Car No.	*Built*	*First Boiler*	*First Engine*	*Tare t - c*	*Steam Heat*	*Incand. Gas*	*4ft Drivers*	*Final Miles*	*Stopped Work*	*To Tr No.*
1	Oct 03	111	0801	38-16	Feb 05	Mar 12	Apr 15	98,934	Jan 17	105
2	Oct 03	112	0802	38-11	Jan 05	Nov 12	-	112,321	Jan 16	106

Diagrams B1, B, C1, C: Nos.3 to 8

Car No. 3 of Diagram B1/C1 fitted with destination board holder, brackets and steps, but is otherwise seen as built.

The first two SRMs had been quickly adjudged as very successful in general terms. On 18th February 1904, twelve more were therefore ordered on Carriage Lot 1054 (curiously, a renewals Lot) and Locomotive Department Lot F37 at an average cost of £718 19s 1d charged to Carriage Department expenses, and £858 18s 7d to Loco Department expenses – a total of £1,577 17s 8d for each car. The first six of these SRMs were delivered in April and May that year, and numbered 3 to 8; the remainder of the Lot had marginally different bodies, and are dealt with below under 'Diagrams D1 and D'.

Those cars under consideration here seem to have had identical bodies and underframes, and only differed in the boilers initially fitted, with consequential differences in weight. The diagrams are considered in more detail below.

DESIGN

SRMs Nos.3–8 were 59ft 6¾in long, 8ft 6¾in wide and 12ft 6in tall from rail to roof. The chimneys were lipped, but did not have the extension as on Nos.1 and 2. These cars were in the same matchboarded style as Nos.1 and 2, but had bow ends – hence the increased length. Steps for low-level halts were not provided, although they did have passenger entrance doors opening directly into the passenger saloon, next to the motor compartment.

The three end windows were all 3ft 1½in tall, and extended from waist level to eaves height, but the central panes no longer seem to have been droplights. A 2ft-wide sliding door with a single fixed light and a ventilator above gave access to the motor compartment, although in practice the cars seem to have always run with these doors open; this doorway was situated next to the corner pillar.

Next to the doorway, the sides of the motor compartment had a droplight with a slatted ventilator above, and panels to either side. Finally, there was the usual three sliding windows arrangement, as on Nos.1 and 2, with three slatted ventilators above them. The general arrangement drawing and the diagrams of these cars incorrectly show two windows here, though (correctly) with three ventilators above.

The motor compartment was 14ft 0⅛in long, and the coal bunker (which was situated just below the front windows) now held 15cwt.

A sliding door was provided in the partition between the passenger and motor compartments, but passenger access to their accommodation was now by means of an outward-opening door next to this partition. The passenger saloon seated 52 in two 13ft 5⅛in lengths of longitudinal bench seating with two 5ft seating bays between them, so the passengers were expected to squash up a little more than in Nos.1 and 2. The gap at the end of the bench seating giving access to the passenger doors was 2ft 4in wide. As well as the droplight in the passenger's door, the saloon had eight large fixed windows, in two groups of four, with twin droplights above each.

The driver's vestibule was 4ft 9in between partition and end, and had an open external doorway, this time protected only by three horizontal bars; these were replaced by doors in due course. There was also a sliding door to the passenger saloon. A handbrake is shown at this end on the diagram, but not in the motor compartment, although one was present.

Underframe details have been dealt with in Chapter 5. Solebars now reached the trailing end headstock, and the headstocks were bowed, with longer buffers fitted. The water tank was now central, and held the usual 450 gallons.

The wheelbase was 48ft 9in, and the usual Dean 8ft 6in trailing bogie was used. The distance between the front headstock and the boiler centre was 10ft 3in, and the distance between the trailing headstock and the trailing bogie centre was 8ft 9in.

In spite of being appreciably larger cars and carrying 5 cwt more coal, Nos.3–5 are shown on diagram B as being over 4 tons lighter than Nos.1 and 2. The reason for this difference could be the smaller-size boiler used on these cars, and the revised underframe arrangement at the trailing end. Diagram C shows a larger, more powerful boiler, and a higher tare weight.

TABLE 16

TARE WEIGHTS: Diagrams A1, B1 & C

	(A1) Nos. 1 & 2	*(B1) Nos. 3 - 5*	*(C) Nos. 6 - 8*
Power Bogie	24t 0cwt	22t 13cwt	24t 16cwt
Trailing Bogie	12t 0cwt	11t 12cwt	11t 10cwt
Total	36t 0cwt	34t 5cwt	36t 6cwt

According to the Lot book, the average weight of Nos.3–8 were 36 tons 6 cwt empty, and 38 tons 19 cwt 2 qtrs laden, while the *Register* gives various weights between 36 tons 16 cwt and 38 tons 13 cwt.

MODIFICATIONS & DISPOSAL

As built, Nos.3–8 had flat flame gas lighting, and one longitudinal rainstrip. Steam heating was fitted new to Nos 7 and 8, and between December 1904 and April 1905 to the others. Incandescent gas lighting was fitted between 1910 and 1913.

Photographs show Nos.6 and 7 (at least) to have very large shell-type ventilators on the roof at an early date (i.e. by the end of 1904), and a hinged door to the driver's vestibule. They also received a pair of steps either side of the vacuum pipe at the motor end; these were almost coincident with the end numbering, and one came partially across the 'N of 'N°', whilst the other was only just to the right of the '7'. These steps were in accordance with drawing 25409 dated 30th June 1904, which shows them to have been 1ft 6in from the top of the bufferbeam and 1ft 11in apart. No.4 also had these steps (which improved access to the

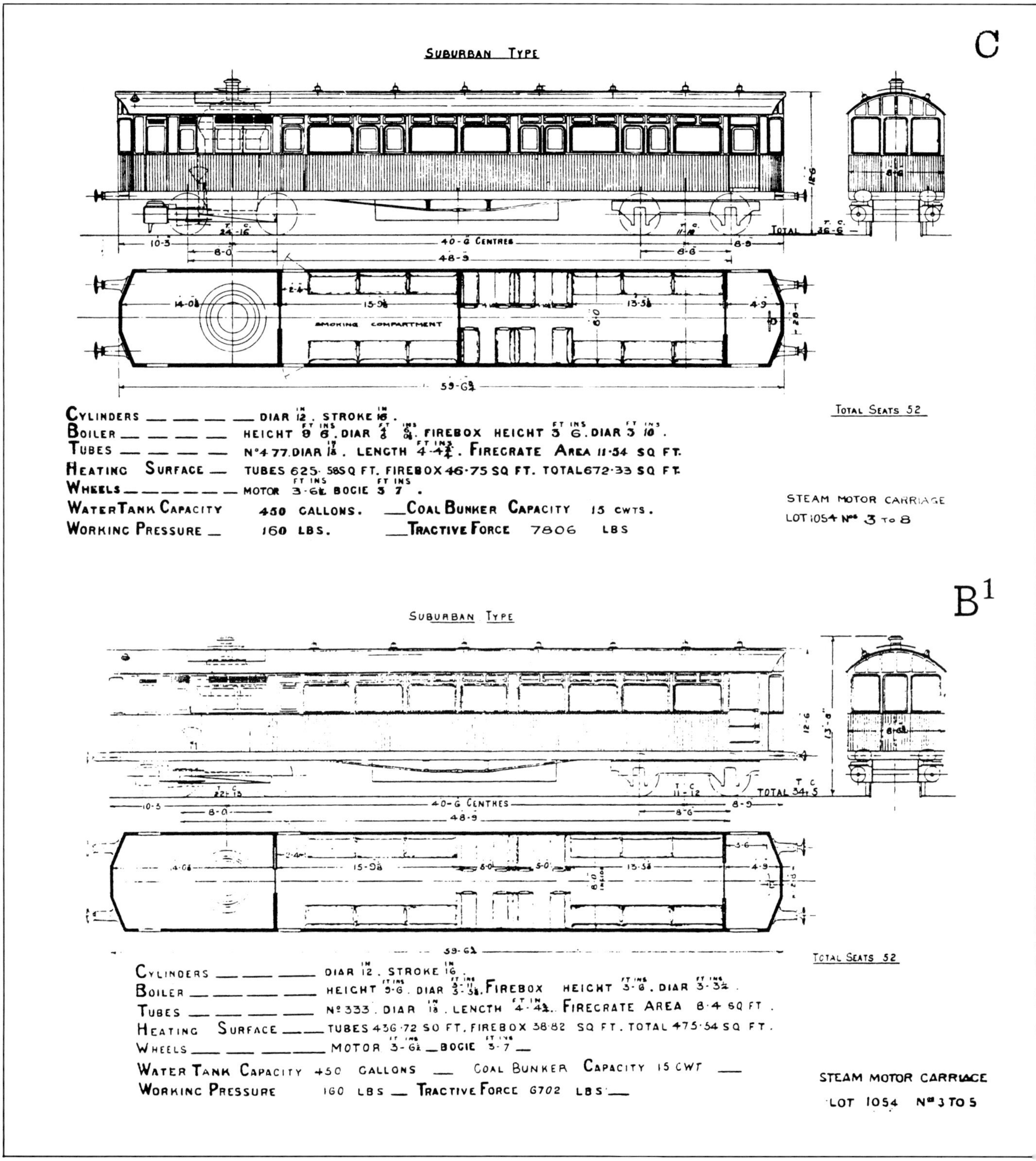

central lamp iron), and this was a modification which would have been applied to all.

Diagrams B and C show the passenger saloon partitioned between the longitudinal seats and the seating bay nearer the power saloon to create a 'smoking' compartment 15ft 9⅛in long. We have a date for this in the case of No.6 – May 1905 – and the others were probably modified thus around this period.

A photograph of car No.5 shows it with the bottom of the motor end windows panelled in to a depth (estimated) of 9 inches; this was presumably to reduce breakages when coaling. The photograph appeared in the January 1906 edition of the *Railway Magazine*, so it was presumably carried out during 1905. A photograph of No.8 at Upwey Wishing Well Halt, possibly in 1906 or 1907, shows a similar modification; in this photograph, No.8 still had all the original large windows in its sides. It is not known if this modification was applied to any other of these cars, but it seems probable. Other probable changes include a second, high-level rainstrip, but this is not confirmed photographically.

Diagrams B and C also show three of the large fixed lights replaced by pairs of droplights so that the saloon window arrangement after the passenger door was

Fxd dd Fxd Fxd dd Fxd dd Fxd

where dd indicates pairs of droplights inserted in place of a large, fixed windows. This condition corresponds reasonably well to the bodies of the Dia. Z trailers, which is what Nos.3–8 became after conversion. It is probable that all received these modifications, but the dates are not recorded – it could well have been from about 1906 because diagrams B and C existed (without their index letters) before the *Diagram Book* was set up about 1907.

The photograph of No.4, mentioned above, also shows that one of the sliding windows in the motor compartment had been replaced by a panel and a water filler cap, still with the slatted ventilator above. Again, this was a modification probably applied to all, and is not recorded in the *Register*.

These SRMs seem to have been very much general purpose units, with frequent changes of locale, although a few spent some time in certain parts of the country. For example, Nos.7 and 8 were to be found mostly in the South West during the years up to 1906, and seem to have been the first in the Plymouth area based on Laira, arriving in July 1904, via Penzance. Nos 5 and 6 replaced Nos.1 and 2 on the Chalford services when the latter pair were hired to the Lambourn Valley Railway, and were themselves later replaced by Nos.3 and 4.

The diagrams still extant which refer to these SRMs again cause a few problems.

Two are labelled 'N^{os}3 to 5'. In one version – a Loco Department diagram showing a small boiler in the motor unit (according to the dimensions recorded below the drawing) – the SRM is shown in 'as built' condition, with

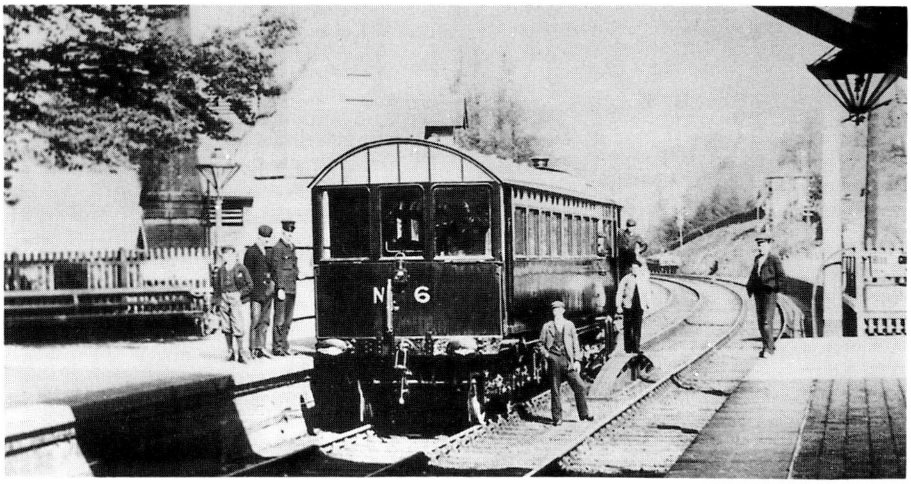

Car No. 6 of Diagram C1 in new condition. COLLECTION LIONEL PADIN

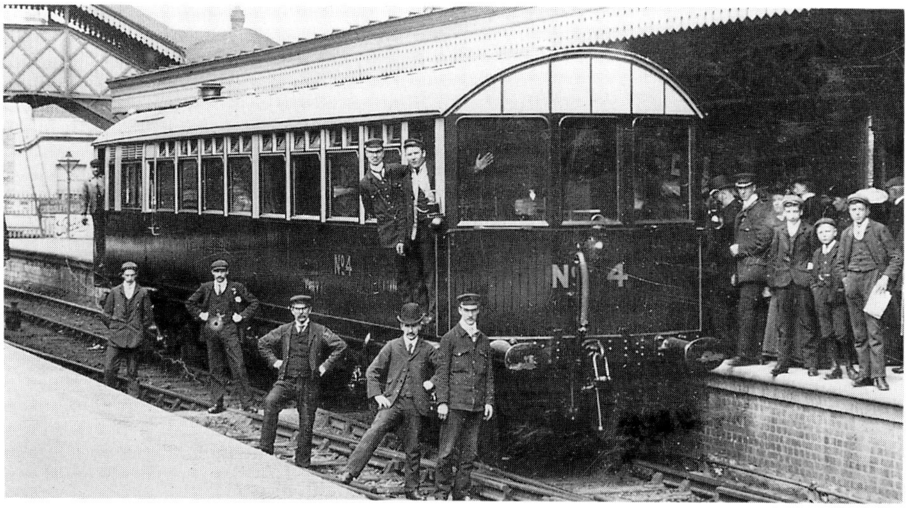

Car No. 4 of Diagram B1 was initially allocated to Southall and moved to Chalford in July 1904. Here it is seen in very clean condition at Stroud station. There does not appear to have been a monogram on the side. COLLECTION R. C. RILEY

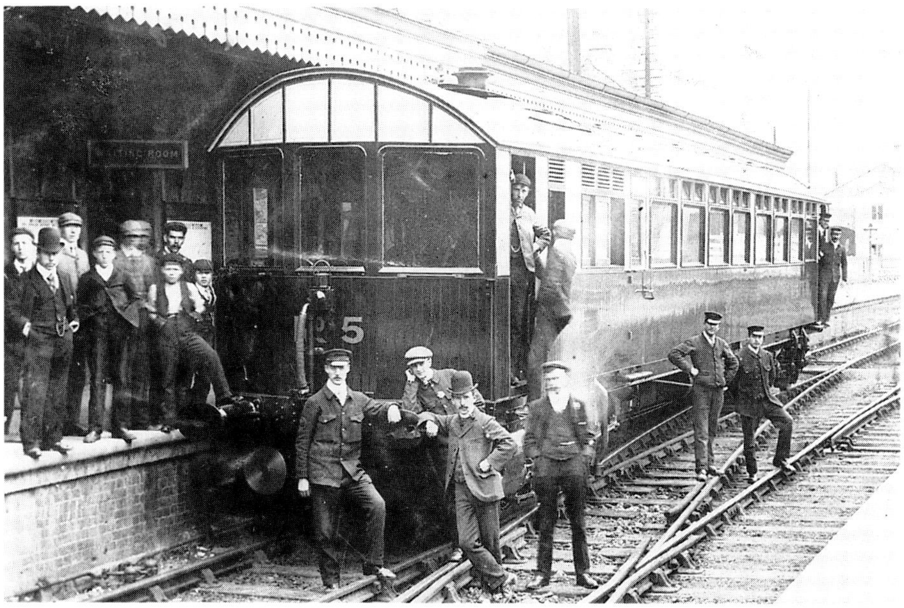

Car No. 5 of Diagram B1, as new at Stroud station, presumably when first allocated to Chalford in May 1904. Notice the absence of steps.

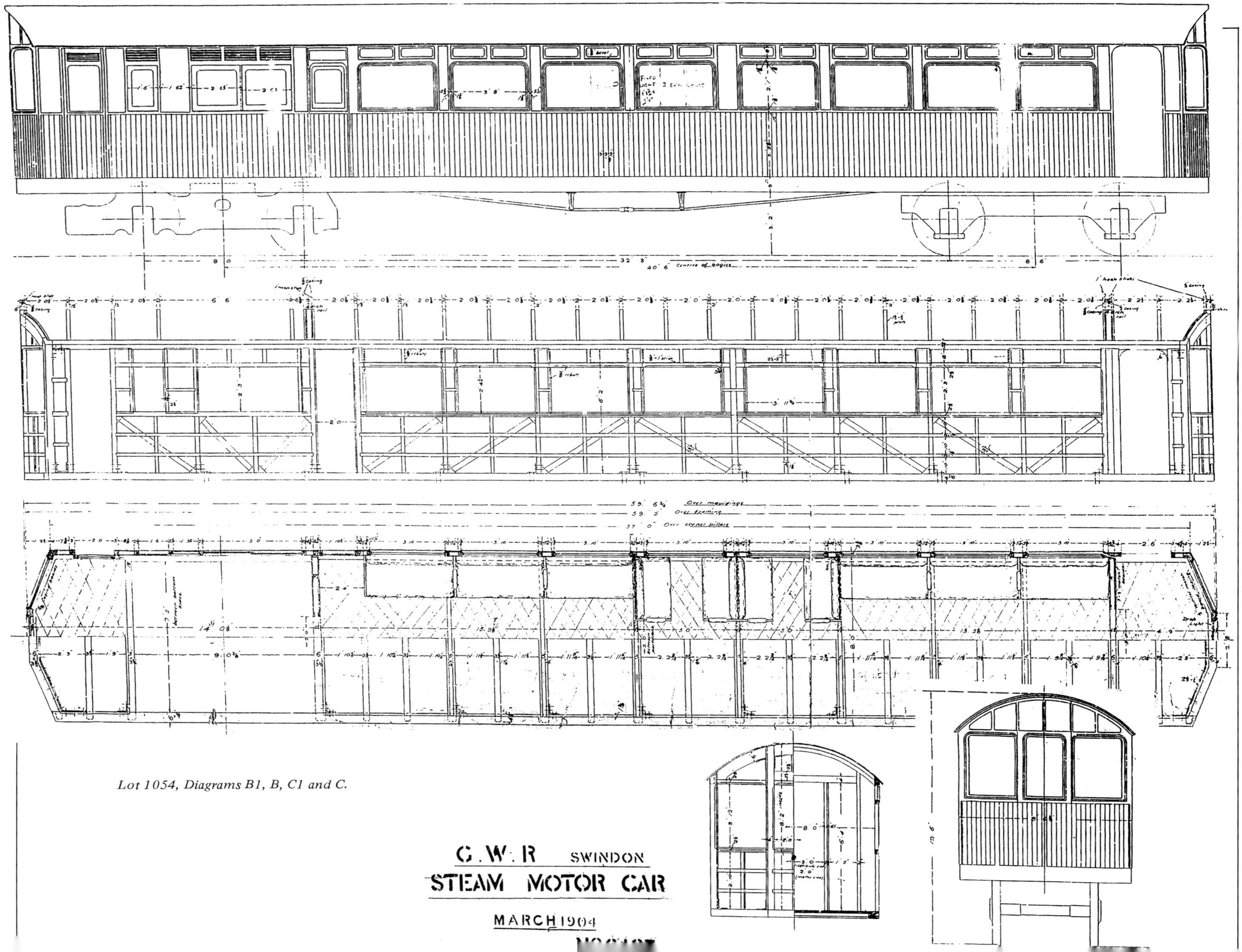

Lot 1054, Diagrams B1, B, C1 and C.

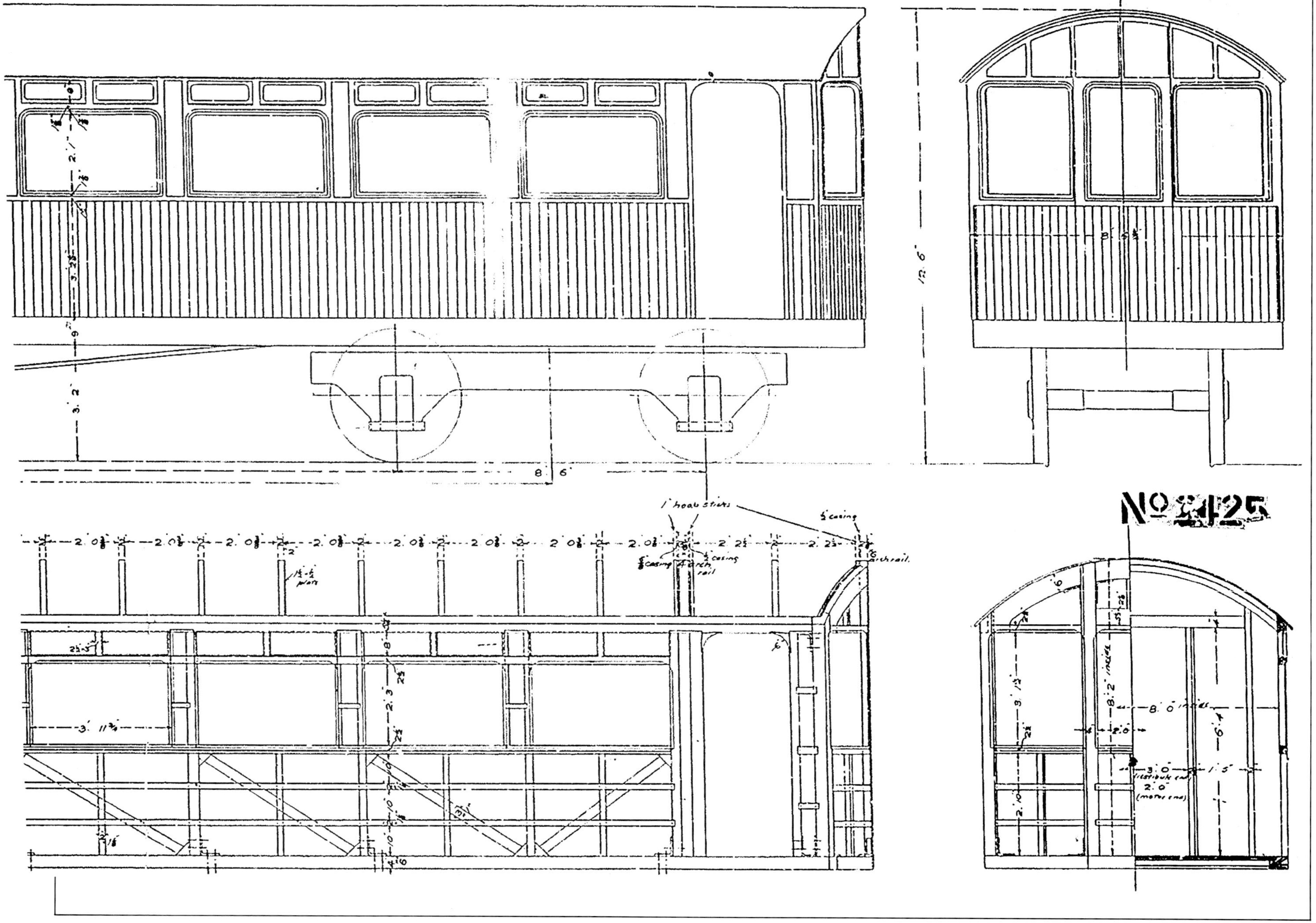

8' 6"
12' 6"
arch rail
8' 0" inside
(motor end)

Underframe for Lot 1054 SRMs 3-14, Diagrams B1, C1 and D1.

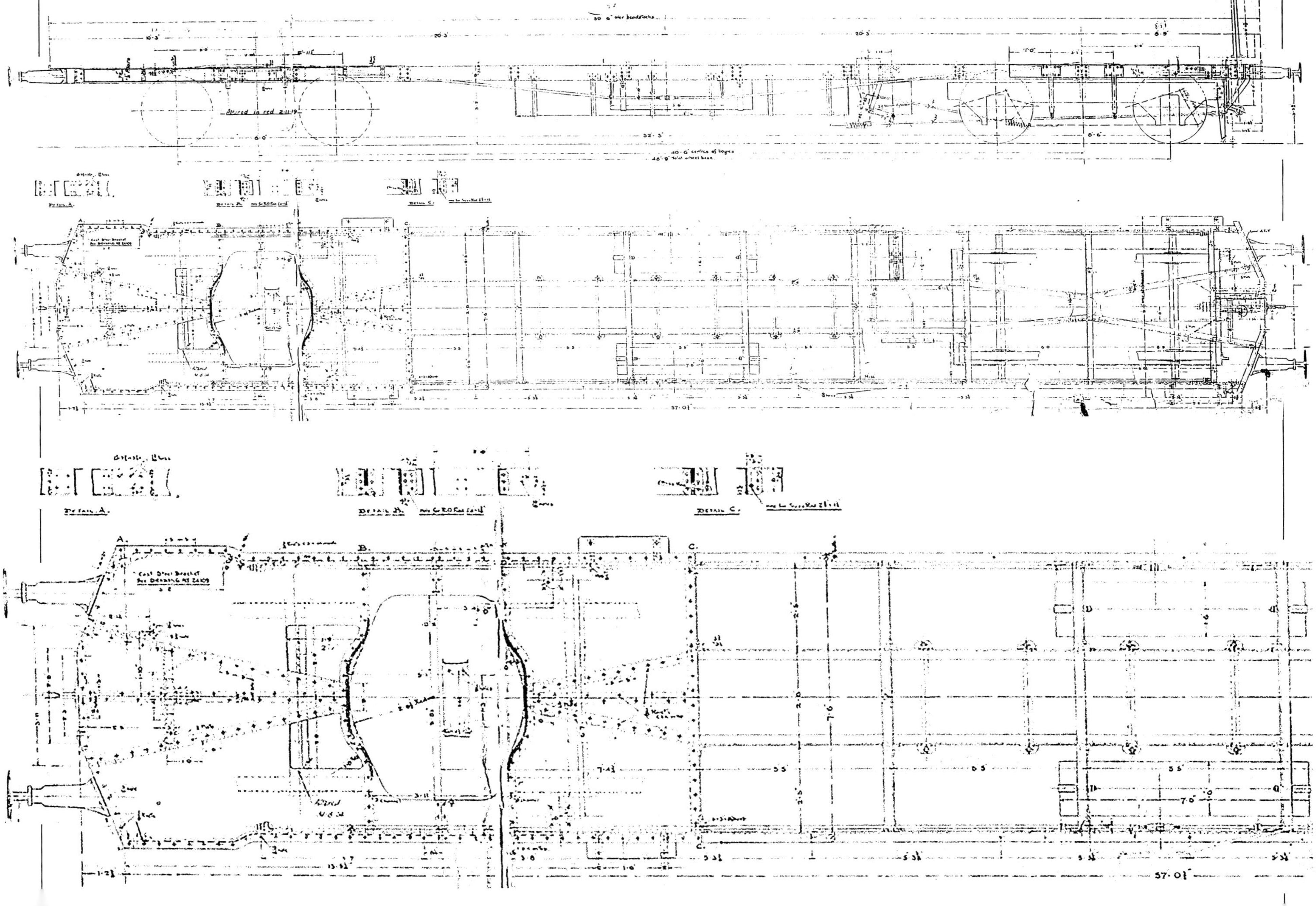

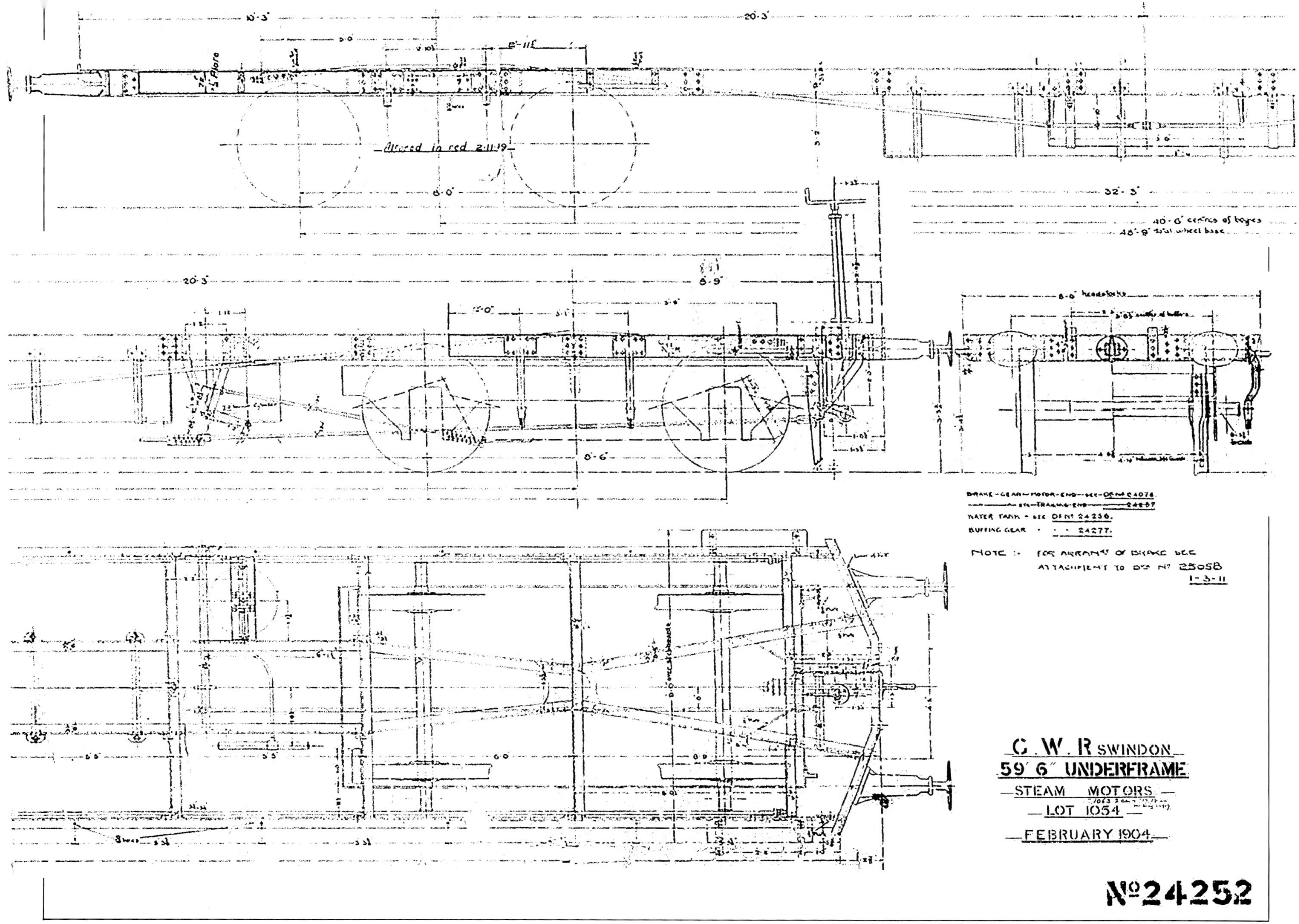
Altered in red 2.11.19
32' 3"
40' 6" centres of bogies
48' 9" total wheel base
BRAKE-GEAR-MOTOR-END-SEE-DGNo 24076.
ETC-TRAILING-END 24287
WATER TANK - SEE DGNo 24236.
BUFFING GEAR " " 24277.
NOTE :- FOR ARRANGT OF BRAKE SEE ATTACHMENT TO DGNo 25058
1-3-11
G.W.R SWINDON
59' 6" UNDERFRAME
STEAM MOTORS
LOT 1054
FEBRUARY 1904
No 24252

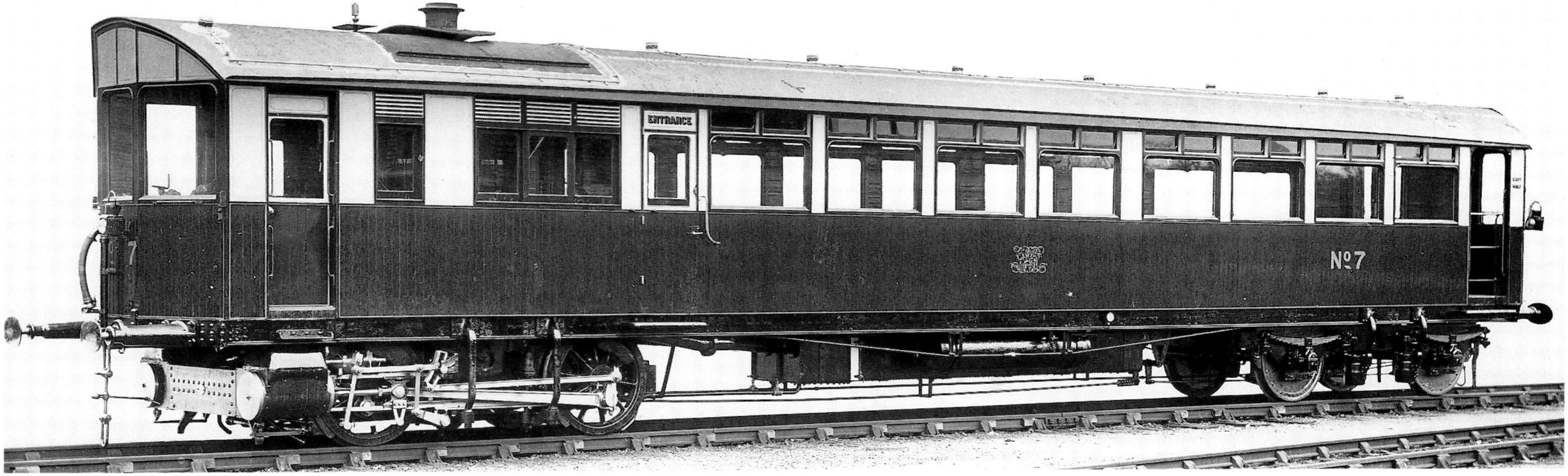

No. 7 of Diagram C1 in the early lined brown and cream livery for SRMs with 'No. 7' on the front, and the entwined monogram and the number again on the side. Notice the large size of the numerals on the matchboarded SRMs and the lettering 'ENTRANCE' over the door. NATIONAL RAILWAY MUSEUM

Car No. 7 was at Laira only from July to October 1904 and in December 1904 to January 1905, but it seems to have been frequently photographed. Here it is seen at Plympton at the eastern end of the Plymouth suburban service, now fitted with brackets for destination boards above the central end window and with handrails between the end windows. COLLECTION R. C. RILEY

Car No. 7 at Melincourt Halt, Resolven.

Early days at Ford Halt, near Plymouth. NATIONAL RAILWAY MUSEUM

Car No. 7 with another SRM coupled together at Plymouth North Road. E. POUTEAU

Below: No. 7 at Plymouth North Road after being fitted with brackets for destination boards above the central end window and handrails between the end windows. Its roof seems to have been repainted and fitted with five roof ventilators which appear to have been of the 'torpedo' type. G. M. MOON, CTY. R. C. RILEY

eight large fixed windows to the passenger saloon. My copy of this diagram is unlettered, but I think this should be regarded as diagram B1, and will be referred to as such.

A second version of this diagram also survives (drawing No.24914), which also refers to '$\mathrm{N^{os}}$3, 4 & 5', illustrating a modified window layout where three of the large, fixed lights had been replaced by pairs of droplights, and with the passenger saloon partitioned into smoking and non-smoking accommodation. The tare weight shown is the same as in diagram B1 but, unlike available copies of the B1, the boiler dimensions are omitted. It also indicates the large window size as 3ft 6in wide by 2ft 1in high. This is a general purpose version of diagram B.

A third diagram, labelled '$\mathrm{N^{os}}$3 to 8', also exists. Like diagram B, this shows the saloon partitioned, three of the large, fixed windows in the saloon replaced by pairs of droplights, and a larger boiler with increased tare weight. The boiler data is given. This is taken to be diagram C.

It is possible that a fourth diagram originally existed – this would have been diagram C1, the same as the original B1 diagram, but with the heavier boiler.

As the boilers of SRMs were subject to regular changes, it is questionable how sensible was the practice of issuing separate SRM diagrams merely to record different boilers in identical bodies. Although boiler records are incomplete, the original boilers of cars Nos.3–5 were 1001–3, which seem to have been mostly confined to Nos.3–6, and not used on 7 or 8 (see Chapter 3). So it would appear that, at various times, Nos.3–6 were represented by diagrams B1 and B, and at other times by diagram C, and assuming it existed, diagram C1. Boilers 1001–3 no longer seem to have been used in SRMs by the end of 1909, and their history cards are not available.

All engines for these cars were built with 3ft 6in driving wheels. Again, engine records are not complete, but it would appear that No.5 was fitted with one having 4ft wheels by July 1912, and No.8 was fitted with another from April to September 1913.

SRMs Nos.3 to 8 all stopped work in 1913–14, and were converted to Dia. Z trailers Nos.99–105, appearing in this form in 1915.

This picture shows what seems to have been Car No. 8 of Diagram C1 hauling a clerestory trailer at Radipole Halt, just north of Weymouth, on an up train to Dorchester. The car was in brown and cream and, although the side windows do not seem to have been altered, the front windows had been shortened by what appears to have been a panel along their lower edges to avoid breakages when loading coal into the bunker. The destination board reads 'RADIPOLE UPWEY UPWEY WISHING WELL CAME BRIDGE DORCHESTER JCN'. The car in this picture has been identified elsewhere as No. 3 but this was at Weymouth from May to December 1905, and May 1905 seems a little early for the modifications to the front windows. Car No. 8 was available for allocation to Weymouth from June 1907 until January 1908. Unfortunately, this is the period when SRMs were omitted from the Locomotive Allocations Register.

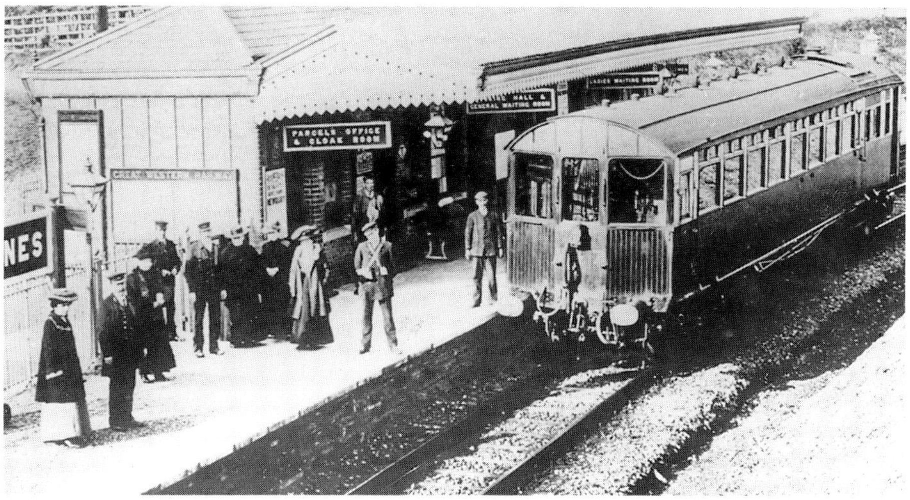

No. 7 spent some time allocated to Truro and Newquay in 1905 and is seen here at St. Agnes on the Truro and Newquay line. By this time it had been fitted with footsteps on the end just below the number. This made it easier and safer to reach the end destination board, when fitted. The roof ventilators can be seen as being fitted in a single line. AUTHOR'S COLLECTION

TABLE 17

SUMMARY: Diagrams B1, B, C1, C (Built on Lot 1054)

Car No.	*Built*	*First Boiler*	*First Engine*	*Tare t - c*	*Partitioned*	*Steam Heat*	*Incand. Gas*	*Final Miles*	*Stopped Work*	*To Trailer No.*	*Dia.*
3	Apr 1904	1001	0803	38-08		Jan 05	Nov 12	185,122	Jan 15	99	Z
4	Apr 1904	1002	0804	38-10	Oct 05	Dec 04	Aug 13	175,006	Jul 14	100	Z
5	Apr 1904	1003	0805	38-16	Jun 05	Apr 05	Nov 13	161,264	Sep 14	101	Z
6	Apr 1904	1004	0806	38-17	May 05	Apr 05	Sep 12	180,585	Jul 14	102	Z
7	May 1904	1007	0809	38-13		Feb 05	Jun 13	193,998	Oct 14	103	Z
8	May 1904	1008	0810	38-15		Feb 05	Apr 13	191,804	Sep 14	104	Z

Diagrams D1, D: Nos.9 to 14

Car No. 9 of Diagram D1 at Cynwyd station, which was between Corwen and Bala on the Ruabon–Dolgelly line. It had been fitted with front destination board brackets and associated handrails and steps, and notice how the car number was in the higher position on the trailing end. No. 9 spent most of its time between June 1904 and July 1907 at Croes Newydd (Wrexham) and this must have been one of the duties of that shed. COLLECTION R. C. RILEY

As well as SRMs Nos.3–8, discussed above, Nos.9–14 were also ordered on Carriage Lot 1054. The power units of Nos.9–11 were built on Locomotive Lot F37, and the remaining three on Lot F44.

These SRMs were almost identical to Nos.3–8 externally, though with a slight difference in the arrangement of windows in the passenger accommodation. The two designs could each be identified because, when new, Nos.3–8 had their large, fixed windows in two distinct groups of four, with a wider panel between them, whilst Nos.9–14 had wider panels between each of the four large, fixed windows nearest the motor end, and narrower panels between the rest.

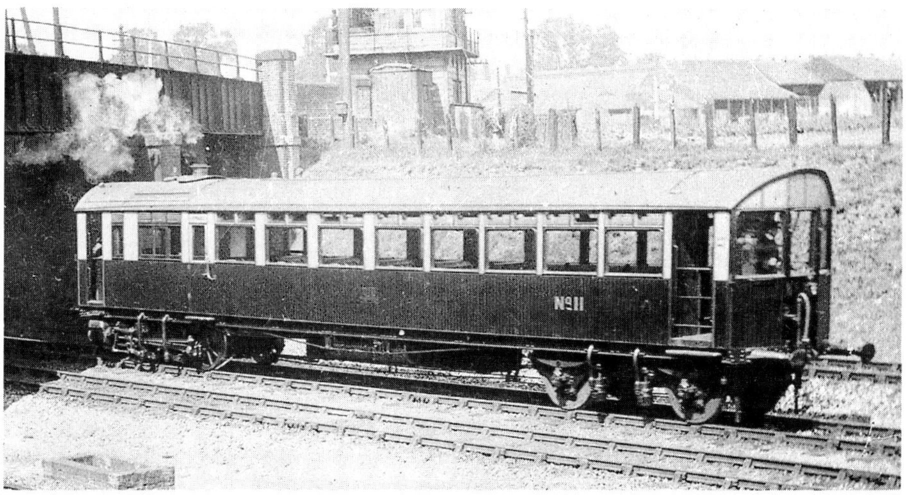

Car No. 11 of Diagram D1 is seen in new condition near Acton. It was allocated to Southall between June and September 1904 when new, so this photograph was probably taken in June 1904 after it had been fitted with destination board brackets, handrails and steps. L&GRP

DESIGN

Internally, Nos.9–14 had four 5ft seating bays at the motor unit end of the saloon, and a 16ft 7in length of longitudinal bench seating at the trailing end. The seating capacity was 54.

According to the Loco Department diagram, the larger boiler shown on diagram C was also originally fitted to those of diagram D1, giving the same tare weight and weight distribution. Except for the overall width and length, which were now 8ft 6in and 59ft 6in respectively, and the internal width (7ft 11in instead of 8ft), these trailers seem to have originally been dimensionally identical to Nos.3–8.

Diagram D1 shows these trailers with doors to the driving vestibule. However, a photograph of No.11, when new, shows it with open doorways protected by three bars, and they were probably all like this to start with. All were built with steam heating, and gas lighting with flat flame burners. From the photograph of No.11, it appears that these SRMs had the footsteps at the front either side of the vacuum pipe from new, and consequently carried their end running number rather higher than before. These steps were fitted to improve access to the lamp bracket just below the central end window (which was fixed). At an early date, shell-type roof ventilators were fitted.

MODIFICATIONS & DISPOSAL

On diagram D, the passenger saloon was shown as divided into 'Smoking' and 'Non-Smoking' compartments by a partition with a sliding door, with two seating bays and the passenger entrance in the smoking compartment. It also illustrates the seating bays as 4ft 11¼in between backs; before partitioning they were 5ft 0in.

D

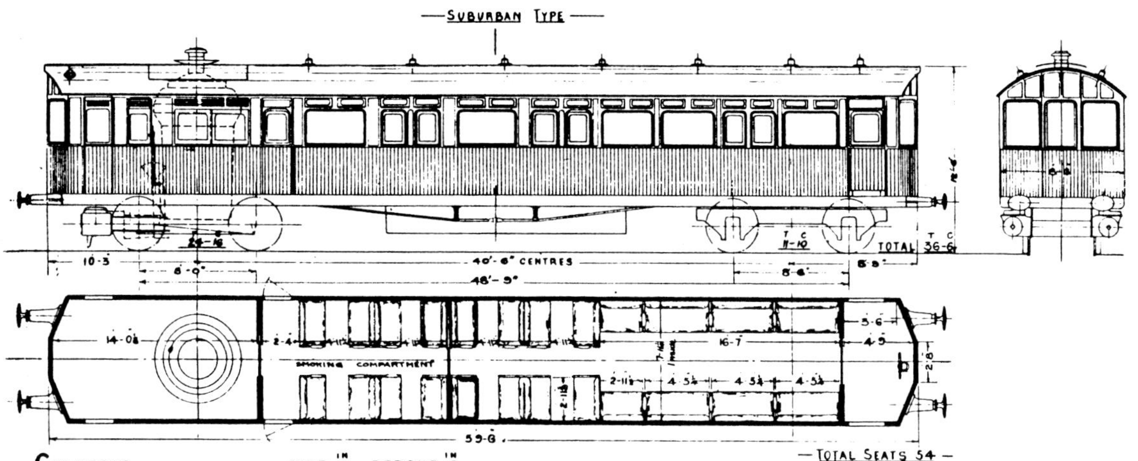

— TOTAL SEATS 54 —

CYLINDERS — DIAR 12 in. STROKE 16 in.
BOILER — HEIGHT 9 ft 6 ins. DIAR 4/3 ft 6/0¼ ins. FIREBOX HEIGHT 5 ft 6 ins. DIAR 3 ft 10 ins.
TUBES — N° 477. DIAR 1⅞ in. LENGTH 4 ft 4½ ins. FIRECRATE AREA 11·54 SQ FT.
HEATING SURFACE — TUBES 625·58 SQ FT. FIREBOX 46·75 SQ FT. TOTAL 672·33 SQ FT.
WHEELS — MOTOR 3 ft 6½ ins. BOGIE 3 ft 7 ins.
WATER TANK CAPACITY 450 GALLONS. — COAL BUNKER CAPACITY 15 CWTS.
WORKING PRESSURE — 160 LBS. — TRACTIVE FORCE 7806 LBS

STEAM MOTOR CARRIAGE
LOT 1054 Nos 9.11.12.13

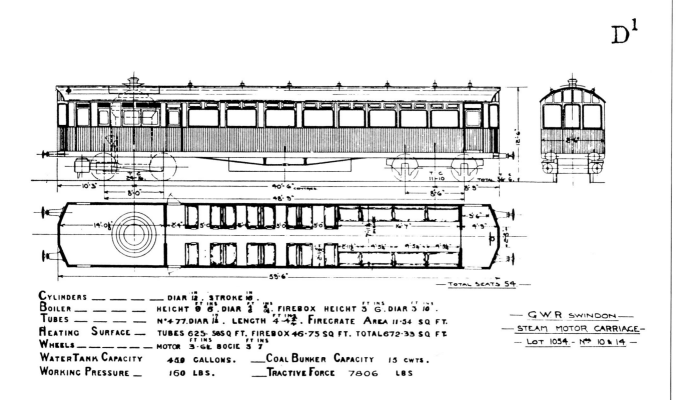

D[1]

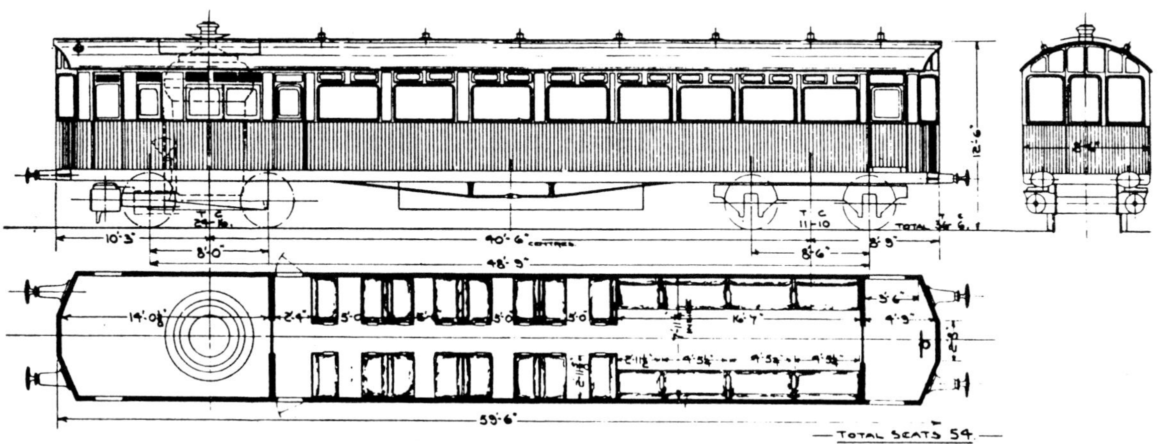

— TOTAL SEATS 54 —

CYLINDERS — DIAR 12 in. STROKE 16 in.
BOILER — HEIGHT 9 ft 6 ins. DIAR 4/3 ft 6/0¼ ins. FIREBOX HEIGHT 5 ft 6 ins. DIAR 3 ft 10 ins.
TUBES — N° 477. DIAR 1⅞ in. LENGTH 4 ft 4½ ins. FIRECRATE AREA 11·54 SQ FT.
HEATING SURFACE — TUBES 625·58 SQ FT. FIREBOX 46·75 SQ FT. TOTAL 672·33 SQ FT.
WHEELS — MOTOR 3 ft 6½ ins. BOGIE 3 ft 7 ins.
WATER TANK CAPACITY 450 GALLONS. — COAL BUNKER CAPACITY 15 CWTS.
WORKING PRESSURE — 160 LBS. — TRACTIVE FORCE 7806 LBS

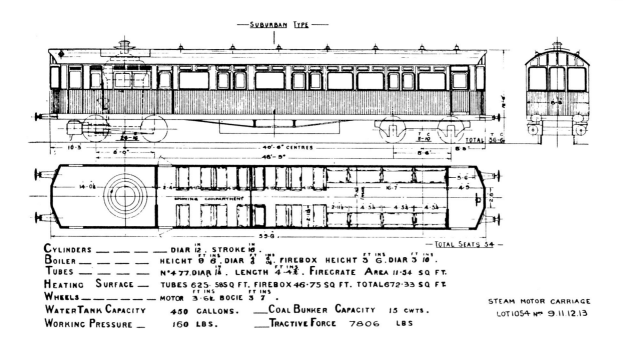

— G.W.R. SWINDON —
— STEAM MOTOR CARRIAGE —
— LOT 1054 - Nos 10 & 14 —

SRM No.9 is recorded as having the saloon partitioned into smoking and non-smoking accommodation, but at an unrecorded date, whilst there is no record for the others. It is likely that this was done from 1906 onwards.

Externally, diagram D shows three of the large fixed windows (Fxd) replaced by double droplights (dd) to give a window arrangement beyond the passenger door of

dd Fxd dd Fxd Fxd dd Fxd,

whereas, beyond the door, diagram C shows

Fxd dd Fxd Fxd dd Fxd dd Fxd.

Diagrams D1 and D both give tare weights of 36 tons 6 cwt, divided 24 tons 16cwt on the power bogie and 11 tons 10 cwt on the trailing bogie, whilst the *Register* gives individual weights of between 37t 15c and 39t 4c.

Both diagrams D and D1 show double sliding windows to the power compartment where there should be triple in the case of diagram D1, and double with a water filler pipe cap in a panel on diagram D.

All received incandescent gas lighting in 1912 or 1913.

A particularly interesting photograph of No.11 at Stonehouse – probably taken in October 1915 – has survived. No.11 is in the lake livery with the number '11' (not 'No 11') in shaded letters on the end. It has droplights in the saloon, as shown on diagram D, but instead of the triple windows in the power compartment, that nearest the passenger saloon has been replaced by a panel with a water filler cap (this looks like a circle with a cross). The motor end had been plated over, and the bottom of the end windows effectively raised, with smaller windows fitted; the tops of these windows remained at eaves level. In fact, the new panelling had even been given decorative beading around the sides and below the end windows. It is also possible to see inside the power compartment: three horizontal protection bars were fitted inside the windows, with the coal piled up against them.

It is probable that all the earlier SRMs had the water filler and end window modifications, but evidence is lacking.

SRM No.14 had an engine (0893) with 4ft driving wheels between November 1911 and November 1913, but otherwise engines with 3ft 6½in drivers were fitted.

Nos.9–14 were stopped between 1915 and 1917 for conversion to trailers Nos.107–112 (Dia. A7) and reappeared in the new guise between 1916 and 1919.

TABLE 18

SUMMARY: Diagrams D1, D (Built on Lot 1054)

Car No.	*Built*	*First Boiler*	*First Engine*	*Tare t - c*	*Incand. Gas*	*Steam Heat*	*Final Miles*	*Stopped Work*	*To Trailer No.*	*Dia.*
9	May 04	1009	0811	39-14	May 13	Feb 05	177,846	Sep 15	107	A7
10	May 04	1010	0812	38-16	Dec 12	Aug 05	204,853	Jul 16	108	A7
11	Jun 04	1012	0814	38-10	Jan 13	Apr 05	202,304	Aug 16	109	A7
12	Jun 04	1019	0815	39-00	Nov 12	Jul 05	204,572	Dec 15	110	A7
13	Jun 04	1020	0816	38-11	Nov 12	Jan 05	241,035	Apr 18	111	A7
14	Jul 04	1022	0818	38-04	Dec 13	Apr 05	225,183	Dec 17	112	A7

NOTE
No.12: Mileage at Oct 14.

Car No. 11 at Stonehouse, probably in 1915 when it was allocated to Chalford. It had been repanelled at the front, possibly with metal sheeting incorporating raised lower edge to the windows, and fitted with protection bars to the windows, a water filler cap with modified sliding windows and droplights had been fitted in the saloon. It is seen here in the lined lake livery. COLLECTION L. PADIN

Diagrams F1, F, G1, G: Nos.17 to 28

The last dozen matchboarded SRMs to be ordered were twelve 'Branch' cars built on Carriage Lot 1063, and ordered on 23rd February 1904. They were delivered between March and September that year at a recorded cost of £1,562 14s 3d each, divided between the Loco Department (£826 2s 8d) and the Carriage Department (£736 11s 7d). Their power units were ordered on Locomotive Department Lots F37 (diagram F) and F44 (diagram G), the difference between the F1/F and G1/G diagrams being that those illustrated by diagrams G1 and G were fitted with retractable steps, and thus had the trailing bogie fitted further forward compared with the other cars.

DESIGN

Externally, the cars were originally very similar to those of SRM diagram D1. They were to the same dimensions: 59ft 6in long by 8ft 6in wide, 12ft 6in high to roof, and 13ft 4½in high to the chimney top. The principal difference between these SRMs and their immediate predecessors was that, instead of having just a single door next to the power compartment partition, these had a luggage compartment instead, so that internally they were arranged thus:

Motor Compartment: 14ft 0⅛in from the SRM front to the partition. The front window arrange-

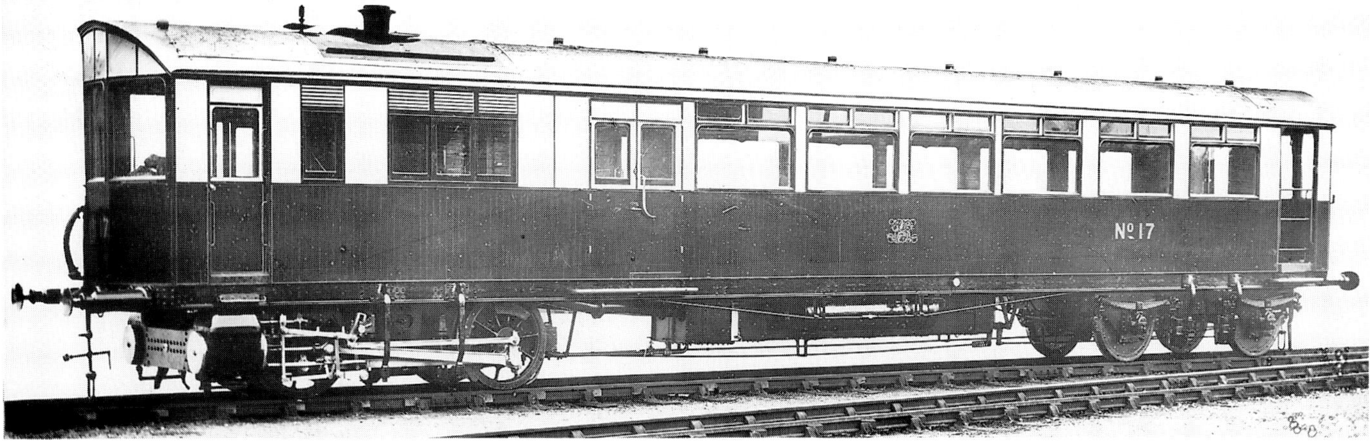

This official photograph of Car No. 17 of Diagram F1 as built without retractable steps shows the original arrangement of three bars hooked across the entrance at the trailing end. NATIONAL RAILWAY MUSEUM

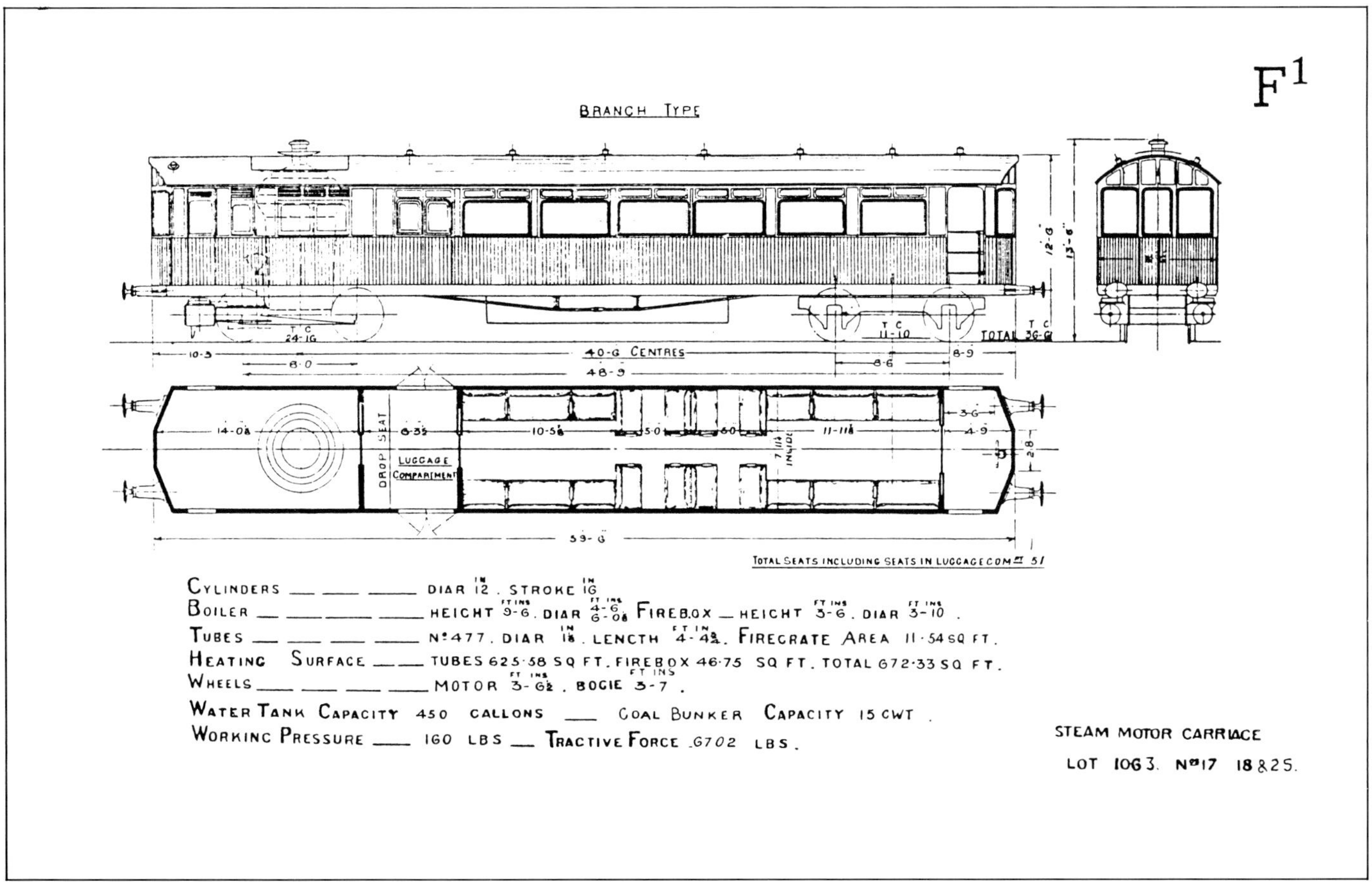

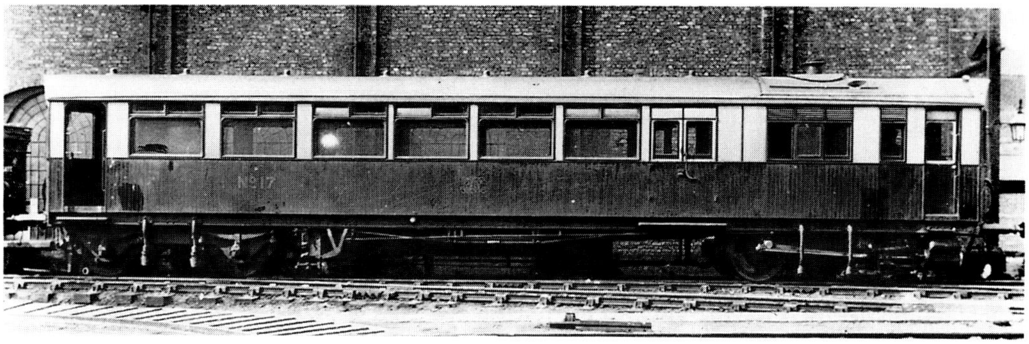

Car No. 17 in early condition, possibly at Southall (the tank engine on the left seems to have an 'ALDGATE' destination board). In this photograph the whistle is not apparent, presumably it sounded through the hole in the removable panel in the roof, which was otherwise for the safety valves. Roof ventilators had not yet been fitted.
COLLECTION J. N. SLINN

Car No. 17 is seen here with end destination board brackets fitted together with the associated steps on the end and handles.
COLLECTION R. C. RILEY

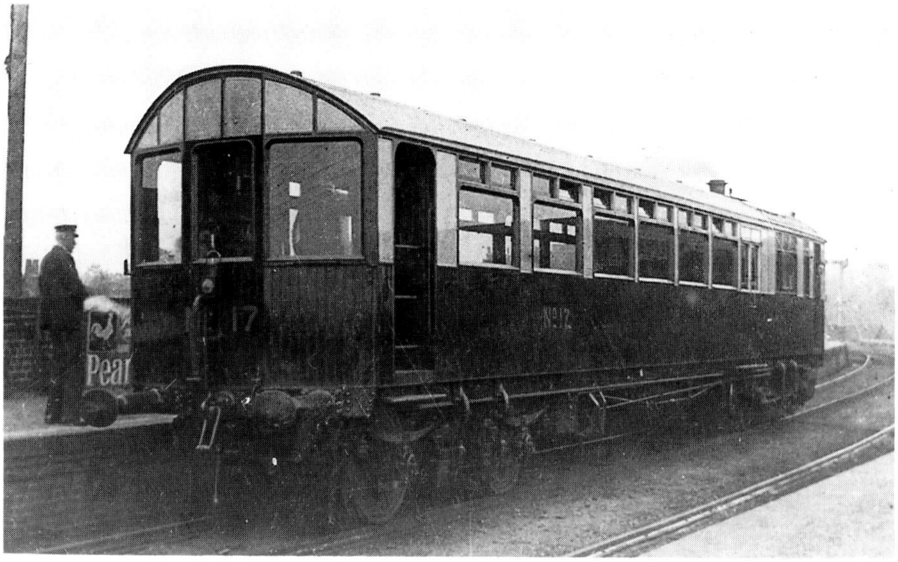

Right: *Car No. 17 was first allocated to Southall in May 1904 and is seen here in as-built condition. Note the guard's compartment double doors further down the car. The location is believed to have been Brentford.*

Car No. 17 with altered side windows, as shown on Diagram F, and front windows modified by panelling to raise the lower edge. The livery was probably lined brown, with the number '17' on the end partly obscured by the lamp, and 'GWR 17' on the side near the driver's door. F. MOORE

ments were as before, whilst the triple sliding windows in the sides were again shown as pairs on the diagrams.

Luggage Compartment: 6ft 3½in between partitions. There were internal sliding doors to both the motor compartment and the passenger saloon. A drop seat across the full width of the compartment against the motor compartment wall is shown on the diagrams. The compartment had double external doors which both opened outwards, each with panels that matched the toplights of the adjacent saloon.

Passenger Saloon: this was rather smaller than before, with a 10ft 5⅞in length of longitudinal bench seating at the motor compartment end, two 5ft seating bays, and an 11ft 11⅞in length of longitudinal bench seating at the trailing end. There was a sliding door in the driving vestibule partition. Originally, the saloon had six large, fixed windows with twin toplights above, though the panel width between them varied. Illustrated on diagrams F1 and G1 in this condition, they seated 51 passengers, including those on the tip-up seat in the luggage compartment.

Driving Vestibule: 4ft 9in maximum between partition and SRM end wall. Diagrams F1 and G1 show these cars with doorway openings protected by three horizontal bars, and it is known that No.17 at least (though probably all) started life like this. No.18 is known to have had doors fitted to this vestibule by August 1908, and all would have had this alteration, although no dates are recorded.

Diagrams F1 and F covered SRMs Nos.17, 18 and 25, which had a total wheelbase of 48ft 9in, including the usual Dean 8ft 6in bogie. The front overhang was 6ft 3in, and the trailing end 4ft 6in.

SRMs Nos.19–24 and 26–28 were shown on diagrams G1 and G, with the Dean 8ft 6in bogie positioned further away from the end so that the total wheelbase became 45ft 9in. These cars had a 6ft 3in overhang at the motor end, and 7ft 6in at the trailing end to allow retractable steps to be fitted beneath the driving vestibule doorway. The steps were of the 'Mk I' type, which retracted under the car as a unit with the treads only horizontal when they

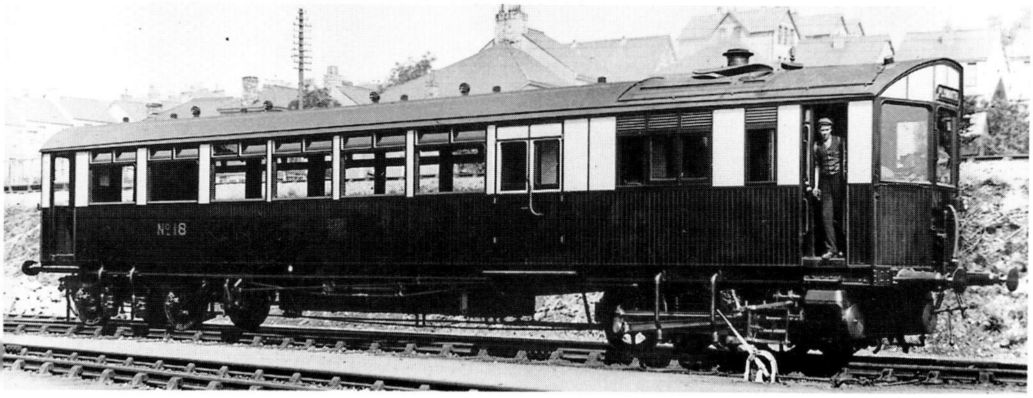

Car No. 18 of Diagram F1 at Plymouth, according to the destination board. It was allocated at Laira from February 1906 to October 1907. The doors to the luggage compartment did not have 'ENTRANCE' over the windows.
COLLECTION R. C. RILEY

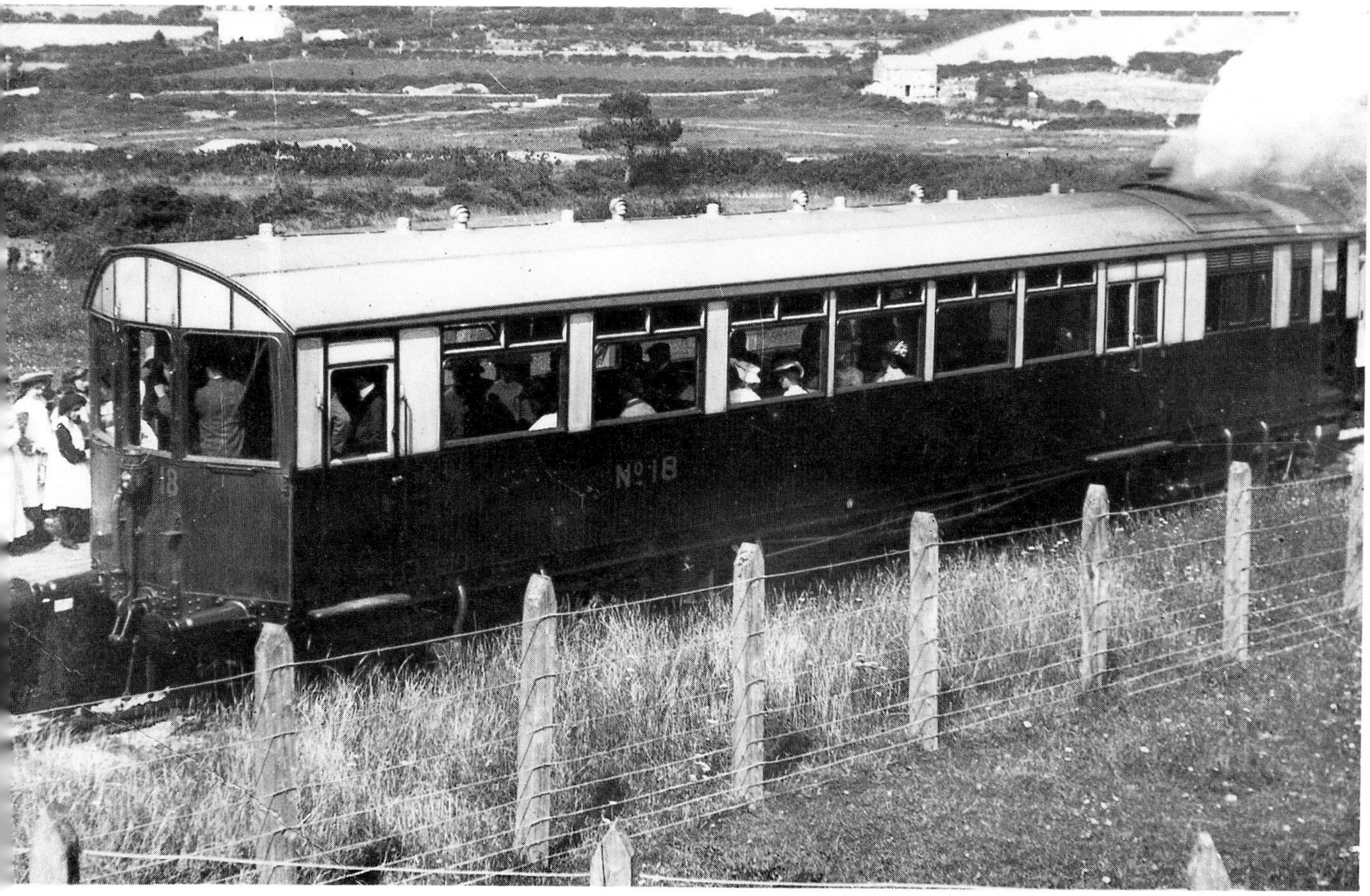

Car No. 18, the first train to call at Goonhaven Halt on the Newquay–Chacewater line on 14th August 1905. It looks as if the car had been repainted for the occasion. Notice the end destination board brackets and the associated steps and handles, also that it had been fitted with shell roof ventilators and a high-level rain strip.
T. DYER, CTY. R. C. RILEY

were fully extended. The diagrams also show another set fitted beneath the trailing end leaf of the luggage compartment doors.

All diagrams give the tare weight distribution as 24 tons 16 cwt on the power bogie and 11 ton 10 cwt on the trailing bogie, a total weight of 36 tons 6 cwt. The register, however, gives figures between 38 and 40 tons.

MODIFICATION & DISPOSAL

An early modification to these trailers was the fitting of shell ventilators, not shown on the diagrams.

Another alteration provided a partition between the bench seats and the seating bays to give a smoking compartment 10ft 5⅞in long at the luggage compartment end of the saloon.

In due course, three of the large windows (Fxd) were replaced by quarterlight, droplight, quarterlight (qdq) units, retaining the twin toplights above. The window arrangement of the saloon now became (from the luggage compartment end):

Fxd qdq Fxd qdq qdq Fxd

G

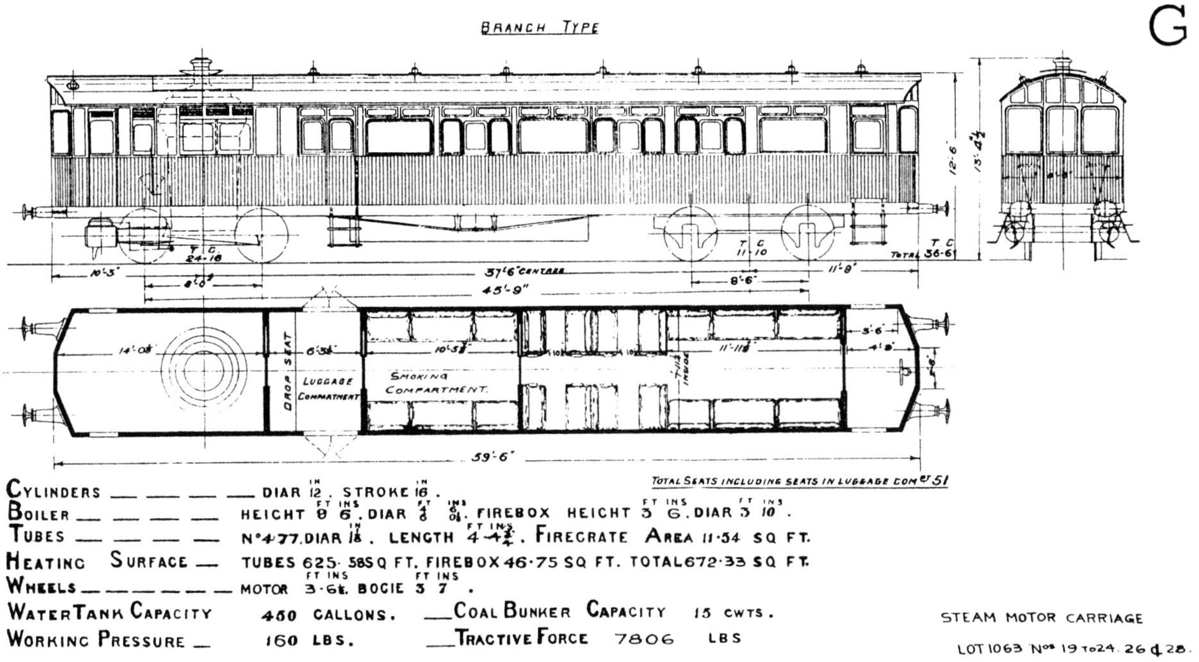

BRANCH TYPE
57'6" CENTRES
45'-9"
59'-6"
LUGGAGE COMPARTMENT
SMOKING COMPARTMENT
DROP SEAT
TOTAL SEATS INCLUDING SEATS IN LUGGAGE COMPT 51
CYLINDERS — DIAR 12. STROKE 16.
BOILER — HEIGHT 9 6. DIAR 4 6. FIREBOX HEIGHT 3 6. DIAR 3 10.
TUBES — N°477. DIAR 1⅛. LENGTH 4-4½. FIRECRATE AREA 11·54 SQ FT.
HEATING SURFACE — TUBES 625·58 SQ FT. FIREBOX 46·75 SQ FT. TOTAL 672·33 SQ FT.
WHEELS — MOTOR 3-6½. BOGIE 3 7.
WATER TANK CAPACITY 450 GALLONS. — COAL BUNKER CAPACITY 15 CWTS.
WORKING PRESSURE — 160 LBS. — TRACTIVE FORCE 7806 LBS
STEAM MOTOR CARRIAGE
LOT 1063 Nos 19 TO 24. 26 & 28.

G[1]

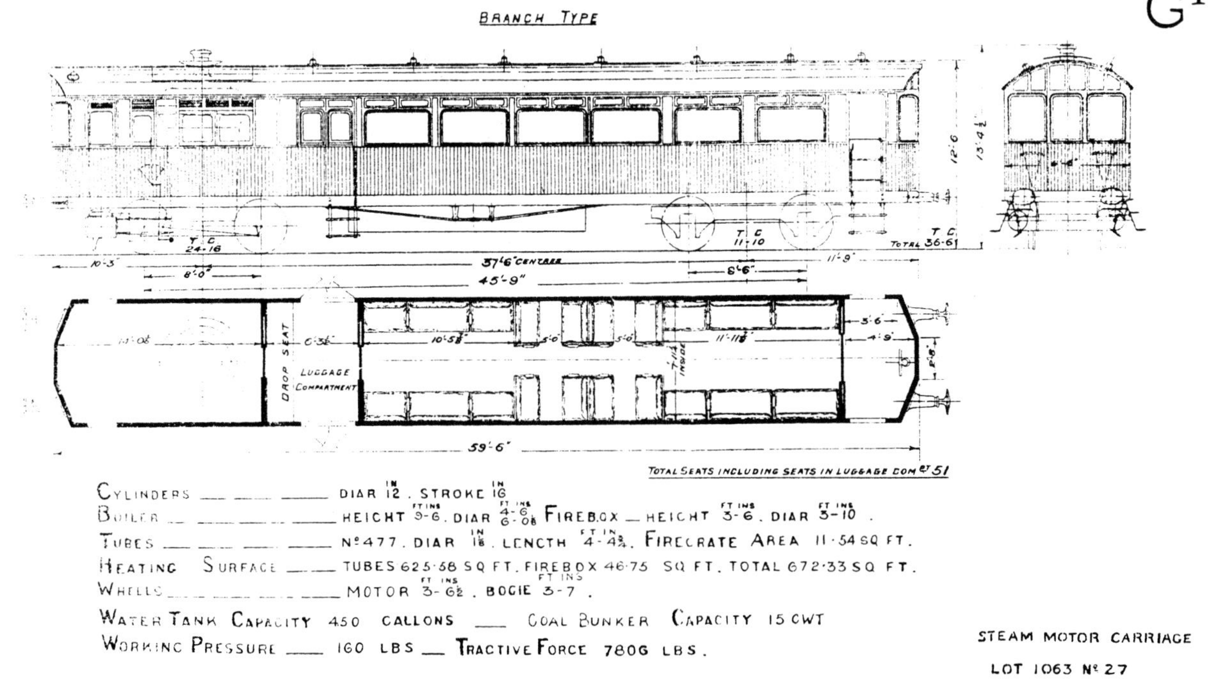

This is borne out by a photograph and by the Dia. A9 trailers. Diagrams F and G show the SRMs in this condition.

Not shown on the diagram, or recorded in the register, are the fitting of upper rainstrips, or the water filler caps and panels in place of one of the sliding windows on each side of the motor compartment. The presence of these are confirmed from a photograph, and probably applied to all. Nos 17, 18 and 25 (at least) received four shell ventilators in the roof above the saloon; this was done by August 1905 in the case of 18. Again, the modification probably applied to all. Again, all the vehicles would have received the steps on their ends, either side of the vacuum pipe.

Incandescent gas lighting replaced the original flat flame burners in all cars between 1911 and 1916.

SRMs 17 and 24 (at least) had smaller windows fitted in the end of the motor compartment, and the area below them was panelled in separately from the matchboarding below.

A number of the cars were fitted with an engine having 4ft wheels from 1910, and these are shown in the summary table below.

The SRMs were stopped for conversion to trailers between 1916 and 1919, and reappeared as Dia. A9 trailers Nos.113–124 in 1919 and 1920.

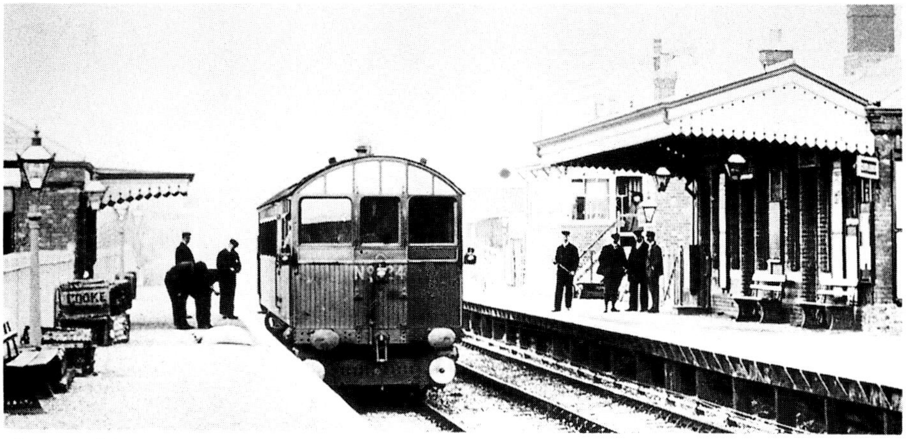

Car No. 24 of Diagram G1 at Shepherds station on the Truro and Newquay line. It is seen in brown and cream livery with modified end windows. Car No. 24 was at Truro from September 1905 and possibly up to July 1907, this picture presumably dating from that period. Notice the side tail lamps. COLLECTION R. C. RILEY

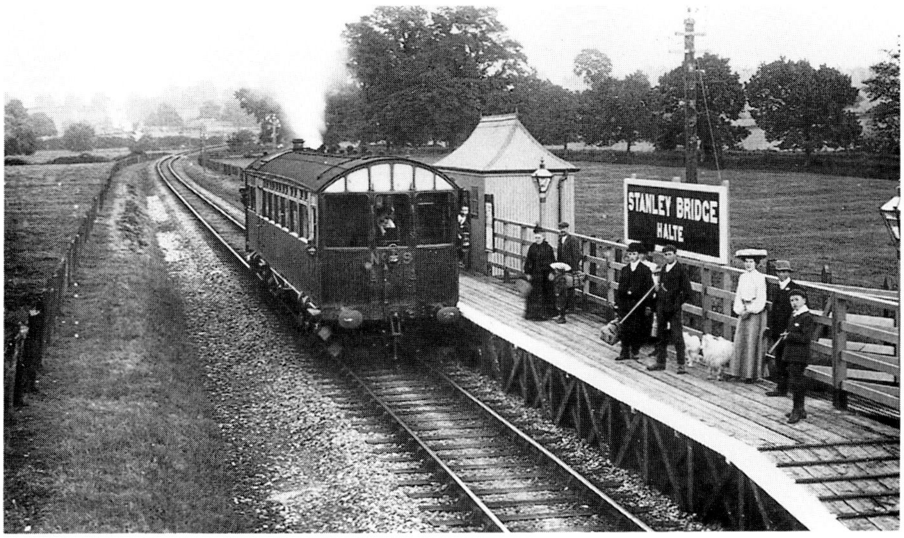

Right: *Car No. 19 of Diagram G1 at Stanley Bridge Halt on the Calne branch. Car No. 19 was allocated to Chippenham from February until September 1905. The halt was opened in April that year. Type 1 steps that swung out as a unit with rigid treads can be seen to the left of and below the buffer. This view also shows the side tail lamps.* AUTHOR'S COLLECTION

TABLE 19

SUMMARY: Diagram F1, F, G1, G (Built on Lot 1063)

Car No.	*Dia.*	*Built*	*First Boiler*	*First Engine*	*Tare t - c*	*Steam Heat*	*Incand. Gas*	*4ft Drivers*	*Final Miles*	*Stopped Work*	*To Trailer No.*	*Dia.*
17	F	Apr 04	1005	0807	38-19	Sep 05	Dec 12	Jan 15	330,146	Dec 17	113	A9
18	F	Apr 04	1006	0808	38-09	Jul 05	Jul 16	Dec 13-Aug 14	228,955	Feb 18	114	A9
19	G	Jul 04	1024	0820	38-17	Feb 05	Jun 15	Jan 10-Apr 11; Jun 15	183,928	Aug 18	115	A9
20	G	Aug 04	1028	0824	39-04	Jul 05	Dec 14		198,418	Mar 19	116	A9
21	G	Jun 04	1021	0817	39-05	Mar 05	Dec 12		238,326	Dec 19	117	A9
22	G	Jul 04	1026	0822	38-16	Jul 05	Apr 13	Nov 14	216,594	Sep 19	118	A9
23	G	Aug 04	1027	0823	38-18	Oct 05	Jun 13		280,346	Feb 19	119	A9
24	G	Jul 04	1025	0821	39-15	+	Aug 12		205,793	Sep 19	120	A9
25	F	May 04	1011	8013	38-16	Jan 05	Oct 11		261,968	Jan 19	121	A9
26	G	Jun 04	1023	0819	38-17	Nov 05	Jun 13	Feb 12-May 13; Oct 14	243,785	Jul 16	122	A9
27	G	Aug 04	1029	0825	39-10	Oct 05	Sep 11		213,449	Dec 16	123	A9
28	G	Sep 04	1030	0826	38-15	Sep 05	Apr 14	Feb 12-Aug 13	249,232	Sep 16	124	A9

H

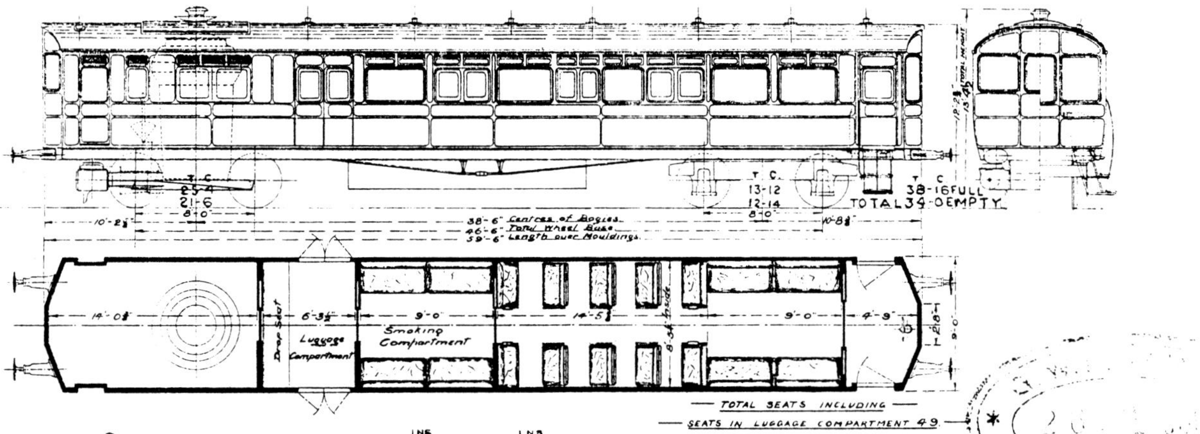

CYLINDERS	DIAR 12 INS. STROKE 16 INS.
BOILER	HEIGHT 9 FT 6 INS. DIAR 4 6 / 6 0¾ FT INS. FIREBOX HEIGHT 3 FT 6 INS. DIAR 3 FT 10 INS.
TUBES	Nº 462. DIAR 1¼ IN. LENGTH 4 FT 5½ INS. FIREGRATE AREA 11·54 SQ FT.
HEATING SURFACE	TUBES 605·9 SQ FT. FIREBOX 46·75 SQ FT. TOTAL 652·65 SQ FT.
WHEELS	MOTOR 3 FT 6½ INS. BOGIE 3 FT 7½ INS.
WATER TANK CAPACITY	450 GALLONS. — COAL BUNKER CAPACITY 15 CWTS.
WORKING PRESSURE	160 LBS. — TRACTIVE FORCE 7806 LBS.

STEAM MOTOR CARRIAGE
LOT 1078 Nos 29, 30, 33, 34, 36.

J[1]

— BRANCH TYPE. —

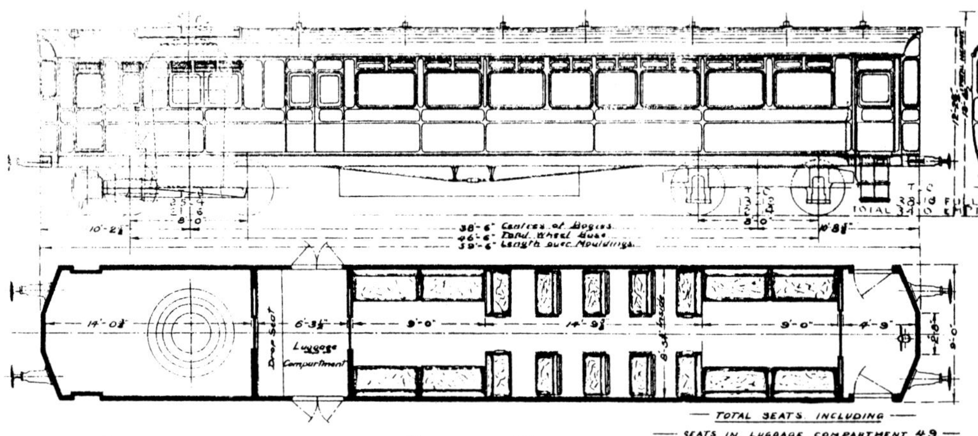

CYLINDERS	DIAR 12 INS. STROKE 16 INS.
BOILER	HEIGHT 9 FT 6 INS. DIAR 4 6 / 6 0¾ FT INS. FIREBOX HEIGHT 3 FT 6 INS. DIAR 3 FT 10 INS.
TUBES	Nº 462. DIAR 1¼ IN. LENGTH 4 FT 5½ INS. FIREGRATE AREA 11·54 SQ FT.
HEATING SURFACE	TUBES 605·9 SQ FT. FIREBOX 46·75 SQ FT. TOTAL 652·65 SQ FT.
WHEELS	MOTOR 3 FT 6½ INS. BOGIE 3 FT 7½ INS.
WATER TANK CAPACITY	450 GALLONS. — COAL BUNKER CAPACITY 15 CWTS.
WORKING PRESSURE	160 LBS. — TRACTIVE FORCE 7806 LBS.

STEAM MOTOR CARRIAGE
LOT 1078 Nº 32

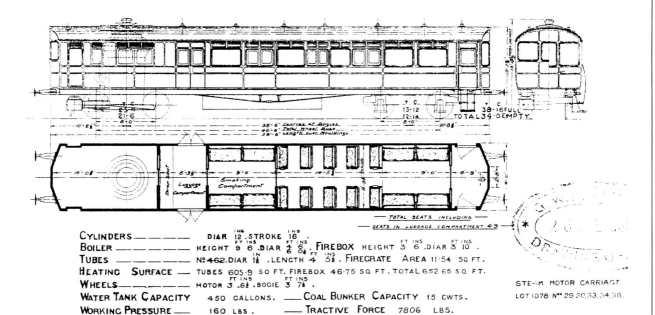

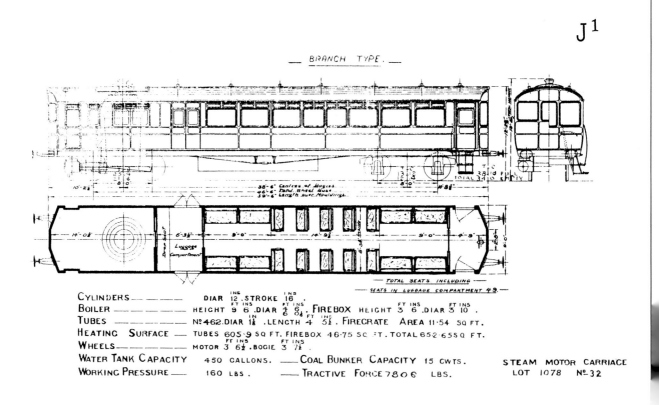

CHAPTER EIGHT

THE 59½FT WOOD PANELLED CARS

Diagrams (H1), H, J1 and J: Nos. 29 to 36

Car No. 29 at Halesowen. J. G. SPENSE, CTY. R. C. RILEY

Lot 1078 was notable: it marked the appearance of the first SRMs with the traditional GWR wood panelled bodies, and included the first 70ft examples. The Lot covered twelve SRMs. In this chapter, only the 59½ft examples, Nos.29–36, will be covered, whilst cars 37–40, which were 70ft long, will be found under diagram K in the next chapter.

There is in existence a *Valuation of Coaching Stock Register* for 1907–8, which divides the cost of Lot 1078 into 8 cars at £1,710 each, presumably the 59½ft vehicles, and 4 cars at £1,860, probably the 70ft cars.

DESIGN

The dimensions of these SRMs compared to the last matchboarded cars (Diagram G) are shown in Table 20.

TABLE 20

COMPARISON: Diagrams 'H/J' with Diagram 'G'

Dimension	*Dia. H J Nos.29-36 Wood-panelled*	*Dia. G Nos 19-24, 26-28 Match-boarded*
Length over Body	59 ft 6 in	59 ft 6 in
Width over Body	9 ft 0 in	8 ft 6 in
Height: Rail-Roof	12 ft 2¾ in	12 ft 6 in
Height: Rail-Chimney	13 ft 4½ in	13 ft 4½ in
Wheelbase	46 ft 6 in	45 ft 9 in
Front - Boiler Centre	10 ft 2⅝ in	10 ft 3 in
Engine Wheelbase	8 ft 0 in	8 ft 0 in
Trailing Bogie Wheelbase	8 ft 0 in	8 ft 6 in
Trailing End - Bogie Centre	10 ft 8⅝ in	11 ft 9 in

The trailing bogie was a bolster design with volute springs – including those over the axle-boxes, which were concealed by semicircular covers. These bogies were of a design new to SRMs. Again, the underframe truss was of the queenpost design, with round-section truss rods and a central turnbuckle for adjustment.

At the motor unit end only, the new cars had an extra deep waist panel, and smaller windows pitched higher than before. This was presumably to reduce the likelihood of breakage when coaling the car, as the bunker was immediately below these windows. The motor compartment was 14ft 0⅜in long internally, and was very similar to most of the matchboarded SRMs. It was provided with external sliding doors, to the rear of which was a droplight with louvred ventilator above, followed by double sliding windows, as shown on the diagrams. These sliding windows had louvred ventilators above, still divided into three.

External access to the luggage compartment was by means of double doors, with internal sliding doors to both the passenger saloon and the motor compartment. This luggage compartment was 6ft 3½in between partitions, and had a drop seat across the width of the SRM against the power compartment partition. The external doors to the luggage compartment did not have retractable steps below.

The passenger saloon contained a 9ft length of longitudinal bench seating at each end, and a 14ft 9⅝in section of walkover seats between; there were five pairs of the latter, including the end seats (which had fixed backs). When partitioned into smoking and non-smoking accommodation, the 9ft length of bench seating nearest the luggage compartment became the smoking saloon.

Including the seats in the luggage compartment, these cars only seated 49 passengers. The last matchboarded SRMs, which also had a luggage compartment, seated 51.

As built, the windows in the saloon were the usual large, fixed type, with two hinged toplights above each, but they came in two distinct sizes, arranged 3 larger, 2 smaller, 3 larger. The smaller windows were more or less square. Because the original fixed windows were of two widths, the central pair of droplights which in due course replaced them were rather narrower than the other droplights – see the diagrams. The pillars between the windows were also of differing thickness.

The driving vestibule appears to have had doors from new; these were recessed slightly, flat, and opened inwards, being hinged on the corner pillars. There were retractable steps for passengers below these doors of the final ('Mk2') pattern, in which the treads were horizontal in all positions. The driving vestibule was 4ft 9in wide (maximum) between partition and end, and contained a sliding door to the passenger saloon.

Interior view of Car No. 31 of Diagram H1 or J1 in as-built condition, i.e. before droplights had been fitted. Note the slatted wood floor, the dark stained woodwork, the 'walkover' seats at the further end of the saloon, the blinds rolled up above the windows, the rails from which the straps hung (the whistle cord passed through one), the gas lights and ventilators between the brackets hanging from the roof. The toplights could be opened by pulling on knobs on their frame above the droplight. The picture frames on the partition at the end each contained three views, whilst the notice above the door reads 'PASSENGERS ARE REQUESTED NOT TO SMOKE OR SPIT IN THIS CAR'.

NATIONAL RAILWAY MUSEUM

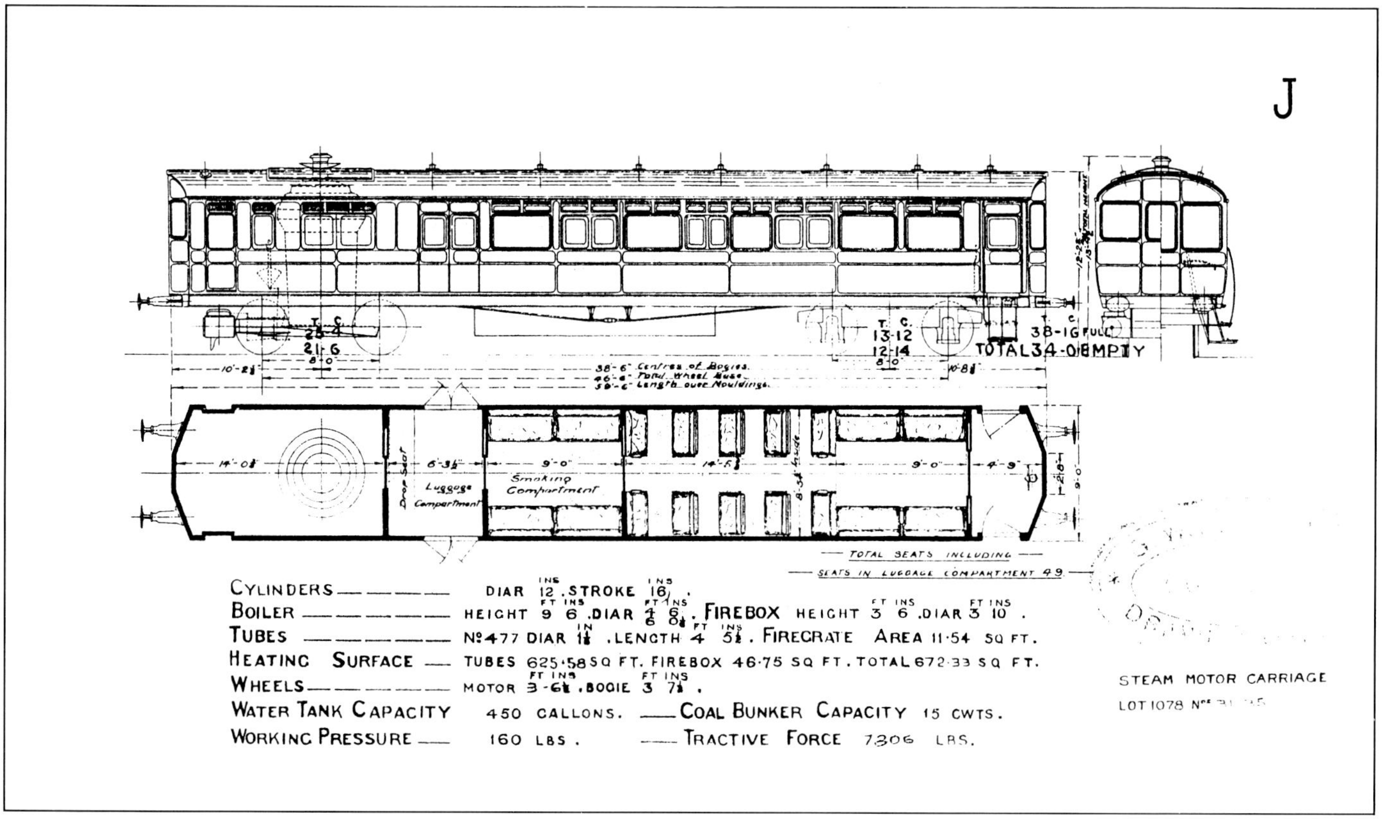

The first motor at Stourport, No. 35 of Diagram H1 or J1 as built.

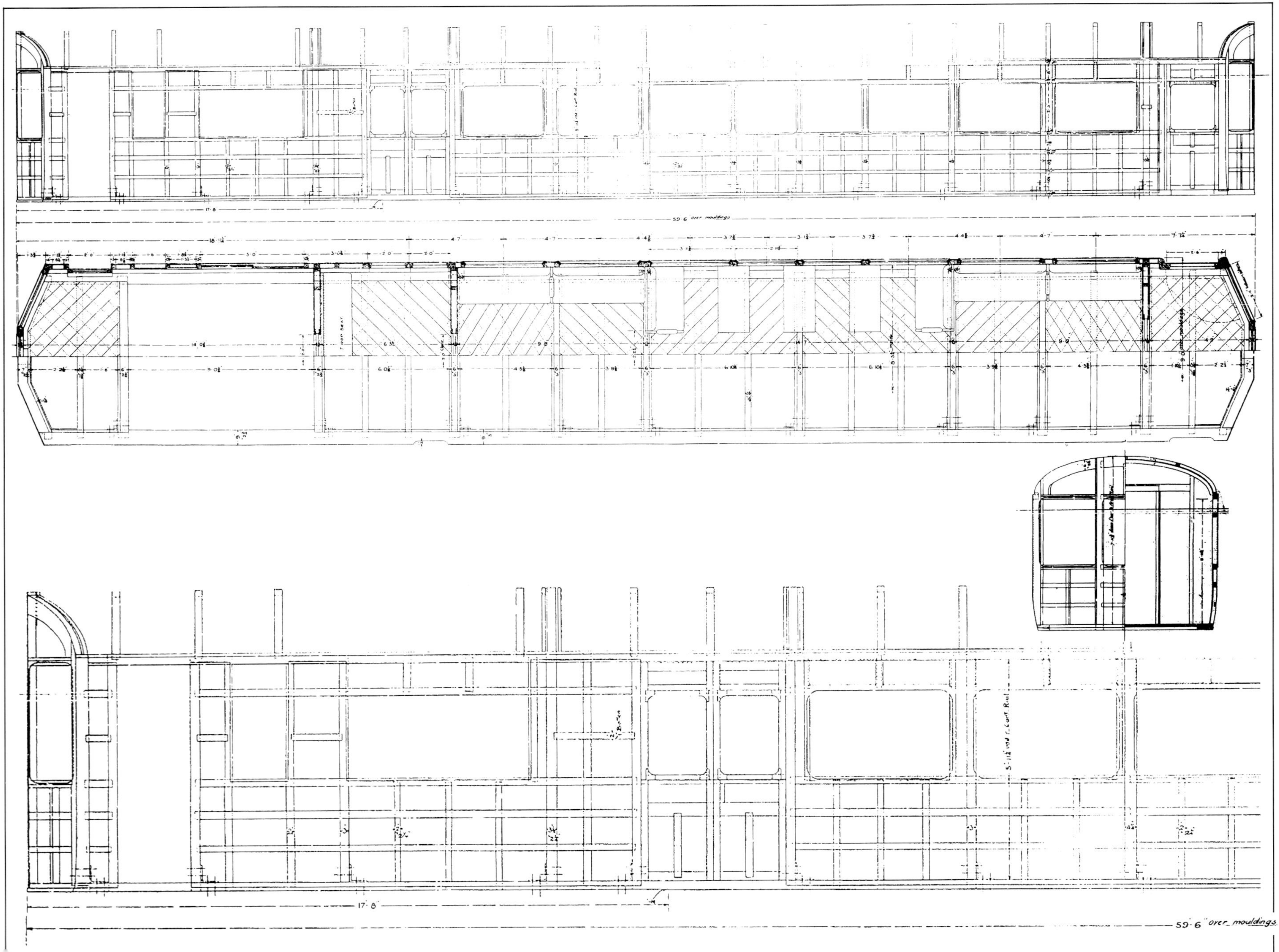
59'6" over mouldings
17'8"

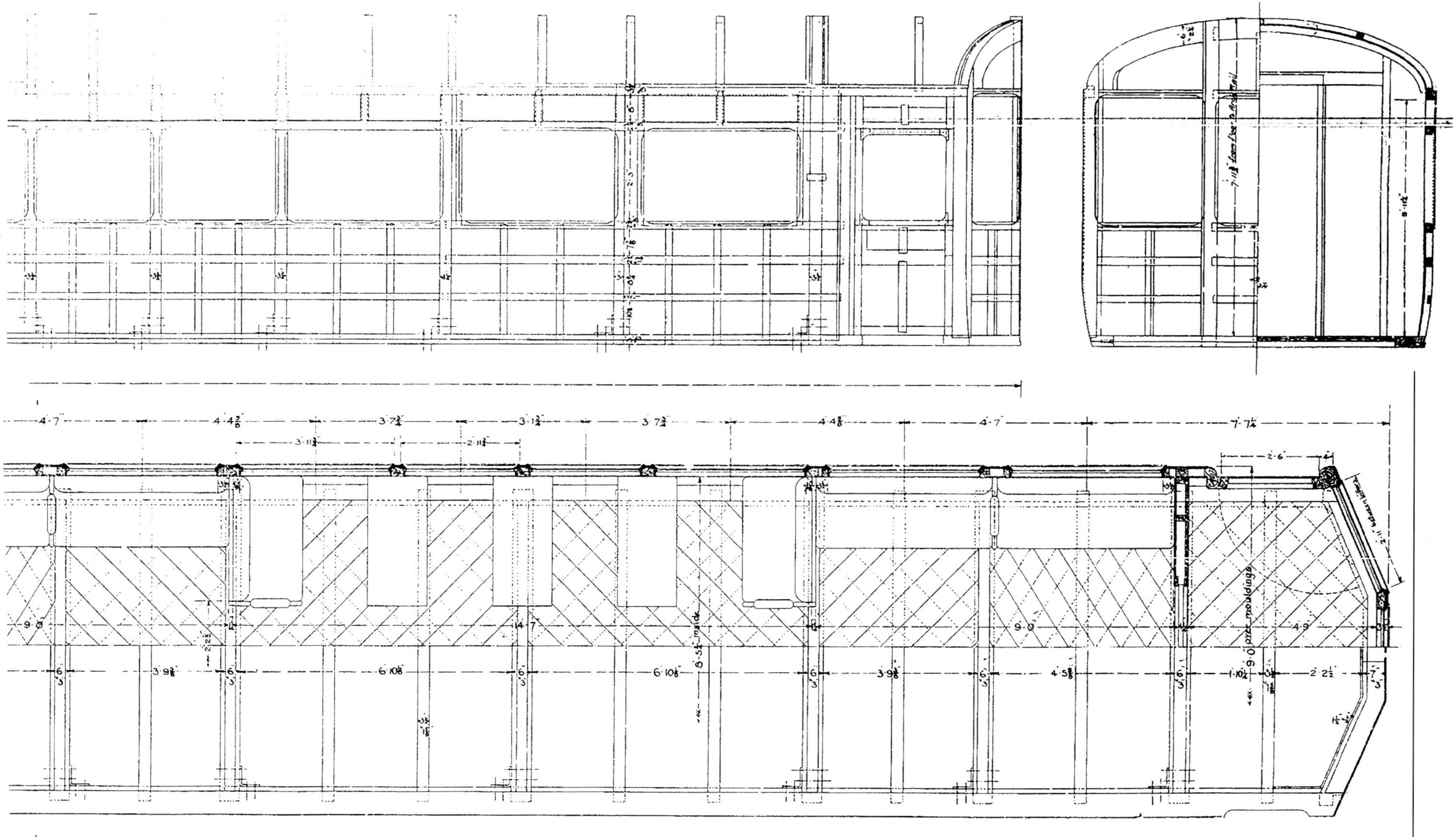

Diagrams H1 and J1 – Construction of body.

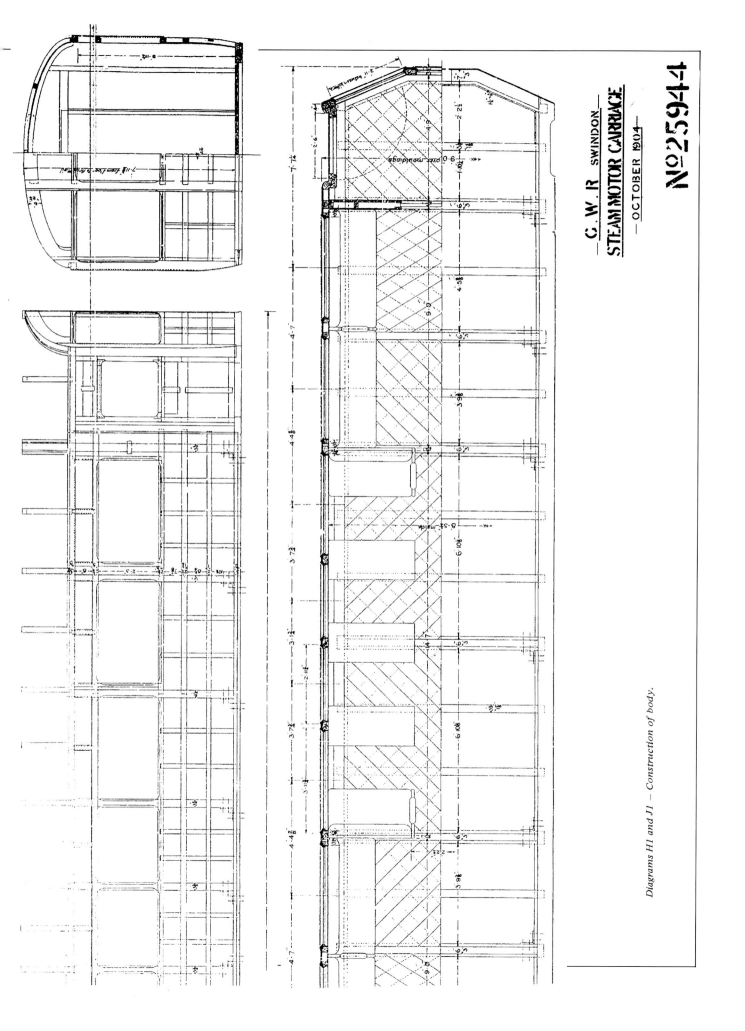

Underframe for Diagram H1 and J1 Cars 29-36.

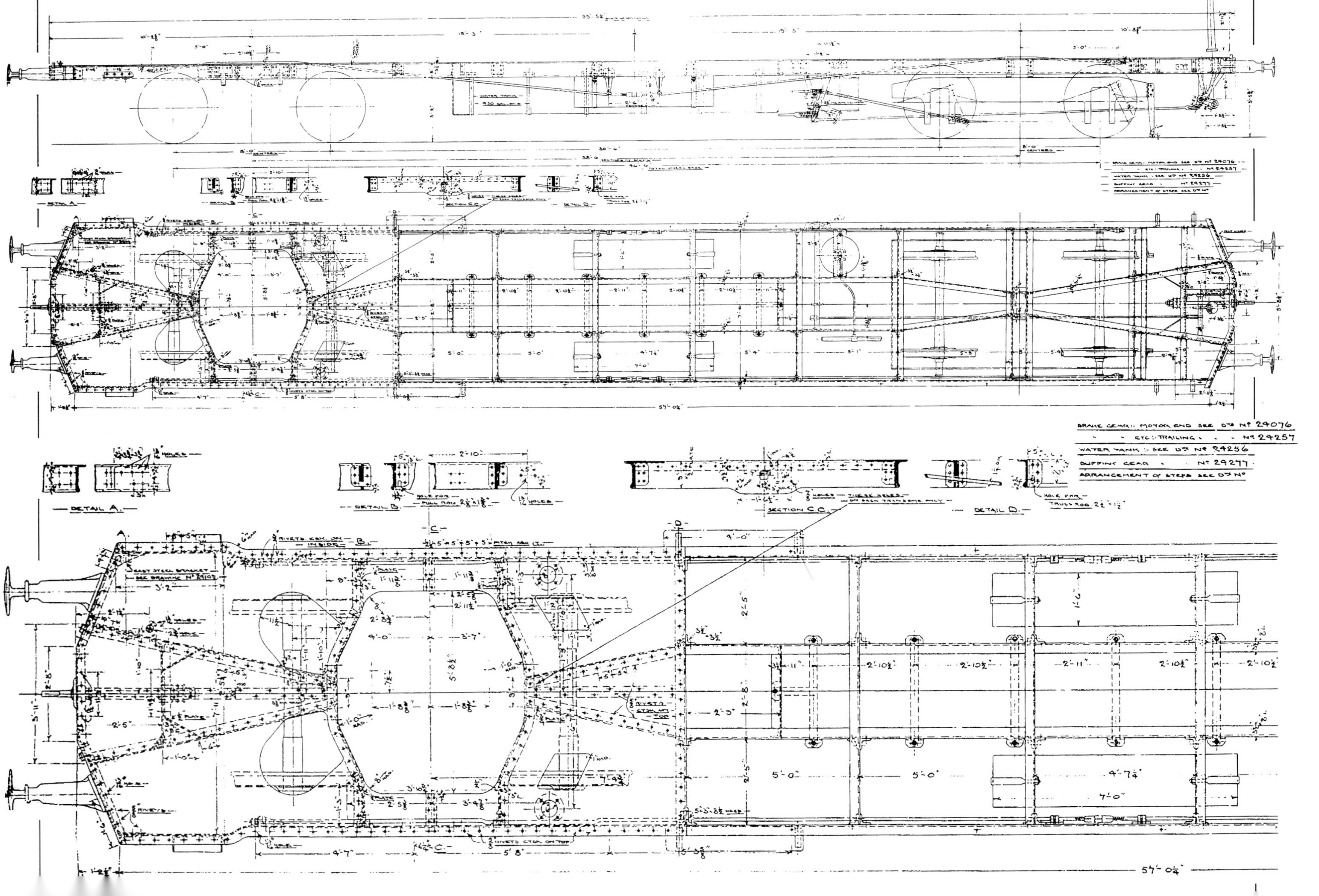

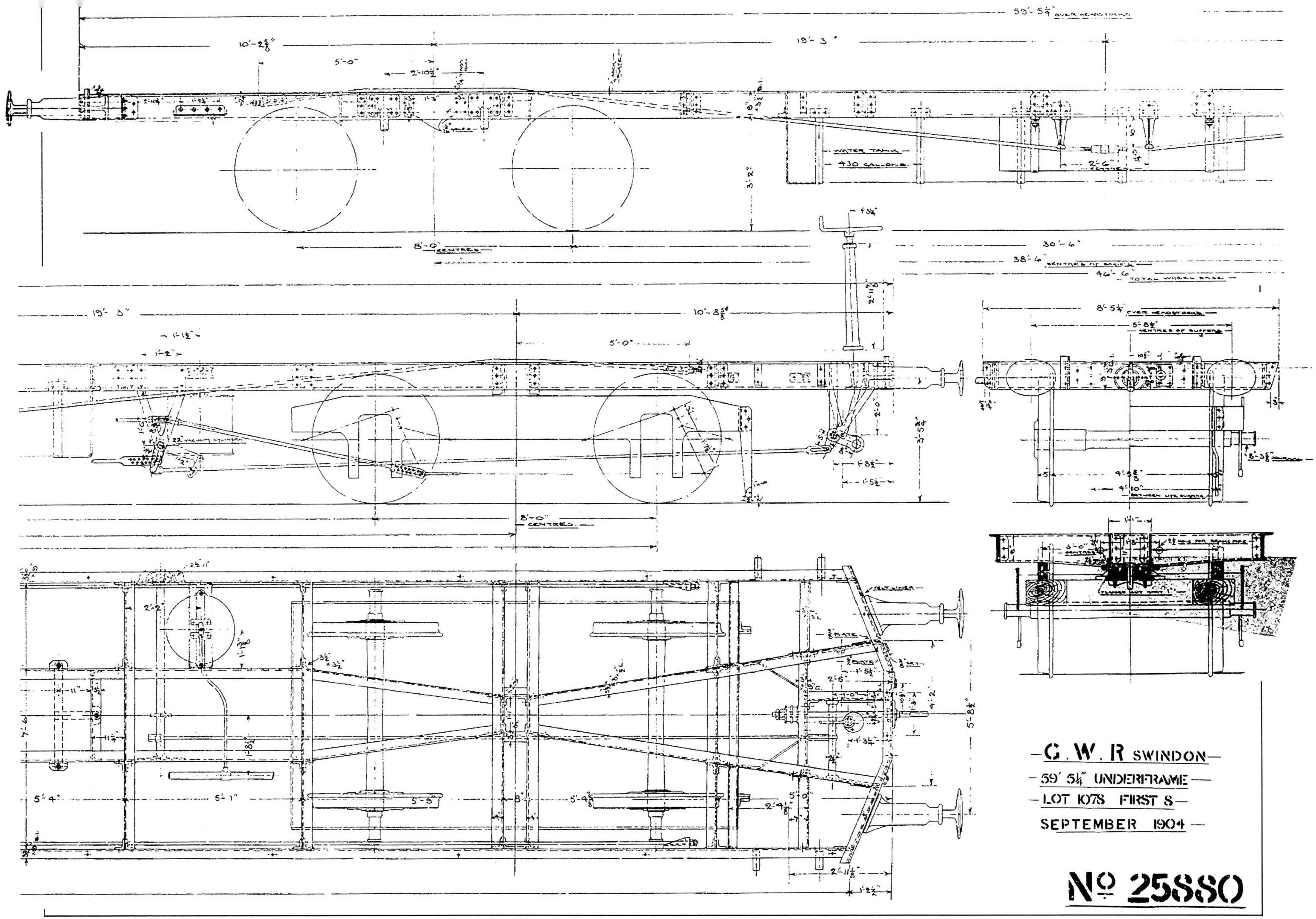
59'-5¼" OVER HEADSTOCKS
10'-2⅞"
19'-3"
5'-0"
2'-10½"
WATER TANK
430 GALLONS
2'-6"
3'-2"
8'-0" CENTRES
30'-6"
38'-6" CENTRES OF BOGIES
46'-6" TOTAL WHEEL BASE
10'-8⅝"
22" VACUUM CYLINDER
8'-5¼" OVER HEADSTOCKS
5'-8¼" CENTRES OF BUFFERS
FELT LINER
5'-9"
5'-1"
5'-4"
7'-6"
G.W.R SWINDON
59' 5¼" UNDERFRAME
LOT 1078 FIRST S
SEPTEMBER 1904
No 25880

As was usual, all these cars had their boilers changed at regular intervals. For example, No.30 was fitted with the following during her early years:

Boiler	*Date*
1045	When new
1025	January 1905
1057	March 1906
1064	October 1906
1049	February 1907

So, the validity of the separate diagrams H and J is questionable. As there are two diagrams, I suspect that by the time the *Diagram Index* was set up, someone had realized that Nos.31 and 35 had boilers with additional tubes, and so a separate diagram for them had been produced, and, being current, it was allocated a different index letter to the others. The other question is why the original diagram was indexed as J1, and not H1?

The weights recorded vary somewhat. The tare weights shown on all the diagrams were:

	Empty	*Full*
	Tons – Cwt	*Tons – Cwt*
Motor Bogie	21 – 6	25 – 4
Trailing Bogie	12 – 14	13 – 12
Total	34 – 0	38 – 16

whilst the Lot book gave an average weight of 35 tons 16 cwt 3 qtrs empty and 38 tons 14 cwt full, and the register gives various weights from 38 tons 11 cwt to 41 tons 4 cwt.

These SRMs were fitted with shell ventilators from an early date, if not from new. There were two rows of seven above the saloon, though not shown on the diagrams.

MODIFICATIONS & DISPOSAL

No.31 was used on the Brynamman branch, and had its chimney height reduced from 13ft 7in to 13ft 0in by March 1905, according to a letter from Mr Waister (Locomotive & Carriage Running Department, Swindon) to Mr Churchward. Quite why its original height is given as 13ft 7in when the diagrams show this as 13ft 4½in is unexplained; I believe 13ft 6in was the maximum height allowed by the standard loading gauge.

The volute spring trailing bogie was not a great success, and was replaced by a very (visually) similar coil spring bolster bogie between 1906 and 1911.

Photographs show only one rain strip; it was of full length, and varied in position from car to car. For example, a photograph of No.29 shows it relatively high up on the roof; No 31, possibly about 1914–5, with a rainstrip that seems to come almost to the corner of the roof; and No.30 had the same arrangement from an early date.

Also fairly early on, the buffers were replaced by a larger, oval-head design. No.29 had this done by August 1911.

The sliding windows to the power compartment were reduced in length by one third, and a panel with water filler was fitted to the rear of the new windows at unrecorded dates.

Car 31 of Diagram H is seen here on the right at Gerrards Cross on the Paddington–Birmingham 'New Line', some time during the winter of 1912/13. It was allocated to Southall between May 1912 and August 1913. It was probably in the lined brown livery of 1908. The white line painted on the end windows is one of the earliest examples seen. The matchboarded car on the left carrying the 'E' sign may have been Car No. 6 of Diagram C which was also allocated to Southall between April 1911 and August 1913. H. GORDON TIDEY/LENS OF SUTTON

With the exception of No.30, all were stopped between 1917 and 1921 for conversion to trailers of Dia.A10.

SRM No.30

No.30 continued in service until October 1935, and was one of the last to be condemned; unlike its sister SRMs, it was broken up. As it lasted so much longer than the others, it went through a number of modifications, revealed by photographs but not in the register – some of the entry for SRM 30 was erased when the number was re-used for a diesel railcar.

A photograph of No.30 taken in the early 1927 two-colour 'simple' livery, shows it to have received a Collett 7ft-wheelbase trailing bogie. The front of the motor end had been steel-panelled below the windows, and these windows had been fitted with protection bars (probably done about 1913). By the time it had received the 1930 two-colour livery with two gold waist lines, it had been fitted with a windscreen wiper (at least at the power end), and the bottom part of the front windows had been painted either brown or black on the inside or – and perhaps more likely – the coal bunker had been extended upwards to conceal the lower third of the windows. Reflecting the changes in passengers' habits, the smoking and non-smoking compartments had been changed round, so that the small saloon next to the luggage compartment was now the 'Non-Smoking', and the other 'Smoking'.

Not apparent from photographs, but related in the engine history cards, No.30 was fitted with engines with 4ft wheels from December 1923 to May 1926 (engine 0892); it then had 0891 until September 1929, and then 0892 again until both car and engine were condemned in April 1935.

No.30 seems to have spent much of the 1920s in Wales, before going to Exeter in December 1932.

DRAWINGS

The surviving diagrams covering these coaches are not too helpful.

1. *Diagram J1* which, according to the appended legend, applied only to SRM No.32. This shows a car in its original state, without droplights to the non-partitioned saloon. It illustrates a power unit with a boiler containing 462 tubes of 1⅛in diameter, 4ft 5½in long, giving 605·9 sq ft of tube steam heating area.
2. *Diagram H* exists in two forms, and both versions I have seen are Locomotive Department prints showing three of the windows in the saloon replaced by pairs of droplights, and the saloon divided into smoking and non-smoking compartments. It pictures the same boiler as diagram J1. One of these diagrams covers Nos.29, 30, 33, 34 and 36, and the other – presumably a later print – all SRMs, Nos.29–36. Apart from the running numbers, the latter differs by showing the width over cylinders as 8ft 5in and the height from rail to the top of the trailing bogie stretcher (apparently) as 3ft 2in.
3. *Diagram J* is the same as diagram H in appearance, but the legend indicates that it covered only Nos.31 and 35. It shows a boiler having 477 tubes of 1⅛in diameter, giving 625·58 sq ft of tube steam heating area, and as far as I can ascertain, this is the only difference from diagram H. Even the weights are the same.

I think they were all built with the body design shown in diagram J1. A photograph of the interior of car No.31 shows it without droplights when new, and the saloon is not partitioned. Their bodies appear to have been altered to the condition shown in diagrams H or J at a fairly early date (circa 1907, which is why No.32 had not been modified by the time the diagram index had been set up). This is partly borne out by the register, as there are two dates surviving for partitioning: No.31 in September 1906, and 32 in March 1907. This also helps to date the setting-up of the SRM diagram index.

The motor end of Car No. 30, possibly at Swindon Works, perhaps in 1907-1909. Its passenger windows had been modified to the form shown in Diagram H, but at this stage it had not had the modification to the power unit windows and the fitting of external lids to the water pipes. COLLECTION J. N. SLINN

TABLE 21

SUMMARY: Diagrams H, J1 & J (Built on Lot 1078)

Car No.	*Built*	*First Boiler*	*First Engine*	*Tare t - c*	*New Bogie Fitted*	*Incand. Gas*	*Final Miles*	*Stopped Work*	*To Trailer No.*	*Dia.*
29	Jan 05	1047	0835	40-05	+	Aug 11	241,907	Jul 19	125	A10
30	Jan 05	1045	0832	40-12	Jul 07	Sep 13	433,034	Feb 35	Condemned	
31	Dec 04	1038	0827	40-08	Mar 06	Mar 13	289,683	Aug 21	129	A10
32	Dec 04	1039	0828	40-06	+	Apr 14	242,863	Jun 17	128	A10
33	Dec 04	1044	0830	39-14	+	Jul 11	293,639	Apr 19	130	A10
34	Jan 05	1043	0832	38-11	+	Feb 13	241,180	Jan 21	131	A10
35	Dec 04	1040	0829	40-02	Feb 09	Mar 14	266,758	Oct 18	132	A10
36	Dec 04	1042	0831	41-04	+	Oct 12	251,275	Jun 17	133	A10

NOTES

Steam heat from new. 8 ft volute bogie replaced by 8 ft coil spring bogie.

No.30: had engines with 4ft drivers from Dec 23.

No.30: 1932 photo shows Collett 7 ft trailing bogie.

No.30: Cond. Oct 1935 and broken up. One of five cars replaced by three diesel railcars.

No.31: Partitioned Nov 1905

Top right: *Car No. 30 again, at Swindon Works on 11th September 1927. It appears to have been newly painted in the first simplified livery of 1927 with the garter crest and supporters. According to the 'stoppages' register, it entered Swindon Works in June 1927 and did not emerge until January 1928, but it must have been repainted early in this visit as the garter crest and supporters were replaced by the coat of arms device. The protection bars on the inside of the front windows are visible.* H. C. CASSERLEY

Above: *The opposite side of Car No. 30 at Swindon Works, probably in 1932, newly painted in the 1930 livery with the coat of arms device on the side and double gold and black lines at the waist. According to the 'stoppages' register, it underwent a heavy repair at Swindon Works between November 1931 and March 1932. The coil spring bogies, seen in the previous photo, had been changed for Collett 7ft ones. This was the last heavy repair it received.* COLLECTION R. C. RILEY

Diagrams (L1), L: Nos.41 and 42

Diagram L covered two 59ft 6in 'Suburban' SRMs ordered on Lot 1079 on 17th August 1904, delivered in January 1905, and numbered 41 and 42. The Lot also covered the building of another 10 cars illustrated on diagrams M and N: these were 70ft long, and their story will be found in the next chapter. The Lot list gives the average cost of the Lot 1079 cars as £850 to the Loco Department and £988 0s 11d to the Carriage Department, a total of £1,838 0s 11d. The 1907–8 *Valuation of Carriage Stock Register* shows 2 cars of Lot 1079 at £1,718 each (presumably these 59½ft vehicles) and 10 at £1,862 (presumably the 70ft cars).

Car No. 41 of Diagram L1 at Winchcombe on 1st February 1905, the day the station opened. No. 41 was allocated new to Evesham on 31st January that year and remained there until June.
WINCHCOMBE RAILWAY MUSEUM

DESIGN

No.41 was used on 1st February 1905, the opening day of the service over the Toddington and Winchcombe section of the new Birmingham, Stratford & Cheltenham route, and was duly photographed several times at Winchcombe on the Honeybourne service. These photographs show it without any drop-lights in the passenger accommodation, although diagram L indicates three pairs on each side. Presumably, there was an earlier version of the diagram showing the cars as built, which had become obsolete by 1907 and was not therefore indexed. No doubt it would have become diagram L1.

Dimensionally, the Dia. L cars were very similar to those of H and J. The differences were largely accounted for by the Dia. L cars being a 'Suburban' type with no luggage compartment, whilst the H and J were 'Branch' types with a requirement to convey luggage and other items.

Two versions of the diagram exist, one of which has the width over cylinders (8ft 5in) and the rail to the lower side of the headstock (3ft 2in) measurements added to it.

The principal dimensions were:

Length over mouldings:	59ft 6in
Width:	9ft 0in
Height: Rail to roof:	12ft 2¾in
Rail to chimney top:	13ft 4½in
Headstock to boiler centre:	10ft 2⅜in
Boiler centre to bogie centre:	38ft 6in
Bogie centre to headstock:	10ft 8⅜in
Trailing bogie:	8ft volute spring
Power unit:	3ft 6½in wheels

The motor compartment was standard at 14ft 0⅛in depth, as was the driver's vestibule at 4ft 9in deep. Both had the standard window and door arrangements. There were 'Mk.2' retractable steps under the trailing vestibule doors.

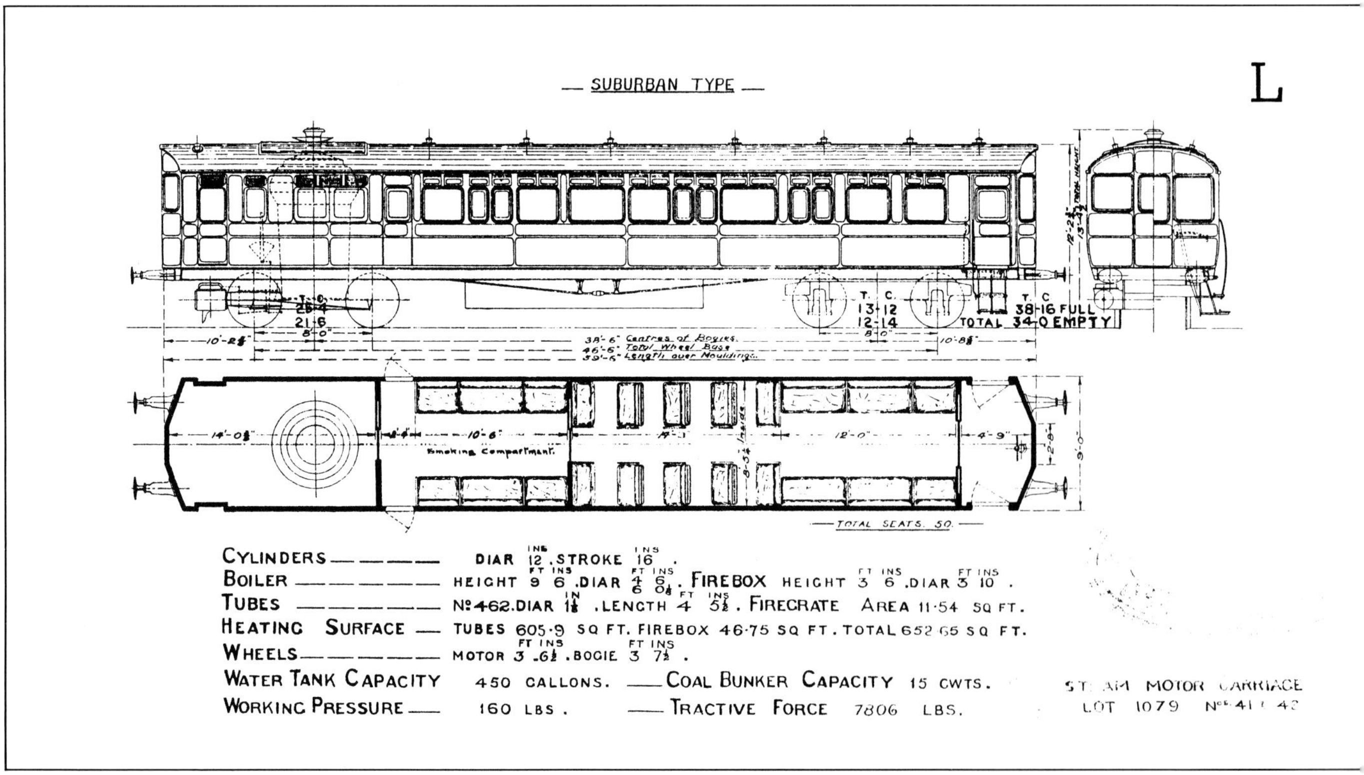

SUBURBAN TYPE
L
Smoking Compartment.
TOTAL SEATS. 50.
CYLINDERS — DIAR 12 INS. STROKE 16 INS.
BOILER — HEIGHT 9 FT 6 INS. DIAR 4 FT 6¼ INS. FIREBOX HEIGHT 3 FT 6 INS. DIAR 3 FT 10 INS.
TUBES — Nº462. DIAR 1⅛ IN. LENGTH 4 FT 5½ INS. FIREGRATE AREA 11·54 SQ FT.
HEATING SURFACE — TUBES 605·9 SQ FT. FIREBOX 46·75 SQ FT. TOTAL 652·65 SQ FT.
WHEELS — MOTOR 3 FT 6½ INS. BOGIE 3 FT 7½ INS.
WATER TANK CAPACITY 450 GALLONS. — COAL BUNKER CAPACITY 15 CWTS.
WORKING PRESSURE — 160 LBS. — TRACTIVE FORCE 7806 LBS.
LOT 1079

Passenger accommodation is shown as divided into smoking and a non-smoking compartments, but this may not have been original; presumably, this was a modification which both cars had received by the time the diagram index was set up.

Starting from the motor compartment end, there was a passenger vestibule across the coach with hinged doors opening outwards in the body sides. This was 2ft 4in deep, and had a sliding door to the power compartment, whilst on the rear side it was open to the smoking compartment, which was 10ft 6in deep, with longitudinal seating. Originally, there were three large, fixed windows each side to the smoking saloon, but the diagram shows the centre one replaced by a pair of droplights.

A partition with a sliding door between the smoking and non-smoking compartments is shown on the diagram. The non-smoking compartment was divided into two areas: a 14ft 3in length with five sets of walkover seats, and a 12ft length of longitudinal seats. Originally, the walkover seat section had four fixed windows, the outer pair being wider than the two in the middle. The diagram shows the smaller window nearer the trailing end to have been replaced by droplights. To the rear, the longitudinal seating section originally had three 'squarish' fixed lights with distinct panels between them, although that nearest to the walkover seats was also later replaced by a pair of droplights.

These cars had the usual underframes with cast queenposts and circular section steel for the trusses, with a central turnbuckle to allow adjustment to be made.

The Lot Book gives the tare weight of these cars as 35 tons 17 cwt empty, and 38 tons 16 cwt full. Diagram L shows:

	Empty *Tons – Cwt*	*Full* *Tons – Cwt*
Power Bogie	21 – 6	25 – 4
Trailing Bogie	12 – 14	13 – 12
Total	34 – 0	38 – 16

The register gives the weight of No.41 as 39 tons 15 cwt, and No.42 as 40 tons 3 cwt.

MODIFICATIONS & DISPOSAL

No.42 had its rail-chimney height reduced to 13ft in 1905 for use on the Brynamman branch in South Wales; according to R.A. Cooke in his *Atlas of the Great Western Railway*, this line was known as the 'Garnant' branch. No.31 also had its chimney height reduced for use on this line at the same time. It is possible that special chimneys were made for cars used on this branch, and that they were removed when the SRM was due to move to another shed. No.42 was specifically allocated to Brynamman only from February to April 1905, when it was 're-allocated' to Garnant, but was perhaps still used on the Brynamman branch for a while. By 1911, the Brynamman branch was worked by engines and 4- or 6-wheel stock, though the adjacent Gwaun-Cae-Gurwen branch had a motor specified, working from Garnant. Meanwhile, No. 42 was transferred to Neath in May, and Whitland in June 1905, so it may have lost its short chimney in May 1905.

The volute trailing bogies on these cars were replaced by coil spring units, but the date is not recorded.

Incandescent gas lighting replaced the original flat flame version in 1912/13. No doubt the other common modifications took place also, but no photographs have come to light to confirm them.

In June 1919, No.42 entered Swindon Works with a recorded mileage of 282,859. After attention and the fitting of electric lighting, it was sold in July 1920 to Mr R. O. Graham for the Port of London Authority. According to the RCTS *History of GWR Locomotives*, it remained in service on the PLA's Millwall Extension Railway until the passenger service over that line was withdrawn in 1926. It was then sold to T. W. Ward & Co. in 1927, who advertised it for sale in August 1928, but finding no buyers it was broken up on the Glanfield siding at the end of that year.

No.41 was stopped for conversion to a trailer on 5th January 1928 with a recorded mileage of 320,261; it reappeared in June 1928 as trailer No.147 of Dia. A24. This trailer had Collett 7ft bogies, so it is possible that the trailing bogie of SRM No.41 was changed to this type, although there is no record of it being carried out.

In use, these two cars wandered over much of the GWR system.

TABLE 22

SUMMARY: Diagram L (Built on Lot 1079)

Car No.	*Built*	*First Boiler*	*First Engine*	*Tare t - c*	*Incand. Gas*	*Final Miles*	*Stopped Work*	*To Trailer No.*	*Dia.*
41	Jan 05	1048	0836	39-15	Oct 13	320,261	Jan 28	147	A24
42	Jan 05	1049	0834	40-03	Oct 12	282,859	Jun 19	Sold	-

NOTES

8 ft volute bogies replaced by 8 ft coil spring bogie at unrecorded dates.

No.42: Sold to Mr Graham for the PLA.

This photograph shows Car No. 41 at Winchcombe again, probably on 1st February 1905. The lettering above the droplight of the nearest door reads 'WAY OUT'. COLLECTION R. C. RILEY

Q

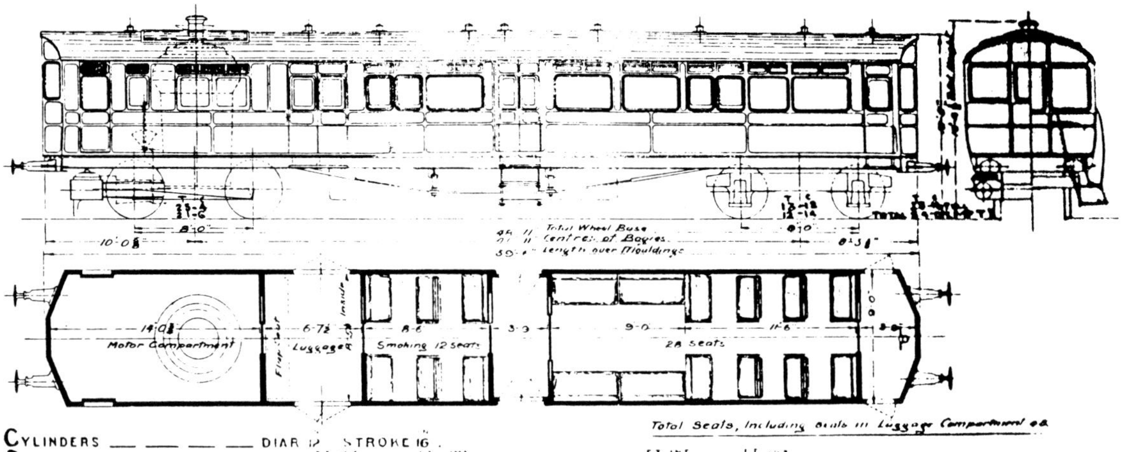

CYLINDERS — DIAR 12 . STROKE 16 .
BOILER — HEIGHT 9 6 . DIAR 4 6 . FIREBOX HEIGHT 3 5⅞ . DIAR 3 10 .
TUBES — N° 420 . DIAR 1¼ . LENGTH 4 5½ . FIRECRATE AREA 11·54 SQ FT.
HEATING SURFACE — TUBES 612·78 SQ FT. FIREBOX 46·46 SQ FT. TOTAL 659·24 SQ FT.
WHEELS — MOTOR 4 0 . BOGIE 3 7½ .
WATER TANK CAPACITY 450 GALLONS. — COAL BUNKER CAPACITY 15 CWTS.
WORKING PRESSURE — 160 LBS. — TRACTIVE FORCE 6912 LBS

STEAM MOTOR CARRIAGE
LOT 1101 N° 73 TO 80

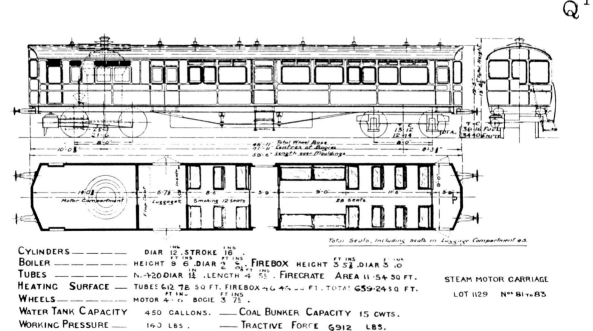

Q[1]

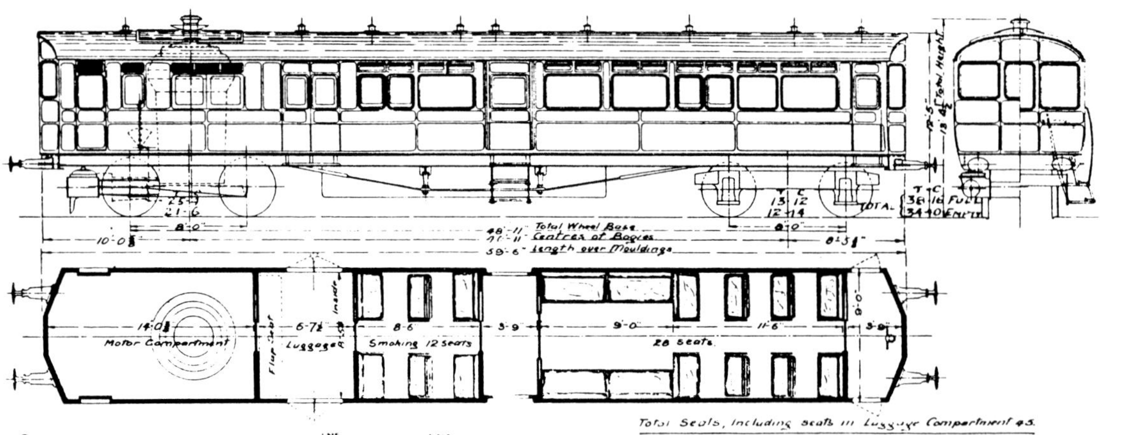

CYLINDERS — DIAR 12 . STROKE 16 .
BOILER — HEIGHT 9 6 . DIAR 4 6 . FIREBOX HEIGHT 3 5⅞ . DIAR 3 10
TUBES — No 420 DIAR 1¼ . LENGTH 4 5½ . FIRECRATE AREA 11·54 SQ FT.
HEATING SURFACE — TUBES 612·78 SQ FT. FIREBOX 46·46 SQ FT. TOTAL 659·24 SQ FT.
WHEELS — MOTOR 4 0 BOGIE 3 7½ .
WATER TANK CAPACITY 450 GALLONS. — COAL BUNKER CAPACITY 15 CWTS.
WORKING PRESSURE — 160 LBS . — TRACTIVE FORCE 6912 LBS.

STEAM MOTOR CARRIAGE
LOT 1129 Nos 81 to 83

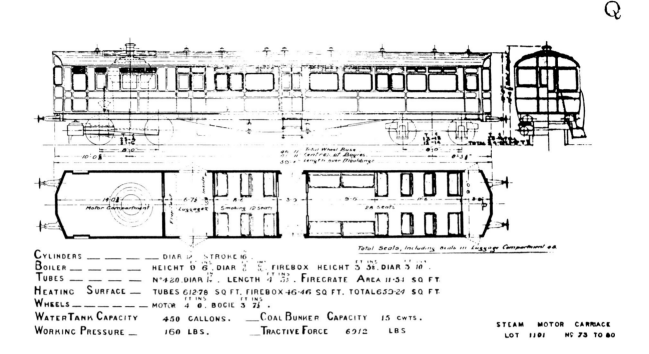

Diagram Q: Nos.73 to 80 & Diagram Q1: Nos. 81 to 83

Car No. 75 of Diagram Q. This is the Gloucester RC&W Co's official photograph of the car, as built, at their works. The wheels and underframe had been painted white with rivets and straps picked out in black for the occasion, and it is possible that the body colour below the waist was a photographic grey. Notice the 'prize monogram'. The boiler and water filler can be seen through the two large-pane windows to the power compartment.
COLLECTION R. C. RILEY

These SRMs were the last of the 'short' branch designs, and were almost identical. The cars covered by diagram Q, with double passenger doors, were built by the Gloucester Carriage & Wagon Co., whilst those on diagram Q1, Nos.81–83, with single passenger doors, were built at Swindon. Unlike earlier types, the Dia. Q SRMs were *not* a subsequent modification of the Q1 cars. The Gloucester-built cars were ordered on Lot 1101 on 27th June 1905 at an average cost of £2,574 11s 2d, and were delivered to Swindon between February and June 1906. The Swindon-built examples were ordered on Lot 1129 on 24th November 1905, and appeared in May 1907, at an average cost of £2,067 18s 4d each.

DESIGN

Two versions of diagram Q exist, both Locomotive Department diagrams, one rubber stamped '27 FEB 1917' with the width over cylinders (8ft 5in) and the height to the bottom of the headstocks/solebars marked (3ft 2¼in), the other without those dimensions. Two Locomotive Department versions of diagram Q1 also exist with the same differences between them. There is also a Carriage Department version of diagram Q which indicates differences between the seating capacity of the cars.

All the diagrams show the cars fitted with 8ft volute spring trailing bogies, although photographs and the register indicate that the Dia. Q cars actually had 8ft bolster bogies with conventional 4ft 6in leaf bearing springs, while Nos.81–83 had 'American' bogies – presumably again 8ft; the photographs I have seen are not clear enough to be absolutely certain on this point. Assuming they were original equipment, this was the first use of the 8ft 'American' bogie.

The principal dimensions of the cars of both diagrams were:

Length over mouldings:	59ft 6in
Width:	9ft 0in
Height: Rail to roof:	12ft 5in
Rail to chimney top	13ft 4½in
Headstock to engine w/b centre:	10ft 0⅝in
Engine w/b centre to bogie centre:	40ft 11in
Bogie centre to headstock:	8ft 5⅝in
Power unit diameter wheels:	4ft 0in

These cars were the only 'short' designs to be built with engines having 4ft 0in wheels.

The motor compartment had the usual deep waist panel and correspondingly shorter windows from new, and was 14ft 0⅜in from front to rear. The sides contained the usual sliding external doors, a single droplight, and two sliding windows giving access to the water filler, these sliding windows had the customary three ventilators above. Both Q and Q1 diagrams show a vertical moulding dividing the waist and bottom panel of the bodyside, directly below the mid point of these sliding windows. In fact, they were built with two of these mouldings, one below each end of these windows; in later years, these were usually removed, but careful study of photographs does sometimes show corresponding joints in the panelling. Internally, the motor compartment had a sliding door to the luggage compartment.

Once more, the luggage compartment, which measured 6ft 7½in between partitions, had a drop-down seat which extended across the compartment against the motor compartment partition; this seems to have seated five passengers. The Carriage Department version of diagram Q has a note that Nos.76–78 had 45 seats, while the remainder had 48, although the Loco. Department version of both Q and Q1 gives the seating capacity of all these cars as 45. If the higher figure is correct, then at some time Nos.73–75, 79 and 80 must have had three additional seats fitted in the luggage compartment. Again, what *may* have occurred is that the original seat was replaced by a pair, on either side of the motor compartment door, each accommodating two persons, whilst another pair of seats were fitted to the smoking compartment partition, facing the first pair. This would have left all the doorways unobstructed. All these seats would have been of the 'drop-down' type, folding up against the partition. The luggage compartment also had external double doors which opened outwards, and an internal sliding door to the smoking saloon.

The smoking saloon was 8ft 6in between partitions, and seated twelve in 2+2 seating: four seats fixed against the partitions, with two walkover seats between them. This compart-

Car No. 74 of Diagram Q is seen here near Wolvercote working the 2.50 p.m. Blenheim–Oxford with gas reservoir truck No. 10 in tow. A copy of the photograph bears the date 13th June 1910 but at that date the car was allocated to Frome. 13th June 1912 is perhaps more likely as the car was then allocated to Oxford. It appears to have been in the 1912 lake livery with a central 'GWR' in the waist panel.
KEN NUNN COLL'N, CTY. LCGB

Car No. 76 at Barmouth in lake livery. It was allocated to the area for much of 1924-6.
COLLECTION R. S. CARPENTER

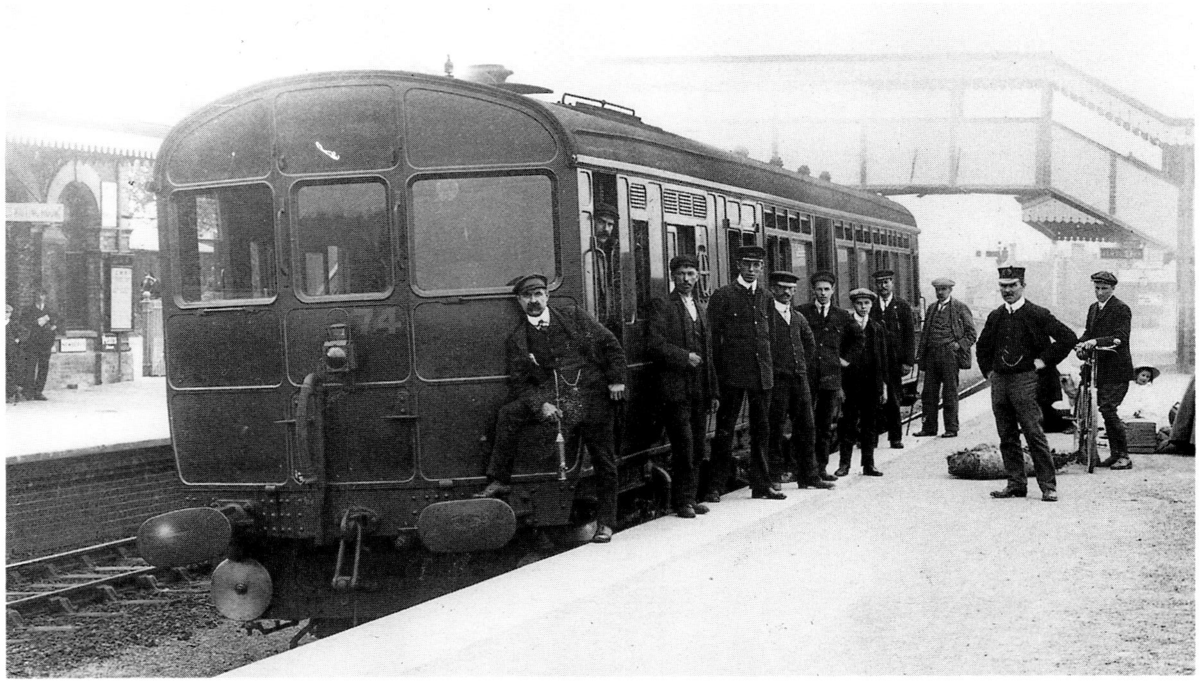

An earlier view of Car No. 74 which was at Frome in 1909-11. It is seen here at Hungerford, presumably during this time, and therefore in the 1908 lined brown livery.
LENS OF SUTTON

ment had a second internal sliding door at the rear, to the vestibule.

A difference between the two designs was apparent at this point: the vestibule, which was 3ft 9in wide between partitions, had double inward-opening doors on the Gloucester-built cars, and single doors in the Swindon-built vehicles. Below these doors were 'Mk 2' retractable steps.

The non-smoking compartment was 20ft 6in long between partitions, and seated 28: twelve on 9ft long longitudinal seats either side of the car, and sixteen on 4 pairs of fixed and walkover seats. This compartment had a sliding door at each end.

Beyond this saloon was the driving compartment, which was a maximum of 3ft 9in deep. It had side-hinged doors that opened outwards, hinged on the bodyside, not the corner pillar.

The smoking compartment had a pair of droplights (next to the luggage compartment) and a single large, fixed light on each side. The non-smoking compartment had two large, fixed lights by the bench seats, then two droplights, and finally two more fixed lights, that next to the droplights being narrower than the others. The Carriage Department version of diagram Q shows the larger, fixed lights to be 3ft 8in wide, and the smaller one 2ft 6¼in. Both types were 2ft 1in high.

On the diagrams for these cars, the underframe as shown does not correspond in some respects to photographs. The underframes had Churchward-type flat trussing with adjustable queenposts (those with nuts on the lower ends, trapping the truss rods), and were the only 'short' railmotors with this type of underframe. On the diagrams, the queenposts are shown as being quite short, and suspended from cross 'H' beams below the solebars. Photographs, however, show the queenposts to be longer, and apparently attached to the underside (or underside and back) of the solebars.

The queen posts were 9ft 6in apart, which is rather more than indicated on the diagrams. The flat truss rod is shown on diagrams Q and Q1 as being twisted from the vertical through 90° near the solebars; according to the diagrams, the twist is shown at a similar distance from the solebars at both ends, but photographs show this twist much nearer the solebar at the trailing bogie end than at the motor unit.

Both brake cylinders were on the same side of the car (the gas cylinders were on the other), and the outer of the 'V' hangers associated with each was positioned outside the truss rod. The 'V' hanger at the motor end had a pronounced joggle to accommodate the truss rod, whilst the other appeared to be almost straight (the truss rod being much lower at this point).

These cars were built with incandescent gas lighting and steam heating. Photographs also show them to have had sanding apparatus from new, applied to the power bogie.

Car No. 73 at Exeter, probably in 1932. COLLECTION G. CARPENTER

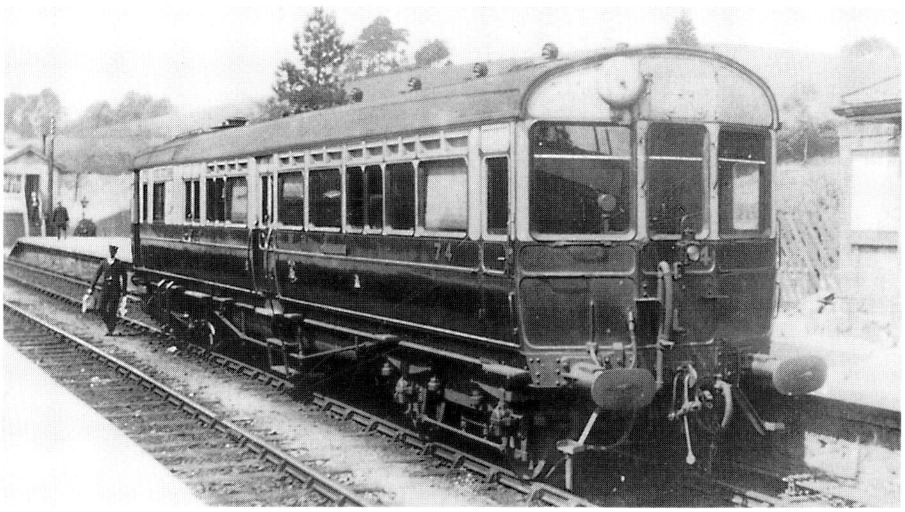

Car No. 74, apparently recently repainted in the 1924 lined livery, was allocated to Exeter during 1925 and 1926. It had been fitted with a gong, but no communication cord apparatus. It has also had the white horizontal line painted across the end windows. G. N. SOUTHERDEN

Car No. 76 of Diagram Q, seen at Swindon in 1931, had been fitted with a warning gong and communication alarm apparatus. Note also the cable for connecting the bell circuits on a trailer attached to this end of the car. HILLSIDE PUBLISHING

Car No. 75 of Diagram Q at Southall on 9th May 1931 is seen in the 1930 livery with the twin shields device and the upper and lower waist gold and black lines. The front window protection bars can be seen, as can a dark-coloured extension to the coal bunker. Although some of the large saloon windows had 'SMOKING' signs, the small saloon seems not to have had 'No Smoking' ones. Car No. 75 was at Southall from August 1930 until October 1931.
W. POTTER

Car No. 77 of Diagram Q at Swindon stock shed, probably between August and October 1931. It is seen in the 1930 double waist lines livery with the twin shields crest. The windscreen wiper pivot had evidently been mounted through a hole in the window glass rather than the bolection moulding. COLLECTION R. C. RILEY

According to the diagrams, the weights of these cars were:

	Empty *Tons – Cwt*	*Full* *Tons – Cwt*
Power Bogie	21 – 6	25 – 4
Trailing Bogie	12 – 14	13 – 12
Total	34 – 0	38 – 16

which is exactly the same as for other 'short' wood-panelled cars. The Lot list gives the average tare weight for Nos.73–80 as 40 tons 16 cwt 3 qtrs, and the Swindon-built cars Nos.81–83 as 41 tons 10 cwt 2 qtrs. The tare weights recorded in the register vary from 40 tons 18cwt (No.75) to 42 tons 13 cwt (No.78).

The Gloucester-built cars seem to have appeared with the 'prize monogram', although it is possible that Nos.78–80 appeared with the garter device with supporters. It is probable, but also not photographically confirmed, that Nos.81–83 had the garter device when new.

MODIFICATIONS & DISPOSAL

These cars had relatively few alterations. Initially, they were provided with a single rain strip high up on the roof, though a second was fitted to all in due course. External water filler covers were also fitted to all, and the sliding windows modified. An official photograph of No.70, dated March 1907, shows this work in progress, so it is *possible* that Nos.81–83 were built with this feature. Other changes included:

Car No. 82 of Diagram Q1 in the earlier 1927 simplified livery. The panels were not lined out, but the garter crest with supporters was present. The photograph was taken at Exeter shed. According to the allocations and stoppages registers, it was sent from Swindon to Exeter on 4th May 1925 after heavy repairs; it was then at Exeter until November 1927 when it was dispatched to Swindon Works. While at Exeter it received heavy repairs at Newton Abbot over five days in November and December 1926. So was it repainted at Swindon or Newton Abbot during its heavy repairs and returned to traffic without being lined out? Or was it repainted at Exeter?
B. Y. WILLIAMS

Car No. 78 of Diagram Q towards the end of its life as an SRM. It is seen in the 1930 livery with twin black and gold lines at the waist.
AUTHOR'S COLLECTION

1. No.74 is recorded as having Gresham Craven vacuum cylinders, but these were changed for standard GWR 22-inch types in September 1912.
2. Protection bars seem to have been fitted in 1912–13.
3. Some cars are recorded as having dry sandboxes fitted – presumably replacements.
4. No. 80 was given new steps in October 1926.
5. The smoking and non-smoking compartments exchanged identity between 1928 and 1930.

Chain communication apparatus was allegedly fitted to all between 1928 and 1933, but the February 1933 date recorded for No.73 is doubtful, as it had finally stopped work by then. Nos.74 and 76 at least were fitted with it. Warning gongs were also fitted to these two cars, and may well have been fitted to the others.

Four of the cars – Nos.74, 76, 77 and 81 – were recorded as being in cream and brown livery with gold lines; see the summary table. No.78 had been painted thus by June 1933.

These were amongst the longest-lasting SRMs: all were condemned during 1933–35, and, except for Nos.77 and 80, all were converted to Dia. A31 trailers. Cars Nos.77 and 80 were scrapped – No.77 was one of five replaced by three diesel rail cars. Nos.73, 74, 82 and 83 were officially condemned in 1933 and 'recovered parts' used in the trailers shown.

Car No. 80 at Christow on the Teign Valley line, hauling a clerestory coach, probably an all-third. This car was at Exeter from May 1933 until March 1934. G. N. SOUTHERDEN

TABLE 23

SUMMARY: Diagrams Q, Q1 (Built on Lots 1101 & 1129)

Car No.	*To Stock/ Built*	*First Boiler*	*First Engine*	*Tare t - c*	*Dry Sand*	*Chain Comm.*	*Smoking Compts. Reversed*	*Cream, Brown & Gold Lines*	*Final Miles*	*Stopped Work*	*To Trailer No.*	*Dia.*
Built on Lot 1101 by the Gloucester Carriage & Wagon Co.: Dia. Q												
73	Apr 06	1065	0878	41-02		Feb 33	Apr 29		425,868	Jun 33	202	A31
74	Apr 06	1086	0879	41-06		Oct 28	Nov 28	Feb 31	364,555	Jun 33	203	A31
75	May 06	1087	0880	40-18		Aug 30	Aug 30		250,365	May 34	207	A31
76	Apr 06	1088	0881	41-05		Nov 28	Feb 29	May 31	409,636	Oct 34	219	A31
77	Apr 06	1089	0882	41-14		Jun 29	Jun 29	Mar 31	399,403	Oct 34	Condemned	
78	Jun 06	1090	0883	42-13		Feb 33	Jun 28		354,245	Feb 34	208	A31
79	Jun 06	1091	0884	41-16	Aug 27	Feb 33	Mar 30		370,148	Apr 34	209	A31
80	Jun 06	1092	0885	42-06	May 28	Aug 30	Aug 30		346,667	Dec 34	Condemned	
Built on Lot 1129 by GWR, Swindon: Dia. Q1												
81	May 07	1083	0890	41-17		Sep 30	Oct 30	Sep 30	483,549	Oct 34	211	A31
82	May 07	1042	0889	42-12	Aug 13	Dec 28	Jun 29		464,795	Mar 33	204	A31
83	May 07	1076	0876	41-07		Mar 29	Apr 29		339,463	Jul 33	205	A31

NOTES

Nos.73-75 may have been delivered in Feb-Mar 06, but not completed. To stock dates shown.

Nos.73, 74, 82 and 83: Officially condemned and recovered parts used in the trailers shown.

No.77: Condemned in Jan 35 and broken up. One of five cars replaced by three diesel rail cars.

No.80: Protection bars fitted, Nov 12. Condemned in Oct 35 and broken up.

No.81: Protection bars fitted, Mar 13.

CHAPTER NINE

THE 70FT WOOD PANELLED CARS

Diagrams K1, K: Nos. 37 to 40

Car No. 38 of Diagram K at Dawlish station. From the registers, it appears that No. 38 was in this area for much of the time between mid-1906 and the end of 1908, and this picture was probably taken during this period. The car had already been fitted with droplights in place of three of the fixed windows. It had also been fitted with a bell cable and connector for use when coupled to a trailer. CHAPMAN & CO.

These four 70ft 'Branch' SRMs were the first examples of that length, and were contemporary with the first 70ft trailers. They were built as part of Lot 1078 together with 59½ft SRMs Nos.29–36 (see Diagrams H and J in Chapter 6) and were delivered between February and April 1905. No.39 is recorded as having its power unit constructed on Locomotive Department Lot 231, and it is possible that the others were also. The 1907–8 *Valuation of Coaching Stock* indicates that the cost of these cars was £1,860 each.

SRMs Nos. 37 to 40 were in the wood panelled style, as were all the GWR 70ft SRMs, and were covered by two diagrams, 'K1' and 'K'.

DESIGN

The motor compartment was the standard 14ft 0⅜in long with the usual three end windows; diagram K1 shows them as having the smaller type of end window with the wide waist panel underneath it. There was the usual external sliding door each side, and the design then followed the normal arrangement for wood panelled SRMs of a panel, a droplight with ventilator over, another panel, and twin sliding windows with three ventilators above.

Next was the luggage compartment, which measured 6ft 3½in between partitions with drop-down seats on the power compartment partition. There were double external doors, opening outwards, and sliding doors to both the main passenger saloon and the motor compartment.

As built, the passenger saloon seating was divided into three:

1. Longitudinal bench seating, 10ft 6in length, at the luggage compartment end. When the saloons were partitioned, this became the 'smoking' accommodation. Originally, the compartment had three fixed lights each side (Dia. K1), but the middle windows were replaced by pairs of droplights (Dia. K).
2. A 20ft 9½in length of seven sets of walkover seats, reduced to 20ft 5in when the saloon was partitioned, according to diagram K. This length originally had seven large fixed lights, and again those in the centre were replaced by double droplights.
3. A 12ft length of longitudinal bench seats. These originally had three fixed lights (Dia. K1); the one furthest from the driver's vestibule each side was changed to a pair of droplights (Dia. K).

The trailing end driving vestibule was 4ft 9in deep (maximum), and provided the main passenger access to the car. It had flat, slightly recessed doors which opened inwards, hinged on the end pillars. These doors were about 2ft 8in wide, and had 'Mk II' retractable steps below. This compartment had the usual full-height end windows with the standard depth waist panel below.

End steps each side of the vacuum pipe were fitted from new.

The underframe was conventional for a 70ft coach, except for the usual modifications at the power unit end. A noteworthy feature were the trusses of the adjustable queenpost type with flat section truss rods, whilst the queenposts had 'H' section cross beams above them, below the solebars, etc. The usual 480-gallon water tank was carried, positioned about the mid-point of the SRM.

On these SRMs, the wheelbase was 57ft 2in. The distance from the front of the vehicle to the mid point of the motor bogie wheelbase measured 10ft 0⅝in, whilst that from the centre of the trailing bogie to the headstock was 11ft 2⅝in. The trailing bogie was of the 9ft volute spring type. The power unit had 4ft diameter wheels, and was of 8ft wheelbase.

Recorded weights in the diagrams were:

	Empty	*Full*
	Tons – Cwt	*Tons – Cwt*
Power Bogie	23 – 0	26 – 18
Trailing Bogie	15 – 7	16 – 5
Total	38 – 7	43 – 3

The total on the Lot List was 40 tons 5 cwt 2 qtr empty, and 43 tons 4 cwt 2 qtr full.

In the register, 'full' weights vary between 45 tons 17 cwt and 43 tons 5 cwt. In some cases, a record of re-weighing was also recorded in the register: e.g. the initial weight recorded for No.39 was 44 tons 6 cwt, but in July 1907 it was re-weighed and found to be 43 tons 5 cwt gross, including the following:

Water: 480 galls = 2 tons 3 cwt (this presumably included some in the boiler).
Coal: 1 ton 2 cwt (presumably included coal in the firebox – the coal bunker is recorded on the diagrams as having 15 cwt capacity).
Sand: 2 cwt.

These items total 3 tons 7 cwt, thus leaving an empty weight of 39 tons 18 cwt. In May 1915 No.39 was weighed again, and 44 tons 16 cwt was recorded. No.40 varied between 43 tons 14 cwt, 44 tons 8 cwt, 40 tons 0 cwt, and 44 tons 18 cwt (at June 1923).

MODIFICATIONS & DISPOSAL

Early modifications included partitioning of the passenger saloon and the fitting of droplights. No dates for these survive in the register, except for No.39, which had two droplights fitted each side in June 1905. No.38 also had the droplights when photographed in the early two-colour livery in about 1908. The existence of diagram K1 indicates that No.37 had probably not been altered by about 1907, when the index was set up.

No.39 is recorded as fitted with two extra lamps to illuminate destination boards, although quite how this was done I do not know. It was also fitted with a 'speaking tube' at the same time, June 1905, presumably between

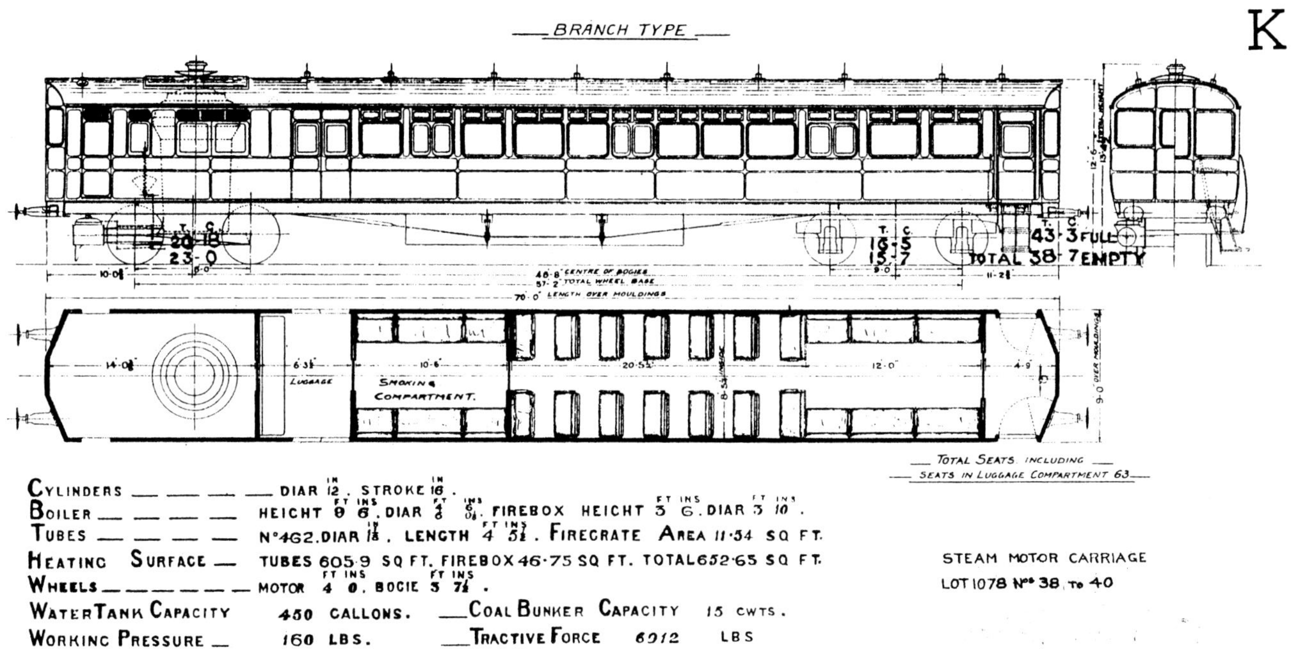

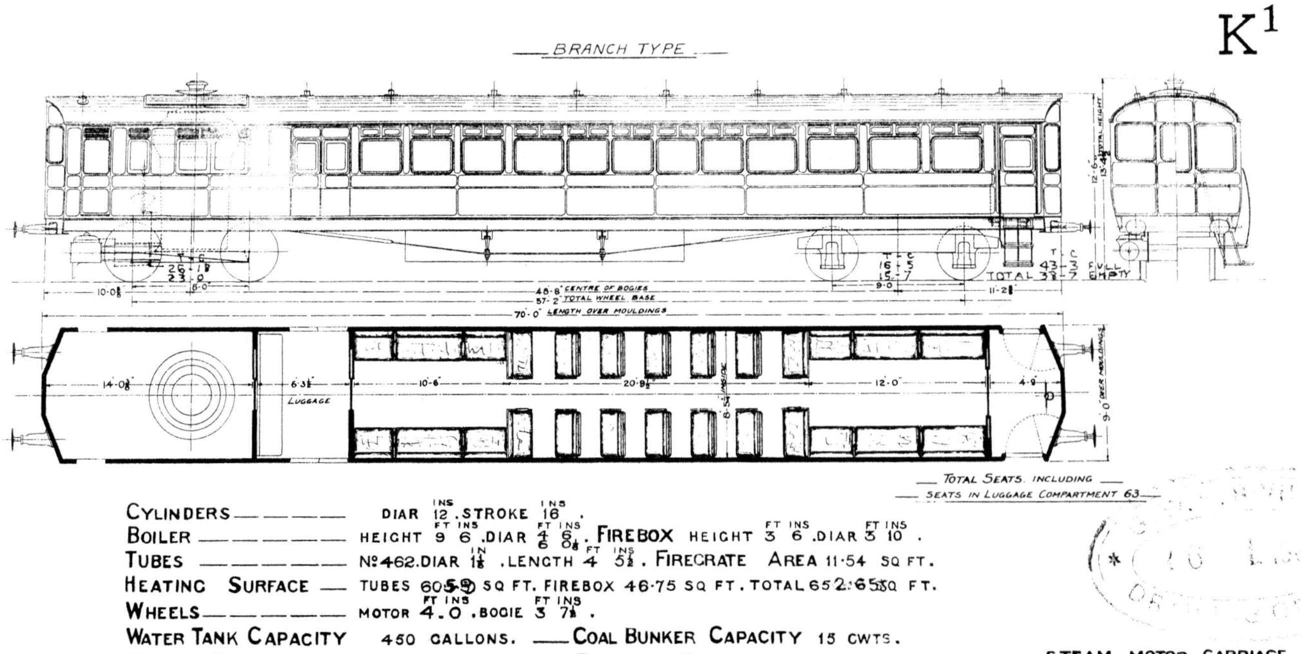

the driving vestibule and the power compartment.

The volute spring trailing bogies were changed at an early date, though the only example known was No.37 in June 1907. There is no record of this being done in the case of No.39, but I think it would have been.

No.39 was apparently built with incandescent gas lighting, whilst the others had flat flame burners; these were changed for the incandescent type between 1909 and 1913.

The usual modifications were made to the motor unit sliding windows, and water filler caps were fitted in new panels adjacent to the reduced-size sliding windows.

In March 1913, No.39 received protection bars, as no doubt did the others.

The coil spring bogies were usually replaced during the 1920s, and No.40 is recorded in the register as being fitted with a 9ft 'American' trailing bogie in 1923. The other three may well have had their trailing bogies changed too, probably for the 9ft 'American' design, but possibly for the Collett 7ft unit. Trailer No.146, converted from SRM No.38, did have Collett 7ft bogies.

No.38 was the first of the cars to be altered to a trailer; this stopped work in July 1927, and re-appeared as trailer No.146 of Dia. A23 in May 1928. Because of the entries relating to diesel railcar No.37 in the register, we do not have details of alterations to SRM No.37, but it would have received the chain communication

Car No. 38 in a single-colour livery, possibly lake or even the khaki brown said to have been used during the Great War. No. 38 was allocated to Gloucester, Cheltenham and Chalford between October 1915 and June 1917, and this photograph may date from that period.
G. H. W. CLIFFORD
CTY. R. C. RILEY

Car No. 38 at Brentford. It appears to have been in the 1908 lined brown livery as 'GWR' is just visible close to the number on the side of the car. There is no sign of any protection bars for the front windows, although the sliding windows to the power compartment had been modified and there was a water filler lid with a cross on the side of the car. It was allocated to Southall during 1910-11.

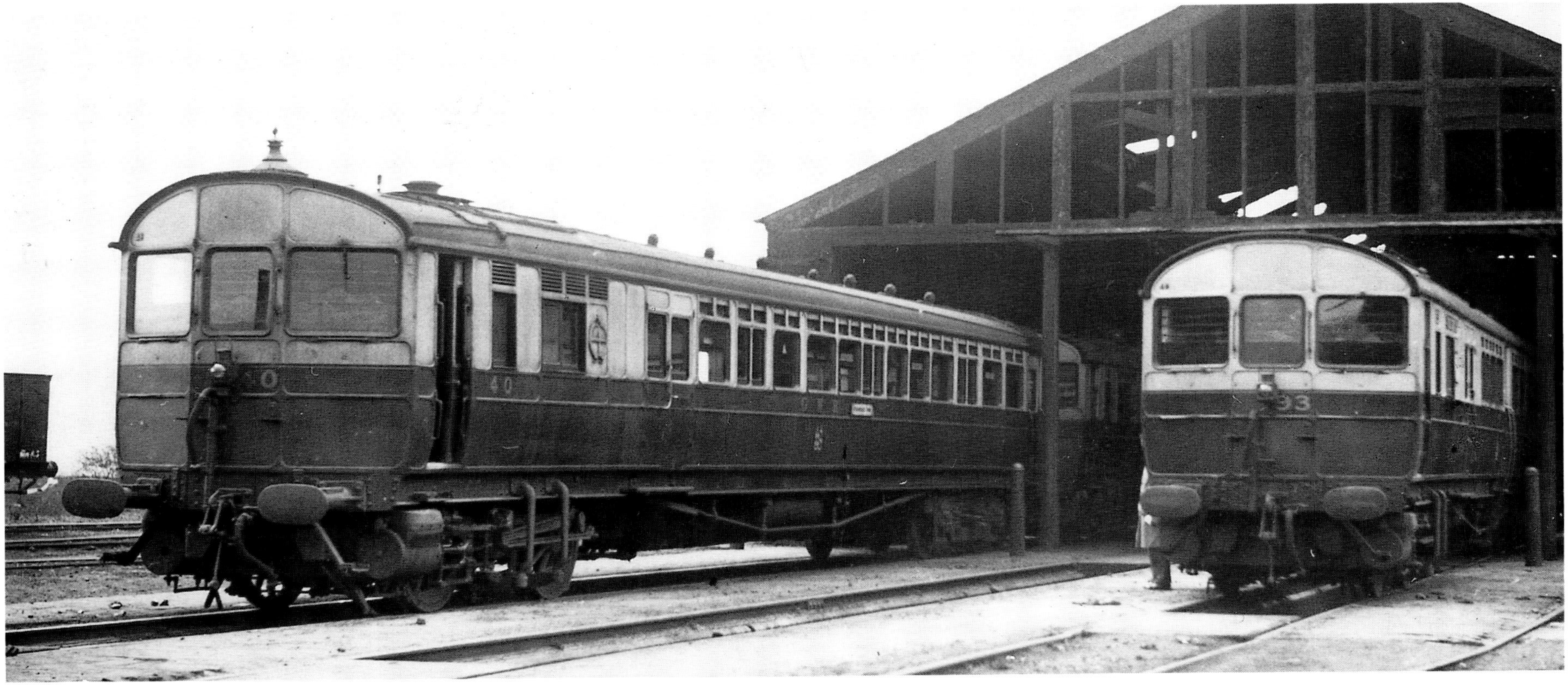

This photograph shows Car No. 40 of Diagram K and Car No. 93 of Diagram R at Stourbridge shed on 24th April 1932. No. 40 spent most of the time between 1926 and 1932 at Stourbridge, while No. 93 was there from 1931 until 1934. Both cars are seen in the 1929 livery with the single gold/black line at the waist, and their weight recorded in cast figures above the left-hand front window. Protection bars and an upwards extension of the bunker (also to protect these windows) are evident on both cars. The side destination board appears to read 'STOURBRIDGE TOWN'.
W. POTTER, CTY. R. C. RILEY

A closer view of Car No. 40 at Stourbridge on 24th April 1932.
H. C. CASSERLEY

alarm system, and the large saloon made into the smoking accommodation. Dates for these do survive in the cases of Nos.39 and 40.

SRMs Nos.39 and 40 stopped work in 1933, and were converted to Dia. A23 trailers Nos.197 and 198. Presumably for accounting reasons in the case of No.39, this was recorded as 'Recovered parts' to be used in trailer No.197.

Car No.37 survived until October 1935, when it was condemned and scrapped.

When new, the cars were widely scattered about the system: No.37 went to Stourbridge and then to Kidderminster; No.38 was initially allocated to Weymouth and went to Trowbridge the following month; No.39 went new to Laira and No.40 to Croes Newydd.

DRAWINGS

Diagram K1 shows the SRMs as built, although its legend only refers to No.37. This shows the windows as all large fixed ones with the usual twin toplights above, and the passenger saloon in a single, unpartitioned state.

Diagram K refers to Nos.37 to 40, and shows the passenger saloon divided into a small smoking compartment and a large non-smoking one, and three of the large fixed windows being replaced with pairs of droplights.

TABLE 24

SUMMARY: Diagrams K1, K (Built on Lot 1078)

Car No.	*Built*	*First Boiler*	*First Engine*	*Tare t - c*	*New Bogie*	*Incand. Gas*	*Chain Comm.*	*Smoking Compts. Reversed*	*Final Miles*	*Stopped Work*	*To Trailer No.*	*Dia.*
37	Feb 05	1056	0844	45-00	Jun 07	Oct 12			513.052	May 35	Condemned	
38	Mar 05	1059	0848	45-17	+	Dec 09			453.689	Jul 27	146	A23
39	Apr 05	1060	0849	44-06	+	+	Feb 33	Jan 28	537.101	Jun 33	197	A23
40	Mar 05	1058	0847	43-14	+	Jun 13	Sep 30	Sep 30	539.980	Dec 32	198	A23

NOTES

Steam heat from new. 9 ft Volute spring bogie changed to 9 ft coil spring bogie.

No.37: Condemned in Oct 35 and broken up.

No.39: Fitted with a speaking tube. Jun 05. Fitted with 2 extra lamps to show destination boards.

No.39: Protection bars fitted. Mar 13. Officially condemned and recovered parts used for trailer 197.

No.40: Also fitted with 9 ft American bogie. Apr 22. Condemned in Mar 33 - then converted to trailer.

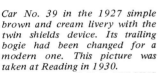

Car No. 39 in the 1927 simple brown and cream livery with the twin shields device. Its trailing bogie had been changed for a modern one. This picture was taken at Reading in 1930.
S. H. P. HIGGINS

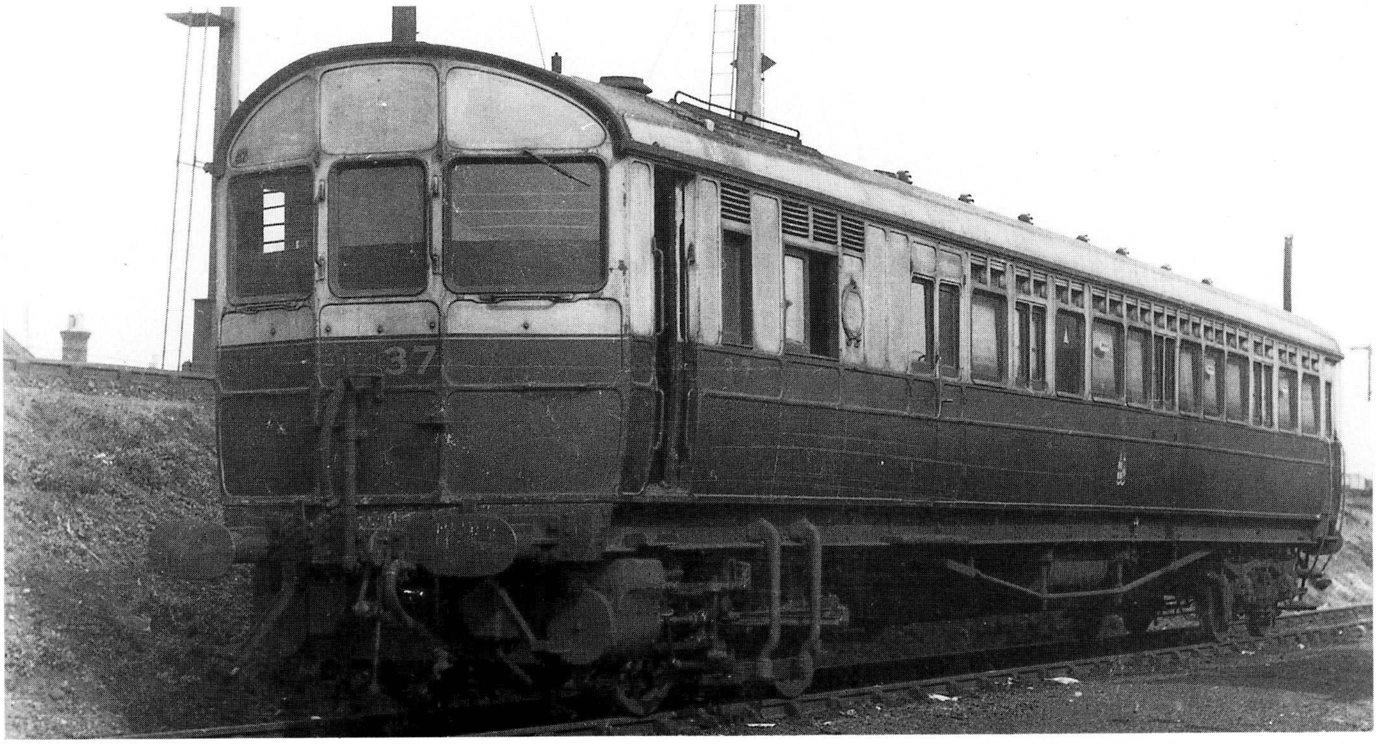

In this view, Car No. 37 of Diagram K is seen in the simple brown and cream livery with a single gold and black line at the waist introduced late in 1929. Again the protection bars to the front windows can be seen, as can the internal strip also protecting these windows, which seems to have been painted black. The water filler lid was of the plain variety. The trailing bogie had been changed to one with leaf springs, possibly a Collett 7ft one. For some reason the roof seems to have been cleaned as far up as the rain strip; perhaps this was as far as the carriage cleaners could reach. No. 37 emerged from Swindon in September 1932 after repairs and was allocated to Reading until the end of 1934. This photograph is believed to have been taken at Reading during this period.
AUTHOR'S COLLECTION

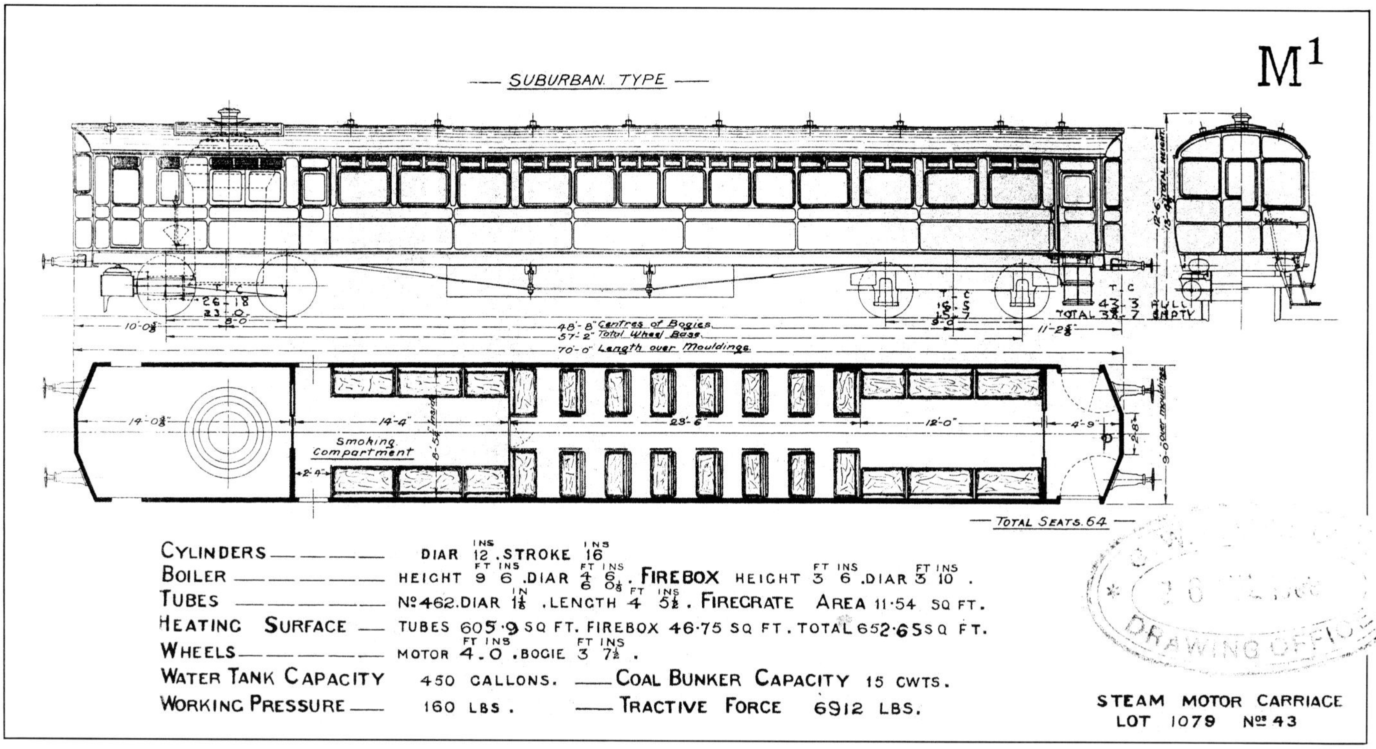

This is the interior of Car No. 43 of Diagram M1, as built (i.e. before droplights had been fitted). Note the slatted wood floor, the dark stained woodwork, the longitudinal seats in the foreground with wooden arm rests and turned legs, the 'walkover' seats beyond the longitudinal seats, the blinds rolled up above the windows, the tubes from which the straps hung (the whistle cord passed through one), the gas lights and the ventilators between the brackets hanging from the roof. The toplights could be opened by pulling on knobs on their frame above the droplight. The notice above the double doors reads 'PASSENGERS ARE REQUESTED NOT TO SMOKE OR SPIT IN THIS CAR'.

NATIONAL RAILWAY MUSEUM

Diagrams M1, M, N: Nos.43 to 52

Car No. 44 of Diagram M at Dawlish Warren Halt. The car is seen in as-built condition, apparently with only a high-level rain strip on the roof. No. 44 was allocated to Exeter from July 1905, possibly until March 1906. B. CHAPMAN, CTY. R. C. RILEY

On 17th August 1904, Lot 1079 was issued for twelve wood panelled steam rail motors – two 59½ft and ten 70ft long. The 1907–8 *Valuation of Carriage Stock* shows two cars of Lot 1079 at £1,718 each (presumably the short ones) and ten at £1,862 (the 70ft vehicles). The long cars were numbered 43–52 and are covered by three surviving diagrams. They were 70ft long, 9ft 0in wide, 12ft 6in high from rail to roof and 13ft 4½in total. The total wheelbase was 57ft 2in, whilst the power end headstock was 10ft 0⅝in from the centre of the engine wheelbase, and the trailing headstock to the bogie's centre was 11ft 2⅜in. A 9ft trailing bogie is shown.

Car No. 45 of Diagram M entering Brent station from the Plymouth direction. Although the side windows to the passenger compartments had been modified and droplights inserted, it had not had the water filler modification or the power compartment sliding windows altered. No. 45 was allocated to Laira by March 1908 (and may have been there for some time before that) and went to Swindon in mid-1909, which serves to date the picture. P. J. T. REED, CTY. R. C. RILEY

DESIGN

The original design was illustrated on diagram M1 which shows a 70ft suburban type SRM.

The motor unit was the usual design with 4ft wheels, and the compartment housing it was 14ft 0⅝in long internally, with the standard arrangement of windows and doors.

Next to the power compartment was the smoking saloon, 14ft 4in long between partitions. It had an external door each side next to the power compartment partition, opening outwards, without retractable steps below them. When the cars were new, these doors had 'SMOKING' in the panel above the droplight. Seating comprised a 12ft length of longitudinal bench on each side. The partition between the smoking and motor compartment contained a sliding door, while that between the smoking and non-smoking compartments had a hinged door that opened into the latter.

In the non-smoking compartment there were 8 pairs of walkover seats, occupying 23ft 6in, and a 12ft length of longitudinal bench seating. The doors to the driver's vestibule at the trailing end were the double sliding type.

The driver's compartment was 4ft 9in deep (maximum), and had the usual flat, slightly recessed, internally-opening doors with retractable steps below.

Windows as shown on diagram M1 were four large, fixed lights at each end of the passenger seating (three at each end next to the longitudinal seats) and five more fixed lights, rather more closely spaced and of a smaller size, next to the central walkover seats.

The diagram has a note on it indicating that it applied to No.43, but I think it originally applied to cars Nos.44–48, and it might have applied to 49–52 as well.

Diagram M exists in two forms. The first is a revision of diagram M1, and shows three of the original fixed lights replaced by pairs of droplights (dd), so the window arrangements from the smoking compartment door became:

Fxd dd Fxd Fxd Fxd dd Fxd Fxd Fxd dd Fxd Fxd Fxd

The centre pair of droplights replaced one of the smaller-size fixed lights and were narrower than the other pairs of droplights.

A second version of diagram M was produced about 1910, and was subsequently amended. On the end elevation, this shows the standard gangway fitted to the trailing end of Nos.43–48 in 1910–11. According to the notes on this version of the diagram, this arrangement applied to 'Nos.43 to 47'. This would indicate an amendment made in 1916, after No.48 was condemned.

As well as these, a diagram N also exists. This shows cars Nos.49–52, and appears to be identical with the first form of diagram M (i.e. it shows the three pairs of droplights fitted, but no gangway connector) and differs only in having a sliding door between the smoking and non-smoking saloons instead of a hinged one. The thicker partition required by the sliding door reduced the length occupied by the walkover seats by 3 inches to 23ft 3in; nevertheless, eight pairs of these were still fitted in. It is quite pos-

M

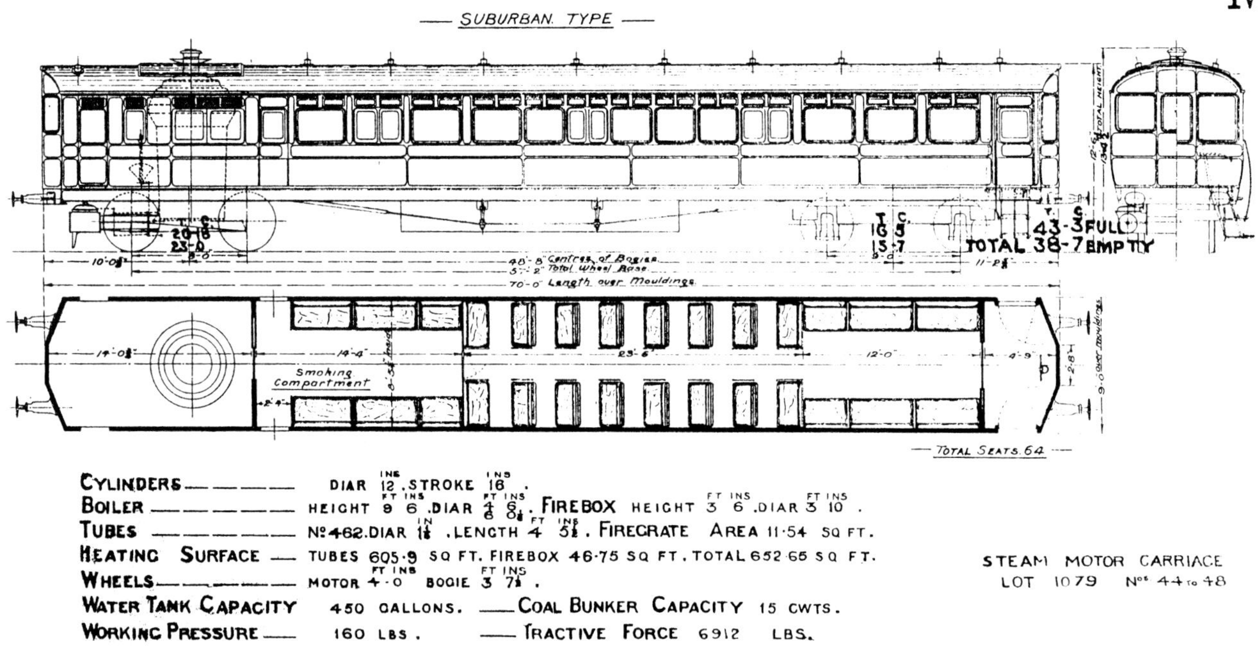

N

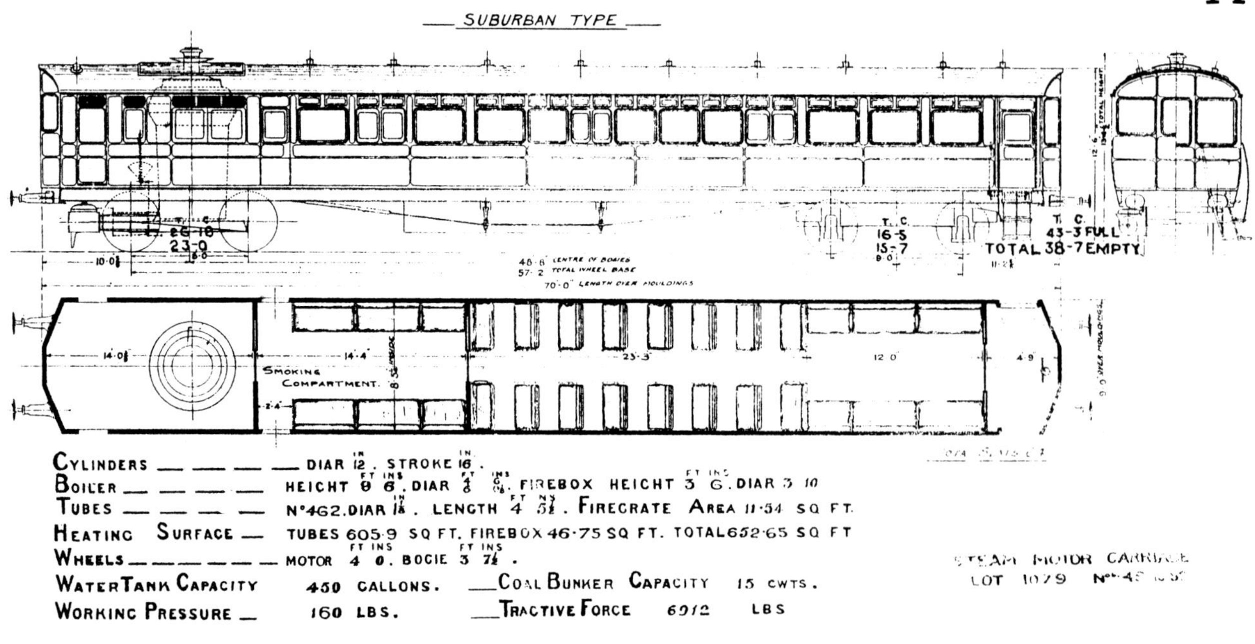

sible that this sliding door was an original feature, so there may have been a diagram N1 (which has not been seen).

Diagrams M1, M and N show a 9ft trailing bogie of the volute or coil spring varieties. This was correct for Nos.43–49, but according to the register, Nos.50–52 were built with 9ft 'American' bogies.

The recorded weights of these SRMs varies depending on the source. However the various diagrams all show the same:

	Empty *Tons – Cwt*	*Full* *Tons – Cwt*
Power Bogie	23 – 0	26 – 18
Trailing Bogie	15 – 7	16 – 5
Total	38 – 7	43 – 3

This is in spite of the variations in bogies, and the addition of the gangway connectors. The register gives various weights between 43 tons 16 cwt and 45 tons 16 cwt.

MODIFICATIONS & DISPOSAL

The subsequent history of these SRMs has been touched upon already. Until 1910, it was much as would be expected with Nos.43–49 inclusive: having been built with 9ft volute spring bogies, they were changed to 9ft coil spring units between October 1905 and June 1907. No change is recorded for No.44, but this is presumably an error of omission in the register.

No records exist of when the fixed lights were replaced by droplights, but this was probably done by about 1907, except in the case of No.43, which had diagram M1 all to itself.

No.43 was fitted with a large coal bunker in April 1907.

The register records the fitting of an additional ventilator in the motor compartment of Nos.43–49 inclusive at unstated dates, but it is not at all clear from photographs where this was fitted. Car No.48 was said to have been fitted with 'drop side light' in May 1907, which could be a date for the fitting of the droplights shown in diagram M in this particular car.

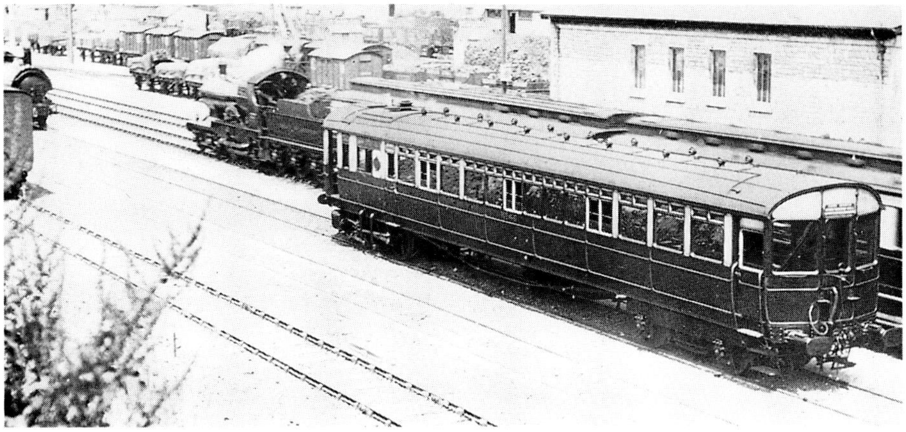

Car No. 46 of Diagram M was allocated to Weymouth for a year from May 1908, and this picture taken at Dorchester probably dates from that period. The car is seen in the fully lined brown and cream livery, although no monogram is visible. Three windows had been replaced by pairs of droplights, the sliding windows to the power compartment had been modified and a tank filler lid fitted, curiously apparently in brown. At the trailing end of the car, nearer the camera, a bell cable had been fitted and the steps cast into the buffer guides are visible.
E. POUTEAU, CTY. J. N. SLINN

This picture of Car No. 47 of Diagram M1, apparently in brand new condition, is believed to have been taken at Cardiff General station from Platform 3. The first allocation of No. 47 was Neath and this photograph raises the question as to how it got there. With its motion in place, was it being delivered under its own power, or was this a crew training run? COLLECTION R. C. RILEY

This picture shows Car No. 48 of Diagram M on the Chalford–Stonehouse service, apparently in the 1912 lake livery. Notice the plain water filler lid but no protection bars at the front windows. No. 48 was allocated to Chalford from 4th September 1915 until it was destroyed by a fire in January the following year, so this may be one of the last photographs of it. P. J. T. REED

Rain strips were fitted fairly early on to all, and the power compartment sliding windows were modified to allow for an external water tank filler to be sited in a panel immediately to the rear of them. This had the usual hinged lid, dropping downwards.

In 1910–1911, standard gangways were fitted to the trailing ends of Nos.43–48 inclusive, but no new diagram index code was issued. On 21st July 1910, the Traffic Committee was asked to recommend the expenditure of £204 for this work – which they did – but no reason for it is quoted in the minutes. These gangways may have enabled two of these SRMs to be coupled back to back, and one conductor would therefore have been able to issue tickets to travellers in both cars. The cars would also have been able to run with trailers fitted with gangways at the trailing end (e.g. Dia. T and U, built in 1911/12) with the gangways connected, but it is not known if this was done regularly.

The presence of the gangway connector also raises the interesting question of what modifications were made to the driving apparatus in the trailing vestibule. Details are not shown on the version of diagram M which shows the gangway connectors. In fact, this diagram still shows the handbrake in a central position, where it would have been in the way of people using the gangway. My guess is that the regulator, vacuum brake setter, handbrake, etc. were moved to the right-hand side of the vestibule, as you look out of the car, but so far I have not found any photographs showing this, or indeed the gangways.

Protection bars were fitted to the quarterlights in the 'Engine Room' in 1912–13.

No.48 was badly damaged in the fire which burnt out Chalford SRM shed on 8th January 1916, and it was formally condemned later that month.

Car No.45 was loaned to the Highland Railway between January 1918 and August 1920, and was allocated to Invergordon, where there was an important naval establishment. It spent about a year at Swindon on its return, but instead of being converted to a trailer it enjoyed a new lease of life as an SRM, running until 1927, and not altered to a trailer until 1928, a lot later than the others.

SRM No.49 was fitted with electric lighting and sold to Mr R.O. Graham of Darlington, on behalf of the Port of London Authority. Like

The trailing end of Car No. 48 before it was fitted with a gangway connector in December 1910. COLLECTION LIONEL PADIN

Car No. 50 of Diagram N, seen here at Ebley Crossing Halt, seems to have been allocated to Gloucester or Chalford from when it was new in 1905 until the end of 1909. This shows the trailing end of the car with the bell cable prominent. The raised, if rather narrow, platforms of the halt were erected in November/December 1905 when the nameboard was still lettered with the word 'Halte'.

Car No. 50 on a Birkenhead–Chester service, possibly at Hooton, is seen in the 1912 lake livery. This shows the power unit end of the car and the protection bars inside the end windows are visible, but the coal bunker had not been extended upwards. The car had been fitted with a plain water filler cap and the droplights can be seen. Notice that the eaves panel of the door next to the power compartment was lettered 'SMOKING'. No. 50 was allocated to Chester from mid-November 1912 until June 1915. LENS OF SUTTON

TABLE 25

SUMMARY: Diagrams M1, M & N (Built on Lot 1079)

Car No.	*Dia.*	*Built*	*First Boiler*	*First Engine*	*Tare t - c*	*Bogie Change*	*Std. G'way*	*Incand. Gas*	*Prot'n Bars*	*Final Miles*	*Stopped Work*	*To Trailer No.*	*Dia.*
43	M	Feb 05	1050	0837	44-15	Apr 07	Oct 10	Apr 14	-	346,888	Oct 22	134	A17
44	M	Feb 05	1052	0839	44-10	+	Dec 10	Mar 14	-	373,664	Nov 22	135	A18
45	M	Feb 05	1053	0840	44-17	Nov 05	May 11	May 11	May 13	414,820	Sep 27	148	A25
46	M	Feb 05	1054	0842	45-16	Oct 10?	Oct 10	Dec 12	-	352,209	Apr 22	136	A15
47	M	Feb 05	1055	0843	45-01	+	Jan 10	May 10	-	281,677	Jan 22	137	A15
48	M	Mar 05	1019	0845	41-02	Mar 06	Dec 10	May 13	May 13	285,634	Jan 16	Condemned	
49	M	Feb 05	1046	0841	43-16	Jun 07	May 11	May 11	-	303,966	Jan 20	Sold	-
50	N	Mar 05	1057	0846	44-07	+	-	+	-	329,420	Nov 22	138	A19
51	N	Apr 05	1061	0850	44-15	+	-	Apr 13	Nov 12	328,550	Jun 22	139	A19
52	N	Feb 05	1051	0838	44-12	+	-	Feb 13	Feb 13	350,567	Sep 22	140	A19

NOTES

Built with 9 ft volute spring bogies. Changed to 9 ft coil spring.

No.43: Fitted with 'large coal bunker', Apr 07.

No.45: Loaned to the Highland Rly, Jan 18 - Aug 20.

No.48: Droplights fitted, May 07. Burnt at Chalford 8 Jan 16 and condemned. Body broken up Apr 18?

No.49: Sold to Mr R. O. Graham for the Port of London Authority, Aug 20.

No.42, it was used on the PLA's Milwall Extension until 1926, when the passenger service was withdrawn, after which it was scrapped.

Apart from Nos.48 and 49, these cars were converted to trailers in 1922, 1923 and 1928. Somewhat unusually, they reappeared as no less than five different types of trailer, as shown below; of these, trailers Nos.134 and 135 ran as a gangwayed pair, whilst the others ran as single units.

TABLE 26

Diagrams M & N: Disposal

Car	*Disposal*	*Date*	*Car*	*Disposal*	*Date*
43	Trailer 134, Dia. A17	Apr 23	48	Burnt at Chalford	8 Jan 16
44	Trailer 135, Dia. A18	Apr 23	49	Sold to the PLA	10 Aug 20
45	Trailer 148, Dia. A25	May 28	50	Trailer 138, Dia. A19	Apr 23
46	Trailer 136, Dia. A15	Nov 22	51	Trailer 139, Dia. A19	Apr 23
47	Trailer 137, Dia. A15	Nov 22	52	Trailer 140, Dia. A19	Apr 23

Car No. 49 of Diagram M after it had been sold to the Port of London Authority. The number and GWR livery had been painted out and electric lighting had been fitted – a battery box is visible. COLLECTION R. C. RILEY

Diagrams O & R: Nos.53 to 58, 61 to 72, 84 to 99

Car No. 71 of Diagram O, apparently new, probably at one of the Langport stations. COLLECTION R. C. RILEY

These 35 cars represent the eventual standard 70ft 'branch' type, and were the most numerous design of SRM on the Great Western. On rebuilding, they gave rise to a near-standard class of trailer.

They were ordered on four Lots in 1905 and 1907, and delivered between September 1905 and February 1908. One Lot, 1100, was contracted to Kerr, Stuart of Stoke on Trent, who in fact only built the power units, the bodies being subcontracted to Hurst, Nelson of Motherwell. Unlike the Dia. E trailers, this time the GWR supplied their own drawings, and these trailers were almost identical to the Swindon-built vehicles.

The recorded costs of the various lots were:

TABLE 27

COSTS: Diagrams O, R

Lot	*Order date*	*Builder*	*Average cost per SRM*	*No. Blt.*	*SRM Nos.*	*Total Cost of Lot.*
1088	14 Mar 05	GWR, Swindon	£1,902 7s 8d	6	53-58	£11,414 6s 0d
1100	13 Jun 05	Kerr, Stewart & Hurst Nelson	£2,743 14s 10d	12	61-72	£32,924 18s 4d
1140	28 May 07	GWR, Swindon	£2,188 0s 3d	7	84-90	£15,316 1s 9d
1142	15 Jul 07	GWR, Swindon	£2,175 6s 6d	10	91-99	£21,753 5s 0d

The only Lot for which the split in costs survives is Lot 1088. This was charged £1,065 1s 8d to the Carriage Department and £837 6s 0d to the Locomotive Department, per SRM. In view of the very much higher figure for the Hurst Nelson cars, it is worth noting that the GWR figures did not include central overheads – an arbitrary 25% would be added to arrive at an 'all-inclusive' cost for valuation purposes, so the Lot 1140 cars each had a total cost of £2,735 applied to them, while the Kerr Stuart cars were valued at cost, although for some reason this is recorded as £2,752.

Lot 1100 power units were delivered direct to Swindon, and the cars were assembled there under the supervision of a fitter from Kerr, Stuart.

DESIGN

These SRMs were almost identical, the principal difference being that those built by Kerr, Stuart (Nos.61–72) had double doors to the passenger vestibule, while the Swindon-built cars had the normal, wider, single doors in this position. Diagram O shows a Kerr, Stuart SRM, but the legend indicates that it was to cover cars ordered on Lot 1088 as well as those of Lot 1100. Diagram R shows a Swindon-built car and is deemed to cover Lots 1140 and 1142. One other difference is shown on the Locomotive Department copies: diagram O shows the usual 15 cwt coal bunker, whilst diagram R shows a coal bunker capacity of 30 cwt. Both diagrams show the cars fitted with 9ft volute or coil spring bogies, but in practice only the Lot 1088 cars had these (rapidly changed from volute to coil spring); those built by Kerr, Stuart & Hurst Nelson had 9ft 'Fishbelly' type bogies with leaf bearing springs, and those of Lots 1140 and 1142 had 9ft 'American' bogies.

A general purpose version of diagram O (drawing No.27052A), which omits the power unit data included on the Locomotive Department diagrams, indicates the window sizes of the large fixed lights: they were all 2ft 1in deep, and were either 2ft 8in or 3ft 2¼in wide.

These cars were 70ft long, 9ft 0in wide and 12ft 6in from rail to roof. Their wheelbase was 59ft 5in, with a distance of 10ft 0⅜in from the headstock to the centre of the engine wheelbase, and at the other end a distance of 8ft 11⅝in from the headstock to the trailing bogie centre.

Their underframe was the standard type for 70ft trailers with four flat-section truss rods and adjustable queenposts. Both diagrams show twists in the truss rods at both ends of the car, but in practice the Dia. R cars (Nos.84–99) are believed to have had the twist only at the power unit end.

The diagrams give the weights of the cars as:

O

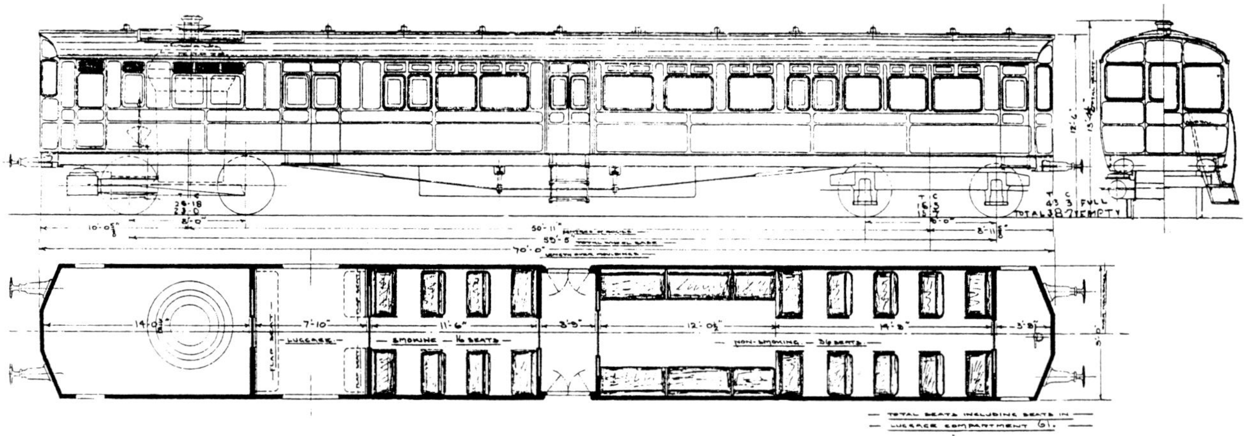

CYLINDERS — DIAR 12 IN. STROKE 16 IN.
BOILER — HEICHT 9 FT 6 INS. DIAR 4/6 FT 6/0¼ INS. FIREBOX HEICHT 3 FT 5⅝ INS. DIAR 3 FT 10 INS.
TUBES — No 420. DIAR 1¼ IN. LENGTH 4 FT 5½ INS. FIRECRATE AREA 11·54 SQ FT.
HEATINC SURFACE — TUBES 612·78 SQ FT. FIREBOX 46·46 SQ FT. TOTAL 659·24 SQ FT.
WHEELS — MOTOR 4 FT 0 INS. BOCIE 3 FT 7½ INS.
WATER TANK CAPACITY 450 CALLONS — COAL BUNKER CAPACITY 15 CWTS.
WORKINC PRESSURE — 160 LBS. — TRACTIVE FORCE 6912 LBS

STEAM MOTOR CARRIACE
LOT 1088 Nos 53 TO 58
1100 " 61 " 72

P

BRANCH TYPE

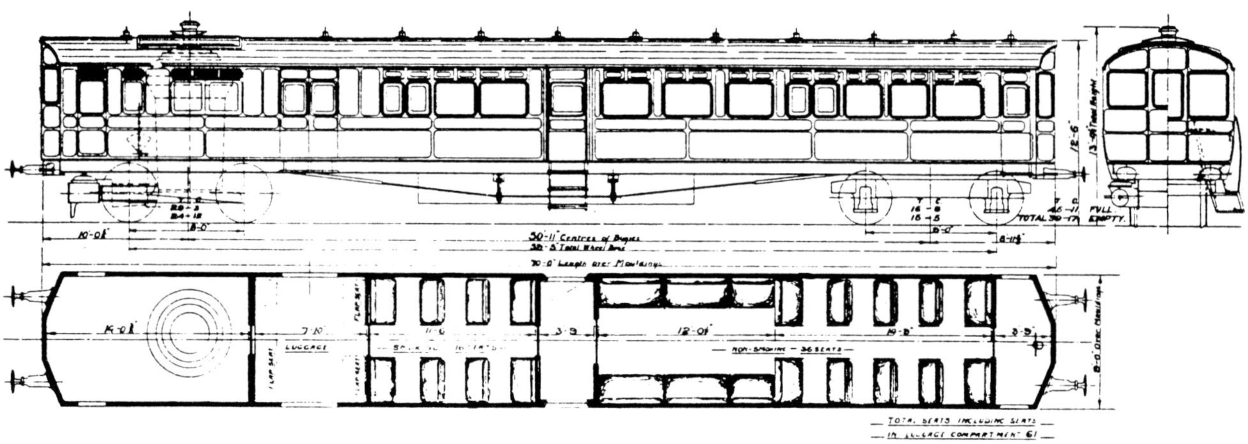

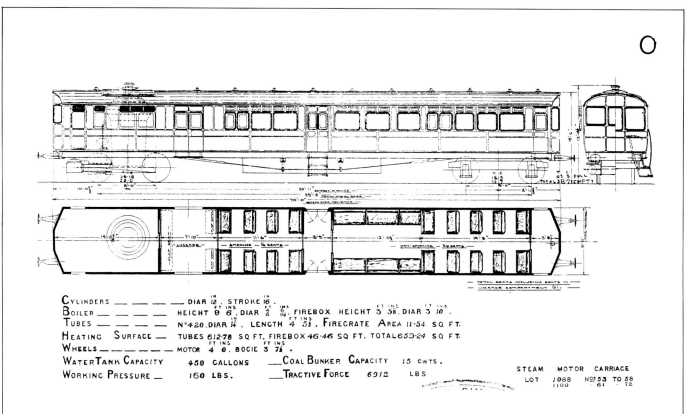

CYLINDERS — DIAR 12 STROKE 16 INS
BOILER — HEICHT 9-6 DIAR 4-6/6-0¼ FT INS. FIREBOX. HEICHT 3-5⅝ FT INS. DIAR 3-10 FT INS
TUBES — No 419. DIAR 1¼ INS. LENCTH 4-5½ FT INS. AREA OF FIRECRATE. 11·54 SQ FT.
HEATINC SURFACE — TUBES 611·32 SQ FT. FIREBOX 46·46 SQ FT. TOTAL 657·78 SQ FT.
WHEELS — MOTOR 4-0 FT INS. BOCIE 3-7½ FT INS.
WATER TANK CAPACITY — 450 CALLONS — COAL BUNKER CAPACITY 30 CWTS.
WORKINC PRESSURE — 160 LBS. — TRACTIVE EFFORT 6912 LBS.

STEAM MOTOR CARRIACE
LOT 1140 Nos 84 TO 90
LOT 1142 Nos 91 TO 99

Dia. O	*Empty* *Tons – Cwt*	*Full* *Tons – Cwt*
Power Bogie	23 – 0	26 – 18
Trailing Bogie	13 – 7	16 – 5
Total	36 – 7	43 – 3

Dia R	*Empty* *Tons – Cwt*	*Full* *Tons – Cwt*
Power Bogie	24 – 12	29 – 3
Trailing Bogie	15 – 5	16 – 8
Total	39 – 17	45 – 11

The *SRM Register* gives various weights for Dia. O cars of between 44 tons 1 cwt and 46 tons 3 cwt, and between 44 tons 16 cwt and 46 tons 10 cwt for Dia. R cars. It should be noted that the weight of cars could vary appreciably over the years, and not always upwards, as may be seen in Table 28.

TABLE 28

WEIGHT VARIATIONS: Diagrams O, R

Car	*Initial Weight*	*Subsequent Wt. (1)*	*Wt. (2)*	*Wt.(3)*
53	46t 2cwt	44t 4cwt (Feb 21)	44t 11cwt (Sep 21)	45t 1cwt (Dec 22)
71	45t 3cwt	44t 13cwt (Sep 21)	46t 4cwt (Mar 34)	-
86	45t 1cwt	45t 16cwt (Mar 21)	-	-
90	45t 17cwt	46t 4cwt	45t 16 cwt (Sep 23)	-
96	46t 1cwt	45t 3cwt	45t 15 cwt	46t 17 cwt (Oct 33)

Some of these variations would have been due to painting or modifications, and some to the amounts of water, coal and sand not being constant each time the car was weighed. No.97 eventually weighed 46 tons 18 cwt, according to the register, and No.96 only one cwt less when weighed in November 1933.

The Hurst, Nelson SRMs Nos.61–72 originally had a different pattern roof ventilator from the GWR standard 'shell' type. They have been described as 'torpedo type, but with hemispheres instead of cones at the sides'. They were a similar size to the GWR standard.

The motor compartment is shown as identical in appearance on both diagrams, and was the standard 14ft 0⅜in length with the usual doors and windows. Most cars had the waist panel and, originally, the main side panel below the waist divided by vertical mouldings below the ends of the sliding windows. However, some cars, and possibly all those of Lot 1088 (Nos.53–58), had instead a single moulding centrally below these windows. Some cars, e.g. 64 and 69, sported roof handrails on or alongside the hatch in the roof through which the boiler could be removed.

Behind this, the luggage compartment measured 7ft 10in between partitions, and had double external doors each side, centrally positioned in relation to the compartment partitions. There was the usual emergency seating against the power compartment partition, plus two shorter seats facing this on the partition between the luggage and the smoking compartments, one either side of the central sliding door.

The smoking compartment was 11ft 6in between partitions, and was provided with 4 pairs of walkover seats. It had a pair of droplights and two large fixed lights, one of each width; these fixed windows were 2ft 8in and 3ft 2¼in wide respectively.

A passenger vestibule, 3ft 9in between partitions, divided the smoking and non-smoking compartments. This had single inward-opening doors on the Swindon built cars, and double

Car No. 69 of Diagram O at Campden station (later Chipping Campden) on the Oxford–Honeybourne line. No. 69 was at Oxford in February–October 1908 and could have been there earlier. T. ELSLEY

A view of the large saloon of Car No. 61 of Diagram O taken from the passenger lobby, looking towards the trailing end of the car. In this view it can be seen that there were picture frames with three photographs on the wider framing between the windows, and three pictures in each of the frames on the partition at the end. The advertisement in a frame below the left-hand pictures was for weekend tickets to resorts – the right-hand one was for express trains direct from the farm dairy to the consumer. NATIONAL RAILWAY MUSEUM

The interior of Car No. 61. The view was taken from the large saloon with the passenger lobby behind the partition, the small saloon behind that and finally the luggage compartment. The droplights can be seen, and there is a good view of the walkover seats in the foreground. The partition had picture frames with two views in each. The poster on the left of the door showed the timetable and fares, probably of the Plymouth suburban services (61 went new to Laira) and the one on the right of the door was an empty leaflet box with 'PLEASE TAKE ONE' and 'GREAT WESTERN PUBLICATIONS'. NATIONAL RAILWAY MUSEUM

doors on those built by Hurst, Nelson. On both, these doors were flat and slightly recessed, and had retractable steps below.

Beyond this, the non-smoking compartment had a 12ft 0½in length of longitudinal bench seating and a 14ft 9in length occupied by five pairs of walkover seats. There were three large fixed lights by the bench seats (all 3ft 2¼in wide), with a pair of droplights and three more fixed lights (widths 2ft 8in, 2ft 8in and 3ft 2¼in) next to the walkover seats.

The cars seated a total of 61 passengers, including the seats in the luggage compartment.

At the trailing end, the driver's vestibule was 3ft 9in deep, maximum, with external, hinged doors each side, 2ft wide. The mouldings at the waist on the diagrams hint that they were hinged on the compartment partition side, but they were actually hinged on the corner pillar, as usual, but opened outwards. There were no retractable steps below these doors.

All these cars had steam heating and incandescent gas lighting from new.

These cars all appeared in the full chocolate and cream livery. Nos.53–58 appeared with the pre-1906 'florid' monogram; some of the Kerr, Stuart cars (Nos.61–69) appeared with the 'prize' monogram, whilst it is believed that Nos.70–72 (KS) and 84–99 (GWR) all had the garter crest with supporters from new.

Photographs indicate that the GWR-built SRMs Nos.84–99 (together with the Kerr, Stuart and Hurst, Nelson cars, and possibly others) not only had sandboxes at both ends of the motor bogie, but also on the outer wheelset of the trailing bogie, perhaps to improve adhesion whilst braking. These trailing end sandboxes seem to have been attached to the car body/underframe, and not to the bogie, while sand was delivered via a long curving pipe attached to the life guard, which pipe was presumably flexible enough to allow for the rotation of the bogie. According to the contract for the Lot 1100 cars, the trailing sandboxes were in the driver's vestibule, operated by foot levers. The register records the fitting of sandboxes to eight of these SRMs at two periods: during 1913–16 and 1927–28. Those fitted in the 1920s were stated to be dry sand boxes, and in all cases these would have been replacements.

MODIFICATIONS & DISPOSAL

Modifications to these cars followed the usual pattern. Nos.53–58 had their 9ft volute spring bogies changed to similar coil spring types at an early date. No subsequent changes are recorded in the *SRM Register*, but a photograph of No.57 in the 1912–22 lake livery shows it as having been fitted with a 9ft 'American' trailing bogie.

SRM	*New bogie*	*Date*
53	9ft coil	Nov 1908
54	9ft coil	Jun 1906
55	9ft coil	Mar 1906
56	9ft coil	Dec 1905
57	9ft coil	+
58	9ft coil	+

Car No. 68 of Diagram O as running in the lined brown livery of 1908. This picture shows several of the window blinds lowered whilst the destination board at the front reads 'TENBURY & WHITLAND'. No. 68 was at Whitland between July and October 1909. F. MOORE

Another view of Car No. 68 in the lined brown livery of 1908, at Lamprey station on a Whitland to Pembroke Dock working. The destination board at the front reads 'PEMBROKE DOCK'. It was hauling a 6-wheel brake third, possibly as shown on Diagram T38 and an 'iron mink' van. F. MOORE

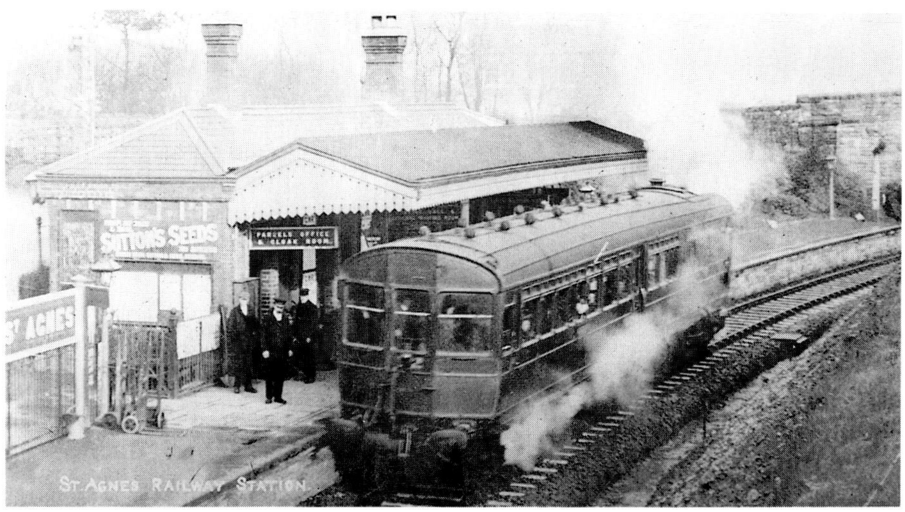

Car No. 72 at St. Agnes in lined brown livery. The windows of the trailing end, nearest the camera, appear to have been given a white line across them. No. 72 was at Newquay or Truro most of the time between June 1909 and May 1913. AUTHOR'S COLLECTION

Car No. 72 of Diagram O at Penzance in what was probably the lined brown livery. It had been given three protection bars to the front windows and a water pipe lid with a cross. The trailer behind was a Diagram L. The picture is dated 'Summer 1912 or 13'; the latter would appear to be correct as it was allocated to Penzance from May to August 1913, then going to Helston.
C. H. FISON, CTY. R. C. RILEY

Dia. O and R cars all had a single 'high level' rain strip along each side of the roof when new, supplemented by a lower one on each side at an early date.

The sliding windows to the power compartment were reduced in length by about a third, and external water fillers were provided on each side of the car, fitted into a panel to the rear of the sliding windows. Some of these had plain filler caps without the cross. It is possible that the last two Lots (Nos.84–99) had this modification from new.

There are records of protection bars being fitted to power compartment windows, and it is probable that all received them.

No.54 was fitted with an 'alarm bell' – presumably a warning gong – in July 1927. With the possible exceptions of those that were withdrawn in 1928, all the others were probably fitted with gongs at about this period.

Those that survived long enough had the smoking and non-smoking compartments changed round, providing additional seating for smokers.

Chain communication apparatus was recorded as fitted to some between 1928 and 1933, a suspiciously large number in February that year.

Several are recorded as appearing in the brown and cream with gold lines livery in 1931/2.

In the Bristol Division *Working of Coaches, Rail Motor or Auto Cars* booklet for September 1930 ('and until further notice'), SRM No.65 was specified as working the Yatton & Clevedon service, and is described as 'chain

Car No. 57 of Diagram O in lined lake livery and fitted with protection bars to the front windows. The right-hand leaf of the double doors had 'LUGGAGE' written on it in the waist.
COLLECTION R. C. RILEY

Car No. 65 at Abbotsbury. It was allocated to Weymouth for most of the period between 1911 and 1914.

Car No. 62 of Diagram O at Reading on 18th February 1922.
A. W. CROUGHTON

Car No. 63 of Diagram O as running in what was presumably the 1908 lined brown livery. As far as can be seen, no modifications had taken place apart from the fitting of water filler pipe covers. Curiously, 'GWR' seems to have been missing from the waist panels and 'LUGGAGE' from the luggage compartment door. This view is believed to have been taken at Oxford.
A. G. ELLIS, CTY. R. C. RILEY

Car No. 64 of Diagram O at Gerrards Cross in 1930 when it was allocated to Southall. It appears to have been in the 1930 livery with the double gold and black lines at the waist. The larger saloon was then the 'smoking' one. T. E. LAYNE, CTY. R. C. RILEY

Another view of Car No. 64 in the 1930 simplified brown and cream livery, but with two gold and black lines at the waist. The middle window in the small saloon had a triangular 'No smoking' sign, whilst two of the windows in the large saloon had 'Smoking' labels. COLLECTION R. C. RILEY

Car No. 69 of Diagram O apparently in the 1929 brown and cream livery with a single gold and black line at the waist. Details include a plain water pipe cover, a coal bunker with raised ends, and driving end windows with protection bars. No. 69 spent the period between December 1929 and September 1930 at Croes Newydd.
AUTHOR'S COLLECTION

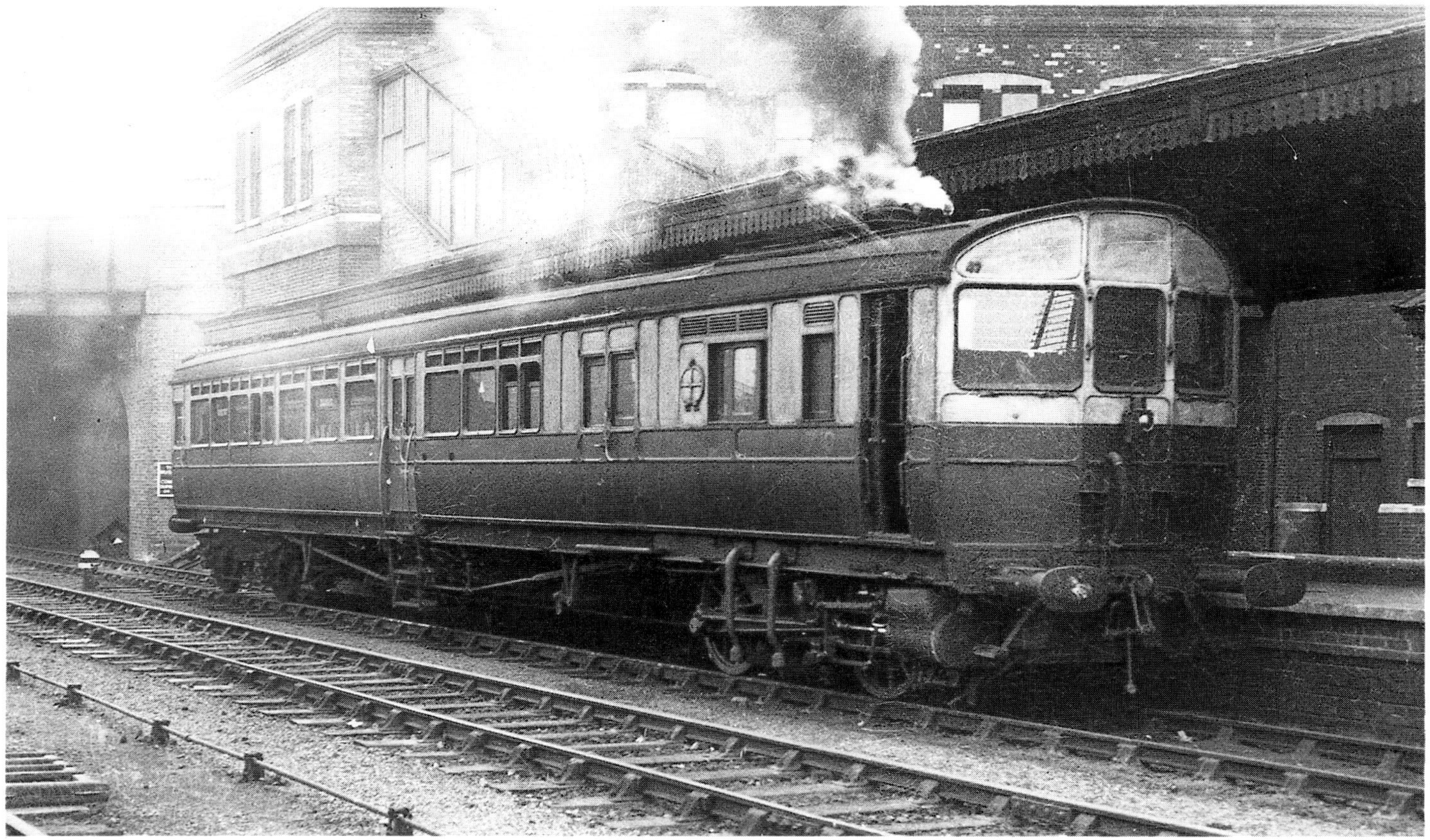

Car No. 70 of Diagram O at Southall on a Brentford service in August 1931. This car is also seen in the 1929 brown and cream livery with a single gold/black line at the waist. No. 70 was allocated to Southall for almost the whole of 1931.
DR. I. C. ALLEN,
CTY. R. C. RILEY

fitted'; trailer No.62, also 'chain fitted', was to be attached as required. It is not certain what was meant by 'chain fitted' in these instances, or why car No.65 and trailer No.62 were specifically allocated to this service – other SRM workings did not have a specific car or trailer allocated in this book, nor did the equivalent London, Birmingham & Worcester, or Exeter & Plymouth Divisional documents. The 'chain-fitted' pair were still shown in the summer 1934 Bristol programme, even though No.65 spent the entire season in Swindon Works; however, an appended note to the four-week allocation register for SRMs indicates 'No change for Yatton'.

Confusion arises over the withdrawal dates for these SRMs and their conversion to trailers, as conflicting records exist. Some of this must be put down to accountancy practice: condemned dates were notional at the end of the appropriate four-week period, whilst 'Out of Stock' dates could be even more arbitrary. A number of record cards survive in the Public Record Office with one date on one side and another on the reverse!

In some periods, SRMs were not 'condemned' when they were altered to trailers.

Car No. 71 of Diagram O at Exeter MPD, in a siding regularly used for steam rail motors. The loco coal wagon next to the car was probably used for coaling it. The car is seen in the 1929 brown and cream livery with a single gold/black line at the waist, although not much is visible along the car's side. The photo shows protection bars behind the front windows, a coal bunker that has been built up and a plain water pipe cover. No. 71 went to Exeter in January 1934 and remained there until May 1935 (except for overhauls). It was withdrawn in June 1935.
J. P. MULLETT
CTY. R. C. RILEY

Car No. 72 at Southall MPD in 1932. J. A. G. H. COLTAS COLLECTION, CTY. R. C. RILEY

They 'stopped work', were 'taken out of stock', 'converted to trailers', and the trailers were 'put into stock'. This had been normal practice, and seems to have happened again in 1929 with Nos.54, 62, 84, 94 and 95. In all five cases, the conversion took place before the 'out of stock' date, and the 'into stock date' of the trailer was the same as the SRM 'out of stock' date. Whether the trailer was actually kept in the Swindon stock sheds until its official 'into stock date' is not known. In other cases during 1927 they stopped work, were formally condemned, converted to a trailer and then, at any time up to six months later, taken out of stock as an SRM and simultaneously taken into stock as a trailer (as with Nos.57, 61, 63, 67, 68, 87, 89, 90).

Up until about 1929, 'New Works Orders' were issued to authorise the expenditure on the conversions, but from that date 'Lot' numbers were issued instead to cover the conversions, in the same way as for new or replacement rolling stock.

Car No. 85 of Diagram R hauling a clerestory trailer, both in the lake livery. On the original print it is possible to see bars fitted to the end windows and boards fitted inside to protect the glass. L&GRP

The interior of Car No. 87 of Diagram R taken in December 1907 when it was new. The view is very similar to those of earlier cars, the main difference being the upholstery of the seats and the arrangement of the posters at the end – the right-hand frame was advertising 'Cornwall and Italy'. NATIONAL RAILWAY MUSEUM

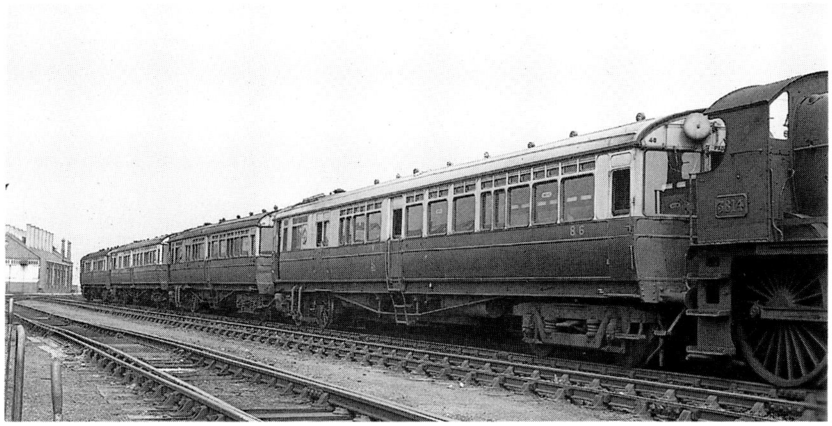

No. 86 of Diagram R which does not appear to have had a gangway connector. This line-up was photographed at Swindon in April 1932.
H. J. STRETTON WARD

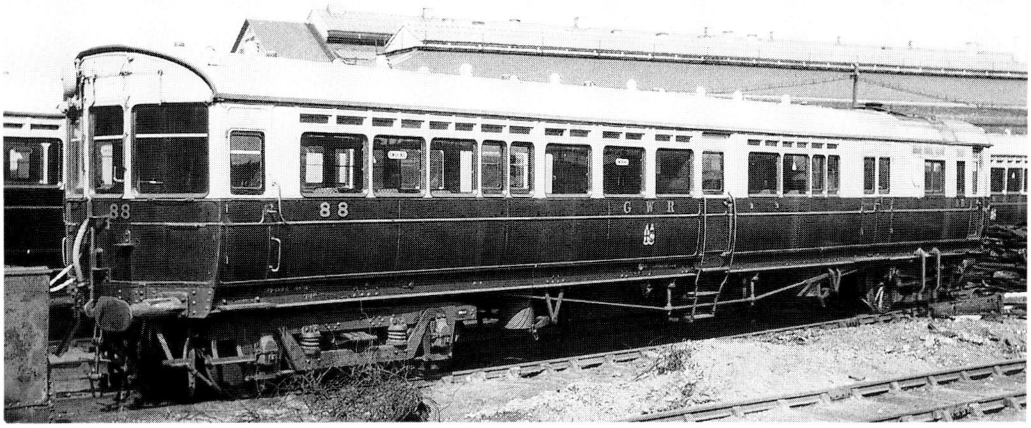

Car No. 88 of Diagram R, seen from the trailing end, in the 1930 livery – the waist panel lined with two gold and black lines. In view of the other cars in the background, all with white roofs, the picture was probably taken outside Swindon stock shed, possibly in May 1931. Car No. 88 had been equipped with a warning gong and passenger alarm apparatus at this end. The end windows and the driver's droplight all had a horizontal white line painted on them. L&GRP

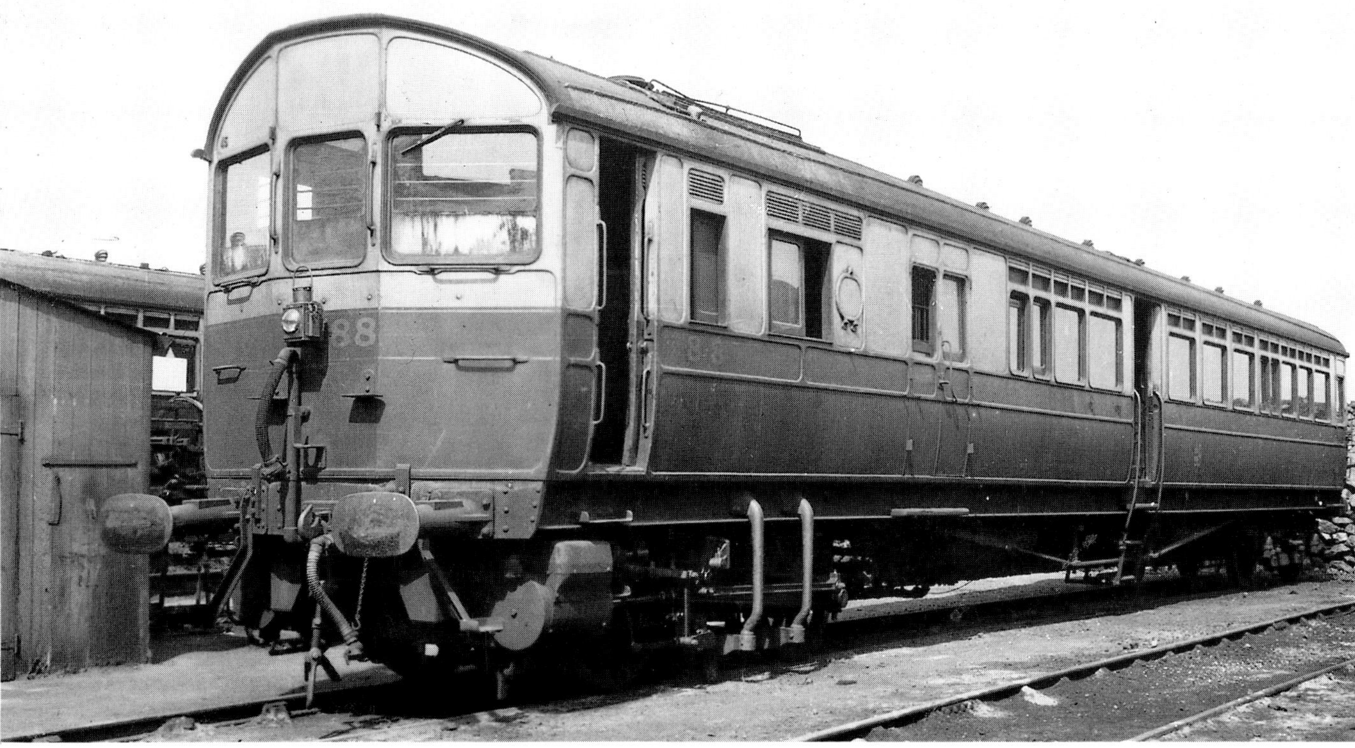

Car No. 88 of Diagram R appears to have been in the late 1929/early 1930 brown and cream livery with a single gold and black line at the waist. The car had been fitted with a windscreen wiper of the newer pattern where the spindle went through the moulding above the window and not through the glass. The protection bars behind the end windows can be seen as well as the sheeting protecting the lower part of the window. In this case it had been painted white or cream. Note the steam heating hose fitted at the front. COLLECTION R. C. RILEY

Another two views of Car No. 88, the upper one showing that part of the coal bunker seems to have been painted cream. The lower view was taken earlier and shows the 1930 livery, apparently outside Swindon stock shed, possibly in 1931.

H. J. STRETTON WARD and AUTHOR'S COLLECTION

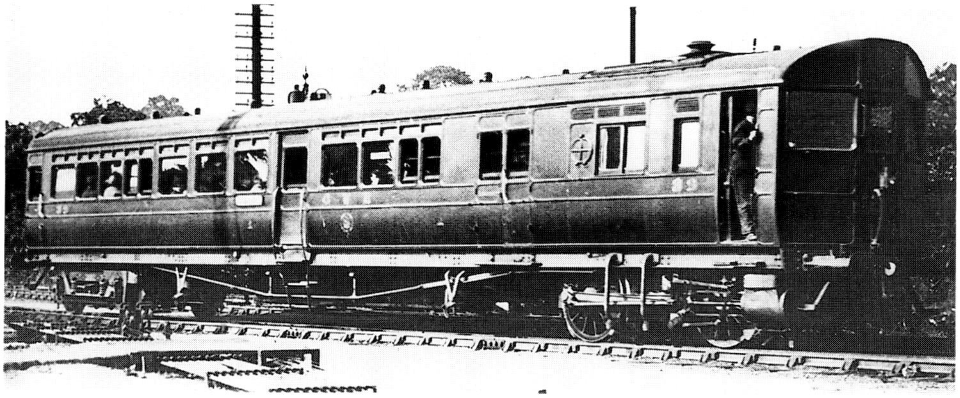

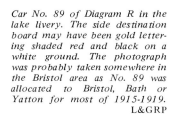

Car No. 89 of Diagram R in the lake livery. The side destination board may have been gold lettering shaded red and black on a white ground. The photograph was probably taken somewhere in the Bristol area as No. 89 was allocated to Bristol, Bath or Yatton for most of 1915-1919. L&GRP

Car No. 91 of Diagram R in the earlier of the simple 1927 brown and cream liveries; this one had the garter crest and supporters. This car looks as if the coal bunker extension behind the front windows had been painted cream, and it is possible that the side window next to the power compartment door had plating behind it — or was this simply a reflection in the low sunlight? COLLECTION J. SCOTT-MORGAN

Car No. 92 of Diagram R hauling a 6-wheel saloon of Diagrams G19 or G20 at Christow in April 1931. It was allocated to Exeter between October 1930 and November 1931 and seems to have gained the lower gold and black waist line of the 1930 livery variant. The cream paint is looking a little worn on the nearest corner. The car's weight, '46' tons, is above the left-hand window. The water filler lid was of the plain type and the coal bunker extension behind the end windows was painted in a dark colour, either black or brown. DR. IAN C. ALLEN, CTY. R. C. RILEY

Car No. 92 at Bath on Friday, 24th May 1929 hauling a 70ft 'Concertina' slip of Diagram F13 and a 56ft or 57ft 'Toplight' corridor composite, quite a load for an SRM. No. 92 is seen in the later 1927 simple brown and cream livery with the twin shields device and had been fitted with the passenger alarm system and a warning gong. No. 92 was allocated to Bristol, St. Philip's Marsh at this period.
H. C. CASSERLEY

Car No. 92 at Exeter shed apparently in the 1930 livery. COLLECTION R. C. RILEY

Car No. 92 hauling a Diagram L or P 70ft trailer. The car appears to have been in the 1929 livery with a single gold and black waist line, which is a little odd in that it was in Swindon Works in 1928 and then in July-October 1930 when the double lines should have been applied. The car's weight, '46' tons, appears above the left-hand window. The water filler lid is seen in the open position and on the original print it can be seen that the coal bunker extension behind the end windows was painted in a dark colour, either black or brown. COLLECTION R. C. RILEY

Car No. 93 of Diagram R at Yatton on Wednesday, 22nd May 1929, is seen in the later 1927 livery with the twin shields device, a plain water filler lid, a side destination board and two 'Smoking' signs in the windows of the large saloon. The end windows had a horizontal white line, and a gong and passenger alarm system had been fitted, but there does not seem to have been a windscreen wiper. During 1929 No. 93's allocation alternated between St. Philip's Marsh and Yatton. In May it was allocated to St. Philip's Marsh. H. C. CASSERLEY

Car No. 96 of Diagram R newly repainted into the 1930 brown and cream livery with twin gold and black waist lines. This photograph was taken in June 1932 after a heavy overhaul at Swindon.
T. E. LAYNE

Below: *Car No. 96 with a short 6-wheel saloon at Tiverton about to leave for Tiverton Junction in May 1933.* G. N. SOUTHERDEN

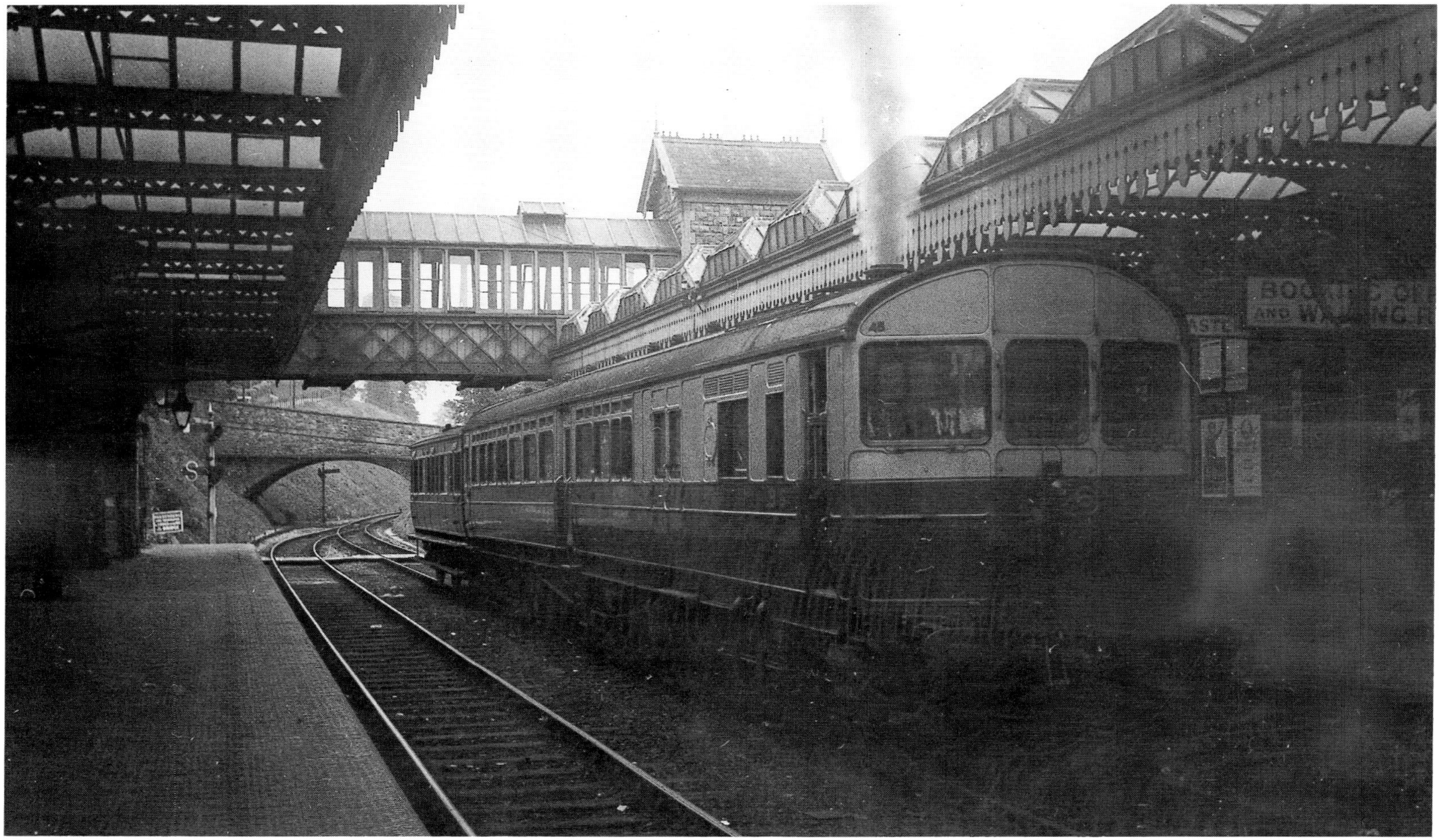

Two further views of steam rail motor No. 96 at Tiverton in May 1933. The lower picture gives a good view of the third-class saloon used to give additional accommodation on this service and contrasts with the modern trailer in the bay platform.

G. N. SOUTHERDEN

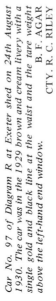

Car No. 97 of Diagram R at Exeter shed on 24th August 1930. The car was in the 1929 brown and cream livery with a single gold and black line at the waist and the tare weight above the left-hand end window. B. F. AGAR
CTY. R. C. RILEY

A second view of Car No. 97 at Exeter on the same day, but from a slightly different angle. H. C. CASSERLEY

In 1933, it would appear that some SRMs were officially condemned and not converted, but trailers *were* built, and happened to use most of the SRM body and underframe. These cars were listed as 'Condemned' in the *Condemned Stock Register*, and 'recovered parts' used in trailers: SRMs Nos.53 (trailer 199), 58 (200) and 86 (206) were involved. In 1934 and 1935, there seems to have been a change in accounting policy, and some SRMs (e.g. Nos.96–98) were officially condemned *and* made into trailers.

Seven cars were condemned without being made into trailers, and three of these (Nos.65, 70 and 71) were amongst the five SRMs condemned in 1935 that were replaced by three diesel railcars. Diagram O and R cars were among the last surviving on the GWR.

SRM No.93 was condemned in November 1934 and altered to trailer 212, appearing in May 1935. In May 1956, it was formally condemned again but was altered into a 'Work Study Coach' and given British Railways internal user number 079014. When BR had finished with it, the vehicle was preserved at the Great Western Society's site at Didcot. In 1998, the GWS launched an appeal to enable restoration of the vehicle back to SRM No.93 once more; this involves not only reconstructing one end of the car, but also building the power unit from scratch. At the time of writing, this major task is ongoing, but one day we may be able to see and experience a Great Western steam rail motor once more.

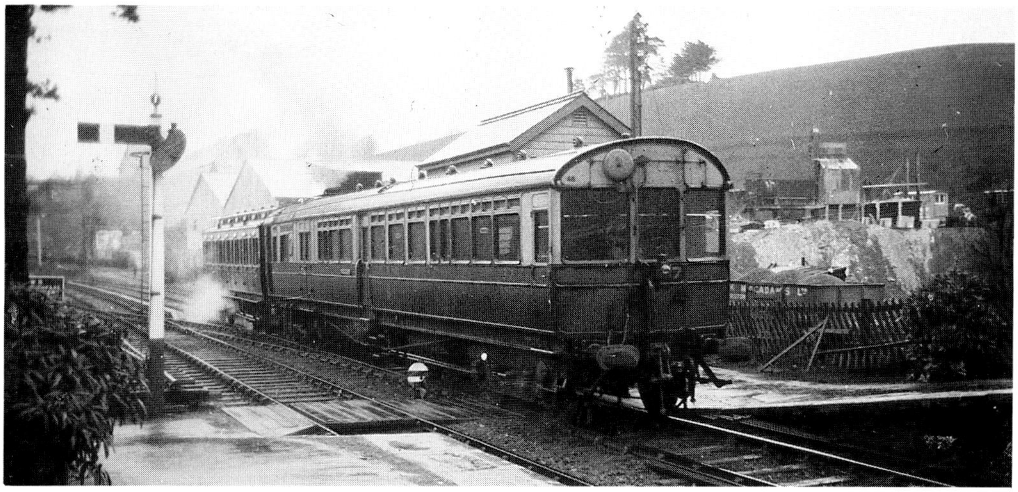

Car No. 97 entering Christow station on the Teign Valley line with a Heathfield–Exeter train. It had to run round the clerestory coach at each end of a journey.
DR. IAN C. ALLEN
CTY. R. C. RILEY

Car No. 97 at Ashton station, also on the Teign Valley line, on 24th July 1930. The car is seen in the 1929 brown and cream livery with a single gold and black line at the waist and the tare weight above the left-hand end window. Again the sheeting of the coal bunker extension seems to have been painted white and there does not seem to be a windscreen wiper at this end. F. M. GATES, CTY. R. C. RILEY

Right: *The steam rail motor shed at Southall. Apparently it was mostly used for trailers.*
NATIONAL RAILWAY MUSEUM

Below: *Car No. 98 being shunted into or out of the rail motor shed at Southall, probably sometime between September 1927 and March 1928. This was common practice when an SRM or any other locomotive, for that matter, was low in steam. A companion view of this car appears on page 49.*
LENS OF SUTTON

TABLE 29

SUMMARY: Diagrams O, R (Built on Lots 1088, 1100, 1140 & 1142)

Car No.	*Built*	*First Boiler*	*First Engine*	*Tare t - c*	*Prot'n Bars*	*Dry Sand*	*Chain Comm.*	*Smoking Compts.*	*Cream, Brown & Gold*	*Final Miles*	*Stopped Work*	*To Trailer No*	*Dia.*
Built on Lot 1088													
53	Sep 05	1030	0859	46-02	Jun 13	Jul 13		Oct 28	May 31	462,884	Jun 33	199	A26
54	Sep 05	1007	0860	45-06						415,980	Jun 29	181	A26
55	Oct 05	1070	0855	45-09		Apr 27	Feb 33	Oct 29	Aug 31	463,101	Apr 35	Condemned	
56	Sep 05	1020	0856	45-04				Jun 28		504,781	Jul 29	182	A26
57	Sep 05	1071	0861	45-03						384,115	Nov 27	149	A26
58	Sep 05	1072	0857	44-19				Jun 29	Nov 31	452,138	Jun 33	200	A26
Built on Lot 1100 by Kerr Stuart & Hurst Nelson													
61	Mar 06	1073	0866	45-17						367,909	Apr 27	151	A29
62	Apr 06	1074	0867	45-11	Dec 12			Nov 28		440,019	Nov 29	186	A29
63	Apr 06	1075	0868	45-07	Nov 12					358,029	Sep 27	151	A29
64	Apr 06	1076	0869	46-01	May 13		Nov 28	Aug 30	Jul 30	452,124	Jun 34	216	A29
65	Apr 06	1077	0870	45-17			Sep 28	Oct 28		538,908	Oct 35	Condemned	
66	May 06	1078	0871	45-11	Feb 13		Feb 33	Nov 28	Apr 31	481,498	Jul 34	217	A29
67	Jun 06	1079	0872	45-04						317,575	Feb 27	152	A29
68	May 06	1080	0873	43-15	Mar 13					327,882	Jun 27	153	A29
69	Jun 06	1081	0874	44-07		Sep 27	Feb 33	Sep 28	Mar 31	419,343	Oct 32	201	A29
70	Jun 06	1082	0875	43-03	Feb 13		Feb 33	Nov 32		456,633	Sep 34	Condemned	
71	Jun 06	1083	0876	45-03			Feb 33	Sep 29	Jan 31	520,169	Jun 35	Condemned	
72	Jul 06	1084	0877	44-17			Jan 29	Jan 29	Feb 31	471,286	Dec 34	218	A29
Built on Lot 1140													
84	Dec 07	1109	0899	45-00	Aug 13	Jan 28		Jan 28		365,949	Sep 29	183	A26
85	Dec 07	1116	0900	46-05		Jul 13				369,060	Apr 27	154	A26
86	Dec 07	1111	0897	45-01			Feb 33	Nov 32		417,181	Jan 33	206	A26
87	Dec 07	1110	0898	45-10						313,946	Jan 28	155	A26
88	Jan 08	1118	0902	45-09			Feb 33	Aug 28	Feb 31	456,375	Oct 35	Condemned	
89	Dec 07	1112	0903	46-01						376,400	Jun 27	156	A26
90	Dec 07	1114	0901	45-17		Jun 13				361,864	Nov 27	157	A26
Built on Lot 1142													
91	Dec 07	1115	0905	46-10			Feb 33	Nov 32	Oct 32	512,641	Jan 35	210	A26
92	Jan 08	1113	0904	46-01	Mar 12		Sep 30	Oct 28		483,696	Oct 35	Condemned	
93	Feb 08	1117	0906	45-07	Dec 12		Feb 29	Feb 29	Jul 31	479,006	Nov 34	212	A26
94	Feb 08	1119	0907	45-11						492,799	Oct 29	185	A26
95	Feb 08	1121	0908	44-16	Dec 12			Nov 28		354,024	Sep 29	184	A26
96	Feb 08	1120	0910	46-01		May 27	Jun 29	Jul 29	Jun 32	490,590	May 34	213	A26
97	Feb 08	1122	0912	45-13			Feb 33	Mar 30		424,247	Mar 35	214	A26
98	Feb 08	1123	0909	45-17		May 27	Feb 33	Jun 28		446,801	Apr 35	215	A26
99	Feb 08	1124	0911	45-09	Nov 12					340,474	Dec 27	158	A26

NOTES

Nos.53, 58 & 86: Officially condemned and recovered parts used in trailers shown.

No.54: Alarm bell fitted, Jul 27.

No.55, 88 & 92: Condemned 19 Oct 35 and broken up

Nos.62, 64, 69, 72, 86, 89, 91, 93, 96 & 97: Officially condemned and converted to the trailers shown

Nos.65, 70 & 71: Condemned Oct 35. Three of five SRMs replaced by three diesel railcars.

No.86: It is possible that this car had a gangway connector fitted. The register has a pencil entry "Corr" against it, and "Wicket gate in gangway 9/13", but there seems to be no other evidence that it was a corridor car.

P

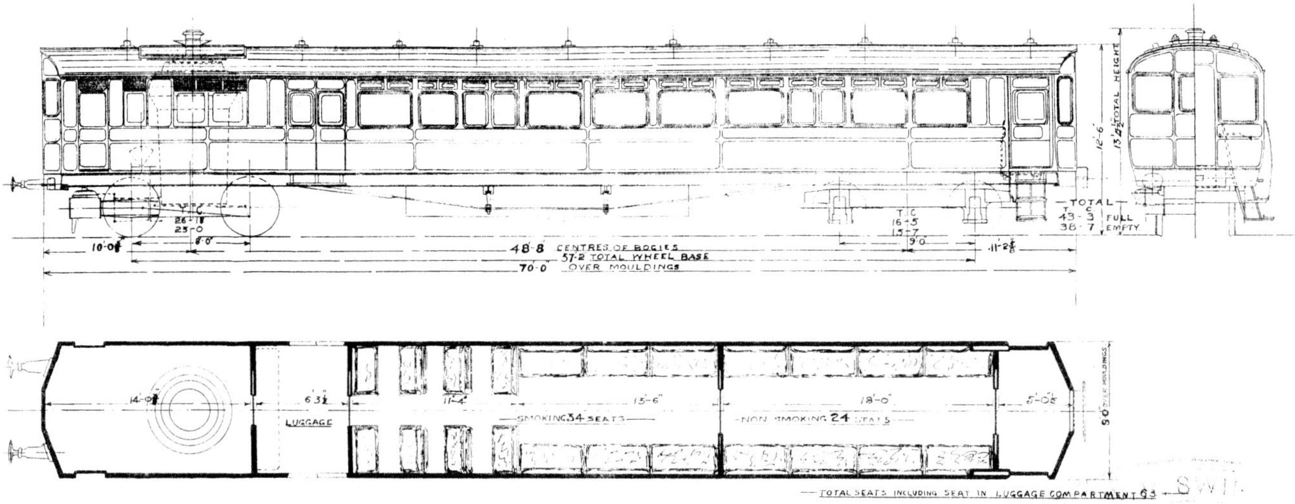

CYLINDERS — DIAR 12 IN. STROKE 16 IN.
BOILER — HEIGHT 9 FT 6 INS. DIAR 4/6 FT 6/0⅛ INS. FIREBOX HEIGHT 3 FT 5⅞ INS. DIAR 3 FT 10 INS.
TUBES — Nº 420. DIAR 1¼ IN. LENGTH 4 FT 5½ INS. FIRECRATE AREA 11·54 SQ FT.
HEATING SURFACE — TUBES 612·78 SQ FT. FIREBOX 46·46 SQ FT. TOTAL 659·24 SQ FT.
WHEELS — MOTOR 4 FT 0 INS. BOCIE 3 FT 7½ INS.
WATER TANK CAPACITY 450 CALLONS. — COAL BUNKER CAPACITY 15 CWTS.
WORKING PRESSURE — 160 LBS. — TRACTIVE FORCE 6912 LBS

STEAM MOTOR CARRIAGE
LOT 1089 Nos 59 TO 60.

T

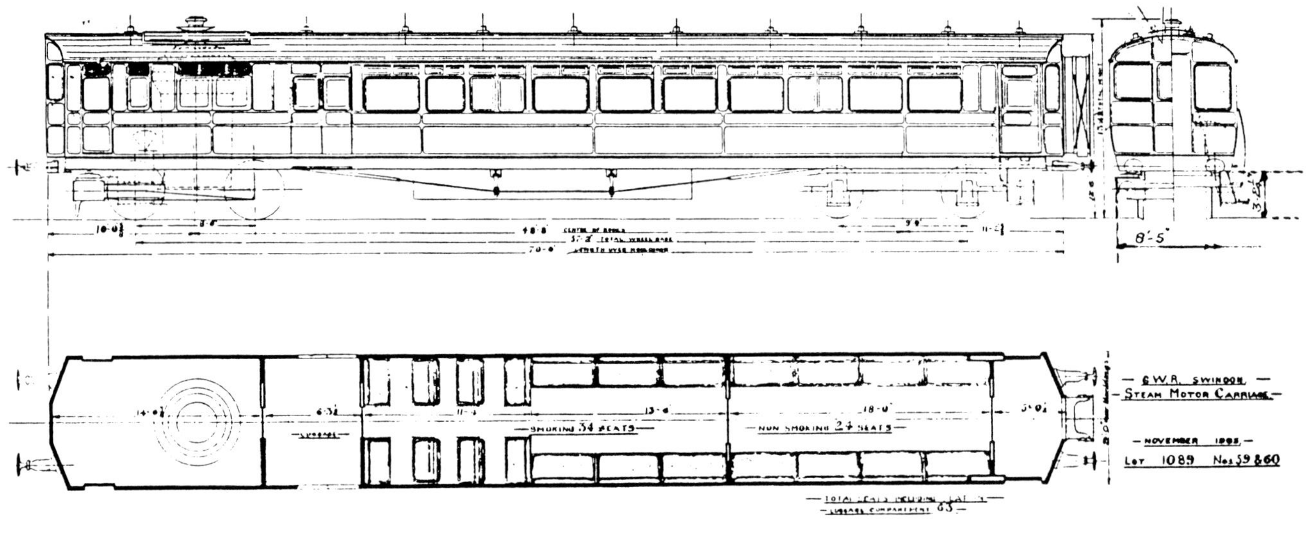

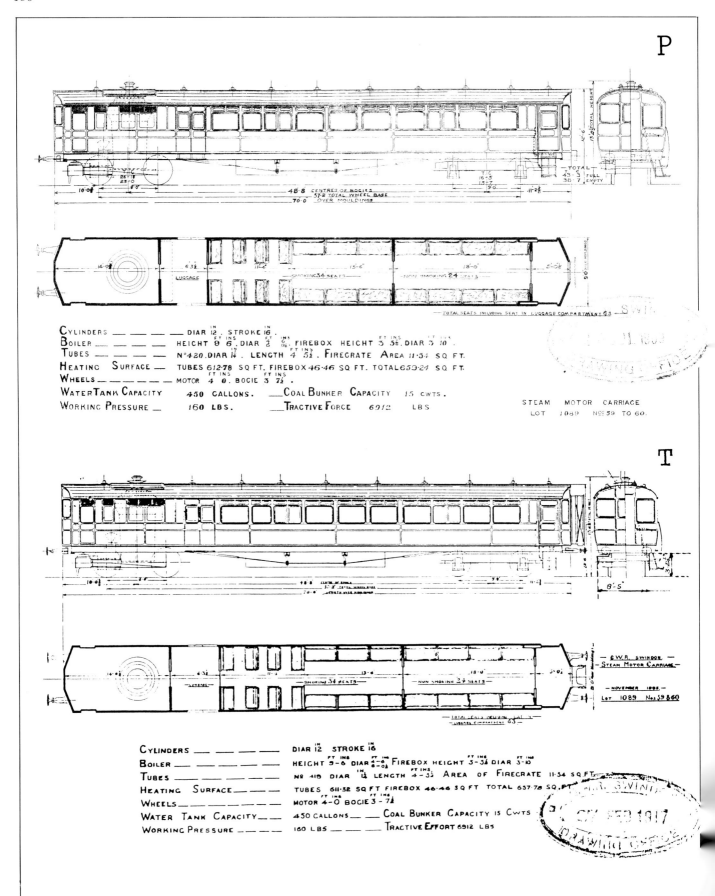

CYLINDERS — DIAR 12 IN STROKE 16 IN
BOILER — HEIGHT 9-6 FT INS DIAR 4-6/6-0⅛ FT INS FIREBOX HEIGHT 3-5⅞ FT INS DIAR 3-10 FT INS
TUBES — Nº 418 DIAR 1¼ IN LENGTH 4-5½ FT INS AREA OF FIRECRATE 11·54 SQ FT
HEATING SURFACE — TUBES 611·32 SQ FT FIREBOX 46·46 SQ FT TOTAL 657·78 SQ FT
WHEELS — MOTOR 4-0 FT INS BOCIE 3-7½ FT INS
WATER TANK CAPACITY — 450 CALLONS — COAL BUNKER CAPACITY 15 CWTS
WORKING PRESSURE — 160 LBS — TRACTIVE EFFORT 6912 LBS

Diagrams P & T: Nos.59 & 60

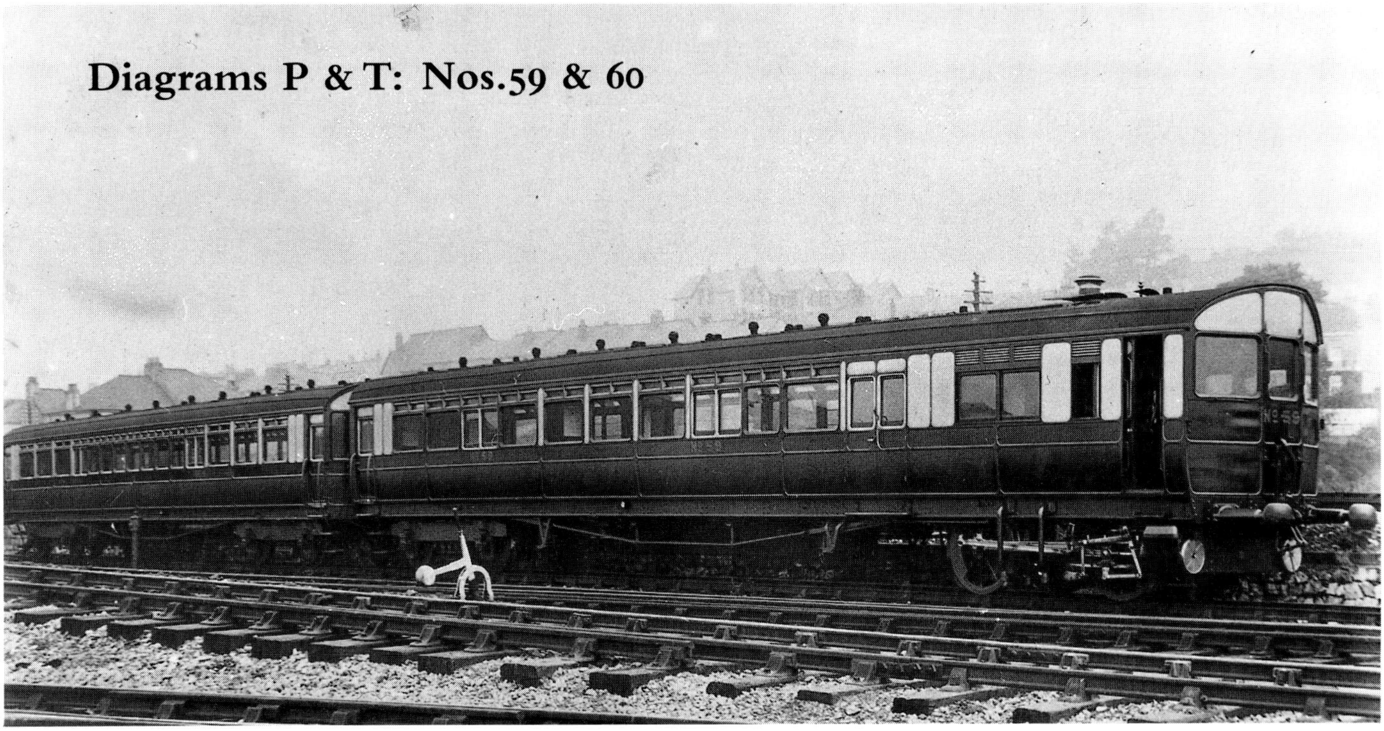

Car No. 59 of Diagram P in as-built condition close-coupled to trailer 9 of Diagram D. Neither had buffers at their adjacent ends. No. 59 seems to have been at Laira from new until 1913 and is believed normally to have run with trailer 9. No. 59 is seen in the fully-lined brown and cream livery, but does not seem to have been carrying any GWR marking or device. COLLECTION R. C. RILEY

On 18th February 1904, in anticipation of heavy traffic in the Plymouth area, two new 70ft SRMs (Nos.59 & 60) were ordered on Carriage Department Lot 1089. These cars were to run with two special trailers (Nos.9 & 10), ordered at the same time. They were all constructed with openings at the trailing end, so that a conductor could easily pass between the two and issue tickets in both. Initially they were close coupled – SRM + trailer – but were not gangwayed together, although standard gangways were fitted later. They were also able to run as a four-coach train: SRM 59 + Trailer 9 + Trailer 10 + SRM 60, which could be divided back into two SRM + trailer trains when traffic requirements necessitated.

Mr. Tom Hurry Riches of the Taff Vale Railway travelled on this train, or one very much like it, in the course of a study of the GWR's auto-train services, and he commented in a report of February 1910 to his General Manager:

> 'Some of the motors and trailers are fitted with close couplings and were designed to run in pairs, each pair consisting of a 74ft motor and a 70ft trailer, an open gangway being provided between the cars. Two sets may be coupled together to form a four vehicle train. When this is done the motor cars are placed at the ends of the trains.'

He further reported that this train ran very smoothly, and without any jerking. Incidentally, his reference to 'a 74ft motor' related to a 70ft SRM, which was 74ft long over buffers.

As these cars and trailers were purpose-built, it is open to speculation as to how control of this particular 4-car train was achieved. Normally, the through regulator gear of two trailers could not be coupled at their driving ends (which were together in this instance), so either there was a special fitting, unrecorded, on trailers Nos.9 and 10 or – which I think more likely – the trailing SRM was driven by its fireman in response to bell signals from the driver in the leading car, in accordance with the instructions for driving two SRMs coupled together.

In theory, SRMs Nos.59 and 60 could be used singly, whilst trailers Nos.9 and 10 could be used with other SRMs or with auto-fitted locomotives if required. However, as built, there seems to have been a gangway-sized 'hole' (Mr Hurry Riches' 'open gangway') in the close-coupled ends of both SRMs and trailers, and these apertures may have inhibited such a practice, at least until standard gangways were fitted and a gangway cover could be used.

DESIGN

SRMs Nos.59 and 60 were delivered in November and October 1905 at an average cost of £1,007 0s 1d to the Locomotive Department, plus £845 11s 9d to the Carriage Department, a total of £1,852 11s 10d each. For some reason, the stock valuation gave a cost of £1,828 each.

In spite of their intended use on Plymouth suburban area services, they were constructed with a luggage compartment – i.e. they were a 'branch' type. They were 70ft long, 9ft wide, 12ft 6in high from rail to roof and 13ft 4½in over chimney. The wheelbase was 57ft 2in, with the centre of the engine wheelbase 10ft 0⅝in from the headstock and the trailing bogie centre 11ft 2⅝in from the other headstock. The trailing bogies were of the 9ft volute spring type, which were changed for the coil spring equivalent at an unrecorded date, but probably within a year or two. They had incandescent gas lighting from new.

As built, they were shown on diagram P. In 1911, they were given gangway connectors at the trailing end and were then shown on diagram T.

The motor compartment was the standard 14ft 0⅜in between the end of the car and the partition, with the usual window, door and ventilation arrangements.

Next to this, the luggage compartment measured 6ft 3½in between partitions, and had double external doors which opened outwards, without retractable steps beneath. A drop-down transverse seat was attached to the motor compartment partition which, when fully in place, blocked the internal sliding door to that compartment.

Passenger accommodation is shown on the diagrams as two compartments, the 'smoking' seating 34 and 'non-smoking' 24. The smoking compartment was next to the luggage compartment, and had four pairs of walkover seats (11ft 4in long) plus a 13ft 6in length of longitudinal bench seats. Adjacent to the walkover seats were two large fixed lights plus a pair of droplights (apparently original equipment), whilst the bench seats had three large, fixed

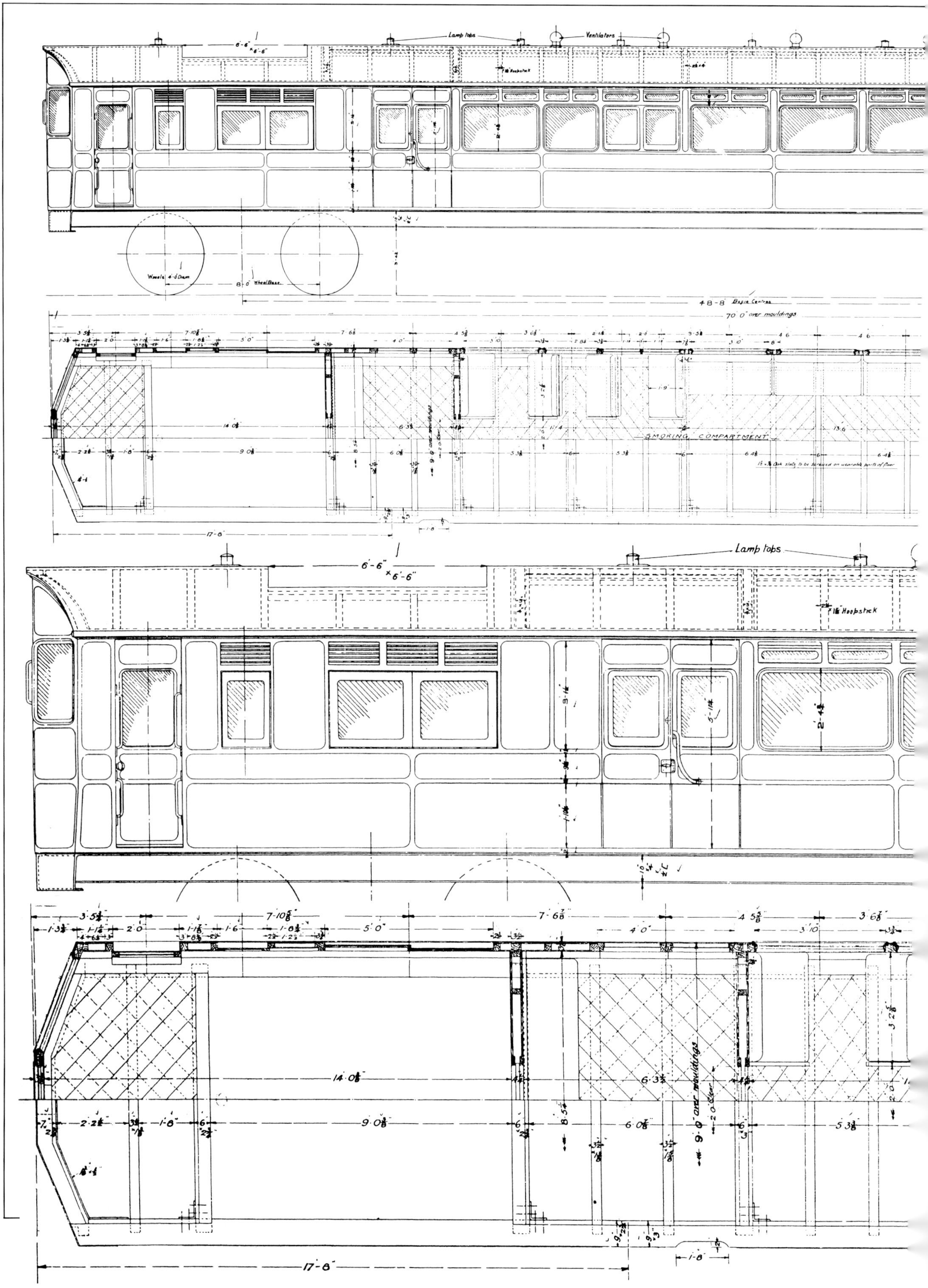
Lamp tops
Ventilators
6'-6" × 6'-6"
8'-0" Wheel Base
48'-8" Bogie Centres
70'-0" over mouldings
SMOKING COMPARTMENT
17'-8"
Lamp tops
6'-6" × 6'-6"
14'-0⅛"
9'-0⅛"
9'-0" over mouldings
17'-8"

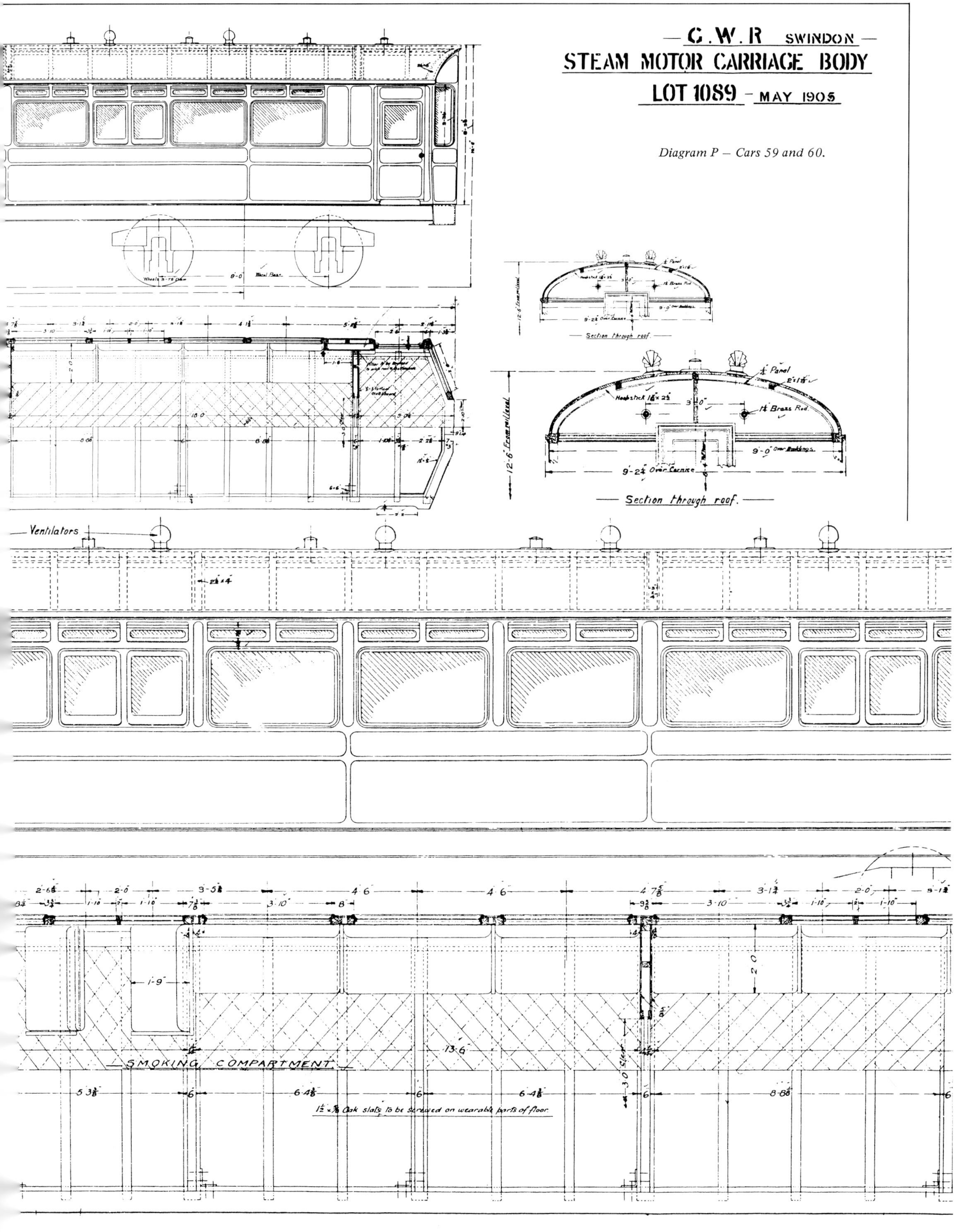
— C.W.R SWINDON —
STEAM MOTOR CARRIAGE BODY
LOT 1089 - MAY 1905
12'-6" From rail level
¼ Panel
Hoodstick 1⅝ × 2¼
3'-0"
1¼ Brass Rod
9'-0" Over Mouldings
9'-2¼ Over Cornice
Section through roof.
Ventilators
SMOKING COMPARTMENT
1½ × ⅞ Oak slats to be screwed on wearable parts of floor.

Diagram P – Cars 59 and 60.

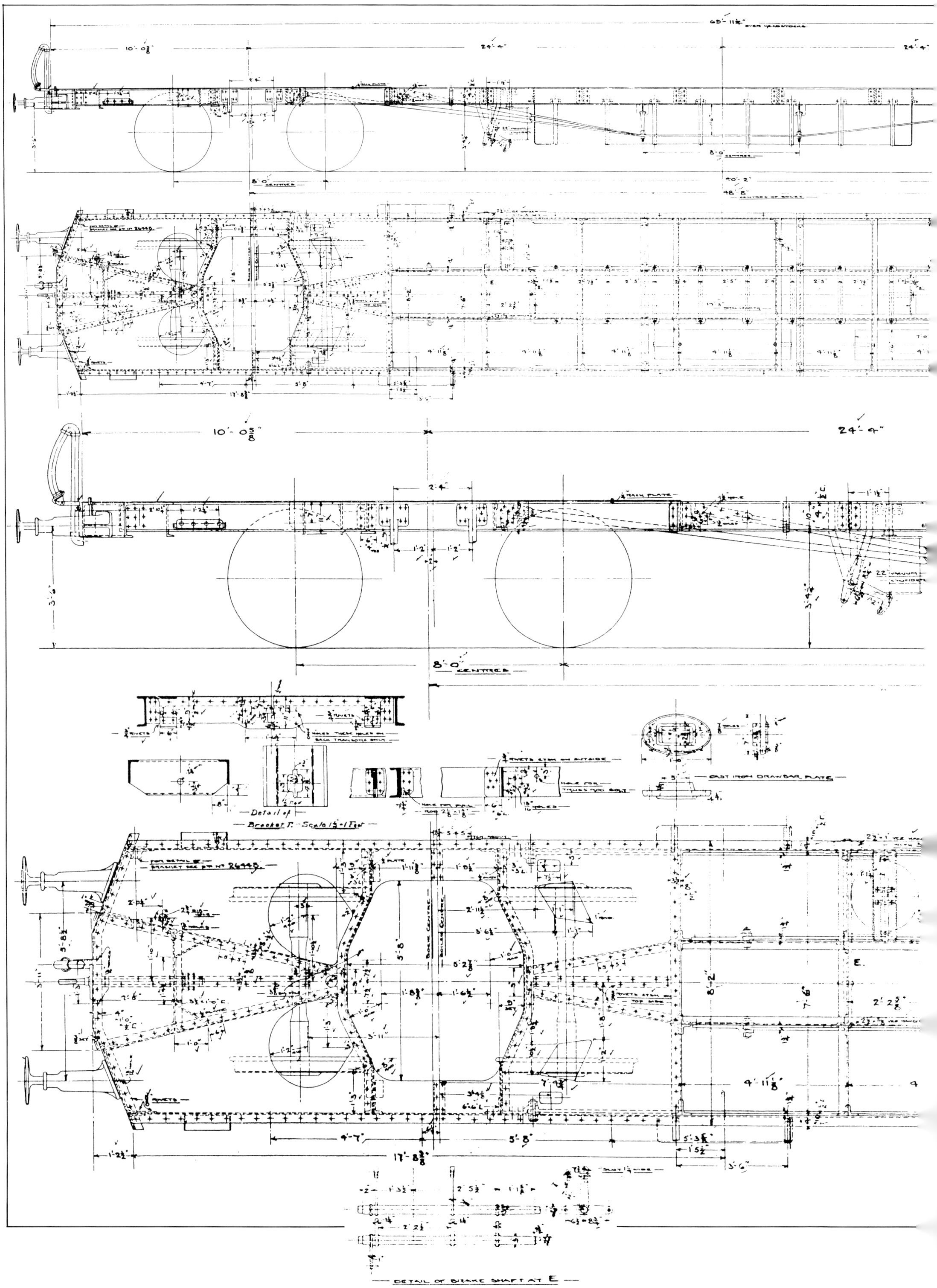

10'-0⅝"
24'-4"
8'-0" CENTRES
4'-7"
5'-8"
17'-8⅜"
Detail of Bracket F - Scale 1½" = 1 Foot
CAST IRON DRAWBAR PLATE
E.
DETAIL OF BRAKE SHAFT AT E

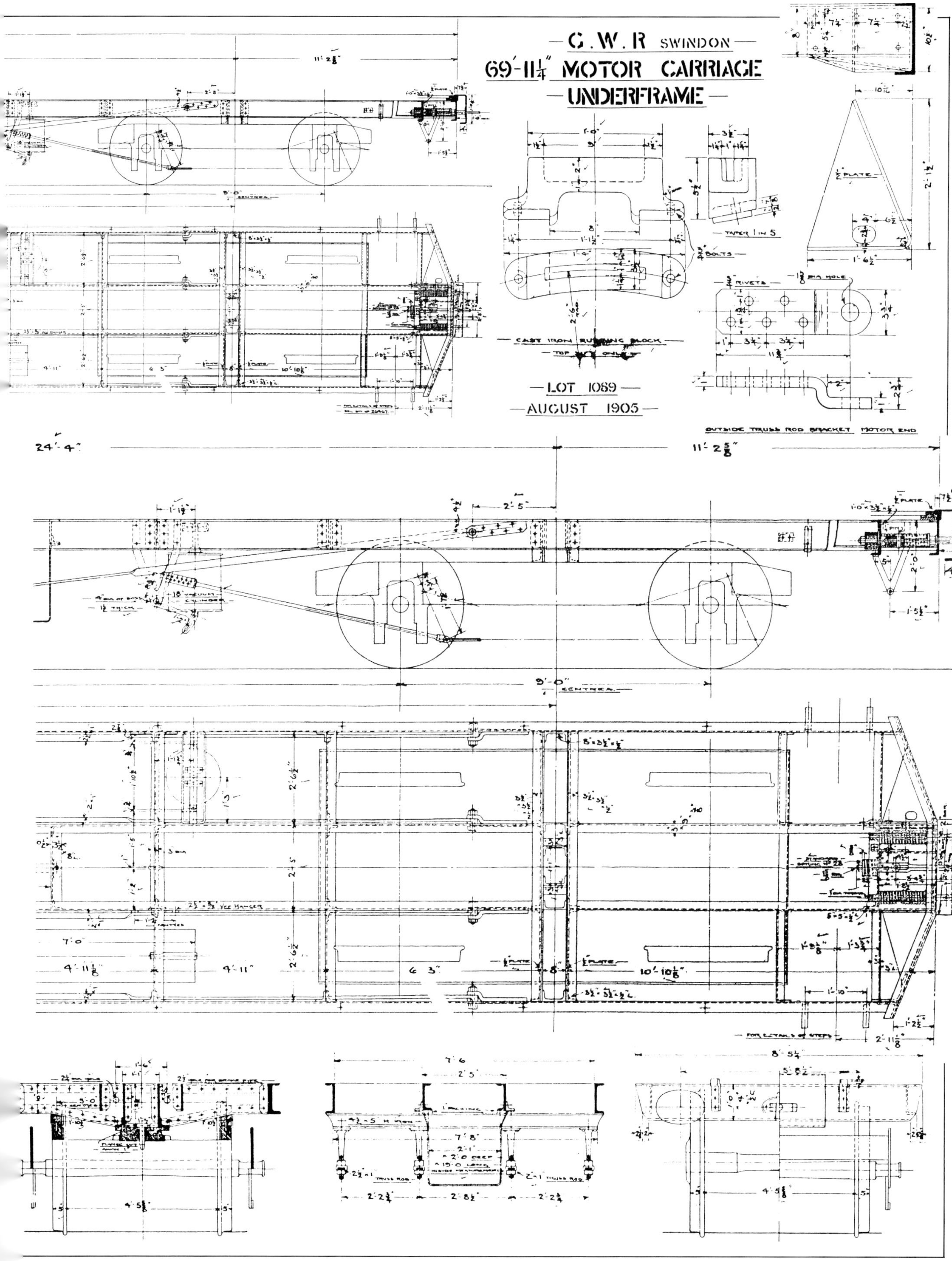

Underframe for Diagram P Cars 59 and 60. Note arrangement for close-coupling at trailing end.

№28384

lights. The non-smoking compartment had an 18ft length of longitudinal bench seating only, and this was served by one large, fixed light, a pair of droplights and another two large, fixed lights.

Seating in the cars accommodated 63 passengers, including those on the seats in the luggage compartment.

The driver's vestibule was 5ft 0½in long, and was provided with sliding doors in the sides and retractable steps below them. This end was normally close coupled to a trailer, and the diagram shows a doorway (or 'hole') in the end that was 2ft 10in wide. Unfortunately, the photographs of these cars do not show either the close coupling (except that no side buffers are visible) or the gangway arrangements.

According to the register, both weighed 45 tons, whilst the weights shown on the diagram P and the Carriage Dept. version of diagram T are both identical:

	Empty *Tons – Cwt*	*Full* *Tons – Cwt*
Power Bogie	23 – 0	26 – 18
Trailing Bogie	15 – 7	16 – 5
Total	38 – 7	43 – 3

MODIFICATIONS & DISPOSAL

These SRMs presumably had their power compartment windows altered so that an external water filler could be fitted in a panel as usual, and rainstrips would have been fitted.

In 1911, they were fitted with standard gangways at the trailing end, and the new diagram, T, was issued showing this modification. It also illustrated the fitting of standard SRM/trailer buffers at the trailing end; the SRMs were no longer close coupled to their trailer. There are two versions of diagram T extant: one, presumably a Carriage Department drawing, shows loaded and empty weights, but no power unit table, whilst the other is a Locomotive Department version, which does include the power unit information, but, unusually, not the weight on each bogie.

In traffic, they were both normally allocated to Plymouth until the end of 1913, after which they went their separate ways. They may have remained attached to their respective trailers until rebuilt, as the trailers were rebuilt at the same time.

The cars stopped work in 1917/18 and were rebuilt as trailers, reappearing in June 1920 as a gangwayed pair for the Plymouth area. Unusually, they were not rebuilt identically, as one was given a luggage compartment and the other not. Their trailers were also rebuilt in 1920 as a gangwayed pair, also spending much of their lives in the Plymouth district.

TABLE 30

SUMMARY: Diagrams P & T (Built on Lot 1089)

Car No.	*Built*	*First Boiler*	*First Engine*	*Tare t - c*	*Steam Heat*	*Std G'way (Dia. T)*	*Final Miles*	*Stopped Work*	*To Trailer No*	*Dia.*
59	Nov 05	1095	0862	45-00	Nov 05	Oct 11	394.817	Dec 18	126	A13
60	Oct 05	1093	0853	45-00	Oct 05	Dec 11	387.653	May 17	127	A14

NOTE

Built with 9 ft volute bogies, replaced by 9 ft coil spring ones at unrecorded dates.

CHAPTER TEN

NON-STANDARD GWR RAIL MOTORS

Kerr, Stuart, Diagram E: Nos.15 and 16

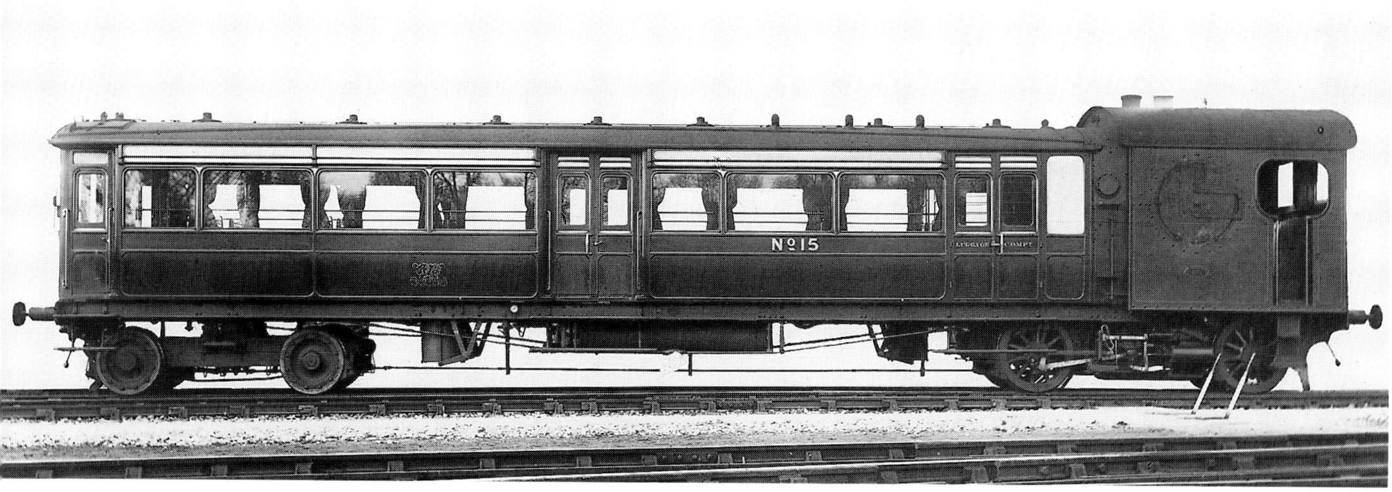

This official photograph of Car 15 of Diagram E as first running on the GWR shows that it has been fitted with gas lighting in place of the electric light with which it was delivered. There appears to have been only one sand pipe to the driving wheel suited to forward motion, although one for reverse running may have been touched out on the negative. The water filler cap appears to have been between the engine and the coach portions. Droplights had not yet been fitted to the passenger saloons and there were bars to all the windows. Unusually for an SRM, the luggage compartment doors had 'LUGGAGE' on one leaf in the waist and 'COMPT' on the other. Curtains at the windows were not provided in GWR design cars.
NATIONAL RAILWAY MUSEUM

SRMs Nos 15 and 16 were ordered from Kerr, Stuart & Co. of Stoke-on-Trent on 15th December 1904. Kerr, Stuart's order number for the GWR cars was 2032, and GWR Carriage Lot 1099 was eventually issued in June 1905 to cover the purchase. This design of SRM was similar in appearance to the Taff Vale Railway's smaller cars Nos.1–7, a further batch of which was being built by Kerr, Stuart & Co. at this time, and both the TVR and GWR cars had the coach portion sub-contracted to the Bristol Carriage & Wagon Co. In fact, the design of the engine portion seems to have been Kerr, Stuart's own, and was based on the three cars they had sold to the 5ft 6in-gauge Buenos Aires Great Southern Railway, while the coach portions and the articulation arrangement were basically of Taff Vale design, and were referred to as such in internal correspondence of Kerr, Stuart.

The most important difference in design between these and the GWR-designed cars was in the way the power unit was incorporated. In the Great Western designs, the motor unit was built into the end of the car, and was positioned within its underframe, whilst in the Kerr, Stuart/TVR design it was semi-independent of the coach portion, and attached to it by an articulated joint. It was therefore much simpler to exchange the power unit of the Kerr, Stuart design when necessary.

There were other significant differences between the TVR and the GWR motor units. The Taff Vale design had a central firebox with a double boiler arranged across the frames in front of the cab, while the cylinders drove the front axle of the power bogie (it was an 0–2–2). The Great Western cars had a single boiler, also positioned across the unit, while the driver's cab was in front of the boiler and the cylinders drove the trailing wheelset of the power unit, so it was a 2–2–0. The GWR cars used Walschaerts valve gear, while the TVR cars had Stephenson's link motion.

These cars were delivered to Swindon in August 1905 at an average cost of £2,071 13s 4d, to which an additional charge of £16 15s 9d was allocated to the Loco Department, and 17s 10d to the Carriage Department, the total cost to the company being £2,089 7s 11d each.

To historians, the purchase of these two SRMs has always posed the question: why did the Great Western acquire them when they were non-standard in so many ways? In particular, they were only about half as powerful as the GWR designs, and the power unit axles were uncoupled, so that slipping was likely to be a problem; these were points that Churchward must surely have noticed from the example the company borrowed from the L & SWR. At least GWR Nos.15 and 16 were over twice as powerful as the L &SWR's car.

Factors which *may* have influenced Churchward included the more intractable problem with the Great Western's design of SRM – the power unit was enclosed by coachwork; if any significant work had to be done on the motor, it had to be removed from the car, which was a fairly major and relatively time-consuming operation. By having the power unit separated from the coach, the two could easily be parted. Hurry Riches, the Locomotive, Carriage & Wagon Superintendent of the TVR, quoted '20 minutes being ample time' to remove the engine from the coach.

Hurry Riches was a very strong proponent of the SRM, and his first effort had only just been preceded by Churchward's. In spite of the lack of coupled wheels, the Taff Vale cars were reputedly very successful: they were able to cope with 1 in 40 gradients, and could haul trailers (but not up 1 in 40 grades). This being the period when the Great Western were experimenting with simple and compound 'Atlantic' locomotives, and comparing them with 4–6–0s, the Great Western's motives for buying these SRMs may have included 'research'.

It is interesting to observe the co-operation between railways in this period, at least on the mechanical engineering side. For example, the TVR were permitted to inspect the L & SWR-built car, and the GWR were able to borrow it. Great Western staff knew that the TVR car would have retractable steps even before that company's directors had seen it. The Lancashire & Yorkshire were able to buy two cars stated to be to the TVR specification from Kerr, Stuart & Co., whilst in 1906 the Great Western's General Manager, James Inglis, asked to see the TVR's specification and drawings for their large rail motors, and a set was loaned to the GWR.

DESIGN

Following their delivery to Swindon, Nos 15 and 16 rated an illustration and a paragraph in the new 'Locomotive, Carriage and Wagons

From this view of the trailing end saloon of Car 16 of Diagram E, it appears that there were windows in the end partition allowing passengers to see into the driving compartment and the line ahead, although the official photographer had either put a screen behind the windows or had retouched the negative. The sliding door to the driver's compartment was open; the handle can be seen on the left of the doorway above the furthest seat. Part of the handbrake wheel can be seen to the left, and the regulator handle is just visible against the glare. The bell pushes for communication with the guard and fireman can be seen to the right of the central window. The compartment was equipped with wooden slatted seats, curtains, a luggage rack and ventilators. The rail across the windows at waist height would appear to have kept the curtains in place.

NATIONAL RAILWAY MUSEUM

Car 15 of Diagram E at Somerton with a clerestory coach in tow. LENS OF SUTTON

Notes' column of the *Great Western Magazine* for October 1905:

> 'Two 56ft cars built by Messrs Kerr, Stuart and Co. have recently been delivered and are here illustrated. The main points of difference between these cars and those constructed by the Company are as follows: The GW motor engines have a vertical boiler; cylinders 12in by 16in, and four coupled wheels 4ft in diameter. The Kerr, Stuart engines have a locomotive type boiler arranged across the frames; the cylinders are 9in by 15in, and drive onto a single pair of wheels. The cars are electrically lighted on the Turbine-Dynamo system. In the case of those of GW construction oil gas is the illuminant; incandescent gas lighting being employed in the later vehicles. The two cars under notice are fitted with steam brake; the GW Co.'s have the vacuum brake. It is expected that the cars will be in service shortly.'

On 31st May 1905, the Traffic Committee had agreed that 'the down line between Castle Cary and Charlton Mackrell on the new railway from Castle Cary to Langport be opened for a rail motor service on 1st July next and [approved] expenditure of £380 in carrying out certain temporary works at Keinton Mandeville and Charlton Mackrell stations and £295 for a Halt at Alford.'

In November 1905, the *GWR Magazine* reported:

> 'One of the Kerr-Stuart railmotor cars (No.15) has been appropriated to Charlton Mackrell. It has been deemed advisable to fit these cars with the vacuum brake; also with the GWR arrangement for working trailers.'

Both cars were actually allocated to Frome shed for this service – No.15 at the end of September, and No.16 at the end of October 1905 – though it appears that the service was opened using other cars. The official 'building' dates for these cars were recorded in the *SRM Register* as October 1905 (No.15) and November 1905 (No.16), but they appear to be the 'set to work' dates.

Over headstocks, both cars were 56ft 3in long, the carriage portion was 8ft 6in wide and the motor unit cover 8ft 11in wide. The height of the coach portion is not recorded on GWR diagram E, but the motor unit is shown to have been 12ft 7in from rail to top of the roof, and 13ft 1½in from rail to chimney top.

The motor unit had a wheelbase of 9ft 9in, and the trailing bogie was of 8ft wheelbase. The total wheelbase was 50ft 0½in, the centre pin of the rear bogie was 6ft 8½in from the adjacent headstock whilst the distance between the leading headstock and the articulation point between the power unit and the coach portion was 9ft 3in. This point was not central in the motor unit, but was about 5ft 9in from the leading axle. The power unit had wheels of 3ft 5in diameter, and are believed to have had 12 spokes. The rear bogie had inside frames, and solid wheels of 2ft 10in diameter.

As reported in the *GWR Magazine*, the cars were fitted with the automatic vacuum brake, and two of the Armstrong type of moving brake cylinders were used. Both were under the coach portion.

The motor unit was housed in a shortened version of the cover used on those Great Western auto tank engines that were 'disguised' as coaches at about this time. From the front, it looks to modern eyes vaguely like a diesel shunter, having two approximately square windows set fairly high up in the end, with a ventilator grille centrally above them. The roof profile was elliptical, with the major radius at the top. In these cars, the boiler was placed behind the driving and firing position, as in the GWR-design cars.

On the side elevation, the motor unit cover had the classical 'keyhole' shape of tank engine cab openings at its leading end, and behind it a half-circle flap giving access to the boiler (on one side – visible when the power unit was to the left). On the other side there was a circular access to the boiler, looking rather like a traditional smokebox door. Below these two access points was a plate, presumably the maker's. The roof had two 'chimneys' poking through it: the rearmost one was the actual chimney, whilst the other hid the safety valves.

Behind the power unit cover there was an extension conforming to the profile of the carriage section, and actually part of it; this contained the water tank and had a filler fairly high up on its side. The tank held 338 gallons.

The power unit cover and the water tank extension were originally painted chocolate brown, with cream lining, whilst the cab interior was also chocolate brown. The frames and wheels were black, but the motion was left bright.

A fairly conventional locomotive-type boiler was provided, with the tubes arranged horizontally across the unit, and the firebox at one end.

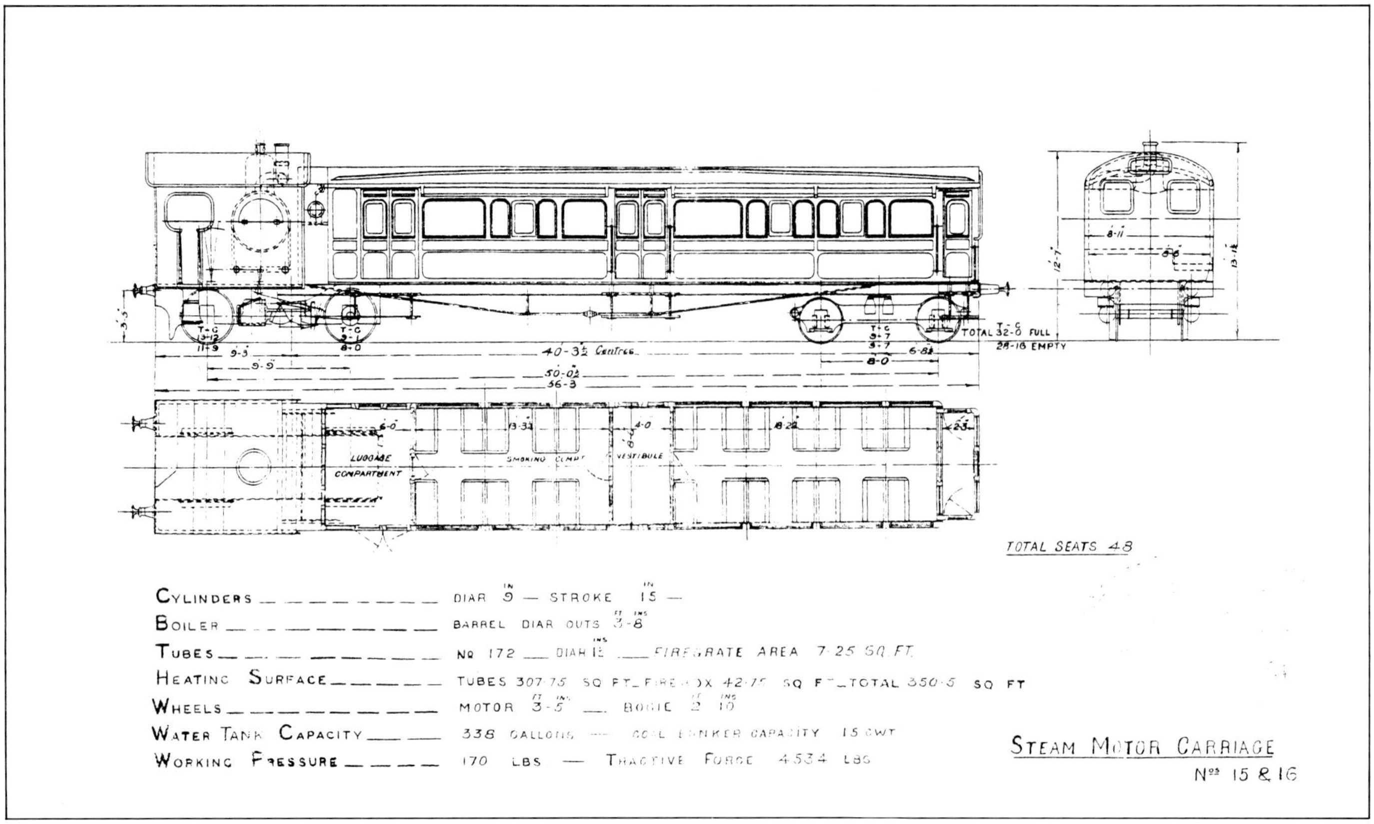

The boiler was 3ft 8in diameter and 6ft 1¼in long with 172 × 1½in tubes. The firegrate had an area of 7·25 sq ft, and the total heating surface was 350·5 sq ft as compared to the normal GWR designs of some 650 – 675 sq ft. The power units of Nos.15 and 16 did, however, work at 170 lbs sq in, a little greater than most of the GWR-built SRMs. The cylinders were much smaller than the GWR standard at 9in diameter × 15in stroke. Like the GWR standard motor units, the cylinders were outside, and Walschaerts valve gear was employed. However, on these two the cylinders were placed just behind the front (undriven) wheelset.

Photographs are not at all clear on the fitting of sandboxes, but Kerr, Stuart correspondence does indicate that sanding apparatus was fitted. The official 'as built' photograph appears to show only one sand pipe feeding a driving wheel, suitable for travel with the power unit leading. However, it is possible that the photographer has retouched the other pipes out of the photograph when he was working on the background.

The motor units of Nos.15 and 16 were numbered 0864 and 0865; they were interchangeable between themselves (only), but in practice seem to have remained with their respective coach units.

Coach units had a wood panelled body with a low arc roof, and a long ventilator above the saloons' windows. There were quadrant corners to the mouldings on the lower panels, and to the tops of the windows and the leading panel that reached the eaves, but square corners to the waist mouldings, and to the bottom corners of the windows.

The trailing end was flat, with three tall windows extending from the waist to the eaves. The handbrake in the driver's compartment at the trailing end was operated by means of a vertical wheel mounted on the end of the coach; its shaft protruded through the end, and operated an external, vertical shaft via bevel gears contained in a prominent housing on the end. Hand rails on the end swept up from the corner pillar at waist height to just below the roof, in Taff Vale style. Also copied from the TVR cars were six end steps, four of which were on the pillars between the end windows (two on each), giving access to the roof.

According to the *Kerr, Stuart Order Book*, electric lighting driven from a steam turbine generator was fitted, making these two cars unique on the Great Western. This is confirmed by the GWR *SRM Register* and the *Great Western Magazine*. However, incandescent gas lighting was substituted for the electric light; from the evidence of photographs this was done at an early date, either before or while they were in use on the Charlton Mackrell service. These two cars were therefore amongst the first GWR SRMs to have incandescent lighting. The roof also carried three rather prominent 'Eros' ventilators above the smoking compartment, and it had a single rainstrip each side.

Curiously, the diagram gives no overall length for the coach portion, possibly because it included the water tank at the motor unit end, as mentioned above. Next to the tank was a 6ft-wide luggage compartment with double doors to the outside, which conformed to the bodyside profile, and opened outwards. There was a single step below these doors. A hinged door provided access to the passenger accommodation.

As built, the cars had large, fixed lights to both saloons, but these were altered so that the 'smoking' saloon had a quarterlight/droplight/quarterlight (qdq) unit substituted for the central fixed light, whilst the 'non-smoking' saloon was given two qdq units in place of the two middle fixed lights. As altered, the windows conformed to those shown on the diagram.

All the doors to the coach portion had a fixed step at solebar height, and a lower fixed step below them.

Next to the luggage compartment was the smoking saloon, 13ft 3¼in long with 2½ seating bays, accommodating 20 passengers.

Beyond, there was a 4ft wide passenger's vestibule with double doors to the outside. These doors were flat, recessed slightly, and opened inwards.

Following the vestibule was the non-smoking saloon, 18ft 2¼in long, with 3½ seating bays accommodating 28; this gave a total of 48 passenger seats in the SRM.

The driver's vestibule was 2ft 3in deep, and was recessed relative to the body sides, with flat doors that opened inwards, hinged on the corner pillars. In this vestibule there was a vertical hand-wheel arranged across the car, operating the handbrake via a spindle through the car end, a pair of bevel gears (hidden under a cover), and a vertical rod reaching down below the headstocks, which presumably carried a screw mechanism.

Underframing to the coach portion was of steel, with queen post trusses. The truss rods were of round section, and there was a turnbuckle positioned centrally on each for adjustment purposes. A gas cylinder, when fitted, was carried centrally. The regulator mechanism under the car seems to have been fitted by the GWR, and not the makers.

The tare weight of these SRMs is given on the diagram as:

	Empty *Tons – Cwt*	*Full* *Tons – Cwt*
Engine		
Leading Wheels	11 – 9	13 – 12
Driven Wheels	8 – 0	9 – 1
Trailing Bogie	9 – 7	9 – 7
Total	28 – 16	32 – 0

The register gives the weight of No.15 as 32 tons 11 cwt 1 qtr, later 33 tons 3 cwt, and No.16 as 32 tons 16 cwt. The Bristol C & W Co. quoted the tare weight of the carriage portion as 17 tons, although a proportion of this would have been carried by the power bogie.

Having the highest axle weight on the non-driven wheelset of the motor unit does seem a little odd, given its implications on adhesion. However, the TVR cars apparently had a weight of 15 tons 13 cwt on their driven axle, which may have provided good adhesion. This weight, together with the small-size driving wheels, was blamed for considerable problems with overheating of the journals, a problem that was only eventually solved by use of forced lubrication.

WORK & DISPOSAL

For some reason, Nos.15 and 16 seem to have almost escaped the attention of photographers while they were at work on the GWR, so it is not known which type of trailer they worked with, or, indeed, if they ever did. It is possible that the Great Western's two 4-wheel trailers, which were produced from old third class coaches, were to run with Nos.15 and 16, but this is speculation.

They did not last long on the Castle Cary & Charlton Mackrell service, and No.16 was transferred to Worcester in January 1906, and then to Stourbridge the following month, presumably for the Stourbridge Junction & Stourbridge Town shuttle service. Nos.15 and 16 were both in store at Swindon in early 1908.

Thereafter, No.15 was based at Stourbridge until May 1915 with a six-month stay in Swindon Stock shed in the first half of 1909. It was not used after April 1915, by which time it had run a recorded mileage of 86,948.

No.16 worked at Southall and Slough as well as Stourbridge. It eventually went to Swindon Works and the Stock shed in December 1919 with a mileage of only 55,054, officially at January 1920.

On 8th April 1920 a minute was drawn up for the Loco. & Stores Committee's meeting on 15th April concerning the sale of these cars:

'SALE OF KERR STUART RAIL MOTOR CARS Nos.15 & 16 to MR. JOHN F. WAKE

'Mr J.F. Wake (Engineer & Machinery Merchant) Darlington, after inspection has offered to purchase the two "Kerr Stuart" rail motor cars Nos.15 & 16 for £1,100 each, delivered free at Swindon.

'The two cars were constructed by Messrs. Kerr Stuart & Company in 1905 to their own design and do not meet the requirements of the Company. They have, therefore, been sold for the sum named above.'

However, the sale of No.16 was not completed, and it was put back into stock in November 1920; the boiler record card says 'Cash not received'. In view of the conversion of the very similar Taff Vale SRMs to trailers or hauled coaches at the grouping – some of which were completed by the GWR – it is perhaps surprising that No.16 was not rebuilt as a trailer or a hauled coach. In the event, it remained in store and seems never to have run again. It was broken up in December 1927.

Meanwhile, No.15 went to the Nidd Valley Light Railway in Yorkshire. This was a private railway, owned by the Bradford Corporation Waterworks, who used the car for a passenger service between Pateley Bridge and Lofthouse-in-Nidderdale. It operated on the line until the passenger service was withdrawn in 1937, by which time, ironically, it was the last Great

Car 15 was sold to the Nidd Valley Railway in Yorkshire, which ran from Pateley Bridge to Lofthouse-in-Nidderdale. In this picture the car is seen at Lofthouse. COLLECTION R. C. RILEY

Car 15 at Pateley Bridge station on the Nidd Valley Railway on 24th September 1923. A. G. ELLIS

Western SRM still in use as such. It was then scrapped, but the coach body – or part of it – was still recognisable in a Leeds scrap yard in September 1961.

It is difficult to decide just how successful these two cars were. No.15 seems to have been distinctly 'better' than No.16, and the mileage it amassed was comparable with conventional SRM No.1, which ran 98,939 miles up to its withdrawal in February 1915 in a life which started about two years earlier than that of No.15. On the other hand, trailers of diagrams B and C typically ran more than twice as far as No.15, though over a slightly longer period (of about 1½ years). Both Nos.15 and 16 spent considerable periods in Swindon works and Swindon stock shed, and this would appear to be a reflection on their non-standard nature, the lack of a spare boiler, and the lack of suitable services for low-power SRMs with their relatively low factor of adhesion.

TABLE 31

SUMMARY: Diagram E (Built on Lot 1099 by Kerr, Stuart & Co.)

Car No.	*Supplied*	*Boiler*	*Engine*	*Tare t - c*	*Steam Heat*	*Incand. Gas*	*Final Miles*	*Stopped Work*	*Sold*	*Re - instated*	*Cond.*
15	Aug 05	894	0864	33-03	Oct 05	Oct 05	86,948	Apr 15	May 20		
16	Aug 05	895	0865	32-16	Nov 05	Nov 05	55,046	Dec 19	[May 20]	Dec 20	Dec 27

NOTE

Not put to work until fitted with steam heating and gas lighting.

Another view of Car 15 at Pateley Bridge station on the Nidd Valley Railway. In the waist can be seen 'NIDD VALLEY LIGHT RAILWAY'. Beyond the centre vestibule door there was 'BRADFORD CORPORATION' in the waist, and 'GUARD' on the guard's door. T. J. EDGINGTON CTY. R. C. RILEY

Car 15 at work on the Nidd Valley Railway. COLLECTION J. N. SLINN

KERR STUART ORDER BOOK

In the National Railway Museum Library there is a photocopy of the *Kerr, Stuart Order Book* which also gives summaries of correspondence. This is a hand written document not suitable for reproduction, but the following has been extracted from it and put into date order. In one or two places I have had to guess missing or unclear words.

NOTES:
BAGS: Buenos Aires Great Southern Railway (then UK owned).
LO: London Office of Kerr Stuart.
d/y: delivery
d/d: delivered.
GWR: Great Western Railway, Swindon

Order Summary

'KS & C° Ltd, London December 15, 1904
[Order No.] 2032
[Vehicle? Ref, presumably to their Stoke Office] 906

'Steam Motor Bogie 4ft 8½in gauge of the type shown on Dwg 11135. The body main frame & carriage bogie will be generally of the Taff Vale design & specfn. The main frame at the motor end will be altered in such a manner that the distance from the end of the body to the centre of the engine bogie pivot will be 2ft 0in instead of 2ft 6in. It will also be altered to permit of the 3ft 5in dia. wheels entering the main frame & giving clearance when rounding a curve. [SRM No.15]

'We will send a Dwg. from the Bristol C° showing this proposed altn in a day or two. If at all possible please make the motor bogie frame suit the pivot end of the Taff Vale frame; with the above mentioned alteration. Electric lighting to be supplied. We will order the dynamo, switch to [be sent to] this office, also the buffers.

'You to supply the top motor bogie centre to the Bristol C°.

'Cross section of coach body to be similar to the TaffVale.

'Further particlrs. to be discussed on Monday next.

'Please send 4 nameplates to the Bristol C° for the bodies. (Done Feb 20)'

[SRM No.16]

'D/y 1 at beginning of April & the other say a month later.'

2032
Additional, 16 Dec 04
'2 plugs and sockets for electric connections between Engine Bogie & bodies of Motor coaches, suitable for 110 volts. No electric light will be needed in Engine Cab. No head or tail lights required. These will be supplied by the Rly. C°.'

2032A
11 Jan 05
'1 Tyre for testing purposes.'

CORRESPONDENCE SUMMARIES 1904/5

The following correspondence was carried out between the various concerns relating to the construction of SRMs 15 and 16:

LO, 15 Dec 04
'Note remarks re. d/y, but we may find later that we shall be able to take parts from say [the motor] bogie of the BAGS to enable us to accelerate d/y. The driving wheels will be as the BAGS. We are aware that the diagonal bracings will be left out. Mr. B will bring the Bristol C°'s dwg showing the revised main frame end. The GWR will send you the loading gauge direct. Copy Orders to Bristol C° enclosed. Are ordering buffers TV type from Turton Platts & dynamo from Greenwood & Bayley.'

LO, 17 Dec 04
'Enclosing dwgs. 6814, 15, 16 which we have received from Bristol C°. You will notice that they have made provision for our driving wheels (3ft 5in dia) clearing the main frame both vertically and laterally. Will you check this and make arrangement suit if possible. The Bristol C° ask us if we shall require any other gusset plates at top of frames [at the] engine end. Please also look into this. With regard to the handbrake on the trailing bogie you will see that the end gangway being only 2ft 3in wide inside against 3ft 9in on the Taff Vale coach there is not room for brake column. What do you suggest?

GWR, 19 Dec 04
'Send herewith print showing maximum loading gauge.'

GWR, 19 Dec 04
'These coaches should be able to go round a curve of at least 3 chains radius.'

Bristol C°, 22 Dec 04
'Are looking into the matter of weights of body & underframe & will let you have same early as possible.'

LO, 24 Dec 04
'The clearance between brakework etc & rail level should be 6in.'

Bristol C°, 29 Dec 04
'We have no accurate weights of the T.V. & coach separate parts, but giving weights in actual working (Empty 32t-1c-0q-0lb loaded ....) we do not think there will be any material difference in the weight of the carriage portion of the GWR coach therefore [these] figures may answer your purpose.

'Note correction required to Dwg 11541. Wrote yesterday re. height of main frame channels.'

LO, 30 Dec 04
'With reference to print 2769 which we enclose of Buffers. We have ordered these & they are the ones shown on same print 602032. The blue dimensions are for the L&Y & red for the GWR. (See same date under [vehicle refs] 904/5).'

GW Ry. 31 Dec 04
'Yours of 28th. Will arrange for my assistants to inspect material at your works.'

LO, 2 Jan 05
'These buffers are ordered exactly in accordance with T.V. Bases are 10¼in sq and bolt holes 8½in centres.'

GWR, 2 Jan 05
'Ref 67302W. Note that if a tyre for testing purposes be required there will be [made ?] charge on this small lot. This is quite in order.'

LO, 3 Jan 05
'Supply ordinary lifeguards instead of cowcatchers.'

LO, 5 Jan 05
'We enclose dwg. of switches etc & turbine dynamo which will be sent from Greenwood & B. You will notice that we have had the switches, voltmeter & ammeter [shown?] on our plan (?).

GWR, 8 Jan 05
'Shall require to make test of tyres. Give notice to makers to put another one in hand.'

LO, 6 Jan 05
'Send soon as possible sketch showing connection of engine cab with carriage body & underframe. Also sketch showing position of steam pipe from engine for steam heating apparatus, so that the Bristol C° may be able to get out the arrgt of the steam pipes on their underframe. We enclose Bristol Dwg 6816. Is this correct?'

LO, 9 Jan 05
'Re. Tyres. We note your remarks & await your price for the extra tyre. Re. Castings. Enclosing letter from Inspector re. d/y. Hope no trouble with Bristol C°.

'The dynamos and switches will be the same as for BAGS but as you will see from the dwg we have sent the switches, voltmeter and ammeter all fastened to one piece.'

LO, 13 Jan 05
'Tail lamps will be to GWR standard, & they will supply & fit them. We have told the Bristol C° this.'

LO, 14 Jan 05
'We enclose dwg 6840 showing the box end of this frame. Is this in order? They have not shown any extra hole, but if they find it necessary they will get them in.

'To the Bristol Wagon & Cge C°'s siding, Bristol for GWR.

'Carriage per GW Ry.: No.15 18/1/05.'

LO, 20 Jan 05
'We enclose sketch 26736 showing the position which the lamp brackets will have to be fixed. These brackets will be supplied by the GWR and will be sent to you direct. They are of the GWR pattern oil lamps.'

Bristol C°, 23 Jan 05
'Acdg tracing showing position of lamp irons. Note GW C° will supply us with these.'

LO, 28 Jan 05
'They inform us that they have dispatched to you the necessary lamp brackets for the motor end of the coaches.'

LO, 1 Feb 05
'Please let us have a sketch arrangement of this early as possible.'

GWR, 1 Feb 05
'The lamp brackets should be fixed in the positions shown on dwg 26736 as per yours of 20th ult.'

Bristol C°. 16 Feb 05
'Have yours of 15th & note the distance between angle iron frames of the cab will be 2ft 3¼in. Re. print showing positions of Reg & whistle [...] we were under the impression that the communication cord apparatus together with the electric bells &c were not required for above coaches as they would only be worked from the engine end. Kindly let us know if such is the case.'

Bristol C°. 18 Feb 05
'Note communication apparatus to be supplied as stated on official order. Re. positions of Reg handle shown on Print 11551.'

LO, 22 Feb 05
'No number plate or monogram are to be placed on these bogies. They will be fixed by the GW Cº. The numbers 15 & 16 are to be painted in 9in letters on the front of the motor bogie. We will ask the Bristol Cº to let me know the height above rail level they will place their numbers at the rear end.

'To the Bristol Wagon & Cge Cº's siding, Bristol for GWR.

'Carriage per GW Ry.: 20 Feb, No.16.'

LO, 22 Feb 05
'We are informed by this Cº that they have sent to you a panel showing the colours used for their Car Bodies. They require the steel cab work to be painted chocolate brown picked out with cream lines. Ends of boiler to be black. Underframe & rear carrying bogie and the engine frame & tyres should also be black, the motion should of course be left bright as usual. The interior of the cab should have one coat of red lead priming & stopping, two coats of brown chocolate & one coat of varnish [wainscot?]. The boiler to have one coat of red lead priming, 2 coats of black overbound & one coat of japan.'

LO, 10 March 05
'If this Ry Cº send you a sample panel of the painting please copy & send on to us to forward to the Bristol Cº.'

LO, 27 Mar 05
'Do not fix electric lamp in the cab for the motor.'

LO, 3 April 05
'Greenwood & B. have forwarded today 2 dynamos & rheostats.'

LO, 4 May 05
'In view of the trouble we are having with the BAGS coach, please see that the clearance on these coaches is correct.'

LO, 5 May 05
'Enclosing dwg 6816. Please check clearances between Motor Bogie & the Carriage frame & return dwg to us. Advise of [position of] 2 double pole switches.'

GWR, 9 May 05
'Am sending sample code board which is placed in end vestibule of the car on right side looking towards luggage compt. Ref. print showing position of writing on the cars. The word "Smoking" should be written on the door dividing centre compt. from the centre vestibule. The side elevation shows the positions of the number of the car, the GWR monogram & the word "Luggage" on the luggage door, also the number of the car on the vestibule end. The number should also be painted on the front of the engine. (Sent to LO)'

LO, 11 May 05
'A number will be required to be painted on the front of this engine. We have asked the Bristol Cº to paint this No. on the front of our engines when they are d/d to them for erection purposes in order that the figures at the rear of the coach and on our engine will be the same shape & form.'

LO, 18 May 05
'We call your attention to the fact that the body of this coach will have electric bells etc fitted in it similar to the Taff Vale. Please arrange connections for these in the cab portion of our motors.'

LO, 20 May 05
'Note you are making electric bell connections similar to T. Vale except that the bell pushes are fixed on the engine end with 2 two pin connectors. We suppose this will not in any way affect the Bristol Cº's work? If so please write them direct. When do you expect to forward the 2 tank ends to Bristol?'

LO, 23 May 05
'Bristol Cº forwarded you y'day the code Board.'

LO, 1 June 05
'Our contract is to deliver free on GW Rails at Bristol. Our engine would have to go to Bristol to be connected to the coach & then simply put on GW rails there. Thus no mileage to be run. From the copy of our order to Bristol which we sent you will see that the Bristol Cº are to make no charge for attaching engine. This engine has to be photographed by the Bristol Cº.'

GWR, 17 June 05
'Our foreman J D Smith will attend on Monday for boiler test.'

GWR, 26 Jun 05
'Enclosing copy of foreman's report.'

LO, 3 July 05
'Re. weights on the 2 axles etc (to JBH)'

LO, 22 July 05
'Re. nameplates to the Bristol Cº.'

Greenwood & Bailey, 1 Aug 05
'Re. position for fixing Turbine Dynamos.'

LO. 4 Aug 05
'See letter re. complaints as to Blower, Reversing shaft, regulator pulley in cab, Regulator, lubricator, Sandboxes, load on leading wheels heavier than on drawing. They wish to make alterations and charge us with cost.'

LO, 14 Aug 05
'Mr Churchward asks for diagrams of these cars; also prints of engine arrgt with boilers. In Feby you sent us tracing 11688 which appears to be a diagram dwg of these coaches.

LO, 17 Aug 05
Awaiting prints 11805, 11688. Note your remarks re difficulty in getting out regulator valve without removing the cab Roof.'

LO, 19 Aug 05
'Are obtaining information desired from the Bristol Cº.'

LO, 24 Aug 05
'Bristol Cº did not have cars weighed but they state their approx weight to be:

	T c q
'1 body complete	9 – 5 – 0 – 0 (about)
'1 underframe	4 – 10 – 0 – 0 (")
'1 trailing bogie	3 – 5 – 0 – 0 (")
	17 – 0 – 0 – 0 (about)'

GWR, 11 Oct 05
'Mr Churchward wants set of prints. Those asked for in ours of 11th should be for 2032 & not 2294.'

The remains of the trailing end of Car 15 in a Leeds scrapyard on 23rd September 1961.
COLLECTION R. C. RILEY

PROPOSED ARTICULATED 0–6–0 STEAM RAIL MOTOR

In 1906, Hawthorne, Leslie & Co. together with Hurst, Nelson & Co., built a large and powerful steam rail motor for the Port Talbot Railway. The power unit was unique in being an 0–6–0, and the coach portion was articulated to it. The car was taken into PTR stock in 1907 – see Chapter 13.

During April 1907, Swindon drawing office produced a Loco. Dept. type diagram of an SRM (side elevation, plus a plan of the coach portion only) showing a small 0–6–0 side tank engine, to which a carriage portion was attached via an articulated joint; the latter seated 52 passengers, and was provided with a luggage compartment. The length of the whole unit would have been 70ft over headstocks.

The locomotive portion was the 'right' way round with the chimney leading, and had a Belpaire boiler working at 150 lbs sq in. It is shown with inside 16in × 24in stroke cylinders driving onto the centre axle, and with small side tanks above the leading driving wheels, holding a total of 600 gallons of water. The wheels were to have been 4ft 1½in diameter. Tractive effort is shown as 16,756 lbs.

This unit's coach portion had the usual longitudinal seating, with central seating bays. The saloon is not shown as partitioned, but it would have been fitted with two droplights flanked with quarterlights each side. The saloon otherwise would have had the usual large, fixed windows with twin toplights above each. There would have been a 5ft luggage compartment and a 3ft 9in driver's compartment with a bow end, and retractable steps below its doors. The underframe would have had queen post trussing, and a 9ft 'American' type bogie is shown.

The reason for this proposal is not known, but in terms of tractive effort it would have been nearly 2½ times as powerful as one of the existing 70ft cars, so it should have been possible to haul short trains. It may have been seen as a possible substitute for an auto engine and one trailer on services such as the Plymouth and London suburban, where trains commonly consisted of an auto-engine with two, three or four trailers. This usage would have required through regulator gear fittings at both ends, but, having a power unit of normal locomotive construction, should not have presented any difficulties. If it was used with conventional passenger stock, the 0–6–0 SRM would have had to run round its train for a return journey, negating the 'bi-directional' capability of such a unit. Again, its value may have been seen on 'mixed' branch services, though shunting in restricted yards may have been difficult. The proposed SRM's water capacity of 600 gallons and its coal capacity of 1½ tons might also have limited its range.

It would, however, have had the advantage of the articulated joint for quick separation into its main component parts. The diagram's drawing number was 32706 (it did not have an index letter), and it has written on it 'Copy supplied to Mr Churchward 25/4/07'.

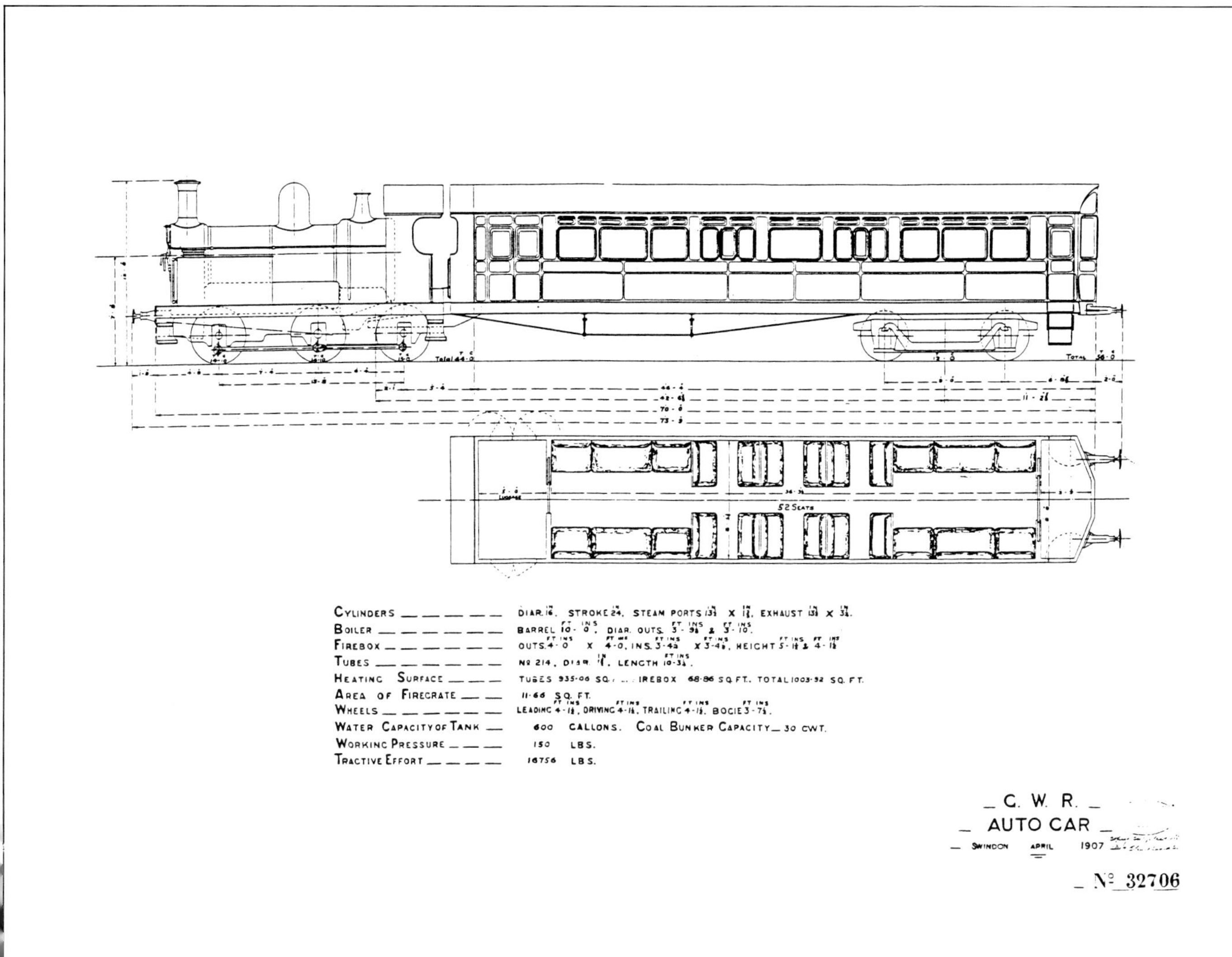

52 Seats
Cylinders — Diar. 16. Stroke 24. Steam ports 13½ x 1¼. Exhaust 13½ x 3¼.
Boiler — Barrel 10-0. Diar. outs. 3-9⅞ & 3-10.
Firebox — Outs. 4-0 x 4-0. Ins. 3-4½ x 3-4½. Height 5-1½ & 4-1½
Tubes — No 214. Diar. 1⅝. Length 10-3¼.
Heating Surface — Tubes 935·06 sq. ft. Firebox 68·86 sq. ft. Total 1003·92 sq. ft.
Area of Firegrate — 11·66 sq. ft.
Wheels — Leading 4-1½. Driving 4-1½. Trailing 4-1½. Bogie 3-7½.
Water Capacity of Tank — 600 gallons. Coal Bunker Capacity — 30 cwt.
Working Pressure — 150 lbs.
Tractive Effort — 16756 lbs.
C. W. R.
AUTO CAR
Swindon April 1907
No 32706

PROPOSED ONLY

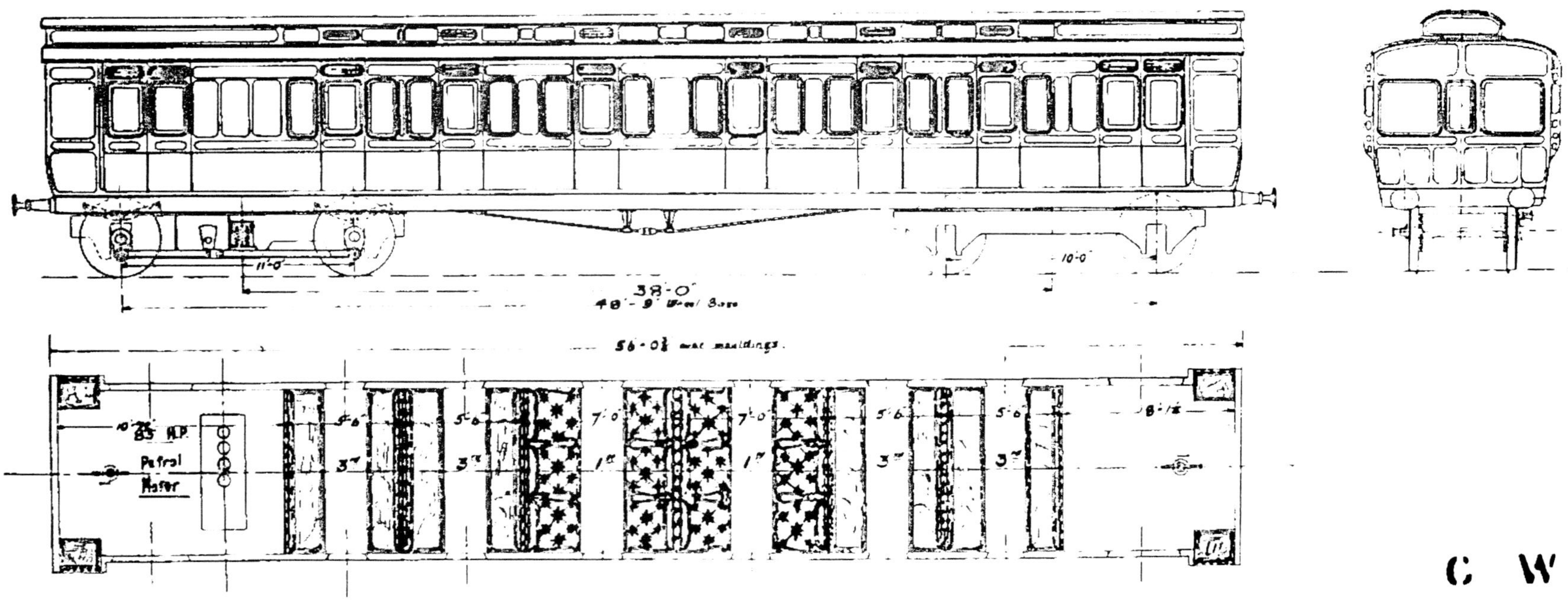

C W

PETROL MOTOR

CHAPTER ELEVEN

INTERNAL COMBUSTION

IN its search for economic train working, the Great Western did not confine its attention to steam, but also considered internal combustion as a source of power. The petrol (or gasoline) engine in a practical form had appeared during the later 1870s with the introduction of a four-stroke machine by the German engineer Nikolaus Otto, and further developed in the following decade by Maybach & Daimler, and Benz.

One petrol-electric car was put into service in 1911, but a much earlier diagram has been seen of a proposed 'Petrol Motor'. Fortunately, the diagram was photographed at Swindon, and I do not know if an original copy has survived. It was dated 'February', but unfortunately the year was not included in the print I have, although the late Jack Slinn told me that the original date was February 1903. I also understand that the original diagram was an octavo print, numbered 22983, which agrees with such a date. This diagram would appear to be in the nature of an early proposal that would have needed a lot more working up, but it is significant that the GWR saw a petrol car at such an early date as one possibility for a 'rail motor'.

To put the proposal into context, the Great Western started to use Milnes Daimler petrol-engined buses ('road motors') in 1903, and by 1904 was using such vehicles of 20 hp. In 1904, the first two GWR-owned Milnes Daimler petrol engine (road) lorries appeared, also powered by 20 hp engines.

As envisaged, the petrol motor (rail) car would have looked rather like a cross between a late 'Dean period' clerestory double-ended slip coach and a saloon. It would have been 56ft 0¾in long, with a driver's compartment at each end, and guard's lookouts (wings) at each corner of the coach. The ends are shown with two large (outer) and one smaller (central) window. The usual waist panels of the Dean period coaches are shown as continuing onto the coach ends, with the ends below the waist mouldings being divided into six apparently similar width panels. The 8ft 6¾in-wide non-gangwayed coaches of the period had ends with six vertical panels, but usually only one waist moulding.

At one end, the driver would have shared a compartment 10ft 7½in long with a transverse 85 HP petrol motor (RAC rating – not output). This rating was calculated thus:

Horsepower = $D^2 \times N/2.5$

where D = piston diameter and N = number of cylinders, and did not take the stroke into account. It is possible that, in the diagram, the four circles drawn on the engine are indications of cylinders. A four-cylinder motor of 85HP capacity would have had pistons of about 7¼in diameter. There is no indication of any radiator for cooling the engine, or of ventilation for the motor compartment.

The motor compartment would have had external double doors next to the wings. Next, there was to be two Third class compartments 5ft 6in between partitions, two First class compartments 7ft 0in wide and two more of Third class, the same size as before. Significantly, no Second class accommodation was to be provided. Finally, there was a luggage/driving compartment 8ft 1¼in long. A hand brake column is shown on the centre line in both driving compartments. I estimate that the car would have seated 40 passengers travelling Third class, plus 12 First class, which was the same capacity as the early steam rail motors, except that the latter were Third class only.

Basically, a standard steel underframe of the period was provided (presumably somewhat modified), with cast queen posts quite close together on each side, and a turnbuckle to adjust the round-section truss rods between the queen posts. The trailing bogie would probably have been a standard Dean 10ft, though only the outline is shown. An inside-framed bogie is shown at the motor end, having 4 coupled wheels at an 11ft wheelbase, the drive to the rail wheels being via a lay shaft and crank driving the coupling rods. The total wheelbase was to be 48ft 9in. There is no indication of how the output of the petrol engine would have reached the lay shaft – presumably via a gear box, including a reversing arrangement, and a clutch – but because the engine was positioned transversely, only spur gears would have been required.

No width or height dimensions are given, but the body would presumably have been the standard widths for clerestory coaches, i.e. 8ft 6¾in wide over the side mouldings and 9ft 3¾in over the lookouts. No indication is given of the estimated weight of the car.

No. 100: The Petrol Electric Car

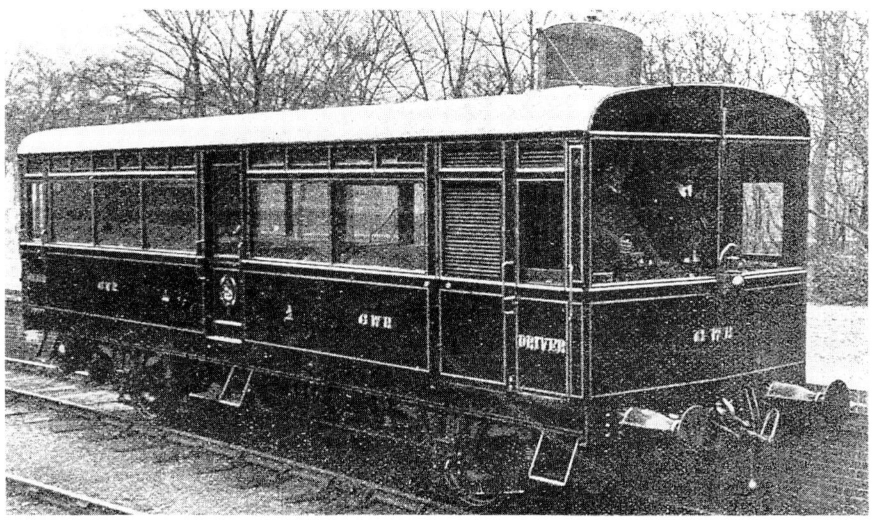

The petrol-electric car, later numbered 100 and shown on Diagram U, on a test run before being purchased by the GWR. This photograph shows the motor end with the radiator visible on the roof.

By 1910, the Great Western were again looking at the possibilities of internal combustion as motive power for a rail car, and negotiations had been taking place with the British Thomas-Houston company with a view to the production of a light rail motor. The minutes of the GWR's Traffic Committee for 3rd November 1910 read:

> 'With a view to ascertain the practicality or otherwise of employing a light rail motor car for the conveyance of passengers on branch lines on steep gradients or on main lines where the traffic is suitable but where one of the Company's ordinary cars cannot be economically worked, it was agreed to recommend [to the Board] that an arrangement be entered into with the British Thomas-Houston Company to build such a car to be driven by a petrol electric engine, this Company giving it facilities for working it upon their line and if found satisfactory to have the option of purchasing it for the sum of £1,437.'

The Board agreed, and the negotiations were successfully concluded; this was announced to readers of the *Great Western Railway Magazine* in the February 1911 issue:

> 'NEW PETROL-ELECTRIC RAIL MOTOR-CAR
>
> 'The Company have entered into an arrangement with the British Thomas-Houston Company of Rugby, to build a rail motor-car, to be driven by a petrol-electric engine, and have arranged to give facilities for this car to be worked on the Great

Western Railway, experimentally. The design of the car is based on the requirements of branch line working where a light self-propelled vehicle is required to run under normal conditions as an independent unit and it is claimed that the petrol-electric system is the most economical form of traction yet designed for such a purpose. The car will seat 45 passengers and will be driven from either end in the same way as the present steam cars. The weight of the car complete without passengers is to be 13½ tons, and fully loaded 16 tons. It will run at a maximum speed of 20 miles per hour.'

The car was duly completed, and about a year later was at work on the system. *The Locomotive* magazine carried a short article in its issue of March 15th, 1912:

'GREAT WESTERN RY. PETROL-ELECTRIC RAIL MOTOR.

'The GWR are running an experimental petrol-electric passenger coach on the Windsor branch. We illustrate the vehicle on this page. The power is supplied by a 40-h.p. Maudslay petrol engine coupled to a dynamo from which the current is supplied to two electric motors on the axle. Accommodation is provided for 46 passengers, the dead weight per passenger being about half that of the GWR steam rail motors of the same carrying capacity. Considerably less space is required for storing the fuel, although sufficient petrol is carried for a run of nearly 250 miles. Only one man is required to drive the car, and a maximum speed approaching 35 miles per hour is attained. The car has been designed by the British Thomas-Houston Co., who have supplied all the electrical equipment. Further developments are awaited with interest in railway circles.'

This was followed by a more detailed article in the *Great Western Railway Magazine* for April 1912:

'PETROL ELECTRIC RAIL CAR

'A good deal of interest has been evinced by passengers on the Windsor and Brentford branches in a new Petrol Electric Rail Car recently delivered to the Company.

'The car was built by the British Thomas-Houston Co. for experimental purposes, and weighs only fourteen tons. The power is supplied by a 40-h.p. Maudslay petrol engine, which drives a dynamo, which, in turn, transmits power to two electric motors on the axles of the rail car. Notwithstanding the light weight of the vehicle, it accommodates 44 passengers, and this in itself is one large advantage of the petrol electric system, the weight of the car, engine, dynamo, &c., per passenger working out to 6 cwt. 1qr., as compared with about 13½ cwt. for the steam rail cars.

'A further advantage is that fuel is carried in a very small area, the petrol tank, which is carried underneath the experimental car, holding sufficient petrol for between 200 and 250 miles running. The car is divided into three compartments:

1. Containing petrol engine, dynamo and controller.
2. Passenger compartment.
3. Conductor's compartment, also containing electrical controller and brake control, the car being driven from either end, according to requirements.

'Only one man is required at the driving end, the conductor riding at the opposite end, and attending to the engine if required, he also being in a position to stop the car in case of emergency.

'The new system should prove, for the above reasons alone, in the case of small cars, considerably more economical than steam power, and with these advantages the development of certain sections of the line which have hitherto not presented the likelihood of paying loads, should be possible – apart from the question of coal consumption.'

Interior and end views

Petrol Engine of new Rail Car.

Expecting the conductor to travel in one of the driving compartments seems a little odd, particularly as he was apparently expected to 'attend to the engine if required' as well as carrying out his other duties, which presumably included seeing to tickets issued at halts. According to the diagram of the car, there was no access to the motor compartment from the passenger saloon.

The Great Western had not purchased the car at this time, which probably accounts for the fact that none of the photographs of the car accompanying the last two articles shows it carrying a number, although it is otherwise in a company livery, carrying 'GWR' twice on each side and once on each end, which is more than the company's SRMs did. However, it would appear that the GWR did acquire the car in 1913, as its first allocation in the *Locomotive Register* is for May that year (at Slough). A diagram was produced, dated December 1913, which shows a number of modifications compared with the earlier photographs. This work may well have been carried out prior to its allocation to Slough, as it appears not to have visited Swindon Works until May 1914. This diagram is said to have been given index letter 'U' in the rail motor series.

DESIGN

A record of the car as No.100 was made in the *Rail Motor Register*, which also indicated that it was built by the British Thomas Houston Company of Rugby in 1911. It is described as being 33ft 0in long, 9ft 0in wide and 7ft 0in high (i.e. the body height), perhaps nominal dimensions, as the diagram shows its external dimensions as 33ft 3in long (maximum), 9ft 0¾in wide, 11ft 5¾in from rail to roof top and 13ft 5¼in from rail to the radiator cap. A 9ft 0¾in exterior width does not agree with an

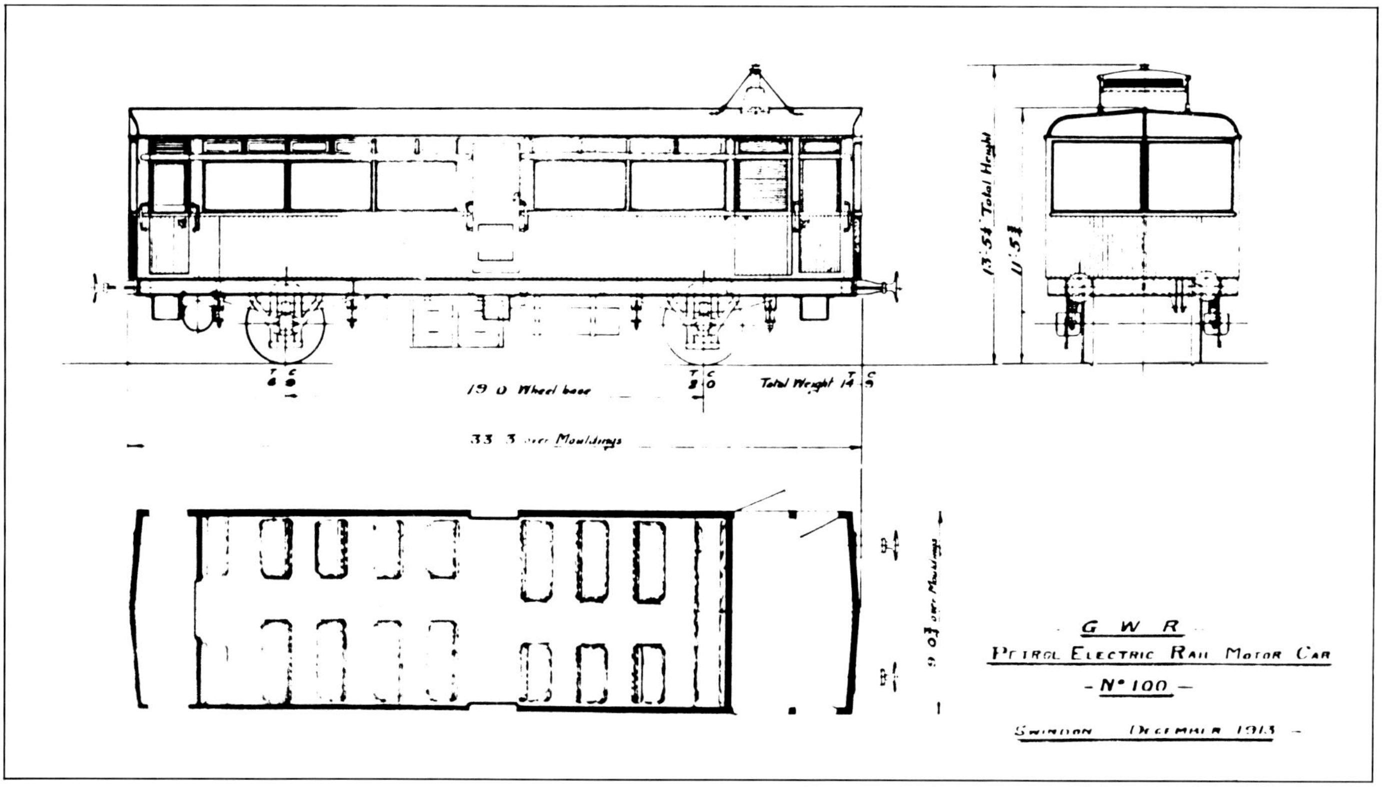

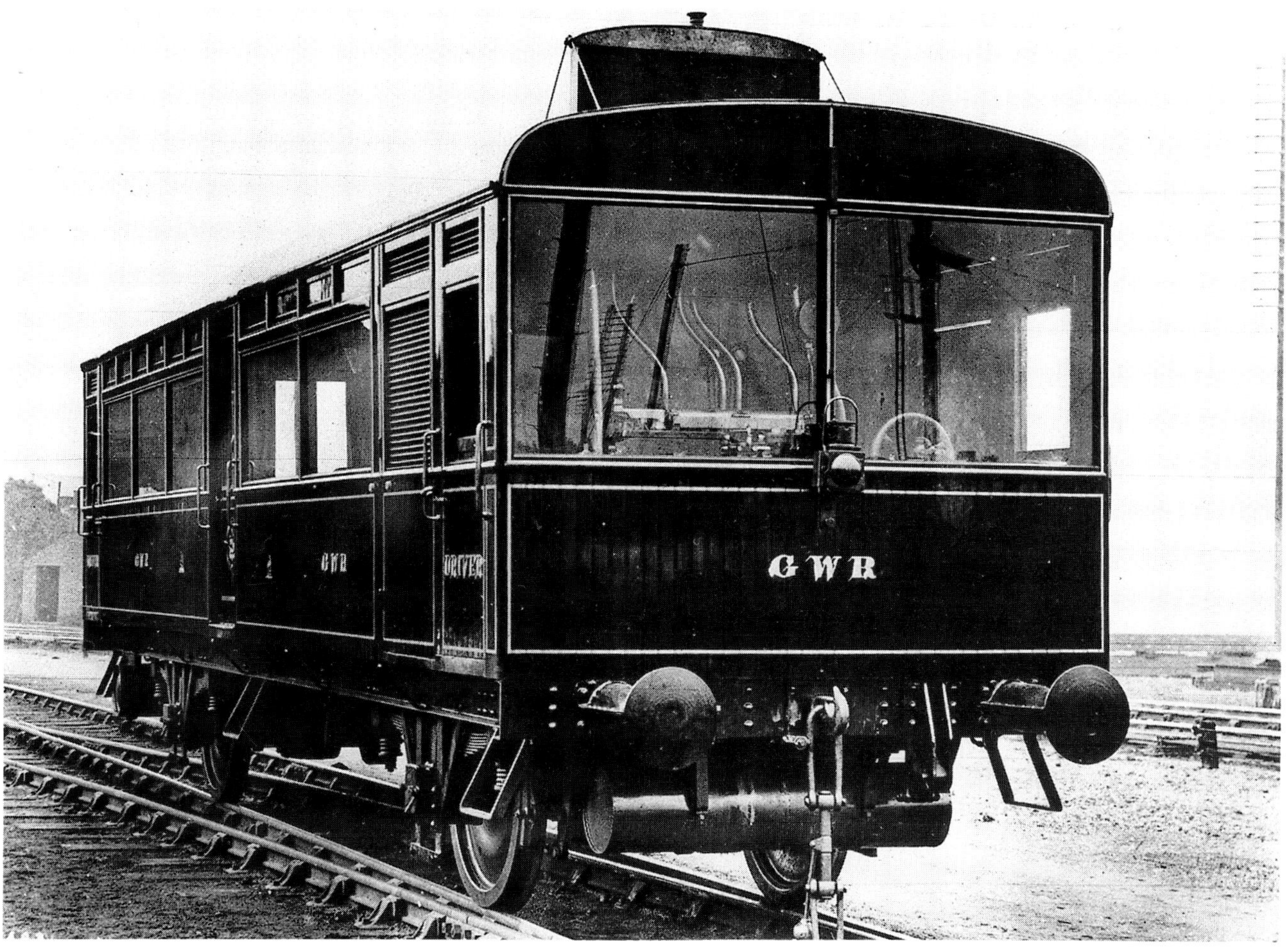

This view shows the power unit end, with various pipes visible in the driver's compartment, and the handbrake wheel. COLLECTION J. N. SLINN

This view from a manufacturer's catalogue shows the power unit end with a driver at the controls. COLLECTION J. N. SLINN

internal width of 9ft 0in: normally, there was 6 or 6¾in difference between the internal and external measurements of a Great Western coach, although this one was probably of lighter construction.

The sides were flat, while the ends were slightly bowed about the central pillar of the end windows to a much smaller degree than most GWR trailers and steam railmotors. Each end contained two large windows for the driver.

A single lamp bracket was placed centrally on each end, and positioned so that the standard head or tail oil lamp was level with the bottom of the end windows. There also appears to be a small whistle placed centrally on the ends, just above the driver's windows, served by an air pipe running up the window frame from waist level.

Externally, below the waist line, the body was covered with vertical matchboarding rather like the early steam rail motors. Above the waist it was mostly windows. The car had a door that opened inwards on each side for the driver at both ends of the car, and immediately behind those at the motor end there was a larger door each side which opened outwards, with louvres above the waist line. There were commode handles at about waist height on either side of the driver's doors and either side of the central passenger doors.

The register gives the capacity of the car's seating as 46 passengers, as did the article in *The Locomotive* magazine, although the diagram gives it as 44. The latter shows the passenger compartment as having a seat the whole width of the bulkhead between the passenger and motor compartments, and this is probably where the discrepancy arose. If you assume this seat accommodated five passengers, like the seats facing it, then the car would have held 44. If it held seven, then the car had 46 seats; it may, in fact, have actually held six, thus giving the 45 passenger seats specified in the *Great Western Magazine* articles. Facing this seat there were three pairs of seats, each pair giving 3+2 places, arranged, as we would now say, airline style. There was an area across the car free of seats, giving access to an external sliding door on each side; these doors slid inside the body, so were slightly recessed. The partition between the passenger and driver's compartments at the end further from the motor had a central sliding door, presumably to allow the conductor access to the compartment while the car was in motion. This partition had double seats backing on to it each side of the door, and 4 pairs of 2+3 seats facing them. A photograph of the interior of the car in the 1912 *Great Western Railway Magazine* seems to show the seats as being made of rattan, or something similar. The seats had grab handles on the top corner nearest the gangway, so it is possible they were walkover seats, tram style.

There were two large, fixed windows in the side of the saloon between the motor compartment and the passenger door, with two hinged toplights above each fixed window. There were three similar window arrangements between the passenger's door and the 'conductor's compartment'. The register indicates that the car had no droplights (which was true of the passenger compartment only), but twelve active ventilators were fitted in the roof, and one large ventilator in the roof of the 'engine room'. However, neither photographs of the new car, nor the diagram, show roof ventilators. Internally, it was electrically-lit with 15 lamps.

The car had a steel underframe, and ran on 4 wheels, 3ft 6in diameter at a 19ft 0in wheelbase. Unusually, the bearing springs were carried inside the axleguards. Self- contained buffers of a tapered type were provided, similar in appearance to those on locomotives. It had screw couplings at each end, but no air pipe connectors or any external control gear connections, so the buffers and drawgear were perhaps only to enable the car to be hauled in an emergency. Footsteps were provided under each door, which appear to have been effectively metal loops; there were no retractable steps.

It was fitted with the Westinghouse brake,

The engine is described in the *SRM Register* as 'a standard 5x5 Maudslay engine with overhead camshaft and valves'; the term '5x5' meant that each piston was 5in diameter, and had a 5in stroke. There were four cylinders. The register also shows that lubrication was forced, using a pump, through oil ways in the crankshaft to the big end and main bearings. The carburettor was duplicated, and a hand-operated valve permitted an instant change from one to the other. Ignition was by a H. I. Magneto, with oil and battery system in reserve.

The most surprising feature to modern eyes is that the radiator was on the roof, which cannot have improved air resistance or fuel efficiency, although at the low speeds involved this was probably not important. However, did they have to drain it each night in frosty weather? The engine was coupled directly to a dynamo,

The front of the petrol-electric car. NATIONAL RAILWAY MUSEUM

which in turn drove the two electrical motors on the axle at the 'non-engine' end.

When new, the car would presumably have been painted in the lined brown livery of the period. Photographs show it to have had 'G W R' (without any stops between the letters) centrally on the end matchboarded area below the windows. There was a garter device on the passenger door, with the supporters either side in the body, and outboard of them was 'G W R'. The word 'DRIVER' was written on the driver's doors. All the lettering was shaded, and appears larger than usual for GWR coaches. The roof was white, and the mouldings around the windows and the edges of the matchboarded areas were lined out. If it was repainted after 1912, it would presumably have been given the new standard lake livery, but the arrangement of the lettering, and the number '100' is not known; it may have substituted for one of the 'G W Rs' on each side.

There are a number of differences between the diagram and 'as built' photographs, which may indicate that the car had been modified by the date the diagram was produced in 1913. According to the diagram, two tanks, of which presumably one at least would have been for fuel, were slung from the underframe, one transversely towards the 'non-motor' end of the car, and the other longitudinally within the wheelbase. However, photographs show it to have originally carried two tanks transversely, one at each end of the car. The tank at the 'motor' end of the car was that which seems to have been removed. Originally, the car carried what appears to be a battery box at the 'non-motor' end, hung transversely across the car just outboard of the tank. The diagram shows that this moved to a central position within the wheelbase, and hung longitudinally from the underframe. This would have improved the weight distribution, and perhaps adhesion.

No details of the brake system is shown on the diagram, and it does not show up very well in photographs. The Westinghouse brake cylinder appears to have been tucked close under the underframe, slightly towards the non-motor end of the car. It would seem that the car had the usual 8 brake shoes in a clasp arrangement, but no 'V' hangers are visible in photographs. There appears to be a vertical hand brake wheel just behind the front windows, and there is a double bracket attached to the headstock near one right-hand buffer, which is presumably for the hand brake mechanism.

The total weight of the car is given by the diagram as 14 tons 8 cwt, split 8 tons on the axle at the motor end, and 6 tons 8 cwt on the other. The *SRM Register* gives the total weight as 14 tons 17 cwt. Comparisons with standard GWR SRMs of similar capacity show Dia. Q1 cars weighing 38 tons 16 cwt full (diagram), or over 41 tons, according to the register, while the non-standard cars of Dia. E (Nos.15 and 16) weighed 32 tons (diagram) or about 33 tons (register) full. In fact, the weight on the power bogie of a GWR-design SRM was greater than the weight of No.100, not helped by over 15 cwt (¾ ton) of coal and 2 tons of water carried when (e.g.) a Dia. Q1 SRM was full. So the claim in *The Locomotive* that the dead weight of the car per passenger was about half that of a similar capacity SRM was, if anything, an understatement.

MODIFICATION & DISPOSAL

In 1912 the car was used on the Windsor branch, providing nine additional return journeys a day between Slough and Windsor; a journey time of 9 minutes was allowed in each direction.

The car seems to have spent its working life on the GWR in the London Division, being allocated first to Slough, and then (in January 1917) to Wormwood Scrubs. It was at Swindon Works from September 1914 until March 1915.

On 9th January 1915, it was reported to have been equipped with a heating system without regulators, employing the exhaust gases to heat cast-iron radiators in the passenger compartment. At the same date, the number of internal lamps was increased from 15 to 16, and 'hand lamps' (possibly 'headlamps'?) were fitted. However, on 18th March 1915, after the car had returned to traffic, the lagging around the heating system pipework caught fire. A report from Mr Armstrong reads:

> 'Before this car went to Swindon for repairs, the exhaust pipes from the engines were connected to the silencer only, but when the car was at Swindon for repairs it was fitted with radiators for heating purposes and branches were put in from the exhaust pipes to the radiators with valves whereby the exhaust could be turned into the silencer or into the radiators as required. These branch pipes were wrapped with felt and canvas which was a mistake, as of course they are liable to become very hot. For the moment these pipes are blanked off, and of course will not be required during the summer season, and I am arranging for the felt and canvas to be stripped from them, and for them to be wrapped with asbestos card which will act as a non-conductor and at the same time is not inflammable.'

Part 11 of the RCTS publication *The Locomotives of the Great Western Railway*, first published in May 1952, records that the Maudslay Motor Co. Ltd. had indicated that the car's engine suffered from overheating of the detachable valve seatings, which affected its performance, but otherwise the engine was entirely satisfactory. This work also records that the car was used by Lever Bros. at Port Sunlight until about 1923, when it was withdrawn. About four years later, the body was sold to a member of their staff and made into a holiday cottage at Gronant Beach, near Prestatyn, where it still sat in 1952.

It was also reported that 'Mr. Collett has noted this letter.'

What its duties at Wormwood Scrubbs were is unclear, but, possibly, it was just stored in the wagon works. No.100 was there from January to August 1917, and at Slough on 1st September, but it was back at Wormwood Scrubbs by the end of that month. At the end of October it was reported at Swindon shed, and was out of action at Swindon works from November 1917 until it was moved, first to Swindon stock shed in August 1919, and then to Wolverhampton on 21st August 1919.

The car was sold to Messrs Lever of Port Sunlight on 20th October 1919 for £1,437 plus the cost of transport to Port Sunlight.

TABLE 32

SUMMARY: Petrol-Electric Car, Diagram U

(Built by British Thomas Huston Co., Rugby)

Built	*To GWR stock*	*Tare t - c*	*Heating (but see text)*	*Stopped Work*	*Sold to Messrs Lever*
1911	May 13	14-17	Jan 15	Nov 17	20 Oct 19

NOTES

Carburettor duplicated with manual switch over valve.

Forced lubrication via oilways in crankshaft to big end and main bearings.

Ignition: HT magneto with coil and battery back up.

Engine room louvres replaced by droplights: no date.

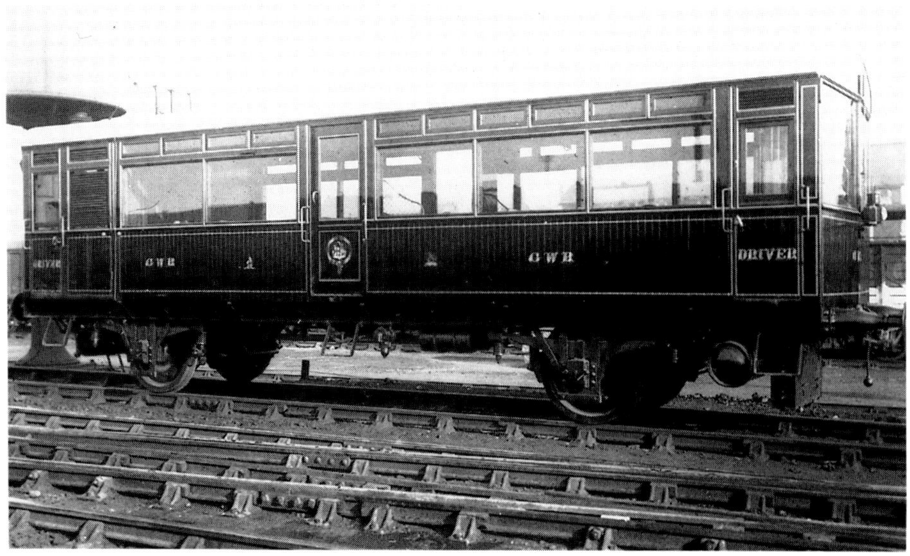

CHAPTER TWELVE

THE TAFF VALE RAILWAY SRMs

THE Taff Vale Railway was one of the earlier users of steam rail motors, their first car entering traffic just a couple of months after the Great Western's Stroud Valley SRMs. The TV company's Locomotive Engineer, Tom Hurry Riches (father of the Rhymney's locomotive engineer), was a strong proponent of their use, and the Taff eventually owned 16 cars and 18 power units.

Motor units were numbered separately from the carriage portions, and each were in their own series. On the GWR, a steam rail motor was known by the number of its coach portion, but on the Taff Vale, rail motors were known by the number of the motor. All the power units could work with any coach portion, although the last batch built were appreciably larger than the earlier ones, both in their coach portions and motor units. The motor units were separate from the coach portion, but the leading end of the coach was carried by the power unit, the rear wheels of which were actually under the luggage compartment doors.

The story of steam rail motors on the Taff Vale seems to have started with the General Manager Ammon Beasley's concern that an electric tramway would be built between Cardiff and Penarth in competition with the TVR's passenger train service; he therefore instructed Hurry Riches to investigate the possibilities of operating the line by electricity, including a review of UK and continental practice. From Hurry Riches' reports, it appears that there were two major problems with electrifying the Penarth line: the infrastructure costs per car were likely to be excessive unless the service required 10–12 power cars; and the GWR owned a mile or so of the line, and would need to agree to its electrification, either on the third rail or on the overhead principle.

One alternative was a battery-electric railcar. Mr. Beasley evidently wanted to be in a position to demonstrate that the Taff Vale was a forward-looking, efficient railway company, and that any competing tramway would have a difficult time; so, in 1902, he sought authority from the Board to invite tenders for a battery-powered railcar for the Cowbridge & Aberthaw branch. This was a section of line where the passenger traffic was poor, and there was little prospect of attracting more, but presumably an area where an experiment like this could be carried out without damaging repercussions if it were not a success. The cost of operating the Aberthaw line was stated to be £1,079 per annum, or £975 if interest on the locomotive and coaches was excluded, as they could be redeployed elsewhere.

Hurry Riches estimated that the cost of a battery-electric car, apparently to include a charging facility, would be about £3,850. Working expenses would be £870 per annum if the batteries were charged using a TV-owned power station, or, if electricity was obtained from the Electric Power Company, the capital costs would be about £2,800 and the annual costs about £770, including 4% interest on capital costs. The power company had quoted a price of 1⅞d per unit, but it was thought that discounts ought to be available if larger quantities of electricity were purchased.

Matters were complicated by the Traffic Department's recommendation that the car should operate over the whole branch – between Llantrisant and Aberthaw – and not just on the Cowbridge to Aberthaw section; this would require a second car, and it would also be necessary to install a charging facility for the batteries at Llantrisant. Initially, tenders were sought for a unit seating 6 First class passengers, 10 in Second and 40 in Third, but the offers came in too high.

Hurry Riches then suggested that a petrol-electric car, with an additional battery, should be used; this was after he had inspected the petrol-electric cars built for the North Eastern Railway. Tenders were again sought, and Witting Bros., a firm of electrical engineers and contractors, enquired of the Board of Trade as to what regulations were in force regarding the carriage of petrol as fuel on trains; they estimated that a 30 gallon tank would be needed. The BoT replied that there were no such regulations. This proposal seems not to have been taken further forward.

The minutes of the TVR Locomotive, Stores & Engineering Committee reveal that, at their meeting on 27th January 1903, tenders for an electric car were submitted, but consideration of them was deferred until the next meeting. Consideration was again postponed until the April meeting, when a report from the Locomotive Superintendent was submitted, to 'come up at the next meeting'. On 5th May 1903, revised tenders for an electric car to run on the Cowbridge branch were opened, and 'referred to the Locomotive Superintendent for a Report'. The Minutes of the 26th May meeting indicate:

> 'Report on tenders for an Electric Car to run on the Cowbridge and Aberthaw branch, and a photograph and description of a self contained steam propelled car as brought into use by the London & South Western Railway Company and as provisionally adopted by the Great Western Company was submitted and a further report was ordered to be brought up at the next meeting.'

Hurry Riches and Beasley had by now inspected the L & SWR's first steam rail motor at Nine Elms, built for the L & SWR and LB & SCR Joint Committee's East Southsea service.

Mr. Hurry Riches' report persuaded the TVR committee that a steam rail motor was the best way forward, for, at their next meeting on 9th June 1903, we read:

> 'Report from the Locomotive Engineer read upon the self-contained steam propelled car which it is proposed to adopt for use on the Company's railway and instructions were given to the Locomotive Engineer to proceed with all dispatch with the construction of one car for experimental purposes.'

Taff Vale SRM No.1

No.1 was the only car to be built by the Taff Vale itself, and its power unit was the last 'locomotive' to be built by that company. The motor was built in the TV Engineering Works, West Yard, Cardiff Docks, and the carriage portion at the company's Cathays Carriage Works.

The Taff was a relatively small company, and material had to be obtained from external suppliers. Hurry Riches had already been in touch with Dougal Drummond of the L & SW to see if that company could supply some parts for the TVR rail motor. The minutes of the Locomotive Committee of the L & SWR for 13th May 1903 read:

> 'The Locomotive Superintendent reported that he had received an application from the Taff Vale Railway asking him to supply them with cylinders and duplicate parts of the engine of the motor car for the Southsea branch.
>
> 'Application may be granted.'

However, this was not proceeded with. Apart from anything else, in the event the TVR design employed larger cylinders than the LSWR one. On 2nd July Hurry Riches reported details of materials ordered, as shown in *Table 33*.

Using standard contracts, the following had also been ordered: woodwork for the carriage and steel for the engine, also 2 piston rod forgings, 318 brass boiler tubes, 4 steel tyres and 'the necessary plate glass'. In addition, through the storekeeper, orders were placed for trimmings from Howell & Co., Cardiff, and 50 yards of lincrusta from Davies & Co., Cardiff.

The committee was told on 22nd August 1903 that it would be at least 5 weeks before the SRM would be ready, and some publicity was obtained, somewhat prematurely as it turned out. However, it was soon evident that there would be problems in completing the unit in time for the committee's meeting on 2nd October 1903, and on 7th September Hurry Riches wrote a letter of explanation to his General Manager as to why the car would not be ready when expected:

TABLE 33
TVR No.1: Material Orders

Items	*Contractor*	*Cost*
Gas fittings for coach	Pintsch's Patent Lighting Co., London	£6 6s 9d
Steel channels for coach	P & W Maclellan Ltd, Glasgow	£7 5s 0d per ton
Plate for angle iron	P & W Maclellan Ltd, Glasgow	£6 5s 0d per ton
Steel plates	P & W Maclellan Ltd, Glasgow	£6 10s 0d per ton
Cylinders	Manning Wardle & Co, Leeds	£48 0s 0d
Copper tube plates	Elliott's Metal Co., Birmingham	£80 10s 0d per ton
Copper Wrapper Plates	Elliott's Metal Co., Birmingham	£72 10s 0d per ton
Carriage wheels (2 pairs)	Leeds Wheel & Axle Co.	£18 16s 0d per pair
Buffers (2 pairs)	Geo Turton Platts & Co.	£11 15s 0d per pair
Collapsible gates (4)	Bayliss Jones & Bayliss	£6 0s 0d the set
1 Lincrusta roof panel	G. D. Peters & Co.	£7 0s 0d
Dome & dome saddle	Chas. M'cNeil	£16 0s 0d
2 flanged smoke box tube plates	Chas. M'cNeil	£3 5s 0d each
2 throat plates (flanged)	Spencer & Sons	£9 15s 0d per ton
2 frame plates		
1 frame cross stay		
1 wrapper plate	Spencer & Sons	£8 10s 0d per ton
1 plate under dome		
2 barrel plates		
4 cast steel wheels		
2 cast steel slide bar brackets	Robert Jones & Co.	19s 6d per ton
plus 43s per wheel for		
rough turning & boring		
2 injectors	Gresham & Craven	£6 10s 0d each

'Dear Sir,

'Self Contained Motor Car

'In reply to your favour of this date. The cause for the Car not being completed by the time stated are various. First of all, I could not get delivery of the necessary material as promised, some portions of which were as much as 8 weeks late. I have had the work pushed on, working day and night wherever I could get it advanced by working overtime, but I regret to say that it is impossible to get it finished in time for the Inspection of the Line. I have done all I possibly could to fulfil the undertaking I gave to you. At that time I had a solemn promise from the Makers that the material would be delivered at once whereas some of it has only just been received. The coach body will be completed by the date, but the engine part of it will not be ready. The boiler has been tested, the engine has been put together, and the cab and tanks are in process of erection, but it is impossible to get the thing to work by the date of the Directors Meeting. I regret this as much as you, but no one could have done more than I have done to endeavour to get the car completed.

'I might further say that another serious reason is that I was disappointed in not getting the drawings which I was promised by the London & South Western people. I only got an outline drawing which you saw, and on the strength of these drawings I ordered a certain amount of materials, but I found afterwards that the details which I received in no way matched the other drawings. We had therefore to make entire drawings ourselves to carry the thing out.

'Further, I took an opportunity of going down to Southsea on the last Friday in August to see the L.&.S.W.R. Car as I had been hearing so many conflicting opinions of the working of this coach. When I reached there I ran with it for two or three trips to see how it worked. I found they had put in another boiler more than double the size of the one we saw at Nine Elms, and they have also made several other material alterations.

'As you will remember I told you when we were at Nine Elms I did not think they had either boiler power or engine power enough. The engine however appears to do its work, but as I have said they have changed the boiler; this however is not anything like as powerful as the one I have built for our engine, and which I think will prove satisfactory.

'I can only add the building of this Car has been more of an anxiety to me than it could possibly have been to anyone else, and had it been possible to finish this in time it would certainly have been done, but the reasons which I have given have absolutely prevented my being able to accomplish this.

'A Beasley Esqre   Yours truly
T. Hurry Riches'

On 2nd October, the committee noted that the Locomotive Engineer reported that he hoped to have the car running in about a week's time, but Hurry Riches had to tell the Chairman that this would not be the case. This produced a rebuke from Beasley on the 7th October:

'The Chairman to whom your letter of the 5th instant was submitted expressed considerable surprise that after having been led to believe that the complete car would be ready for the inspection of the line on September 15th, he is now told that some of the drawings are not even ready.

'This is a fact which certainly ought to have been stated before. However there is now no help for it but to complete the car with the utmost possible dispatch, and the Directors are relying upon being able to see it at their next meeting.

'We have been talking about this car for so long that people will not believe that we have any real intention of constructing it. You know that my great object was to get the car running before notices of application to Parliament for next Session are due. With this object in view I urge you to complete the thing without a moment's delay.'

Eventually the car was ready, and running trials commenced late in October 1903. This fact was reported in the *Western Mail* of 29th October, accompanied by a moderately accurate sketch of the car, and in the *South Wales Daily News* on the same day, accompanied by a rather less accurate sketch. The Locomotive (&c.) Committee minutes of 3rd November 1903 noted that the car had been inspected by the committee at Cardiff Queen Street, and that at the meeting 'letters were read out from the GWR and the L & SWR setting out the conditions imposed by the Board of Trade upon the working of similar vehicles on those lines'.

On 1st December 1903, Hurry Riches reported to the committee that the cost of the steam car running between Penarth and Cadoxton was about 40% of that of 'ordinary trains', and that the car would start work between Penarth and Cardiff on 21st December 1903. Figures published in the February 1904 *Railway News* compared the running costs of the TVR car with an ordinary train of an engine and four coaches. This was further reported in the *Western Mail* on 23rd February 1904 in pence per train-mile:

	SRM	*Train*
Running costs	2·09	5·31
Repairs, renewals	1·46	6·22
Wages	1·93	3·47
Total	5·48d	15·00d

The validity of the comparison is questionable – the SRM seated 12 passengers in the First class saloon and 40 in the Third class, while the conventional train would have seated something like 24 in First class, 20 in Second and 110–130 in Third. It was only when passenger numbers were within the capacity of the SRM that the figures quoted held any real significance. Nevertheless, the directors were evidently already sufficiently impressed by the new car that they decided that the company should go out to tender for a further six.

No.1 was put into stock in December 1903. Its first public service was on an experimental basis, announced as between Cardiff and Cadoxton, although in practice Cadoxton was only served by one return journey – the 8.15 a.m. from Cardiff Riverside and the 9.0 a.m. return from Cadoxton. These two journeys were in lieu of an ordinary train, all others by the car were in addition to the normal train service. The first journey of the day started

MOTOR CARS ON RAILWAYS.

TO-DAY'S EXPERIMENT ON THE TAFF VALE LINE.

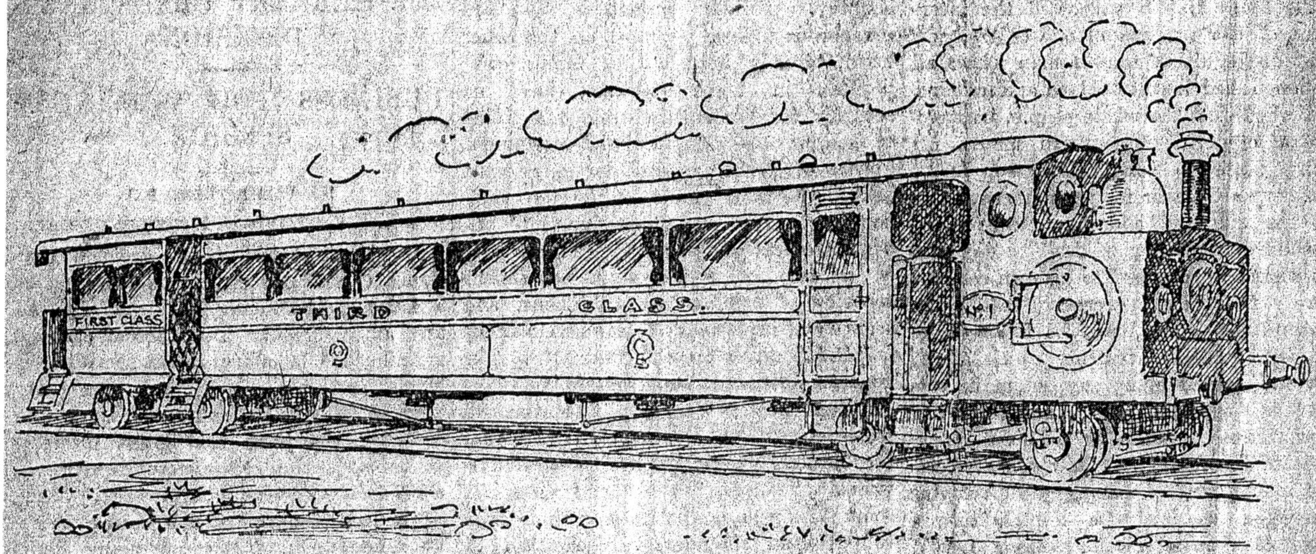

The accompanying sketch represents a steam motor-coach with which the Taff Vale Railway Company are going to experiment upon certain sections of their lines to-day (Thursday). It was constructed from designs by Mr. T. Hurry Riches, M.I.C.E. (locomotive engineer to the Taff Vale Railway Company), the locomotive at the Taff Vale Engineering Works, West Yard, Cardiff Docks, and the coach at the Cathays Carriage Works. It is designed to carry fifty-two people, twelve first-class and forty third-class, and has also a luggage compartment. The engine has cylinders 9½ in. by 14in. stroke. The wheels are 2ft. 10in. diameter. The boiler, which is multitubular, has about 300ft. of heating surface, and carries 160lb. pressure. The coach is constructed to experimentally test the value of this description of carriage, and it will probably be tried on the various sections of the line to see where it suits best. The carriage is arranged with movable steps, so that passengers may board it or alight from it at a platform or from the ground level. It is so arranged that one end of the carriage is carried on the centre of the bogie which carries the engine, and the other end is carried on a four-wheel bogie in the ordinary way.

How the press saw the first TVR rail motor – 'Western Mail' of 29th October 1903.

from Cardiff Queen Street and ran to Penarth, whilst the last returned from Penarth to Queen Street. In between, there was the one return working to Cadoxton, otherwise the service ran between Penarth and Cardiff (Riverside or Clarence Road). Daily operations (Sundays excepted) commenced on Monday, 21st December 1903, a total of 24 single journeys being run.

SRM No.1 offered First and Third class accommodation only; this could perhaps be regarded as a first step towards the abolition of Second class on the railway – except that the TVR never did, leaving the GWR to do so on 1st July 1923. The public notice announcing the service stated that passengers holding Second class tickets could travel in First class, if there was room. If not, they were to use Third class – or wait for the next train with Second class accommodation!

DESIGN

The completed SRM was described at some length in the *Locomotive* of 15th January 1904, in *Engineering*, in *The Railway Engineer* for February 1904, and in the *Railway Magazine*. As well as First and Third class accommodation, the carriage portion had a trailing driving position and a small luggage compartment at the motor unit end. The carriage portion was 45ft long, 8ft 6in wide (both external) and the height from floor to roof was 7ft 2½in.

A description of the First class compartment indicated that it was 'furnished with longitudinal seats, upholstered with figured velvet plush, the roof being of lincrusta Walton'. This compartment was 8ft 11in long, seated 12 passengers, and contained two largish, fixed windows each side.

The Third class compartment was 26ft 1¼in between partitions, and seated 40 passengers in

> 'Transverse seats arranged in pairs divided by a central gangway. The seats are constructed of teak frames with oak bars [i.e. no upholstery]. The roof is of bird's-eye maple veneer. Racks are provided for light articles. Ample ventilation is provided, and both compartments are heated by steam from the engine by means of G. D. Peters & Co's system.'

The description continued:

> 'Entrance to the car is effected by gangways [vestibules], one at the guard's [trailing] end and the other at the centre leading into both the First and Third class compartments. Each gangway is fitted with collapsible gates, and is provided with steps, to enable passengers to enter from the road level.'

These were retractable steps, which seem to have been attached below or behind the solebars.

The trailing driver's position was originally open to the elements above the waist – apart from the roof, which appeared to be supported by pillars at the outer side of the entrance. However, the trials established that this was unsatisfactory, and on 17th November, the Locomotive Committee approved a recommendation that a screen be constructed for the open end of the car.

In the luggage compartment, No.1 had a single door with droplight, and ventilator above. The passenger compartments had longitudinal ventilators above the windows, that above the Third class compartment being divided in two.

The car was gas lit.

> 'The car underframe is constructed of steel, and is carried at one end on an ordinary carriage bogie, the wheels of which are of Kitson's patent wood cushioned type. The other end of the car is supported on the engine bogie. The advantage of this arrangement is that the vibration of the engine is not transmitted to the car.'

In spite of the description of the trailing bogie as 'conventional', it actually had inside frames, and the solid wheels were of only 2ft 10in diameter at 8ft wheelbase; they appear to have had only one brake shoe per wheel. The car's total wheelbase was 49ft 3½in.

Underframe trusses were of the queenpost type, with round-section truss rods, adjustable by means of a central turnbuckle.

The locomotive portion appeared to be a rather boxed-in 0–2–2 tank engine.

Taff Vale Railway SRM No. 1 (engine 1 + coach portion 1) as built with an open vestibule at the far end. The luggage door appears to have had a ventilator panel which had been left in a light colour.
COLLECTION R. C. RILEY

There were smokebox doors either side as well as at the front; this was because the boiler had a central firebox, with two short horizontal barrels arranged across the unit, one on either side. The boiler, which contained a total of 312 tubes, 1¾in diameter and 2ft 3 5/16in long, was of steel plate, whilst the firebox was of copper.

Cylinders were 9in diameter by 14in stroke, the driving wheels were 2ft 10in diameter and the working pressure was 160lb sq in, giving a tractive effort of 4,803 lbs at 90% efficiency, although the technical press only claimed a more modest (and precise) 4,263·2 lbs 'at 80% working pressure'. Inside Stevenson's link motion was provided. The outside cylinders were within the wheelbase, and drove onto the leading pair of wheels.

The cab roof seems to have been extended backwards, so a short portion of it ran above the coach roof.

Other matters of note are that the car carried 10 cwt of coal in a bunker inside the cab, and 530 gallons of water in two tanks. The car's weight in working order was 33 tons 2 cwt.

It was reported that, as built:

> 'To ensure proper control of the car when the engine is the rear end, the guard can communicate with the driver by means of an electric bell, shut off steam, and sound the whistle, also apply a hand brake on the carriage bogie.'

There were two bells in communication between the locomotive portion and the trailing 'driving' position, and also two cords – one for the whistle, and the other to operate the throttle valve. According to a drawing, these should have run along the roof of the coach portion, but are not visible in photographs.

The original intention was that the guard on these cars – referred to by the TVR as the 'conductor – should (more or less) drive the car when the engine was at the rear, whilst the driver, called the 'motorman', would stay in the motor unit and fire it, as well as attending to his other duties. However, the Board of Trade would not sanction this, and referred the TVR to the example of the Great Western Railway, where the driver was at the controls at the leading end of the car in whichever direction it was travelling. Mr. Beasley pressed the Board of Trade on the number of men required to operate a rail motor, and wrote to them three times. In his third letter, of 23rd January 1904, he said that having the driver at the leading end was all very well on a main line, but circumstances were different on the TVR branches.

> 'The conductor of the car whose place will be at the leading end will be well acquainted with the signals and the road as any driver could possibly be, and as he will be provided with the means of sounding the whistle, shutting off steam, and applying the brakes, it is submitted that all the requirements making for safety will be complied with without rendering it necessary for the driver to be at the leading end. In such a case as that described [Cowbridge to Aberthaw] the traffic would not justify the employment of three men on the car, and I am therefore to strongly urge upon the Board of Trade that the requirement should be so varied as to enable us to dispense with the third man.'

Herbert Jekyll of the Board of Trade replied on 6th February 1904 that they had 'carefully considered the views expressed therein, but are unable, as advised, to vary the opinion which has been previously communicated to you in regard to the position of the driver in the car.'

Shortly after its introduction into traffic, the *Locomotive Magazine* reported that car No.1 had been running 'with success'.

Avonside/Bristol SRMs Nos. 2 to 7

Mr Hurry Riches and the Taff Vale Board were satisfied by the performance of No.1 in tests, and in January 1904 the company invited tenders for a further six 'Steam cars for Passenger Traffic "Class A"'. The principal dimensions of the engine were to be:

The tendering process was swift, and at the Locomotive &c. Committee's meeting of 9th February, in Bristol, 'Tenders for six steam Rail Motors were opened'. The lowest bid was from the Bristol Wagon Co. & Avonside Engine Co. Ltd. of Bristol, for £2,200, on which 'The General Manager and the Locomotive Superintendent were to seek modification of the price and were authorised to conclude the contract.' This was done, and the final price was '£2,100 less 2½% = £2,047 10s 0d per car = £12,285', though there was a penalty for non-delivery of £10 per car per week beyond the

TABLE 34
TVR CARS: Dimensions & Details

Inside diameter of cylinders:	9 in
Piston stroke:	1 ft 2 in
Length of boiler barrel between tube plates:	2 ft 13/16 in
Outside diameter of barrel plates:	3 ft 4⅛ in
Length of firebox shell outside:	3 ft 10¾ in
Width of firebox shell at bottom:	3 ft. 0⅛ in
Number of tubes:	304 (152 in each barrel)
(Altered in manuscript from 312 and 156 respectively)	
Outside diameter of tubes:	1¾ in
Height from centre of boiler barrels from rails:	6 ft 11 in (Altered from 6 ft 9¼ in)
Length of engine frame:	13 ft 10½ in
Thickness of engine frame:	⅞ in
Distance between frame:	4 ft 2 in
Diameter of driving wheels on tread:	2 ft 10 in
Diameter of trailing wheels on tread:	2 ft 10 in
Wheelbase, total:	9 ft 6 in
Centre of driving to centre of trailing wheels:	9 ft 6 in
Height of centre of buffers from rails:	3 ft 5 in
Working steam pressure:	160 lbs psi
Capacity of water tanks:	550 gallons

Taff Vale Railway SRM No. 3 as built. Each leaf of the luggage door appears to have a ventilator panel which had been left in a light colour. The driver's vestibule at the trailing end is enclosed. Coach portion 1 was soon enclosed like this. COLLECTION R. C. RILEY

due date. These SRMs were to be supplied between 24th May and 22nd July 1904, but they were delayed, and were delivered at about one month intervals between 16th July and 11th December. The TVR initially paid the Bristol Wagon Co. the sum of £11,427 18s 8d, having retained £812 16s 11d because of late deliveries, and £44 4s 5d for repairs, but after negotiations waived the penalty for late deliveries. In spite of what had happened with Car No.1, once again there was some premature publicity over the introduction of the new cars and the services they would operate.

DESIGN

Carriage portions of the new SRMs were similar to No.1, but had a few significant alterations. The luggage compartment was now 3ft 11½in between partitions, and had double doors each side, opening outwards. It also had a side-hinged door with frosted glass, which opened into the Third class saloon; this saloon was now 24ft 2in long, had 4½ seating bays each side, and seated 36 passengers on wooden slatted seats ('garden seat pattern', made of oak and teak). The reduction in length and seating, and the length of the window nearest to the luggage compartment, compensated for the larger luggage compartment. There was a sliding door between the Third class compartment and the vestibule.

The vestibule ('gangway', according to the Taff Vale) was slightly recessed into the body sides, and had 2ft 8in doorways each side, closed off by collapsible gates 'the same as supplied to this company by Messrs. Bayliss, Jones & Bayliss, Ltd., Victoria Works, Wolverhampton'.

First class accommodation was similar to that of No.1, and seated 12 on longitudinal bench seats.

The driving compartment was enclosed from new, and had full doors with droplights each side, as well as a narrow window. There were the usual three front windows, the centre one of which was a droplight. All these droplights are shown on the drawing to have 'Telling's Draught Excluders' fitted. The driver's compartment was 4ft between partitions, though this part of the coach was only 7ft 4¾in wide.

Lighting was by gas (double burners in the First class saloon, single in the Third class), and the cars were fitted with torpedo roof ventilators. Also on the roof were brass loops for the communication wires.

In working order, they weighed 35 tons 14cwt.

WORK AND DISPOSAL

On 26th April 1904, the TVR Traffic Committee considered possible sites for new stopping places on the services to be operated by the new cars. The costs were set out, both for rail level halts and for platforms with surfaces 3ft above rail level, and were approved 'subject to the Chairman determining whether the folding steps fitted to the car now running [No.1] are satisfactory'. Some revised figures were approved at the next meeting of the committee on 10th May.

The revised costs were mostly for standard 40ft-long raised platforms without any other facilities. Although no revised costing was given for Alberta Place, Penarth, this was constructed. On the other hand, the Taff Vale did not build Duffryn Crossing, although a halt of that name was eventually built by the GWR on the line between Mountain Ash and Aberdare High Level. On 4th October, four other stopping places were authorised:

Coke Ovens	£247	(not built)
Tylacoch	£ 75	Treherbert branch
Wattstown	£260	Maerdy branch
Pontygwaith	£300	Maerdy branch

On 30th July, the *Pontypridd Chronicle* reported the arrival of the first of the new cars, and said that trial trips had been run with it. When the stopping places had been completed, the car was to be placed on the Penarth route so as to allow a regular service to Cadoxton.

Services using the new cars began between Pontypridd and Nelson on Monday, 10th October 1904, with eight trips each way. A new platform at Llanfarbon Road was also opened.

TABLE 35

TVR: Costs of New Stations for Motor Services

Stopping place	*Cost of Platform* £	*Cost of Rail - Level Halt* £	*Revised Cost.* £
Berw Road, Main Line	308	145	257
Abernant, Nelson Branch	155	71	127
Robertstown, Ynysybwl Branch	118	40	90
Old Ynysybwl, Ynysybwl Branch	117	20	95
Pontycynon, Aberdare Branch	124	33	95
Duffryn Crossing	237	44	193
Mill Street, Aberdare	126	44	106
Tonteg, Llantrisant branch	-	-	89
Maendy, Cowbridge Branch	114	43	81
Aberthin, Cowbridge Branch	119	46	91
St. Hilary, Cowbridge Branch	123	45	96
Llanbethery, Cowbridge Branch	121	41	98
Alberta Place, Penarth	196	51	-
TOTALS	1,964	653	1,398

A report of the commencement of the service in the *Glamorgan Free Press* on 15th October said that the First class portion was to be reserved for 'ladies and season ticket holders'. It also stated that 'the engine driver can work from either end of the car'. The newspaper also recorded that the SRM carried 13 cwt of coal, which lasted 8 hours (Hurry Riches later reported that the cars were in service each day for between over 12 and over 17 hours), and that it developed 160 horsepower. It appears that the first run by the car was treated almost like the opening of a new railway, with crowds gathering and fog signals exploded at each station en route!

The Nelson service was followed by the introduction of one between the Ynysybwl branch and Pontypridd on Monday 17th October 1904, which completely replaced the existing train service between Ynysybwl and Abercynon. New platforms were provided at Old Ynysybwl and Robertstown on the Ynysybwl branch, and at Berw Road on the Abercynon & Pontypridd main line. The official notice indicated that 'Third class tickets only will be issued, and all First and Second class bookings to, from and upon the Ynysybwl Branch will be discontinued' – yet the cars used initially had First class accommodation.

A local service in Aberdare between Commercial Street Crossing and Mill Street commenced on 26th November 1904.

TAFF VALE RAILWAY.

INTRODUCTION OF MOTOR CAR SERVICE

BETWEEN

PONTYPRIDD AND YNYSYBWL.

COMMENCING ON MONDAY, OCTOBER 17, 1904,

The Passenger Train Service between YNYSYBWL and ABERCYNON will be discontinued, and a Service of Steam Motor Cars will be introduced beween YNYSYBWL and PONTYPRIDD; also New Platforms will be opened at Old Ynysybwl, Robertstown and Berw Road.

The Cars will start from Ynysybwl for Pontypridd at 7.56, 8.52, 10.40 a.m., 12.3, 12.55, 2a8, 2.53, 3.38, 4.40, 5.50, 6b40, 7.35, 9.18, 10b18 p.m., and from Pontypridd to Ynysybwl at 7.20, 8.28, 9.36, 11.33 a.m., 12.38, 1.45, 2a25, 3.22, 4.10, 5.7, 6.25, 7b0, 8.20, 9b50 p.m.

(*a*) Thursdays and Saturdays only. (*b*) Saturdays only.

Third class tickets only will be issued, and all First and Second class bookings to, from upon the Ynysybwl Branch will be discontinued.

For further Particulars see Posters.

A. BEASLEY, General Manager.

Cardiff, October 1904.

Announcement of the new service in the 'Glamorgan Free Press' of 15th October 1904.

Taff Vale Railway SRM engine 6 and one of the short coach portions hauling a 6-wheel brake third. A. G. ELLIS, CTY. R. C. RILEY

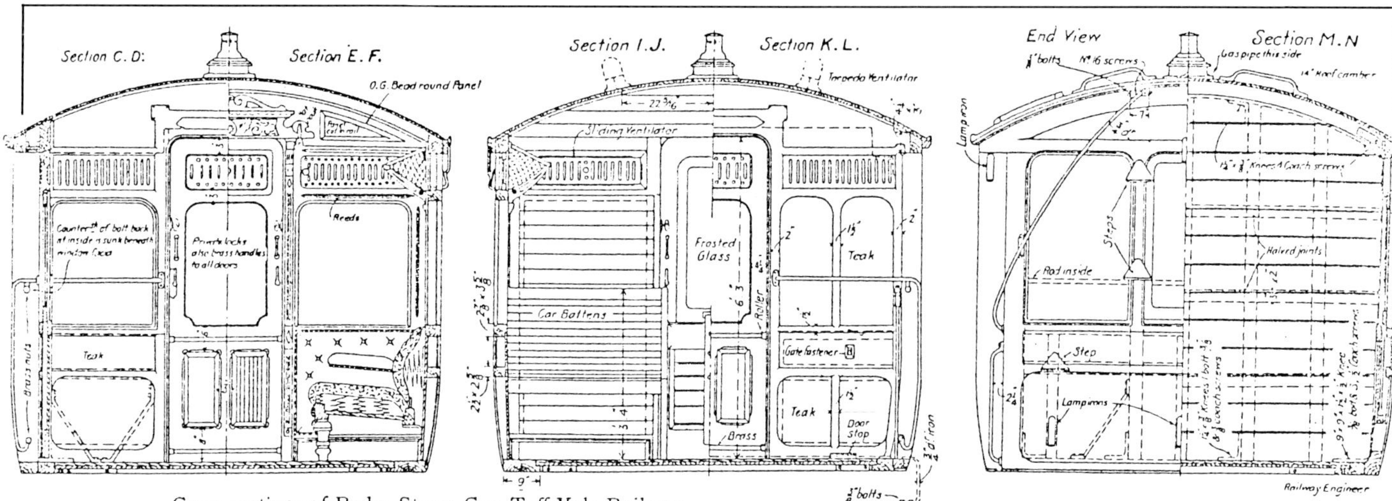

Cross sections of Body, Steam Car, Taff Vale Railway.

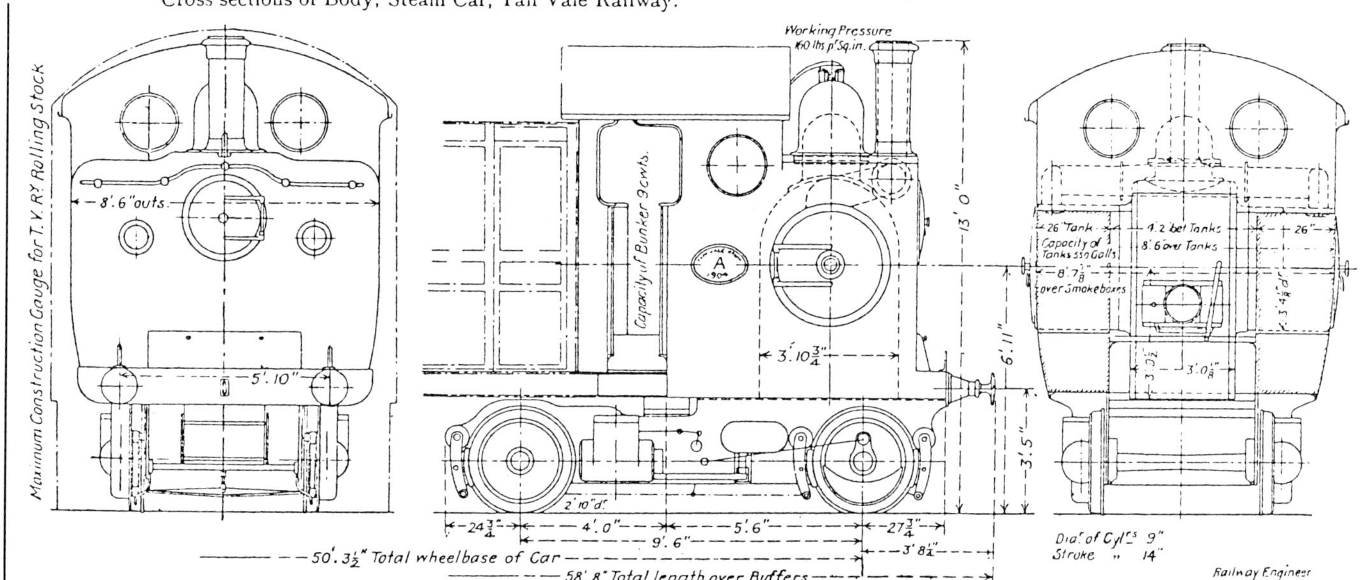

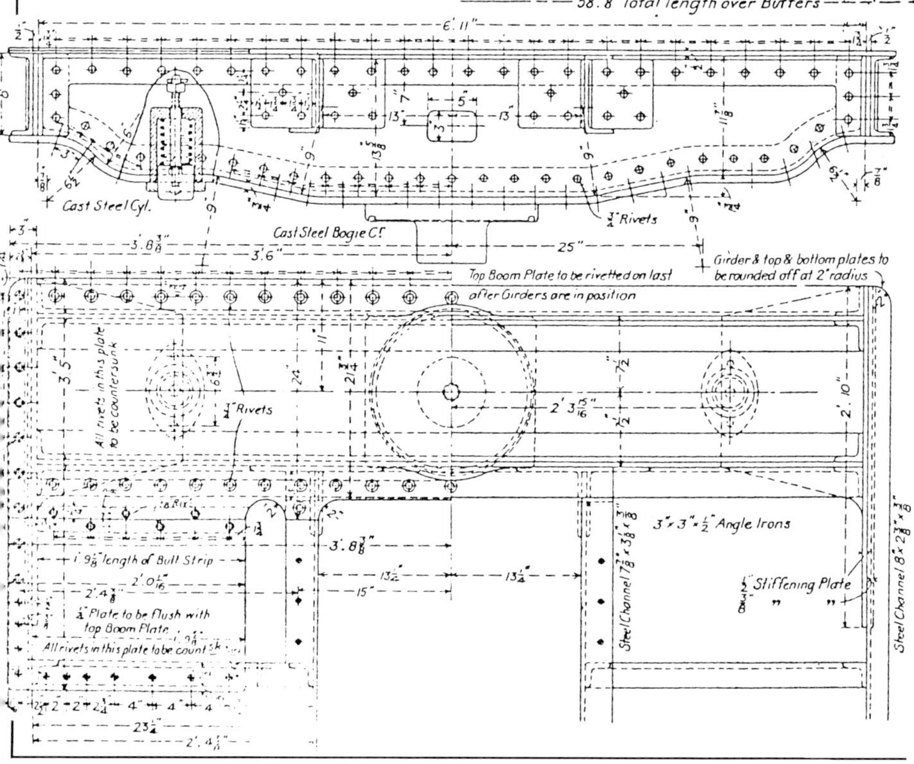

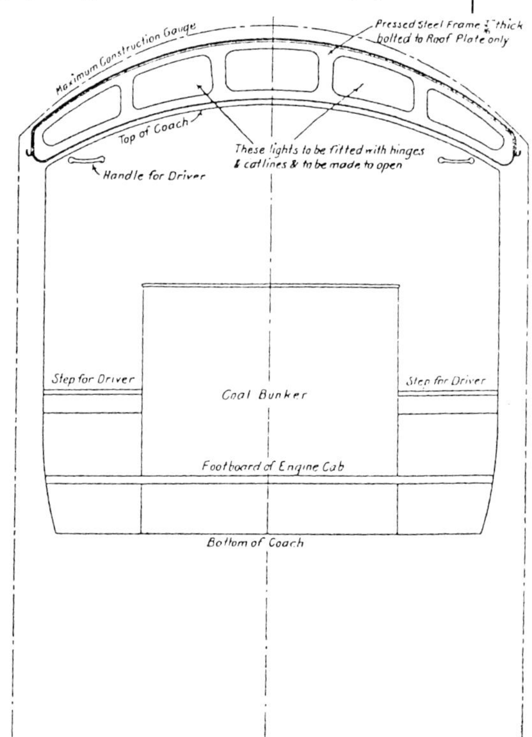

Taken from The Railway Engineer *of November 1904.*

Pressed Steel Frame for Back of Cab, Steam Car, Taff Vale Railway.

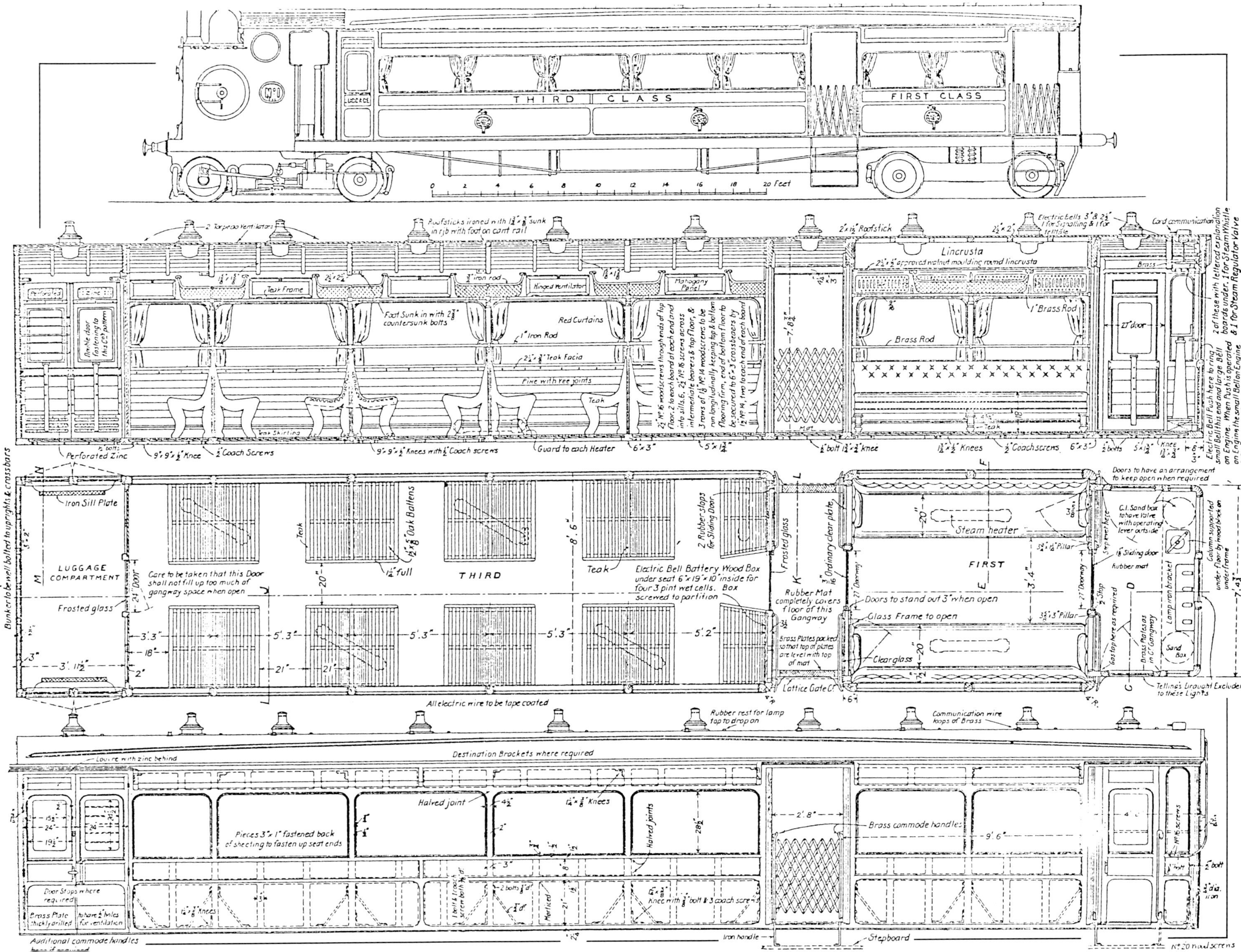
THIRD CLASS
FIRST CLASS
LUGGAGE
0 2 4 6 8 10 12 14 16 18 20 Feet
2 Torpedo Ventilators
Roofsticks ironed with 1¾" x ⅝" sunk in rib with foot on cant rail
Lincrusta
Red Curtains
1" Iron Rod
Teak Frame
Hinged Ventilator
Mahogany Panel
Brass Rod
1" Brass Rod
27" door
Pine with vee joints
Teak Skirting
Perforated Zinc
Guard to each Heater
Coach Screws
LUGGAGE COMPARTMENT
Iron Sill Plate
Frosted glass
Care to be taken that this Door shall not fill up too much of gangway space when open
THIRD
FIRST
Steam heater
Oak Battens
Electric Bell Battery Wood Box under seat 6" x 19" x 10" inside for four 3 pint wet cells. Box screwed to partition
2 Rubber stops for Sliding Door
Frosted glass
Ordinary clear plate
Rubber Mat completely covers floor of this Gangway
Doors to stand out 3" when open
Glass Frame to open
Clearglass
Lattice Gate
Doors to have an arrangement to keep open when required
C.I. Sand box to have valve with operating lever outside
Sliding door
Rubber mat
Lamp iron bracket
Sand Box
Column supported under floor by wood block on underframe
Telling's Draught Excluders to these Lights
Bunker to be well bolted to uprights & crossbars
All electric wire to be tape coated
Rubber rest for lamp tap to drop on
Communication wire loops of Brass
Destination Brackets where required
Louvre with zinc behind
Halved joint
Halved joints
Pieces 3" x 1" fastened back of sheeting to fasten up seat ends
Brass commode handles
Door Stops where required
Brass Plate thickly drilled for ventilation
Additional commode handles
Iron handle
Stepboard
Morticed

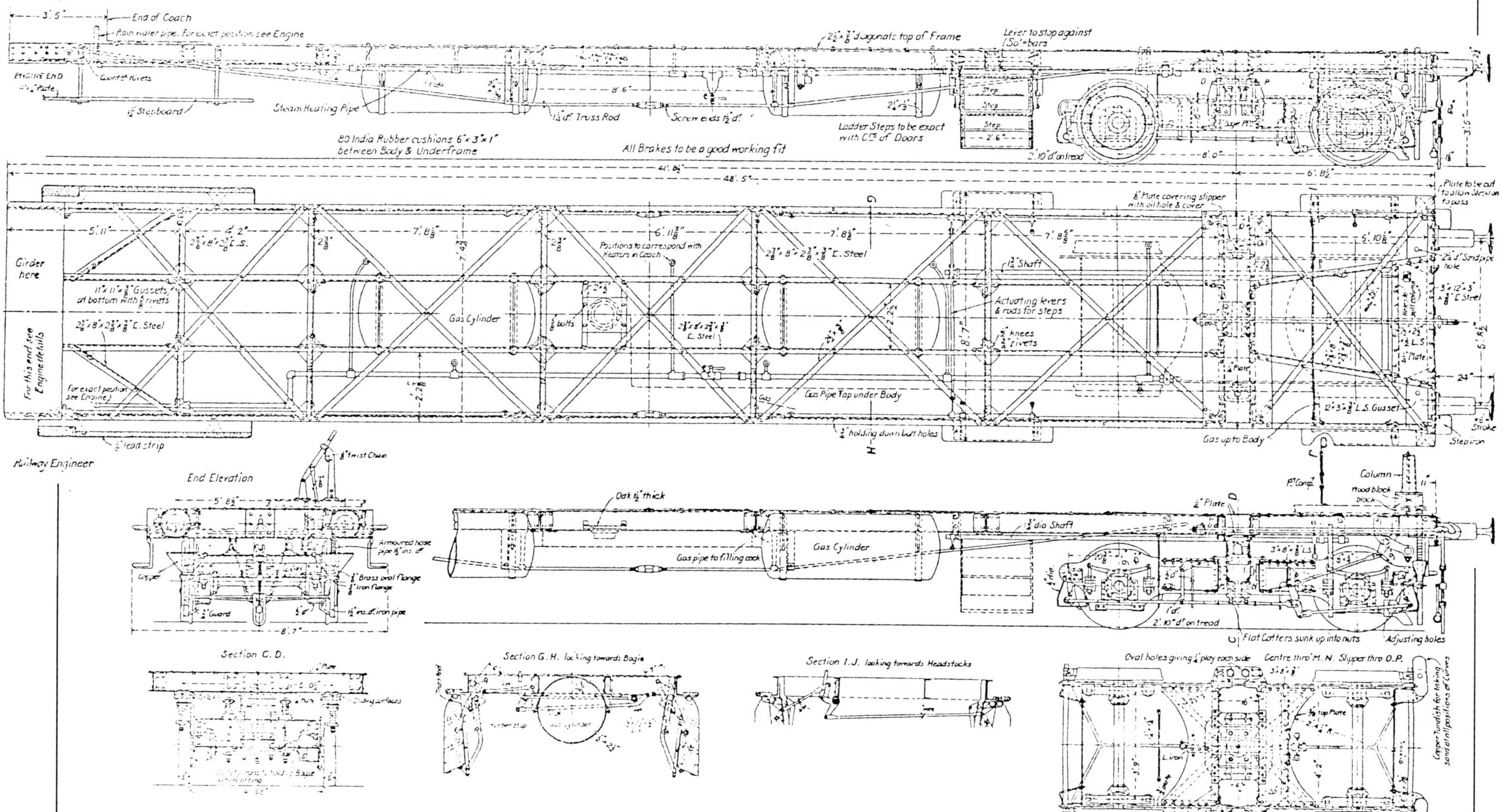

Underframe Steam Passenger Car, Taff Vale Railway.

Taken from The Railway Engineer *of November 1904.*

An article in *The Railway Engineer* of November 1904 stated that

'The ease with which these cars stop and start on gradients of 1 in 40, e.g. between Cardiff and Penarth, is most remarkable. Vibration is practically non-existent, and the result is no doubt due to the carriage frame being connected to the engine bogie ... In working these cars have been very successful. Their popularity is so great that passengers commonly allow the ordinary train to pass, and wait for the following car, which is, therefore, often over-crowded, but without complaints from the passengers.'

This last statement was not entirely true. The following letter appeared in the Cardiff *Evening Express* for 2nd November 1904 under the heading 'MEDITATIONS ON THE T.V.R.':

'To the Editor of the Evening Express

'SIR – Anyone who has had the misfortune to travel on the South Eastern and Chatham Railway will not rashly condemn "an enterprising" line, but in my ten years of travel on the "Chatham" I have never experienced such want of consideration as exists for the Penarth passengers of the Taff Vale Railway.

'We have the choice of dirty trains or steam motor-cars! The most marvellous outcome of human ingenuity as applied to the railway engineering and management is the Taff Vale Railway steam motor-car! It is either very drafty or dreadfully stuffy, according to the weather; it jolts and jumps over the points like a "thing possessed"; it has a happy knack of over-running its stopping place; and, as a rule, it will seat about one-half its passengers, and under the most favourable circumstances will not be many minutes late.

'But those who travelled on the 5.30 p.m. car this evening spent the ten minutes travelling to Dingle-road discussing who is responsible for running the cars, which will not seat more than 60 people, when morning after morning, and night after night, there are over 100 passengers to go by it. Is it humorous to pay £7 per annum for a first class season and every other journey to be squeezed into the luggage compartment or left behind to await the next dirty train?

'To return to the tale of tonight's journey. We arrived at Dingle-road, and then the fun commenced. The cars have a short iron lever (placed in the most inconvenient position), which is supposed to raise or lower the steps (Dingle-road has no platform, it would cost too much, I presume). These steps have often struck me as a marvel of ingenuity, especially when watching a fat guard struggling with the lever until the perspiration rolls off him.

'Well, after some trouble the steps were lowered, and the passengers alighted, the guard attempted to raise them, and after three or four futile attempts another assisted him, but, no, the lever would not budge. Then an official got down and examined the mechanism with a lamp, and stated that the avoirdupois of human flesh in the car was jamming the rods underneath!

'We were asked to move to the other end of the car, which was an impossibility owing to it already being full.

'Many of us then got out and watched these poor fellows struggling with the monstrosity, and we pitied them. After a few minutes, in which people were getting out and in – not knowing if they would get any further or not – away went this clean, but slothful invention. I have not heard whether it reached Penarth! We lit our pipes and walked home, wondering why the manager criticises the tramway and never uses the Taff Vale Railway motors.

'In conclusion I would say that the 9.4 and 9.45 from Penarth are always crowded out, and when I was foolish enough to travel by them in preference to a dirty train I could never get a seat, not even in the luggage van. Now I use the train and travel smoking!

'On Saturday the 2.48 car arrived at 3.15 p.m., but one gets used to that. The trains often take fifty minutes to cover four miles.

'The 5.30 and 8.40 cars from Cardiff are analogous to sardine tins, and when Sir Henry Irving was at Cardiff – but I'll spare the "powers that be"!

'I shall be glad if you will insert this letter to warn those thinking of residing at Penarth.

'I am, &c. A VICTIM.
P.S. – I enclose my card
Penarth, Oct 31.'

The TVR seems to have taken this sort of complaint to heart, because the following year the company acquired two small six-wheel trailers for use with their rail motors. However, as recounted below, their trials on the Penarth line were unsuccessful, and eventually larger railcars were used. From 1907, locomotive-operated auto trains became available.

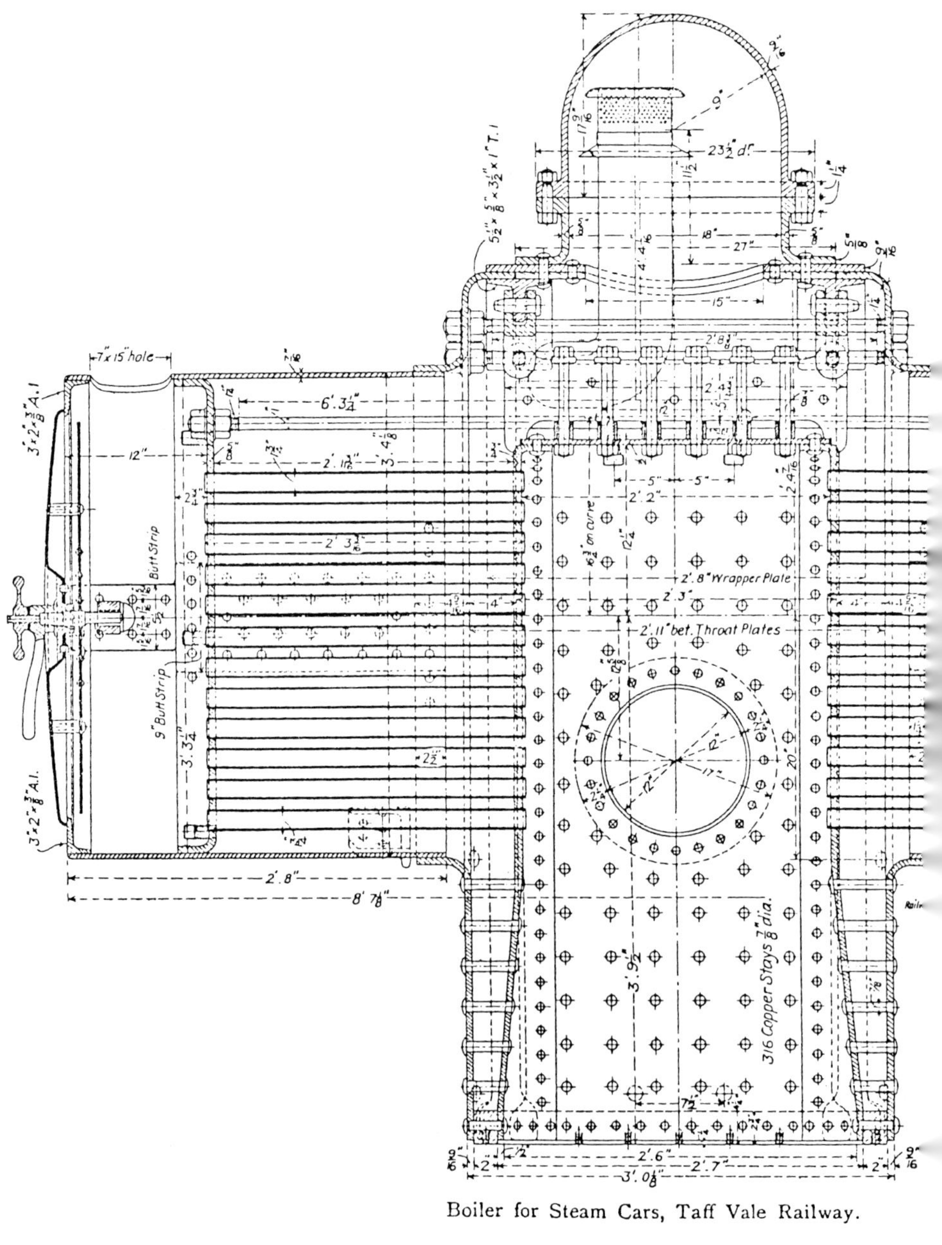

Boiler for Steam Cars, Taff Vale Railway.

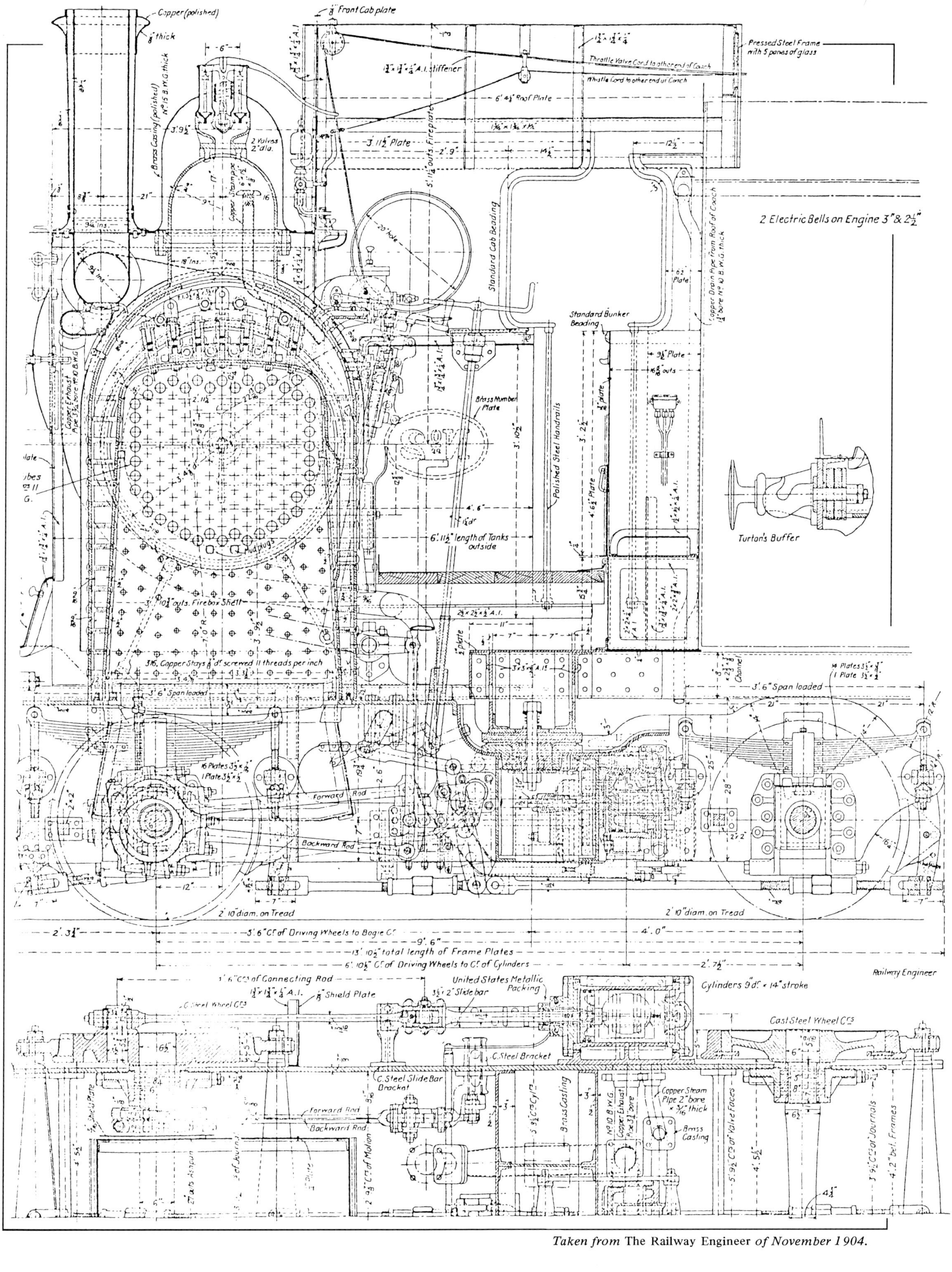

Taken from The Railway Engineer *of November 1904.*

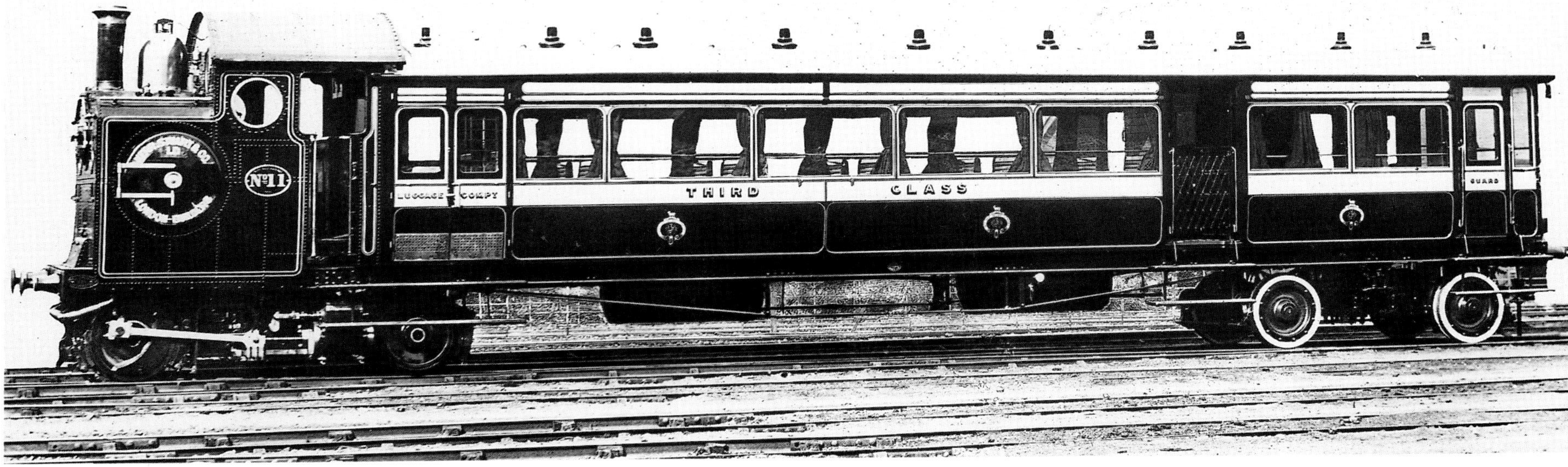

Taff Vale Railway SRM No. 11 (engine 11 + probably coach portion 11) as built. Note the 'KERR STUART LD LONDON BUILDERS' round the smokebox, possibly on a removable sticker, as it did not run in service with this embellishment.
LPC, CTY. R. C. RILEY

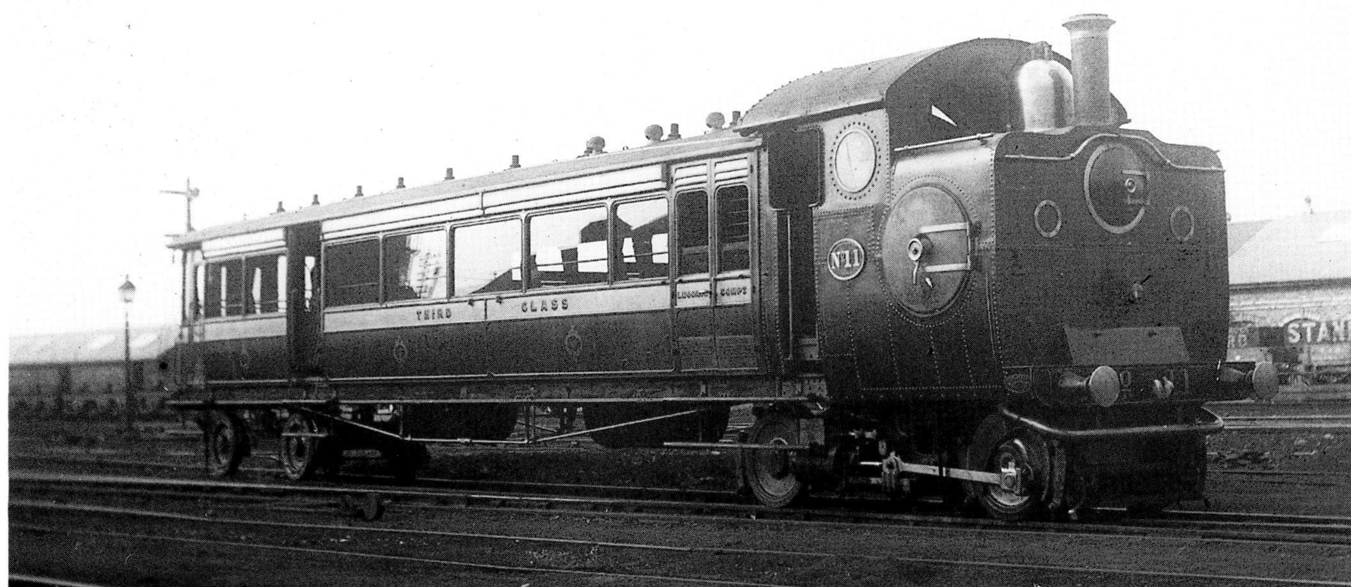

Taff Vale Railway SRM engine 11 with an all-third class coach portion, possibly at Cardiff, 28th July 1905.
KEN NUNN COLLECTION
CTY. LCGB

Taff Vale Railway SRM engine 11 with composite coach portion No. 4. The destination board reads 'YNYSYBWL'. COLLECTION R. C. RILEY

Kerr, Stuart/Bristol SRMs Nos.8 to 13

On 4th October 1904, the Traffic Committee 'recommended that six additional motor cars of the same design as now in use be sought', but Third class only, with separate compartments for ladies and non-smokers. In due course, these cars were supplied – Kerr Stuart of Stoke-on-Trent built their engine portions, whilst the coach portions were again supplied by the Bristol Wagon & Carriage Co. Ltd. It would appear that the only material difference between Nos.2–7 and these cars was that the later batch were all Third class only, and seated 48 passengers. Presumably, the small saloon now had wooden seats and its ceiling was no longer covered with lincrusta Walton. These cars were delivered between March and May 1905 – again, late. Disagreements over payment by the TVR, who tried to enforce penalties for late delivery, led Kerr, Stuart to retain certain patterns supplied by the Taff Vale, and there were threats of court action.

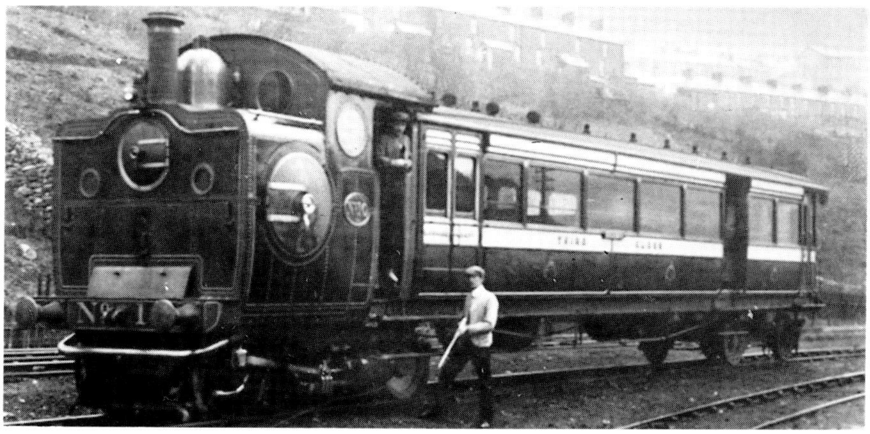

TVR Engine Unit 10 with an all-third class coach portion. COLLECTION R. C. RILEY

Taff Vale Railway SRM engine 8 + coach portion 7 at Cathays shed.
G. H. W. CLIFFORD
CTY. R. C. RILEY

Manning, Wardle/Brush SRMs/Motors Nos.14 to 18

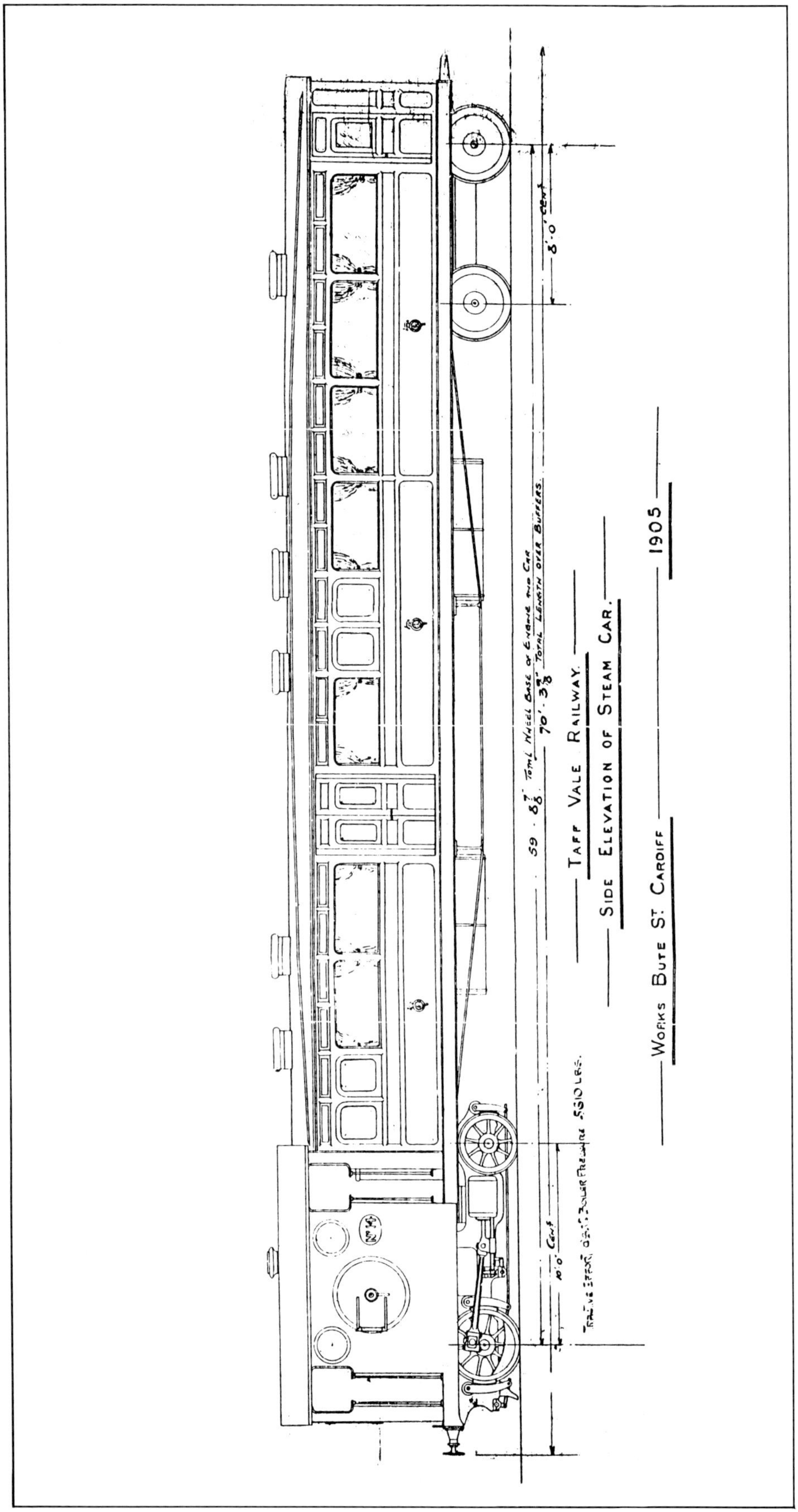

The Traffic Committee authorised the purchase of three additional cars plus two extra engines on 26th September 1905; three complete cars with motor units were numbered 14–16 when delivered, and the two additional power units became 17 and 18. These were supplied by Manning, Wardle & Co. Ltd., of Leeds, with carriage portions subcontracted to the Brush Electrical Engineering Company of Loughborough. They were built between April and June 1906, and the *Railway Times* of 5th May 1906 reported that they were to be used on the Penarth branch.

These cars and their motor units were rather larger than the earlier designs: they were 70ft 3⅞in long over buffers and weighed 44 tons 11 cwt, nearly 9 tons more than Nos.2–13.

Unlike Nos.8–13, they were composites, seating 16 First class passengers and 57 Third in a rather different arrangement of passenger accommodation. Now, the Third class saloon was next to the power unit, and was provided with a pair of droplights and a pair of large, fixed windows. Then came a vestibule with double doors to the outside – flat and slightly recessed, as on the earlier cars. Next, another saloon, divided into Third and First class areas, the First class being subdivided into 'Smoking' and 'Non-smoking' accommodation.

The driver's vestibule had single doors and a quarterlight as before, also recessed.

There were two other notable features of the coach unit: instead of ventilators above the windows, there were now toplights, and instead of torpedo ventilators, the coach had some raised ventilators giving the appearance of a number of short clerestory roofs.

It was reported in *The Railway Times* for 24th August 1907 that the interior of the First class compartment was in polished teak and walnut, with Lincrusta on the ceilings painted white and bordered with polished walnut bands. Wood's wire seats were provided, framed in polished teak and upholstered in moquette to match the exterior finish (purple brown and white). An accompanying photograph shows the moquette to have a floral pattern.

The *Railway Times* further indicated that the 'carriage underframe is of steel throughout, being built of steel channels kneed together and stiffened by gusset plates and diagonal braces. It is trussed with four 1½in diameter truss rods.' There were two gas cylinders, and 'a coupling loop and link for attaching a trailer when required'. The exterior of the carriage portion was reported to have the lower panels painted purple brown, the upper panels white, and the finish completed with gold and vermilion lines.

Motor units were enclosed in a different casing than before: they now had three windows at the front, the tops of which were curved in a similar profile to the roof, with two 'keyhole' type doorways in each of the sides,

Taff Vale Railway large SRM No. 14 (engine 14 + coach portion 14) being delivered from Brush. Notice the discreet Manning Wardle works plate just in front of the front cab steps. It would appear that these large engine units were driven from the front cab, but fired from the rear one. The coal bunker here appears to have been fitted with additional coal rails. NATIONAL RAILWAY MUSEUM

The interior of the first-class section of a large TVR SRM. NATIONAL RAILWAY MUSEUM

TVR large SRM consisting of large engine unit 15 with large composite carriage unit 14 at Mountain Ash. Note the signal cable to the left of the vacuum pipe for when a trailer was in use, and safety chains fitted to the front buffer beam. The train seems to have been carrying 'C' headlamps for some reason. COLLECTION J. N. SLINN

The interior of the third-class section of a large TVR SRM. NATIONAL RAILWAY MUSEUM

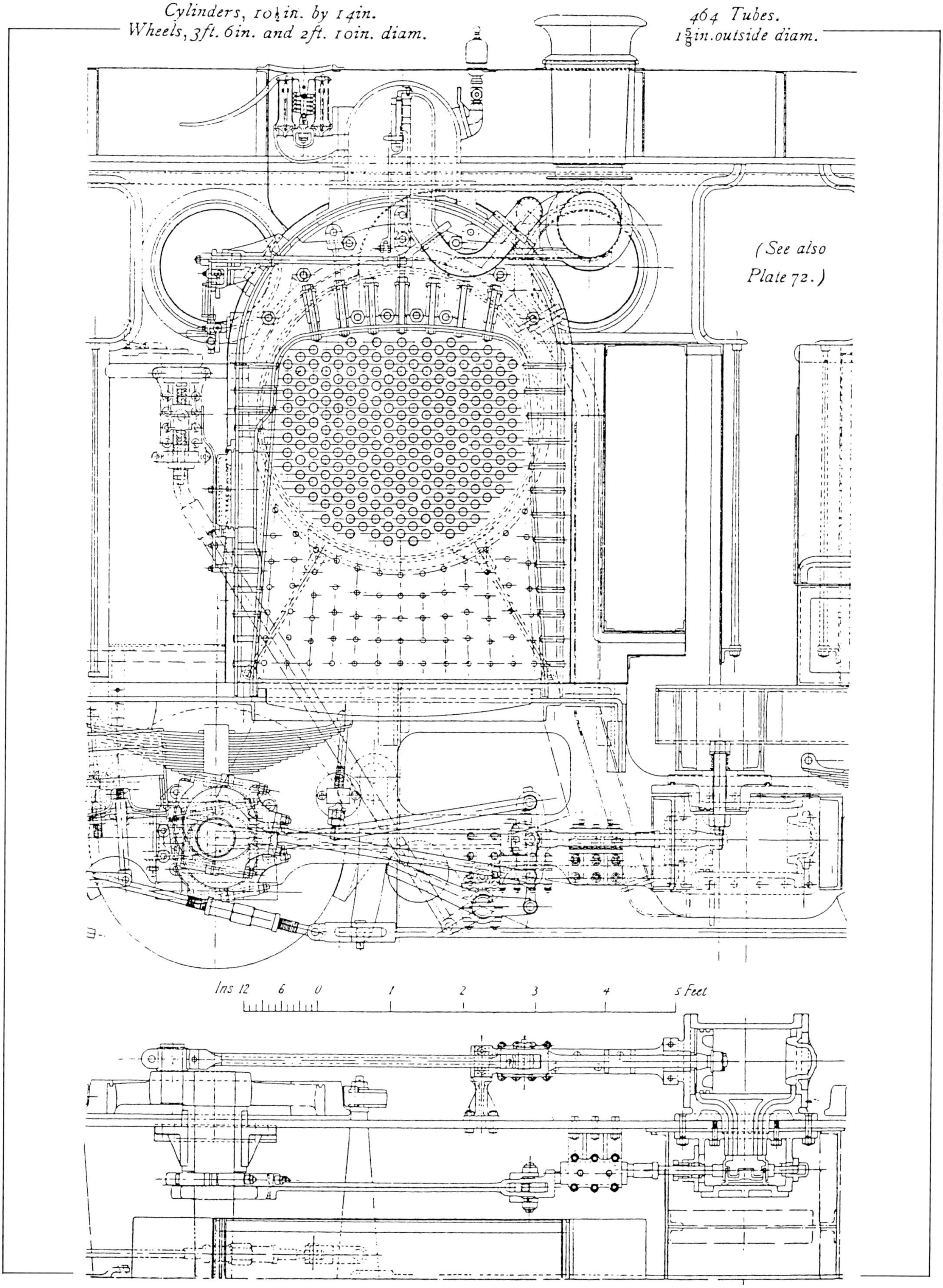

Taken from Mechanical Engineers *1906.*

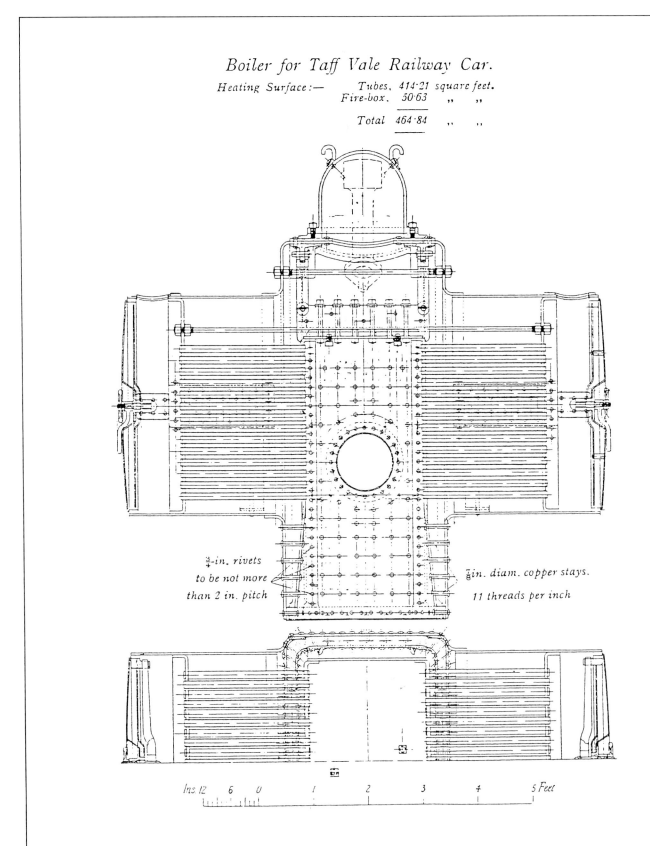

Boiler for Taff Vale Railway Car.

Heating Surface:— Tubes, 414·21 square feet.
Fire-box, 50·63 ,, ,,
Total 464·84 ,, ,,

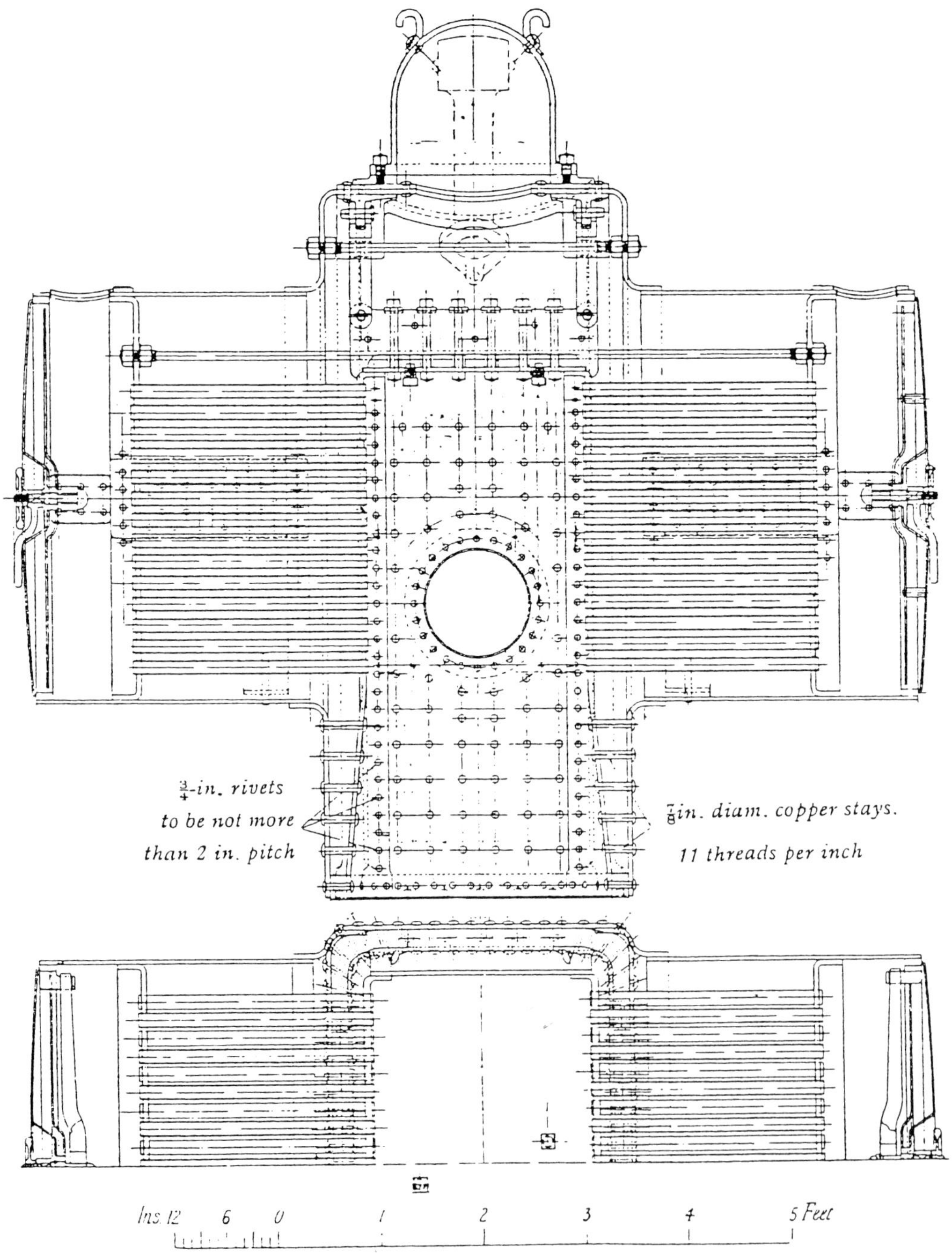

Taken from Mechanical Engineers *1906.*

similar to many tank locomotives, although the rear one appeared to be partly formed by an extension to the coach sides. There was a smokebox door on each side of the power unit casing, between the side doors, but there was no longer one at the front. Cylinders were now 10½in × 14in stroke, but the driving wheels (and the carrying wheels on the power bogie) were now 3ft 6in diameter. With the boiler pressure now increased to 180 lbs sq in, the tractive effort at 90% efficiency was 5,954 lbs as against 4,803 lbs of the older cars. Motor units Nos.14–18 still had the 0–2–2 wheel arrangement, with the cylinders next to the trailing wheels.

The boilers were of a similar type to those on the earlier cars, but were a little larger at 3ft 9½in diameter, and 464 tubes of 1⅝in diameter. The heating area of 476 sq ft was appreciably greater than before. In spite of the new arrangement of the cabs, it appears that they were still fired from the rear of the boiler, as in the earlier cars, although now they were driven from the front.

Their water tanks were still attached to the end of the coach portion.

The 'spare' TVR large SRM engine unit 18 in use with large coach portion 15. This picture was taken in the Maerdy Branch platform at Porth, about 1912-14.
C. W. HARRIS, COLLECTION R. C. RILEY

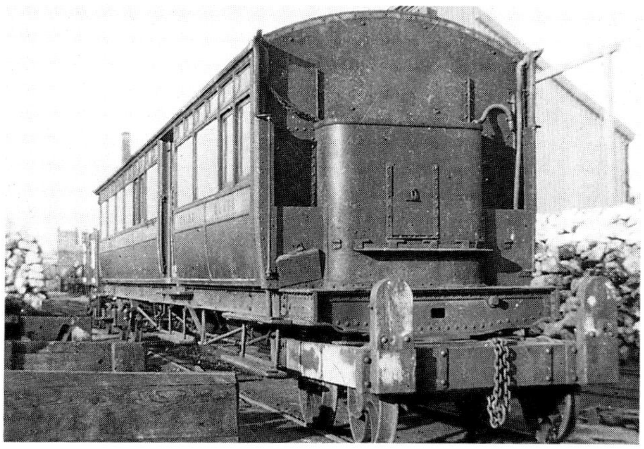

This shows the end of one of the large SRM coach portions which had been separated from the engine and rested on some accommodation bogies. The tanklike structure in the centre of the end was the coal bunker.
G. H. W. CLIFFORD
CTY. R. C. RILEY

Below: *The 'spare' TVR large SRM engine unit 18, the large additional Manning Wardle's plate showing it to be their No. 1680. The usual plate is seen at the right-hand end of the solebar. The large plate may well have been for this photograph only.*
COLLECTION R. C. RILEY

TAFF VALE SRM OPERATIONS

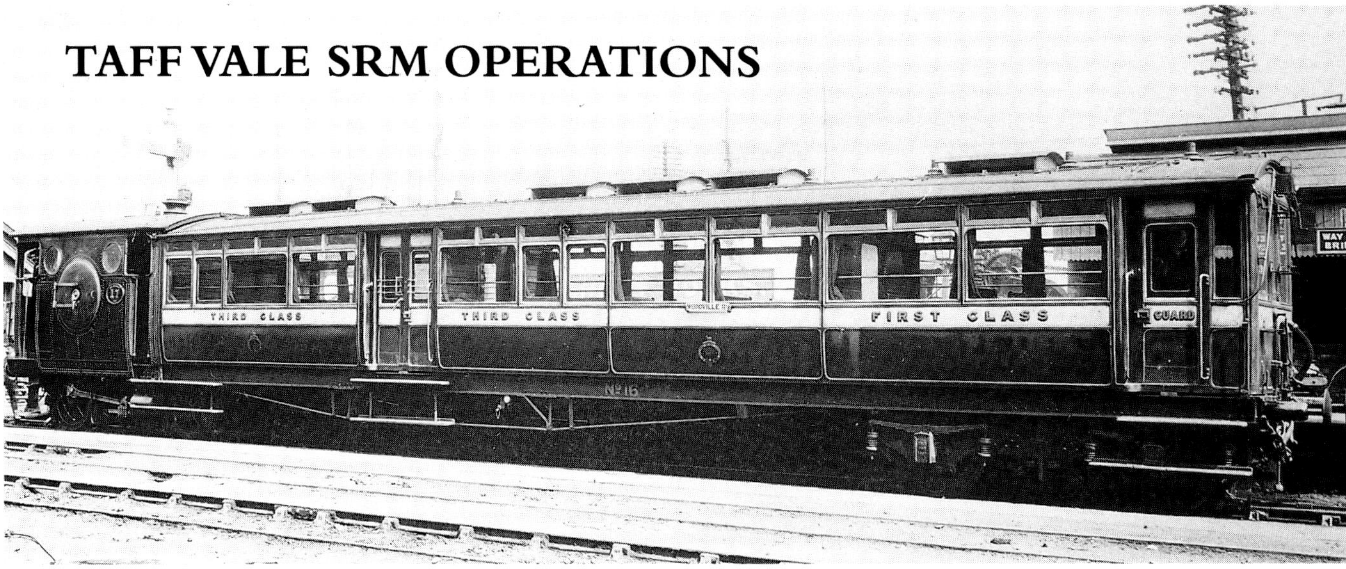

A TVR large SRM, consisting of large engine unit 17 with large composite carriage unit 16, at Cardiff Docks. COLLECTION R. C. RILEY

The SRMs were to be found running over the majority of Taff Vale regular passenger-carrying routes during the years leading up to the Great War, in most cases in conjunction with ordinary trains.

SERVICES

In 1907, the Taff Vale SRMs were used on the following services:

Aberdare (Mill Street) & Aberdare (Low Level)
Aberdare (Mill Street) & Pontypridd
Cardiff & Pontypridd
Cardiff (Bute Road) & Maindy
Cardiff, Penarth & Cadoxton
Pontypridd & Nelson
Pontypridd & Old Ynysbwl (SRMs only)
Pontypridd, Llantrisant, Cowbridge & Aberthaw
Pontypridd & Treherbert (& Blaencwm Platform).

Blaencwm Platform was about 1½ miles north-west of Treherbert at the end of what was known as the Dunraven Siding, not far from the R & SB Blaenrhondda station. It is shown in the TVR 1907 timetable, but no trains are indicated as stopping there. It is not certain that it was ever opened. The RCTS *History of GWR Locomotives* also lists Aberdare (Mill Street) & Nantmelyn Platform, which was situated at the end of the TVR's Dare Valley branch; it appears this was an unadvertised miners' service.

By 1910, the cars were being used on the Maerdy service: No.6 broke down at Maerdy Platform on 6th August 1910, with the 'Key to rocking shaft breaking', whilst No.16 broke down there on 26th June 1913 with a defective blower pipe. I believe that, by this time, the TVR auto trains tended to be used on their main line services, leaving the less flexible and (probably) less reliable SRMs on branch services.

TRAILER TESTS

In July 1905, haulage trials took place on the 1 in 40 Penarth bank involving a railcar and a trailer. The first attempt was made with the car carrying a load of 5½ tons and the trailer (which weighed 13½ tons empty) carrying 3½ tons. The half-mile up the incline from Penarth Dock to Dingle Road took 4½ minutes, and having stopped at Dingle Road the car failed to restart on the heavy gradient, and the train had to be pushed on to Penarth by a locomotive. A second attempt from Penarth Dock with the load reduced by 1 ton was then made, and the car and trailer reached Dingle Road in 4¼ minutes, but again could not be successfully restarted from Dingle Road. A further one ton of the load was thrown out at Dingle Road and the train was then successfully restarted, but took a further 4 minutes to reach Penarth (a distance of 28 chains). The conclusions drawn from this exercise were that the time taken of 8¼ minutes from Penarth Dock to Penarth with a brief stop at Dingle Road would be excessive, even with a lightweight trailer, and that 'It may be desirable when designing the proposed additional cars to construct them in a manner suitable for the Penarth Bank. If we can get 70 seats it would be a great help.'

A Pontypridd–Aberdare train at Pontypridd on 15th August 1913 showing one of the TVR short driving trailers leading the train which otherwise consisted of one of the large SRM engines with a short coach portion. KEN NUNN COLLECTION, CTY. LCGB

PROBLEMS IN TRAFFIC

At each meeting of the TVR's Traffic Committee, a list of locomotive, carriage and wagon derailments and failures was presented, and these also included the reasons for the incidents. To these regular items on the agenda was added a separate list of motor car failures, and these became quite numerous, sometimes exceeding the number of locomotive failures. Of the problems affecting the 'small' SRM's reliability, the most significant were inadequate axlebox journals – which overheated – and poor quality steam pipes on the earlier motor units supplied by the Avonside Engine Co. Mr. Hurry Riches had to explain the problems to the General Manager and the Traffic Committee; he wrote on 21st October 1905:

'Dear Sir,

'Failures of Motor Cars

'Referring to your letter of the 11th instant. As to the Traffic comments upon the failure of the motor cars so far as running hot is concerned, I have already reported several times that the cause is due to the heavy weight upon the bearings, and the high speed of the journal.

'I altered No 1 Car when she came in for heavy repairs recently, and since then we have had no serious trouble with her, and she has the heaviest journals of any motor car that we have.

'No 3 is now in the West Yard and I am altering her journals in the same way as No.1, and I think we shall probably have no further trouble with her.

'As I take the others in I will alter them in the same way.

'The failures in the steam pipes that have occurred up to now have taken place on the cars built at Bristol, and I have personally investigated the matter and find the pipes are thinner than what is stipulated in our specification. This ought to have been found out when the cars were delivered. I have written to the Avonside Coy. about it but have not yet had their reply.

'Further than that the copper appears to be rather softer than should be the case.

'I will have these pipes changed as soon as I can then I think we shall have no further trouble in that respect.

'As to the one case of a nut breaking which is reported as having caused a failure. This was a mistake on the part of the driver. It was only the washer at the end of the brake screw that came off but this did not affect the efficiency of the brake at all, and was not a sufficient cause for stopping the car. I have taken up strongly with the driver for his stupidity in this matter.

'Yours faithfully
T. Hurry Riches

A. Beasley Esqre.'

This letter was followed by another on 12th November 1905, setting out the reasons for the failures over the three weeks from 21st October to 11th November:

Motor Car No.1: 21st October

'The failure of this Car was through the injectors failing to pick up the water. The injectors were examined, and cleaned on Sunday the 22nd ulto., and tested in the Shed when they appeared to work alright. On Monday the 23rd ulto. the injectors again failed, but as we could not trace the cause the injectors were taken off, and a new pair were tried. These appeared to work perfectly satisfactorily in the Shed, and the Car was sent out on the 24th October when it again failed on the 7.55 a.m. trip from Queen Street to Cadoxton. The water was emptied out of the tanks and an examination was made when it was found that some waste had accumulated round the strainer of the suction pipe and this obstructed the free flow of the water and gave all the trouble. This is not a failure that is likely to occur again as the cause has been ascertained. How the waste got there it has been impossible to trace but very special precautions are being taken to see that waste does not get into the other tanks. Someone has reported that this car has failed several times, this is wrong, the car has only failed on three occasions since September 15th 1905.'

Motor Car No. 2: 23rd October

'This car had been under the lift having the boxes remetalled, and on Saturday 21st and Sunday 22nd the Car had been run on trial over the Sidings at Cathays. The bearings seemed to run so well that there was every confidence in placing the Car on the service on Monday 23rd ulto. It ran the service until 3.2 p.m. when the right driving box gradually got worse from the time it started in the morning until about 3 o'clock when the Motorman felt it so hot that it was undesirable to run the car longer. The great weight per square inch on these boxes make them extremely liable to run hot, and a plentiful supply of oil has to be given to ensure them running.'

Motor Car No.8: 25th October

'This failure was caused by the accidental working out of one of the keys securing the arm of the rocking shaft. This was an accident which was almost impossible to have foreseen, but steps have been taken to prevent a repetition.'

Motor Car No. 7: 25th October

'The above car failed at 11.23 a.m. owing to the two driving axleboxes running warm. The boxes were cooled down and the motorman again tried the Car at 1.14 p.m. but the boxes continued to run hot. This car had been under the lift and the Motorman assures me that he gave the bearings every attention but they continued to get hot. The cause of running hot I can only repeat is the same as in the case of No.2 Motor Car.'

Motor Car No.4: 25th October

'This failure was caused by the steam pipe bursting. These steam pipes were put in thinner than specified. It was not observed namely 1/8th of an inch. As soon as this was discovered it was taken up with the Avonside Company who replied that they ordered them the right thickness but had not noticed that they were under the thickness and they have offered to supply new pipes of the proper thickness, and have done so. These will be changed gradually as we can get at the Cars.'

Motor Car No.11: 28th October

'While this car was at Llantrisant it was discovered that one of the boxes was running warm. The car had run a considerable time, and on opening up the pipes supplying oil to the axleboxes some fluff from the trimmings had accumulated in the pipe and had evidently obstructed the free flow of oil to the bearing. Under ordinary circumstances this large accumulation of fluff in the pipe would not occur. It is caused by the large quantity of oil being used to keep the bearings cool and the constant pulling out and in of the trimmings to supplement the ordinary automatic supply of oil.

Motor Car No.11: 30th October

'No.11 Car was lifted and tested and to all appearances seemed to be right but on her working on the Penarth Branch the right bearing gradually got hot and the Motorman had no alternative but to withdraw the car from service. It is a tedious matter to get these Cars to run with the present bearing when once they get hot.'

Motor Car No.2: 30th October

'This failure occurred after the Car had been lifted and tested. When a Car is put on the service the work is rather more severe that we can give them in testing at Cathays mainly because of the cants in the roads. These cants cause the weight to be from one box to the other and this additional weight seems at times to start the boxes to get hot.'

Motor Car No.7: 1st November

'This car had been under the lift, and had been run for several days at Cathays on the Siding and she appeared to be running so well that we had every confidence in her running the service but at 4.10 p.m. the box got so hot that it was necessary to stop the car for relifting.'

Motor Car No. 5: 2nd November

'This Car had been working the Penarth service from October 25th to November 2nd. The boxes had each been a little warm, but not unusually warm. The Motorman attributes the box hot to a small quantity of sand coming in contact with the journal. It is very difficult to say whether this was the cause or not because the same result would have happened had the supplementary oiling been temporarily neglected.

Motor Car No.13: 11th November

'This car was running on the Aberdare section and there was no report that the axlebox was giving

---

'Dear Sir,

No.2 Motor Car taking the wrong road August 27th 1904.

Motorman D. Evans, Assistant Motorman Walter Wheeler

'I regret to report that this car was going up No.2 Road at Cathays Shed, the Motorman D. Evans at the Guards end, and the Assistant Motorman W. Wheeler being on the Engine. As the Engine approached the points leading to the Down Running Road, the Motorman signalled to the Assistant Motorman to stop which was done, the wheels of the Carriage bogie was over the points leading to the Coal Stage Road. The Assistant Motorman on looking out noticed an Engine coming towards him, and thinking that the Guards end of the Car was foul of the adjoining road he reversed the Engine, and commenced to run down with the result that the Engine of the Car remained on No 2 Road while the bogie wheels passed onto the Coal Stage Road, then ran for about 28 yards, and the cross straining damaged one of the folding steps, strained the Car Bogie and also strained the Engine. It has been necessary to send the Carriage bogie to Cathays for repairs to the steps, and the same will be necessary to the Engine. Assistant Motorman W. Wheeler is suspended.

'Yours faithfully'

Letter from Mr T. Hurry Riches to Mr A. Beasley, dated 30th August 1904. The original copy is in the Public Record Office, Kew.

trouble but it suddenly through the crown of the axlebox gave way at 11.48 a.m. while running from Aberdare to Pontypridd and the Car had to be brought to Cathays for the box to be replaced.'

This was not the end of the saga. On 5th January 1906, Tom Hurry Riches again wrote to Ammon Beesley, making the case that the cars were overworked and there were insufficient spare units. He pointed out that there were 13 cars to cover 11 diagrams, although at this time the cars were being taken into the works one after the other to have their axles changed, leaving only one unit spare to cover any contingencies. The working diagrams required the cars to be out for between 12 and 18 hours each day, during which time they averaged about 150 miles. Given the 2½ times differences in wheel diameter between an SRM and a 'large' engine, this was the equivalent of an engine running 375 miles per day – and the TVR considered 100 miles to be a good day's work for a large engine. Hurry Riches also reported that three cars (Nos.1–3) had their axles changed, and there had only been one failure of these due to an axlebox running hot.

TABLE 36

TVR SRM FAILURES

Car	*Location*	*Date*	*Cause*
15	Cardiff Queen Street	10 May 10	Tubes leaking.
11	Pontypridd	11 May 10	Hot bearings.
16	Pontypridd	16 May 10	Right branch steam pipe giving out.
15	Cardiff Queen Street	18 May 10	Left hand driving axlebox hot.
6	Llantrisant - Pontypridd	27 May 10	Steam pipe joint blew out.
16	Pontypridd - Cross Inn	31 May 10	Bridle rod broken.
16	Llantrisant	16 Jun 10	Bridle rod broken.
11	Pontypridd	17 Jun 10	Right hand driving spring broke.
8	Ynysywbl	18 Jun 10	Right hand driving axlebox hot.
18	Pontypridd - Nelson	18 Jun 10	Boiler tubes leaking badly.
15	Cardiff Dock	21 Jun 10	Broken spring.
15	Llandough - Grangemouth	25 Jun 10	Spring pillar broke.
18	Cadoxton - Penarth	11 Jul 10	Main steam pipe and left spindle gland blowing badly.
14	Aberdare	12 Jul 10	Tube breaking.
5	Aberdare	27 Jul 10	Union nut to whistle pipe broke.
9	Dinas	1 Aug 10	Eccentric rod disconnected owing to bolt and nut working off.
15	Lavernock - Swanbridge	2 Aug 10	Right driving spring hanger broke.
15	Penarth	9 Aug 10	Right hand driving axlebox hot
16	Pontypridd	13 Aug 10	Bridle rod broken.
6	Maerdy Platform	15 Aug 10	Key to rocking shaft breaking.
14	Pontypridd	27 Aug 10	Driving spring breaking.
17	Cathays service	27 Aug 10	Short of steam. Assistant Motorman admonished.
16	Aberdare	12 Sep 10	Right hand driving axlebox hot.
5	Aberdare	20 Sep 10	Right hand driving axlebox hot.
6	Cowbridge	21 Nov 10	Blowing of dome joint of boiler.
13	Queen Street - Penarth	10 Dec 10	Radial bearing hot.
7	Coke Ovens	25 Dec 10	Left rails owing to Motorman wrongly turning the points.
16	Penarth, Dock St.	27 Dec 10	Short of steam - inexperience of fireman.
17	Cardiff Queen Street	12 Jan 11	Defective firing by Assistant Motorman.
8	Nelson service	16 Jan 11	Steam chest cover blowing out.
3	Pontypridd	20 Jan 11	Defective firing by motor prepareman.
1	Aberdare	9 Feb 11	Left hand driving axlebox hot.
5	Llantrisant - Pontypridd	21 Feb 11	Short of steam - fireman blamed.
4	Cowbridge	14 Mar 11	Left hand driving axlebox hot.
4	Llantrisant	23 Mar 11	Seam in firebox leaking.
16	Cowbridge	25 Apr 11	Driving axlebox hot.
3	Pontypridd	1 May 11	Nearside spiral spring broke.
2	Pontypridd	11 May 11	Whistle pipe broke.
2	Pontypridd	16 May 11	Whistle pipe broke.
13	Aberdare	22 Jun 11	Spring hanger broke.
17	Cockherbertown	27 Jun 11	Brake block sticking.
2	Cowbridge section	9 Aug 11	Shortness of steam.
6	New Road Pfm. - Ynysybwl	18 Nov 11	Shortness of steam.
14	Penarth	26 Dec 11	Breaking of boiler tubes.
10	Cowbridge service	3 Feb 12	Shortage of steam.
12	Aberdare	14 Feb 12	Right hand driving spring.
4	Cowbridge	6 May 12	Right hand driving axlebox hot.
9	Clydach Vale - Windsor	12 Jun 12	Fire overloaded with coal.
17	Pontypridd	12 Jul 12	Left hand driving spring defective.
18	Cardiff Dock	16 Oct 12	Nut on brake gear slack.
13	Pontypridd	18 Oct 12	Left hand driving spring broke.
16	Cardiff Dock	18 Oct 12	Not enough time to get up steam to replace defective No.18.
16	Maerdy	26 Jun 13	Defective blower pipe.
5	Sully	21 Jul 13	Broken suspension link.
16	Taffs Well - Pontypridd	21 Jul 13	Leaking tubes.
18	Cardiff - Penarth	8 Sep 13	Auxillary valve on regulator jammed.
14	Cardiff Docks - Pontypridd	24 Sep 13	Leaking tubes.
8	Pontypridd - Nelson	7 Oct 13	Want of steam.
2	Clydach Court - Windsor Passing Siding.	15 Oct 13	Want of steam.
8	Pontypridd	22 Oct 13	Leaking tubes.
8	Mountain Ash	4 Dec 13	Fractured exhaust pipe.
17	Pontypridd - Aberdare	29 Dec 13	Brake problems.
11	Pontypridd - Old Ynysybwl	29 Dec 13	Exhaust pipe defective.
13	Nelson - Pontypridd	18 Mar 14	Short of steam.
6	Pontypridd - Nelson	19 Mar 14	Short of steam.
9	Llanfarbon	6 Apr 14	Short of steam - poor coal.
16	Taffs Well	23 Sep 14	Leaking tubes.
11	Rhondda Cutting	1 Oct 14	Big end bolt stripped.
17	Pontypridd - Aberdare, Gyfeillon Lower	1 Oct 14	Poor firing.
16	Cardiff Docks - Pontypridd	14 Oct 14	Engine in need of repairs.
6	Pontypridd - Ysynybwl	28 Oct 14	Not powerful enough for large coach.
17	Aberdare - Pontypridd	29 Oct 14	Poor firing.
17	Pontypridd - Old Ynysybwl	23 Nov 14	Leaking tubes.
17	Windsor Siding	24 Nov 14	Leaking tubes.
6	Cilfynydd	7 Jan 15	Leaking stays.
17	Pontypridd	18 Jan 15	Leaking stays.
18	Pontypridd - Nelson	6 Feb 15	Poor firing.
17	Mountain Ash	24 Feb 15	Failure of blower pipe
13	Aberdare - Coke Ovens	13 Mar 15	Poor firing.
14	Taffs Well	15 Mar 15	Injector not working properly.
14	Cathays Shed	29 Mar 15	Auxillary valve on regulator jammed - trailer car not coupled.
14	Llantrisant Jct - Treforest (Barry Rly. Jct)	8 Dec 15	Poor firing.
12	Pontypridd	10 Mar 16	Mudguard knocked off by locking bar, which had become elevated above rail level.
16	Pontypridd	20 Mar 16	Left trailing bearing running hot.

Despite these improvements, the number of failures of the cars continued at a significant rate, although Hurry Riches does not seem to have been asked to explain why to the Traffic Committee again. Eventually he seems to have cured the tendency of the driving axleboxes to run hot by fitting them with forced lubrication, using a pair of oil pumps on each car (one for forward running, the other for reverse), which were belt driven from the axle. The axleboxes were fitted with a reservoir to collect the used oil, which was then pumped back into the axleboxes. According to a paper read before the Institution of Mechanical Engineers by Hurry Riches and Mr Bertie Reynolds – also of the TVR – and reported in the November 1908 issue of *The Railway Engineer*, the TVR cars had driving axleboxes with 6in diameter and 9½in length, the weight of a loaded car upon the driving axle was 15 tons 13 cwt, giving a weight upon the bearing area of the axleboxes of 466 lbs sq ft. At 30 mph, the axle rotated at almost 300 rpm. The relatively high axle weight on the driving wheelset was perhaps to ensure adequate adhesion on steep gradients, such as the 1 in 40 on the approach to Penarth Town.

The list of failures (Table 36) is taken from the Minutes of the Traffic Committee, and is a valuable indicator as to which car (or rather, which power unit) was working which service.

Taff Vale's SRMs do seem to have become more reliable, with no failures being reported in the first part of 1913, whilst a number of the later failures were down to poor firing or poor preparation, as opposed to mechanical failure.

THE END OF THE TVR RAIL MOTORS

The minutes of the TVR Traffic Committee meeting of 24th October 1913 reveal that 'A formal report by the Locomotive Superintendent and the Superintendent of the Line recommending conversion of eight small motor cars into four auto trains at an estimated cost of £2,300 and subject to slight alteration in detail was approved'. On 7th November the matter was considered by the Locomotive & Stores Committee, who also approved the proposal. The eight coach portions altered to auto trains were Nos.1, 3, and 8 to13, and this was done between August 1914 and May 1916.

At their meeting on 23rd July 1916, the Traffic Committee recorded:

> 'A suggestion by the Locomotive Superintendent that the carriage portion of eight steam motor cars be converted to auto train coaches at an estimated cost (including repairs) of £6,050 and that 18 engines be disposed of or broken up was submitted for consideration, but having regard to existing conditions arising out of the war, the Committee came to no conclusion thereon and ordered that it be deferred.'

However, it would seem likely that the remaining steam rail motors had been taken out of traffic by about this time as the last recorded failure was dated 20th March 1916, when No.16 failed with its left trailing bearing running hot at Pontypridd.

There the matter rested for two years, until the TVR's Engineering & Stores Committee met on 24th July 1919. It was recorded:

> 'A joint report dated 19 July 1919 was submitted from the Locomotive Superintendent and the Superintendent of the Line in which it is suggested that eight motor cars should be converted into passenger coaches for use on ordinary passenger trains at an estimated cost of £9,500. It was recommended that the proposed conversion be carried out. The question of the allocation of the costs being deferred for consideration later.'

Eventually this was done; the remaining rail motor coach portions were altered to hauled coaches between December 1921 and May 1922, and the locomotive portions scrapped.

Taff Vale Railway SRM engine 6 + large composite coach portion 16. The combination of a large car with a small engine could give rise to problems. COLLECTION WELSH RAILWAYS RESEARCH CIRCLE

Alexandra (Newport and South Wales) Docks and Railway.

On and from September 1st, 1904, this Company will run A MOTOR CAR SERVICE between PONTYPRIDD AND CAERPHILLY and Intermediate Stations, as under:—

Week Days Only.

DOWN TRAINS.		a.m.	a.m.	a.m.	p.m.	p.m.	p.m.	p.m.
Pontypridd	dep.	8 45	10 5	11 30	1 45	2 52	5 3	6 30
Glyntaff	„	8 48	10 8	11 33	1 48	2 54	5 6	6 33
Treforest	„	8 50	10 10	11 35	1 50	2 56	5 8	6 35
Rhyd-y-felen	„	9 53	10 13	11 38	1 53	2 58	5 11	6 38
Dynea	„	8 56	10 16	11 41	1 56	3 1	5 14	6 41
Upper Boat	„	8 59	10 19	11 44	1 59	3 4	5 17	6 44
Groeswen	„	9 2	10 22	11 47	2 2	3 7	5 20	6 47
Nantgarw	„	9 5	10 25	11 50	2 5	3 10	5 23	6 50
Caerphilly	arr.	9 12	10 32	11 57	2 12	3 17	5 30	6 57
UP TRAINS.								
Caerphilly	dep.	9 15	10 35	12 2	2 27	3 20	5 33	7 0
Nantgarw	„	9 22	10 42	12 9	2 32	3 25	5 40	7 7
Groeswen	„	9 25	10 45	12 12	2 35	3 28	5 48	7 10
Upper Boat	„	9 28	10 48	12 15	2 38	3 31	5 46	7 13
Dynea	„	9 31	10 51	12 18	2 41	3 34	5 49	7 16
Rhyd-y-felen	„	9 34	10 54	12 21	2 43	3 36	5 52	7 19
Treforest	„	9 37	10 57	12 24	2 45	3 38	5 55	7 22
Glyntaff	„	9 39	10 59	12 26	2 47	3 40	5 57	7 24
Pontypridd	arr.	9 42	11 2	12 29	2 50	3 43	6 0	7 27

SINGLE JOURNEY FARES TO

FROM	Glyntaff	Tre-forest	Rhyd-y-felin	Dynea	Upper Boat	Groes-wen	Nant-garw	Caer-philly
Pontypridd	1d.	1d.	1d.	1d.	1½d.	2d.	2½d.	4d.
Glyntaff		1d.	1d.	1d.	1½d.	2d.	2½d.	4d.
Treforest			1d.	1d.	1d.	1½d.	2d.	4d.
Rhyd-y-felin				1d.	1d.	1½d.	2d.	3d.
Dynea					1d.	1d.	1½d.	3d.
Upper Boat						1d.	1d.	2½d.
Groeswen							1d.	2d.
Nantgarw								1½d.

The Issuing of Tickets is subject to the Conditions and Regulations referred to in the Time Tables, Bills, and Notices of the Company.

JOHN MACAULAY,
General Manager.

Press cutting from the 'Pontypridd Observer' of 27th August 1904: an official notice of the ADR's new Pontypridd–Caerphilly service.

CHAPTER THIRTEEN

THE STEAM RAIL MOTORS OF THE OTHER ABSORBED COMPANIES

AS well as the Taff Vale, several other Welsh companies that became part of the Great Western at the grouping had tried out steam rail motors on certain passenger services, though not to the same extent. However, by 1922 the GWR was the only railway of the Western group to have examples still running on their lines, although the Port Talbot Railway's only SRM had been sold to the Port of London Authority in 1920, and was running on that system.

The Alexandra (Newport & South Wales) Dock & Railway Company – often abbreviated to ADR – was originally a docks company, owning the Alexandra Dock at Newport. In 1897, it absorbed the Pontypridd, Caerphilly & Newport Railway, which was predominantly a freight line, built to divert some of the coal traffic from the Rhondda and Cynon Valleys of South Wales to the docks at Newport. Amalgamated into the Great Western group on 25th March 1922, the ADR had effectively two separate sections of main line which had formed the Pontypridd, Caerphilly & Newport Railway: the first section ran from Pontypridd (from a junction with the Taff Vale Railway) to Penrhos Junction, near Caerphilly. Thence, its trains ran over the Rhymney Railway to Caerphilly, and the Brecon & Merthyr Railway from Caerphilly to Bassaleg Junction, near Newport. The second section of the ADR ran from Bassaleg Junction, over the 'Park Mile' owned by Lord Tredegar alongside the GWR tracks to Park Junction, Newport, and thence to Mendalgief West Junction and the docks complex. The ADR's motor train service, introduced in 1904, ran between the ADR station at Pontypridd (Tram Road) and Caerphilly, and supplemented a GWR Pontypridd & Newport service.

Whilst the Barry Railway was predominantly concerned with mineral and goods traffic, owning the comprehensive docks system at Barry, it also worked considerable passenger traffic, particularly in the summer months; the sandy beach at Whitmore Bay, Barry Island, was a very popular venue. Its everyday passenger working was centred around the main line between Barry and Trehafod, which was extended over Taff Vale metals to Porth, and to Cogan Jct., from whence it continued over Taff Vale and Great Western lines into Cardiff. Another branch served Bridgend.

The Cardiff Railway was another owner of a major docks system in South Wales; its extensive site at Bute handled the greatest tonnage of minerals and goods in the Principality. Passenger services operated by the company were limited, comprising SRM workings between the Rhymney Railway station in Cardiff and Heath Jct., thence over their own metals to Rhydyfelin Halt, near Treforest, which commenced in 1911.

Another company with dock interests was the Port Talbot Railway. This concern also ran passenger services from Port Talbot (Central, and PT/Aberavon) to Pontyrhyll, thence over the Great Western line to Blaengarw. The Great Western managed its railway operations from 1908.

In common with the other railways serving the valleys around Cardiff, the Rhymney company was primarily concerned with mineral and goods traffic. Nevertheless, it operated a busy passenger service over its main line between Cardiff and Rhymney or Rhymney Bridge, with branch trains from Caerphilly to Machen (largely over Brecon & Merthyr metals) and to Senghenydd (the Aber branch).

Although SRMs were found on all of these lines, most of the cars were converted to trailers or hauled coaches by their owners before the grouping, and their subsequent history has been covered in detail in Volume 2 of *Great Western Auto Trailers*.

The Alexandra (Newport & South Wales) Dock & Railway Co. : Glasgow Railway & Engineering SRMs Nos.1 & 2

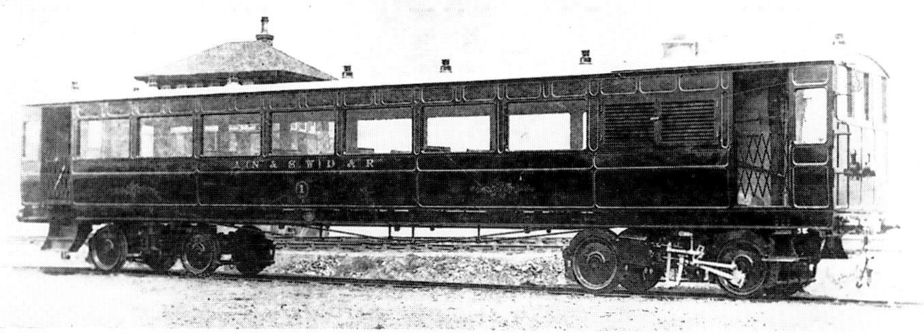

ADR Car No. 1 showing the power unit end. CTY. HMRS

On 1st September 1904, the ADR instituted a passenger service between Caerphilly and Pontypridd (Tram Road), along a 6½-mile stretch of line provided with rail-level halts, supplementing a GWR Newport, Caerphilly & Pontypridd service. For this, the ADR purchased a steam rail motor from the Glasgow Railway & Engineering Company in 1904, and a second, larger steam rail motor car from the Glasgow company in 1905, which can be regarded as an enlarged version of No.1.

The Glasgow company had been founded by Dougal Drummond as 'D. Drummond & Son' after he had resigned from the Caledonian Railway, but when he was appointed to the L & SWR, the firm was taken over by his son as the Glasgow Railway & Engineering Co. Ltd.

DESIGN: NO.1

The first ADR steam rail motor was reported as 59ft long over buffers, although as a trailer it is recorded as being 58ft 5in long over buffers, with a body length (over headstocks) of 55ft 5in. It was 8ft 7in wide. The vehicle had a low arc roof, flat ends and sides with tumblehome.

Each end contained three windows, extending down from the eaves to a level rather above the waist, of which the central windows were droplights, the other two fixed. The ends were divided into four vertical panels below the windows, and the sides were also panelled below their windows, there being a deep waist panel and a bottom panel, both divided by vertical mouldings.

The car had a single passenger compartment with seven quite large, fixed windows on each side, each window surmounted by two prominent ventilators. There were longitudinal bench seats each end of the passenger compartment (each 10ft 8½in long) and between them three fixed seating bays (16ft 2½in total). The seats were wooden, and seated 52 passengers.

There was a vestibule at the trailing end of the car, 5ft 2in between the end and the passenger saloon wall. In this vestibule were fitted access steps each side, with a very narrow driving area in the centre; the steps appear to have been fixed, and they left only 3ft 6in floor space between them. However, from photographs, it would appear that they could be covered with flaps, thus giving a conventional height floor, required for Caerphilly station, and, from early 1906, Tram Road, too. The doorways for the steps were 2ft 8¾in wide, and were closed by lazy-tong-type doors extending just above waist level. The driver thus had a 'compartment' about 2ft 3½in deep with an almost central handbrake. The driving area could not be shut off from the open passenger vestibule behind; however, it did have a quarterlight-sized fixed side window.

At the other end of the car was the motor unit. The car body had two large, louvred ventilators with three smaller ones above. There was another doorway closed by a lazy-tongs arrangement, and a side window to the driving area.

The underframe of the car was of steel, and had a circular section, adjustable truss rod each side, the adjustment being provided by a central turnbuckle. There were two queen posts each side.

ADR Car No. 2 viewed from the trailing end. CTY. HMRS

Clerestory-roofed ADR Car No. 2 showing the power unit end. CTY. HMRS

The trailing end of ADR Car No. 2.

An unusual, inside frame trailing bogie was provided, with no obvious springs, and with solid wheels, 3ft 0in diameter. Its wheelbase was 8ft.

The power unit had a 'locomotive type' boiler (i.e. horizontal) with a barrel 6ft 10⅞in long and 3ft 6in diameter. It had 274 tubes, 1½in diameter, a 7 sq ft grate area, and operated at a maximum pressure of 160 lbs sq in. The cylinders were 9in diameter by 14in stroke, and operated onto the leading wheelset only, thus producing an 0–2–2 arrangement. Walschaert's valve gear was employed, the motion looking rather spindly, to say the least. The power bogie had the same 3ft diameter solid wheels on an 8ft wheelbase as the trailing bogie, with a total wheelbase of 43ft 10in. The tractive effort was 4,788 lbs at 90% efficiency.

A water tank was built into the body, and had a capacity of 350 gallons, whilst the coal bunker held 1 ton. The weight of the car in working order was 40 tons exactly. It was said to have been capable of 30 mph, but does not seem to have been used with a trailer.

No.1 carried what looked like an oil head/tail lamp.

DESIGN: NO.2

According to the *Railway News* of 7th October 1905, this car was 64ft 11in long, although the Great Western's trailer diagram quotes 64ft 10in over buffers, and 61ft 3in over headstocks. It was 8ft 7in wide over body mouldings. The body height was 7ft 6in, plus a clerestory of 10in; this clerestory was what the GWR termed a 'royal clerestory', sloping down at each end of the car to the level of the main roof, which had an arc profile like No.1. As with No.1, the ends were flat and contained three windows, whilst the ends and sides were panelled in a similar way.

The passenger saloon was 42ft 2½in long, and seated 54 passengers on longitudinal bench seating along the sides. *Railway News* waxed quite lyrical about the passenger accommodation:

> 'The interior of the passenger compartment is panelled with bird's-eye maple, finished with teak and mahogany, a great improvement on the decoration of the first car. The roof, of the clerestory type, lined with lincrusta, having a gilded moulding, is very handsome in appearance. The seats, which are placed longitudinally, are of plaited rush matting over springs, and are very comfortable and sanitary. Ample ventilation is secured by ordinary sliding ventilators placed over side lights, and swing ventilators in the sides of the clerestory roof. Passengers enter by a sliding door from a vestibule at the rear end, and in addition, doors on each side of the carriage at the end next the motor compartment, to facilitate dealing expeditiously with exceptionally heavy traffic. The vestibule is also fitted with steps for taking up passengers from the level of the permanent way, and hinged platforms for railway stations. The rear end driving compartments are fitted with a sliding door, so that the driver is separated from the passengers entering and leaving the carriage, while a speaking tube communicates between the driving

compartment and the motor compartment, and electric bells are available for communicating between those compartments and the passenger compartment. Electricity, generated by a De Laval steam turbine dynamo placed on the footplate, is used for lighting the car, each of the headlamps being of 50 candle-power The car can also be heated by steam.'

Apart from the longitudinal seating, the internal arrangement seems to have been arranged rather better than in No.1. The driving and passenger vestibule was 6ft 1in long, of which the passenger exit had doorways 3ft 5in wide, containing an ordinary door with a droplight, and a narrow 'blind' door. Both opened inwards. The driver's area had a side droplight, and he may even have been able to close himself off from the passengers in the vestibule. The vestibule seems to have had the same arrangement of fixed steps as before.

The passenger compartment had seven large, fixed lights, each with a ventilator above. At the power unit end of the passenger compartment, there was another door with, it appears, a fixed step below, not recessed into the body.

In the motor compartment there were two large, louvred ventilators in the bodyside. There was also a side door to the power compartment, which seems to have been open in all the photographs I have seen, so I cannot be sure how – or if – it was closed. There was another side window to the motor compartment next to the corner pillar.

The power unit was apparently very similar to that of No.1, and had a locomotive-type boiler with Drummond water tubes, working at a pressure of 160 lbs sq in. The cylinders again were of 9in diameter by 14in stroke, giving a TE of 4,788 lbs at 90% efficiency. Walschaert's valve gear was used, and the bogie was again uncoupled, and thus of the 0–2–2 arrangement. The trailing wheelbase was 8ft, and the same type of inside-framed bogie with 3ft diameter solid wheels were used. No.2 had a 48ft 8in total wheelbase and, according to *Railway News*, weighed 35 tons in working order; this seems rather low, especially when compared with No.1. However, other sources, quoted in the RCTS *History of GWR Locomotives*, give 43 tons.

DETAILS & DISPOSAL

Car No.1 seems to have been quite successful, because it lasted as a steam rail motor until 1917. However, the ADR purchased three second-hand bogie coaches (Barnum & Bailey) in 1909 for their passenger service, so I cannot help wondering just how much work it did after that date.

No.2 was altered to a trailer in 1911. I am not sure that this indicates that it was appreciably less successful than No.1, but perhaps it was more attractive for conversion to a trailer.

According to Eric Mountford, in his book *GWR Absorbed Coaching Stock*, the colour of these cars is not known, but was probably a darkish brown or red-brown. Photographs of these cars when new indicate that the mouldings were picked out in yellow or gold, and that they carried the company's initials, 'A. (N. & S.W.) D. & R.', in gold upper case letters centrally in the waist panel. No.1 also carried the company's 'coat of arms' below the initials; the coat of arms consisted of the company's initials intertwined, and surrounded by a red belt with the company's name, in full, in gold. No.2 had a vertical moulding dividing the bottom panel into two (and not divided, as the trailer diagram indicates). The coat of arms seems to have been displayed in the bottom panel below the second window of the saloon, and possibly also below the last large window nearest to the motor compartment. Both cars had 'N°' on the headstock to the left of the coupling hook, and the figure on the other side. The headstocks were lined out.

Both No.1 and No.2 would have been allocated to the ADR's Glyntaff engine shed, Pontypridd, for the services to Caerphilly.

ADR REGULATIONS

The Alexandra (Newport & South Wales) Docks and Railway Company's *Appendix to the Working Timetables and Supplementary Instructions to the General Rules and Regulations* of May 1906 contained working instructions pertaining to their SRMs:

'Regulations for Rail Motor Car Service

1. The Motor Cars must be dealt with in all respects as Ordinary Passenger trains and must be signalled accordingly.
2. The cars must be worked by motorman, assistant motorman, and conductor. The motorman must always be at the leading end of the car, which when running must be under his control as regards keeping a look out for signals, and stopping as and when required.
3. At the furthest end from the engine there are levers for shutting off steam, whistling and applying brakes. Should the motorman require additional brakes to be applied he may call for them by pressing the electric bell **once** or by giving two short whistles.
4. While the motorman is riding at the car end, the engine must be in charge of the assistant motorman, who must promptly obey the instructions of the motorman.
5. Before giving the signal to start, the conductor must see that all passengers are aboard, and that the collapsible gates are closed and fastened. At intermediate stations or platforms it may be necessary for passengers to alight from and join cars by means of the same doorway, passengers requiring to alight must be given precedence over those requiring to join the cars.
6. The gates of the motor car platforms must be kept locked except when opened by the conductors for passengers to pass on and off the platforms.
7. The collapsible gates must not be removed for passengers to alight until the car has been brought to a stand.
8. The conductor must always give the motorman the signal to start.
9. When not otherwise engaged inside the car, the conductor must ride on the rear platform, when running engine first, and be prepared to apply the hand brake when it is asked for.
10. The conductor must collect the fares from and issue tickets to all passengers joining the cars at the platforms. Tickets for stations must be collected from the passengers by the ticket collecting staff at the stations in the usual way, except in the case of open stations and motor car platforms, when they must be collected by the conductor either upon the journey or as the passengers leave the cars. The tickets collected by the conductor must be handed over to the Glyntaff Agent who must compare the collected tickets with those in the conductor's ticket case.
11. The cash collected by the conductor must be paid to the Glyntaff Agent at the end of each turn of duty. The particulars of the tickets issued must be recorded by the conductor in the book provided for the purpose, and the cash paid in must be signed for by the person to whom it is paid.
12. Privilege tickets will be available by the cars. Workmen in dirty clothes are to be permitted to ride only in the cars specially reserved for them.
13. No extra vehicles of any description are to be attached to the motor cars for the conveyance of passengers unless specially authorised by the General Manager. Where this authority has been given the extra vehicle must have a brake, and a competent man must be appointed to ride in the brake compartment.
14. Special trains or trains run to relieve motor cars must not stop at the motor car platforms unless special authority is given.

'The inspector at Interchange Sidings [Pontypridd] will be in charge of the Motor Car Service, and in cases where it may be necessary to run special cars at short notice will be held responsible for advising the line.'

In traffic, the SRMs were to carry a white head light and a red tail light in the centre of the ends.

Barry Railway: North British/Pickering SRMs Nos.1 & 2

Barry Railway SRM No. 1. COLLECTION R. C. RILEY

The Barry Railway purchased two steam rail motors in 1905, in which the power units were built by the North British Locomotive Co. of Glasgow, whilst the coach bodies were constructed by R. Y. Pickering & Co. of Wishaw. These were bow-ended cars with prominent roof ventilators, as well as ventilators above most windows. They were 60ft 10½in long over headstocks, 8ft 11in wide, and 12ft 0in high from rail to roof.

DESIGN

In summary, from the rear, these cars had:

Driver's Compartment
Small Saloon, with two fixed lights
Doorway (open in the photographs) which seems to have retractable steps below it
Passenger Saloon, with 5 large lights, the middle one of which did not have a ventilator above it
Luggage Compartment with double doors, one leaf of which was blind, although it incorporated a ventilator.
Motor Compartment, with two large windows, a sliding door (which also had two windows – narrow ones) and a fairly large side window.

There were three windows in each end.

These cars seated 10 First class and 40 Third class passengers.

Barry Railway livery was lake (red-brown) with gold lining. The company's armorial bearing – a Welsh dragon in a garter with 'Barry Railway Company 1884' on it, and with a stag's head and antlers above – appeared twice in the bottom panels towards the middle of the car, and the running number appeared twice on each end: once, centrally above the driver's windows as '2', and once in the centre bottom panel where it was enclosed in the company's armorial device, but with 'Nº2' substituted for the dragon. The luggage compartment had 'LUGGAGE' in the waist panel on both door leaves.

End view of Barry Railway SRM No. 2. R. Y. PICKERING CTY. HMRS

The SRMs had a steel underframe with queen post trusses, with truss rods of round section with a central adjustable turnbuckle.

They were electrically lit, using Stone's system.

One curiosity was a lamp bracket centrally on the ends, just below roof level – presumably the equivalent of the bracket below the chimney on a locomotive. There were also two lamp brackets on the front of the corner pillars, just above waist height, and one either side just above the buffers.

Wheelbase was 46ft, with an 8ft 0in wheelbase power bogie with 4ft diameter wheels, and a trailing bogie wheelbase of 8ft 6in with 3ft 7½in diameter wheels. Both bogies were attached to the solebars by suspension units, as on the earlier GWR cars.

The boiler was 9ft 1in long and 4ft 11in diameter, with a maximum working pressure of

160 lbs sq in. This engine was one of the more powerful ones. The cylinders were 12in diameter × 16in stroke of the 0–4–0 type, with the cylinders ahead of the wheels, and Walschaert's valve gear utilised. Tractive effort at 90% was 7,680 lbs. Water capacity was 500 gallons, but only 15 cwt of coal was carried. The weight in working order was 50 tons 15 cwt.

DISPOSAL

These cars seem to have been mainly used on the Vale of Glamorgan line services between Cardiff, Barry and Bridgend, but were later also seen on the Pontypridd line. They only survived as steam rail motors until 1911, and in that year they were both considerably rebuilt as a gangwayed trailer pair, Barry Railway Nos.177 and 178. As trailers, they continued in traffic on the Vale of Glamorgan line.

Barry Railway SRM No. 2. COLLECTION J. N. SLINN

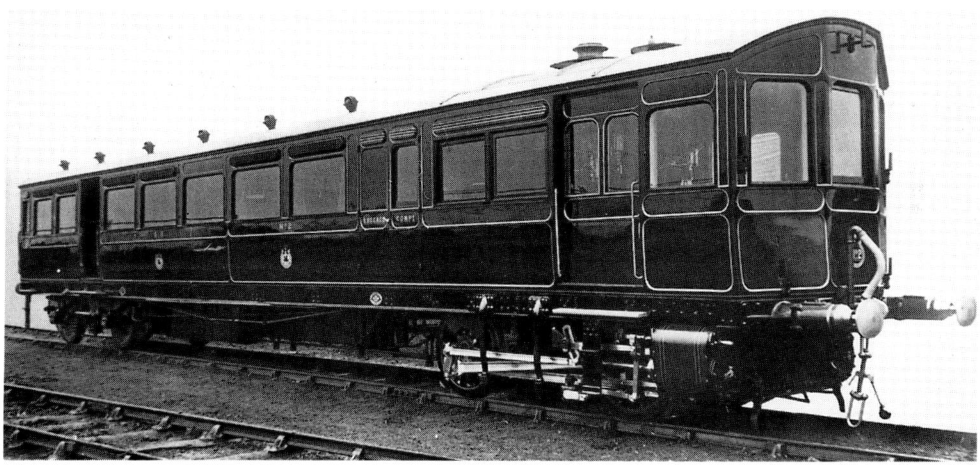

Barry Railway SRM No. 2 from a maker's advertisement. COLLECTION R. C. RILEY

Below: *Barry Railway SRM No. 2.* COLLECTION R. C. RILEY

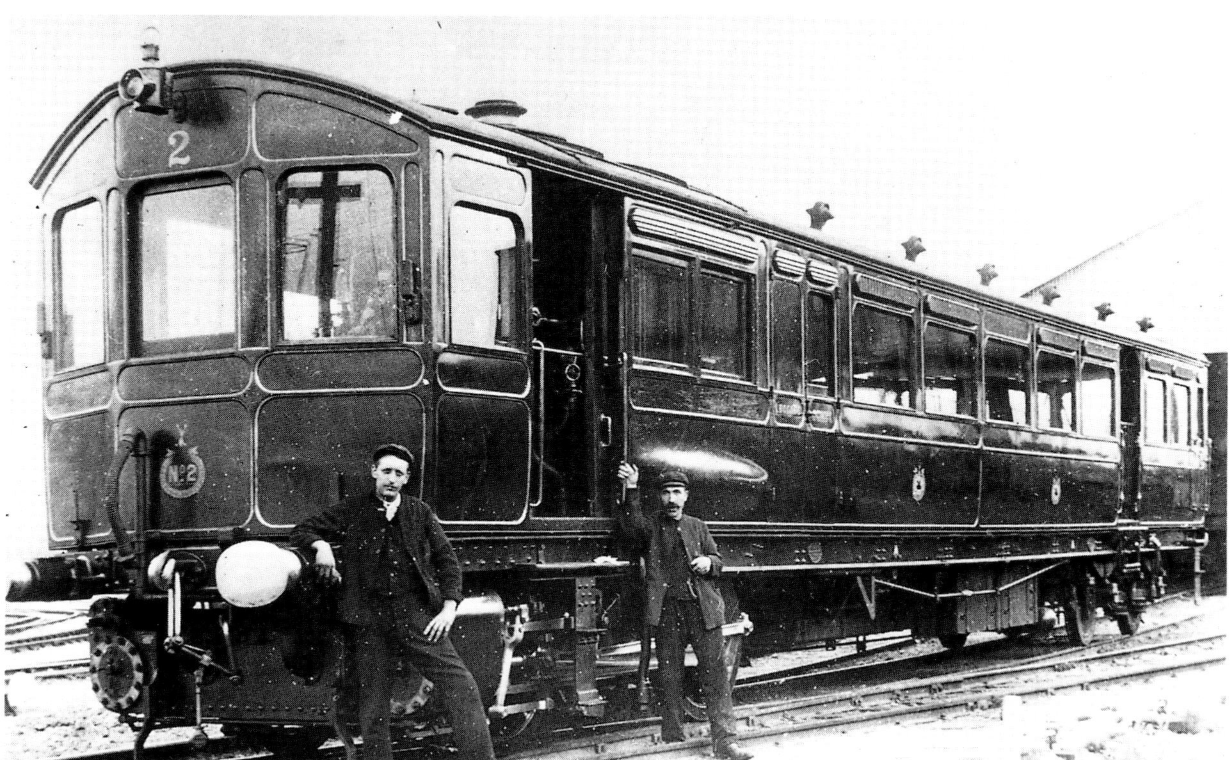

Cardiff Railway: Gloucester C & W SRMs Nos.2 & 3

Cardiff Railway No. 3. COLLECTION HMRS

SRM engine for a Cardiff Railway SRM. The boiler was not tapered like the GWR ones. COLLECTION HMRS

The Cardiff Railway had two steam rail motors. In the context of Great Western, these had two particular points of note: firstly, they were the last SRMs built for what became the GWR group, and were the last steam rail motors to be built for any railway of Great Britain until the Sentinel and Clayton cars of the later 1920s and 1930s; and secondly, they were very similar indeed to the GWR 70ft cars.

These cars were built by the Gloucester Carriage & Wagon Co. together with two trailers, and were numbered 2 and 3, with the trailers as Nos.4 and 5. According to the RCTS *History of GWR Locomotives*, Part 11, the construction of the motor units was subcontracted to Messrs. W. Sisson & Co. of Gloucester, who supplied three power units – one spare. There is an official photograph of trailer No.4 dated 1910, but SRM No.3 was not photographed at the Gloucester works until February 1911. What was presumably the spare motor unit (which seems to have been No.1) was also photographed by – or for – the Gloucester Carriage & Wagon Co. on multi-gauge track, probably at their works (the background has been retouched out), in June 1911.

The Cardiff Railway does not seem to have had a No.1 passenger coach or railcar, although it did have an inspection car of that number, which did not survive until the grouping.

DESIGN

These SRMs were 65ft long, 9ft wide over the body and 12ft 4in from rail to roof. Their trailing and motor bogies were both of 8ft wheelbase, with 3ft 7in diameter wheels in the trailing bogie, and 4ft 0in under the power bogie. The trailing bogies were of Gloucester design. The total wheelbase was 54ft 9in.

The driving compartment – which was 4ft from partition to end – had an external side door which opened outwards, being hinged on the body side, not the corner pillar.

Then came a First class saloon 12ft 11¾in long, which seated 16. This had a pair of large, fixed windows with a pair of droplights in between. All the droplights in the car seem to have had a pair of protection bars across them.

Next was a 3ft 3in vestibule with a set of retractable steps underneath the single, inward-opening doors.

Third class accommodation was in a single saloon 28ft 9in long, seating 48 passengers. This had droplights and large, fixed lights alternately. The saloon windows all had toplights above them, double toplights in the case of the large, fixed windows.

The motor compartment was 14ft 6⅝in long, with a side door that opened outwards, a single droplight, and a pair of sliding windows with a water filler in the panel immediately behind them. Just like the Great Western's filler caps, the Cardiff Railway's were oval in shape and hinged at the bottom.

Both ends of the car were bowed, and had three windows. Like the later GWR cars, the windows at the power unit end were shorter than at the trailing end, with a correspondingly deeper waist panel. The top of the coal bunker presumably resided behind the wide waist panels. Side windows to the motor compartment all had ventilators above them, as did the panel containing the water filler lid.

The power unit had a vertical multitubular boiler, as on the Great Western cars, which worked at 160 lbs sq in. The shape, however, was slightly different to the GWR's, whose boilers had a cylindrical lower part which then tapered rapidly outwards to a maximum diameter, after which it tapered inwards to the top. Boilers for the Cardiff Railway, however, had a step outwards, so that the boiler was effectively of two diameters, and not tapered, whilst the top was domed. The engine had 12in diameter cylinders of 16in stroke; the tractive effort was therefore 6,912 lbs at 90% efficiency. Cylinders were ahead of the leading wheels, which were coupled, giving an 0–4–0 arrangement. Walschaert's valve gear was employed. This motor was fastened to the car's underframe with scroll irons, but photographs of the power unit show it to have had rubbing plates (presumably fore and aft of the boiler) to take up the tractive force. According to a Gloucester C & W photograph, a Cardiff Railway power unit complete weighed 14 tons 12 cwt.

Just how similar the Cardiff Railway's motor units were to those of the GWR's can been seen from the following table:

	Cardiff Rly	*GWR (Dia. R)*
Boiler: height	9ft 6in	9ft 6in
Diameter, max.	6ft 0in	6ft 0⅛in
Diameter, min.	4ft 6in	4ft 6in
Tubes, number	420	419
Tubes, dia.	1¼in	1¼in
Grate area	11½ sq ft	11·54 sq ft
Heating surface	660 sq ft	657·78 sq ft
Working pressure	160 lbs sq in	160 lbs sq in
Cylinders	12in × 16in	12in × 16in
Wheel diameter	4ft 0in	4ft 0in
Coal bunker capacity	30 cwt	30 cwt
Water tank capacity	Not known	450 gallons

The underframe of the car had four queen-post trusses with adjustable queenposts, the truss rod itself being of flat strip, twisted to the vertical outboard of the vacuum cylinders. There were 'H' section cross members below the solebars, to which the queenposts were attached. The water tank was suspended centrally from the underframe, GWR style, and measured 2ft 1in wide, 2ft 8in deep and 17ft 6in long, holding 490 gallons. According to the underframe drawing, there were two vacuum cylinders to one side of the water tank and two gas cylinders on the other side, but photographs indicate one gas cylinder, and that on the same side as the vacuum cylinders. I am not aware of a clear photograph of the other side of the car.

Cardiff Railway livery for the SRMs was lake for the lower side and end panels, and cream for the waist panels upwards. The mouldings seem to have been lake, lined out. The Cardiff Railway insignia was placed twice on each side in the bottom panels: once below the sliding windows of the power compartment, and once below the droplights in the First class saloon. Central in the bottom panel of the Third class saloon, next to the passenger vestibule door, was 'C. R.' with 'Nº 2' beneath. In the waist panel, painted in gold and possibly shaded in red, was 'FIRST CLASS' and 'THIRD CLASS' below their respective saloon windows. Gloucester C & W maker's plates were placed on the underframe below the 'THIRD CLASS' lettering and on the side frames of the trailing bogies.

DISPOSAL

As discussed, the cars and trailers were used on the services from Cardiff (Rhymney Railway) to Rhydyfelin Halt, which was introduced on 1st March 1911.

The two Cardiff Railway SRMs worked until 1920, when they were converted into trailers with the same running numbers. In the process, the motor unit ends were rebuilt with square panelling and gangway connectors, and conventional Gloucester bogies were fitted in place of the engine bogie.

There are a couple of points about the GWR trailer diagrams relating to them – A20 and A21 – that are worth making. Firstly, these drawings show the original, deep waist panel at the ex-motor unit end, although this feature does not seem to have been present – at least by the mid 1930s. Then there is the rather odd feature of the A21 diagram, which purports to illustrate CR trailer No. 3, and which, if accurate, indicates that it ran as a trailer with seats occupying what had been the motor compartment, but with the motor compartment sides still intact, except for the ventilators and water filler caps, which are absent. It is not known if this was the case.

Cardiff Railway No. 3 – a remarkably close copy of a GWR SRM. COLLECTION R. C. RILEY

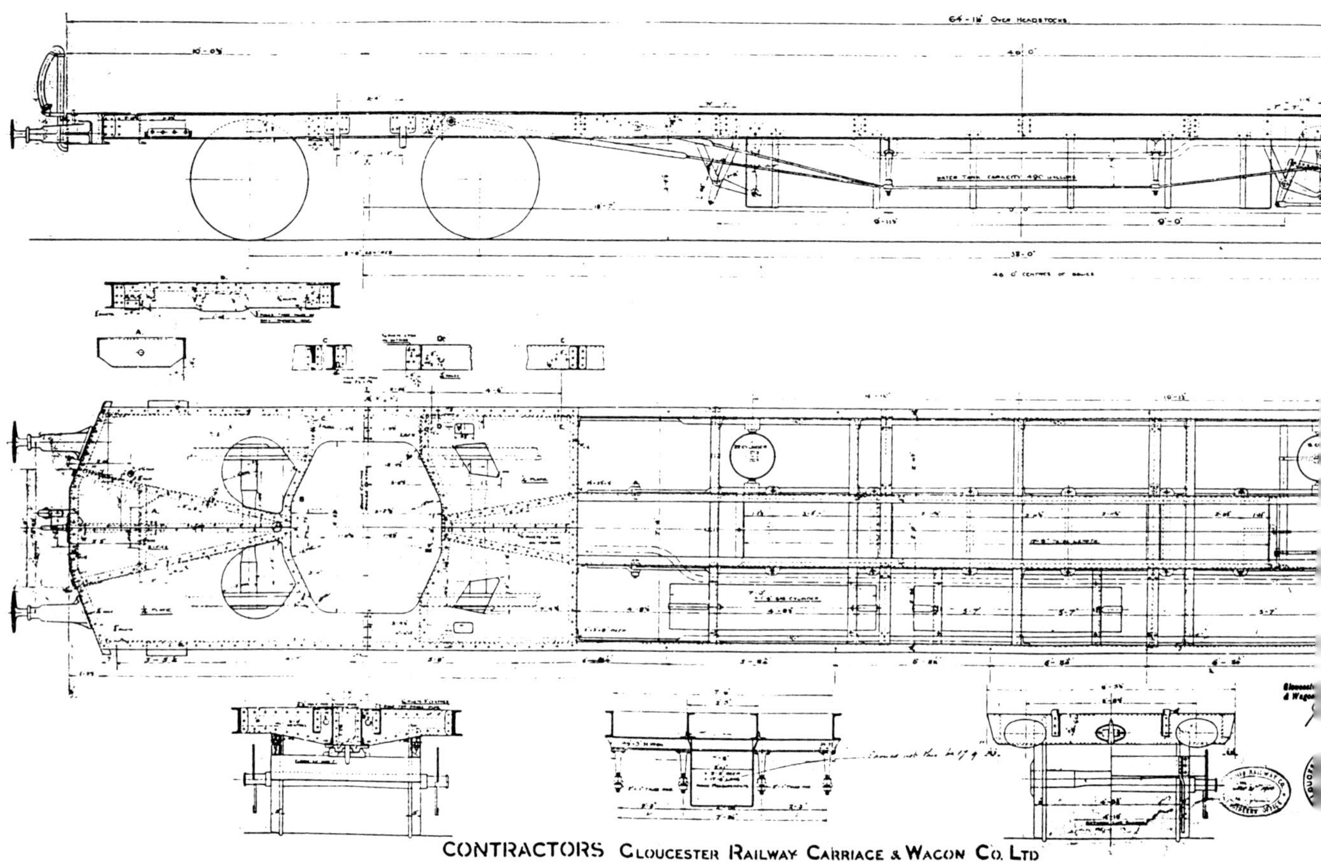

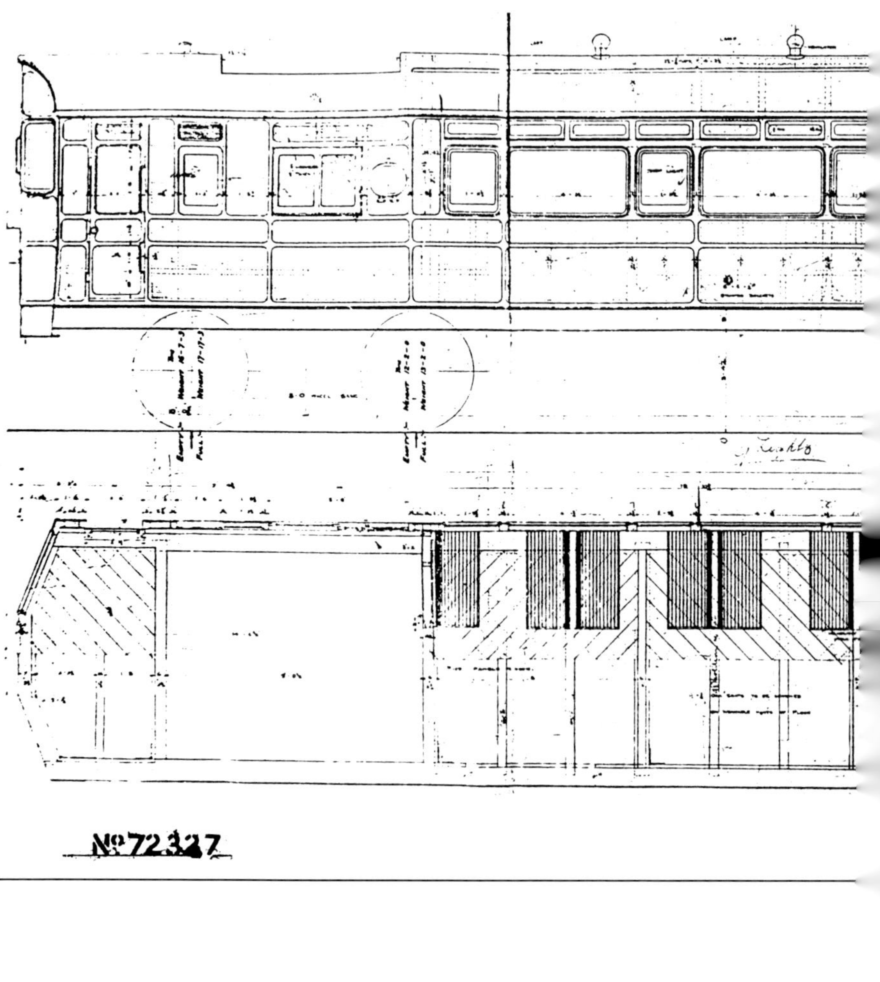

Cardiff Railway SRM body.

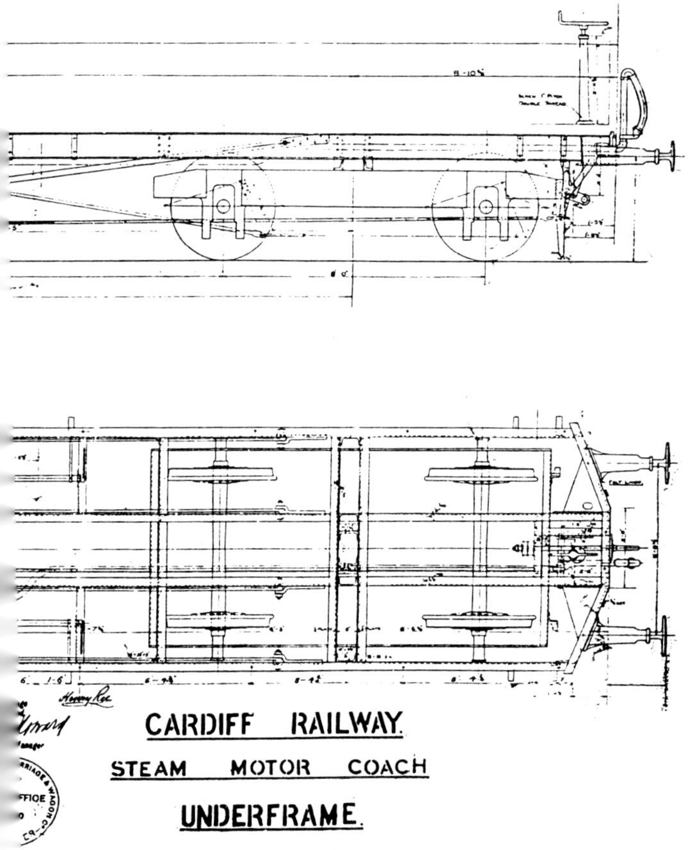

Cardiff Railway SRM underframe.

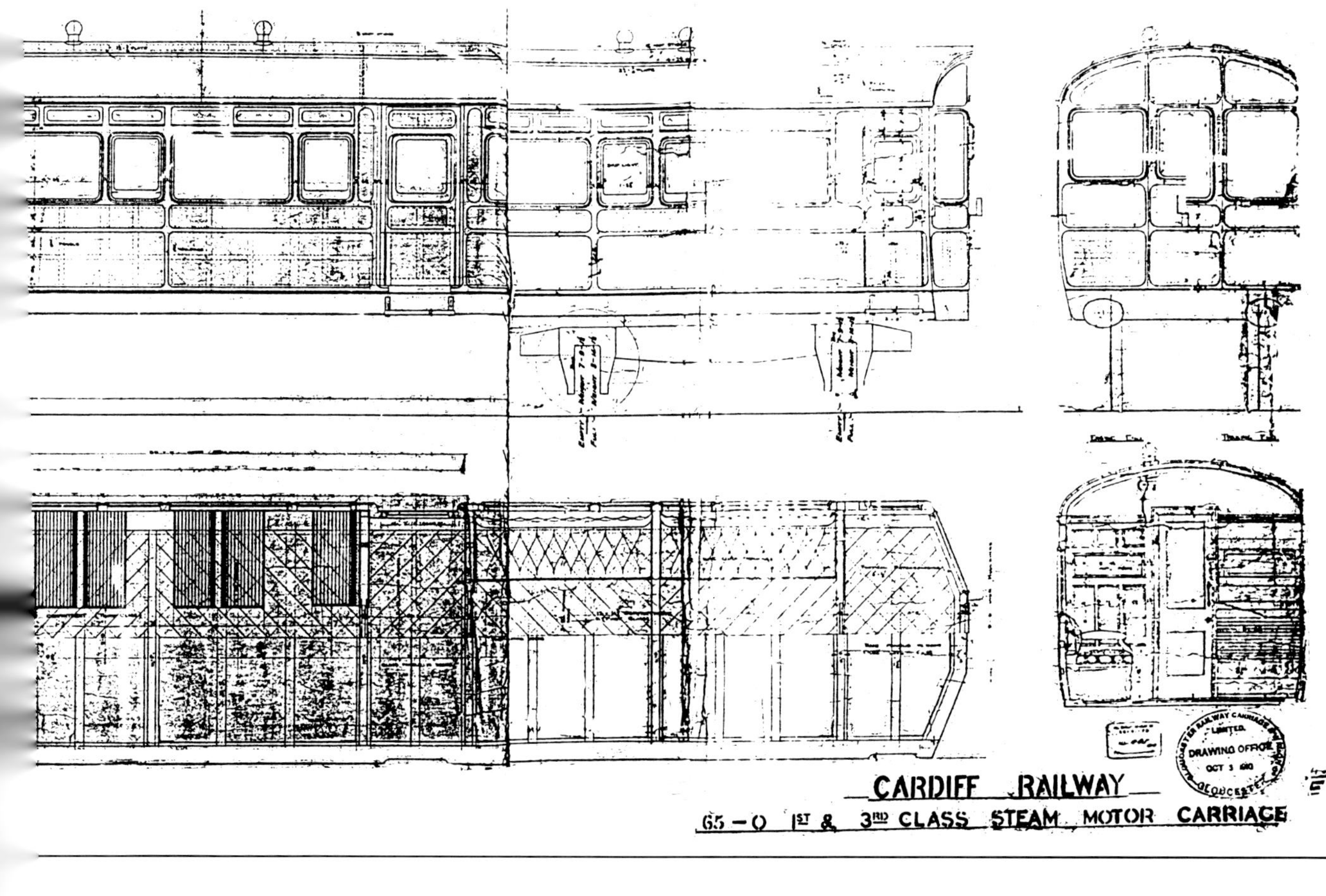

S

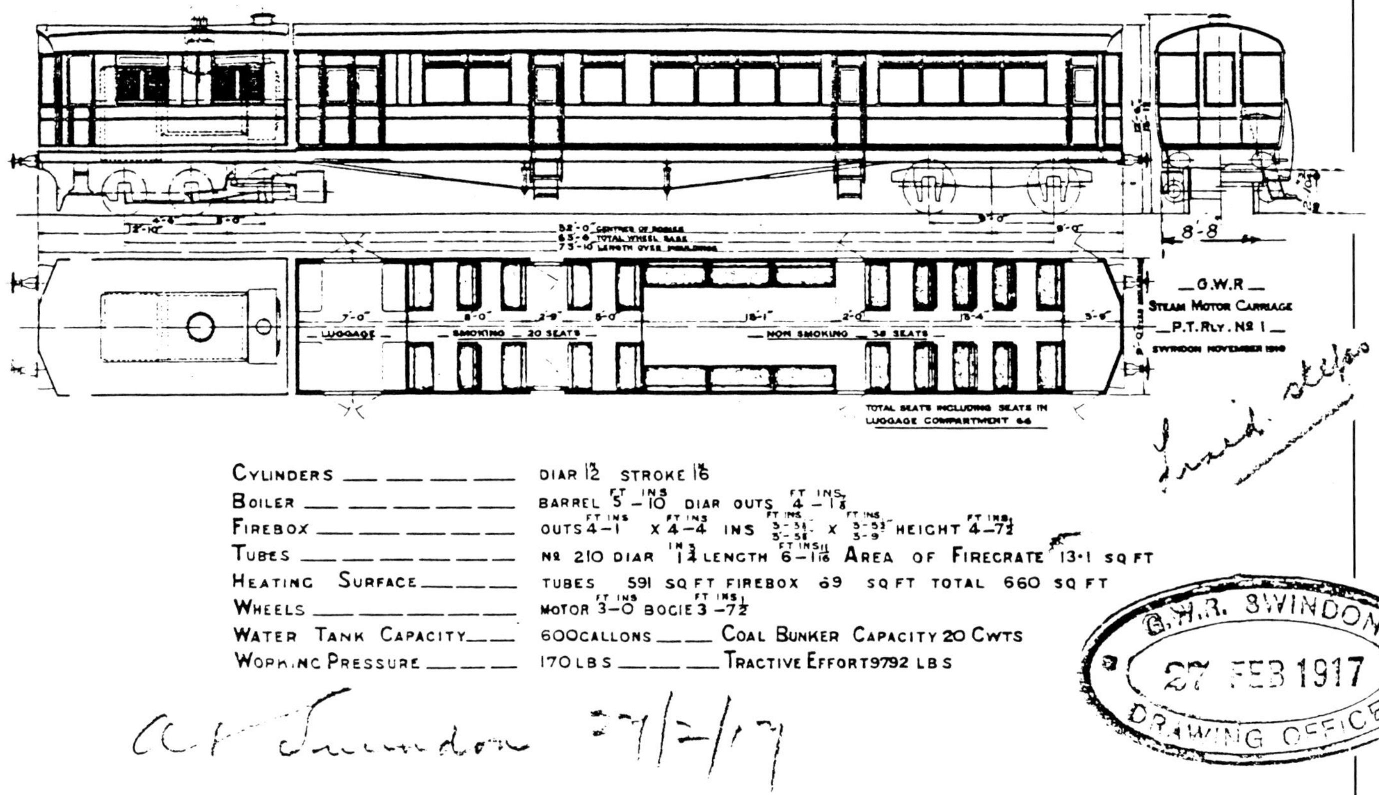

R. & W. HAWTHORN, LESLIE & CO., LTD.,

STEAM RAIL MOTOR COACH.

Gauge of Railway .. .. 4-ft. 8½-ins.

PRINCIPAL DIMENSIONS.

CYLINDERS—Diameter	12-ins.	HEATING SURFACE—Tubes	590.0 sq. ft.
Stroke	16-ins.	Fire Box	67.2 sq. ft.
WHEELS (Diameter of Coupled)	3-ft. 0-ins.	Total	657.2 sq. ft.
WHEEL-BASE—Fixed	9-ft. 6-ins.	GRATE AREA	12.9 sq. ft.
„ Total	9-ft. 6-ins.	WORKING PRESSURE	170-lbs. per sq. inch
WATER CAPACITY	550 galls. (Imperial)	WEIGHT on Coupled Wheels	27 tons
FUEL „	68 cu. ft. = 1½ tons	TOTAL WEIGHT in Working Order, Engine and Coach	57.5 tons
TOTAL WHEEL-BASE of Coach	63-ft. 6-ins.		

TRACTIVE FORCE taking 90% of the Working Pressure .. .. 9792-lbs.
„ „ „ 75% „ „ „ .. .. 8160-lbs.

HAULING CAPACITY—Load 111 tons—Speed on level, 40 m.p.h. ; up 1 in 200, 32 m.p.h. ; up 1 in 100, 22 m.p.h. ; up 1 in 50, 12 m.p.h.

SEATING ACCOMMODATION for 70 Passengers.

Code Word - - TALBOT.

FORTH BANKS LOCOMOTIVE WORKS, NEWCASTLE-ON-TYNE.

Port Talbot Railway: Hawthorn Leslie/Hurst Nelson SRM No.1

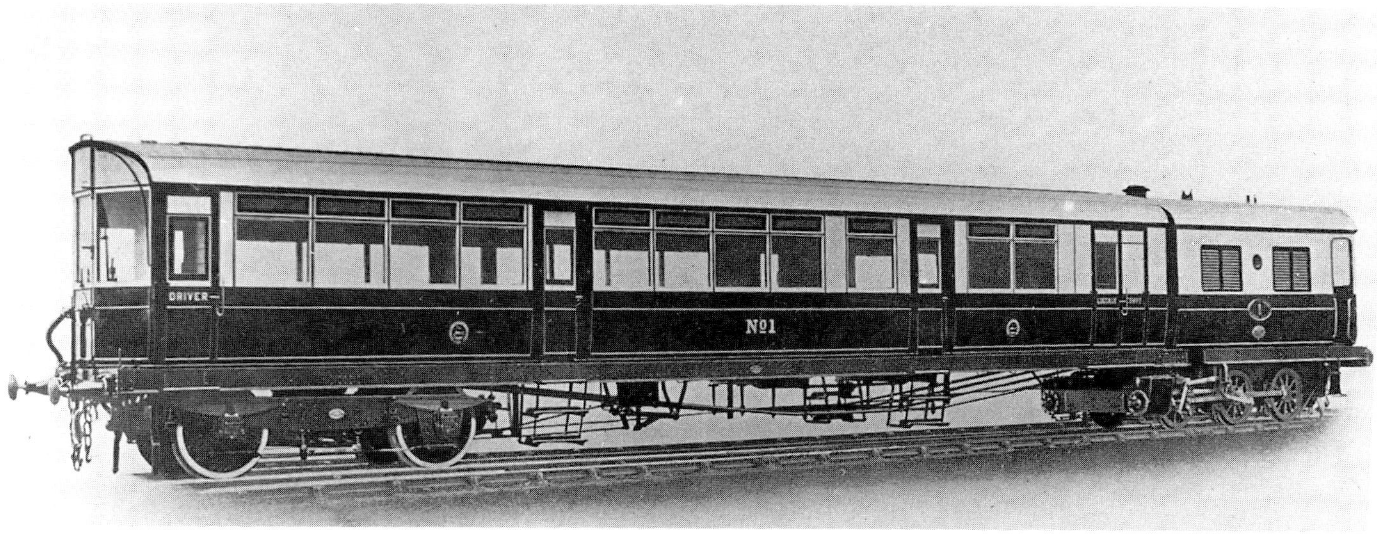

Manufacturer's photograph.

With effect from 30th March 1908, the Great Western entered into an agreement with the Port Talbot Railway & Docks Co. to take control of the latter company's railway interests, although the docks remained under PTR & D control until that company was absorbed by the GWR on 9th May 1922. From March 1908, the PTR rolling stock was thus effectively treated as the GWR's , although it was separately identified in that company's documents, and retained its PTR numbers until the grouping. The Port Talbot Railway had one steam rail motor, which the GWR recorded in its *Register of Monthly Shed Allocations of Locomotive Stock*, along with its own SRMs. The Great Western also issued its own diagram for the PTR car, which was included in the GWR SRM binder as 'diagram S', although the car remained as No.1, the solitary example in the PTR SRM series.

DESIGN

PTR No.1 had a motor unit that was unique in the United Kingdom, as it was an 0–6–0 with trailing cylinders, enclosed in coachwork, but was articulated to the remainder of the car. It was built by R. & W. Hawthorn Leslie & Co. of Newcastle-upon-Tyne, whilst the attached car was built by Hurst Nelson & Co. of Motherwell. The railmotor was constructed in 1906 and taken into PTR stock the following year.

The motor unit had a bow end with three windows, and a flat inner end. The body was seemingly constructed of sheet metal, at least above the waist, although there was a waist panel on the sides and outer end; it is possible that this was for decorative purposes only, to match the passenger portion of the car. A very prominent oval number plate was carried centrally on both sides, at the level of the lower waist moulding. Each side of the unit had a crew door, the top of which only came up to waist height – rather like a locomotive – and also two large, double-louvred ventilators, which could be slid open.

A conventional, small locomotive-type boiler was arranged with the firebox leading, and the chimney protruding through the roof towards the end of the motor unit. Its barrel was 5ft 10in long and 4ft 1⅞in outside diameter, with 210 tubes 6ft 1¹¹⁄₁₆in long and 1¾in diameter. The boiler carried a dome on which was mounted the safety valves, which also protruded through the unit's roof. The area of the fire grate is given as 13·1 sq ft on the diagram, although a specification in a Hawthorn, Leslie catalogue gives it as 12·9 sq ft. The total heating area was 660 sq ft (catalogue 657·2 sq ft) and the maximum working pressure was 170 lbs sq in. Cylinders were 12in diameter and 16in stroke. The driving wheels were 3ft 0in diameter, at 4ft 6in + 5ft 0in wheelbase. The tractive effort is shown as 9,792 lbs.

Next to the motor, the passenger portion had a 7ft luggage compartment fitted with passenger seats, and external double doors that opened outwards; only one leaf of these doors had a droplight, although the diagram shows droplights in both. The diagram also shows three narrow, window-height panels between the luggage doors and the passenger saloon windows, but as built there were only two, rather wider, panels. The panelling, incidentally, was square cornered.

The smoking saloon seated 20, comprising an 8ft length with 1½ seating bays (the middle pair of seats may have been of the walkover type), a 2ft 9in cross vestibule with inward-opening doors each side, and a further 5ft 0in length with another seating bay. The external doors had what appear to be retractable steps below them, although someone has written 'Fixed steps' on a copy of the diagram.

Beyond, the non-smoking saloon seated 38, with a 13ft 1in length of longitudinal seating, a 2ft-wide cross passage between the seat ends, and a 13ft 4in length with 5 pairs of seats arranged each side of the central corridor; the middle three pairs again may well have been walkover seats. The central, open vestibule is shown with an outward-opening door on each side, again with retractable steps below. However, photographs show that the car had flat, slightly recessed doors here that opened inwards. According to the diagram, the smoking compartment doors were slightly recessed and flat, while the non-smoking compartment ones were the same profile as the body sides. I suspect the diagram may show some of the features of the car 'as proposed', instead of 'as built'.

Seating was provided for a total of 66 passengers, including the seats in the luggage compartment, although Hawthorn, Leslie's catalogue gave the figure of 70. It was electrically lit by means of a steam turbine-driven dynamo.

The driver's compartment had a maximum length of 3ft 9in between the partition and the end of the car, and had side doors which opened outwards, hinged on the corner pillars. The trailing end was also bow ended, with the usual three large windows.

PTR No.1's car unit was 9ft 0in wide over mouldings, 12ft 6in from rail to roof, and 13ft 1½in from rail to chimney top. The total length of the SRM was 73ft 10in over mouldings; there are no separate lengths given for the coach portion or the power unit. The diagram shows the SRM to have one rain strip high up on the roof, and this is confirmed by a photograph of the car in use.

The passenger portion of the car had four queen post trusses, with adjustable queen posts suspended from cross 'H' beams, and flat truss rods which had a twist towards each end. As shown in the maker's photograph, and as running on the PTR, the car had safety chains in addition to screw couplings, as well as steam heating pipes.

No weight is shown on the diagram for the car, but Hawthorn, Leslie's catalogue gives the weight on the coupled wheels as 27 tons, and the total weight in working order, engine and coach, as 57·5 tons. According to the catalogue, its haulage capacity was 111 tons, whilst its speed was 40 mph on the level; 32 mph up 1 in 200; 22 mph up 1 in 100; and 12 mph up 1 in 50 gradients.

Apparently, the original colours of the car were dark green and cream, but GWR lined brown was used later. According to the maker's photograph, the motor unit had what was possibly a maker's plate under the PTR number plate, but this is missing from photographs of the car in action, as are PTR insignia shown twice on the car sides. The maker's photograph also shows a 'N°1' in about the middle of the car, and that is missing, too

DISPOSAL

The arrival of the car on the PTR system was indicated in a list of passenger train alterations for 1907, which stated:

'For running the Passenger Service from Port Talbot to Blaengarw and Blaengarw to Port Talbot, a New Rail Motor Car (Saturdays and special occasions excepted) has been provided. The New Motor Car is fitted with Electric Light and has separate compartments for smokers and non-smokers.'

According to the GWR allocation registers, the car was normally stationed at Duffryn Yard. It was repaired a number of times at Swindon, the final time being on 7th August 1916.

PTR No.1 was sent to the Swindon Stock Shed on 30th October 1916 and remained there until it was sold to Mr R. O. Graham for the Port of London Authority, probably in July 1920, together with GWR SRMs Nos.42 and 49. Like them, it seems to have survived in use on the PTA's Millwall Extension Railway until 1926. It is reported as being broken up in 1928.

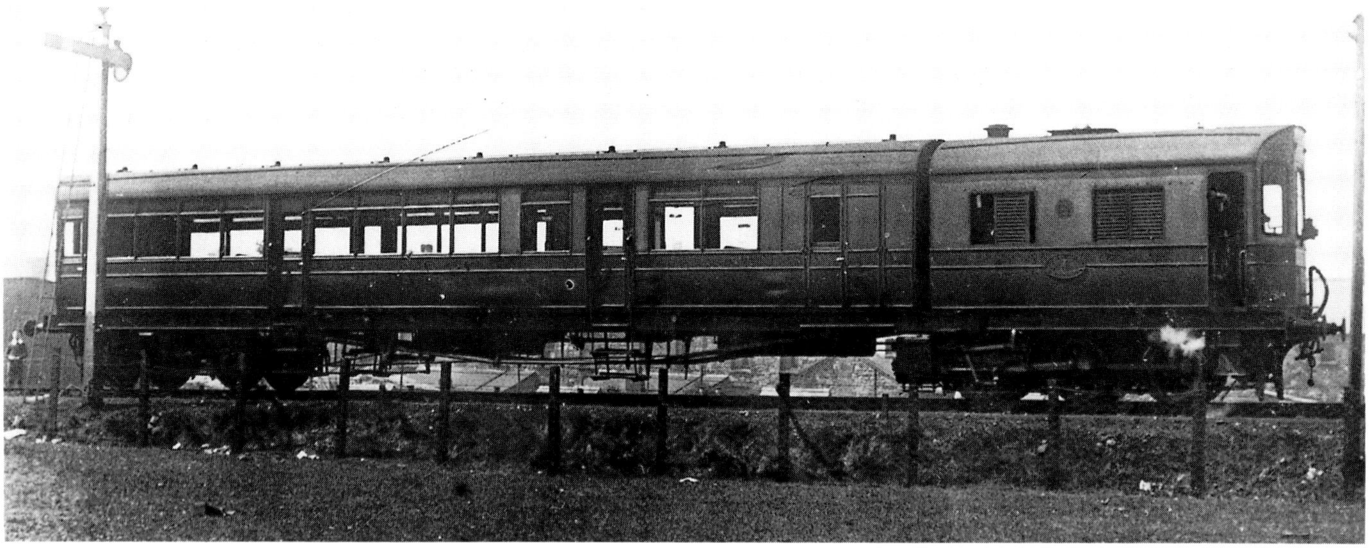

Port Talbot SRM No. 1.
HOPWOOD
CTY. R. C. RILEY

Port Talbot SRM No. 1 at Port Talbot.
HOPWOOD
CTY. R. C. RILEY

Rhymney Railway: Hudswell Clarke/Cravens SRMs Nos.1 & 2

Rhymney Railway SRM No. 1 as built with an 0–4–0 engine. HUDSWELL, CLARKE & CO., CTY HMRS

Close-up of Rhymney Railway SRM No. 1 engine unit. Note that in this view the numberplate on the side had been removed and 'R No. 1 R' in shaded letters had been substituted. Presumably it was in its 0–4–2 state. COLLECTION R. C. RILEY

The Rhymney Railway had two SRMs, designed by its Locomotive Superintendent, Mr Carlton Hurry Riches, and numbered 1 and 2 in their own series. The Rhymney cars were notable in the GWR group by having power units that looked like conventional, small 0–4–0 side tank locomotives, articulated to the coach portions of the car.

DESIGN

The locomotives of these units were built by Hudswell Clarke & Co. of Leeds, and the coach portions by Cravens Ltd. of Sheffield, in September 1907. Other noteworthy features of these SRMs included the provision of electric lighting; the Westinghouse air brake (it was standard on Rhymney Railway coaching stock); and the means of operating the locomotive controls from the trailing end driver's vestibules, which was said to be by cables along the top of the car roof, although this does not show in photographs.

Unlike many SRMs, not only did the power unit look like a locomotive, it was attached to the coach portion the 'right way' round with the chimney and cylinders at the front end, and its cab and controls next to the coach portion. The boiler was 5ft 11½in long, and had a diameter of 4ft 7⅛in, containing 210 tubes of 1¾in diameter; it worked at 175 lb sq in. Cylinders were 12in diameter by 16in stroke, and the driving wheels were 3ft 6in diameter at 8ft wheelbase, giving a T.E. of 8,640 lbs at 90% efficiency. Walschaert's valve gear was employed. Twin cylindrical tanks under the coach portion carried 700 gallons of water, and storage for 20 cwt of coal was probably located behind what looked like short side tanks. The Westinghouse pump was on the right-hand side of the smokebox, as the driver looked forward.

The saloon seated 64 passengers, and featured a quite wide door at each end with retractable steps below; these had three treads which appear to have folded upwards when the steps were retracted. The car had a rather narrow window inboard of the doors (the one at the locomotive end appearing to be narrower than the one at the trailing end), and between these were seven practically square fixed windows, each with a short, louvred ventilator above.

Access to the driver's compartment at the trailing end was via the adjacent passenger door, though the vestibule was provided with a narrow side window on each side.

The coach body had no waist panel, only a single, horizontal moulding at this height, and the bottom panel was subdivided into short panels by vertical mouldings.

On the roof, there seems to have been two rows of 9 prominent roof ventilators. The roof also carried what were presumably the light fittings, and had short rainstrips above each door, although these may well have been later additions.

The underframe had queenpost trusses, and round-section truss rods with a central turnbuckle for adjustment. As well as the water tanks, battery boxes were hung from the underframe, and it is possible that a coach dynamo was driven from the trailing bogie. This bogie had 3ft 7in wheels at an 8ft wheelbase, giving a total wheelbase of 55ft 10in. The whole car was

71ft 9½in long over buffers, and weighed 55 tons 2 cwt.

Cars were painted in lake, picked out in yellow, and were amongst the first new stock to carry this livery. Its roof appears to have been a medium grey.

The standard colour for locomotives on the Rhymney was a dark Brunswick green, while chimney, running plates and cab roofs were black; this was also the case with the locomotive portion of these SRMs. The locomotive also had bright (brass?) domes and safety valve mountings, at least before the Great War, whilst the smokebox hinges and locking handles were also bright, as was the beading round the spectacle glasses. They were introduced with large oval number plates on the side sheets, with 'RHYMNEY' around the top and 'RAILWAY' around the bottom, and the car number in the middle. A maker's plate was fitted to the smokebox sides, just above the running plate. A maker's photograph, featuring No.1's locomotive portion in works grey, showed the carriage part with the Rhymney Railway armorial device under each narrow window next to the doors, and two intertwined 'RR' monograms equidistant between those devices. One picture of No.1 in use shows it to have had a destination board on the side, immediately below the centre window.

WORK & DISPOSAL

The SRMs were used for services between Senghenydd, Caerphilly and Machen; between Rhymney and Ystrad Mynach; and between Ystrad Mynach and Merthyr. They were designed to work with a 6-wheel trailer on reverse gradients of 1 in 35, or, according to the late Eric Mountford, to haul up to three ordinary 6-wheel carriages.

It was found that these cars were very rough riding 'as the front end of the carriage portion

Rhymney Railway SRM No. 2 as built.
COLLECTION R. C. RILEY

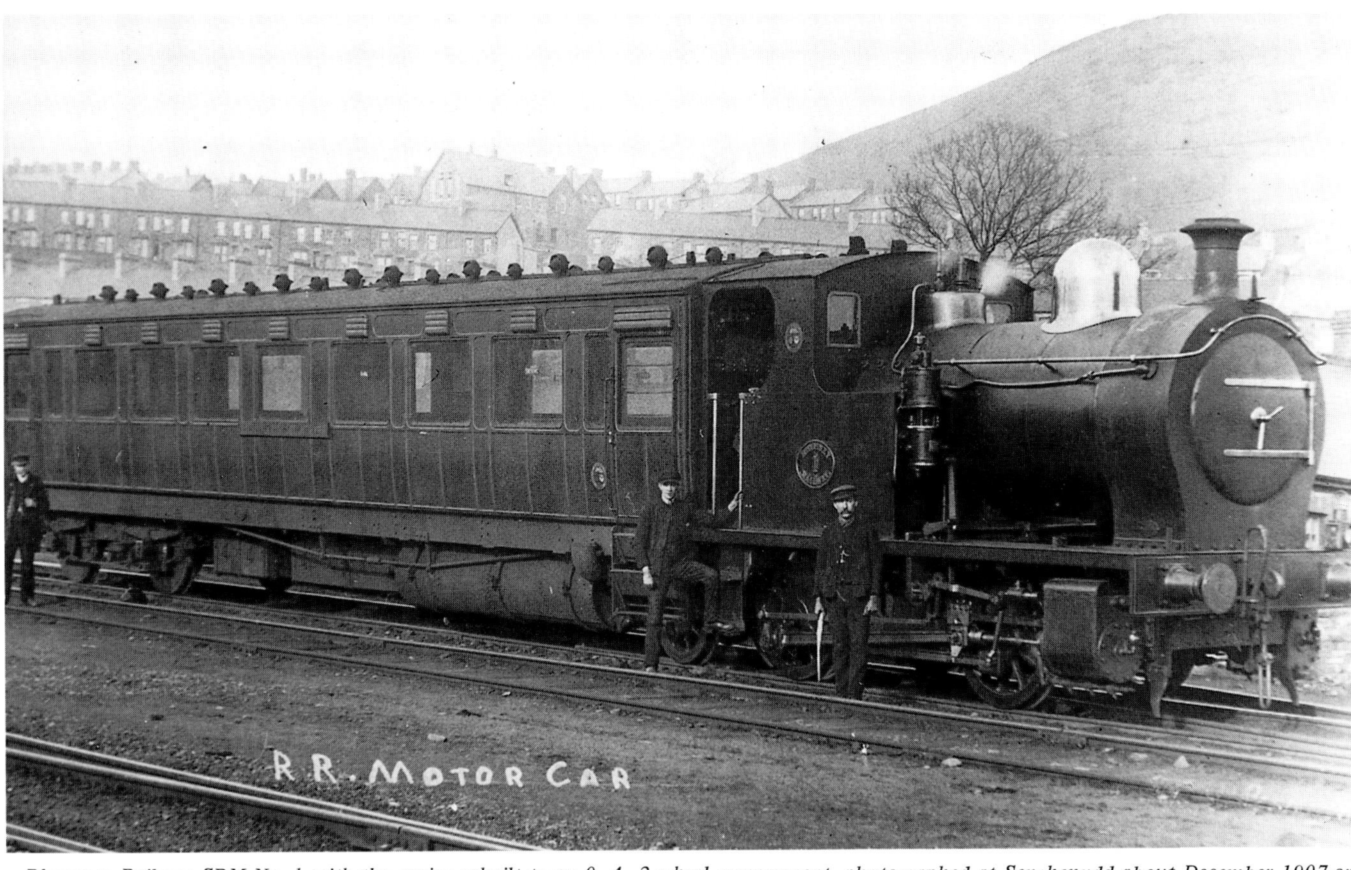

Rhymney Railway SRM No. 1 with the engine rebuilt to an 0–4–2 wheel arrangement, photographed at Senghenydd about December 1907 or January 1908.
COLLECTION R. C. RILEY

Rhymney Railway SRM 1 running as an 0–4–2 in service at Bargoed, hauling a short trailer. COLLECTION R. C. RILEY

was not sufficiently supported by the engine frame' (Eric. Mountford, *Caerphilly Works*). The solution adopted was to extend the locomotive underframe back under the carriage, and to add a wheelset, so the power unit became an 0–4–2; this was done at the Caerphilly Works of the RR in late 1907 or early 1908, and cured the problem. It would appear from photographs that the Westinghouse pump was moved from the smokebox to the front of the side sheet, probably at this time.

In 1910, it was decided that one steam rail motor was sufficient, and this worked the Senghenydd branch; the Rhymney, Ystrad and Merthyr routes were now deemed to be adequately served by main line trains. So, SRM No.2 was taken into Caerphilly Works in 1910 and divided into a coach portion – bogie Brake Third No.114 – and an 0–6–0T, No.120. This involved new rear extension frames for the locomotive, which was fitted with a relatively large combined coal and water bunker, while the side sheets were removed; all this did nothing for its appearance.

Meanwhile, No.1 continued in traffic. A photograph shows the locomotive portion to have lost its number plate, which was replaced by 'R Nº1 R' in block lettering – probably gold, shaded red.

In 1919, No.1 was withdrawn and rebuilt at Caerphilly into Brake Third No.119 and 0–6–0T No.121. Like No.120, the locomotive had the water tank below the coal space in the bunker. Brake Thirds Nos.114 and 119 became GWR coaches 1234 and 1236 respectively, though in 1927 they became trailers, and were given through regulator gear.

After Rhymney Railway SRM 1 had been split up, its engine was further rebuilt to an 0–6–0 back tank engine and renumbered 121 by the RR. LPC POSTCARD

After the grouping the engine portion of RR SRM 1 was renumbered 662 by the GWR. It is seen here at Cardiff. A. W. CROUGHTON, CTY. R. C. RILEY

STATIONS & HALTS.

WE

STATIONS & HALTS.		a.m.	a.m.	a.m.	a.m.	a.m.	a.m.	a.m.	p.m.	p.m.	p.m.
Dudley - -	dep.	6 15	8 32	9 0	9 43	-	11 1	11 42	12 45	1 20	2 15
Dudley (S.S.) & Nethert'n	,,	6 18	8 36	9 3	9 49	10 25	11 4	11 45	12 48	1 23	2 18
Baptist End Halt	,,	6 20	-	9 5	9 51	10 27	11 6	11 47	12 50	1 25	2 20
Windmill End - -	,,	6 23	8 40	9 8	9 54	10 30	11 9	11 50	12 53	1 28	2 23
Darby End Halt -	,,	6 25	-	9 10	9 56	10 32	11 11	11 52	12 55	1 30	2 25
Old Hill (High St.) Halt	,,	6 27	-	9 12	9 58	10 34	11 13	11 54	12 57	1 32	2 27
Old Hill - -	arr.	6 29	8 43	9 14	10 0	10 36	11 15	11 56	12 59	1 34	2 2
Old Hill -	d				10 6	-	11 30	11 58	1 5	1 40	2 4
									1 8	1 43	2 4

Old Hill -
Coombes Hollo'y Halt
Halesowen -

Old Hill -
Birmingham (S. Hill)

Birmingham (S. Hill)
Old Hill - -

Halesowen
Coombes Hollo'y Hal
Old Hill -

Old Hill -
Old Hill (High St.) Ha
Darby End Halt -
Windmill End -
Baptist End Halt
Dudley (S.S.) & Nethe
Dudley -

FROM

Halesowen
Coombes Hollo
Old Hill ...
Old Hill (High
Darby End Hal
Windmill End
Baptist End H
Dudley (S.S.) a
Dudley ...

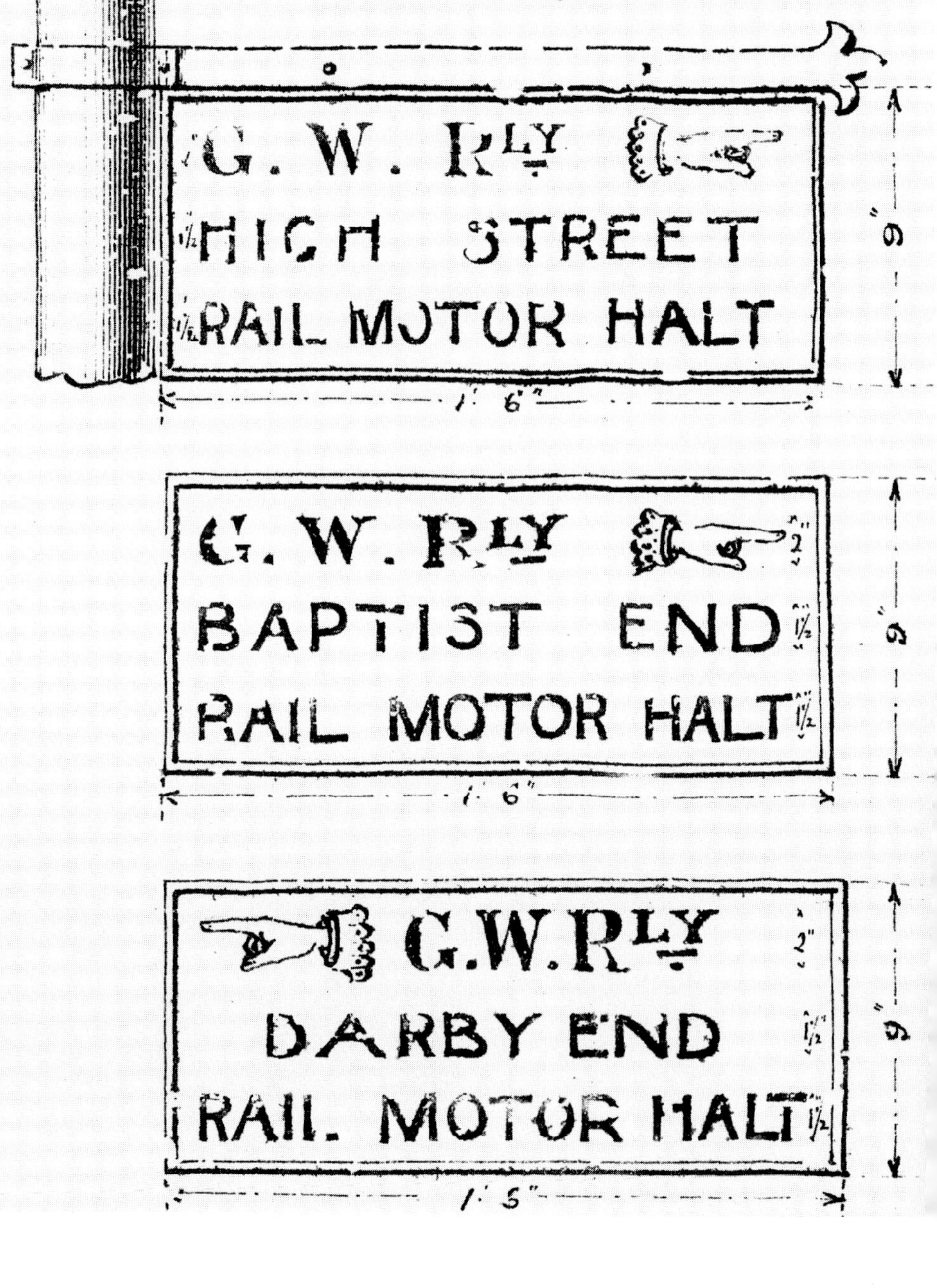

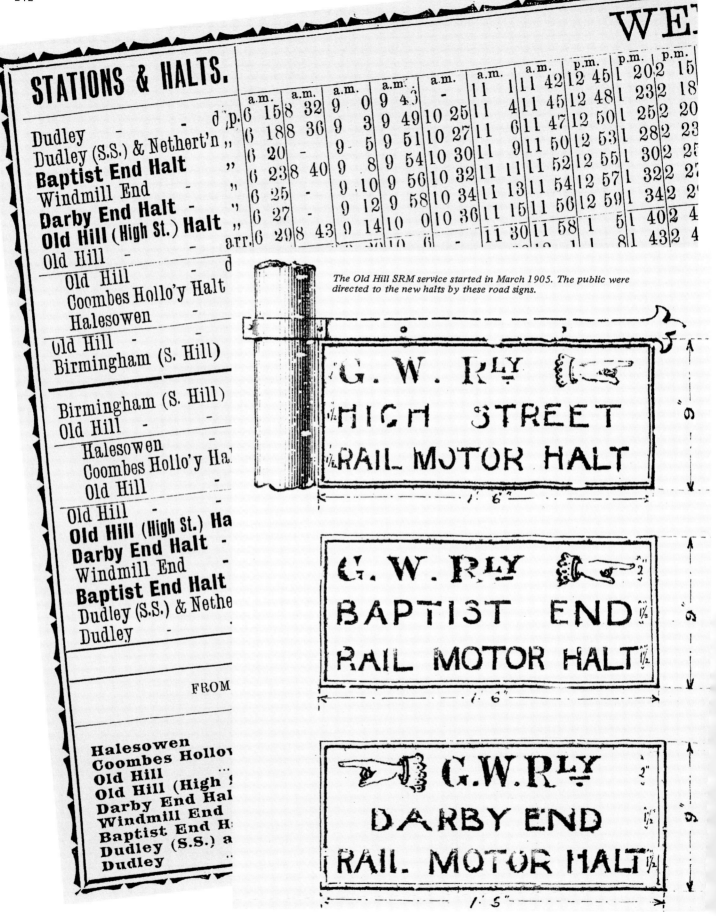

The Old Hill SRM service started in March 1905. The public were directed to the new halts by these road signs.

APPENDIX A

CONTRACTUAL CORRESPONDENCE & SPECIFICATION, KERR, STUART & CO. AND THE GREAT WESTERN RAILWAY

This is the contract between the GWR and Kerr, Stuart & Co for the building of the 12 steam rail motors of Lot 1100. It includes the specification for the various components, and how some of them were to be fitted. The title page was originally in a copperplate hand with 'Contract' in a gothic-type style. The second page was typewritten with some hand writing for the costs, signature etc.

Dated June 22nd 1905
Rail Motor Cars

Kerr Stuart & Co. Ltd.
—— and ——
The Great Western
Railway Company

Contract

Form of Tender.
Great Western Railway Company.
Specification of Rail Motor cars with Engines and Boilers complete.

Drawing Nos.
27052, 25648, 27539, 25715, 27342 for 70' 0" Cars
27396, 25648, 27540, 26747, 27541, for 59' 6" Cars.

To the
Chairman and Directors of the Great Western Railway Company,
PADDINGTON.

Gentlemen,

Having examined the Specification and Drawings along with the Great Western Railway standard specifications mentioned on page 2 of this specification, we hereby offer to supply and carry out the whole of the work for twelve 70' 0" Motor Cars according to the said specification, drawings and Great Western Railway standard specifications for the sum of £2,688 each for 70' 0" Cars.

We hereby undertake to deliver the first motor car with engine and boiler complete, in running order, within ..20.. weeks from the date of the acceptance of our Tender, and further to deliver the whole of the cars complete and in running order within ..32.. weeks from the date of the acceptance of our Tender, under a liability for damage of £.30.. per car per week for each and every week the work remains incomplete after the expiration of such times, except in so far as such delays may be caused by fire or by strikes of workmen.

In case this tender is accepted, we undertake to execute a Contract Deed, and to provide two good and satisfactory sureties, who with us jointly and severally will enter into a bond to the amount of £5,000, conditional on the due fulfilment of the Contract.

We remain, Gentlemen,
Your obedient servants,
Name ..**KERR STUART & CO, LTD**...
Geo Glass Hooper
M. Director
Address ..Broad Street Place..
..London E.C..

Date ..May 22nd..1905.

Great Western Railway
Secretary's Office
Paddington Station
London, W.
13th June 1905
Gentlemen,

With reference to the interview which your Representative had with Mr Dean's on the 9th instant when he agreed to amend your tender price for the supply of twelve 70 feet Rail Motor Cars to £2,500 each, I beg to inform you that the Directors have agreed to place the Contract with you for the supply of the cars at that price, the Contract in all other respects to be in accordance with your tender of the 22nd ultimo.

I will instruct the Company's Solicitor to prepare the Contract Deed accordingly and in the meantime will ask you to be good enough to furnish me with the names of the two sureties to join in the Bond for £5,000 together with Bankers references as to their responsibility.

As regards your letter to Mr Inglis of the 9th instant and his reply of the 10th, the question of the sub-contractor for the Carriage Bodies to which you refer must, of course, be subject to the approval of the Locomotive & Carriage Superintendent in accordance with Clause 7 of the Specification and you will no doubt place yourselves in communication with him on the subject at once.

The period of delivery will date from to day in accordance with the tender.

Yours faithfully,
(signed) A. E. Bolter
Assist. Sec^y.

Messrs. Kerr, Stuart & Co. Lt^d.,
Broad Street Place
London. E.C.

Great Western Railway
Secretary's Office
Paddington Station
London, W.
21st June 1905
Gentlemen,

I am in receipt of your letter of the 19th instant the contents of which I note.

The question of the period for completion of the Cars starting from the 22nd instant is perhaps not very material and under the circumstances we will agree to the former date.

Yours faithfully,
(signed) A. E. Bolter

Messrs. Kerr, Stuart & Co. Ld,
1 & 2 Broad Street Place
E.C.

GREAT WESTERN RAILWAY
Specification of Rail Motor cars with Engines and Boilers complete.
Drawing Nos.
27052, 25648, 27539, 25715, 27342 for 70' 0" Cars
27396, 25648, 27540, 26747, 27541, for 59' 6" Cars.

General Conditions
The Motor cars must be made in strict accordance with the terms and specification and to the general and detailed description and dimensions given

on the drawings to be supplied by the Railway Company's Locomotive & Carriage Superintendent, except in cases where his consent to an alteration has been obtained in writing.

Erection and Delivery

The whole of the motor cars are to be erected, finished and painted at the contractor's Works. They are to be consigned via the Great Western Railway Company's route and delivered free of charge to the Company at their Works at Swindon.

Time for delivery and completion

When preparing their tenders, contractors are to remember that time of delivery and completion will be [??..s] of the essence of the contract, and as being in every way of the utmost importance, and the Company in making their decision as to the tender to be accepted will specially consider the guarantees the Contractors are able to give as the time of delivery and completion of the work. Contractors must state in their tender the earliest date at which they can guarantee to finish and deliver the first car. They are further to state the total time within which they can finish and deliver the whole of the cars from the date of the acceptance of their tender.

Drawings and Great Western Railway Standard Specifications

The following drawings accompany this specification:-

Nos. 27052, 25648, 27539, 25715, 27342, – 70' 0" Cars

Nos. 27396, 25648, 27540, 26747, 27541, – 59' 6" Cars.

The whole of the work is to be made to the Great Western Co.'s standard specifications below, copies of which are annexed hereto:

Boiler and Firebox Shell plates		Specification	No. 8
Mild steel rivet bars	... ...	"	No. 7
Mild steel sections	... ...	"	No. 7a
Copper pipes	... ...	"	No. 24
Steel tubes	... ...	"	No. 17
Mild steel frame plates	... ...	"	No. 6
Mild steel plates	... ...	"	No. 6a
Steel castings	... ...	"	No. 5
Cast steel	wheel bosses	Class A	
"	wheel centres	Class E	
"	motion plates	Class C	
"	crossheads	Class C	
"	link brackets	Class C	
"	brake shaft brackets	Class B	
Wheels axles	... ...	Specification	No.2
Steel tyres	... ...	"	No. 4 Class C
Laminated springs	... ...	"	No. 15a
Spiral springs	... ...	"	No. 16a
Steel crank pins	... ...	"	No. 22 Clause 7
Reversing shafts	... ...	"	No. 22 Clause 9
Motion bars	... ...	"	No. 22 Clause 10
Truss Rods	... ...	"	No. 10
Drawbar hooks and screw couplings		"	No. 20 Clause 6
Buffers	... ...	"	No. 20 clause 4
Iron castings	... ...	"	No. 21

No advantage whatever is to be taken of any omission or discrepancy in the drawings or specification, or both. The Locomotive and Carriage Superintendent will supply [all] necessary information upon application, and explain any points that may not be fully understood.

Inspection and Testing

The motor cars must be finished in every respect to the entire satisfaction of the Locomotive & Carriage Superintendent, who shall at any and at all times during the progress of the work be at liberty to inspect the same, either personally or by deputy, and to reject anything which he, or his deputy may consider deficient or defective, either as regards material or workmanship. He also reserves to himself the right of testing from time to time as specified or by additional tests as he may select any portion of material used under this contract either at the contractor's works, the Company's works, the works of any firm supplying material to be used in construction of the motor cars, or at any [places] for testing purposes which may hereafter be decided [by him], and should any test not be to his entire satisfaction, he has the right to reject any or the whole of such material so tested. The entire cost of tests of material, chemical or mechanical, he may desire to make, [to be] borne by the contractor, including both cost of material and preparation of same for testing.

Quality of material and workmanship

The material is to be of the best make and quality specified in each case, and where not defined or instructions given, both material and workmanship must be of the very best of their respective kinds.

Subcontractor &c.

Before any material is ordered the Locomotive and Carriage Superintendent shall have approved in writing the names of the firms from whom the contractor proposes to purchase, and after selection he must be duly used.

Patent Royalties

The contractor is to hold the Company absolutely free from all claims for patent royalties or other such payments of any kind whatever in respect of the construction or use of any apparatus or methods included in the works for which he tenders.

Disputes &c.

In case of any dispute arising in connection with the construction of these motor cars, either during the progress of contract or at its termination, the decision of the Locomotive and Carriage Superintendent is to be taken as final and binding in every respect.

Form of Tender

The contractor is to give in the Form of Tender a lump sum for which he is prepared to carry out and deliver the whole of the work as shown on the drawings and specification above, complete and in every respect ready for work. The price named in the Tender is to include everything required to be done by the General Conditions, Specification and Drawings, and all such work as is necessary to the proper completion of the contract, notwithstanding that special mention thereof may have been omitted in the specification or drawings. The attached Form of Tender is to be filled in, signed and dated, and sent to the Secretary of the Great Western Railway Company, together with the Specification and drawings, subject to which the whole of the work is to be carried out.

A second copy of the Specification and Drawings can be obtained from the Locomotive and Carriage Superintendent for the convenience of the contractor when preparing his tender. If an extra copy of the Specification has been obtained, it must be immediately returned on the receipt of an intimation that the Tender has not been accepted.

Payment for Work

Payment for the work will only become due on the completion of the Contract, and will be made by a gross sum to be named in the Tender, subject to all payments and deductions which by any of the terms of the Specification are to be made or allowed to the Great Western Railway Company by the contractor.

During the progress of the work advances or payments on account will be made on the application in writing of the contractor subject to the certificate of the Locomotive and Carriage Superintendent. It is intended that such advances and payments shall not exceed 85% of the value, as estimated by the Locomotive and Carriage Superintendent, of the cars delivered.

May, 1905.

Motor Car Engine and Boiler

Boiler and Firebox

The boiler, firebox shell, angles and rivets are to be made of steel to the Great Western Railway Company's standard specifications. The lower part of boiler is to be tapered as shewn, made up of one plate with a treble riveted butt joint. The top of the boiler is to be made up of two cone plates, each brought to the required shape under hydraulic press, with no joint. The smokebox and firebox are to be cylindrical, each made up of one plate with single riveted joint. The smokebox and firebox tube plates are to be flanged and secured to their respective shells with single riveted joints, and the firebox is to be stayed with two rows of Taylor's iron stays. The ring for the firedoor must of the best Yorkshire iron, riveted to boiler and firebox shells, and to be of elliptical shape. Mudhole doors and washout plugs must be arranged as shewn. The brackets on front and back of boiler must have their rubbing faces casehardened, and be perfectly parallel to centre line of boiler. The carrying brackets on sides of boiler must have their under surfaces perfectly square with the centre line of boiler. The firebox foundation ring is to be made of the best Yorkshire iron with holes drilled and tapped to size and depth for ashpan studs. All flanges must be accurately faced so that perfectly steam tight joints may be made. All rivets must completely fill the holes, which must be drilled 1/16" larger than rivets. All holes in plates and angles must have the burrs cleaned off before riveting and be perfectly fair with each other, and no drifting will be allowed on any consideration whatever. Should any of the holes not be perfectly fair with each other, they should be carefully reamered until they become so, but not beyond 1/16" in excess of the diameter of the rivet. Care must be taken that after reamering, the rivets completely fill the holes to the satisfaction of the Locomotive and Carriage Superintendent or his deputy. All the plates are to be brought well together before any rivets are put in, and hydraulic riveting and steel rivets must be used throughout. Holes in angles must be marked off from the plates and drilled not punched. Any caulking which may be required must be done with broad faced or other approved tools, care being taken that the plates are not damaged by so doing. The boiler must be carefully covered with an approved clothing, and steel plates 14 S.W.G. thick.

Tubes
The boiler tubes are to be of solid drawn steel to the Great Western Railway Company's specification, 1⅛" outside diameter, 13 S.W.G. thick, expanded 1/16" for 3" diameter at one end.

Stays
Great care must be taken that the stays have full tight fitting threads. They must be well screwed into boiler barrel and firebox shell, and every precaution must be observed to see that the threads are not damaged by the ends being cut off, and the holes of both plates must be perfectly fair with each other.

Smokebox
The smokebox is to be made up of a steel plate riveted to the flange of the smokebox tube plate, and to the top cone plate. An angle iron in halves must be riveted at four places, and tapped for bolts to fix the top plate, which is to be of mild steel, with a flanged hole for the door. This is to be of mild steel, with a hole cut in the centre for the chimney. Great care must be taken that the door, when closed, makes a perfectly air-tight joint. This must be made by four levers secured to the smokebox top plate by collar studs, sliding on four taper casehardened strips on the door, which must be hinged as shewn.

Internal steam pipes
The boiler is to be fitted with internal copper steam pipes reaching to within ¾" of top of boiler from the regulator, water gauge, injector cocks, ejector, blower and safety valve seatings. The clack box seating must be fitted with a nozzle to direct the flow of water downwards towards the foundation ring.

The normal water line is to be 5" below the under surface of smokebox tube plate.

Manhole
The manhole door is to be made of two steel plates riveted together, the outside plate to fit an oval hole in the boiler and the inside plate to overlap this hole all round. A stiffening plate must be riveted to the boiler on the outside.

Firehole door
The firedoors are to be made of steel plate with three air holes in each. Knobs must be fixed for sliding them in grooved racks secured to the boiler with two studs in each rack.

Firegrate
The firebars must be of wrought iron of the section shewn and be supported on a wrought iron ring made in halves, and carried by wrought iron brackets, riveted to the ashpan.

Ashpan
The ashpan is to be circular, with doors at the front and back, arranged so as to be worked from the front of the boiler. The manhole in the bottom is to have a cover steel plate studded on to a stiffening ring riveted to the pan. The pan must be fixed to the boiler by angle irons carried on studs screwed into the foundation ring.

Chimney
The chimney is to be made of mild steel plates with an outer and inner casing. Around the top of the outer casing a copper plate of the shape shewn must be riveted. A flanged plate is to be secured to chimney, and a cover plate must be bolted to the flanged plate. The chimney is to be fastened to the smokebox door through the hole provided for it, by an angle iron.

Tests
Each boiler is to be tested in the presence of the Locomotive and Carriage Superintendent or his deputy, to a hydraulic pressure of 220 pounds per square inch, and with steam to the full working pressure – 160 pounds per square inch, this latter pressure to be maintained for four consecutive hours. The boiler must be perfectly tight under these pressures, and must be thoroughly cleaned and receive a coat of red lead whilst warm.

All studs to be screwed with Whitworth standard thread and to be in place before testing. The boiler must be left perfectly clean inside, free from all chippings &c.

Frames
The main frames and frame stay plates are to be made of mild steel to the Great Western Railway Company's standard specification. They must be very carefully set as shewn, to clear the boiler. All holes must be drilled and reamered out to the exact sizes given before the frames are set. The cylinder, motion plate and cheek block bolts must be turned to gauge and driven into place a good driving fit. The frames are to be set 4' 1¾" between and stayed at the leading end by a flanged racking plate, two cross stay plates and angle irons, as shewn. Behind the leading wheel and on each side of the driving wheel cross stay plates are required with box angle irons riveted to them and to the frames. Horn plates must be riveted to the main frames as shewn. Two square holes must be cut in the flanged racking plate to carry the leading sand boxes. An angle iron must be riveted to the bottom of frames to support the set, and at the top a forged angle bracket is to be riveted, having a buffing surface as shewn. The boiler must be secured to these brackets by twelve studs in each with clearing holes in boiler brackets to allow for expansion. Great importance is attached to the cross staying of frames, which must be a thoroughly good job.

The cheek blocks are to be made of cast iron, casehardened on rubbing surfaces as shewn, their flanges being planed all over and fitted to template, and when in position must be perfectly parallel, and square with the engine in all directions. The horn ties are to be attached to the cheek blocks as shewn, and secured by studs and nuts.

Cylinders
The cylinders are to be 12" diameter when finished, with a stroke of 16", and are to be of close grained hard cast iron; they must be as hard as they can be made to allow of their being properly fitted and finished, and must be perfectly free from honeycomb or any other defect of material or workmanship; they must be truly bored out, the front and back end being bell-mouthed, as shewn. All joints, covers and faces are to be planed, turned or scraped to a true surface, so that a perfect joint can be obtained. All the studs are to be screwed tight home. The cylinders are to be made with loose covers at both ends, provision being made on the back cover for carrying the motion bars. They are to set in a horizontal line, exactly 1" below the wheel centres and placed at a distance apart of 6' 7" from centre to centre. The steam chest is to be on the top and secured to the cylinder by studs. When the cylinders are correctly set to their places they are to be firmly secured to the frames by turned bolts driven home a tight fit. They are to be covered with an approved clothing and steel plates 14 S.W.G. thick. The front and back cylinder covers are to be protected by polished cleating plates. The cylinders, before being fixed in position, must be tested in the presence of the Locomotive and Carriage Superintendent, or his deputy, by hydraulic pressure to 225 lbs. per square inch, and all joints must be perfectly tight under this pressure.

Steam pipes
The steam pipes are to be of solid drawn copper and to be made up in two lengths to each cylinder, the flanges against the regulator and steam chest to be of brazing metal, the intermediate flanges to be of flexible design.

Regulator
The regulator is to be of cast iron with two steam pipe connections. The main valve is to be of gun metal with a cast iron 'jockey' valve working on the back.

Blast pipes
The blast pipes are to be of solid drawn copper, two lengths from the cylinder to be led to a breeches pipe on the left hand side, from which one pipe must be led to the front of smokebox at the top. The blast pipe inside the smokebox is to be of copper, and 3¼" diameter at the tip.

Piston and rod
The piston heads are to be of cast iron, free from honeycomb or any other defects, cored out with five 1" ribs supporting the sides as shewn. They must be turned and finished 1/32" smaller in diameter than the cylinder bore. The packing rings are to be turned larger than the diameter of the cylinders, then to be cut and sprung in position, the joints to come on opposite sides of piston. The piston rod is to be enlarged at its connection with the crosshead and tapered [down] as shewn, and a spring steel cotter must be used to secure it.

Slide valves
The valves are to be of gun metal and balanced with Richardson strips. The steam lap is to be 1⅛", exhaust lap 1/16", and constant lead 5/32".

Valve Spindles
The valve spindles and straps are to be of the best Yorkshire iron, secured to valve spindle crosshead by a cotter of spring steel.

Metallic packing
The piston rods and valve spindles are to be fitted with metallic packing of the Great Western Railway Company's design.

Motion bars
The motion bars are to be of steel to the Great Western Railway Company's specification and tapered towards the ends as shewn. They are to be studded to the back cylinder covers, which must be recessed to take the lug and bolted to the motion plate, which must be accurately fitted to receive them A brass liner is to be placed at each end between the bar and the carriers. Each top bar is to have three cast iron syphons, two for the crosshead, and one for the piston rod, each bottom bar to have two lubricating recesses, and both top and bottom bars to have a recess across them at the ends of stroke to allow for wear. Each bar to have a perfectly smooth, true, polished face all over the bearing surface.

Motion plates
The motion plates are to be of cast steel to the Great Western Railway Company's specification. They must be faced perfectly square for the attachment to frames, motion bars and valve gear brackets, and secured to frame by 12 rivets, ⅞" diameter in each plate, countersunk where shewn; and four bolts ¾" diameter countersunk outside which also carry the cast iron reversing shaft bracket.

Crossheads
These are to be of cast steel to the Great Western Railway Company's standard specification. The rubbing surfaces are to have recesses filled with white metal, and bosses at the bottom for the connection of valve gear arm. The gudgeon pins are to be of best Yorkshire iron casehardened, and are to be a taper fit in the outside and inside bosses of crosshead, kept in position by a nut on the inside, and prevented from turning round in the crosshead by a feather fitted in the outer boss. On the bottom is to be fitted a cast iron lubricator for the bottom bar. Great care must be taken that the crosshead works freely between the bars.

Connecting rods
The connecting rods are to be forged of steel, to be of H section, and are to be fitted with adjustable bushes of bronze at big end. The small ends are to be accurately fitted with bronze bushes, pressed in so as to ensure a perfectly tight fit, and to be secured by a gun metal pin, riveted over. The bushes are to be lined with white metal as shewn. Oil cups are to be forged solid with both ends of rod. The cotters are to be of spring steel accurately fitted in the taper, and provided with set screws and cross cotters.

Coupling rods
The coupling rods are to be forged of steel, to be of H section, and are to be fitted with adjustable bushes of bronze at one end, the other ends to be accurately fitted with bronze bushes, pressed in and finished the same as the connecting rod bushes. Oil cups are to be forged solid with both ends of rod. The cotters are to be made of spring steel and accurately fitted in the taper and provided with set screws and cross cotters.

Crank pins
The crank pins are to be of steel to the Company's standard specification, and are to be accurately turned and pressed to the wheels by hydraulic pressure of not less than 40 tons and riveted over on the inside.

Wheel centres
The wheel centres are to be of cast steel to the Great Western Railway Company's standard specification. They must be bored and turned and have keyways cut strictly to template and turned correctly to gauge to receive the tyres. Each wheel must be forced on the axle before the tyre is shrunk on, by hydraulic pressure of not less than 80 tons. The crank pin bosses are to be cast solid with the axle bosses, and bored out parallel to fit the connecting and coupling rod crank pins. The crank pin holes are to be bored in a suitable quartering machine.

Tyres
The tyres are to be of steel to the Great Western Railway Company's standard specification. They must be turned to the Great Western Railway standard contour and must measure 4' 5⅜" between backs when secured to wheel centre and axle. Great Western Railway standard fastening must be used. All tyres must be bored to gauge before being shrunk on the wheel centres and must be turned so that the diameters are exact to size.

Balance weights
All the revolving and 75% of the reciprocating weight must be balanced, one half of the reciprocating balance to be in the leading wheels, and one half in the drivers. The balance weight to be of steel plates, one on each side of spoke, filled in with lead and riveted together.

Valve gear
The valve gear is to be of the Walschaerts type. All levers, expansion link, valve rod and return crank to be of best Yorkshire iron.

The return crank is to be shrunk on to the crank pin and secured by a retaining stud and set at 90° to the main crank to follow in fore gear. The eccentric rod leading from return crank to expansion link to be of steel, and of fluted section. The expansion link support to work in cast steel brackets bolted to motion plate. The valve rod is to work in a cast iron guide, lined with a gun metal bush bolted to the motion bars. All pins are to be of the best Yorkshire iron, casehardened, a taper fit in the jaws, and kept in position by castle nuts. All bearings for the pins to be bushed with bronze metal, great care being taken with the methods of lubrication for each working surface.

Axles
All axles to be of steel to the Great Western Railway Company's standard specification. The inside wheel bosses must be machined to gauge, and axle end faced off flush with wheel boss when in position.

Axle boxes
All axle boxes and keeps are to be of gun metal, with bearing surfaces of anti-friction metal, and oil recesses in crown of bearing. The keeps must have lubricating pads oiled from the bottom. Cheek blocks must be lubricated from the top of axle box. The boxes must be a working fit on the flanges for a length of 2" at the centre, tapering off to the top and bottom as shewn.

Springs
The springs are to be made of steel to the Great Western Railway Company's standard specification. The plates are to be prevented from moving on each other by nibs stamped on them, which must fit the slots properly. The buckles must be of Yorkshire iron, must fit the springs accurately, and be prevented from shifting on the springs by a steel pin driven into a hole through the buckle and plates end riveted over at each end.

Spring gear
Each spring to have two links at each end attached by pins to adjustable hangers with washers bearing against rubber pads enclosed in spring cups, on the top of which must be placed knife edge washers bearing on brackets fixed to the frame.

The bottom of the buckles on the springs must be turned to fit the hole in the top of the axle boxes.

Reversing gear
The motion is to be reversed by a hand lever arrangement, secured to a quadrant plate attached to an angle iron on the boiler above the footplate. The reversing shaft is to be turned from one bar of high tensile steel to the Great Western Railway Company's standard specification, which is to be placed below the motion and carried by two cast iron brackets with loose caps bolted to the frame and motion plate.

The shaft must also be supported by two wrought iron brackets bolted to the frame, and the lifting link levers must be shrunk on shaft and secured by studs as shewn. The reversing lever is to be secured by a square key and the weight of motion and levers must be counteracted by a flat spiral spring, the resistance being taken by an eye bolt attached to a bracket bolted to the frame stay.

Brake gear
The engines are to be fitted with the vacuum and hand brakes, the cylinders to be attached to the carriage underframe. The ejector will be supplied by the Great Western Railway Company.

Cylinder cock gear
Each cylinder is to be provided with two cylinder cocks, worked by suitable gear from the footplate.

Buffing gear between boiler and underframe
The tractive effort of the engine is to be transmitted by the boiler shell through buffing gear to cross girders of the underframe. The leading buffer is to consist of a spiral spring on an adjustable plunger as shewn, while the other side of boiler bears against a laminated spring steel plate.

Scroll irons, suspension bolts, &c.
The weight of the car at the engine end must be taken through wrought scroll irons riveted to the solebars, two on each side, secured to cross girders carried by suspension bolts attached to the engine frames. Four wrought iron brackets must be riveted to the frames and fitted with casehardened cup bearings and spiral springs, to carry the suspension bolts.

Sand boxes
Four boxes for 'dry sand' are to be provided, one on each side at leading end for the leading wheels, and one on each side attached to the trailing frame stay for the driving wheels. They are to be made of mild steel plate, and so arranged that the leading and driving gear respectively can be worked simultaneously by suitable rods from the footplate. The sand to be led within 2" of the rails by wrought iron pipes. The general arrangement of sand boxes and gear to be as shewn.

Injectors
Two No.6 restarting injectors of Messrs. Davis and Metcalfe's make are to be fixed one on each side of boiler. The delivery pipes are to be of wrought iron leading to the trailing end of bogie, where they must couple by flexible connections to wrought iron pipes from the tank. Two 1½" Lambert valves must be used at the injector inlet to regulate the supply; and also two underneath the tanks to disconnect the water supply when necessary. The steam pipes to the injectors must be of copper 1" in diameter. The overflow pipes are to be of wrought iron. Care must be taken that the pipes are so set that the flanges of all joints come fairly to their places without any spring upon them.

Water pipes
The pipes are to be of copper, so arranged as to fill the tank from either side of the coach. The mouths of the pipes must be in the back corners of motor compartment, covered with a hinged cover of mild steel plate. The least area of pipes must be 28 sq. ins.

Coal bunker
The coal bunker is to be made of mild steel plate with a carrying capacity of 15 cwt. The front must fit the shape of the car body and the back is to have a sliding door for coal. The length to be 6' 6" leaving a space at the ends to be utilised for toolboxes. Inside the bunker at the right hand side must be fixed the hand brake gear column and handle.

General Mountings
Each engine is to be supplied with the following:

- Two Ashton muffler pop safety valves, the springs to be set for a pressure of 160 lbs per square inch.
- One vacuum gauge, 6" diameter, to the Great Western Company's pattern.
- One Bourdon's pressure gauge, 7" in diameter, to indicate up to 220 lbs. pressure to the Great Western Railway Company's pattern.
- One Water Gauge, complete, with glass guard and pipes leading to the ashpan.
- One small whistle, so arranged as to be operated from each end of car.
- Two steam cocks for the supply of the injectors, fixed on seatings on the front of boiler.
- One blower cock placed on right hand side of boiler.
- Steam heating cock and reducing valve.
- Two clack boxes, one on each side of boiler.
- Sight feed lubricator.
- One watering cock attached to the injector delivery pipe on left side of boiler.
- Washout plugs and mud doors as shewn.
- Four toolboxes with locks and keys, one placed in each corner of engine room.
- Lamp irons.
- Driver's book case.

All plugs and mountings are to be of gun metal, and must be of first class finish. The whistle seatings and valves, blower cock, clack boxes, water gauges and cylinder lubricators are to be of the Great Western Railway Company's pattern.

Painting
Before any paint is applied the surfaces must be cleaned and free from all scale and rust. The boiler is to receive one coat of red lead whilst warm. The outside of cleating, plates, wheels, frames, chimney, brake work and springs must have one coat of lead colour, one coat japan black and one coat best engine varnish. Great care must be taken that all parts of the engines are, where possible, duplicates of each other.

Underframe
The underframe is to be built of rolled steel sections. The headstocks and boiler transoms must be carefully made to their respective shapes. The connection of transoms, longitudinals and diagonals must be made of angle brackets or bent plate as shewn. At the right hand corner of the leading end the connection must be made by a specially forged wrought iron bracket which must also carry the brake shaft. This bracket must be planed and faced to the required angle, and the boss for the brake shaft must be faced and bored. The frame bolster is to be formed of two steel plates with top and bottom angles, cut to shape as shewn. Two channels with angles must be riveted to the two bolster plates to carry the upper centre casting and the connection of the bolster to the sole bars must be made as shewn.

Truss rods
The truss rods must be made of special quality iron. They must be fixed at the ends to the sole bars and fitted with the adjusting arrangement shewn.

Racking plates
Racking plates butt jointed with holes as shewn must be riveted over the engine end of underframe and all rivets must be countersunk in the top of plate.

Draw Gear and screw couplings
Great Western Railway standard draw bar hooks and screw couplings with rubber pads and washers must be used. Cast iron draw bar plates must be bolted to the headstock to give the necessary horizontal clearance.

Buffing gear
The buffers are to be self-contained, with heads of elliptical shape as shewn. The heads and shanks are to be made of wrought iron and the casing of cast iron. The spiral springs and washers are to be to the dimensions given and bear on a cast iron packing piece against the headstock. The shank must be square in section where passing through this packing piece to prevent rotation.

Body Brackets and holding down bolts
Two wrought iron body brackets must be riveted to the headstocks. The holding down bolts for the body are to be pitched as shewn and must pass through the 'bottom sides' and top flanges of the sole bars.

Scroll irons
The weight of the car at the engine end must be taken through wrought scroll irons riveted to sole bars. See clause 39.

Water tank
The water tank is to be made of mild steel plate. It must be fixed in the position shewn by wrought iron straps riveted to the tank and bolted to angle brackets on longitudinals and transoms of the underframe A manhole is to be provided in the bottom of the tank, and stiffening plates as shewn with holes to afford facility for repairs. Air pipes must be fixed as shewn.

Carrying bogies, frames &c.
The carrying bogie is to be of the bolster type, built up of plates and rolled sections. The flanges of the end cross members must be cut away where shewn to clear the brake block hanger brackets. Two transoms of channel section must be fixed to the frame plates by angle brackets, and bent plates as shewn. Each of these channels must be connected to the end cross members by two diagonals. Buffing plates of bent plate must be riveted, and cast iron wearing plates and sling carrying brackets must be bolted to the transoms as shewn. Angle pieces must be riveted in the positions shewn to carry the brake fulcrum brackets, and axle safety brackets of bent plate must be riveted to the diagonals. The axle guards are to be of mild steel and must be riveted to the outside of the frame plates. Wrought iron cheek blocks of the section shewn must be riveted to the axle guards and those on each side must be held together at their openings by horn ties of wrought iron. Brake block hanger brackets must be carried on plates riveted between diagonals and frame plates.

Centre castings
The centre castings are to be of good sound cast iron with bearing surfaces turned and holes bored for the centre pin. The top casting is to be faced and bolted to the frame bolster and the bottom casting to be faced and bolted to the bogie bolster. A groove must be turned in the bottom casting as shewn for a dust guard of leather which must bear against the top casting when in position. The centre must be lubricated by means of small oil feed pipes, leading from oil boxes fixed to the outside of the sole bars, to a drilled hole in the top centre casting as shewn. The bogie pin must be of wrought iron turned and cottered.

Rubbing blocks
The rubbing blocks are to be of good sound cast iron and, when bolted in position, $\frac{1}{4}$" clearance is required between top and bottom blocks.

Bogie bolster
The bogie bolster is to be made up of rolled sections as shewn, bolted at ends to cast iron spring bearing blocks, and riveted at the bottom to two mild steel plates. Angle bearing plates must be riveted at the centre as shewn to assist in carrying the bottom centre casting.

Spring gear
The suspension links must be of best wrought iron, slung from cast iron carrying brackets bolted to the transoms. The brackets must be bushed with wrought iron casehardened, to carry a wrought iron casehardened pin, fixed in suspension link. The suspension links must carry wrought iron rocking bars of the section shewn, to bear in cast iron brackets bolted to the spring plank. The spring plank is to be of channel section and must carry a cast iron spring bearing plate at each end, having lugs similar in form and position to lugs on the top bearing block. These lugs must hold the bolster springs in position and act as spring stops limiting the range to $1\frac{1}{4}$".

The side springs are to be of the laminated type. The spring buckle must fit into the axle box top and the spring hangers are to have India rubber pads and plates in a spring cup as shewn. The brackets are to be of wrought iron riveted to the frame plates.

Wheels
The wheels of the carrying bogie are to be of the 'Mansell' type. The wheel bosses must be of cast steel and bolted to the teak segments with bolts countersunk in the washer plates as shewn. The bosses must be faced, turned and bored, and the wheel forced on to the axle by hydraulic pressure of not less than 60 tons. The washer plates must be of wrought iron.

Tyres
The tyres are to be of steel. They must be turned to the Great Western Railway standard contour and must measure 4' $5\frac{5}{8}$" between backs when secured to wheel centre and axle. They must be bored out and turned for key rings and put on the teak blocks while hot with an allowance of $\frac{5}{32}$" in diameter for contraction.

Axles
The axles are to be of steel. There must be no shoulder behind the boss so that the wheel may be forced on with the required pressure.

Axle boxes
The axleboxes are to be of good sound cast iron of the open front type. The load must be taken by a phosphor bronze bearing fitting in a cast iron wedge piece shaped to a radius as shewn. The boxes must have lubricating pads of

the Great Western Railway pattern oiled from the bottom. The back of the box must be fitted with wood and leather shields as shewn.

Brake gear

Vacuum brake cylinders of the diameters given are to be carried in the positions shewn, fitted with release valves, which must be capable of being opened from each side of the car. The vacuum brake will be worked from both ends of car; and for this purpose a brake setter and vacuum gauge must be fixed in suitable positions in the driver's compartment, and a vacuum gauge in the motor compartment. A hand brake column and handle must be fixed in the driver's compartment, and pull through a bell crank and brake rods on to the main brake shaft worked by the vacuum cylinder, independent working of hand and vacuum brake must be provided for.

Steps

Plate steps must be riveted to the solebars at the driver's and motor compartment, and wrought iron brackets must be bolted to the sole bars at the vestibule to carry the step boards. Swing steps are to be provided at the vestibule doorways hung in brackets fixed to the inside of the sole bars, and actuated by a lever working in a notched quadrant fixed to the vestibule partition. The handle must have a spring catch which can be locked with an ordinary carriage key. A commode handle must be hinged to the door pillar on each side, and must not project more than 2½" beyond the outside of the car when the steps are swung back.

Sand gear

A sand box must be provided in the driver's compartment for the wheels of the carrying bogie. It must be made of mild steel plate and operated by levers at the driver's foot.

Gas reservoirs

Gas reservoirs must be attached to the underframe by plate slings as shewn. They must be made of wrought iron or mild steel plate and must be of exact dimensions and form given. The wrapper plates must be welded throughout their whole length and the ends must be dished and welded to the reservoirs. They must be capable of standing a pressure of 200 lbs. per square inch without leakage.

Motor Car Body

Body framing and interior

The structure framing must be of teak or Canadian or Baltic oak, the panelling of Honduras mahogany canvassed and blocked, and the roof, floor and interior casing must be of pine. The bottom sides must have one box splice only in each, secured by wrought iron plates let in and screwed to the underside. All floor members must be tenoned into the bottom sides, the bearing floor members having wrought iron corner plates in addition. The end bars must each be made in two parts, lap jointed at the middle and plated on the inside. This plate must extend all round the end bar and be bolted to it and the bottom sides. The bottom sides, end bars and main floor bearers must be rebated to receive the floor boards. Double floor boards must be used, placed diagonally and screwed down to bottom sides and floor bearers; the bottom boards must be tongued and grooved and the top boards square edged and all joints levelled The cant rails must have one lap splice only in each, and the splice must be in such a position that a pillar may be tenoned through the half lap. All main pillars must be tenoned into bottom sides and cant rail, and additionally secured to bottom sides by wrought iron box brackets. Intermediate pillars must be tenoned into bottom sides and bottom light rails. The end arch rails are to be in three parts, tenoned into corner and end pillars, and the partition and intermediate arch rails must be lap jointed in the middle. The hoop sticks are to be of oak, steamed and bent to shape without a break, and to be thoroughly dry before being fixed in position. The roof boards are to be tongued and screwed to the hoop sticks. The interior of the roof must be cased with three ply panelling which must have a coat of priming on the back before being fixed. Double doors, hinged to open outwards, are required at each side of luggage compartment, double doors, hinged to open inwards, at the vestibule, and single doors, hinged to open inwards, at the driver's compartment. A sliding door is required on each side of motor compartment, and between the compartments as shewn. All side doors, except in the motor compartment, must have drop lights. The inside doors must be hung on ball bearing rollers and guided by grooved plates let in the floor.

Seating and finishing

The seats must be arranged as shewn. The walk-over seats are to be of Hale and Kilburn's patent, and all seats must be covered with rattan. The seat divisions and ends and all internal wood finishing must be of polished oak and plain flap seats are to be provided in the luggage compartment.

The outside light mouldings are to be of polished mahogany, screwed to pillars and light rails from the inside and so arranged that the light frame can be removed bodily.

The vestibule must be cased with narrow vertical vee-jointed matching.

All wearing parts of the floor must be covered with chamfered oak strips.

Lighting

The cars must be lighted by incandescent oil gas compressed to 140 lbs. per square inch, and carried in reservoirs attached to underframe. See clause 66. Pressure gauges must be bolted to the sole bars. High and low pressure gas governors are to be provided and fixed to the underframe in a convenient position.

The main and bye-pass pipes must pass through regulating cocks in the driver's vestibule and motor compartments, and pass along the top of the roof with a branch to each lamp. The lamps are to be 20 c.p., and arranged as shewn.

Hand loops

Two brass tubes supported by brass hanging brackets to the hoopsticks are required, running from the motor compartment to the other end of car. These tubes must carry leather hand loops, and through the right hand one the whistle chain must be passed.

Ventilators

Ventilators of Acme pattern must be provided in the roof of the non-smoking, and in the smoking compartment, fitted with internal caps with perforated sides.

Electric communication

An electric bell must be fixed in the motor and driver's compartments and the necessary cells carried in a wood box in the driver's compartment.

Driving gear

A regulator handle must be fixed in the driver's compartment to work the regulator at the engine end through a bell crank, shaft and rod, and the necessary gear provided, so that the car may be worked from the end of a trailer when required.

Painting

The roof boards, after joints have been levelled, must be well puttied, painted and given a coat of thick white lead paint. Stout canvas of good quality must then be strained over and held in position by a suitable cornice screwed to the cant rails. The canvas must then be given four coats of thick white lead paint.

The interior of the roof is to have one coat of priming, two coats of white, and one coat of Perline and the mouldings picked out in blue. The sides and ends of car must be properly cleaned off and given two coats of lead colour, four coats of filling, then to be rubbed down, one coat of lead colour and faced, one coat of lead colour, one coat of chocolate brown and a second coat of half varnish half colour below the light rails, and four coats of white above the rails. The mouldings are then to have two coats of brown, and the whole given one coat of varnish; the round of mouldings is then to have two coats of gold colour finished with three coats of varnish flattened down after the first coat. The inside of car below the roof is to be oak grained.

Furnishing

Locks, commode handles and catches for sliding doors of approved patterns, and all inside metal furnishing must be of burnished brass. The outside doors are to be provided with carriage locks, private locks, hinges, commode handles and escutcheons of gun metal of approved patterns. Spring roller blinds with brass heads must be fixed over each light in the passenger compartments, and pressed window blind brackets on each light moulding.

Lamp brackets, steps &c.

Wrought iron lamp brackets made to the Great Western Railway template must be fixed in the positions required.

Destination board brackets are to be fixed above the centre end lights.

Plate steps and wrought iron commode handles are to be fixed to the ends of car as shewn.

A flag box must be provided and fixed in the driver's compartment.

Steam heating

The cars must be heated by steam from the motor car boiler on the storage system, a pipe to run through with Great Western Railway standard diaphragm steam traps and hose pipe connection.

APPENDIX B
CORRESPONDENCE SUMMARIES KERR, STUART LTD.

The correspondence between the Great Western, Kerr, Stuart Ltd. and Hurst, Nelson Ltd. concerning the Lot 1100 SRMs (61–72) survives in hand-written summary form in a copy of Kerr, Stuart's Order Book, kept at the National Railway Museum Library. There are also many communications with their works at Stoke. It provides a valuable insight into the pressures and difficulties involved in the fulfilment of a contract.

Within the pages, Harrison appears to have been the Kerr, Stuart fitter sent to Swindon to superintend their part of the car assembly; Hurst Nelson seem also to have sent men for this purpose, even though the tender documents originally required the cars to be assembled at the manufacturer's works.

1905

Correspondence records started on 16th June with the transfer of drawings from Churchward to Kerr, Stuart. In these, an early letter gives 'Boiler complete without water weighs 5T. Engine 8T 10c. Total 13T 10c.' These were followed by a formal instruction to Stoke on 20th June:

> 'Order No. 2294 KS & Co. Ltd., London. ½ pl photo 1092.
>
> 'Motor Bogie in accordance with the GWR Co's Specfn dated April 1905 and to drgs. sent to you June 16th & later. [Marginal Note: "See 6903: 3 cone plates; 6987: Tank Gauges; 7285: Regulator Handles etc.; 7010: Hearth (?); 7353: Brake pull rods, Pins for whistle etc. Invoiced (24.1.06); 7541: Regulator (?) etc."] To be finished to the satisfaction of the GWR Co's Engineer or Inspector.
>
> 'Your portion to include the boiler & fittings, engine & engine bogie, coal bunker, filling and suction pipes up to tank under carriage main frame, the cross beams and springs under the engine bogie up to but not including the four scroll irons hanging from the mainframe. You will send a template to Hurst Nelsons showing the centres of the four holes for the scroll irons. The tank under the mainframe will be made by either Hurst Nelsons or yourselves, as will be arranged later. The whole of the brakework up to the engine bogie connection will be supplied by Hurst Nelsons, and they will also supply all connections from one end of the coach to the other.
>
> 'Please inform us when the patterns are ready as Mr Churchward desires them to be inspected.
>
> 'Please submit list of proposed suppliers of material as soon as possible and later, copies of the orders in duplicate. Please note that all materials are to be ordered strictly in accordance with the specfn & tests.
>
> 'We enclose herewith copy of our order to Hurst Nelson.
>
> 'Mr Churchward will entertain any suggestion you may make with a view to improving the coaches or to effect economies, which will not depreciate their efficiency.
>
> 'The fireboxes, tubes & stays to be made of copper. We will do this, however.
>
> 'D/y The first in 20 weeks from June 19th (Nov. 6th)
>
> 'The rest at rate of 1 per week thereafter (complete by Jan 22nd) Under penalty of £30 each per week.
>
> 'To the Great Western Railway Co., Swindon, over their system as far [as possible].'

Hurst, Nelson and Kerr, Stuart exchanged a great deal of correspondence about the drawings at this stage, with particular reference to that of an amended roof plate.

On 25th July, Churchward confirmed details of chimney and other fittings that had been the subject of queries:

> 'The angle iron for carrying the chimney should be riveted to the smokebox door & the chimney bolted to the angle iron by 11 bolts ⅜" dia. The mud plugs should be of one size only, am sending sample today. Enclosing rough sketch showing method of attachment of boiler to bogie frame.'

As planning progressed, correspondence increasingly covered a larger number of items, as shown by a letter from Kerr, Stuart's London office of 2nd August:

> 'We have arranged with HN & Co. for them to supply Tanks at [given in cipher, believed to be £15] less 2½%. We shall supply water gauge levels, so advise us when you have them ready. Enclosing drg 28310 showing argt of pipes. Please take what information you require and send direct to HN when you have finished with it. Enclosing drg 24077A showing details of valve gear. We believe you have had this argt before, but there may be modifications on it. Enclosing drg 28320 showing exhaust steam pipe. We believe this is a detail of the pipe which Mr Beache [?] arranged with you when at Stoke, last should be made on the flat & not on the curve. If this is so please ignore this drg. Note you have ordered lubricators & that you had 2 quotes. Vacuum & Wakefields. Are telling Mr Churchward that we are putting Vacuum in hand. The drg. of tank you sent us the other day does not show the copper sieve inside the tank, which HN supply. Did you send it to them?'

Another point under discussion in early August was the use of asbestos mattress for boiler covering, instead of a fossil meal composition. Mr Churchward accepted the use of the asbestos mattresses, and also the Vacuum company's lubricator. Regarding the exhaust steam bend mentioned in the correspondence of 2nd August, Kerr Stuart resolved: 'we could safely make it on the straight as originally decided'.

On 17th August, it was recorded that 'Mr. Churchward has sent 6 ejectors complete'. The packing case they had arrived in had to be returned before the remaining six were sent. The Great Western never ceased to look for economies. Having received his empty ejector box back from Kerr Stuart, Churchward later advised the company that the remainder of the ejectors had been sent from Swindon on 8th September.

In another sub-contract, some platework was being provided by Stewarts & Lloyds. On 22nd August, Mr. Churchward indicated that some of the boiler plates were to hand, but two had been found defective. He required the remainder, and also replacement plates before commencing flanging. A few days later, Kerr, Stuart received another letter from Mr Churchward stating that 13 plates had not withstood the examination; these plates were tested by the GWR Inspector at Stewarts & Lloyds works. It was found that an important clause had been omitted when ordering the plates from S & L, and replacement plates were instantly ordered. On receipt, a test piece was to be sent to Mr. Nash. Soon, re-flanged plates were received, and the office advised the works: 'Think you may use them.'

In the daily correspondence during construction, other items requiring clarification during early September included spring cups, flexible pipe connections and valve cord. The Great Western were also asked to send samples of other fittings, including their required pattern of steam reducing valve.

The arrangement of dampers was also causing some concern at Kerr, Stuart, and Churchward duly sent another drawing. He drew attention to the safety clip:

> 'this is correctly shown on drg. It should fit loosely round the suspension bolt, its object being to prevent the bolt falling in the event of a breakage. The nut has a split cone & therefore requires nothing to prevent slacking back.'

Although the Great Western had finalised the design before the contract had been let, occasionally it was necessary to make alterations as work proceeded. The scroll irons were a case in point, and Churchward ordered some alterations made, supplying a part drawing of the amended section. Whilst Kerr, Stuart were doubtless happy to comply, their London office asked of the works: 'Inform us if this will necessitate any delay, expense or alteration'. The Great Western would of course be immediately asked to re-imburse the company for any additional work. As they were also involved, Hurst, Nelson were advised of the alterations.

Close co-operation was obviously required between the London office and works of the company, and in late September we see a flow of correspondence from the office, including the following examples:

> '25th September
> Enclosing drg 22/9/05 showing positions of notches in the reversing quadrant. This drg should be strictly adhered to. HN & Co. ask us to send them a set of the engine bogie crossbars and taper pins as soon as possible. They will require these as a template for their scroll irons so kindly see that all the crossbars are identical with those you send to Motherwell.'
>
> '27th September
> We note that you will send a set of bogie cross bars to Motherwell in a day or two. Mr Churchward's letter was not enclosed in yours. He wrote us about 11th inst. re scroll irons & enclosed drg 25501 which we sent to HN & Co. We have asked them to return the drg direct to you as we are not sure if the alteration as shown has also been made to the ends of the bogie bars.'

On 29th September, Mr. Churchward advised the company on the required arrangement of component parts of the SRMs:

Car No.	*Engine No.*	*Boiler No.*
61	866	1073
62	867	1074
63	868	1075
64	869	1076
65	870	1077
66	871	1078
67	872	1079
68	873	1080
69	874	1081
70	875	1082
71	876	1083
72	877	1084

In the formal order above, Churchward indicated that he would 'entertain suggestions' on improvements, and Kerr, Stuart duly offered one concerning the location of a plug on the boiler. The office duly advised the works on 2nd October:

> 'We are submitting your proposal regarding the position of the plug on the boiler to Mr Churchward. We are sending our papers to HN & Co & we return to you the schedule calling for particulars of the engine portion, which return in due course. We have informed Mr Churchward that we are arranging to fit the number [?] plug in the position shown in red on drg 28699 which we have today returned to him. We presume you have taken particulars of this.'

Two days later, the office again advised the works that 'there is no objection to you fitting the plug in the position indicated in red on print No 28699 – So writes Mr Churchward.'

Whilst letters seem to have been remarkably speedy in transit, urgent messages were often sent by telegraph (or 'wire'). Such a message was received from Hurst, Nelson on 4th October to say that non-arrival of the bogie cross bars was delaying work: 'Kindly forward immediately.'

Another alteration became apparent in mid-October concerning the use of reducing valves on the steam heating system. The office wrote to Stoke: 'Do not fit reducing valves for the steam heating.' Two days later, a letter from Churchward confirmed the arrangement: 'The steam heating cock is used as the reducing valve on Motor cars & as it would appear that you have completed these fittings, nothing further is required.'

The occasional movement of special materials and fittings continued from Swindon to Stoke. On October 13th, Churchward wired: '10 top cone plates forwarded last night, in trucks 25796, 54474.'

Another modification was forwarded by Churchward concerning boiler tubes. The office advised the works on 19th October that 'Mr Churchward orders these tubes to be beaded. Kindly do. We have applied for 10 days extension of time in consequence – give cost.' A few days later, the works had responded, Churchward had agreed, and the word went out to Stoke: 'Please bead the tubes in all twelve boilers'.

During construction, Hurst, Nelson had run across a minor problem with the positioning of the heating pipe, and on 20th October wrote with a suggestion to Kerr, Stuart:

> 'Enclosing sketch 9931 showing how we are moving the heating pipe at the point where connection will be made with the boiler. The pressure gauge pipe will pass thorough a hole in the nock [?] plate – please let us know in which position this hole will be best suit.'

Kerr, Stuart responded, and Hurst, Nelson confirmed 'we note position in which the hole in the nock back plate for pressure gauge is to be put & we will arrange accordingly.'

As the first car neared completion, Churchward wrote to Kerr, Stuart on 21st October concerning the livery:

> 'Enclosing print (28948) showing the positions of the monograms & numbers. Am arranging for the necessary monograms of our standard design to be sent you. I understand your foreman painter has visited our works & observed our method of numbering, so presume it will not now be necessary to send you the panel promised. If however you still wish to have it I will on hearing from you arrange for one to be sent.'

On 1st November, Churchward wrote to the London office, arranging for an inspection of the first engine on 3rd. He went on: 'Cannot accept engine until coach complete.' He had also sent a sample painted panel 'to HN & Co.'

As the components were completed, delivery details were confirmed by Kerr, Stuart: 'Our arrangement with the GWR is that we shall deliver the engine bogies to them purely for storage & unload them from the trucks & cover with tarpaulins, keeping note of the time occupied in doing so.'

A further ongoing problem concerned the supply of the regulator gear. On 8th November, the London office wrote to Hurst, Nelson:

> 'We assume we are right in assuming that you have supplied the Regulator Gear in accordance with our instructions to you on June 26th last?'

Having received Hurst, Nelson's reply, the office wrote to Stoke on 13th November:

> 'We are in receipt of HN's letter re. Regulator Gear. It is true they sent us a letter on June 28, reading as per your enclosed copy to us, but this letter we did not acknowledge, having had some controversy on the point, & our last letter on this matter to HN & Co. on June 26 reads as follows:
> "Hurst Nelson to supply Regulator Gear in accordance with GWR Drg 27730A excepting the parts marked in red as being supplied by KS & Co. In addition to this KS & Co will supply the handle on the Regulator valve and the rod connecting this up to, but not including the first bell crank connection on the underframe at the engine end."
> This you will see is very clear & definite & is quite in accordance with the instructions we gave you on the same date. In view of this we do not know what HN mean by saying "and in addition Regulator Handle and pull rod only", except that they are labouring under the assumption that we are to supply them with the handling gear at the carriage end which from our letter of 26 June you will see is clearly defined as being supplied at the engine end only. We are replying to the letter enclosed.'

The situation dragged on, and the London office eventually advised Stoke of its resolution on 23rd November:

> 'We have been having a wordy correspondence with HN & Co. & to save any further delay in the motor, we have informed them that we are putting in hand 12 sets of Reg Handles & pull rods only at the Coach End. This does not, of course, include the first bell crank on the underframe. We shall of course deduct the cost of this from their a/c.'

With the imminent delivery of the first components to the GWR, arrangements were finalised and the works informed on 14th November:

> 'In view of fact that first 4 Motor Engines will be lying in sidings at Swindon for a number of weeks covered by tarpaulins only, please protect the bright parts & any other parts susceptible to damp as much as possible. We cannot ask Mr. Churchward to unpack & return cases[!!]. When man gets [receipt of?] first coach portion he can unpack 2 or 3 sets of crates.'

During mid-November, there was obviously a delay in the preparation of certain parts at Stoke works. The office suggested an approach to the neighbouring North Staffs Railway: 'Do you think N.S. Co. could help you with machining of the rods: & do you think it absolutely necessary to mill out quite so much material as shown?'

The question of the boiler tubes arose once more, and following an appeal to Churchward, he responded on 17th November: 'Will accept the 3 boilers with tubes ferruled. Not necessary to ferrule tubes of other boilers.'

During November, the first components were delivered to the GWR. Churchward advised the company on 1st December: 'Engines to Swindon Nov 7 & Nov 17 were d/d to our Loco Dept on Nov 9th and Nov 20th respectively'.

In early December, the regulator components were again the subject of much correspondence. The London office advised their works:

> 'Please note that in our order to you we ordered 12 sets of Regulating Handles and Pull Rods only. These are HN & Co's exact words & this does not include the brackets: so note that we wish to work exactly in accordance with their words & we mentioned this to Mr Hidd on the 'phone & in Stoke letter of Nov 22.'

A couple of days later, following a response from Stoke, the office again confirmed:

> 'We are afraid our 'phone message was not quite clearly understood – you are to supply 12 sets of Reg Handles & Pull Rods only. This does not include brackets of any kind.'

This obviously caused some difficulty with the works, who had presumably made an alternative suggestion. The office responded thus:

> 'We note your remarks & under the circumstances we confirm your decision for the brackets as well as the Regulating Handles and Pull Rods, in other words all as shown on drg.12490. Enclosing revised Order.'

Another letter on the same subject was dispatched on 6th December to the works:

> 'Mr. Beache was at Motherwell y'day & they say they have not yet rec'd. the 3 sets Reg. gear dispatched pass. train. We have hopes that Nos.1 & 2 coaches will be d/d to Swindon by the end of next week.'

Even when they did arrive at Hurst, Nelson, this particular saga was not concluded:

> 'We have a letter from HN & Co. who say:
>
> "We beg to advise you that the small jaw couplings between the Regulator Rod & the Bell Crank on the underframe have been sent us with the slot for the feather of the pin in the wrong position. We shall be glad if you will arrange to correct the matter immediately by sending either new pins or couplings."
>
> Please look into this matter immediately & let us know if this is correct as we have no means of verifying it from this end. We trust that there is no fault & that HN & Co. are labouring under a delusion. Please phone your reply.'

New jaws for the regulator gear were arranged.

On 18th December, the office received a telegraph from Hurst, Nelson 'informing us that the first 2 coaches will be dispatched tomorrow & we expect they will be best part of 3 days on the way.' They phoned Stoke with the news, and confirmed by letter, advising the works to 'send a man to Swindon immediately & that Mr Beache will be there tomorrow & will make all arrangements'.

Further deliveries of engines took place during December, and were confirmed by Churchward: 'Engines to Swindon Nov 29, Dec 8, Dec 14 were d/d to our Loco Dept on Dec 1, Dec 11 & Dec 16.'

Another complaint was received from Hurst, Nelson after Christmas; on 27th December, the London office informed Stoke:

> 'We have a letter from HN & Co. informing us that you have not sent them the whistle connections, which we informed you in our letter of June 29 we should supply & that these would be fitted to the coaches by HN & Co. We regret that you should have omitted to send these because it is too late now for us to send them to HN as they would undoubtedly make this a claim for delay. Please send the 12 sets to Swindon with instructions to our man there to fit these to the coaches at the same time sending him all particulars to enable him to do so.'

Churchward forwarded a sample chain for whistle connection at this time.

Mr. T. Harrison had in the meantime arrived at Swindon, and wrote to the London office on 29th December: 'Sending sample of whistle connection. Re progress: Enclosing sketch of altn. to boiler frame. They require boiler number in a different place.'

Meanwhile, the office took issue with Stoke over the whistle connections on 29th December:

> 'We return drgs.12063, 28096. On the latter drg. we have marked the operating handle & bracket at driver's end, which HN & Co. are to supply. The whole of the remainder of the whistle connections are to be supplied by us in accordance with our letter of 29 June last. As we have already informed you in this letter, these should have been d/d to HN & Co. & their contract was to fit them to the coaches. The instructions given to you regarding these appear to us to be quite clear. It is a pity, however, as they did not appear so to you that you did not communicate with us on this point at the time.'

The following day they wired the works:

> 'Forward communicating cords, bell cranks, guide pulleys for whistle to Harrison Swindon, to fit. Send Harrison all the information necessary.
>
> 'Coaches arrived Swindon 10.30 a.m. today.'

1906

Part of the whistle operating equipment had been contracted out. On 1st January, the London office wired the Passenger Communication Co. at 35, Queen Victoria Street, London: 'Send whistle chains only. Hurst Nelson have supplied 2 pulleys & bell cranks.'

Churchward confirmed the position: 'Chain to the sample sent you should be fitted from one end of the coach to the other on the RH side looking towards the engine.'

It was confirmed that Hurst Nelson had forwarded 3 coaches in that week.

Mr. Beache had also arrived in Swindon for the assembly operations, and from the information received by the London office, they advised Stoke of a number of ongoing requirements:

> 'Confirming Mr Beache's wire from Swindon that whistle chains only are required.
>
> 'Re condition of work at Swindon, the tank ends with the two holes for the suction & delivery pipes are not level. It appears that it will be necessary to put in if possible an extra thick India rubber washer. This we instructed Harrison to do.
>
> 'Regulator gear. The GW people informed Mr B. that the Regulator Quadrant should have been case hardened. The wear caused by the spring stud in the regulator handle is noticeable even now. Please inform us if it was specified on drgs or Specification to be case hardened.
>
> 'Re. whistle gear sent to Harrison &c &c &c. Mr Beache noticed that HN & Co. have been very liberal in placing their nameplates on these coaches. They have one on each side at centre of underframe and one on each side of the carriage bogie. We intend to remove the nameplates on the centre of the underframe & fit our own, which please send to Harrison at very earliest moment. The plates that HN have put on at the present moment are oval 7½" × 4" & are held in position by two screws 6⅞" centres. Please pick out this nameplate in red. We shall require two per coach to be fitted to the underframe in the centre. These are of

course in addition to the nameplates on the engine bogie. Note find 2 sets dispatched to Motherwell without being case hardened & that remaining 10 sets have been.

'It is not the spring buffers that are wearing at Swindon, but the Reg. quadrants themselves in which the spring button wearing a groove &c &c &c. Instructing Harrison to get them hardened. Confirming wire to supply only chains for whistle connections as HN & Co. have supplied with 2 coaches already sent 2 pulleys & bell crank &c &c &c.'

The third coach arrived at Swindon on 4th January. Harrison was required to obtain the services of a GWR fitter 'in order that there would be as little delay as possible in coupling the engine to this coach'.

As the assembly got under way at Swindon, many questions arose from the works as to responsibilities. The office wrote to Stoke on 6th January with responses:

'HN must of course supply the sheet steel on the flooring in front of the boiler. This is undoubtedly part of their contract.'

'HN are to supply the pull rods from the Motor Bogie to the rocking shaft under the coach. (See our drg 12033) &c &c &c.

'Regulator Connecting Rod Hangers. You have not sent us a detail of this but we should certainly say that this is also part of HN's contract.

'Drg 12033 clearly shows the whole of the brakework which we have to supply under this contract &c &c &c.

'Please take up the various points with them & send man to Swindon to help Harrison. Hopes he will complete the 3 coaches by end of next week. We note that in spite of our supplying new jaws they [H & N] have sent the original ones with the keyway cut in the wrong position.'

A further batch of questions were answered on 9th January:

'We have a letter from HN informing us that the steel sheet plate on floor was neither shown on our drg & not mentioned on Specfn. & we have written to Mr Churchward to this effect & asked for his instructions.

'Brake pull rods. We have informed HN that we have sent the 3 rods for the coaches now at Swindon & they must obtain the length of these rods from their man & make the remainder (9) & deliver them fitted to the coaches they belong to.

'Regulator Rod Carriers HN say they will supply these if you will let them have particulars. Note you have no particulars. So have instructed HN to apply to Swindon.

'We note that Harrison has not made any return of time worked by GWR man. Mr Beache asked him to keep a careful note of time worked by Ry. Co's man and to check their a/c.'

On 11th January, Harrison advised the office that 'Nº.62 complete as far as we can go. Rest of items on G.W. Motors and not on our drgs &c .'

The London office had corresponded with Hurst, Nelson on the question of supplying regulator connecting rod hanger brackets, for which a specific drawing would be required: 'Have wired Harrison to send sketch. Put 3 sets in hand.' Two days later, Harrison's sketch of the rod hanger arrived. Hurst Nelson confirmed the arrival of the drawings, to which Kerr, Stuart replied: 'We note Harrison sent you sketches of Reg. carriers & informed you at same time that GWR are making & putting these on coaches themselves.'

Although Harrison was doing a good job at Swindon, he may have been overawed by the Great Western works' administration. The London office noticed this, and told Harrison he must not be afraid to ask for what he wants.

It was found necessary to produce a new bend in the vacuum pipe for all the cars. On 24th January, the office wrote to Stoke expressing some concern about the timing: 'Do not think injector pipes for 4th coach can be returned to Stoke as this might delay d/y. Those for 935 – 40 might be.'

The roof cover plate over the boiler also needed adjustment: 'Am telling Harrison to ask HN men to cut away the plate in a similar manner to that done by GWR Co.' However, Hurst Nelson took exception to this, and the office reported the matter to Stoke:

'HN & Co. inform us that carefully checking the dimensions of the roof plates & also their position on the carriages they find that they are in accordance with the drgs supplied to them – there seems to be a variance of opinion. Please look into this further.'

On 26th January, the London office advised that, for the present, the injector pipes had better be left at Swindon. 'Harrison has got some stocks and dies. Not able to try Vacuum pipe bend on a/c of shaking [?]' The office indicated that it was 'Acquiring print of actual position of cover plate'.

The office reported that assembly work was proceeding well, but following 'Mr B's report of a visit to Swindon, had better have 2 gangs working'.

There was a considerable movement of items to Swindon, and not all arrived in a good condition. Churchward wrote to Kerr Stuart on 2nd February with the news that 'The motor boiler recd. here in NS wagon 2787 on 30th ult. had cladding slightly damaged due to packing having shifted & ropes getting slack.'

Occasionally, shortages were discovered. On 10th February, Hurst, Nelson declared 'Coach 64 buffer & spring short. We are not responsible.'

Harrison wrote on 19th February 'that 3 Regulator jaws are required per coach – one at top of down rod & 2 underneath'. Two days later, the office confirmed with Stoke that it 'Noted remarks re. jaws & that you have put it in hand.'

By early March, Harrison had contacted the office and notified them that he only required one man now for the delivery of the remaining coaches.

On 9th March, a problem with the slide valves had materialised, possibly involving the integrity of the steam supply. The Great Western had contacted Kerr, Stuart, but that company seemed reluctant to become involved; the office advised Stoke: 'We want Harrison not to examine slide valves.' They further reported: 'GWR have found it necessary to take out the slide valves of one or two coaches to be scraped'. Some excuse was presumably then given to Churchward, who was not impressed:

'I am in receipt of your letter of yesterday & note that your works people have found it impossible to make the balance strips steam tight. It may be of interest to you to know that it is one of the simplest & commonest forms of balancing & that the making of the strips tight is also one of the simplest & commonest operations at the hands of a decent mechanic.'

Indeed, he found fault with another aspect of Kerr, Stuart's work, and on 15th March made his concern known: 'I find that in each of the cars you have built the head of the boiler buffer & the buffing brackets have not been case hardened in accordance with drgs.'

This apparently involved coaches 61 to 67 inclusive.

In late March, Harrison reported other problems with the new cars: 'Harrison writes that 6 M [6th motor?] steam pipe blowing very bad at middle joint.' And a couple of days later: 'Harrison writes that firebars all loose & short & after "working" tend to fall out.'

On 28th March, the office responded that: 'copy letter sent to Mr Churchward that Centre Boiler Buffers *were* case hardened. Also to replace firebars that were unsatisfactory.'

A serious problem surfaced in May, and Churchward wrote on 26th:

'We are surprised & alarmed to find that the steam pipe flanges on these cars are not properly brazed, but only fastened [?] on the top further from the pipes. Further, that the pipes are not expanded or laid over on the flanges. I regret to say that we have had a case of one blowout nearly killing one man & seriously injuring another in the cab. We have had, of course, to stop all the cars at most serious loss & inconvenience in order to put these pipes right.'

On the other hand, Mr Churchward praised another aspect, and on 11th June the office asked Stoke: 'the white metal used in the axleboxes of our Motor Cars is giving good results. Please give us information as to makers.' The Great Western doubtless wanted to take advantage of a good supplier of a material that could prove troublesome at times.

After this, the problems with the new cars seemed to decrease, and by May 1907, the flow of contract correspondence had largely ceased.

APPENDIX C

SRM WORKING DIAGRAMS, SUMMER 1911

by JOHN LEWIS and JOHN COPSEY

On completion of its SRM-building programme in February 1908, the Great Western had 99 cars in service, plus the Port Talbot vehicle it had acquired in the assumption of control over that company's railway interests during the following month. This number did not remain intact for very long; in July 1914, No.4 was withdrawn for conversion to trailer, a fate that, as we have seen, overtook the majority of the cars in the following years.

During their first eighteen months in traffic – and shortly before the introduction of the auto engines – the following SRM services had been established:

Car Base	*Route*	*Commenced*
Chalford	Stonehouse	12 Oct 03
Southall	Westbourne Park	1 May 04
	West Ealing, Park Royal, Willesden	1 Oct 04
	Brentford	1 May 04
	Clapham Jct., West Ealing (Suns)	16 Apr 05
Lambourn	Lambourn (on hire)	15 May 05
Plymouth	Plympton, Saltash	1 Jun 04
	Yealmpton	1 Jun 04
	Tavistock (Suns)	19 Jun 04
Croes Newydd	Gobowen, Llangollen, Llanuwchllyn	1 Jul 04
(Wrexham)	Coed Poeth	1 Oct 04
	Rhos	1 Oct 04
Ashburton	Totnes	1 Oct 04
Penzance	Truro	1 Oct 04
Honeybourne	Winchcombe	1 Oct 04
Kidderminster	Bewdley, Stourport	1 Jan 05
Stourbridge	Town branch	1 Jan 05
	Old Hill, Halesowen	1 Mar 05
	Langley Green, Oldbury	1 Mar 05
	Stourport (Suns)	2 Apr 05
Chippenham	Calne	1 Feb 05
Truro	Newquay	1 Feb 05
Brynamman	Llandilo	1 Mar 05
Swansea ED	Glyn Neath	3 Apr 05

By the end of April 1905, the first 50 motors were in operation.

There were 60 SRMs in traffic in March 1906, whilst 15 auto engines were tabulated in the four-weekly allocations. Whilst the SRMs continued to increase in numbers, the expansion of auto engines at this time was rather more modest.

SRM services reached their peak after 1908, with 99 SRMs and the Port Talbot motor on the GWR's books, and the years 1909-13 saw the greatest number of scheduled operations. Thereafter, the availability of additional auto engines and trailers – rather more versatile than their railmotor equivalents – spelt the beginning of the end of SRM dominance on 'motor' services on the Great Western. At the same time, conversion of SRMs into trailers began.

In January 1922, there were 57 SRMs available for traffic, but the number of auto engines had increased to 79. With the reduction of SRM numbers, many of their turns were now operated by alternative motive power, and some sheds no longer had any motors allocated.

The following tabular details illustrate the full summer services of 1911, in which the SRM operations were around their zenith. Some 59 SRM diagrams were in operation at this time, as opposed to around 15 auto train services, but the picture would soon change. Although certain services were designated for motors, they were obviously unavailable at times, and were temporarily replaced by conventional trains, or auto units if available. It was also known for SRMs to substitute for an unavailable auto train, but with increasing rarity. The SRMs also operated a number of 'summer only' diagrams.

LONDON DIVISION

In April 1904, the new SRMs Nos.3 and 4 were transferred from Swindon to Southall for their impending suburban duties. These turns began in May 1904 on a new route from Hanwell, running northwards over the West Ealing Loop line to a point just short of Greenford, then turning south-eastwards (over the Greenford East Curve, between the as yet unopened Greenford South and East Junctions) through Perivale to Park Royal. At the latter point it joined the recently-opened section to Old Oak Common, and ran thence along the old main line to Westbourne Park; owing to the congested state of Paddington, it was decided to terminate services at Westbourne Park (apart from Sundays, when space was available at the terminus).

SRM No.17 was also allocated to Southall with effect from 1st May 1904, and may initially have been utilised on the Brentford branch, the motor service over which started on that day. The notice announcing the commencement of that service indicated that parcels (etc.) would be carried; No.17 had a guard/luggage compartment, whereas Nos 3 and 4 did not. However, the Brentford branch soon went over primarily to autotrailer operation.

Building work on the new line towards High Wycombe continued with the opening of the two loops at Greenford – together with its station – in October 1904, and on to Northolt Junction, High Wycombe and beyond in November 1905. It was over the southern part of this new line, to the south of Gerrard's Cross, and on the West Ealing Loop, that the Southall cars found most of their employment. The working diagrams of SRMs (and later, auto trains) from Southall over the 'New Line' via Park Royal (etc.) were each designated by a letter; in due course these letters, in the form of a large metal cut-out, were carried on the front of the appropriate train.

The Lambourn branch, not then owned by the GWR, was also briefly operated by SRMs from 15th May 1904. One car sufficed for the basic service, joined by a second on Thursday and Saturday afternoons. During the 15-month period, five different cars were used over the branch, including Nos.1 and 2.

In July 1905, there were two daily workings from Southall on weekdays, and a third on Saturday afternoons. There were no less than five duties on Sundays, including a number of workings over the West London line.

The Uxbridge High Street branch opened in May 1907, and a service using SRMs was instituted.

Oxford received two cars in January 1908, and these were to be found over the Princes Risborough branch, along the OW & W line to Shipton, the Northern line to Kidlington, with a couple of trips over the Woodstock branch.

A car was allocated to Didcot for main-line trips in April 1911.

1911

In July 1911, SRMs were shedded at Southall, Didcot and Oxford.

Shed	*Cars*
Southall	6, 17, 35 (59 ft); 38, 43, 56, 62 (70 ft)
Didcot	37 (70 ft)
Oxford	41, 82 (59 ft); 97 (70 ft)

Seven cars were allocated to Southall to operate its four weekday diagrams. An auto engine and trailer was also to be seen in the early morning within the Paddington & Southall sector at this time, although this unit was scheduled for the Brentford branch from about 7.15 a.m., releasing Southall SRM 'D' on that line.

The cars were utilised even more fully on Sundays, with six in operation during the afternoon within the Paddington – Clapham Jct. – Victoria – Gerrard's Cross – Southall area. To reach Victoria, the cars ran over the West London line to Longhedge Junction, and then exercised running rights under joint leasing powers over the LC & D line into that station.

Didcot had a 70 ft car for its service over the main lines between Basingstoke, Reading and Oxford, with a spare car shared with Oxford, and located at the latter shed.

Oxford had two 'short' and one 70 ft cars, working for the most part over the main line to the north and over the branch to Princes Risborough.

LONDON DIVISION

SOUTHALL CAR 'A'

Dly	6 48 Southall	West Ealing	6 55
..	6 58 West Ealing	Greenford	7 6
..	7 41 Greenford	Westbourne Park	8 4
..	8 5 Westbourne Park	Greenford & West Ealing	8 36
..	8 52 West Ealing	Willesden	9 5
..	9 10 Willesden	Ruislip	9 43
..	9 58 Ruislip	West Ealing	10 16
..	10 36 West Ealing	Hayes	10 49
..	10 55 Hayes	Southall	11 0
..	11 15 Southall	West Ealing	11 25
..	11 27 West Ealing	Greenford	11 34
SX	12/32 Greenford	Westbourne Park	12/54
..	12/55 Westbourne Park	Greenford & Willesden	1/32
..	1/42 Willesden	West Ealing	1/53
..	2/14 West Ealing	Gerrard's Cross	2/47
..	3/3 Gerrard's Cross	Uxbridge	3/19
..	3/22 Uxbridge	Gerrard's Cross	3/35
..	3/50 Gerrard's Cross	Uxbridge	4/5
..	4/16 Uxbridge	Gerrard's Cross	4/29
..	4/35 Gerrard's Cross	West Ealing	5/1
..	5/23 West Ealing	Greenford	5/34
..	5/35 Greenford	Ealing Broadway	5/43
..	5/46 Ealing Broadway	Greenford	5/58
..	6/3 Greenford	Willesden	6/27
..	6/38 Willesden	Ruislip	7/7
..	7/12 Ruislip	Willesden	7/44
..	8/8 Willesden	Greenford & Westbourne Park	8/49
..	8/50 Westbourne Park	Greenford & West Ealing	9/18
..	9/55 West Ealing	Kensington	10/15
..	10/43 Kensington	Southall	11/10
SO	12/15 Greenford	Southall (Empty)	12/30
..	1/5 Southall	Hayes (Empty)	1/10
..	1/15 Hayes	Westbourne Park	1/41
..	1/50 Westbourne Park	Greenford	2/10
..	2/27 Greenford	Westbourne Park	2/52
..	2/53 Westbourne Park	Bishop's Road (Empty)	3/0
..	3/14 Bishop's Road	Gerrard's Cross	3/59
..	4/14 Gerrard's Cross	Uxbridge	4/29
..	5/28 Uxbridge	Gerrard's Cross	5/41
..	6/5 Gerrard's Cross	Uxbridge	6/20
..	6/25 Uxbridge	Gerrard's Cross	6/38
..	6/55 Gerrard's Cross	Uxbridge	7/7
..	7/32 Uxbridge	Gerrard's Cross	7/45
..	8/57 Gerrard's Cross	Uxbridge	9/12
..	9/20 Uxbridge	Gerrard's Cross	9/33
..	9/48 Gerrard's Cross	West Ealing	10/18
..	10/30 West Ealing	Southall (Empty)	10/38

Mileage: 190 miles 31 chains (SX): 159 miles 17 chains (SO)

SOUTHALL CAR 'B'

Dly	7 25 Southall	Gerrard's Cross	8 1
..	8 9 Gerrard's Cross	Uxbridge	8 20
..	8 22 Uxbridge	Gerrard's Cross	8 35
..	9 10 Gerrard's Cross	Uxbridge	9 25
..	9 40 Uxbridge	Gerrard's Cross	9 53
..	9 55 Gerrard's Cross	Uxbridge	10 10
..	10 25 Uxbridge	Gerrard's Cross	10 38
..	10 46 Gerrard's Cross	Acton	11 23
..	12/8 Acton	Gerrard's Cross	12/52
..	1/10 Gerrard's Cross	Uxbridge	1/25
..	1/35 Uxbridge	Gerrard's Cross	1/48
..	1/57 Gerrard's Cross	West Ealing	2/26
SX	2/43 West Ealing	Willesden	2/57
..	3/8 Willesden	Greenford & Westbourne Park	3/49
..	3/52 Westbourne Park	Greenford	4/16
..	4/25 Greenford	Westbourne Park	4/58
..	5/0 Westbourne Park	Greenford & Acton	5/42
..	6/12 Acton	Greenford	6/26
..	6/46 Greenford	Westbourne Park	7/7
..	7/8 Westbourne Park	Greenford & West Ealing	7/36
..	8/8 West Ealing	Ruislip	8/26
..	8/40 Ruislip	West Ealing	8/58
..	9/28 West Ealing	Gerrard's Cross	9/59
..	10/5 Gerrard's Cross	Uxbridge	10/20
..	10/36 Uxbridge	Gerrard's Cross	10/49
..	11/8 Gerrard's Cross	West Ealing	11/38
WX	11/45 West Ealing	Southall (Empty)	11/53
ThO	12 4 West Ealing	Denham	12 27
..	12 30 Denham	West Ealing & Southall (Empty)	1 0
SO	2/35 West Ealing	Westbourne Park (Empty)	2/47
..	2/50 Westbourne Park	Greenford	3/10
..	3/18 Greenford	Westbourne Park	3/39
..	3/40 Westbourne Park	Greenford & Willesden	4/25
..	4/37 Willesden	Greenford	4/56
..	5/10 Greenford	Westbourne Park	5/32
..	5/34 Westbourne Park	Greenford	5/58
..	6/48 Greenford	West Ealing	6/55
..	7/13 West Ealing	Greenford & Westbourne Park	7/42
..	7/43 Westbourne Park	Greenford & West Ealing	8/11
..	9/6 West Ealing	Greenford & Westbourne Park	9/39
..	9/40 Westbourne Park	Greenford & West Ealing	10/7
..	10/26 West Ealing	Denham	10/48
..	10/52 Denham	West Ealing	11/14
..	11/20 West Ealing	Southall (Empty)	11/28

Mileage: 213 miles 17 chains (WX): 232 miles 41 chains (WO): 213 miles 7 chains (SO)

SOUTHALL CAR 'C'

Dly	7 25 Southall	Ruislip	7 48
..	7 56 Ruislip	Greenford	8 9
..	8 39 Greenford	Westbourne Park	8 47
..	8 48 Westbourne Park	Greenford	9 5
..	9 18 Greenford	Westbourne Park	9 38
..	9 39 Westbourne Park	West Ealing	9 51
..	10 5 West Ealing	Westbourne Park	10 18
..	10 40 Westbourne Park	Greenford	11 0
..	11/37 Greenford	Westbourne Park	11 59
..	12/0 Westbourne Park	Greenford	12/20
SX	1/27 Greenford	Westbourne Park	1/49
..	1/50 Westbourne Park	Greenford	2/10
..	3/18 Greenford	Westbourne Park	3/39
..	3/40 Westbourne Park	Greenford & Willesden	4/25
..	4/37 Willesden	Greenford	4/56
..	5/10 Greenford	Westbourne Park	5/32
..	5/34 Westbourne Park	West Ealing	5/56
..	6/0 West Ealing	Westbourne Park (Empty)	6/12
..	6/14 Westbourne Park	West Ealing	6/36
..	7/13 West Ealing	Greenford & Westbourne Park	7/42
..	7/43 Westbourne Park	Greenford & West Ealing	8/11
..	9/6 West Ealing	Greenford & Westbourne Park	9/39
..	9/40 Westbourne Park	Greenford & West Ealing	10/7
..	10/26 West Ealing	Denham	10/48
..	10/52 Denham	West Ealing	11/14
..	11/20 West Ealing	Southall (Empty)	11/28
SO	12/32 Greenford	Westbourne Park	12/54
..	12/55 Westbourne Park	Greenford & Willesden	1/32
..	1/42 Willesden	West Ealing	1/53
..	2/14 West Ealing	Gerrard's Cross	2/47
..	3/3 Gerrard's Cross	Uxbridge	3/19
..	3/22 Uxbridge	Gerrard's Cross	3/35
..	3/50 Gerrard's Cross	Uxbridge	4/5
..	4/16 Uxbridge	Gerrard's Cross	4/29
..	4/35 Gerrard's Cross	West Ealing	5/1
..	5/5 West Ealing	Ruislip	5/23
..	5/52 Ruislip	Willesden	6/27
..	6/38 Willesden	Ruislip	7/7
..	7/12 Ruislip	Willesden	7/44
..	8/8 Willesden	Greenford & Westbourne Park	8/49
..	8/52 Westbourne Park	Greenford & West Ealing	9/18
..	9/55 West Ealing	Kensington	10/15
..	10/43 Kensington	Southall	11/10

Mileage: 190 miles 22 chains (SX): 207 miles 72 chains (SO)

SOUTHALL CAR 'D'

Dly	5 45 Southall	Brentford & return	6 9
..	6 15 Southall	Brentford & return	6 39
..	6 45 Southall	Brentford & return	7 9
..	7 53 Southall	Willesden	8 11
..	8 23 Willesden	Ruislip	8 51
..	9 11 Ruislip	West Ealing	9 28
..	9 33 West Ealing	Greenford & Westburne Park	10 9
..	10 10 Westbourne Park	Acton (Empty)	10 16
..	10 27 Acton	Gerrard's Cross	11 0
..	11 6 Gerrard's Cross	Uxbridge	11 22
..	11 40 Uxbridge	Gerrard's Cross	11 53
..	12/0nn Gerrard's Cross	West Ealing	12/30
SX	1/15 West Ealing	Greenford	1/24
..	2/27 Greenford	Westbourne Park	2/49
..	2/50 Westbourne Park	Greenford	3/10
..	3/34 Greenford	Ruislip	3/46
..	4/20 Ruislip	Acton	4/44
..	4/58 Acton	Gerrard's Cross	5/34
..	6/5 Gerrard's Cross	Uxbridge	6/20
..	6/25 Uxbridge	Gerrard's Cross	6/38
..	6/55 Gerrard's Cross	Uxbridge	7/7
..	7/32 Uxbridge	Gerrard's Cross	7/45
..	8/57 Gerrard's Cross	Uxbridge	9/12
..	9/20 Uxbridge	Gerrard's Cross	9/33
..	9/48 Gerrard's Cross	West Ealing	10/18
..	10/30 West Ealing	Southall (Empty)	10/38
SO	1/15 West Ealing	Greenford & Westbourne Park	1/52
..	2/15 Westbourne Park	Greenford & Willesden	2/57
..	3/8 Willesden	Greenford & Westbourne Park	3/49
..	3/52 Westbourne Park	Greenford	4/16
..	4/25 Greenford	Westbourne Park	4/58
..	5/0 Westbourne Park	Greenford & Acton	5/42
..	6/12 Acton	Greenford	6/26
..	6/46 Greenford	Westbourne Park	7/7
..	7/8 Westbourne Park	Greenford & West Ealing	7/36
..	8/8 West Ealing	Ruislip	8/26
..	8/40 Ruislip	West Ealing	8/58
..	9/28 West Ealing	Gerrard's Cross	9/59
..	10/5 Gerrard's Cross	Uxbridge	10/20
..	10/36 Uxbridge	Gerrard's Cross	10/49
..	11/8 Gerrard's Cross	West Ealing	11/38
..	12 4 West Ealing	Denham	12 27
..	12 30 Denham	West Ealing & Southall (Empty)	1 0

Mileage: 184 miles 61 chains(SX): 246 miles 62 chains (SO)

SRM TRAILERS (SO)

No 1 7 50 Southall — West Ealing (at rear)
Car 'D' 1/15 Ealing until 8/15 Greenford
Car 'C' 8/27 Greenford until finish

No 2 7 50 Southall — West Ealing (at rear)
Car 'B' 2/35 West Ealing until 10/7 West Ealing

Nos 3/- Car 'A' 1/15 Southall until finishh

DIDCOT CAR

Dly	10 5 Didcot	Reading	10 50
..	11 5 Reading	Oxford	12 /25
..	2/18 Oxford	Reading	3/35
..	4/25 Reading	Basingstoke	5/5
..	5/35 Basingstoke	Reading	6/15
..	7/7 Reading	Didcot	7/52

Mileage: 120 miles 22 chains

NOTE
Spare car for Didcot service will be stabled at Oxford

OXFORD CAR 'A'

ThX	8 12 Oxford	Heyford	8 44
..	9 20 Heyford	Oxford	9 52
ThO	9 24 Oxford	Kidlington	9 39
..	9 41 Kidlington	Oxford	9 55
Dly	10 25 Oxford	Wheatley	10 51
..	11 3 Wheatley	Oxford	11 38
..	12/17 Oxford	Heyford	12/48
..	12/53 Heyford	Oxford	1/25
..	1/57 Oxford	Blenheim & Woodstock	2/19
..	2/50 Blenheim & Woodstock	Oxford	3/15
..	5/35 Oxford	Kidlington	5/49
..	5/55 Kidlington	Oxford	6/10

Mileage: 92 miles 26 chains (ThX): 79 miles 70 chains (ThO)

OXFORD CAR 'B'

Dly	1/5 Oxford	Princes Risborough	2/5
..	2/13 Princes Risborough	Wheatley	2/49
..	3/3 Wheatley	Oxford	3/30
..	4/3 Oxford	Kidlington	4/19
..	4/23 Kidlington	Oxford	4/38
..	4/50 Oxford	Princes Risborough	5/55
..	6/30 Princes Risborough*	Thame	6/50
..	7/10 Thame*	Oxford	7/57
ThSO	8/50 Oxford	Princes Risborough	9/54
..	10/20 Princes Risborough	Oxford	11/25
ThSX	8/50 Oxford	Thame	9/36
	9/45 Thame	Oxford	10/32

Mileage: 125 miles 66 chains (ThSX): 137 miles 28 chains (ThSO)

NOTES
* Milk Truck Aylesbury to Oxford
Cars to be strengthened with ordinary stock as required by Oxford
Cars to work with engines towards London

Later Years

Southall

The SRMs were operating similar diagrams in summer 1912, although their trips to Willesden and over the Kensington line had been discontinued. In summer 1913 there were five daily SRM diagrams over and between the two main lines, whilst on Sundays, six motors were in operation, five of which visited Victoria or Clapham Junction.

In the summer of 1922, scheduled SRM services from Southall had decreased to just one car, primarily for the Gerrard's Cross & Uxbridge (High St.) service, whilst the remainder of the intensive services were now worked by autocars.

The SRMs operated two turns daily from Southall in September 1929: Car 'A', again largely over the Gerrard's Cross and Uxbridge line, Car 'F' (SX) mostly on the Northolt, Westbourne Park and Ealing routes, and Car 'K' (SO) on a similar working. In September 1931, Car 'A' again worked the Uxbridge (High St) duty, with a second car running duty 'E' (SX) until 30th April 1932, and 'F' (SX) from 2nd May of that year; both the latter duties covered the Ealing, Northolt/Ruislip and Westbourne Park routes.

In the summer of 1933, the Uxbridge (High St.) diagram was still nominally held by an SRM, though auto cars were increasingly used on the other turns.

During 1934, SRMs Nos.30, 91, 97 and 98 were at Southall, by which time the 'Oil Engine Rail Car' in the form of No.1 had appeared on the scene. The last motor at Southall was No.98, which was taken out of service on 18th April 1935.

Slough

In October 1912, the petrol-electric car No.100 was apparently in use at Slough, running extra trips over the Windsor branch; although the car was not specifically nominated, a poster shows 'Rail Motor – One class only'. Slough received an SRM for the Windsor branch services in March 1913; starting with the 10.45 a.m. Slough, the car worked 14 return trips daily, supplementing the conventional trains. It is likely that the SRM either covered for, or replaced, No.100.

From about January 1916, ordinary stock would seem to have been used on the Windsor branch workings, although a motor was shown as being present until December 1919.

SRMs returned to Slough in summer 1929, with the coach programme of September 1929 showing 15 return trips on weekdays, and 9 on Sundays. The motors, Nos. 54 and 64, provided a short-lived service on the Windsor branch, incorporating a call at the newly-opened Chalvey Halt. They left Slough in August 1930.

Reading

Although the first SRM at Reading arrived in the spring of 1914, the presence was short. It was not until 1921 that a permanent working allocation was established, and two motors worked services to Maidenhead, Henley-on-Thames, Basingstoke and Didcot.

By the late 1920s, 2-car auto trains were scheduled for these duties, although a motor remained on the allocation. Reading held No.39, later changed to No.37, until November 1934, probably as a backup to its fleet of autocars.

Basingstoke housed an SRM in the spring and summer of 1914, commencing a diagram with the 9.32 a.m. to Reading, working on the Henley branch as well as trips over the Basingstoke line.

Didcot

The Didcot SRM's services over the main line ceased in the early months of the Great War, and the car was transferred away in March 1915.

Oxford

As with the Didcot motors, the Oxford allocation terminated in early 1915.

BRISTOL DIVISION

The first SRM duty in the Bristol Division was over the Chippenham & Calne branch, commencing on 1st February 1905, in place of the former 3-coach four-wheel train. Motor No.42, then No.21, was transferred in to Chippenham for this duty initially.

In the spring of 1905, Nos.3 and 5 were sent to Trowbridge for local services around the area, including trips over the Warminster, Devizes and Bath lines.

Also in April 1905, Weymouth received Nos.38 and 51 for the local services to Dorchester.

Bath was provided with a motor at this time for main-line duties.

The Dia. E cars – Nos.15 and 16 – were sent to Frome in the autumn of 1905 for duties on the new line via Charlton Mackrell, although the service may have been operated by GW-built cars before this. The Dia. E motors were soon replaced on this line by 'conventional' SRMs.

By May 1907, there were seven daily workings in the division, utilising cars from Trowbridge (2), Frome (2), Bath, Chippenham and Weymouth.

The first Trowbridge SRM started with the 6.5 a.m. (MX) to Warminster, and worked throughout the day on a Patney, Lavington, Devizes & Westbury schedule, whilst the second commenced as the 6.35 a.m. to Devizes, and thereafter ran out as far as Bath, Calne, and Frome.

From its departure as the 6.30 a.m. to Bristol, the first of the Frome motors then operated within the Chippenham, Patney, and Trowbridge area until it returned to its home shed in the late afternoon. The second motor worked the 8.47 a.m. to Bridgwater, then covered part of the Castle Cary & Taunton service with the Taunton motor.

The Bath motor started at 6.15 a.m. and ran variously to Bristol, Chipping Sodbury (via Filton) and Trowbridge. Chippenham's motor generally worked over the Calne branch, and out as far as Bath and Trowbridge.

In the south, the Weymouth SRM ran the 7.40 a.m. to Abbotsbury and back, then the nine return trips of the Dorchester schedule. The former branch was mainly operated by an auto train.

It does not appear that any allocation of SRMs to Swindon was made specifically to carry out any regular workings, but one regular Monday afternoon turn to Cirencester was largely the preserve of the motors. These trips were doubtless worked by cars in Swindon Stock, or perhaps before entering or after emerging from the factory. They were certainly operating the 2.10 p.m. turn from Swindon in May 1907, and continued to do so afterwards.

In May 1909, motor No.67, followed in June by No.76, were transferred to Bristol, primarily for services around the city, but including the Portishead and Clevedon branches.

Yatton received a car, No.34, in September 1909, and this worked on main-line and Clevedon branch trips.

SRM services over the Camerton branch (and beyond) commenced on Monday, 9th May 1910.

1911

SRMs were allocated to the following sheds in July 1911 for workings around the division:

Shed	*Cars*
Bath	30, 42 (59 ft)
Bristol	12 (59 ft); 44, 46 (70 ft); 80 (59 ft)
Frome	10, 78 (59 ft)
Radstock	81 (59 ft)
Trowbridge	26, 76, 79 (59 ft)
Weymouth	40 (70 ft); 75 (59 ft); 86 (70 ft)
Yatton	48 (70 ft)

Swindon Stock shed held a couple, from which the Monday Cirencester working was probably operated, whilst there were invariably a few in the factory:

Swindon Stock	1, 4
Swindon Works	13, 16, 25, 27, 29, 53, 63, 67, 83, 89

Bath had two of the shorter cars for its pair of duties out as far as Bristol, Chipping Sodbury, Clevedon, Swindon and Trowbridge. On Sundays, both cars were in operation, working from Bath to Winterbourne and Charlton Mackrell in one case, and to Winterbourne and Avonmouth in the other.

Bristol had two duties, and was provided with two 59 ft and two 70 ft cars. The workings were mostly in the local area, although one car did make its way to Devizes and Trowbridge. On Sundays, two cars worked on the afternoon Clifton Down service, each running seven return trips.

The two cars at Frome were both of the shorter variety, one of which was used on the Bridgwater/Taunton service via Durston, and the other on a Patney, Warminster and Hungerford diagram.

Radstock was provided with a 59 ft vehicle for use over the Camerton branch, though with forays through to Trowbridge and Westbury.

Three of the motors were allocated to Trowbridge for the two workings. The first ran as far as Bath, Chippenham, Patney and Frome, whilst the second operated out to Bristol, Calne and Patney. Two cars (each with a trailer) were used on Sundays, the first on a Bristol, Portishead, Bath and Salisbury diagram, and the other a Bristol, Westbury, Chippenham and Bath turn; the former car stayed overnight at Salisbury and commenced its Monday duty with a trip to Trowbridge to take up the usual weekday working.

Weymouth had one SRM and one auto duty, both of which were involved with Upwey, Abbotsbury and Dorchester working, though the motor carried out more runs to Dorchester, leaving the Abbotsbury branch to be covered more by the auto. The motor was used on Sundays for various return trips to Abbotsbury, Dorchester and Maiden Newton.

It is reasonable to suppose that the Yatton car had been provided for working along one of the adjacent branch lines, but in 1911 its duties took it out along the main line to Bath and Swindon, calling at Avonmouth on the way back. On Sundays, however, it did find work on the Clevedon branch from 11.25 a.m. until the late evening.

BRISTOL DIVISION

TROWBRIDGE CAR 'A'

MO	5.55 Salisbury	Westbury	6.53
..	7.50 Westbury	Trowbridge	7.58
	(from Sunday working - Trailer attached)		
Dly	8.36 Trowbridge	Bath	9.10
..	9.35 Bath	Frome	10.44
..	10.52 Frome	Westbury	11.3
WO	11.36 Westbury	Frome	11.47
..	12/20 Frome	Westbury	12/52
Dly	12/35 Westbury	Devizes	1/20
MWO	2/20 Devizes	Trowbridge	2/48
..	3/20 Trowbridge	Chippenham	3/51
..	4/10 Chippenham	Trowbridge	4/38
..	4/50 Trowbridge	Chippenham	5/10
..	6/10 Chippenham	Trowbridge	6/41
MWX	2/20 Devizes	Westbury	3/2
ThSO	3/6 Westbury	Warminster	3/17
..	3/55 Warminster	Westbury	4/5
MWX	4/15 Westbury	Patney	5/5
..	5/44 Patney	Westbury	6/16
..	6/40 Westbury	Patney	7/32
..	8/27 Patney	Trowbridge	9/15
..	9/35 Trowbridge	Devizes	10/05
..	10/40 Devizes	Trowbridge	11/10

Mileage: 143 miles 13 chains (MO); 153 miles 29 chains (TFO)
126 miles 6 chains (WO); 162 miles 59 chains (ThSO)

TROWBRIDGE CAR 'B'

Dly	7.12 Trowbridge §‡	Bristol	8.17
..	8.30 Bristol §	Chippenham	9.31
..	10.10 Chippenham §	Trowbridge	10.43
..	10.52 Trowbridge	Chippenham	11.20
..	12/20 Chippenham	Calne	12/35
MWO	1/15 Calne	Westbury	2/15
..	2/25 Westbury	Lavington	2/45
..	3/12 Lavington	Westbury	3/30
..	4/15 Westbury	Patney	5/5
..	5/44 Patney	Westbury	6/16
..	6/40 Westbury	Patney	7/32
..	8/27 Patney	Trowbridge	9/15
..	9/35 Trowbridge	Devizes	10/5
..	10/40 Devizes	Trowbridge	11/10
MWX	1/15 Calne	Trowbridge	2/1
..	3/20 Trowbridge	Chippenham	3/51
..	4/10 Chippenham	Trowbridge	4/38
..	4/50 Trowbridge	Chippenham	5/20
..	6/10 Chippenham	Trowbridge	6/41
SO	8/16 Trowbridge §	Devizes	8/45
..	9/30 Devizes	Trowbridge	10/2

Mileage: 198 miles 26 chains (MWO); 142 miles 15 chains (TThFO)
164 miles 51 chains (SO)

NOTES
§ with Trailer
‡ with Third from Bath (MO)

FROME CAR 'A'

Dly	7.55 Frome §	Bridgwater	9.48
..	11.35 Bridgwater	Castle Cary	12/52
..	2/12 Castle Cary	Taunton	3/20
..	3/30 Taunton	Frome	6/5

Mileage: 139 miles 34 chains
NOTE
§ with Third (MThO)

FROME CAR 'B'

Dly	6.45 Frome ‡	Devizes	7.46
..	7.55 Devizes	Westbury	8.37
..	9.10 Westbury	Patney (via Lavington)	9.43
..	10.3 Patney	Warminster (via Lavington)	10.57
..	11.23 Warminster	Savernake	12/58
..	1/30 Savernake	Hungerford	1/50
..	2/7 Hungerford	Frome (via Devizes)	4/12

Mileage: 159 miles 42 chains
NOTE
‡ Set 222 (Brake Third & Compo. 4/6-wheel stock) attached Holt to Devizes

BATH CAR 'A'

Dly	6.16 Bath	Chipping Sodbury	7.37
..	7.45 Chipping Sodbury	Bristol	8.20
..	9.50 Bristol	Swindon	11.46
..	1/0 Swindon	Bath	2/48
..	3/30 Bath	Chippenham	4/3
..	5/3 Chippenham	Bath	5/36
..	6/21 Bath	Yatton	7/31
..	8/28 Yatton	Clevedon	8/36
..	Clevedon	Yatton	8/55
..	9/5 Yatton	Clevedon	9/13
..	9/17 Clevedon	Bristol	10/12
SX	10/20 Bristol	Bath	10/50
SO	11/30 Bristol	Bath	11/8

Mileage: 195 miles 18 chains

BATH CAR 'B'

MO	5.45 Bath	Chippenham	6.15
..	6.31 Chippenham	Bath	7.2
Dly	7.7 Bath	Bristol	7.56
..	7.58 Bristol	Patchway & return	8.30
..	9.15 Bristol	Bath	9.40
..	11.47 Bath	Nailsea	1/1
..	1/5 Nailsea	Chipping Sodbury	2/42
..	3/18 Chipping Sodbury	Bath	5/0
..	5/27 Bath	Trowbridge	6/2
..	8/12 Trowbridge	Bristol	9/23
..	9/40 Bristol	Bath	10/10
SO	11/15 Bath	Chippenham	11/47
..	Chippenham	Bath (Empty)	12.22

Mileage: 201 miles 34 chains (MSO); 149 miles 66 chains (T-F)
NOTE
Services with Trailer throughout

WEYMOUTH CAR

Dly	7.40 Weymouth	Abbotsbury	8.4
..	8.23 Abbotsbury	Weymouth	8.47
..	9.10 Weymouth	Upwey Jct. & return	9.35
..	9.54 Weymouth	Dorchester	10.14
..	10.30 Dorchester	Weymouth	10.52
..	11.5 Weymouth	Dorchester	11.27
..	11.45 Dorchester	Weymouth	12/5
..	12/15 Weymouth	Dorchester	12.37
..	1/10 Dorchester	Weymouth	1/30
..	2/30 Weymouth	Dorchester	2/52
..	3/15 Dorchester	Weymouth	3/35
..	3/50 Weymouth	Dorchester	4/12
..	4/30 Dorchester	Weymouth	4/50
..	5/5 Weymouth	Dorchester	5/27
..	5/40 Dorchester	Weymouth	6/0
..	6/25 Weymouth	Dorchester	6/47
..	7/8 Dorchester	Weymouth	7/28
..	7/42 Weymouth	Dorchester	8/4
..	8/15 Dorchester	Weymouth	8/35
..	9/20 Weymouth	Dorchester	9/43
..	9/50 Dorchester	Weymouth	10/13
..	11/15 Weymouth	Dorchester	11/38
..	11/45 Dorchester	Weymouth	12.7

Mileage: 161 miles 6 chains

RADSTOCK CAR

Dly	8.0 Radstock	Hallatrow	8.13
..	8.16 Hallatrow	Limpley Stoke	8.50
..	10.0 Lompley Stoke	Hallatrow	10.37
..	10.55 Hallatrow	Trowbridge	11/51
..	12/5 Trowbridge	Hallatrow	1/0
..	1/20 Hallatrow	Westbury	2/26
..	2/45 Westbury	Hallatrow	3/55
..	4/8 Hallatrow	Limpley Stoke	4/40
..	5/0 Limpley Stoke	Hallatrow	5/35
..	5/50 Hallatrow	Camerton	6/0
..	6/15 Camerton	Radstock	6/50

Mileage: 141 miles 18 chains

YATTON CAR

Dly	11.20 Yatton	Bath	12/22
..	1/31 Bath	Swindon	2/44
..	3/15 Swindon	Bristol	5/7
..	7/8 Bristol	Avonmouth (via Filton Jct.)	7/42
..	8/50 Avonmouth	Yatton (via Filton Jct.)	10/6

Mileage: 132 miles 4 chains

BRISTOL CAR 'A'

Dly	4.55 Bristol	Keynsham (Empty)	5.7
..	5.26 Keynsham	Bristol	5.42
..	6.50 Bristol	Lawrence Hill (Empty)	6.55
..	7.3 Lawrence Hill	Avonmouth	7.40
..	8.5 Avonmouth	Filton Jct	8.27
..	8.32 Filton Jct	Avonmouth	8.53
..	9.25 Avonmouth	Lawrence Hill	10.0
..	10.20 Lawrence Hill	Avonmouth	10.53
..	11.0 Avonmouth	Lawrence Hill	11.33
..	12/33 Lawrence Hill	Avonmouth	1/5
..	1/40 Avonmouth	Lawrence Hill	2/13
..	2/25 Lawrence Hill	Avonmouth	3/3
WO	3/15 Avonmouth	Lawrence Hill	3/49
..	3/55 Lawrence Hill	Avonmouth	4/30
Dly	4/50 Avonmouth	Lawrence Hill	5/23
..	5/40 Lawrence Hill	Avonmouth	6/18
..	6/30 Avonmouth	Bristol	7/10
..	7/30 Bristol	Clifton Down	7/46
..	7/55 Clifton Down	Bristol	8/11
..	8/20 Bristol	Saltford & return	9/11
WX	9/15 Bristol	Portishead	9/50
..	10/0 Portishead	Bristol	10/35
WO	9/30 Bristol	Winterbourne	9/57
..	10/10 Winterbourne	Bristol	10/35
Dly	10/45 Bristol	Clifton Down	11/2
..	11/10 Clifton Down	Bristol	11/25

Mileage: 215 miles 72 chains (WO); 199 54 chains (WX)
NOTE
Trailer attached when required

BRISTOL CAR 'B'

Dly	8.25 Bristol	Pilning	8/55
..	9.5 Pilning	Portishead	10/20
..	10.30 Portishead	Bristol	11/3
..	11/13 Bristol	Portishead	11/44
..	11/52 Portishead	Bristol	12/25
SX	1/15 Bristol	Keynsham	1/29
SO	1/15 Bristol	Saltford	1/35
..	1/39 Saltford	Keynsham (Empty)	1/45
Dly	2/35 Keynsham	Bristol	2/49
..	3/12 Bristol ‡	Devizes	4/42
..	5/29 Devizes	Trowbridge	5/55
..	6/18 Trowbridge	Bath	6/53
..	8/12 Bath	Chippenham	8/45
..	8/55 Chippenham §	Bristol	10/02
ThO	10/10 Bristol	Pilning	10/45
..	Pilning	Bristol	11/27
SO	10/20 Bristol	Bath	10/50
..	11/6 Bath	Bristol	11/35

Mileage: 177 miles 49 chains (ThO); 195 miles 69 chains (SO)
168 miles 7 chains (M-W, F

NOTES
Trailer attached to services
‡ with Third to Bath (SO)
§ with Brake Third

SWINDON CAR

MO	2/10 Swindon	Cirencester	2/47
..	4/0 Cirencester	Swindon	4/40

Mileage: 35 miles 70 chains

Later Years

Trowbridge

By the autumn of 1914, auto trains had taken over the two former daily SRM duties at Trowbridge, although motors were still present there. On Sundays, the motor (with a trailer) was used for a round trip to Bristol, Westbury, Chippenham and Bath.

In the later part of the Great War, this was changed to an afternoon trip to Keinton Mandeville and back, formerly operated by a Bath motor.

By 1920, this Sunday duty was scheduled for a Trowbridge auto, though an SRM remained until July 1922. The shed closed in June 1923.

Bath

In October 1914, one Bath SRM carried out an early visit to Bristol and Chipping Sodbury, a late morning trip to Portishead and Chipping Sodbury, and an evening sequence between Bath, Trowbridge and Bristol. The second motor ran to Bristol and Patchway, and to Swindon, an afternoon return trip to Chippenham, with an evening journey to Bristol and Avonmouth. On Sundays, an SRM was used on trips from Bath to Winterbourne and Charlton Mackrell.

By January 1919 the one Bath working had been simplified to operations between Bristol, Chippenham and Trowbridge. Gone were the trips around the Badminton cut-off to Chipping Sodbury, and there was no longer a Sunday working.

In summer 1920, the motor ran to Pilning, Portishead, and Calne, with an evening sequence between Chippenham, Bristol and Clifton Down, with Trailer 79 attached. By 1923, the evening sequence was between Chippenham, Trowbridge and Bristol.

By 1928, the single Bath car ran to Bristol, Chippenham (and Calne) and Swindon, with an evening run to Trowbridge, terminating for the day at Bristol (St. Philip's Marsh). This was balanced by the Bristol car, which ended the day at Bath.

The allocation at Bath ended in September 1929 with the transfer of No.92, although working of the Bristol/Bath pair continued, with both nominally allocated to Bristol. The working continued into the winter of 1930/31, and probably a little beyond, though it had ceased by summer 1933.

Bristol

Bristol's 1912 motor duties were similar to those of 1911, with trailers again much in evidence. They were not utilised on Sundays at this time. The SRM workings of October 1914 were again of a very local nature, much as they had been in 1911, with one venturing no further afield than Bath, though the second did reach Devizes and Trowbridge in the evening.

In January 1919, the single Bristol motor diagram covered trips to Bath, Pilning and Portishead, with an afternoon sequence over the Calne branch, and in the evening to Bath.

Bristol's SRM spent most of its day away from the city and environs in summer 1920, running out to Bath, Chippenham (and Calne), and Trowbridge. Trailer No.83 was scheduled to be attached.

During summer 1922, there were two motor diagrams in operation again. The first covered an area encompassed by Swindon, Calne, Devizes and Trowbridge, with little time spent in or around Bristol, whilst the second duty at Bristol worked out to Calne, Swindon and Clevedon.

The years up to 1928 saw a gradual erosion of SRM duties in the division, and by the summer of that year there was one which ran to Bath and back with a Third and Van in tow, then continued with trips to Severn Beach and Portishead before running out to Calne and Trowbridge, ending the day at Bath.

By September 1930, the SRM workings had been reduced to the alternating Bristol/Bath pair, stationed at SPM. This ceased soon afterwards.

Motors were present at St. Philip's Marsh throughout 1934, with the last one – No.92 – leaving in July 1935.

Frome

During 1912, Frome's SRM duties were still much as in 1911, and little changed up to the outbreak of war in 1914.

By January 1918, one of Frome's two duties (the easterly, towards Newbury, etc.) was now worked by an auto, but the motor continued with the Taunton diagram, although now running no further north than Durston.

A major rearrangement had occurred by the summer of 1920, with both duties again worked by SRMs. The first operated to Trowbridge, Devizes, Bath, Patney and Warminster, whilst the second carried out trips to Bridgwater, Durston, Castle Cary and Westbury.

By summer 1922, the easterly duty had again been taken over by an auto train, whilst the SRM continued with the Bridgwater and Taunton diagram.

In the summer of 1928, the motor was still scheduled to work the Taunton turn, although autos were increasingly to be seen. The last SRM at Frome was No.80 which left in October 1928. Both Frome diagrams were marked for auto trains by September 1930.

Weymouth

A change in arrangements at Weymouth by October 1914 saw two SRMs operating both the Abbotsbury and Dorchester duties on weekdays, with one car on duties to Bridport and Dorchester on Sundays.

In January 1919, the Weymouth motor now divided its day between Abbotsbury and Dorchester turns, though a Thursdays-only trip saw the car at Bridport. An auto train worked the duty by October 1919.

Reinstatement of two cars had taken place by summer 1920, and the two motors shared the Abbotsbury and Dorchester trains. A trip to Yeovil was also included. On Sundays, an auto now worked the Dorchester turn.

By summer 1922, an auto train had once more taken over one of the Abbotsbury and Dorchester diagrams, leaving a motor on the Abbotsbury, Yeovil and Dorchester turn. The last recorded SRM at Weymouth was No.69, which left in December 1923.

Thereafter, Weymouth duties were scheduled entirely for auto and non-auto engine/trailer combinations, with all five of the turns visiting Dorchester in the summer of 1928, for so long the preserve of the SRMs. However, a Sunday afternoon duty from Weymouth at this time is shown for an SRM, working an extensive service to Dorchester, though it is probable that this was a misprint in the coach programme, and it was worked by an auto, unless a car from elsewhere was utilised.

Yatton

In October 1914, Yatton had two SRM diagrams, running largely on the Clevedon branch, but with a trip to Cheddar, and another to Swindon, as previously. On Sundays, one car worked on the Clevedon branch.

Yatton's two cars still worked the Clevedon and Swindon turns in January 1919, though the mileage had dropped considerably from the prewar diagrams. One ran solely to Swindon and back (with trailer), whilst the other worked six return trips to Clevedon. These continued into the early 1920s, and in 1922 the Clevedon motor additionally worked out to Blagdon and Bristol in addition to six branch trips. One car was in operation in summer 1923, running nine (ten on Saturdays) return trips down the branch, with Trailer No.85 attached when required.

The Yatton car in 1928 was again largely involved in Clevedon branch duties, working seven return trips (eight on Saturdays), though with an afternoon trip to Blagdon incorporated. On Sundays, the car was utilised for Blagdon, Clevedon and Cheddar trips, followed by the four afternoon and evening return runs over the Clevedon branch.

The last regular allocation of motors to Yatton occurred in 1930, with No.65 leaving in August after a fairly long association (some twenty months). However, cars were still seen over the Clevedon line, and No.82 (SPM) worked the branch on Sunday, 28th August 1932.

It is likely that, by July 1933, the Yatton & Clevedon service was mostly operated by more 'conventional' means, or by an auto. The SRM working was still shown in the divisional coach programme at the time for 'Car No.65, chain fitted', although it had moved away from Yatton three years previously.

However, this was not quite the end of the SRMs – No.77 was shedded at Yatton in April 1934, possibly for the Clevedon branch duty.

Radstock

In October 1911, the car worked the Trowbridge and Westbury trips as in the summer schedule, but by February 1912 there were just four trips along the Camerton branch only. In the summer of 1912, the motor took up two return trips to Trowbridge.

By October 1914, the 'off-branch' workings had been reduced to one early afternoon return trip to Trowbridge.

The last allocation was in February 1915; a *Suspension and Alteration of Ordinary Passenger Trains* notice of 22nd March 1915 indicates 'Rail Motor Car Service Suspended'.

For a service that lasted for less than five years, the Camerton branch saw a remarkable number of the SRMs over its metals: no less than 23 different motors were allocated to Radstock over the currency of operations.

Swindon

The Monday afternoon Swindon to Cirencester trip with an SRM continued to October 1914, though it was suspended shortly afterwards. The service was re-introduced in the post-Great War years as a normal passenger turn.

Yeovil

SRM No.68 was transferred to Yeovil in October 1921 for working the 11.30 a.m. trip to Durston (via Martock), the 1.25 p.m. Durston return, then the 2.50 p.m. Yeovil to Hungerford, 5.55 p.m. Hungerford to Westbury and the 8.10 p.m. Westbury to Yeovil. This working continued until September 1923.

EXETER DIVISION

SRMs did not work regularly within the Exeter Division at the very beginning, though in the summer of 1905 a motor service between Exeter and Teignmouth was introduced. In March 1908, the motor ran six return trips between St. Thomas and Teignmouth, starting at 7.50 a.m., one early evening return journey to Dawlish, and finished with the 9.40 p.m. St. David's to Newton and the 10.55 p.m. return.

Newton Abbot had dealt with a number of SRMs during 1904, though primarily as the works and headquarters of the Loco Division. It did appear to have one or two on an operational basis in 1904/5, and these may have been cover for the Exeter and the Ashburton branch services; although the latter lay in the neighbouring Plymouth Traffic Division, it was a lot closer to Newton than to Plymouth.

Taunton received its first motor in the summer of 1906, and by May 1907 it was working out as the 8.25 a.m. Taunton to Castle Cary, returning to Bridgwater on the first trip, running the 3.55 p.m. Castle Cary to Durston and return on the second, and the 7.55 p.m. Castle Cary to Taunton on the final leg.

1911

The allocation within the Exeter Division for July 1911 was:

Shed	*Cars*
Exeter	94 (70 ft)
Newton Abbot	24 (59 ft); 58 (70 ft)
Taunton	23 (59 ft); 91 (70 ft)

SRMs in the area could be dealt with at Newton works, as was the case at this time:

Newton Abbot Works	72

The Taunton motor's working was much the same as in 1907, with visits to Bridgwater and Durston on succeeding trips from Castle Cary.

Exeter's allocation comprised one 70 ft SRM for the St. Thomas & Teignmouth service, and the eight return trips (though one to Dawlish only) amassed a total of over 220 miles during the day, the approximate equivalent of a run between Paddington and Plymouth (via Lavington).

Newton's diagram shows that the motor spent the whole day running between various locations along the Kingswear branch, and included a trip to Brixham. During the turn, the motor made only two intermediate visits to Newton.

EXETER DIVISION

EXETER CAR

Dly	7.45 Exeter	Teignmouth	8.24
..	8.32 Teignmouth	St. Thomas	9.8
..	9.40 St. Thomas	Teignmouth	10.14
..	10.20 Teignmouth	St. Thomas	10.56
..	11.35 St. Thomas	Teignmouth	12/9
..	12/25 Teignmouth	St. Thomas	12/56
..	1/1 St. Thomas	Teignmouth	1/37
..	3/7 Teignmouth	St. Thomas	3/43
..	4/15 St. Thomas	Teignmouth	4/49
..	5/20 Teignmouth	St. Thomas	5/56
..	6/10 St. Thomas	Dawlish	6/36
..	6/40 Dawlish	St. Thomas	7/8
..	7/45 St. Thomas	Teignmouth	8/19
..	8/25 Teignmouth	St. Thomas	9/3
..	9/10 St. Thomas	Teignmouth	9/45
..	10/12 Teignmouth	Exeter	10/51

Mileage: 221 miles 76 chains

NEWTON ABBOT CAR

Dly	7.50 Newton Abbot	Paignton	8.15
..	8.18 Paignton	Newton Abbot	8.42
..	9.17 Newton Abbot	Paignton	9.44
..	10.55 Paignton	Brixham	11.18
..	11.25 Brixham	Torre	11.55
..	12/0nn Torre	Kingswear	12/35
..	1/35 Kingswear	Torre	2/6
..	3/20 Torre	Paignton	3/32
..	3/45 Paignton	Newton Abbot	4/10
..	4/20 Newton Abbot	Paignton	4/47
..	5/25 Paignton	Torre	5/37
..	6/45 Torre	Paignton	6/57
..	7/5 Paignton	Torre	7/18
..	8/30 Torre	Paignton	8/56
..	9/35 Paignton	Torre	9/47
..	10/13 Torre	Kingswear	10/45
..	11/0 Kingswear	Newton Abbot	11/46

Mileage: 114 miles 30 chains

TAUNTON CAR

Dly	8.25 Taunton	Castle Cary	9.46
..	11.15 Castle Cary	Bridgwater	1/2
..	1/25 Bridgwater	Castle Cary	2/34
..	4/8 Castle Cary	Durston	5/25
..	6/55 Durston	Castle Cary	7/55
..	8/15 Castle Cary	Taunton	9/26

Mileage: 155 miles 42 chains

Later Years

Newton

Considerable changes had occurred by the summer of 1912 with the withdrawal of the dedicated Exeter & Teignmouth SRM service. However, following a morning trip to Paignton, the Newton car now worked an abridged version between St. Thomas, Dawlish and Teignmouth, including a mid-afternoon working through to Paignton to carry out part of the old schedule. Its working day started with the 7.50 a.m. Newton to Paignton, and finished with the 11.46 p.m. Dawlish to Newton, covering 206 miles in the process. The Torbay services formerly worked by the motor were now, where appropriate, largely covered by 6- or 8-wheel hauled stock, operating almost entirely to and from Newton.

This schedule was in force during the summer of 1914, and in October of that year. The last recorded motor left Newton shed in May 1915.

Exeter

After the cessation of Exeter's motor working around May 1912, the car was transferred away. Another was provided in late 1915, and this is believed to have run the 7.5 a.m. to Newton and the 8.45 a.m. return.

By the summer of 1921, the motor was working over the Teign Valley line with the 12.55 p.m. Exeter to Heathfield, the 3.55 p.m. Heathfield to Christow and return, and the 5.45 p.m. Heathfield to Exeter, a working that continued into the winter timetable, and the summer 1922 schedule; the latter also included a Thursdays- and Saturdays-only evening trip to Dulverton.

The summer 1921 schedules included the reinstatement of the Exeter & Teignmouth SRM, which worked the 10.0 and 11.55 a.m., the 3.20 and 6.45 p.m. departures from Exeter (St. David's or St. Thomas) and the return workings. Again, these were in force during the winter 1921/2 and summer 1922 timetables.

SRM working over the Teign Valley line further expanded in the 1920s to utilise two diagrams.

The 1929 coach programme shows two duties at Exeter: one car ran the 7.0 and 10.55 a.m. Exeter to Heathfield and return, the 2.45 p.m. Exeter to Chudleigh, Christow and Heathfield, and the 5.10 p.m. return, followed by the 7.10 p.m. Exeter to Hele & Bradninch and return. The second motor started with the 7.50 a.m. Exeter to Tiverton Jct. and return, the 9.25 a.m. to Heathfield and return, the 12.55 p.m. to Heathfield (Newton on Wednesdays and Saturdays) and return, finishing with the 4.38 and 6.8 p.m. trips to Tiverton. Trailers were attached to nearly all the Teign Valley trains.

Working over the Teign Valley line continued into the 1930s, and did not cease until the last SRMs left in May 1935.

Taunton

The Taunton motor continued throughout the pre-Great War years with its three return-trip shuttle out to Castle Cary, incorporating intermediate return trips to Bridgwater and Durston respectively.

An alteration late in the war saw the car operate a Taunton – Westbury – Castle Cary – Durston – Castle Cary and Taunton schedule, though in 1920 this changed again to the 8.10 a.m. to Castle Cary, 10.40 a.m. thence to Durston, 1.40 p.m. Durston to Castle Cary, the 3.15 p.m. thence to Taunton, finishing with the 4.35 p.m. Taunton and the 6.45 p.m. Castle Cary return. In summer 1922, all three trips returned to Taunton.

In 1928, the intermediate returns were made to Taunton and Durston respectively, with an early afternoon Durston & Athelney return trip incorporated. The SRMs left Taunton in the latter part of 1928.

PLYMOUTH DIVISION

To many, the Plymouth suburban workings epitomised SRM operations, though their time in Devon was relatively short. The first SRM duties in the division were at Plymouth, commencing on 1st June 1904 on Plympton & Saltash, and Yealmpton branch services. The Plymouth services in the summer of 1905 comprised two diagrams for the Saltash & Plympton trains, and one primarily for use on the Yealmpton branch. Even as early as this, there were two auto engines at Laira for similar duties.

In October 1904, the Penzance & Truro service was instigated. Later in the decade, the Penzance car was also utilised over the Helston branch, though from 1908 until 1913, a motor spent the summer and autumn working out of Helston. The Penzance motor in March 1908 ran variously between Penzance, Gwinear Road, Camborne and Redruth, with a late afternoon trip over the Helston branch.

A service over the Ashburton branch from Totnes was instigated in October 1904, but in June 1905 the branch SRM was withdrawn after only about eight months operation. The branch timetable reverted to loco-hauled 4-wheel stock.

These services were followed in February 1905 by the Truro & Newquay (via Perranporth), whose cars also later worked on the main line to Redruth and Camborne.

In the early summer of 1905, an SRM was allocated to Newquay for the Chacewater and Truro service, working with the Truro car, and also running down the main line to Camborne in the morning.

1911

The allocation of motors in summer 1911 was:

Laira	39, 47, 49, 59, 60 (70 ft)
Truro	61, 90 (70 ft)
Helston	96 (70 ft)

Plymouth services were covered by 70 ft motors, though the number of duties worked by SRMs had now been equalled by autos. At this time, the SRMs worked three Saturdays-excepted and two Saturdays-only diagrams, with the autos operating three 'SO' and two 'SX'. The cars worked the usual intensive sequences between Wearde, Saltash (etc.) and Plympton, though with visits to Tavistock and Yealmpton; the latter branch was now mainly operated with auto trains. On Sundays, two SRM units and two auto trains worked the suburban services, with one of the motors incorporating two trips to Brent, and the other one duty to Kingsbridge. Otherwise, the cars were to be found largely on the Saltash & Plympton route, though with visits to Yelverton and Tavistock.

The Truro and Newquay cars were largely employed on the Newquay line via Chacewater and Perranporth, but both also worked down over the main line to Redruth and Camborne.

With a car stationed at Helston, it could be assumed that its primary work was over the branch, but this was not the case. Having gained the main line at Gwinear Road on its first leg, the car then worked up to Truro, then back to Penzance, both in a series of workings, and finally up to Redruth before returning to Gwinear Road and Helston. Only on Monday, Friday and Saturday nights did the car work an evening return trip over the branch.

PLYMOUTH DIVISION

PLYMOUTH SET 1 - CAR & TRAILER (SX), TWIN CARS (SO)

Dly	5.50 Laira Jct †	Plympton (Empty)	5.53	WO	3/15 Plymouth	Yelverton	3/50	WO	10/52 Plymouth	Plympton	11/6
..	6.0 Plympton †	Keyham	6.22	..	3/55 Yelverton	Plymouth	4/30	..	11/23 Plympton	Laira Jct (Empty)	11/28
..	6.27 Keyham †	Plymouth	6.38	WX	3/3 Plymouth	Saltash	3/20	SO	5/25 Plymouth	Plympton	5/42
..	6.45 Plymouth †	Wearde	7.7	..	3/31 Saltash	Plymouth	3/48	..	5/50 Plympton	Plymouth	6/7
..	7.28 Wearde	Plymouth	7.48	..	3/58 Plymouth	Laira Jct	4/10	..	6/8 Plymouth	St. Budeaux (Empty)	6/17
..	7.54 Plymouth	Laira Jct	8.4	..	4/20 Laira Jct	Plymouth	4/35	..	6/29 St. Budeaux	Plymouth	6/44
..	8.10 Laira Jct	Plymouth	8.23	SX	4/40 Plymouth	Saltash	4/58	..	6/46 Plymouth	Keyham	6/54
..	8.32 Plymouth	Wearde	8.54	..	5/5 Saltash	Plymouth	5/23	..	7/5 Keyham	Plymouth	7/17
..	9.4 Wearde	Plymouth	9.27	..	5/35 Plymouth	Saltash	5/51	..	8/20 Plymouth	Yelverton	8/55
..	9.40 Plymouth	Plympton	9.55	..	6/0 Saltash	Plymouth	6/17	..	9/5 Yelverton	Plymouth	9/36
..	10.0 Plympton	Plymouth	10.14	..	6/22 Plymouth	Saltash	6/40	..	9/43 Plymouth	Tavistock	10/39
..	10.20 Plymouth	Saltash	10.38	..	6/53 Saltash	Plymouth	7/12	..	10/50 Tavistock	Plymouth	11/35
..	10.40 Saltash	Plymouth	10.58	..	7/50 Plymouth	Wearde	8/11	..	11/40 Plymouth	Laira Jct (Empty)	11/55
..	11.3 Plymouth	Plympton	11.19	..	8/40 Wearde	Plymouth	9/6				
..	11.30 Plympton	Plymouth	11.45	..	9/20 Plymouth	Plympton	9/35				
..	11.55 Plymouth	Tavistock	12/52	..	9/55 Plympton	Plymouth	10/10				
..	1/0 Tavistock §	Plymouth	1/48	..	10/15 Plymouth	Saltash	10/32				
..	1/52 Plymouth	Plympton	2/9	..	10/33 Saltash	Plymouth	10/51				
..	2/40 Plympton	Plymouth	2/58	WX	10/52 Plymouth	Laira Jct (Empty)	11/4				

Mileage 196 miles 3 chains (MTThF), 178 miles 29 chains (WO)
204 miles 37 chains (SO)

NOTES
† Coupled to Set 2
§ 8-wheel Third added SO

PLYMOUTH SET 2 - CAR & TRAILER

Dly	5.50 Laira Jct †	Plympton (Empty)	5.53
..	6.0 Plympton †	Keyham	6.22
..	6.27 Keyham †	Plymouth	6.38
..	6.45 Plymouth †	Wearde	7.7
..	7.13 Wearde	Plympton	7.46
..	7.50 Plympton	Plymouth	8.5
..	8.7 Plymouth	Saltash	8.24
..	8.30 Saltash	Plymouth	8.49
SX	8.55 Plymouth	Laira Jct	9.7
..	9.8 Laira Jct	Plymouth	9.19
..	9.27 Plymouth	Saltash	9.45
..	10.5 Saltash	Plympton	10.35
..	10.35 Plympton	Plymouth	10.50
..	10.55 Plymouth	Wearde	11.17
..	11.20 Wearde	Plymouth	11.44
..	12/47 Plymouth	Laira Jct	12/58
..	1/0 Laira Jct	Plymouth	1/12
..	1/25 Plymouth	Plympton	1/42
..	1/48 Plympton	Plymouth	2/4
..	2/10 Plymouth	Wearde	2/31
..	2/40 Wearde	Plymouth	3/4
..	3/25 Plymouth	Plympton	3/43
..	3/50 Plympton	Plymouth	4/7
..	4/21 Plymouth	Wearde	4/42
..	4/43 Wearde	Plymouth	5/7
..	5/20 Plymouth	Wearde	5/42
..	5/43 Wearde	Plympton	6/16
..	6/25 Plympton	Plymouth	6/40
..	6/50 Plymouth	Saltash	7/8
..	7/24 Saltash	Plymouth	7/42
..	8/3 Plymouth	Plympton	8/18
..	8/32 Plympton	Plymouth	8/46
..	8/48 Plymouth	Wearde	9/10
..	9/11 Wearde	Plymouth	9/33
..	9/37 Plymouth	Saltash	9/55
..	9/57 Saltash	Plymouth	10/16
..	10/32 Plymouth	Plympton	10/47
..	10/50 Plympton	Plymouth	11/6
..	11/10 Plymouth	Wearde	11/33
..	11/36 Wearde	Laira Jct	12.8
SO	9.8 Plymouth	Yealmpton	9.44
..	10.0 Yealmpton	Plymouth	10.36
..	10.50 Plymouth	Yealmpton	11.26
..	11.32 Yealmpton	Plymouth	12/5
..	12/13 Plymouth	Plympton	12/30
..	12/40 Plympton	Plymouth	12/56
..	1/2 Plymouth	Yealmpton	1/38
..	2/0 Yealmpton	Plymouth	2/34
..	2/47 Plymouth	Saltash	3/5
..	3/9 Saltash	Plymouth	3/27
..	3/42 Plymouth	Wearde	4/0
..	4/1 Wearde	Plymouth	4/24
..	6/10 Plymouth	Wearde	6/31
..	6/35 Wearde	Plymouth	6/56
..	6/59 Plymouth	Plympton	7/14
..	7/16 Plympton	Plymouth	7/32
..	7/50 Plymouth	Wearde	8/10
..	8/42 Wearde	Plymouth	9/4
..	9/20 Plymouth	Plympton	9/35
..	9/55 Plympton	Plymouth	10/10
..	10/13 Plymouth	Plympton	10/29
..	10/35 Plympton	Laira Jct	11/4

Mileage: 203 miles 62 chains (SX); 180 miles 61 chains (SO)

NOTES

† Coupled to Set 1

PLYMOUTH SET 5 - TWIN CARS

SX	1/39 Laira Jct	Plymouth	1/52
..	2/47 Plymouth	Saltash	3/5
..	3/9 Saltash	Plymouth	3/27
..	3/42 Plymouth	Wearde	4/0
..	4/1 Wearde	Plymouth	4/24
WX	4/29 Plymouth	Yelverton	5/9
..	5/20 Yelverton	Plymouth	5/59
SX	6/10 Plymouth	Wearde	6/31
..	6/35 Wearde	Plymouth	6/56
..	7/18 Plymouth	Saltash	7/36
..	8/0 Saltash	Plymouth	8/18
..	8/28 Plymouth	Saltash	8/46
..	8/55 Saltash	Plymouth	9/12
..	9/25 Plymouth	Saltash	9/41
..	9/47 Saltash	Plymouth	10/5
..	10/13 Plymouth	Plympton	10/29
..	10/35 Plympton	Plymouth	10/50
..	10/54 Plymouth	Saltash	11/20
..	11/25 Saltash	Laira Jct	12.0mn

Mileage: 110 miles 5 chains(WSX); 87 miles 61 chains (WO)

TRURO CAR

Dly	7.43 Truro	Newquay	8.48
..	9.0 Newquay	Chacewater	9.52
..	10.6 Chacewater	Truro	10.17
..	11.15 Truro	Penzance	12/29
..	12/35 Penzance	Redruth	1/25
..	1/30 Redruth	Camborne	1/42
..	2/5 Camborne	Truro	2/46
..	3/22 Truro	Camborne	4/0
..	4/26 Camborne	Chacewater	4/51
..	4/57 Chacewater	Perranporth	5/20
..	5/25 Perranporth ‡	Blackwater Jct	5/46
..	5/50 Blackwater Jct	Chacewater	5/53
..	5/55 Chacewater	Truro	6/5

Mileage: 159 miles 7 chains

NOTE

‡ Attached to 4/55 Newquay to Redruth Car

NEWQUAY CAR

Dly	7.50 Newquay	Chacewater	8.53
..	8.54 Chacewater	Camborne	9.18
..	9.40 Camborne	Chacewater	10.4
..	10.10 Chacewater	Newquay	11.1
..	11.40 Newquay	Chacewater	12/33
..	1/10 Chacewater	Newquay	2/6
..	2/32 Newquay	Chacewater	3/31
..	3/44 Chacewater	Newquay	4/38
..	4/55 Newquay ‡	Redruth	6/0
..	6/5 Redruth	Newquay	7/7
..	7/16 Newquay	Truro	8/27
..	8/50 Truro	Newquay	10/2

Mileage: 216 miles 14 chains

NOTE

‡ Truro Car attached Perranporth to Blackwater Jct

HELSTON CAR

Dly	9.50 Helston	Gwinear Road	10.15
..	10.32 Gwinear Road	Redruth	10.50
..	10.53 Redruth	Camborne	11.6
..	11.45 Camborne	Truro	12/25
..	12/43 Truro	Camborne	1/21
..	1/25 Camborne	Redruth	1/36
..	1/40 Redruth	Penzance	2/30
..	3/0 Penzance	Redruth	3/45
..	4/15 Redruth	Gwinear Road	4/32
..	5/20 Gwinear Road	Helston	5/48
MFSO	6/22 Helston	Gwinear Road	6/50
..	7/25 Gwinear Road	Helston	7/53

Mileage: 96 miles 4 chains (TWThO); 113 miles 58 chains (MFSO)

Later Years

Plymouth

The gradual erosion of SRM services continued into the summer of 1912, when the number at Plymouth dropped to two workings throughout the week ('SX' and 'SO'), whilst the auto trains increased to three. On Sundays, the balance was now one motor and two auto units.

SRM working ceased in the Plymouth area after the 1913 summer service, although a pair were to be seen throughout most of 1929.

Truro & Newquay

A greater change took place on the Truro & Newquay services for the summer 1912 timetable, and both duties were now shown to be worked by auto trains. Nevertheless, motors continued to appear occasionally up to 1913. At Truro, an allocation was provided in 1919/20, with cars running over the Newquay branch, and on main line trips to Penzance, Gwinear Road and Camborne.

Helston & Penzance

The Penzance motor services continued into 1916, with a minor renaissance in 1921/22. Working from Helston effectively ceased in 1913, although very brief allocations were made in 1914, and again in the summer of 1921. In the latter, the 10.5 a.m. Helston car ran firstly to Newquay (via Perranporth), 12.26 p.m. Newquay to Penzance, 3.5 p.m. Penzance to Redruth and finished on the 4.5 p.m. Redruth to Helston.

GLOUCESTER DIVISION

To the Gloucester Division fell the honour of the first SRM working, commencing on 12th October 1903 over the Chalford & Stonehouse route, as discussed in some detail in Chapter 1. There were hourly departures from Chalford between 8.0 a.m. and 7.0 p.m., then 8.30, 9.30 (Fridays and Saturdays) and 10.30 p.m. (Saturdays only). Return from Stonehouse was on the half-hour, and at 9.0, 10.0 and 11.0 p.m. on the late evening services.

A similar arrangement was found in March 1906, though the 8.30 and 9.30 p.m. departures were now Thursdays to Saturdays.

Cheltenham received its first car in the summer of 1908, and this was put to work on a morning return trip to Moreton-in-Marsh, and two afternoon trains to and from Honeybourne.

Gloucester had a regular allocation of SRMs from 1907, and, given the transfer of motors between them, it probably acted as a form of 'home' base for the Cheltenham and Chalford cars, also providing additional cars when traffic dictated. It also worked a duty, details of which are unknown.

1911

The allocation of motors in July 1911 was:

Chalford	52 (70 ft)
Gloucester	51 (70 ft)
Cheltenham	65 (70 ft)

A single motor sufficed for the Chalford & Stonehouse services, although on Saturday evenings it was joined by the Gloucester car, which worked as a relief service from Stroud ahead of the Stonehouse departures. It is believed that the 'stale' Chalford car became the 'spare' at this point, and returned to Gloucester when released, whilst the Gloucester car remained at Chalford for the following week's working. On Sundays, trips were worked in the afternoon and evening during summer months.

The Cheltenham motor operated its duties over the Honeybourne line, working through to Moreton-in-Marsh on its first run to connect with a London-bound express that did not call at Honeybourne.

GLOUCESTER DIVISION

CHALFORD CAR

Dly	8.0 Chalford	Stonehouse	8.25
..	8.30 Stonehouse	Chalford	8.55
..	9.0 Chalford	Stonehouse	9.25
..	9.30 Stonehouse	Chalford	9.55
..	10.5 Chalford	Stonehouse	10.28
..	10.30 Stonehouse	Chalford	10.55
..	11.0 Chalford	Stonehouse	11.25
..	11.30 Stonehouse	Chalford	11.55
..	12/0nn Chalford	Stonehouse	12/25
..	12/30 Stonehouse	Chalford	12/55
..	1/0 Chalford	Stonehouse	1/25
..	1/30 Stonehouse	Chalford	1/55
..	2/0 Chalford	Stonehouse	2/25
..	2/30 Stonehouse	Chalford	2/53
..	3/0 Chalford	Stonehouse	3/25
..	3/30 Stonehouse	Chalford	3/55
..	4/0 Chalford	Stonehouse †	4/25
..	4/30 Stonehouse	Chalford	4/55
..	5/0 Chalford	Stonehouse	5/25
..	5/30 Stonehouse	Chalford	5/55
..	6/2 Chalford	Stonehouse	6/27
..	6/30 Stonehouse	Chalford	6/55
SX	7/0 Chalford	Stonehouse	7/29
SO	7/3 Chalford	Stonehouse	7/30
SX	7/32 Stonehouse	Chalford	7/57
SO	7/34 Stonehouse	Chalford	7/59
Dly	8/30 Chalford	Stonehouse	8/55
..	9/0 Stonehouse	Chalford	9/25
TFO	9/30 Chalford	Stonehouse	9/55
SO	9/35 Chalford	Stonehouse	10/0
TFSO	10/0 Stonehouse	Chalford	10/25
SO	10/35 Chalford	Stonehouse	10/58
..	11/2 Stonehouse	Chalford	11/28

Mileage: 180 miles 4 chains (MWThO); 193 miles 72 chains (TFO)
207 miles 60 chains (SO)

NOTE
† Trailer attached

GLOUCESTER CAR & Trailer

SO	4/45 Gloucester	Stonehouse or Stroud	-
..	5/30 Stonehouse (attached)	Chalford, or	5/55
..	5/30 Stroud	Chalford (Relief Service)	5/45
..	7/0 Chalford (attached)	Stroud	7/15
..	7/30 Stroud	Chalford (Relief Service)	7/45
..	8/30 Chalford (attached)	Stroud	8/45
..	9/0 Stroud	Chalford (Relief Service)	9/15
..	A/R Chalford	Gloucester (Spare Car), or	-
..	9/30 Chalford (attached)	Stroud	9/45
..	10/0 Stroud	Chalford (Relief Service)	10/15
..	A/R Chalford	Gloucester (Spare Car)	

Mileage: 57 miles 8 chains or 48 miles 64 chains

CHELTENHAM CAR

Dly	7.55 Cheltenham St James†*	Moreton-in-Marsh	9.49
..	10.0 Moreton-in-Marsh†	Cheltenham St James	11.33
..	12/32 Cheltenham St. James ‡	Honeybourne	1/37
..	1/55 Honeybourne‡	Cheltenham St James	3/2
..	3/37 Cheltenham St James	Honeybourne	4/42
..	5/57 Honeybourne*	Cheltenham St James	7/4

Mileage: 152 miles 44 chains

NOTES
† Trailer MThSO
‡ Trailer ThSO
* Brake Van to work between Birmingham and Bishop's Cleeve on these trips

Later Years

Chalford & Gloucester

The working arrangements as in 1911 continued with minor adjustments until the Great War, though the 9.30 p.m. Chalford working became daily in the summer timetables, reverting to Thursdays to Saturdays during the winter.

By January 1916, the 10.30 p.m. SRM service from Chalford had been withdrawn.

In April 1918, the Chalford services were given over to auto train operation, and it was not until July 1921 that the SRMs returned. With the takeover came the first of the daily through workings to and from Gloucester for the Chalford SRM, which was now joined by a Gloucester car for other trips in the Stroud Valley. In October 1921, the traditional hourly return service was in operation from Chalford between 8.0 a.m. and 9.0 p.m., with a 10.0 p.m. Saturdays-only train.

Additional workings were in hand for the summer 1922 timetable, and the Chalford motor was again joined by a Gloucester SRM on a daily basis, with an additional car on Saturdays.

By the summer of 1925, the Chalford and Gloucester motors were working a full timetable between them, with the Chalford car working the 7.0 and 11.0 a.m., 3.0 and 7.0 p.m. departures through to Gloucester, with the 8.10 a.m., 1.12, 5.7 and 8.7 p.m. Gloucester departures back to Chalford. It also operated the 9.0, 10.2 a.m., 2.2, 6.2 and 9.10 p.m. departures from Chalford to Stonehouse, with the balancing trips back to Chalford.

The Gloucester motor worked the 7.8 and 11.10 a.m., 3.10, 6.37 (to Stroud) and 9.20 p.m. departures from Gloucester to Chalford, and the 8.0 a.m., 1.0, 4.0, 8.0 and 10.10 p.m. Chalford trains to Gloucester, as well as the 12.39, 4.30 and 7.30 p.m. Stonehouse to Chalford services with their balances. On Saturdays, an additional Gloucester motor ran the 12.20 and 1.50 p.m. return trips to Stroud, then the 3.40 p.m. Gloucester to Chalford, five return Chalford and Stonehouse relief trips, and the 9.45 p.m. Chalford to Gloucester.

SRM working from Chalford ceased in May 1928 with the transfer of No.70. This car remained at Gloucester for another eight months, though the auto trains were now in control over the Stroud Valley.

Cheltenham

As far as can be seen, the Cheltenham SRM workings over the Honeybourne line continued through until the summer of 1918. In January 1917, it commenced with the 7.25 a.m. return trip to Moreton, and the 12.37, 3.42 and 6.6 p.m. round trips to Honeybourne. The 7.0 a.m. Stratford motor made two visits to Cheltenham in the course of its duties to complete the timetable. The Cheltenham car made one morning and one evening trip to Honeybourne on Sundays. As usual, auto services replaced the SRMs.

PONTYPOOL ROAD (LATER NEWPORT) DIVISION

One of the first motors in the district came to Newport in December 1905, though it soon moved to Merthyr for the new service. A 1906 internal notice recorded the commencement of the SRM service between Merthyr and Newport over the 26-mile route – and a problem with the LNWR:

'Merthyr And Newport Rail Motor Car Service

'On Monday, March 12th 1906 a Rail Motor Car Service was inaugurated between Merthyr and Newport via Nine Mile Point.

'Four trips in each direction are run, leaving

Merthyr at	8.40 a.m.	12.3 p.m.	4.2 p.m.	7.40 p.m.
and				
Newport at	10.36 a.m.	2.22 p.m.	6.20 p.m.	9.5 p.m.

'Since the commencement of this service, which passes over a portion of the London and North Western Co.'s line, it has been necessary to attach a trailer car to accommodate the persons, which in one direction is propelled by the Motor Car, but that Co. object to Cars being propelled over their line, and where it is necessary for a trailer to be used, the Motor Car must run round the former vehicle at the terminal points.'

Newport had a motor allocation for a year or so at this time, probably as a backup for the Merthyr car.

December 1905 saw another SRM transferred into the division with the establishment of an allocation at Aberdare for the Black Lion & Cwmaman Colliery service. The first two motors to arrive included No.2, which had already seen service in the Stroud and Lambourn Valleys, and had worked briefly on suburban traffic from Southall.

The allocation at Aberdare was doubled in May 1911, a motor being used on the Swansea service in addition to conventional trains. This new service ran mostly to and from Cwmbach Halt, the next station east of Aberdare.

1911

Allocation of SRMs in the division in July 1911 was:

Aberdare	2 (57 ft), 7, 8, 11 (59 ft)
Merthyr	54, 92 (70 ft)
Monmouth Troy	22 (59 ft)

Aberdare's duties comprised one motor (Saturdays excepted) or two (Saturdays only, attached) running a timetable over the 2½-mile long branch between Black Lion Crossing and Cwmaman Colliery. The cars gained access to this line via Gelli Tawr Jct., to the north-west of Aberdare. Curiously, it was operated in isolation, as there were no passenger trains over the section between Gelli Tarw Junction and Black Lion Crossing.

Another Aberdare duty was the car for the Mountain Ash & Swansea East Dock, running along the Vale of Neath line via Neath (Low Level).

PONTYPOOL ROAD (later NEWPORT) DIVISION

ABERDARE CAR 'A'

Dly	7.20 Aberdare	Black Lion Crossing (Empty)	
..	8.5 Black Lion Crossing	Cwmaman Colliery & return	8.40
..	9.25 Black Lion Crossing	Cwmaman Colliery & return	9.55
..	11.5 Black Lion Crossing	Cwmaman Colliery & return	11.40
..	1/35 Black Lion Crossing	Cwmaman Colliery & return	2/15
SO	3/25 Black Lion Crossing	Cwmaman Colliery & return	4/0
Dly	4/45 Black Lion Crossing	Cwmaman Colliery & return	5/25
..	6/10 Black Lion Crossing	Cwmaman Colliery & return	6/50
..	7/10 Black Lion Crossing	Cwmaman Colliery & return	7/50
..	8/20 Black Lion Crossing	Cwmaman Colliery & return	8/48
SO	9/15 Black Lion Crossing	Cwmaman Colliery & return	9/50
Dly	10/0 Black Lion Crossing	Cwmaman Colliery & return	10/35
..	11/0 Black Lion Crossing	Cwmaman Colliery & return	11/35
..	11/40 Black Lion Crossing	Aberdare (Empty)	

Mileage: 52 miles 20 chains (SX); 62 miles 56 chains (SO)

NOTE

Car 'B' attached 1/35 Black Lion until finish (SO)

ABERDARE CAR 'B'

SO	1/35 Black Lion Crossing	Cwmaman Colliery & return	2/15
..	3/25 Black Lion Crossing	Cwmaman Colliery & return	4/0
..	4/45 Black Lion Crossing	Cwmaman Colliery & return	5/25
..	6/10 Black Lion Crossing	Cwmaman Colliery & return	6/50
..	7/10 Black Lion Crossing	Cwmaman Colliery & return	7/50
..	8/20 Black Lion Crossing	Cwmaman Colliery & return	8/48
..	9/15 Black Lion Crossing	Cwmaman Colliery & return	9/50
..	10/0 Black Lion Crossing	Cwmaman Colliery & return	10/35
..	11/0 Black Lion Crossing	Cwmaman Colliery & return	11/35
..	11/40 Black Lion Crossing	Aberdare (Empty)	

Mileage: 47 miles 2 chains

NOTE

Attached to Car 'A'

ABERDARE CAR 'C'

Dly	8.5 Aberdare	Hirwain	8.15
..	8.20 Hirwain	Mountain Ash	8.42
..	9.15 Mountain Ash	Swansea ED	10.38
..	10.48 Swansea ED	Mountain Ash	12/15
..	1/20 Mountain Ash	Swansea ED	2/47
..	2/52 Swansea ED	Glyn Neath	3/39
..	5/0 Glyn Neath	Swansea ED	5/44
..	6/0 Swansea ED	Mountain Ash	7/31
..	7/40 Mountain Ash	Aberdare	7/50

Mileage: 166 miles 42 chains

MERTHYR CAR

Dly	8.35 Merthyr	Llanwern	10.5
..	10.13 Llanwern	Merthyr	11.48
..	12/3 Merthyr §	Newport	1/18
..	2/8 Newport §	Merthyr	3/30
..	3/55 Merthyr	Newport	5/8
..	6/20 Newport ‡	Merthyr	7/40
..	8/5 Merthyr †	Newport	9/25
..	9/50 Newport	Merthyr	11/0

Mileage: 214 miles 60 chains

NOTES

§ Trailer (MSO)

‡ 8w Third (MSO) Quaker's Yard to Merthyr

† 8w Third & Brake Third (SO)

MONMOUTH CAR

Dly	7.30 Monmouth	Ross	8.3
..	8.31 Ross	Gloucester	9.20
..	10.52 Gloucester	Ross	11.45
..	12/0nn Ross	Lydbrook	12/15
..	12/25 Lydbrook	Ross	12/43
..	1/35 Ross	Monmouth	2/17
..	2/35 Monmouth	Chepstow	3/55
..	5/0 Chepstow	Monmouth	5/52

Mileage: 102 miles 30 chains

Merthyr retained its rather tortuous diagram from High Street station, via the Rhymney joint line to Quaker's Yard (High Level), the Vale of Neath to Hengoed & Maesycwmmer, the L & NW line to Nine Mile Point, then via Risca and Bassaleg into Newport. In fact, the first of the four return trips ran beyond Newport along the main line to Llanwern.

One of the most beautiful routes on the system must surely have been that along the Wye Valley between Chepstow and Ross, and this was the venue for much of the Monmouth SRM's turn. Its first trip in the morning was via Ross and on to Gloucester, then to Lydbrook, Ross and back to Monmouth. In mid-afternoon, the car worked a return trip along the other portion of the valley, down to Chepstow.

Later Years

Aberdare

The allocation dropped to two again after the Great War, with the motors running the Cwmaman Colliery service. '517' and '2021' class auto engines and trailers now ran the Swansea trains.

The Cwmaman motors continued into early 1925, when 'workmen's trains' took over the schedule.

Merthyr & Newport

The Merthyr & Newport operation continued until April 1915, when the Merthyr motors were transferred away and the service suspended. Newport retained an allocation until 1920.

Monmouth

SRMs continued to operate on the Wye Valley service until September 1914.

Pontypool Road

In 1912, a new allocation to Pontypool Road saw two intensive SRM diagrams worked, encompassing Pontypool, Brynmawr, Talywain, Panteg and Blaenavon. This probably continued until late 1916, with the last of the cars transferred away in January 1917. By the early 1920s, these were all shown as auto train duties.

SRMs returned to Pontypool Road in June 1923, with a continuous allocation of one until spring 1927, two until summer 1930, and mostly one until September 1932. These motors worked alongside the auto trains on Blaenavon and Talywain services, in particular on an overnight turn: this involved late evening trips between Panteg or Pontypool and those places, and an early morning trip to Talywain and back.

SWANSEA DIVISION

The first SRMs into the Swansea Division were those on the Brynamman & Llandilo service, which commenced on 1st March 1905. Nos.31 and 42 were stationed at Brynamman between February and April of that year, moving then to Garnant for a couple of months. The SRM allocation ceased in June 1905.

Further introductions during that year saw two SRMs at Neath, operating from 3rd April 1905 on the Swansea & Vale of Neath service, initially out to Glyn Neath.

In June 1905, Whitland received a car for the Pembroke Dock branch service, with a second residing at Tenby. The SRM service over the branch appeared to be summers only, and by 1908 both motors were at Tenby. In summer 1909, Whitland and Tenby shared the cars, but from summer 1910, three motors were allocated to Whitland.

The SRMs arrived back in the Llanelly area in September 1907, a motor being stationed there until May 1908, when 'Gwaun-cae-Gurwen', then Garnant (June), took over the allocation for the new G-C-G branch. In June 1910, the allocation is shown as moving back to 'G-C-G'. Connections to conventional trains were made at Garnant, for Pantyffynnon and beyond.

Two motors were transferred to Fishguard/Goodwick in the summer of 1907 for local services over the Neyland and Milford Haven lines, and along the main line to Whitland.

Aberystwyth received two cars for each summer service commencing July 1908, and operated along the Carmarthen line.

1911

The allocation of motors to the Swansea Division in July 1911 was as follows:

Duffryn	PT No.1
Neath	14 (59 ft), 50 (70 ft)
Garnant	21, 34 (59 ft)
Whitland	3 (59 ft), 71 (70 ft), 77 (59 ft)
Goodwick	33, 36 (59 ft)
Aberystwyth	74 (59 ft), 99 (70 ft)

The Port Talbot car, based at Duffryn Yard shed, worked between Port Talbot (Central or Aberavon) and Blaengarw, with five daily return trips (with an additional late-night trip on Wednesdays and Saturdays) shown in the autumn schedule. Although the Great Western was now responsible for operating the service, it was not shown in the GWR coach programmes, but had its own documentation. When PT No.1 was sent to Swindon for overhaul, a GWR car was sometimes provided as a substitute: for example, No.21 was allocated to Duffryn in November 1911, and remained there until June 1912.

Neath had two SRMs with one diagram working out as far east as Quaker's Yard, on the Vale of Neath line, and into Swansea East Dock station, balancing the Aberdare car's operations (see

Pontypool Division). The two cars' workings were in addition to conventional trains over the line.

Garnant had a pair of 59 ft motors available for its Gwaun-cae-Gurwen branch duty.

Whitland's SRMs were provided for two duties, one of which worked along the main line to Fishguard Harbour, whilst the other worked over the Pembroke Dock branch, mostly between Tenby and the terminus.

Fishguard's SRMs were shedded at nearby Goodwick, and the single duty took it onto the Neyland line, as well as along the main line to Whitland and Clynderwen.

The Aberystwyth working was a summer-only arrangement, and ran along the Carmarthen line as far as Lampeter, Tregaron and Trawscoed (twice).

Later Years

Neath

Apart from a period around 1919, the Neath allocation continued almost uninterrupted to October 1935, when No.65 was sent to Swindon factory for disposal.

In 1922, the motor schedule started with the 8.15 a.m. return trip from Neath (Low Level) to Glyn Neath, followed by the 11.5 a.m. Neath to Resolven, which worked back to Swansea East Dock. A return trip, 12.55 p.m. from Swansea to Resolven, was next, then the 4.0 p.m. East Dock to Glyn Neath, which returned to Neath Town. The last trip was the 9.35 p.m. Town to Glyn Neath and return. An Aberdare auto train worked other trips over the route.

The 1930 motor diagram was rather different, starting with an 8.30 a.m. departure from Neath Riverside for Glyn Neath, returning to Swansea East Dock. Thereafter, there were three services from Swansea to Resolven, Glyn Neath and Cwmbach respectively, the last of which returned to Neath Riverside. The day finished with three return trips from Neath to Glyn Neath. An auto train was still working alongside the SRM at this time over the Vale of Neath, and a second auto increasingly took over the motor's schedule.

The last regular GWR SRM service operated between Neath and Court Sart station (ex-R & SB). It was discontinued on 16th September 1935.

Garnant/G-C-G

From 1912 until September 1917, the allocation for the Gwaun-cae-Gurwen branch was shown as being largely at 'G-C-G', after which the motors were shown entirely at Garnant. Garnant shed was very small, sited on the Cawdor mineral branch just over half-a-mile from Garnant station. In view of the very restricted facilities at this shed, it may be that the car was parked at either Garnant station or G-C-G. Alternatively, the Locomotive Department clerks may have used the term 'GCG' to signify an allocation to the branch, or even for Garnant shed, although the GWR clerical abbreviation for the shed was 'Gar'. Certainly, all trips in service and public timetables, and in coach working programmes, are shown as commencing and ending at Garnant.

In 1922, the Garnant duty to Gwaun-cae-Gurwen involved nine daily trips (ten on Saturdays, extending to Ammanford), though with one morning leg from Brynamman to Pantyffynnon. The motors remained at Garnant – or Llanelly – until the end of 1926.

Whitland/Tenby

The SRM summer services continued over the Pembroke branch until 1914, when they ceased. Three motors returned briefly to Tenby from December 1918, though one remained until February 1920.

Fishguard/Goodwick

The Goodwick motor continued to work into the Great War period, finally finishing around June 1917; after this, the services to Neyland and Clarbeston Road were worked by an auto train.

Aberystwyth

The summer SRM service to Trawscoed, Tregaron and Lampeter ceased after the 1914 season.

BIRMINGHAM DIVISION

Stourbridge established itself as a centre for SRMs in the early months of 1905 with the commencement of services to the Town station in January, and over the Old Hill & Halesowen and the Langley Green & Oldbury branches in March. The shed worked a motor to Kidderminster and Stourport on Sundays from April 1905.

The opening of the North Warwicks line between Tyseley and Bearley in July 1908 brought about the need for a local service to cater for the new and rebuilt stations between Birmingham and Stratford. Three SRMs were allocated to Tyseley and two to Stratford, working variously between the two ends, with starting and terminating services at various intermediate stations. The allocation at Tyseley was soon increased to four, then five in 1910, allowing three, or even four, diagrams to be regularly operated. An auto train was in service along the line by October 1910.

SWANSEA DIVISION

NEATH CAR

Dly	7.50 Neath (Engine Shed Jct.)	Neath Jct	8.2
..	8.25 Neath Jct*	Swansea East Dock	8.44
..	8.55 Swansea East Dock	Quaker's Yard	10.50
..	11.5 Quaker's Yard	Swansea East Dock	12/42
..	1/0 Swansea East Dock	Mountain Ash	2/31
..	2/40 Mountain Ash	Swansea East Dock	4/8
..	4/20 Swansea East Dock ‡	Quaker's Yard	6/0
..	6/20 Quaker's Yard	Swansea East Dock	7/56
..	8/15 Swansea East Dock	Neath Jct	8/34
..	8/37 Neath Jct	Neath (Empty)	8/56
SO	10/50 Neath	Rhigos Halt	11/33
..	Rhigos Halt	Neath (Empty)	12/20

Mileage: 204 miles (SX); 231 miles 70 chains

NOTES

* Conveys Merthyr to Swansea Through Coach

‡ Brake Third East Dock to Glyn Neath (SO)

GWAUN-CAE-GURWEN (GARNANT) CAR

Dly	7.25 Garnant Halt	Gwaun-Cae-Gurwen & return	7.50
..	9.20 Garnant Halt	Gwaun-Cae-Gurwen & return	9.55
..	11.1 Granant Halt	Gwaun-Cae-Gurwen & return	11.22
..	12/19 Garnant Halt	Gwaun-Cae-Gurwen & return	2/0
..	2/15 Garnant Halt	Gwaun-Cae-Gurwen & return	3/45
..	4/10 Garnant Halt	Gwaun-Cae-Gurwen & return	5/43
..	6/10 Garnant Halt	Gwaun-Cae-Gurwen & return	6/50
..	7/28 Garnant Halt	Gwaun-Cae-Gurwen & return	7/53
ThSO	8/15 Garnant Halt	Gwaun-Cae-Gurwen & return	8/40
..	8/45 Garnant Halt	Pontardulais	9/10
..	9/35 Pontardulais	Garnant Halt	10/10
..	10/20 Garnant Halt	Gwaun-Cae-Gurwen & return	10/43
SO	11/44 Garnant Halt	Gwaun-Cae-Gurwen	11/54
..	11/58 Gwaun-Cae-Gurwen	Garnant Halt (Empty)	12.6

Mileage: 21 miles 32 chains(ThSX); 45 miles 58 chains (ThO)
48 miles 32 chains (SO)

ABERYSTWYTH CAR

Dly	8.7 Aberystwyth	Lampeter	8.27
..	9.42 Lampeter	Aberystwyth	11.0
..	12/15 Aberystwyth	Trawscoed	12/39
..	1/10 Trawscoed	Aberystwyth	1/36
..	2/0 Aberystwyth	Tregaron	2/54
..	3/53 Tregaron	Aberystwyth	4/42
..	5/30 Aberystwyth	Trawscoed	5/52
..	5/55 Trawscoed	Aberystwyth	6/18

Mileage: 131 miles 40 chains

WHITLAND CAR 'A'

Dly	11.5 Whitland	Fishguard Harbour	12/12
..	12/25 Fishguard Harbour	Goodwick	12/27
..	12/35 Goodwick	Fishguard Harbour	12/37
..	1/50 Fishguard Harbour	Clarbeston	2/30
..	3/0 Clarbeston	Fishguard Harbour	3/40
..	4/45 Fishguard Harbour	Goodwick	4/47
..	4/50 Goodwick	Fishguard Harbour	4/52
..	6/45 Fishguard Harbour	Whitland	7/46

Mileage: 88 miles 64 chains

WHITLAND CAR 'B'

Dly	9.30 Whitland	Pembroke Dock	11.2
..	11.40 Pembroke Dock	Tenby	12/17
..	12/22 Tenby	Pembroke Dock	12/58
..	1/35 Pembroke Dock	Tenby	2/9
..	2/45 Tenby	Pembroke Dock	3/19
..	4/0 Pembroke Dock	Tenby	4/33
..	4/38 Tenby	Pembroke Dock	5/10
..	5/15 Pembroke Dock †	Tenby	5/50
..	6/5 Tenby †	Pembroke Dock	6/40
..	6/55 Pembroke Dock	Whitland	8/15

Mileage: 124 miles 48 chains; 147 miles 62 chains (from 22nd July)

NOTE

Service as from 15th July

† From 22nd July

FISHGUARD CAR

Dly	7.5 Goodwick	Neyland	8.20
..	8.25 Neyland	Haverfordwest	8.46
..	8.50 Haverfordwest	Johnston	9.0
..	9.15 Johnston	Goodwick	10.13
..	10.35 Goodwick	Whitland	11.37
..	12/10 Whitland	Fishguard Harbour	1/17
..	1/20 Fishguard Harbour	Goodwick	1/22
..	1/58 Goodwick	Fishguard Harbour	2/0
..	2/30 Fishguard Harbour	Goodwick	2/32
..	3/40 Goodwick	Fishguard Harbour	3/42
..	4/15 Fishguard Harbour	Clynderwen	4/55
..	6/0 Clynderwen	Fishguard Harbour	6/50
..	Fishguard Harbour	Goodwick (Empty)	-

Mileage: 170 miles 72 chains

1911

Allocation of motors in July 1911 was:

Stourbridge Jct.	15, 31 (57ft); 64, 68, 69, 93 (70ft)
Stratford-u-Avon	57 (70ft), 73 (59ft)
Tyseley	55, 84, 87, 95 (70ft)

Stourbridge Junction had four diagrams in operation, three of which covered the Halesowen and Dudley branches from Old Hill, and the Oldbury branch from Langley Green or Smethwick Jct., with intermediate visits to Wolverhampton and Hagley. The fourth car worked the Stourbridge Town branch, including an early visit to Snow Hill. On Sundays, the one car operated the Town branch, whilst another ran a Halesowen and Dudley diagram; the Town car also visited Severn Valley stations on three occasions during the day.

Two Tyseley schedules covered working along the North Warwicks line between Moor Street, Henley-in-Arden, Bearley and Stratford-on-Avon, with one car in operation on Sundays. A Tyseley auto train shared the duties on weekdays; an SRM was attached to this for a Saturday night service from Danzey to Moor Street, presenting a rather unusual spectacle.

Stratford-on-Avon also worked two diagrams, the first mainly on Moor Street line duties, and the second in the opposite direction, to Honeybourne, Cheltenham and Evesham.

BIRMINGHAM DIVISION

STOURBRIDGE CAR 'A'

Dly	5.15 Stourbridge Jct	Stourbridge Town (Empty)	5.18
..	5.28 Stourbridge Town	Stourbridge Junction	5.31
..	5.33 Stourbridge Jct	Dudley	5.56
..	6.0 Dudley	Old Hill	6.14
..	6.25 Old Hill	Halesowen & return	6.41
..	6.50 Old Hill	Halesowen	6.55
..	7.8 Halesowen §	Old Hill	7.13
..	7.22 Old Hill §	Halesowen	7.27
..	7.30 Halesowen	Old Hill	7.35
..	7.37 Old Hill	Halesowen & return	8.7
..	8.10 Old Hill	Dudley	8.27
..	8.38 Dudley	Old Hill	8.52
..	9.6 Old Hill	Halesowen & return	9.36
..	9.40 Old Hill	Halesowen & return	9.55
..	10.4 Old Hill	Halesowen & return	10.18
..	10.27 Old Hill	Halesowen & return	11.12
..	11.22 Old Hill	Halesowen & return	11.35
..	11.38 Old Hill	Halesowen & return	12/5
..	12/24 Old Hill	Dudley	12/39
..	12/43 Dudley	Old Hill	12/57
..	1/3 Old Hill	Halesowen & return	1/25
..	1/35 Old Hill	Halesowen & return	1/58
..	2/8 Old Hill	Halesowen & return	2/25
..	2/28 Old Hill	Dudley	2/44
..	2/50 Dudley	Old Hill	3/4
..	3/15 Old Hill	Halesowen & return	3/35
..	3/50 Old Hill	Dudley	4/6
..	4/36 Dudley	Old Hill	4/50
..	4/56 Old Hill	Halesowen	5/1
..	5/15 Halesowen §	Old Hill	5/20
..	5/37 Old Hill §	Halesowen & return	6/17
..	6/30 Old Hill §	Halesowen & return	6/55
..	7/5 Old Hill §	Halesowen	7/10
..	7/15 Halesowen	Old Hill	7/20
..	7/47 Old Hill	Halesowen & return	8/30
..	8/45 Old Hill	Halesowen & return	9/7
..	9/10 Old Hill	Stourbridge Jct	9/25
..	9/40 Stourbridge Jct	Old Hill	9/55
..	10/0 Old Hill	Dudley	10/16
..	10/22 Dudley	Old Hill	10/36
..	10/50 Old Hill	Stourbridge Jct	11/3

Mileage: 119 miles 9 chains

NOTE

§ Trailer attached

STOURBRIDGE CAR 'B'

Dly	5.45 Stourbridge Jct	Old Hill	5.58
..	6.0 Old Hill	Halesowen & return	6.15
..	6.17 Old Hill	Dudley	6.33
..	6.55 Dudley	Old Hill	7.9
..	7.18 Old Hill	Stourbridge Jct	7.32
..	7.45 Stourbridge Jct	Hagley & return	8.0
..	8.1 Stourbridge Jct	Stourbridge Town & return	8.9
..	8.11 Stourbridge Jct	Stourbridge Town & return	8.18
..	8.20 Stourbridge Jct	Old Hill	8.38
..	8.43 Old Hill	Halesowen & return	9.0
..	9.10 Old Hill	Dudley	9.26
..	9.46 Dudley	Old Hill	10.0
..	10.30 Old Hill	Dudley	10.46
..	11.6 Dudley	Old Hill	11.20
..	11.39 Old Hill	Dudley	11.54
..	12/20 Dudley	Wolverhampton	12/42
..	12/50 Wolverhampton	Dudley	1/10
..	1/11 Dudley	Old Hill	1/26
..	1/35 Old Hill	Dudley	1/49
..	2/20 Dudley	Old Hill	2/34
..	2/43 Old Hill	Halesowen & return	2/57
..	3/6 Old Hill	Dudley	3/22
..	3/28 Dudley	Old Hill	3/42
..	3/50 Old Hill	Halesowen & return	4/20
..	4/28 Old Hill	Dudley	4/44
..	5/2 Dudley	Old Hill	5/16
..	5/26 Old Hill	Stourbridge Jct	5/40
..	5/45 Stourbridge Jct	Dudley	6/10
..	6/13 Dudley	Old Hill	6/27
..	6/30 Old Hill	Dudley	6/46
..	6/50 Dudley	Old Hill	7/4
..	7/7 Old Hill	Dudley	7/23
..	7/30 Dudley	Old Hill	7/44
..	7/50 Old Hill	Dudley	8/6
..	8/15 Dudley	Old Hill	8/29
..	8/42 Old Hill	Dudley	8/58
..	9/3 Dudley	Old Hill	9/17
..	9/40 Old Hill	Halesowen & return	9/55
..	10/2 Old Hill	Halesowen & return	10/15
..	10/20 Old Hill	Halesowen	10/25
SX	10/35 Halesowen	Old Hill	10/40
..	10/50 Old Hill	Stourbridge Jct	11/3
SO	10/42 Halesowen	Old Hill	10/47
..	10/50 Old Hill	Dudley	11/6
..	11/10 Dudley	Old Hill	11/25
..	11/30 Old Hill	Halesowen & return	11/45
..	11/47 Old Hill	Halesowen & return	12.0mn
Sun	12.2 Old Hill	Stourbridge Jct	12.17

Mileage: 151 miles 37 chains (SX): 168 miles 60 chains (SO)

STOURBRIDGE CAR 'C'

Dly	5.0 Stourbridge Jct †	Stourbridge Town (Empty)	5.3
..	5.10 Stourbridge Town †	Langley Green	5.40
..	5.45 Langley Green	Oldbury	5.48
..	13 return branch trips, to		
..	1/5 Oldbury	Smethwick Jct	1/11
..	1/13 Smethwick Jct	Oldbury	1/20
..	6 return branch trips, to		
..	4/0 Oldbury	Smethwick Jct	4/7
..	4/15 Smethwick Jct	Oldbury	4/22
..	11 return branch trips, to		
..	10/7 Oldbury	Langley Green	10/10
..	10/12 Langley Green	Stourbridge Jct	10/35

Mileage: 68 miles 59 chains

NOTE

† Attached to Car 'D' as far as Langley Green

STOURBRIDGE CAR 'D'

Dly	5.0 Stourbridge Jct †	Stourbridge Town (Empty)	5.3
..	5.10 Stourbridge Town †	Birmingham	6.2
..	6.15 Birmingham	Stourbridge Jct	6.58
..	7.10 Stourbridge Jct	Stourbridge Town	7.13
..	54 return branch trips, to		
..	11/45 Stourbridge Town	Stourbridge Jct	11/48

Mileage: 107 miles

NOTE

† Car 'C' attached as far as Langley Green

TYSELEY CAR 'A'

Dly	6.50 Tyseley ‡	Bearley	8.9
..	8.28 Bearley ‡	Birmingham Moor St	9.30
..	9.35 Birmingham Moor St ‡	Henley-in-Arden	10.23
..	10.40 Henley-in-Arden	Stratford	11.0
..	11.30 Stratford	Henley-in-Arden	11.56
..	12/22 Henley-in-Arden	Birmingham Moor St	1/11
SX	1/19 Birmingham Moor St	Bearley	2/21
..	2/40 Bearley	Birmingham Moor St	3/46
..	4/20 Birmingham Moor St	Bearley	5/23
..	5/28 Bearley	Henley-in-Arden	5/39
..	5/40 Henley-in-Arden	Bearley	5/51
..	6/54 Bearley	Birmingham Moor St	8/12
..	8/30 Birmingham Moor St	Danzey	9/12
..	9/48 Danzey	Birmingham Moor St	10/34
..	10/45 Birmingham Moor St	Shirley	11/8
..	11/15 Shirley	Tyseley (Empty)	11/27
SO	1/35 Birmingham Moor St	Danzey	2/15
..	2/35 Danzey	Birmingham Moor St	3/14
..	3/20 Birmingham Moor St	Danzey	4/2
..	4/13 Danzey	Birmingham Moor St	4/54
..	5/15 Birmingham Moor St §	Henley-in-Arden	6/3
..	6/28 Henley-in-Arden	Bearley	6/39
..	6/43 Bearley	Stratford	6/53
..	8/5 Stratford §	Henley-in-Arden	8/32
..	8/42 Henley-in-Arden	Birmingham Moor St	9/33
..	9/40 Birmingham Moor St §	Henley-in-Arden	10/28
..	10/44 Henley-in-Arden §‡	Tyseley	11/22

Mileage: 237 miles 61 chains (SX): 220 miles 41 chains (SO)

NOTES

§ Trailer No.1 from Moor Street to Earlswood and return, then attached to 9/40 Moor Street and 10/44 Henley services throughout

‡ Trailer No.2 attached to 6.50 Tyseley and 8.28 Bearley throughout, then to 9.35 Moor St. as far as Shirley; 10/44 Henley from Earlswood

TYSELEY CAR 'B'

Dly	7.31 Tyseley ¶	Henley-in-Arden	8.5
..	8.15 Henley-in-Arden ¶	Birmingham Moor St	9.0
..	9.10 Birmingham Moor St ¶	Tyseley (Empty)	9.17
..	10.20 Tyseley	Shirley	10.34
..	10.55 Shirley	Birmingham Moor St	11.18
..	12/25 Birmingham Moor St †	Henley-in-Arden	1/12
..	1/39 Henley-in-Arden †	Birmingham Moor St	2/28
SX	3/10 Birmingham Moor St	Danzey	3/52
..	4/13 Danzey	Birmingham Moor St	4/54
..	5/15 Birmingham Moor St	Henley-in-Arden	6/3
..	6/28 Henley-in-Arden	Bearley	6/39
..	6/43 Bearley	Stratford	6/53
..	8/5 Stratford	Henley-in-Arden	8/32
..	8/42 Henley-in-Arden	Birmingham Moor St	9/33
..	9/40 Birmingham Moor St	Henley-in-Arden	10/28
..	10/44 Henley-in-Arden	Tyseley	11/22
SO	2/30 Birmingham Moor St	Stratford	3/45
..	4/45 Stratford	Bearley	4/56
..	5/3 Bearley	Henley-in-Arden	5/14
..	5/43 Henley-in-Arden §	Birmingham Moor St	6/31
..	6/40 Birmingham Moor St §	Shirley	7/3
..	7/10 Shirley §	Birmingham Moor St	7/33
..	7/40 Birmingham Moor St §	Henley-in-Arden	8/28
..	9/40 Henley-in-Arden	Danzey	9/46
..	9/48 Danzey ‡	Birmingham Moor St	10/34
..	11/10 Birmingham Moor St	Henley-in-Arden	11/58
Sun	12.5 Henley-in-Arden	Tyseley (Empty)	12.35

Mileage: 180 miles 54 chains (SX): 197 miles 38 chains (SO)

NOTES

‡ Attached to 9/48 Danzey to Moor St. Auto

§ Trailer No.2 attached at Shirley, then works 6/40 Moor St. and 7/10 Shirley throughout, attached to 7/40 Moor St. as far as Earlswood

¶ Trailer No.3 attached

† Stratford Trailer attached

STRATFORD CAR 'A'

Dly	6.45 Stratford §	Hatton	7.8
..	7.12 Hatton §	Bearley	7.23
..	7.26 Bearley §	Birmingham Moor St	8.28
..	8.40 Birmingham Moor St §	Henley-in-Arden	9.28
..	9.40 Henley-in-Arden §	Birmingham Moor St	10.29
..	10.45 Birmingham Moor St	Stratford	12/0nn
..	4/15 Stratford	Tyseley	5/20
..	5/48 Tyseley §	Hall Green	5/54
..	5/57 Hall Green §	Birmingham Moor St	6/12
..	6/17 Birmingham Moor St §	Henley-in-Arden	7/5
..	7/55 Henley-in-Arden	Lapworth	8/5
..	8/22 Lapworth	Henley-in-Arden	8/32
..	8/43 Henley-in-Arden §	Bearley	8/54
..	8/59 Bearley §	Stratford	9/10

Mileage: 154 miles 65 chains

NOTES

§ Trailer attached, on 8.40 Moor St as far as Danzey, then by 9.40 Henley to Moor St and empty to Tyseley; 5/48 thence as shown

STRATFORD CAR 'B'

Dly	7.15 Stratford	Cheltenham	8.55
..	9.42 Cheltenham	Honeybourne	11.3
..	11.11 Honeybourne	Broadway	11.22
..	12/3 Broadway	Honeybourne	12/18
..	12/36 Honeybourne	Cheltenham	1/56
..	2/39 Cheltenham	Evesham	4/0
..	4/38 Evesham	Cheltenham	6/6
..	6/10 Cheltenham	Honeybourne	7/16
..	7/39 Honeybourne	Cheltenham	8/50
..	9/0 Cheltenham	Stratford	10/42

Mileage: 207 miles 40 chains

Later Years

Stourbridge

A similar arrangement to the summer 1911 was in force for Stourbridge motors during 1912, with two cars on the Old Hill, Halesowen and Dudley services, one on the Oldbury branch, and a fourth on the Stourbridge Town trains.

In 1922, two Stourbridge motors are shown in charge of the Old Hill, Halesowen and Dudley services, another on the Town branch, and a fourth on the Birmingham (Snow Hill) & Dudley trains. However, it is likely that auto trains were now used on at least two of these, as Stourbridge Jct's allocation of motors during that summer never exceeded two; however, the shed had four auto-fitted '517' and '2021' locomotives in that year. The Town service was, however, clearly labelled 'Rail Motor'.

On 11th May 1925, a new passenger service using SRMs was introduced between Wolverhampton and Stourbridge Junction, via Wombourn, using the recently-opened Oxley & Himley line. For this, two motors were required, one of which came from Stourbridge, the other from Wolverhampton. The Stourbridge car started the day with the 7.22 a.m. Stourbridge Junction service, and made a total of four round trips to Wolverhampton, one of which terminated at Brettell Lane on its return, and left again from that station for Wolverhampton. The SRM ended its day with the 8.50 p.m. Wolverhampton to Stourbridge Jct.

By 1929, Stourbridge's allocation of SRMs had climbed to three, and in the coach programme a pair were shown as operating the Dudley services out of Old Hill, a third on the Stourbridge, Wombourn & Wolverhampton duty, and a fourth on the Town branch. Again, there was probably a mix with auto trains as operational circumstances and availability dictated. The Wombourn branch was now operated solely by a Stourbridge 'motor', starting at 6.50 a.m. with four round trips to Wolverhampton, but intermediately working three return journeys from Wolverhampton to Wombourn, and one from Stourbridge Jct. to Hagley. This duty was suspended in 1932.

Three motors survived at Stourbridge on local services until the early summer of 1934, when all three were sent to Swindon. They had probably worked on the Halesowen duty, though that ceased in 1933 with the substitution of a 'road motor car service' from Old Hill, but the workmen's trains continued to run. The motors also ran the Town service to their departure.

In June 1934, No.88 was transferred in, and this probably spent most of its serviceable time on the Town service. The removal of No.88 in October 1935 severed a thirty-year association with the SRMs.

Stratford

The summer 1912 arrangement was similar, though Stratford is shown with an additional SRM diagram, working variously to Honeybourne, Evesham, Hatton and Leamington.

A pair of motors remained at Stratford on the services until August 1917, after which auto and conventional trains ran the originating diagrams. The SRM continued on its Cheltenham duty until that time.

Tyseley

Tyseley retained its two SRM and one auto duties in summer 1912, though the last pair of motors left the shed in February 1914. Autos presumably took over the diagrams from that time; the 1922 coach programme certainly shows four auto workings over the line.

Wolverhampton

When the Wombourn and Stourbridge service commenced in May 1925, the timetable required two cars, one of which was based on Wolverhampton; this started the day with the 6.55 a.m. return trip to Wombourn, followed by four round trips to Stourbridge Junction, finishing with the 8.40 p.m. Stourbridge to Wolverhampton. Motors Nos.40 (which was the car on the first train from Wolverhampton) and 95 were amongst those allocated to Stafford Road shed, presumably for this service, and were photographed on the line.

Passenger numbers were not as great as had been hoped for, and as an economy move, the timetable was modified so that it could be worked from the Stourbridge end by a single car (see under Stourbridge). The service was withdrawn in 1932.

WORCESTER DIVISION

The earliest SRMs into the division were allocated to Evesham for the service along the uncompleted section of the Cheltenham line, working from October 1904. They also visited Stratford.

This was followed by an allocation to Kidderminster for the services to Bewdley and Stourport, which commenced in January 1905.

In 1909, the Evesham motor set out at 7.30 a.m. for Honeybourne, working the 7.47 a.m. thence to Cheltenham, and return, then the 11.10 a.m. Honeybourne to Broadway and Evesham. The motor then worked the 12.37 p.m. Evesham to Cheltenham and back, the 4.25 p.m. Evesham to Cheltenham with a return to Honeybourne, the 7.34 p.m. return trip Honeybourne to Cheltenham, and finally the 9.57 p.m. Honeybourne to Evesham. The Cheltenham car worked the 8.0 a.m. Cheltenham to Moreton-in-Marsh and return, and the 12.34 and 3.36 p.m. return trips to Honeybourne.

The SRMs were transferred away from Evesham in July 1911.

Worcester had spasmodic allocations in 1905/6, and a more permanent presence from 1908. The motors may have been utilised on the Malvern services at that time, but little evidence is available. The cars may have been held as spares for Evesham and Kidderminster.

1911

Allocation of SRMs in July 1911 was:

Kidderminster	85, 98 (70 ft)
Worcester	66 (70 ft)

Most of the work in two Kidderminster SRM diagrams was based around the Kidderminster, Bewdley & Hartlebury triangle, though with extensions to Stourbridge Jct., Bridgnorth, Woofferton and Worcester.

Although a car was allocated to Worcester, no workings are shown for it in the coach programme.

WORCESTER DIVISION

KIDDERMINSTER CAR 'A'

Dly	5.42 Kidderminster	Stourbridge Jct.	6.0
..	6.20 Stourbridge Jct	Stourbridge Town	6.23
..	6.26 Stourbridge Town	Stourbridge Jct.	6.29
..	6.33 Stourbridge Jct. †	Kidderminster	6.50
..	7.5 Kidderminster	Stourport (via Bewdley)	7.25
..	7.30 Stourport	Bewdley	7.37
..	7.46 Bewdley	Hartlebury	8.22
..	8.40 Hartlebury	Kidderminster (via Bewdley)	9.10
..	9.26 Kidderminster	Hartlebury (via Bewdley)	9.53
..	9.56 Hartlebury	Kidderminster (via Main Line)	10.4
..	10.35 Kidderminster	Hartlebury (via Bewdley)	11.5
..	11.8 Hartlebury	Kidderminster (via Main Line)	11.17
..	11.50 Kidderminster	Hartlebury (via Bewdley)	12/16
..	12/19 Hartlebury	Kidderminster (via Main Line)	12/28
..	1/23 Kidderminster	Bewdley	1/35
..	2/20 Bewdley	Hartlebury	2/40
..	4/5 Hartlebury	Kidderminster (via Bewdley)	4/34
..	4/46 Kidderminster	Hartlebury (via Bewdley)	5/16
..	5/20 Hartlebury	Bewdley	5/35
..	5/45 Bewdley	Stourport (Empty)	5/52
..	6/4 Stourport	Bewdley	6/10
..	6/14 Bewdley	Kidderminster	6/26
..	6/45 Kidderminster	Hartlebury (via Bewdley)	7/13
..	7/17 Hartlebury	Bridgnorth	8/7
..	9/25 Bridgnorth	Kidderminster	10/16
WSO	10/50 Kidderminster	Hartlebury (via Bewdley)	11/17
..	11/30 Hartlebury	Kidderminster (via Main Line)	11/39

Mileage: 161½ miles (WSX). 174¼ miles (WSO)

NOTE: † Brake Van ex-Birmingham attached

KIDDERMINSTER CAR 'B'

Dly	7.30 Kidderminster	Bewdley	7.40
..	8.40 Bewdley	Kidderminster	8.50
..	9.10 Kidderminster	Worcester (via Bewdley)	10.13
..	10.40 Worcester	Bridgnorth (via Stourport)	12/0nn
..	1/25 Bridgnorth ‡	Kidderminster	2/17
..	2/30 Kidderminster	Stourport (via Bewdley)	2/52
..	3/5 Stourport	Kidderminster (via Bewdley)	3/27
..	4/10 Kidderminster	Woofferton	5/42
..	6/5 Woofferton	Kidderminster	7/50
..	8/10 Kidderminster	Hartlebury (via Bewdley)	8/40
..	8/45 Hartlebury	Kidderminster (via Bewdley)	9/16
..	9/25 Kidderminster	Stourport (via Bewdley)	9/47
..	9/50 Stourport	Kidderminster (via Bewdley)	10/16
..	10/45 Kidderminster	Worcester (via Main Line)	11/17
SX	11/25 Worcester	Kidderminster (via Main Line)	12.0mn
SO	11/25 Worcester	Stourbridge Jct (via Main Line)	12.19
Sun	12.20 Stourbridge Jct	Kidderminster (Empty)	12.34

Mileage: 201 miles (SX); 213½ miles (SO)

NOTE

‡ 8w Third attached

Later Years

Worcester

By 1922, the Worcester SRM had found 'official' employment, and was used on an afternoon and evening, five return-trip sequence to the Malverns (Great and Wells). The last motor left in February 1925, and the summer 1925 schedules were marked for an auto train.

Kidderminster

The SRM diagrams continued into the spring of 1918, after which one working was carried out by an auto train.

Malvern Wells

An SRM was allocated to Malvern Wells from April 1917 until December 1919. This may have been for storage purposes, or for some local services.

NORTHERN DIVISION

One of the greatest concentrations of SRMs during the pre-Great War years was at Wrexham, Croes Newydd shed. The first duty, commencing in July 1904, worked to Gobowen, Llangollen (and, it is officially recorded, 'Llanuwchllyn'). The operating pamphlet produced by the Chester Division prior to commencement of the services shows the first motor working the 9.55 a.m. Wrexham to Gobowen, then back to Ruabon for a 90-mile return trip to Dolgelly, and finally the 3.49 p.m. Ruabon and Wrexham. The second car again worked mostly on the Dolgelly branch, and started with the 1.50 p.m. Wrexham to Bala, and return to Ruabon. A return trip from Ruabon to Bala, then Llangollen, was carried out before finally working the 9.20 p.m. Ruabon to Llangollen and the 9.50 p.m. thence back to Wrexham. Three SRMs were initially stationed at Croes Newydd, two in use and one spare. One coach could be attached to a motor for strengthening, and these were located at Ruabon, Llangollen, Corwen, Bala and Dolgelly for that purpose.

More motors were transferred by October of that year for diagrams involving the Coed Poeth and Rhos lines.

By the summer of 1905, the Croes Newydd allocation had risen from the initial three to ten motors, with six daily diagrams, and a seventh on Mondays, Thursdays and Saturdays. These covered workings along the main line as far south as Oswestry, the Llangollen line, and on the Wrexham and Coed Poeth/Berwig, Wynne Hall, Ponkey and Moss branches.

A Corwen motor also worked to Ruabon and the main line during 1905/6, and the shed was diagrammed in once more from 1910. The official Corwen allocation seems to have been dependent upon the Croes Newydd diagrams; in early summer 1909, for example, a Croes Newydd car stopped overnight on weekdays, and departed again mid-morning, though it was nominally part of a Wrexham schedule as no car was shown for Corwen at that time. It also worked two return trips from Corwen to Ruabon on Sundays.

The branch from Wellington to Buildwas, Much Wenlock and Craven Arms (Wellington & Severn Junction), together with the connecting line between Shifnal, the Madeley branch and Coalbrookdale, was the scene of intense SRM operation in the summer and autumn of 1906, starting on 1st May. There were three daily motor diagrams based on Much Wenlock, and these ran out to the three limits of the lines, and intermediately to Coalbrookdale, Buildwas, Much Wenlock and Presthope. The first motor left Wenlock at 6.45 a.m. for Craven Arms, then ran eleven intermediate legs before completing the day with the 7.5 p.m. Wellington to Much Wenlock. The second departed at 7.30 a.m. from Wenlock to Wellington, worked eight intermediate legs, and finished with the 9.10 p.m. Wellington to Much Wenlock. The shortest diagram was operated by the third SRM, which started with the 8.20 a.m. Much Wenlock to Shifnal, ran six intermediate legs, and completed its turn with the 5.44 p.m. Wellington to Much Wenlock. All three motors visited Wellington (ten times, eleven on Saturdays), Shifnal (five) and Craven Arms (four) in the course of their duties. However, with large numbers of passengers travelling on market days – but not on other days – and the steep gradients on the line, it was soon apparent that circumstances were not best suited to SRM operation. At peak periods, two SRMs sandwiching a trailer were used, and this incurred additional crew and operating costs.

Between September and November 1906, no less than 19 failures occurred on seven different cars used from Much Wenlock, and the cars were withdrawn in 1907. The branch went back to conventional operation, using three 3-coach sets on much the same workings as the motors, though the Shifnal visits decreased as time passed.

1911

The allocation in July 1911 was:

Shed	*Cars*
Croes Newydd	5, 9, 18, 19, 20, 28, 32 (59 ft), 70, 88 (70 ft)
(Corwen	88)

There were at this time five duties for Croes Newydd motors, with a sixth working from Corwen (with motor No.88 from August). The first two diagrams at Croes Newydd and that from Corwen worked within the Wrexham, Corwen and Oswestry area, whilst the other three from Croes Newydd operated the Ponkey, Moss and Wynn Hall turns. With the exception of a visit by the Ponkey motor in the afternoon, the Coed Poeth and Berwig Sidings Halt branch was worked by an auto train at the time.

NORTHERN DIVISION

CROES NEWYDD CAR 'A'

Dly	6.10 Wrexham	Llangollen	6.45
..	6.55 Llangollen	Ruabon	7.13
..	7.28 Ruabon	Oswestry	7.57
..	8.0 Oswestry	Ruabon & Corwen	9.23
..	9.40 Corwen	Ruabon	10.25
..	10.42 Ruabon	Llangollen	11.2
..	11.25 Llangollen	Ruabon	11.43
..	12/28 Ruabon	Gobowen	12/55
..	1/15 Gobowen	Ruabon	1/38
..	2/10 Ruabon	Corwen	2/55
..	4/0 Corwen	Ruabon	4/53
..	5/10 Ruabon	Oswestry	5/40
..	6/0 Oswestry	Gobowen	6/6
..	6/19 Gobowen	Oswestry	6/25
..	6/30 Oswestry	Gobowen	6/36
..	8/26 Gobowen	Oswestry	8/32
..	9/33 Oswestry	Wrexham	10/22

Mileage: 163 miles 8 chains

CROES NEWYDD CAR 'B'

Dly	9.35 Wrexham	Oswestry	10.29
..	10.33 Oswestry	Gobowen	10.39
..	10.55 Gobowen	Oswestry	11.1
..	11.6 Oswestry	Ruabon	11.35
..	11.45 Ruabon	Chester	12/28
..	12/45 Chester	Ruabon	1/31
..	1/40 Ruabon*	Llangollen	1/58
..	2/20 Llangollen	Ruabon (Empty)	2/35
..	4/10 Ruabon	Corwen	4/55
..	5/10 Corwen	Ruabon	5/56
..	6/12 Ruabon	Corwen	6/57
..	7/40 Corwen	Wrexham	8/45

Mileage: 145 miles 25 chains

NOTE

* Strengthened as required

CORWEN MOTOR

Dly	12/48 Corwen	Ruabon	1/40
..	2/20 Ruabon ‡	Oswestry	2/50
..	2/58 Oswestry	Gobowen	3/4
..	3/23 Gobowen	Oswestry	3/29
..	3/40 Oswestry	Gobowen	3/46
..	4/0 Gobowen	Oswestry	4/6
..	4/25 Oswestry ‡	Ruabon	5/2
..	6/10 Ruabon	Oswestry	6/48
..	7/15 Oswestry	Wrexham	8/0
..	8/16 Wrexham	Llangollen	8/50
..	9/0 Llangollen	Ruabon	9/18
MTFO	9/52 Ruabon	Corwen	10/40
WThSO	9/52 Ruabon	Llangollen	10/10
..	10/18 Llangollen	Ruabon	10/35
..	10/50 Ruabon	Corwen	11/35

Mileage: 103 miles 24 chains (MTFO); 115 miles 52 chains (WThSO)

NOTE

‡ Four-bodied Brake Third attached

CROES NEWYDD CAR 'C'

Dly	8.0 Wrexham	Ponkey	8.17
..	8.30 Ponkey	Wrexham	8.47
..	10.0 Wrexham	Ponkey	10.20
..	10.33 Ponkey	Wrexham	10.53
..	12/5 Wrexham	Ponkey	12/23
..	12/35 Ponkey	Wrexham	12/52
..	1/10 Wreham	Ponkey	1/29
..	1/35 Ponkey	Wrexham	1/55
..	2/3 Wrexham	Ponkey	2/23
..	2/45 Ponkey	Wrexham	3/5
..	4/15 Wrexham	Ponkey	4/34
..	4/40 Ponkey	Wrexham	5/0
..	5/38 Wrexham	Ponkey	5/54
..	5/57 Ponkey	Wrexham	6/12
SX	6/20 Wrexham	Coed Poeth	6/48
..	6/57 Coed Poeth	Wrexham	7/23
ThSX	7/40 Wrexham	Moss	7/53
..	7/57 Moss	Wrexham	8/10
..	8/45 Wrexham	Moss	8/58
..	9/3 Moss	Wrexham	9/20
SO	8/20 Wrexham	Ponkey	8/40
..	8/50 Ponkey	Wrexham	9/10
..	9/28 Wrexham	Ponkey	9/45
..	9/55 Ponkey	Wrexham	10/15
..	10/40 Wrexham	Ponkey	10/59
..	11/2 Ponkey	Wrexham	11/21

Mileage: 74 miles 78 chains (ThO); 87 miles 50 chains (ThSX); 89 miles 40 chains (SO)

CROES NEWYDD CAR 'D'

SX	7.55 Wrexham ‡	Moss	8.8
..	8.10 Moss ‡	Wrexham	8.25
MO	8.32 Wrexham	Brymbo West	8.48
..	8.53 Brymbo West	Wrexham	9.10
SX	9.40 Wrexham ‡	Moss	9.53
..	9.58 Moss ‡	Wrexham	10.13
..	11.20 Wrexham	Moss	11.33
..	11.36 Moss	Wrexham	11.51
..	12/50 Wrexham	Moss	1/3
..	1/5 Moss	Wrexham	1/20
..	2/5 Wrexham	Moss	2/18
..	2/21 Moss	Wrexham	2/36
..	3/5 Wrexham	Moss	3/18
..	3/30 Moss	Wrexham	3/45
MThO	4/20 Wrexham ‡	Brymbo West	4/36
..	4/48 Brymbo West ‡	Wrexham	5/5
SX	6/0 Wrexham ‡	Moss	6/13
..	6/15 Moss ‡	Wrexham	6/30
..	6/50 Wrexham	Chester	7/26
..	8/50 Chester	Ruabon	9/35
WSX	10/3 Ruabon	Croes Newydd (Empty)	10/15
WO	10/40 Ruabon	Wrexham	10/52

Mileage: 93 miles 1 chain (MO); 77 miles 53 chains(TFO); 78 miles 6 chains (WO); 85 miles 27 chains (ThO)

NOTE

‡ Trailer (MThO)

SO	7.55 Wrexham	Moss	8.8
..	8.11 Moss	Wrexham	8.25
..	9.40 Wrexham	Moss	9.53
..	10.0 Moss	Wrexham	10.13
..	11.20 Wrexham	Moss	11.33
..	11.38 Moss	Wrexham	11.51
..	12/50 Wrexham	Moss	1/3
..	1/5 Moss	Wrexham	1/18
..	2/5 Wrexham	Moss	2/18
..	2/23 Moss	Wrexham	2/36
..	3/5 Wrexham	Moss	3/18
..	3/30 Moss	Wrexham	3/43
..	4/25 Wrexham	Moss	4/38
..	4/42 Moss	Wrexham	4/55
..	5/20 Wrexham	Moss	5/33
..	5/35 Moss	Wrexham	5/50
..	6/0 Wrexham	Moss	6/13
..	6/18 Moss	Wrexham	6/31
..	7/40 Wrexham	Moss	7/53
..	7/55 Moss	Wrexham	8/10
..	8/30 Wrexham	Moss	8/43
..	8/47 Moss	Wrexham	9/0
..	9/10 Wrexham	Moss	9/23
..	9/25 Moss	Wrexham	9/40
..	9/55 Wrexham	Moss	10/8
..	10/15 Moss	Wrexham	10/30
..	10/50 Wrexham	Moss	11.3
..	11/5 Moss	Croes Newydd (Empty)	1/15

Mileage: 88 miles 16 chains

NOTE

One Car and one Trailer up to 3/43 Wrexham arrival. Two Cars and two Trailers from 4/25 Wrexham departure until finish

CROES NEWYDD CAR 'E'

Dly	7.40 Wrexham	Wynn Hall	8.3
..	8.8 Wynn Hall	Wrexham	8.30
..	9.0 Wrexham	Wynn Hall	9.25
..	9.28 Wynn Hall	Wrexham	9.53
..	10.0 Wrexham	Wynn Hall	10.25
..	10.28 Wynn Hall	Wrexham	10.53
..	11.0 Wrexham	Wynn Hall	11.25
..	11.30 Wynn Hall	Wrexham	11.54
..	12/5 Wrexham	Rhos	12/20
..	12/25 Rhos	Wrexham	12/37
..	1/10 Wrexham	Wynn Hall	1/32
..	1/35 Wynn Hall	Wrexham	1/55
..	2/3 Wrexham	Wynn Hall	2/25
..	2/40 Wynn Hall	Wrexham	3/5
..	3/15 Wrexham	Rhos	3/29
..	3/37 Rhos	Wrexham	3/52
..	4/15 Wrexham	Wynn Hall	4/36
..	4/38 Wynn Hall	Wrexham	5/0
..	5/13 Wrexham	Wynn Hall	5/35
..	5/43 Wynn Hall	Wrexham	6/5
..	6/10 Wrexham	Wynn Hall	6/30
..	6/35 Wynn Hall	Wrexham	6/57
..	7/5 Wrexham	Wynn Hall	7/30
..	7/33 Wynn Hall	Wrexham	7/55
SX	8/20 Wrexham	Rhos	8/36
..	8/55 Rhos	Wrexham	9/10
..	9/28 Wrexham	Rhos	9/40
..	9/43 Rhos	Wrexham	10/2
SO	8/20 Wrexham	Wynn Hall	8/44
..	8/46 Wynn Hall	Wrexham	9/10
..	9/28 Wrexham	Wynn Hall	9/47
..	9/50 Wynn Hall	Wrexham	10/15
..	10/40 Wrexham	Rhos	10/56
..	11/5 Rhos	Wrexham	11/21

Mileage: 143 miles 12 chains (SX); 156 miles 42 chains (SO)

NOTE

Trailer attached 3/15 Wrexham until finish (SO)

Later Years

Croes Newydd

In 1912, the working of Croes Newydd SRM 'A' (see Tables) was transferred to an auto.

Ponkey branch motors ceased in 1915, and in the post-Great War era, the adjacent Wynn Hall services were terminated short, at Rhos.

In 1921, a motor was involved on the Berwig/Coed Poeth branch, with most trains now turning round at Coed Poeth. Most of the trips over the Moss branch was worked by a motor, although an auto train was used for one return trip.

The run-down in the use of SRMs at Croes Newydd had commenced during the Great War, and continued into the 1920s. By mid-1922, there were just four motors left at the shed, reduced to two in September, and one from 1924. From 1928 to 1930 there were two SRMs at the shed. The two diagrams in the latter 1920s were divided for one motor to work eleven daily return trips between Wrexham, Brymbo West, Coed Poeth or Berwig, whilst the second operated eleven from Wrexham to Rhos and five to Moss, totalling 16. In the summer 1928 season, these had been reduced to eight on the Berwig line, and five Rhos/Moss.

There was just one motor at Croes Newydd from 1931 to 1933. The branches along which the SRMs had carried out much of their work were closed in January 1931, although the resident car could still be seen on an occasional main-line stopping train. No.78 left Wrexham in December 1933 to sever the long connection.

Cambrian

Following the amalgamation with the Cambrian Railways in January 1922, the Great Western decided to use SRMs on parts of the system, and particularly in the Barmouth & Dolgelly district. Since the amalgamation, it had become possible to run many of the trains from the east through Dolgelly onto former Cambrian metals, rather than make a change of trains at that place, as had previously been the norm. From September 1922, a motor was stationed at Dolgelly or Penmaenpool for the 'branch' service, though this car was also used for intermediate services on the main Pwllheli line. The day started with the 8.45 a.m. Dolgelly to Barmouth and return, then the 10.45 a.m. Dolgelly to Dyffryn, the 11.35 a.m. thence to Barmouth, and the 12.30 p.m. back to Dolgelly. The afternoon sequence started with the 1.25 p.m. Dolgelly to Dyffryn, then back along the main line with the 2.55 p.m. Dyffryn, through Barmouth to Llwyngwril, the 3.55 p.m. Llwyngwril to Harlech, and finally the 5.10 p.m. Harlech to Dolgelly. SRMs remained in the area until the summer of 1927.

A car was also tried on the Llanidloes line from September 1922, working the 11.20 a.m. Llanidloes to Moat Lane, the 12.35 p.m. Moat Lane to Builth Wells and back, the 4.50 p.m. Moat Lane to Llanidloes and return, and finally the 6.0 p.m. Moat Lane to Llanidloes. The motors were perhaps not seen as successful, and the allocation ceased in summer 1924, although 'motor' services are shown over the line for a while longer. In summer 1928, these services were scheduled for auto working, and may well have been so earlier.

Other cars are shown as allocated to 'Cambrian Line' (e.g. Nos.74 and 84 in July 1922) rather than to any specific shed. No.74 is shown at Oswestry in August 1922. A note from Ifor Higgon to Ken Davies indicates that an Oswestry motor was used on the Ellesmere & Wrexham service, the first journey starting at Oswestry and the last finishing there; he saw Nos.39, 40, 73, 78, 84 and 85 on this service.

Several cars are recorded as being allocated to Machynlleth: Nos.74 and 75 at various times in 1922/3, 76 in 1924-5, and 81 in 1926-7. There are no details of any services worked, and they may have been spares for the Dolgelly duty.

GW & LNW JOINT

The only service worked by SRMs over the joint line between Chester and Birkenhead, and along the Helsby branch, was based at Chester, and commenced around May 1911.

1911

One car was allocated in summer 1911:

Shed	*Car*
Chester	45 (70 ft)

The Chester car worked a modest service on the Hooton & Helsby branch at this time, with one extension to Birkenhead.

GWR and L & NWR JOINT

CHESTER CAR

Dly	10.45 Chester	Hooton	11 1
..	11 3 Hooton	Ellesmere Port	11 12
..	11 50 Ellesmere Port	Birkenhead	12/16
..	12/40 Birkenhead	Hooton	12/56
SO	12/57 Hooton	Ellesmere Port	1/6
..	1/15 Ellesmere Port	Hooton	1/25
Dly	4/0 Hooton	Helsby	4/21
..	4/35 Helsby	Hooton	4/57
..	5/10 Hooton	Ellesmere Port	5/19
..	5/45 Ellesmere Port	Chester	6/10

Mileage 63 miles 28 chains (SX) 70 miles 72 chains (SO)

Later Years

Chester

In 1912, the diagram was much the same, except the 5.10 p.m. Hooton now ran through to Helsby instead of Ellesmere Port.

The Chester SRM duty continued through to December 1919, with two motors permanently in residence from 1915. A rather more complex diagram was now in operation. In 1917, this started with the 6.20 a.m. Chester (via Helsby) to Ellesmere Port, then the 8.35 a.m. Helsby to Birkenhead. Two round trips from Birkenhead (departing 9.8 and 10.45 a.m.) to Ellesmere Port came next, with the unit returning from Birkenhead to Hooton at 12.35 p.m. The afternoon schedule commenced with the 4.50 p.m. Hooton, Helsby and Chester trip, followed by the 6.20 p.m. Chester to Hooton by the same route, and finally the 7.5 p.m. Hooton to Helsby and Chester.

Another brief allocation was made in the summer of 1924, by which time the motors were primarily shedded at Birkenhead.

Birkenhead

Two motors returned to the area again in July 1923, but this time allocated to Birkenhead, though one was briefly held at Chester in the summer 1924 schedule. This schedule was completely different from that of the previous decade in that its service was based heavily on Mersey Railway connections between Rock Ferry and Liverpool (Central and St. James's St.). In 1927, The car ran empty at 6.10 a.m. from Birkenhead shed to Ledsham, worked the 6.42 a.m. Ledsham to Rock Ferry, then ran eight return trips out to Hooton (for connections to West Kirby and Helsby branches), and one to Spital. The working expanded after this, with the 3.5 p.m. Rock Ferry to Hooton returning to Birkenhead, forming the 4.38 p.m. Birkenhead to Hooton and back, and the 5.26 p.m. Birkenhead to Heswall with a return to Rock Ferry. The 7.27 p.m. Rock Ferry to Hooton returned to Birkenhead, with the last trip, the 8.40 p.m. Birkenhead to Hooton and return, then to shed.

Motor No.98 was the last to work in the area, from October 1929 to April 1933, after which it returned to Swindon Pool.

APPENDIX D
STEAM RAIL MOTOR ALLOCATIONS AND STOPPAGES

This Appendix had been compiled principally from material in the National Archives (Public Record Office): the *Registers of Monthly Shed Allocations of Locomotive Stock* (RAIL 254/61-93), the *Rail Motor (Stoppages) Register* (RAIL 254/210) and the *History Sheets for Condemned Locomotives* (RAIL 254/224-331), which effectively take over from the stoppages register as far as SRMs are concerned. SRMs were not recorded in the allocations registers from April 1906 until April 1908, although some allocations during this period can be deduced. The allocations registers for 1920 and 1933 are not in the PRO's collection.

GWR accountancy seems to have been carried out on the basis of four-week periods. Thus, there were 13 periods and 1 day in a normal year (2 days in a leap year), so one month every year had two period end-dates falling within it. For example, in 1905 allocations were recorded on 7th January, 4th February, 4th March, 1st April, 29th April, etc. Because the number of four-week periods in a year is not exact, the dates on which the allocations were recorded slipped each year; in 1906 they were on 6th Jan, 3rd Feb, 3rd Mar, 31st Mar, 28th Apr, etc. There were adjustments to the four-week dates from time to time. Allocations where only the month and year are given should be read as allocated during (one of) the four week periods ending in that month.

Repairs were categorized in the stoppages register and the history sheets as:

L = Light (or Slight)
G = General
H = Heavy
BC = Boiler Change

Boiler changes were listed in the stoppages register, but owing to repairs made to the register over the years, many of these have been lost. For some reason, engine changes were not listed in the stoppages register, although some are given on the surviving engine, boiler and car history sheets. Because of the incomplete nature of the surviving records, neither boiler or engine changes are listed here.

The number of days a car was stopped for repairs was recorded. These have been recalculated on the most common basis used ('Date set to work' minus 'Date stopped') for consistency, and to eliminate the occasional error. It seems that the 'Date set to work' would have been better defined as 'Date available for work', because there was quite often a period between this date and the date when a car was allocated to a depot. Short delays like this (e.g. for a car to get to its new depot) have been ignored. Swindon had a Stock Shed to which cars could be allocated when there was an appreciable delay between the repairs being completed and the car going to a depot.

SHED/FACTORY ABBREVIATIONS

				NEA	Neath	RDG	Reading	STB	Stourbridge Jct.
ABDR	Aberdare	Cnstr	Cirencester Stock	NEY	Neyland	SDN	Swindon Loco	Sltny	Saltney Shops
BAN	Banbury	CNYD	Croes Newydd	NPT	Ebbw Jct.	SDst	Swindon District	SWks	Swindon Works
BHD	Birkenhead	DYD	Duffryn Yard	N/R	Not Recorded	SFPl	Swindon Factory Pool	TN	Taunton
Bgwtr	Bridgwater	EXE	Exeter	OOC	Old Oak Common	SHL	Southall	TR	Truro
BTL	Bristol	FGD	Goodwick	OSW	Oswestry	SLO	Slough	TYS	Tyseley
Chlfd	Chalford	GLO	Gloucester	OXY	Oxley	SLP	Shrewsbury	WES	Westbury
Chphm	Chippenham	LLY	Llanelly	PDN	Paddington	SPM	St. Philip's Marsh	WEY	Weymouth
CHR	Chester	MCH	Machynlleth	PPRD	Pontypool Road	SRD	Stafford Road (Factory/Shed)	WOS	Worcester
Clhm	Coleham Shops	MtSdg	Military Sidings	PZ	Penzance	SStk	Swindon Stock	WPN	Wolverhampton

SRM ALLOCATIONS

No.1 (Diagrams A1, A)

Allocation	*Date*	*Stop'd*	*Date*	*Days Stop'd*	*Catgy. Repair*	*Miles Run*
New	Oct 03					
Chalford	12 Oct 03	SWks	9 May 04	5		
Lambourn Valley	14 May 04	SWks	26 Nov 04	62	G	
Swindon Stock	27 Jan 05					
Lambourn Valley	19 Feb 05	SWks	4 Sep 05	131	G	
Swindon Stock	13 Jan 06					
Trowbridge	23 Jan 06	SWks	10 Feb 06	16		
Aberdare	26 Feb 06	SWks	5 Nov 06	78	G	
Aberdare?	22 Jan 07					
At Aberdare	25 Apr 08	SWks	6 Oct 08	119	G	
Swindon Stock	2 Feb 09					
Weymouth	21 Feb 10					
Swindon Stock	Mar 10	SWks	23 Mar 10	17		
Swindon Stock	9 Apr 10					
Southall	9 May 10					
Swindon Stock	Jun 10					
Gloucester	12 Jul 11	GLO	11 Aug 11	223		
		SWks	13 Sep 11		G	
Swindon Stock	21 Mar 12					
Neath	4 Jul 12					
Aberystwyth	Aug 12					
Neath	Oct 12					
Swindon Stock	Nov 12					
Stourbridge Jn.	6 Nov 12					
Swindon Stock	Dec 12					
Bristol	23 May 13	SWks	18 Aug 13	66	H, BC	
Swindon Stock	23 Oct 13					
Chalford	16 May 14					
Swindon Stock	Jun 14					
Neath	23 Jun 14	SWks	26 Aug 14	16	L	
Swindon Stock	11 Sep 14					
Aberdare	25 Sep 14	SWks	15 Oct 14	23	H	
Swindon Stock	7 Nov 14					
Aberdare	20 Nov 14	SWks	16 Feb 15	44	H, BC	
Swindon Stock	1 Apr 15					
Newport	16 Oct 15					
Swindon Stock	Nov 15					
Aberdare	Dec 15	SWks	15 Jan 17			

(Converted to Trailer No.105 (Dia. A6)

No.2 (Diagrams A1, A)

Allocation	*Date*	*Stop'd*	*Date*	*Days Stop'd*	*Catgy. Repair*	*Miles Run*
New	Oct 03					
Chalford	10 Oct 03	SWks	9 May 04	5		
Lambourn Valley	14 May 04	SWks	29 Oct 04	76	G	24,226
Lambourn Valley	13 Jan 05	SWks	16 Aug 05	64	G	38,487
Southall	19 Oct 05					
Aberdare	29 Dec 05	SWks	14 Aug 07	75	G	57,940
Swindon Stock?	28 Oct 07					
Croes Newydd	27 Jan 08					
Swindon Stock	May 08	SWks	29 Jan 10	4		
Swindon Stock	2 Feb 10					
Aberdare	16 Feb 10	SWks	11 Jul 12	106	G	91,878
Swindon Stock	25 Oct 12					
Gloucester	16 Jan 13					
Swindon Stock	Feb 13					
Yatton	23 May 13					
Bristol	Jul 13					
Radstock	Sep 13					
Bristol	Nov 13	SWks	15 Jan 14	133	H	105,841
Swindon Stock	28 May 14					
Southall Jn	26 Jun 14	SWks	10 Oct 14	89	H, BC	111,920
Swindon Stock	7 Jan 15					
Southall	26 Jan 15					
Swindon Stock	Apr 15	SWks	11 Jan 16			112,321

Converted to Trailer No.106, (Dia. A6)

No.3 (Diagrams B1, B, C)

Allocation	*Date*	*Stop'd*	*Date*	*Days Stop'd*	*Catgy. Repair*	*Miles Run*
New	Apr 04					
Southall	14 Apr 04	SWks	29 Jul 04	21	-	
Swindon Stock	19 Aug 04					
Chalford	24 Aug 04	SWks	1 Nov 04	8	L	
Chalford	9 Nov 04	SWks	10 Dec 04	14	L	
Swindon Stock	24 Dec 04					
Chalford	25 Jan 05	SWks	18 Feb 05	55	-	
Swindon Stock	14 Apr 05					
Trowbridge	27 Apr 05					
Weymouth	May 05	SDst	9 Aug 05	37	L	
Weymouth	15 Sep 05	SWks	16 Dec 05	34	G, BC	29,417
Swindon Stock	19 Jan 06					
Swindon Stock	19 Jan 06					
Laira	24 Jan 06	SWks	27 Nov 06	22	G, BC	41,698
Laira?	19 Dec 06	SWks	25 Jan 07	3	L, BC	42,745
?	28 Jan 07	SWks	7 Sep 07	54	G, BC	63,925
Swindon Stock	31 Oct 07					
Laira?	16 Dec 07					
At Laira	25 Apr 08					
Newton Abbot	Feb 09	NA	5 Mar 09	20	L	
Laira	25 Mar 09	NA	9 Aug 10	59	L	
Exeter	7 Oct 10	NA	2 Nov 10	16	L, BC	115,616
Laira	18 Nov 10					
Swindon Stock	Jun 11					
Whitland	4 Jul 11					
Neath	Oct 11	SWks	30 Aug 12	84	L, BC	144,216
Swindon Stock	22 Nov 12					
Bristol	6 Jan 13					
Yatton	Mar 13	SWks	23 May 13	88	H, BC	153,267
Swindon Stock	19 Aug 13					
Aberdare	3 Sep 13	SWks	19 Jan 15			185,122

(Converted to Trailer No 99 (Dia. Z)

No.4 (Diagrams B1, B, C)

Allocation	*Date*	*Stop'd*	*Date*	*Days Stop'd*	*Catgy. Repair*	*Miles Run*
New	Apr 04					
Southall	23 Apr 04	SWks	8 Jul 04	14	-	
Swindon Stock	22 Jul 04					
Chalford	15 Aug 04	SWks	21 Oct 04	49	G	20,158
Chalford	9 Dec 04	SWks	17 Mar 05	47	L	
Swindon Stock	3 May 05					
Trowbridge	13 May 05	SWks	23 Jun 05	3	L	
Trowbridge	26 Jun 05	SWks	1 Jul 05	11	L	
Trowbridge	12 Jul 05	SWks	2 Sep 05	32	L, BC	37,944
Southall	4 Oct 05	PDN	29 Jan 06	5	L	
Southall	3 Feb 06	SWks	16 Jun 06	69	G	48,767
Swindon Stock	24 Aug 06	SWks	30 Aug 06	4	G, BC	48,767
Southall?	3 Sep 06	SWks	28 Jan 07	32	G	61,392
Southall?	1 Mar 07	SWks	8 Apr 07	10	L, BC	61,533
?	18 Apr 07	SWks	28 Feb 08	81	G, BC	81,835
Swindon Stock	19 May 08					
Weymouth	8 Jun 08	SWks	21 Feb 10	93	G, BC	102,363
Swindon Stock	25 May 10					
Southall	2 Jul 10					
Swindon Stock	Aug 10					
Southall	11 Jan 11	OOC	1 May 12	5		
Southall	6 May 12	SWks	11 Jul 12	47	G, BC	138,512
Swindon Stock	27 Aug 12					
Croes Newydd	8 Sep 12					
Radstock	17 Sep 12					
Yatton	Nov 12					
Bath	Nov 12					
Bristol	Dec 12					
Bath	Feb 13					
Bristol	Apr 13	BTL	15 Apr 13	21	L	
Bristol	6 May 13	SWks	5 Jun 13	56	L, BC	156,964

Allocation	Date	Stop'd	Date	Days Stop'd	Catgy. Repair	Miles Run
Swindon Stock	31 Jul 13					
Bath	Sep 13					
Yatton	Oct 13					
Bath	Nov 13					
Bristol	Nov 13	BTL	4 Feb 14	14	L	
Bristol	18 Feb 14					
Yatton	Mar 14	SWks	6 Apr 14	52	H, BC	171,221
Southall	28 May 14	SWks	6 Jul 14			175,006

Converted to Trailer No.100 (Dia. Z)

No.5 (Diagrams B1, B, C)

Allocation	Date	Stop'd	Date	Days Stop'd	Catgy. Repair	Miles Run
New	Apr 04					
Chalford	29 May 04	SWks	14 Jul 04	16	-	
Chalford	30 Jul 04	SWks	27 Sep 04	14	-	
Swindon Stock	11 Oct 04				-	24,159
Chalford	22 Oct 04	SWks	25 Jan 05	73		
Swindon Stock	8 Apr 05					
Trowbridge	27 Apr 05	SWks	12 May 05	18	L, BC	25,717
Swindon Stock	30 May 05					
Southall	9 Jun 05	SWks	24 Nov 05	29	G, BC	35,202
Aberdare	27 Dec 05	SWks	27 Feb 06	6	G	37,392
Chippenham	3 Mar 06	SWks	21 Apr 06	21	L, BC	41,991
?	12 May 06	SWks	16 Jun 06	42	*No loco work.*	
?	28 Jul 06	SWks	4 Dec 06	46	G, BC	55,378
Weymouth?	19 Jan 07					
At Weymouth	25 Apr 08	SWks	9 Jun 08	83	G, BC	71,090
Swindon Stock	31 Aug 08					
Croes Newydd	7 Sep 08	SRD	25 Oct 09	12	G, BC	95,752
Croes Newydd	6 Nov 09	SRD	14 Dec 09	37	G, BC	97,083
Croes Newydd	20 Jan 10	SRD	28 Jun 10	32	G, BC	103,232
Croes Newydd	30 Jul 10	SRD	15 Feb 11	23	G, BC	108,828
Croes Newydd	10 Mar 11					
Chester	Jan 12					
Croes Newydd	Feb 12	SWks	3 May 12	62	G, BC	121,131
Swindon Stock	4 Jul 12					
Aberdare	9 Jul 12	SWks	3 Sep 13	85	H, BC	148,947
Swindon Stock	27 Nov 13					
Merthyr	26 Mar 14					
Aberdare	May 14	SWks	25 Sep 14			161,264

Converted to Trailer No.101 (Dia. Z)

No.6 (Diagrams C1, C)

Allocation	Date	Stop'd	Date	Days Stop'd	Catgy. Repair	Miles Run
New	Apr 04					
Chalford	30 Apr 04					
Southall	9 Jul 04	SWks	16 Sep 04	75	G	15,614
Southall	30 Nov 04	SWks	17 Feb 05	38	-	
Southall	27 Mar 05	SWks	15 Apr 05	27	L, BC	27,642
Swindon Stock	12 May 05					
Garnant	24 May 05					
Chippenham	22 Jun 05					
Croes Newydd	30 Jun 05	SRD	25 Jul 05	7	L, BC	31,230
Croes Newydd	1 Aug 05	SRD	25 Sep 05	10	G, BC	38,378
Croes Newydd	5 Oct 05	SRD	19 Dec 05	3	L, BC	42,313
Croes Newydd	22 Dec 05	SRD	12 Mar 06	17	L, BC	44,585
Croes Newydd	29 Mar 06	SRD	11 Apr 06	10	L, BC	45,471
Croes Newydd?	21 Apr 06	SRD	11 Jul 06	20	G, BC	49,941
Croes Newydd?	31 Jul 06	SRD	22 Nov 06	22	G, BC	54,373
Croes Newydd?	14 Dec 06	SRD	2 Apr 07	48	G, BC	59,201
Croes Newydd?	20 May 07	SWks	19 Jul 07	49	G, BC	62,392
?	6 Sep 07	SWks	4 Nov 07	21		
Swindon Stock	25 Nov 07					
Southall?	9 Jan 08					
At Southall	25 Apr 08	SWks	20 Nov 08	62	G, BC	80,881
Swindon Stock	21 Jan 09					
Neath	20 Feb 09	SWks	20 Apr 09	9	G, BC	84,776
Swindon Stock	29 Apr 09					
Neath	5 Jul 09	SWks	13 Oct 09	91	G, BC	91,223
Swindon Stock	12 Jan 10					
Croes Newydd	28 Jan 10	CNYD	5 Jul 10	65		
		SWks	30 Jul 10		?, BC	97,964
Swindon Stock	8 Sep 10					
Southall	12 Apr 11	SHL	7 Oct 11	28	L	
Southall	4 Nov 11	SHL	20 Mar 12	21	L	
Southall	10 Apr 12	SHL	6 May 12	5	L	
Southall	11 May 12	SWks	16 Jul 12	58	G, BC	124,520
Southall	12 Sep 12	SWks	29 May 13	49	H, BC	157,734
Southall	17 Jul 13	SWks				
Swindon Stock	Nov 13					
Bristol	14 Jan 14					
Bath	Feb 14					
Yatton	Apr 14					
Reading	30 Apr 14					
Southall	Jun 14	SWks	27 Jul 14			180,585

Converted to Trailer No.102 (Dia. Z)

No.7 (Diagrams C1, C)

Allocation	Date	Stop'd	Date	Days Stop'd	Catgy. Repair	Miles Run
New	May 04					
Newton Abbot	29 Jun 04					
Penzance	Jun 04					
Laira	Jul 04					
Newton Abbot	Oct 04					
Ashburton	Nov 04					
Laira	Dec 04					
Penzance	Jan 05					
Newton Abbot	Feb 05					
Truro	Apr 05					
Newton Abbot	May 05	SWks	2 Jun 05	20	G, BC	28,429
Ashburton	22 Jun 05					
Truro	Jul 05					
Newquay	Sep 05					
Truro	Oct 05	NA	9 Dec 05	49	G, BC	41,103
Exeter	27 Jan 06	SWks	24 Oct 06	24	G, BC	61,356
Exeter	17 Nov 06	SWks	17 Dec 07	42	?, BC	75,176
Swindon Stock	28 Jan 08					
At Swindon Stock	25 Apr 08					
Neath	15 May 08	SWks	20 Feb 09	41	G, BC	98,248
Swindon Stock	2 Apr 09					
Neath	16 Apr 09	SWks	6 Jul 09	34	G, BC	105,002
Swindon Stock	9 Aug 09					
Trowbridge	8 Sep 09					
Swindon Stock	Oct 09					
Stratford on Avon	20 Dec 09	SWks	6 Jul 10	76	G, BC	117,184
Swindon Stock	20 Sep 10					
Aberdare	17 May 11	SWks	8 May 13	30	H, BC	160,581
Swindon Stock	7 Jun 13					
Monmouth	8 Jul 13					
Swindon Stock	Aug 13					
Bath	18 Aug 13					
Bristol	Nov 13					
Yatton	Nov 13					
Bath	Dec 13					
Bristol	Jan 14					
Bath	Apr 14					
Yatton	May 14					
Bristol	Jun 14	SWks	3 Oct 14			193,998

Converted to Trailer No.103 (Dia. Z)

No.8 Diagrams (C1, C)

Allocation	Date	Stop'd	Date	Days Stop'd	Catgy. Repair	Miles Run
New	May 04					
Newton Abbot	29 May 04					
Penzance	Jun 04					
Laira	Jul 04					
Truro	Feb 05					
Penzance	Mar 05					
Newton Abbot	May 05					
Penzance	Jun 05	NA	Jul 05		BC	31,946
Exeter	Aug 05					
Laira	Sep 05					
Newton Abbot	Jan 06	SWks	12 Feb 06	22	G, BC	41,042
Swindon Stock	6 Mar 06	SWks	20 Sep 06	29	G, BC	57,178
Swindon Stock	19 Oct 06	SWks	19 Jun 07	10	BC	72,783
Weymouth?	29 Jun 07	SWks	31 Jan 08	58	G, BC	84,723
Swindon Stock	29 Mar 08					
Croes Newydd	11 May 08	SRD	17 Aug 08	10	G, BC	91,336
Croes Newydd	27 Aug 08	SRD	24 Sep 08	7	L, BC	92,490
Croes Newydd	1 Oct 08	SRD	21 Dec 08	3	L, BC	95,834

Allocation	Date	Stop'd	Date	Days Stop'd	Catgy. Repair	Miles Run
Croes Newydd	24 Dec 08	SRD	2 Mar 09	16	L, BC	99,590
Croes Newydd	18 Mar 09	SRD	25 May 09	4	L, BC	101,905
Croes Newydd	29 May 09	CNYD	23 Dec 09	91		
		SWks	4 Jan 10		G, BC	112,181
Swindon Stock	24 Mar 10					
Southall	9 May 10					
Swindon Stock	Jun 10					
Southall	2 Jul 10					
Swindon Stock	Aug 10					
Bristol	9 Nov 10					
Yatton	Dec 10					
Bath	Jan 11	SWks	22 Feb 11	30	G, BC	123,781
Swindon Stock	24 Mar 11					
Aberdare	17 May 11	SWks	19 Feb 13	49	H, BC	161,551
Neath	9 Apr 13					
Whitland	Jul 13	SWks	18 Sep 13	70	H, BC	193,198
Swindon Stock	27 Nov 13					
Bristol	15 Jan 14					
Southall	19 Feb 14	SHL	3 Jun 14	19	L	
Southall	22 Jun 14	SWks	21 Sep 14			191,804

Converted to Trailer No.104 (Dia. Z)

No.9 (Diagrams D1, D)

Allocation	Date	Stop'd	Date	Days Stop'd	Catgy. Repair	Miles Run
New	May 04					
Croes Newydd	25 Jun 04	CNYD	Oct. 04			
Croes Newydd	28 Oct 04	CHR	6 Feb 05	45	L	
Croes Newydd	23 Mar 05	SRD	19 Jul 05	14	LG, BC	20,743
Croes Newydd	2 Aug 05	SRD	30 Aug 05	3	L, BC	21,520
Croes Newydd	2 Sep 05	SRD	6 Dec 05	6	L, BC	27,329
Croes Newydd	12 Dec 05	SRD	23 May 06	9	G, BC	39,948
Croes Newydd?	1 Jun 06	SRD	31 Aug 06	5	L, BC	45,320
Croes Newydd?	5 Sep 06	SRD	2 Jan 07	28	G	49,538
Croes Newydd?	30 Jan 07	SWks	11 Jul 07	26	?, BC	53,710
?	6 Aug 07					
At Aberdare	25 Apr 08	SWks	16 Feb 10	85	G, BC	85,533
Swindon Stock	12 May 10					
Croes Newydd	28 Jul 10	CNYD	25 Apr 11	17	L	
Croes Newydd	12 May 11	CNYD	20 Feb 12	6		
Croes Newydd	26 Feb 12	SRD	18 Jul 12	13	G, BC	111,099
Croes Newydd	31 Jul 12					
Southall	14 Sep 12	OOC	24 Dec 12	29		
Paddington	22 Jan 13	OOC	19 Feb 13	7	L	
Paddington	26 Feb 13					
Southall	Mar 13	SWks	7 Apr 13	22	?, BC	125,284
Swindon Stock	29 Apr 13					
Southall	6 May 13	SWks	21 Jul 13	5	L, BC	134,049
Swindon Stock	26 Jul 13					
Neath	Sep 13	SWks	24 Jun 14	72	H, BC	153,426
Swindon Stock	4 Sep 14					
Bristol	10 Sep 14	BTL	18 Jan 15	37	L	
Bristol	24 Feb 15					
Yatton	May 15					
Bristol	Jul 15					
Yatton	Aug 15					
Bristol	Sep 15	SWks	10 Sep 15			177,846

Converted to Trailer 107 (Dia. A7)

No.10 (Diagrams D1, D)

Allocation	Date	Stop'd	Date	Days Stop'd	Catgy. Repair	Miles Run
New	May 04					
Croes Newydd	25 Jun 04	SWks	12 Sep 04	3		
Swindon Stock	15 Sep 04					
Southall	17 Sep 04					
Newton Abbot	29 Sep 04					
Penzance	Feb 05					
Truro	Mar 05	SWks	18 Mar 05	31	BC	15,137
Swindon Stock	18 Apr 05					
Swindon	May 05					
Trowbridge	Jun 05	SWks	17 Jul 05	9	L, BC	20,214
Swindon Stock	26 Jul 05					
Lambourn Valley	16 Aug 05	SWks	2 Sep 05	5	L	
Chippenham	7 Sep 05					
Swindon	Oct 05					
Chalford	Nov 05					
Weymouth	Jan 06	SWks	19 Jan 07	51	G, BC	45,618
Croes Newydd?	11 Mar 07					
At Croes Newydd	25 Apr 08	SRD	25 Jun 08	9	L, BC	69,027
Croes Newydd	4 Jul 08	SRD	14 Dec 08	26	G, BC	77,058
Croes Newydd	9 Jan 09	CNYD	20 Dec 09	107		
		SWks	4 Jan 10		G, BC	94,745
Swindon Stock	6 Apr 10					
Southall	10 May 10					
Swindon Stock	Jun 10					
Worcester	16 Jul 10					
Kidderminster	Aug 10					
Worcester	Oct 10					
Stratford on Avon	Nov 10					
Swindon Stock	Dec 10					
Bristol	22 Feb 11	SWks	1 Jun 11	35	G, BC	106,243
Swindon Stock	6 Jul 11					
Frome	10 Jul 11					
Swindon Stock	1 Dec 11					
Bath	6 Jan 12					
Bristol	Mar 12					
Radstock	Jun 12					
Yatton	Jul 12					
Radstock	Aug 12					
Yatton	Sep 12	SWks	30 Sep 12	82	G, BC	138,221
Swindon Stock	21 Dec 12					
Pontypool Road	Jan 13					
Aberdare	Feb 13	SWks	6 May 14	56	H, BC	179,187
Southall	1 Jul 14	SHL	28 Dec 14	56		
		SWks	26 Jan 15		L, BC	200,606
Swindon Stock	22 Feb 15					
Gloucester	19 Mar 15					
Swindon Stock	Apr 15					
Exeter	20 Dec 15					
Newton Abbot	Apr 16					
Stopped Work	13 Jul 16	SWks	13 Jul 16			204,853

Converted to Trailer No.108 (Dia. A7)

No.11 (Diagrams D1, D)

Allocation	Date	Stop'd	Date	Days Stop'd	Catgy. Repair	Miles Run
New	Jun 04					
Southall	30 Jun 04	SWks	29 Sep 04	1	L	
Croes Newydd	30 Sep 04	SRD	4 Nov 04	14	L, BC	9,960
Croes Newydd	18 Nov 04	SRD	22 Aug 05	56	G, BC	25,318
Croes Newydd	17 Oct 05	SRD	6 Dec 05	14	L, BC	27,867
Croes Newydd	20 Dec 05	SRD	16 Mar 06	7	L, BC	32,132
Croes Newydd	23 Mar 06	SRD	18 Aug 06	42	G, BC	36,116
Croes Newydd?	29 Sep 06	SWks	8 Dec 06	42	G, BC	40,720
?	19 Jan 07	SWks	9 Jan 08	60	G, BC	64,952
Neath	9 Mar 08	SWks	16 May 08	12	L, BC	70,429
Swindon Stock	28 May 08					
Oxford	31 Jul 08					
Swindon Stock	Sep 08					
Aberdare	2 Oct 08	SWks	3 Feb 12	119	G, BC	117,265
Swindon Stock	1 Jun 12					
Bristol	8 Jun 12					
Bath	Jul 12					
Bristol	Aug 12					
Radstock	Sep 12					
Bristol	Oct 12	SWks	30 Oct 12	78	H, BC	130,246
Swindon Stock	16 Jan 13					
Neath	4 Mar 13	SWks	9 Apr 13	26	NR	
Swindon Stock	5 May 13					
Aberdare	7 May 13	SWks	13 Jan 15	138	H, BC	179,840
Swindon Stock	31 May 15					
Chalford	7 Oct 15					
Swindon Stock	Jan 16					
Bristol	28 Jan 16					
Bath	Jun 16					
Bristol	Jul 16	BTL	21 Aug 16			
		SWks	9 Sep 16			202,304

Converted to Trailer No.109 (Dia. A7)

No.12 (Diagrams D1, D)

Allocation	Date	Stop'd	Date	Days Stop'd	Catgy. Repair	Miles Run
New	Jun 04					
Southall	30 Jun 04	SWks	29 Sep 04	1	L	
Croes Newydd	30 Sep 04	SRD	18 Nov 04	34	BC	19,923
Croes Newydd	22 Dec 04	SRD	4 Sep 05	38	G, BC	32,350
Croes Newydd	12 Oct 05	SRD	29 Nov 05	9	L, BC	33,544
Stafford Road	8 Dec 05	SRD	29 Dec 05	9	L, BC	33,544
Croes Newydd	7 Jan 06	SRD	28 Feb 06	4	L, BC	36,516
Croes Newydd	4 Mar 06	SRD	19 Apr 06	27	L, BC	39,936
Croes Newydd?	16 May 06	SRD	2 Oct 06	27	G, BC	45,619
Croes Newydd?	29 Oct 06	SRD	9 Mar 07	14	L, BC	52,840
Croes Newydd?	23 Mar 07	SWks	9 Jul 07	291	G, BC	56,509
Croes Newydd?	14 Aug 07					
At Croes Newydd	25 Apr 08	SRD	21 May 08	14	L, BC	73,699
Croes Newydd	4 Jun 08	SRD	24 Sep 08	9	L, BC	81,115
Croes Newydd	3 Oct 08	SRD	5 Feb 09	20	L, BC	87,436
Croes Newydd	25 Feb 09	SWks	21 Dec 09	134	G, BC	103,969
Swindon Stock	4 May 10					
Southall	10 May 10					
Swindon Stock	Jun 10					
Whitland	4 Jul 10					
Chalford	6 Oct 10					
Swindon Stock	Nov 10					
Trowbridge	6 Mar 11					
Yatton	10 Apr 11					
Bristol	May 11					
Yatton	Aug 11	SWks	28 Aug 11	37	G, BC	124,485
Swindon Stock	4 Oct 11					
Yatton	15 Dec 11					
Bristol	Jan 12					
Bath	Mar 12					
Bristol	Apr 12					
Yatton	May 12					
Bristol	Jun 12	SWks	16 Sep 12	58	L, BC	151,861
Swindon Stock	13 Nov 12					
Bristol	9 Dec 12					
Yatton	Jan 13					
Bath	Mar 13					
Bristol	May 13	SWks	31 Oct 13	75	H, BC	186,955
Swindon Stock	14 Jan 14					
Wrexham	21 Jan 14					
Southall	30 Apr 14	SWks	29 Jun 14	51	H, BC	198,393
Swindon Stock	19 Aug 14					
Southall	21 Aug 14	SWks	26 Oct 14	44	H, BC	204,572
Swindon Stock	9 Dec 14					
Aberdare	14 Jan 15	SWks	21 Dec 15			N/R

Converted to Trailer No.110 (Dia. A7)

No.13 (Diagrams D1, D)

Allocation	Date	Stop'd	Date	Days Stop'd	Catgy. Repair	Miles Run
New	Jun 04					
Croes Newydd	1 Jul 04	SRD	18 Nov 04	19	?	
Croes Newydd	7 Dec 04	CHR	9 Dec 04	3	?	
Croes Newydd	12 Dec 04	CNYD	6 Feb 05	16	?	
Croes Newydd	22 Feb 05	SRD	20 Mar 05	17	?	
Croes Newydd	6 Apr 05	SRD	11 Jul 05	14	L, BC	19,249
Croes Newydd	25 Jul 05	SRD	9 Jun 06	48	G, BC	43,428
Croes Newydd	27 Jul 06	SRD	22 Nov 06	21	G, BC	48,986
Croes Newydd	13 Dec 06	SRD	15 Jul 07	12	G, BC	60,699
Croes Newydd?	27 Jul 07	SRD	29 Jan 08	10	G, BC	68,364
Croes Newydd?	8 Feb 08					
At Croes Newydd	25 Apr 08	SWks	8 Sep 08	46	G, BC	81,980
Swindon Stock	24 Oct 08					
Stratford on Avon	25 Jul 09	SWks	20 Dec 09	56	G, BC	89,136
Swindon Stock	14 Feb 10					
Neath	7 Apr 10	SWks	22 Mar 11	129	G, BC	115,552
Southall	29 Jul 11	SHL	11 Apr 12	21		
Southall	2 May 12	SHL	8 Jul 12	2		
Southall	10 Jul 12	OOC	20 Jul 12	27	L	
Southall	16 Aug 12	SWks	26 Sep 12	29	G, BC	159,362
Swindon Stock	25 Oct 12					
Bristol	30 Oct 12					
Bath	Nov 12					
Bristol	Dec 12	SWks	6 Jan 13	46	L	
Swindon Stock	21 Feb 13					
Southall	7 Apr 13					
Duffryn	5 Jun 13					
Whitland	Jul 13					
Swindon Stock	Oct 13					
Bristol	21 Oct 13					
Yatton	Jan 14					
Bristol	Feb 14	BTL	18 Mar 14	14	L	
Bristol	1 Apr 14	BTL	4 Aug 14	105		
		SWks	12 Sep 14		H, BC	206,277
Swindon Stock	17 Nov 14					
Aberdare	14 Jan 15	ABDR	2 Mar 15	17		
Aberdare	19 Mar 15	NPT	20 Apr 18			241,035
		SWks	22 Apr 18			

Converted to Trailer No.111 (Dia. A7)

No.14 (Diagrams D1, D)

Allocation	Date	Stop'd	Date	Days Stop'd	Catgy. Repair	Miles Run
New	Jul 04					
Chalford	20 Jul 04					
Southall	5 Aug 04	PDN	16 Dec 04	8	L	
Southall	24 Dec 04	PDN	6 Feb 05	5	L	
Southall	11 Feb 05	SWks	30 Mar 05	30	G, BC	31,740
Croes Newydd	29 Apr 05	CHR	25 Sep 05	54		
		SWks	18 Oct 05		G, BC	42,807
Croes Newydd	18 Nov 05	SRD	12 Dec 05	3	L, BC	46,634
Croes Newydd	15 Dec 05	SRD	5 Mar 06	17	L, BC	49,192
Croes Newydd	22 Mar 06	SRD	11 May 06	18	LG, BC	52,753
Croes Newydd	29 May 06	SRD	27 Jun 06	3	L, BC	55,401
Croes Newydd?	30 Jun 06	SRD	24 Jul 06	51	G, BC	55,401
Croes Newydd?	13 Sep 06	SRD	14 Dec 06	8	L, BC	62,712
Croes Newydd?	22 Dec 06	SRD	9 Mar 07	18	L, BC	64,532
Croes Newydd?	27 Mar 07	SRD	5 Jul 07	15	G, BC	69,080
Croes Newydd?	20 Jul 07	SWks	24 Oct 07	100	G, BC	72,424
Swindon Stock	1 Feb 08					
Tenby	23 Jun 08					
Neath	Oct 08					
Swindon Stock	Nov 08					
Tenby	27 Jun 09					
Swindon Stock	Oct 09					
Neath	5 Nov 09	SWks	20 Nov 09	9	L	
Swindon Stock	29 Nov 09					
Croes Newydd	3 Jan 10	SWks	30 Jul 10	81	G, BC	91,423
Swindon Stock	19 Oct 10					
Neath	21 Mar 11	NEA	1 Sep 11	24		
		SWks	10 Oct 11		G, BC	107,889
Swindon Stock	3 Nov 11					
Gloucester	17 Dec 11					
Chalford	Jan 12					
Gloucester	Feb 12					
Chalford	Mar 12					
Gloucester	May 12					
Swindon Stock	Jun 12					
Radstock	20 Jul 12					
Bath	Aug 12					
Bristol	Sep 12					
Yatton	Oct 12					
Bath	Nov 12					
Radstock	Nov 12					
Bath	Jan 13					
Bristol	Feb 13					
Yatton	Jul 13					
Swindon	2 Aug 13					
Yatton	12 Sep 13					
Bath	Nov 13	SWks	17 Nov 13	36	H, BC	160,137
Swindon Stock	23 Dec 13					
Southall	16 Feb 14	OOC	8 Aug 14	66		
		SWks	11 Aug 14		H, BC	179,311
Swindon Stock	13 Oct 14					
Southall	12 Nov 14	SWks	11 Nov 15	536	H, BC	212,060
Swindon Stock	30 Apr 17					
Bristol	20 Jun 17					
Bath	Sep 17					
Bristol	Oct 17					
Bath	Nov 17					
Bristol	Dec 17	SPM	5 Dec 17			225,183
		SWks	20 Apr 18			

Converted to Trailer No.112 (Dia. A7)

Allocation	*Date*	*Stop'd*	*Date*	*Days Stop'd*	*Catgy. Repair*	*Miles Run*
No.15 (Diagram E)						
New	10 Aug 05	SWks	10 Aug 05	43	LG	
Swindon Stock	22 Sep 05					
Frome	30 Sep 05	SWks	15 Nov 05	36	L	
Frome	21 Dec 05	SWks	15 Sep 06	90	G	25,466
?	14 Dec 06	SWks	25 Oct 07	161	G	38,616
Swindon Stock	3 Apr 08					
Stourbridge	2 Nov 08					
Swindon Stock	Jan 09					
Stourbridge	28 Jun 09	SWks	19 Aug 10	175		50,086
Swindon Stock	10 Feb 11					
Stourbridge	2 Mar 11	SRD	21 Apr 11	14		
Stourbridge	5 May 11	SRD	18 Sep 11	24	L	56,924
Stourbridge	12 Oct 11	STB	26 Feb 12	29	L	
Stourbridge	26 Mar 12	SRD	20 Aug 12	45		
Stourbridge	4 Oct 12	STB	13 Apr 13	53		
		SRD	9 May 13		H	75,883
Stourbridge	5 Jun 13	STB	2 Aug 13	108		
		SRD	25 Aug 13		L	
Stourbridge	18 Nov 13	SRD	23 Jan 14	61		
Stourbridge	25 Mar 14	STB	11 Sep 14	36		
Stourbridge	17 Oct 14	SRD	19 Nov 14	34		
Stourbridge	23 Dec 14	SRD	19 Feb 15	19	L	
Stourbridge	10 Mar 15	SWks	26 Apr 15	1,834	H	86,948
		SWks/SStk				
Sold to J.F. Wake, Darlington.			3 May 20			

Then to Nidd Valley Rly.
NOTE
Boiler and engine never changed.

Allocation	*Date*	*Stop'd*	*Date*	*Days Stop'd*	*Catgy. Repair*	*Miles Run*
No.16 (Diagram E)						
New	10 Aug 05	SWks	10 Aug 05	112	LG	0
Frome	30 Nov 05	SWks	13 Dec 05	21	L	
Wolverhampton	3 Jan 06					
Stourbridge	Feb 06	SWks	13 Feb 06	56	L	
Stourbridge	10 Apr 06	SRD	27 May 07	66	G	21,371
Stourbridge ?	1 Aug 07	SWks	30 Oct 07	140	L	21,593
Swindon Stock	18 Mar 08	SWks	10 Dec 08	19		
Swindon Stock	29 Dec 08					
Stourbridge	28 Jun 09	STB	5 Sep 10	11		
Stourbridge	16 Sep 10	SWks	2 Dec 10	193	G	32,789
Swindon Stock	13 Jun 11	SWks	11 Jul 12	5		
Swindon Stock	16 Jul 12					
Southall	19 Jul 12					
Swindon Stock	Oct 12					
Southall	8 Jan 13					
Slough	1 Mar 13					
Swindon Stock	May 13					
Stourbridge	20 Aug 13	SWks	11 Nov 13	268	H	42,559
Slough	6 Aug 14	SWks	29 Apr 15	89	L	
Swindon Stock	27 Jul 15					
Slough	25 Oct 15					
Stopped Work	15 Dec 19	SWks	15 Dec 19	42	L	55,046
Swindon Stock	26 Jan 20					
Out of Stock	15 Apr 20					
'Sold' to J.F. Wake, Darlington, 3 May 20, but money not received						
Back into Stock	Dec 20					
Swindon Works/Swindon Stock						
Condemned 22 Dec 27 and broken up.						55,046

NOTE
Boiler and engine never changed.

Allocation	*Date*	*Stop'd*	*Date*	*Days Stop'd*	*Catgy. Repair*	*Miles Run*
No.17 (Diagrams F1, F)						
New	Apr 04					
Southall	1 May 04	SWks	25 Aug 04	22		
Southall	16 Sep 04	SWks	19 Nov 04	20	G, BC	22,330
Southall	9 Dec 04	SHL	13 Mar 05	5	L	
Southall	18 Mar 05					
Chipppenham	13 Jun 05	SWks	26 Jun 05	1	BC	47,364
Corwen	27 Jun 05					
Croes Newydd	Sep 05					
Corwen	Oct 05	CNYD	22 Feb 06	5	L	
Corwen ?	27 Feb 06	SRD	5 May 06	27	G, BC	73,650
?	1 Jun 06	SRD	16 Nov 06	20	L, BC	76,219
?	6 Dec 06	SRD	12 Jan 07	20	G, BC	78,603
?	1 Feb 07	SWks	7 Sep 07	37	G, BC	93,049
Frome ?	14 Oct 07	SDst	18 Nov 08	20	L	
Frome?	8 Dec 08					
At Frome	25 Apr 08	SWks	13 Jan 10	85	G, BC	160,057
Swindon Stock	8 Apr 10					
Whitland	21 Jun 10					
Swindon Stock	Oct 10					
Yatton	18 Oct 10					
Bath	Dec 10					
Yatton	Feb 11					
Bristol	Mar 11	SWks	1 Apr 11	56	BC	181,025
Swindon Stock	27 May 11					
Southall	30 May 11	SHL	27 Nov 11	9		
Southall	6 Dec 11	SHL	25 Jan 12	7		
Southall	1 Feb 12	SHL	26 Feb 12	12		
Southall	9 Mar 12	SHL	25 Mar 12	18		
Southall	12 Apr 12	OOC	11 Jun 12	12		
Southall	23 Jun 12	OOC	4 Jul 12	14		
Southall	18 Jul 12	OOC	22 Jul 12	5		
Southall	27 Jul 12	SWks	18 Sep 12	87	G, BC	232,608
Swindon Stock	14 Dec 12					
Bath	18 Dec 12					
Radstock	1 Jan 13	BTL	19 Feb 13	78		
		SWks	11 Apr 13		G, BC	240,979
Bristol	8 May 13					
Radstock	Jun 13					
Bristol	Jul 13					
Radstock	Aug 13					
Bristol	Sep 13					
Yatton	Oct 13					
Radstock	Nov 13					
Bristol	Nov 13					
Yatton	Dec 13	BTL	17 Jan 14	14	L	
Radstock	31 Jan 14					
Bristol	Mar 14					
Radstock	May 14					
Bristol	Jun 14					
Radstock	Sep 14					
Bristol	Oct 14	SWks	12 Oct 14	107	H, BC	284,408
Swindon Stock	27 Jan 15					
Aberdare	16 Feb 15	SWks	8 Jun 15	69	L	
Swindon Stock	16 Aug 15					
Newport	16 Oct 15					
Aberdare	Dec 15					
Frome	13 Apr 16					
Trowbridge	May 16					
Frome	Sep 16	Frome	2 Feb 17	42	R	
Frome	16 Mar 17	SDst	16 Dec 17			
		SWks	22 Apr 18			330,146

Converted to Trailer No.113 (Dia. A9)

Allocation	*Date*	*Stop'd*	*Date*	*Days Stop'd*	*Catgy. Repair*	*Miles Run*
No.18 (Diagrams F1, F)						
New	Apr 04					
Newton Abbot	29 Apr 04					
Penzance	Jun 04					
Laira	Jul 04					
Ashburton	Oct 04					
Newton Abbot	Nov 04					
Ashburton	8 Dec 04					
Newton Abbot	Feb 05					
Ashburton	Apr 05					
Newton Abbot	May 05					
Newquay	Aug 05					
Truro	Sep 05					
Newquay	Oct 05	NA	7 Feb 06	20	G, BC	37,736
Laira	27 Feb 06	SWks	5 Jul 06	64	G, BC	47,319
Laira?	7 Sep 06	SWks	11 Oct 07	39	G, BC	83,360
Swindon Stock?	19 Nov 07					
Southall	24 Feb 08	SWks	20 Nov 08	61	G, BC	94,207
Swindon Stock	20 Jan 09					
Worcester	10 Jun 09					

Allocation	*Date*	*Stop'd*	*Date*	*Days Stop'd*	*Catgy. Repair*	*Miles Run*
Kidderminster	Jul 09					
Evesham	Aug 09	SWks	19 Nov 09	66	G, BC	107,585
Swindon Stock	24 Jan 10					
Croes Newydd	25 May 10	CNYD	19 Sep 10	5	L	114,659
Croes Newydd	24 Sep 10	SRD	9 Feb 11	26	G, BC	124,197
Croes Newydd	7 Mar 11	CNYD	9 Aug 11	7		
Croes Newydd	16 Aug 11	CNYD	4 Oct 11	6	L	144,655
Croes Newydd	10 Oct 11	CNYD	9 Mar 12	114		
		SRD	12 Apr 12		G, BC	146,601
Croes Newydd	1 Jul 12	Clhm	2 Oct 12	5		
Croes Newydd	7 Oct 12	SRD	17 Dec 13	7	L,BC	173,610
Croes Newydd	24 Dec 13	SRD	12 Aug 14	12	L,BC	183,895
Croes Newydd	24 Aug 14					
Stourbridge	Jan 14	STB	25 Jan 15	43	L	
Stourbridge	9 Mar 15	SWks	26 Apr 15	444	H, BC	192,867
Swindon Stock	13 Jul 16					
Southall	8 Aug 16	OOC	18 Jun 17	23	R	
Southall	11 Jul 17	OOC	22 Feb 18			
		RDG	Jul 18			
		SWks	6 Aug 18			228,955

Converted to Trailer No.114 (Dia. A9)

No.19 (Diagrams G1, G)

Allocation	*Date*	*Stop'd*	*Date*	*Days Stop'd*	*Catgy. Repair*	*Miles Run*
New	Jul 04					
Southall	20 Aug 04	SWks				
Lambourn Valley	2 Dec 04	SWks	16 Jan 05	3	BC	14,136
Lambourn Valley	19 Jan 05	SWks	1 Feb 05	6		
Swindon Stock	7 Feb 05					
Chippenham	14 Feb 05	SWks	23 Mar 05	18		
Swindon Stock	10 Apr 05					
Chippenham	14 Apr 05	SWks	13 Jun 05	14	G, BC	27,077
Swindon Stock	27 Jun 05					
Chippenham	3 Jul 05	SWks	2 Sep 05	20	L, BC	34,895
Swindon Stock	22 Sep 05					
Southall	22 Oct 05	SWks	23 May 06	73	G, BC	49,093
Southall?	4 Aug 06	SWks	23 Oct 07	99	G, BC	74,529
Swindon Stock	30 Jan 08					
Croes Newydd	26 Feb 08	SWks	8 Sep 08	31	L, BC	88,569
Swindon Stock	9 Oct 08					
Frome	18 Nov 08					
Swindon Stock	Jan 09					
Taunton	6 Feb 09	SWks	12 Oct 09	105	G, BC	107,239
Worcester	25 Jan 10					
Kidderminster	Feb 10					
Worcester	May 10					
Kidderminster	Jun 10					
Worcester	Aug 10					
Kidderminster	Oct 10					
Stourbridge	29 Nov 10	CNYD	27 Dec 10	32		
Croes Newydd	28 Jan 11	SRD	5 Apr 11	16	G, BC	138,157
Croes Newydd	21 Apr 11	CNYD	5 Jan 12	14	G	
Croes Newydd	19 Jan 12	SWks	5 Feb 12	178	G, BC	156,026
Swindon Stock	1 Aug 12	SWks	6 Aug 12	6		
Didcot	12 Aug 12					
Swindon Stock	Aug 12					
Gwaun-Cae-Gurwen	30 Oct 12	SWks	18 Jan 15	149	H, BC	173,539
Swindon Stock	16 Jun 15					
Neath	25 Oct 15					
Gwaun-Cae-Gurwen	Apr 16					
Neath	Jun 17	SWks	12 Aug 18			183,928

Converted to Trailer No.115 (Dia. A9)

No.20 (Diagrams G1, G)

Allocation	*Date*	*Stop'd*	*Date*	*Days Stop'd*	*Catgy. Repair*	*Miles Run*
New	Aug 04					
Croes Newydd	9 Sep 04	SRD	30 Sep 04	20		
Croes Newydd	20 Oct 04	SWks	26 Oct 04	99	G	2,640
Croes Newydd	2 Feb 05	SRD	16 May 05	9		
Croes Newydd	25 May 05	SRD	11 Aug 05	15	G, BC	21,191
Croes Newydd	26 Aug 05	SRD	24 Nov 05	15	L, BC	27,321
Croes Newydd	9 Dec 05	CHR	14 Jan 06	41		
		SRD	N/R		L, BC	29,243
Croes Newydd	24 Feb 06	SRD	29 Mar 06	26	G, BC	31,810
Croes Newydd	24 Apr 06	SWks	21 Nov 06	28	G, BC	43,210
Croes Newydd?	19 Dec 06	SWks	23 Mar 08	57	G, BC	75,745
Swindon Stock	19 May 08					
Duffryn	23 Jun 08					
Croes Newydd	7 Sep 08	SWks	15 Sep 09	54	G, BC	101,372
Croes Newydd	8 Nov 09	SRD	31 Oct 10	18	G, BC	125,128
Croes Newydd	18 Nov 10	SRD	14 Jan 11	11	G, BC	128,503
Croes Newydd	25 Jan 11	CNYD	18 Apr 11	7		
Croes Newydd	25 Apr 11	CNYD	11 Aug 11	18		
		SRD	N/R		BC	139,960
Croes Newydd	29 Aug 11	SRD	28 May 12	34	G, BC	155,489
Croes Newydd	1 Jul 12	CNYD	19 May 13	28		
Croes Newydd	16 Jun 13	CNYD	29 Sep 13	15		
Croes Newydd	14 Oct 13	CNYD	1 Nov 13	25	BC	178,517
Croes Newydd	26 Nov 13					
Wrexham	Feb 14	SRD	1 May 14	11	H, BC	187,664
Croes Newydd	12 May 14	SWks	14 Oct 14	73	H, BC	188,620
Swindon Stock	26 Dec 14					
Garnant	18 Jan 15	NEA	15 Apr 15	12	L	
Garnant	27 Apr 15					
Gwaun-Cae-Gurwen	Jan 16	NEA	16 Apr 16	19		
Gwaun-Cae-Gurwen	5 May 16					
Neath	Sep 16	LLY	16 Oct 16	19	R	
Gwaun-Cae-Gurwen	4 Nov 16					
Neath	Sep 17					
Tenby	Dec 18	SWks	4 Mar 19			198,418

Converted to Trailer No.116 (Dia. A9)

No.21 (Diagrams G1, G)

Allocation	*Date*	*Stop'd*	*Date*	*Days Stop'd*	*Catgy. Repair*	*Miles Run*
New	Jun 04					
Southall	26 Jul 04	SWks	Oct 04			
Lambourn Valley	29 Oct 04	SWks	9 Feb 05	26	BC	11,630
Swindon Stock	7 Mar 05					
Chippenham	23 Mar 05					
Southall	14 Apr 05	SWks	11 Oct 05	51	G, BC	33,485
Swindon Stock	1 Dec 05					
Frome	4 Dec 05					
Wolverhampton	4 Jan 06					
Croes Newydd	Feb 06	SRD	17 May 06	4	L, BC	46,395
Croes Newydd?	21 May 06	Sltny	25 Jul 06			
Croes Newydd?	25 Jul 06	SRD	24 Sep 06	23	G, BC	50,900
Croes Newydd?	17 Oct 06	SRD	14 Dec 06	6	L, BC	53,825
Croes Newydd?	20 Dec 06	SRD	5 Apr 07	14	G, BC	58,012
Croes Newydd?	19 Apr 07	SRD	26 Aug 07	11	L, BC	60,539
Stourbridge?	6 Sep 07	STB	11 Mar 08	23	L	
Stourbridge	3 Apr 08	SWks	29 May 08	64	G, BC	79,941
Swindon Stock	1 Aug 08					
Duffryn	17 Aug 08					
Swindon Stock	Dec 08					
Duffryn	1 Feb 09	SWks	23 Mar 09	31	G, BC	88,937
Swindon Stock	23 Apr 09					
Evesham	10 Jun 09					
Worcester	Aug 09					
Kidderminster	Sep 09	SWks	27 Sep 09	51	G, BC	100,473
Stourbridge	17 Nov 09					
Croes Newydd	Jun 10					
Duffryn	23 Dec 10	SWks	23 Jan 11	75	G, BC	118,352
Swindon Stock	8 Apr 11					
Oxford	13 Apr 11					
Stourbridge	9 May 11					
Gwaun-Cae-Gurwen	3 Jun 11					
Duffryn	24 Nov 11					
Goodwick	4 Jun 12	NEA	10 Jun 12	24		
Goodwick	4 Jul 12	FGD	30 Sep 12	11		
Goodwick	11 Oct 12	SWks	23 Oct 12	37	G, BC	136,866
Swindon Stock	29 Nov 12					
Worcester	3 Dec 12					
Kidderminster	Jan 13					
Duffryn	6 Jun 13	SWks	6 Jun 13	54	H, BC	148,274
Southall	30 Jul 13	SHL	7 Aug 13	7	L	
Slough	14 Aug 13					
Southall	Nov 13	SHL	2 Jun 14	100		
		SWks	23 Jun 14		H, BC	177,248

Allocation	*Date*	*Stop'd*	*Date*	*Days Stop'd*	*Catgy. Repair*	*Miles Run*
Swindon Stock	10 Sep 14					
Frome	19 Sep 14					
Westbury	Sep 15	SWks	14 Sep 15	1,026	H, BC	204,729
Swindon Stock	6 Jul 18					
Croes Newydd	15 Jul 18	SWks	3 Dec 19			228,326

Converted to Trailer No.117 (Dia. A9)

No.22 (Diagrams G1, G)

New	Jul 04					
Croes Newydd	12 Sep 04	SRD	27 Jun 05	14	G	23,918
Croes Newydd	11 Jul 05	SRD	18 Nov 05	5	L, BC	30,578
Croes Newydd	23 Nov 05	SRD	16 Jan 06	24	LG, BC	32,534
Croes Newydd	9 Feb 06	SWks	2 Nov 06	11	G, BC	44,555
Croes Newydd?	13 Nov 06	SRD	27 May 07	30	L	
Croes Newydd?	26 Jun 07	SRD	8 Oct 07	11	G, BC	60,591
Croes Newydd?	19 Oct 07					
At Croes Newydd	25 Apr 08	SRD	8 May 08	22	G, BC	71,215
Croes Newydd	30 May 08	SRD	15 Jun 08	28	LG	
Croes Newydd	13 Jul 08	SRD	26 Jan 09	14	L, BC	82,237
Croes Newydd	9 Feb 09	SRD	3 Jun 09	9	G, BC	88,226
Croes Newydd	12 Jun 09	SWks	17 Nov 09	80	G, BC	96,829
Swindon Stock	5 Feb 10					
Taunton	13 May 10	SWks	17 Feb 11	77	G, BC	114,621
Swindon Stock	5 May 11					
Monmouth Troy	7 Jul 11					
Pontypool Road	Oct 11					
Trowbridge	14 Oct 11	SWks	8 Jan 13	83	H, BC	148,781
Swindon Stock	1 Apr 13					
Southall	6 May 13	SHL	30 Sep 13	30	L	
Southall	30 Oct 13	SHL	27 Dec 13	85		
		SWks	1 Jan 14		H, BC	175,188
Swindon Stock	27 Mar 14					
Trowbridge	3 Apr 14					
Rogerstone	19 May 14					
Basingstoke	Jul 14					
Rogerstone	Aug 14					
Southall	Oct 14	SWks	26 Oct 14	19	H, BC	187,580
Swindon Stock	14 Nov 14					
Kidderminster	18 Nov 14					
Swindon Stock	Apr 15					
Neath	3 Nov 15					
Goodwick	Aug 16					
Neath	Jun 17					
Tenby	Dec 18	SWks	15 Sep 19			216,594

Converted to Trailer No.118 (Dia. A9)

No.23 (Diagrams G1, G)

New	Aug 04	SWks	Sep 04			
Evesham	30 Sep 04					
Worcester	Feb 05					
Evesham	Mar 05	WOS	11 Apr 05	20	G	14,787
Evesham	1 May 05	WOS	5 Oct 05	18	#	
Evesham	23 Oct 05	WOS	13 May 06	94		
?		SWks	11 Jun 06		G, BC	51,026
Much Wenlock?	15 Aug 06	SRD	29 Jan 07	21	L	
?	19 Feb 07	SRD	29 Apr 07	36	G, BC	65,623
?	4 Jun 07	SRD	30 Dec 07	10	#, BC	78,623
Stourbridge?	9 Jan 08					
At Stourbridge	25 Apr 08	SRD	2 Jun 08	11	L, BC	91,133
Stourbridge	13 Jun 08	SWks	15 Jul 08	42	G, BC	92,670
Swindon Stock	26 Aug 08					
Croes Newydd	7 Sep 08	SRD	18 Feb 09	15	L, BC	100,754
Croes Newydd	5 Mar 09	CNYD	17 May 10	100		
		SWks	26 May 10		G, BC	127,747
Swindon Stock	25 Aug 10					
Evesham	4 Sep 10					
Swindon Stock	Nov 10					
Bristol	6 Nov 10	SWks	13 Dec 10	57	L	134,530
Swindon Stock	8 Feb 11					
Taunton	16 Feb 11	BTL	27 Feb 12	45		
Bristol	12 Apr 12	SWks	29 May 12	43	L, BC	162,020
Southall	11 Jul 12	OOC	30 Sep 12	25		
Southall	25 Oct 12	SHL	16 Jan 13	29	L	
Southall	14 Feb 13	SWks	17 Dec 13	113	H, BC	215,792
Swindon Stock	9 Apr 14					
Trowbridge	21 Apr 14					
Frome	Jun 14					
Trowbridge	Jul 14					
Frome	Oct 14					
Trowbridge	Nov 14					
Swindon Stock	Jul 15					
Frome	23 Aug 15					
Trowbridge	Nov 15	SWks	14 Mar 16	246	H, BC	247,717
Swindon Stock	15 Nov 16					
Croes Newydd	22 Dec 16	CNYD	22 Nov 17	15	L, BC	
Croes Newydd	7 Dec 17	CNYD	22 Jul 18	28	CR	
Croes Newydd	19 Aug 18	SRD	3 Feb 19			
		TYS	3 Jul 19			
		SWks	25 Sep 19			280,346

Converted to Trailer No.119 (Dia. A9)

NOTES

'L & T' - light repairs and tyres?

CR Carriage repairs only

No.24 (Diagrams G1, G)

New	Jul 04					
Laira	25 Aug 04					
Newton Abbot	5 Dec 04					
Laira	Jan 05					
Newquay	Feb 05					
Newton Abbot	Jun 05					
Laira	Jul 05	N/R	N/R		BC	24,231
Laira	1 Sep 05					
Truro	30 Sep 05	SWks	16 Feb 06	69	G, BC	33,946
?	26 Apr 06	SWks	3 Sep 06	26	G, BC	51,402
?	29 Sep 06	SWks	19 Jul 07	47	G, BC	69,634
Llanelly?	4 Sep 07					
At Llanelly	28 Mar 08					
Gwaun-Cae-Gurwen	May 08					
Garnant	Jun 08	SWks	4 Jun 09	49	G, BC	79,007
Kidderminster	23 Jul 09					
Worcester	Nov 09	SWks	25 Jan 10	53	G, BC	96,991
Swindon Stock	19 Mar 10					
Bristol	21 Jun 10	SWks	17 Sep 10	35	G, BC	105,436
Bristol?	22 Oct 10					
Newton Abbot	12 Nov 10	NA	18 Sep 11	0	BC	114,449
Newton Abbot	18 Sep 11					
Newton Abbot	Jan 12	SWks	8 May 12	111	G, BC	119,554
Swindon Stock	27 Aug 12					
Croes Newydd	8 Sep 12	CNYD	12 Nov 13	6	L	
Croes Newydd	18 Nov 13	WPN	16 Feb 14	23	H, BC	149,371
Croes Newydd	11 Mar 14					
Corwen	Jan 15					
Croes Newydd	Feb 15	SWks	15 May 15	502	H, BC	165,589
Swindon Stock	28 Sep 16					
Southall	10 Oct 16	OOC	16 Apr 17	24	R	
Southall	10 May 17					
Slough	Dec 17					
Southall	Apr 18	SHL	26 Jul 18	71	R	
Southall	5 Oct 18	OOC	18 Dec 18	23	R	
Southall	10 Jan 19	OOC	23 Jan 19	100	R	
Southall	3 May 19	SWks	8 Sep 19			205,793

Converted to Trailer No.120 (Dia. A9)

No.25 (Diagrams F1, F)

New	May 04					
Helston	28 Jun 04					
Penzance	Oct 04					
Newton Abbot	Jan 05					
Ashburton	Feb 05					
Newton Abbot	23 Feb 05	SWks	27 Mar 05	46	BC	5,855
Truro	12 May 05					
Newquay	Jul 05	SWks	18 Aug 05	43	G	26,662
Stourbridge	30 Sep 05	SRD	27 Jan 06	24	L, BC	40,624
Stourbridge	20 Feb 06	SRD	21 Jul 06	5	L, BC	51,937
Stourbridge?	26 Jul 06	SRD	8 Dec 06	14	G, BC	60,807

Allocation	*Date*	*Stop'd*	*Date*	*Days Stop'd*	*Catgy. Repair*	*Miles Run*
Stourbridge?	22 Dec 06	SRD	25 Jun 07	15	G, BC	71,779
Stourbridge?	10 Jul 07	SRD	27 Jul 07	21	L	
Stourbridge?	17 Aug 07	SRD	27 Jan 08	23	L	
Stourbridge/	19 Feb 08					
At Stourbridge	25 Apr 08	SRD	28 Apr 08	17	L	
Stourbridge	15 May 08	SRD	29 May 08	27	LG	
Stourbridge	25 Jun 08	SRD	21 Jul 08	23	L	
Stourbridge	13 Aug 08	SRD	2 Nov 08	9	L, BC	99,744
Stourbridge?	11 Nov 08	SRD	25 Nov 08	26	G, BC	100,055
Stourbridge	21 Dec 08	SRD	28 May 09	19	L	
Stourbridge	16 Jun 09	SRD	1 Nov 09	18	G, BC	115,379
Stourbridge	19 Nov 09	SRD	7 May 10	7	LB, BC	122,576
Stourbridge	14 May 10	SRD	4 Nov 10	19	L?, BC	129,292
Stourbridge	23 Nov 10	SWks	11 May 11	149	G, BC	136,572
Swindon Stock	7 Oct 11					
Frome	14 Oct 11	SWks	14 Apr 13	26	H, BC	176,031
Swindon Stock	10 May 13					
Frome	13 May 13					
Taunton	1 Nov 13					
Frome	Dec 13	SWks	14 Feb 14	24	L	
Frome	10 Mar 14					
Trowbridge	Jun 14					
Frome	Jul 14	SWks	28 Sep 14	79	H, BC	210,869
Swindon Stock	16 Dec 14					
Radstock	26 Jan 15					
Swindon Stock	Feb 15					
Slough	22 Feb 15					
Southall	Apr 15	SWks	11 Nov 15	783	H, BC	243,081
Swindon Stock	2 Jan 18					
Yatton	18 Feb 18					
Bristol	Apr 18					
Yatton	May 18					
Bristol	Jun 18	BTL	16 Dec 18	30	R	
Bristol	15 Jan 19	BTL	22 Jan 19			
		SWks	11 Sep 19			261,968

Converted to Trailer No.121 (Dia. A9)

No.26 (Diagrams G1, G)

New	Jun 04					
Southall	3 Aug 04	PDN	26 Dec 04	13	L	
Southall	8 Jan 05	SWks	4 Mar 05	34	G, BC	22,106
Swindon Stock	7 Apr 05					
Southall	14 Apr 05	SWks	11 Aug 05	88	G, BC	35,622
Trowbridge	7 Nov 05	SWks	31 Jan 06	16	L	
Trowbridge	16 Feb 06	SWks	26 Apr 06	85	G, BC	59,123
?	20 Jul 06	SRD	18 Aug 06	11	L	
Much Wenlock?	29 Aug 06	SRD	12 Oct 06	17	L, BC	63,876
Much Wenlock?	29 Oct 06	SRD	8 Jan 07	10	L, BC	67,284
?	18 Jan 07	SRD	10 Jun 07	25	L, BC	73,601
?	5 Jul 07	SWks	28 Feb 08	41	G, BC	82,924
Swindon Stock	9 Apr 08					
Taunton	24 Apr 08	SWks	6 Feb 09	23	G, BC	99,739
Swindon Stock	1 Mar 09					
Worcester	10 Apr 09					
Swindon Stock	May 09					
Gwaun-Cae-Gurwen	26 May 09					
Garnant	Dec 09					
Neath	Jun 10	SWks	21 Jun 10	79	G, BC	106,353
Swindon Stock	8 Sep 10					
Bristol	12 Sep 10					
Radstock	Nov 10					
Bristol	Dec 10					
Trowbridge	24 Apr 11	SWks	5 Aug 11	17	G, BC	130,007
Swindon Stock	22 Aug 11					
Trowbridge	29 Aug 11	SDst	20 Dec 11	52		
		SWks	1 Jan 12		G, BC	138,735
Swindon Stock	10 Feb 12					
Trowbridge	20 Feb 12	SWks	9 May 13	29	H, BC	177,203
Trowbridge	7 Jun 13	SWks	1 Oct 13	71	H, BC	187,794
Swindon Stock	11 Dec 13					
Penzance	13 Jan 14					
Newton Abbot	Apr 14					
Bristol	12 Apr 14					

Allocation	*Date*	*Stop'd*	*Date*	*Days Stop'd*	*Catgy. Repair*	*Miles Run*
Yatton	Aug 14					
Bristol	Sep 14	SWks	12 Sep 14	19	H, BC	208,170
Swindon Stock	1 Oct 14					
Bristol	12 Oct 14					
Bath	Dec 14					
Bristol	Jan 15					
Bath	Feb 15					
Bristol	Mar 15					
Swindon Stock	Apr 15					
Bristol	11 Oct 15					
Yatton	Jan 16					
Bath	Mar 16					
Bristol	May 16					
Yatton	Jun 16					
Bristol	Jul 16	SWks	10 Jul 16			243,785

Converted to Trailer No.122 (Dia. A9)

No.27 (Diagrams G1, G)

New	Aug 04					
Swindon Works	Sep 04					
Evesham	30 Sep 04	WOS	7 Mar 05	25		
Evesham	1 Apr 05	SRD	8 Oct 05	20	L, BC	29,124
Stourbridge	28 Oct 05					
Kidderminster	Dec 05	SRD	3 Jan 06	9	L, BC	32,887
Stourbridge	12 Jan 06	SRD	18 Apr 06	19	LG	
Stourbridge ?	7 May 06	SRD	21 Aug 06	24	L, BC	48,330
Stourbridge ?	14 Sep 06	SRD	31 Dec 06	15	G, BC	55,595
Stourbridge ?	15 Jan 07	SRD	5 Feb 07	10	G	57,531
Stourbridge ?	15 Feb 07	SWks	15 Aug 07	35	BC	68,056
Swindon Stock?	19 Sep 07					
At Llanelly	25 Apr 08					
Gwaun-Cae-Gurwen	May 08					
Garnant	Jun 08					
Gwaun-Cae-Gurwen	Dec 09	SWks	9 Jun 11	94	G, BC	85,003
Swindon Stock	11 Sep 11					
Bristol	25 Sep 11					
Yatton	Jan 12					
Radstock	Feb 12					
Bristol	Mar 12					
Bath	Apr 12					
Bristol	Jun 12	SWks	9 Dec 12	80	H, BC	132,694
Swindon Stock	27 Feb 13					
Pontypool Road	3 Mar 13					
Swindon Stock	Apr 13					
Trowbridge	23 Apr 13	Trwbg	28 Jun 13	30	L	
Trowbridge	28 Jul 13	Trwbg	31 Oct 13	18	L	
Trowbridge	18 Nov 13	SWks	4 Apr 14	82	H, BC	161,414
Swindon Stock	25 Jun 14					
Whitland	7 Jul 14					
Oxford	19 Sep 14					
Didcot	Oct 14					
Oxford	Nov 14					
Swindon Stock	Apr 15					
Southall	11 Nov 15	SHL	25 May 16	30	R	
Southall	24 Jun 16	OOC	7 Jul 16	39	L	202,907
Southall	15 Aug 16	SHL	15 Dec 16			213,449
		RDG	Jul 18			
		SWks	1 Sep 19			

Converted to Trailer No.123 (Dia. A9)

No.28 (Diagrams G1, G)

New	Sep 04					
Laira	8 Oct 04	SWks	23 Dec 04	8	BC	12,064
Croes Newydd	31 Dec 04	SRD	14 Jan 05	17	L	20,630
Croes Newydd	31 Jan 05	SRD	13 Jun 05	10	BC	24,115
Croes Newydd	23 Jun 05					
Corwen	Sep 05					
Croes Newydd	Oct 05	SRD	15 Dec 05	34	G	
Croes Newydd	18 Jan 06	SRD	5 Apr 06	7	L, BC	45,656
Croes Newydd	12 Apr 06	SRD	26 Apr 06	46	L, BC	46,124
Croes Newydd?	11 Jun 06	SRD	18 Aug 06	4	L, BC	49,670
Croes Newydd?	22 Aug 06	SRD	29 Oct 06	15	G, BC	51,833
Croes Newydd?	13 Nov 06	SRD	18 Jan 07	25	L, BC	54,163

Allocation	*Date*	*Stop'd*	*Date*	*Days Stop'd*	*Catgy. Repair*	*Miles Run*
Croes Newydd?	12 Feb 07	SRD	14 Mar 07	14	L, BC	54,249
Croes Newydd?	28 Mar 07	SRD	15 Jul 07	16	L, BC	60,436
Croes Newydd?	31 Jul 07	SRD	14 Nov 07	14	BC	63,625
Croes Newydd?	28 Nov 07	SRD	16 May 08	12	L, BC	71,419
At Croes Newydd	25 Apr 08					
Croes Newydd	28 May 08	SWks	11 Sep 08	103	G, BC	76,107
by Jan 07?	23 Dec 08					
Stourbridge	1 Jan 09	SRD	9 Mar 09	11	L, BC	82,558
Stourbridge	20 Mar 09	SRD	1 Nov 09	18	L, BC	100,733
Stourbridge	19 Nov 09	SRD	11 May 10	2	#, BC	114,800
Stourbridge	13 May 10					
Croes Newydd	Jul 10	CNYD	29 Oct 10	14		
Croes Newydd	12 Nov 10	CNYD	25 Jan 11	7		
Croes Newydd	1 Feb 11	SRD	3 May 11	15	G, BC	133,088
Croes Newydd	18 May 11	SRD	2 Feb 12	52		
		Clhm	29 Feb 12		G, BC	150,288
Croes Newydd	25 Mar 12	CNYD	3 Jul 12	13		
Croes Newydd	16 Jul 12					
Corwen	Oct 12	SRD	31 Mar 13	11	H, BC	167,351
Croes Newydd	11 Apr 13	CNYD	8 Sep 13	4	L	
Croes Newydd	12 Sep 13	CNYD	7 Nov 13	6	L	
Croes Newydd	13 Nov 13	CNYD	31 Dec 13	2	L	
Croes Newydd	2 Jan 14	SWks	17 Jan 14	82	H, BC	178,154
Swindon Stock	9 Apr 14					
Southall	26 Apr 14	SHL	1 Feb 15	134		
		SWks	22 Feb 15		H, BC	211,946
Swindon Stock	15 Jun 15					
Paddington	25 Oct 15					
Southall	Nov 15	SHL	29 Sep 16			
		RDG	Jul 18			
		SWks	1 Sep 19			249,232

Converted to Trailer No.124 (Dia. A9)

NOTE:

'L&B' - Light repairs & Boiler?

No.29 (Diagrams H1, H)

New	Jan 05					
Laira	26 Jan 05					
Stourbridge	27 Feb 05	STB	18 May 05	10		
Stourbridge	28 May 05					
Kidderminster	Sep 05	SRD	14 Oct 05	31	LG, BC	20,664
Stourbridge	14 Nov 05	STB	6 Jan 06	18	L, BC	22,639
Stourbridge	24 Jan 06					
Kidderminster	Mar 06	SRD	5 Jun 06	36	G, BC	33,053
Kidderminster ?	11 Jul 06	SWks	11 Jan 07	35	G, BC	45,669
Evesham ?	15 Feb 07	SWks	5 Oct 07	39	G, BC	64,610
Evensham ?	13 Nov 07					
At Evesham	25 Apr 08	SWks	11 May 08	46	G, BC	76,780
Swindon Stock	26 Jun 08					
Stourbridge	14 Jul 08	SWks	13 Nov 09	104	G, BC	96,951
Swindon Stock	25 Feb 10					
Oxley	13 Apr 10					
Trowbridge	Jun 10					
Frome	Jul 10	SWks	12 Jul 11	40	L, BC	130,886
Swindon Stock	21 Aug 11					
Trowbridge	30 Aug 11					
Frome	Oct 11	SWks	6 May 12	89	G, BC	145,917
Swindon Stock	3 Aug 12					
Frome	21 Aug 12	SWks	19 Mar 14	20	H, BC	188,069
Swindon Stock	8 Apr 14					
Stourbridge	11 Apr 14					
Croes Newydd	May 14	SWks	19 May 15	493	H, BC	208,729
Croes Newydd	23 Sep 16	CNYD	12 Feb 18	13	R	
Croes Newydd	25 Feb 18	SWks	22 Jul 19			241,907

Converted to Trailer No.125 (Dia. A10)

No.30 (Diagrams H1, H)

New	Jan 05					
Laira	26 Jan 05	NA	5 Sep 05		BC	24,802
Laira	Oct 05					
Newton Abbot	Dec 05					
Truro	Jan 06					
Newquay	Feb 06	NA	26 Mar 06	3	L, BC	47,475

Allocation	*Date*	*Stop'd*	*Date*	*Days Stop'd*	*Catgy. Repair*	*Miles Run*
?	29 Mar 06	NA	1 Oct 06	30	G, BC	61,775
?	31 Oct 06	NA	15 Feb 07		BC	72,052
?	?	SWks	14 May 07	30	G, BC	76,700
Croes Newydd?	13 Jun 07					
At Croes Newydd	25 Apr 08	SWks	8 Sep 08	46	G, BC	102,968
Swindon Stock	24 Oct 08					
Stourbridge	26 Nov 08	SRD	18 Aug 09	12	L, BC	115,311
Stourbridge	30 Aug 09	SWks	24 Nov 09	83	G, BC	120,083
Swindon Stock	15 Feb 10					
Southall	23 Feb 10	SWks	9 May 10	24	G, BC	126,098
Swindon Stock	2 Jun 10					
Yatton	16 Jun 10					
Bristol	Sep 10					
Yatton	Oct 10	SWks	17 Oct 10	39	BC	136,622
Swindon Stock	25 Nov 10					
Radstock	13 Dec 10					
Bath	Feb 11					
Radstock	Mar 11					
Yatton	Jun 11					
Bath	Jul 11					
Bristol	Aug 11					
Bath	Oct 11					
Radstock	Nov 11					
Bristol	Dec 11	SWks	30 Dec 11	38	G, BC	174,809
Swindon Stock	6 Feb 12					
Stourbridge	14 Feb 12	STB	30 Sep 12	6		
Stourbridge	6 Oct 12	SRD	14 May 13	21	H, BC	198,454
Stourbridge	4 Jun 13	SWks	25 Jul 13	56	H, BC	201,989
Swindon Stock	19 Sep 13					
Stourbridge	24 Sep 13					
Croes Newydd	Nov 13	Sltny	18 Feb 14	8	L	
Croes Newydd	26 Feb 14					
Saltney	May 15					
Croes Newydd	Jun 15	CNYD	17 Jan 16	38		
Croes Newydd	24 Feb 16	SWks	30 Mar 16	1112	H, BC	247,729
Swindon Stock	16 Apr 19					
Bristol	3 May 19					
Yatton	Feb 20	SPM	20 Feb 20	297		
		SWks	7 Apr 20		H, BC	273,003
Swindon Stock	13 Dec 20					
Croes Newydd	1 Feb 21	SRD	3 Apr 22	81	H, BC	286,100
Croes Newydd	23 Jun 22	Clhm	27 Jun 22	34	R	
Croes Newydd	31 Jul 22	SRD	13 Nov 23	36	H, BC	308,713
Croes Newydd	19 Dec 23	SWks	18 Mar 24	150	H, BC	312,383
Swindon Stock	15 Aug 24					
Penmaenpool	20 Aug 24	OSW	6 Jul 25	4	L	
Machynlleth	10 Jul 25					
Penmaenpool	30 Sep 25	SWks	30 Oct 25	216	H, BC	338,267
Swindon Stock	3 Jun 26	SWks	25 Aug 26	23	L	
Swindon Stock	14 Sep 26					
Penmaenpool	17 Sep 26					
Machynlleth	Oct 26					
Penmaenpool	Dec 26	SWks	15 Jun 27	220	L	
Swindon Stock	21 Jan 28	SWks	3 Feb 28	13	L	
Pontypool Road	16 Feb 28	SWks	27 Mar 29	201	H, BC	374,116
Neath	14 Oct 29	NEA	27 Jul 31	12	R	
Neath	8 Aug 31	NEA	21 Oct 31	9	R	
Stourbridge	30 Oct 31	SWks	18 Nov 31	117	G, BC	411,352
Swindon Stock	14 Mar 32					
Exeter	10 Dec 32	EXE	30 Jan 33	18	R	
Exeter	17 Feb 33	SFPI	27 May 33	37		
		SWks	6 Jun 33		L	
Swindon Stock	3 Jul 33					
Southall	Dec 33	SHL	18 Jun 34	23	R	
Southall	11 Jul 34	SHL	20 Jul 34	42	R	
Southall	31 Aug 34	SHL	19 Feb 35			
		SFPI	18 Mar 35			433,034
Condemned	19 Oct 35					

Broken up. One of five cars replaced by three diesel cars.

No.31 (Diagrams J1, J/H)

Allocation	Date	Stop'd	Date	Days Stop'd	Catgy. Repair	Miles Run
New	Dec 04					
Laira	26 Dec 04	SWks	18 Feb 05	5		
Brynamman	23 Feb 05					
Garnant	Apr 05					
Neath	Jun 05					
Whitland	Jul 05					
Tenby	Sep 05	SWks	30 Sep 05	38	G	17,254
Trowbridge	7 Nov 05	SWks	16 Feb 06	35	LG, BC	27,920
?	23 Mar 06	SWks	12 Jul 06	52	G, BC	41,531
?	2 Sep 06	SWks	28 Feb 08	52	G, BC	78,137
Swindon Stock	20 Apr 08					
Stourbridge	28 May 08	SRD	5 May 09	9	L, BC	87,879
Weymouth	14 May 09	SRD	25 Nov 09	23	G, BC	95,609
Stourbridge	18 Dec 09	SRD	2 Mar 11	28	L, BC	114,405
Stourbridge	30 Mar 11	SRD	5 Jan 12	14	BC	
Stourbridge	19 Jan 12	SWks	19 Jan 12	84	G, BC	129,119
Swindon Stock	12 Apr 12					
Southall	4 May 12	OOC	19 Aug 12	5		
Southall	24 Aug 12	OOC	23 Sep 12	5		
Southall	28 Sep 12	OOC	23 Dec 12	79		
		SWks	2 Jan 13		H, BC	156,248
Swindon Stock	12 Mar 13	SWks	15 May 13	12	L, BC	159,152
Southall	27 May 13	SWks	12 Aug 13	10	L	
Croes Newydd	22 Aug 13	SWks	23 Jun 14	56	H, BC	201,512
Croes Newydd	18 Aug 14	SWks	15 Dec 16	890	L, BC	245,014
Swindon Stock	24 May 19					
Bath	25 Jun 19					
Yatton	Nov 19					
Bristol	Dec 19					
Bath	Feb 20					
Bristol	Apr 20					
Yatton	May 20					
Bristol	Jul 20					
Bath	Aug 20					
Bristol	Sep 20					
Bath	Nov 20					
Yatton	Dec 20					
Bristol	Jan 21					
Yatton	May 21					
Bristol	Aug 21	BTL	18 Aug 21			
		SWks	8 Oct 21			289,683

Converted to Trailer No.129 (Dia. A10)

No.32 (Diagrams J1, J/H)

Allocation	Date	Stop'd	Date	Days Stop'd	Catgy. Repair	Miles Run
New	Dec 04					
Stourbridge	28 Dec 04	STB	18 May 05	10		
Stourbridge	28 May 05	SRD	5 Jul 05	7	L, BC	9,295
Stourbridge	12 Jul 05	STB	7 Sep 05	14		
Stourbridge	21 Sep 05	STB	21 Nov 05	21		
Stourbridge	12 Dec 05	SRD	9 Feb 06	22	LG, BC	24,462
Stourbridge?	3 Mar 06	SRD	6 Sep 06	23	G, BC	35,892
Stourbridge?	29 Sep 06	SWks	9 Jan 07	45	BC	44,304
?	23 Feb 07	SWks	5 Apr 07	21	BC	48,481
Swindon Stock?	26 Apr 07	SWks	4 May 07	26	G	48,481
?	30 May 07	SWks	30 Oct 07	48	BC	62,239
?	17 Dec 07	SWks	23 Mar 08	22	G	64,424
Swindon Stock	14 Apr 08					
Evesham	11 May 08					
Worcester	Sep 08	SWks	9 Oct 08	75	BC	74,079
Swindon Stock	23 Dec 08					
Stratford on Avon	20 Jan 09					
Kidderminster	Feb 09					
Worcester	Mar 09					
Kidderminster	May 09	SWks	10 Jun 09	12	G, BC	84,988
Trowbridge	22 Jun 09	SWks	11 Oct 09	67	G, BC	94,748
Swindon Stock	17 Dec 09					
Croes Newydd	30 Dec 09	CNYD	2 Dec 10	35		
Croes Newydd	6 Jan 11	SRD	11 Mar 11	16	G, BC	125,666
Croes Newydd	27 Mar 11	SRD	10 Jun 11	33	G, BC	129,879
Croes Newydd	13 Jul 11	CNYD	9 Sep 11	5		
Croes Newydd	14 Sep 11	CNYD	24 Jan 12	6		
Croes Newydd	30 Jan 12	TYS	9 Mar 12	48	G, BC	145,259
Croes Newydd	26 Apr 12	CNYD	7 Sep 12	9		
Croes Newydd	16 Sep 12	SRD	18 Feb 13	16	G, BC	158,714
Croes Newydd	6 Mar 13	SRD	17 Sep 13	2	G, BC	167,814
Croes Newydd	19 Sep 13	SWks	14 Jan 14	77	H, BC	174,164
Frome	1 Apr 14	SWks	27 Oct 14	16	H, BC	189,837
Frome	12 Nov 14					
Trowbridge	Sep 16	Trwbg	9 Jun 17			
		BTL	Dec 18			
		SDN	Jan 19			
		SWks	27 Aug 19			242,863

Converted to Trailer No.128 (Dia. A10)

No.33 (Diagrams H1, H)

Allocation	Date	Stop'd	Date	Days Stop'd	Catgy. Repair	Miles Run
New	Dec 04					
Southall	6 Jan 05	SHL	10 Apr 05	5	LT	
Southall	15 Apr 05	SWks	4 Jul 05	30	G	23,810
Southall	3 Aug 05	SHL	22 Jan 06	5	L	
Southall	27 Jan 06	SWks	10 May 06	57	G, BC	47,983
?	6 Jul 06	NA	2 Sep 06	4	BC	57,711
?	6 Sep 06	SWks	14 Jan 07	32	G	69,516
?	15 Feb 07	SWks	27 Jul 07	49	G, BC	77,588
?	14 Sep 07	SWks	22 Nov 07	59	G, BC	82,149
Swindon Stock	20 Jan 08					
Worcester	17 Feb 08					
Evesham	Sep 08					
Worcester	Nov 08	SWks	13 Nov 08	46	G, BC	100,869
Swindon Stock	29 Dec 08					
Evesham	27 Jan 09	SWks	10 Jun 09	20	L, BC	112,152
Swindon Stock	30 Jun 09					
Frome	4 Jul 09	SWks	19 Aug 09	46	L, BC	115,179
Swindon Stock	4 Oct 09					
Trowbridge	9 Oct 09					
Weymouth	16 Nov 09	SWks	21 Jan 10	13	L, BC	122,013
Goodwick	3 Feb 10	NEA	19 May 11	8		
Goodwick	27 May 11	NEA	7 Aug 11	108		
		SWks	10 Oct 11		G, BC	160,178
Swindon Stock	23 Nov 11					
Gwaun-Cae-Gurwen	27 Nov 11	NEA	6 Mar 13	120		
		SWks	31 Mar 13		BC	166,522
Swindon Stock	4 Jul 13					
Whitland	7 Jul 13	SWks	4 Oct 13	18	L	
Swindon Stock	22 Oct 13					
Kidderminster	3 Nov 13					
Worcester	Apr 14					
Kidderminster	Sep 14	SWks	3 Nov 14	67	H, BC	203,522
Swindon Stock	9 Jan 15					
Goodwick	18 Jan 15	NEA	1 Jul 16	262		
		SWks	10 Jul 16		H, BC	239,469
Swindon Stock	20 Mar 17					
Bath	17 Apr 17					
Bristol	Jul 17					
Yatton	Aug 17					
Bristol	Sep 17					
Bath	Sep 17					
Yatton	Oct 17					
Bristol	Dec 17					
Bath	Jan 18	BTL	7 Feb 18	37	R	
Bristol	16 Mar 18					
Bath	Jun 18					
Bristol	Jul 18					
Yatton	Feb 19					
Bristol	Mar 19					
Yatton	Apr 19	BTL	23 Apr 19			293,639
		SWks	29 Dec 19			

Converted to Trailer No.130 (Dia. A10)

No.34 (Diagrams H1, H)

Allocation	Date	Stop'd	Date	Days Stop'd	Catgy. Repair	Miles Run
New	Jan 05					
Truro	26 Jan 05					
Laira	Aug 05	NA	17 Oct 05	18	LG, BC	28,603
Laira	4 Nov 05					
Truro	Dec 05	NA	26 Apr 06	13	G, BC	47,193
?	9 May 06	NA	17 Aug 06	48	G, BC	59,267
?	4 Oct 06	NA	17 Jan 07	2	L, BC	68,246

Allocation	Date	Stop'd	Date	Days Stop'd	Catgy. Repair	Miles Run
?	19 Jan 07	SWks	15 Jun 07	46	G, BC	80,561
Stourbridge?	31 Jul 07					
At Stourbridge	25 Apr 08	SRD	19 Sep 08	7	L, BC	98,553
Stourbridge	26 Sep 08	SWks	4 Jan 09	81	G, BC	104,062
Swindon Stock	26 Mar 09					
Trowbridge	7 Jun 09	SWks	8 Sep 09	20	G, BC	115,841
Yatton	28 Sep 09					
Taunton	Oct 09	SWks	17 May 10	62	G, BC	133,397
Swindon Stock	18 Jul 10					
Gwaun-Cae-Gurwen	26 Jul 10					
Llanelly	Nov 12	SWks	7 Nov 12	93	H, BC	144,042
Westbury	8 Feb 13					
Kidderminster	Jun13					
Worcester	Aug 13					
Kidderminster	Nov 13	SWks	4 Nov 13	28	H, BC	163,713
Swindon Stock	2 Dec 13					
Wrexham	15 Jan 14					
Croes Newydd	May 14					
Corwen	Aug 14	SRD	17 Aug 14	12	BC	176,615
Stourbridge	29 Aug 14					
Croes Newydd	Oct 14					
Saltney	Apr 15					
Croes Newydd	May 15	SWks	30 Sep 16	752	H, BC	212,032
Swindon Stock	22 Oct 18					
Trowbridge	30 Oct 18					
Swindon Stock	Dec 20	SWks	5 Jan 21			241,180

Converted to Trailer No.131 (Dia. A10)

No.35 (Diagrams J1, J/H)

Allocation	Date	Stop'd	Date	Days Stop'd	Catgy. Repair	Miles Run
New	Dec 04					
Kidderminster	28 Dec 04	SRD	15 May 05	19	L	
Kidderminster	3 Jun 05	SRD	12 Jul 05	6	L, BC	18,661
Kidderminster	18 Jul 05	SRD	6 Sep 05	16	L	
Stourbridge	22 Sep 05	SRD	30 Oct 05	29	L	
Stourbridge	28 Nov 05	SRD	23 Mar 06	10	LG, BC	35,029
Stourbridge?	2 Apr 06	SRD	26 May 06	5	L, BC	39,263
Stourbridge?	31 May 06	SRD	9 Oct 06	29	G	46,705
Stourbridge?	7 Nov 06	SRD	2 Mar 07	10	L, BC	55,559
Stourbridge?	12 Mar 07	SRD	10 Jan 08	18	G,BC	65,543
Stourbridge?	28 Jan 08					
At Stourbridge	25 Apr 08	SWks	31 Oct 08	94	G,BC	82,880
Swindon Stock	2 Feb 09					
Southall	19 Feb 09	SWks	23 Mar 09	2	G,BC	84,247
Swindon Stock	25 Mar 09					
Southall	29 Mar 09	SWks	23 Feb 10	24	G,BC	109,018
Swindon Stock	19 Mar 10					
Southall	8 Apr 10	SHL	27 Mar 11	12		
Southall	8 Apr 11	SHL	31 Jan 12	153		
		SWks	26 Feb 12		G,BC	162,374
Pontypool Road	2 Jul 12					
Merthyr	Jan 13					
Pontypool Road	Feb 13	SWks	13 Nov 13	123	H, BC	194,808
Swindon Stock	16 Mar 14					
Weymouth	23 Mar 14	SWks	15 Jan 15	18	H, BC	207,549
Swindon Stock	2 Feb 15					
Aberdare	8 Jun 15					
Newport	Nov 15					
Southall	22 Feb 16	SHL	7 Jul 16	382		
		SWks	13 Jul 16		H, BC	234,584
Trowbridge	24 Jul 17					
Frome	Sep 17					
Trowbridge	Nov 17	Trwbg	14 Jun 18	31	R	
Frome	15 Jul 18					
Swindon Stock	24 Oct 18	SWks	13 Dec 18			
		SStk	Jan 19			
		SDN	Feb 19			
		SWks	Oct 19			266,758

Converted to Trailer No.132 (Dia. A10)

No.36 (Diagrams H1, H)

Allocation	Date	Stop'd	Date	Days Stop'd	Catgy. Repair	Miles Run
New	Dec 04					
Stourbridge	1 Jan 05	SRD	31 Aug 05	5	L, BC	15,296
Stourbridge	5 Sep 05	STB	2 Dec 05	21	L, BC	24,132
Stourbridge	23 Dec 05	SRD	5 Mar 06	4	L, BC	27,892
Stourbridge	9 Mar 06	SRD	19 Apr 06	7	G	31,770
Stourbridge	26 Apr 06	SRD	20 Jun 06	5	L, BC	35,995
Stourbridge?	25 Jun 06	Clhm	14 Aug 06	56	L	
		SRD	17 Sep 06			
Stourbridge?	9 Oct 06	SWks	4 Feb 07	35	BC	45,820
Stourbridge?	11 Mar 07	SWks	24 May 07	6	G	52,629
Stourbridge?	30 May 07	SRD	27 Feb 08	6	L, BC	62,625
Stourbridge	4 Mar 08	SWks	31 Oct 08	86	G, BC	71,948
Swindon Stock	25 Jan 09					
Chippenham	17 Jun 09					
Weymouth	Jul 09	SWks	16 Nov 09	90	G, BC	78,894
Swindon Stock	14 Feb 10					
Weymouth	16 Mar 10	SWks	29 Sep 10	25	G, BC	92,405
Swindon Stock	24 Oct 10					
Goodwick	28 Oct 10	SWks	5 Jun 12	119	G	136,682
Southall	2 Oct 12	SHL	15 Sep 13	23	L	
Southall	8 Oct 13	SWks	7 Nov 13	40	H, BC	186,483
Swindon Stock	17 Dec 13	SWks	12 Jan 14	65	H	186,591
Swindon Stock	18 Mar 14					
Trowbridge	21 Mar 14	SWks	9 Dec 14	98	H, BC	207,994
Swindon Stock	17 Mar 15					
Bristol	11 Oct 15					
Bath	Jan 16					
Bristol	Feb 16	SPM	25 Aug 16	18	R	
Bristol	12 Sep 16					
Bath	Apr 17					
Bristol	May 17	SPM	8 Jun 17			
		SWks	24 Oct 19			251,275

Converted to Trailer No.133 (Dia. A10)

No.37 (Diagrams K1, K)

Allocation	Date	Stop'd	Date	Days Stop'd	Catgy. Repair	Miles Run
New	Feb 05					
Stourbridge	27 Feb 05					
Kidderminster	Oct 05	STB	2 Dec 05	55		
		SRD	19 Dec 05		G, BC	20,981
Kidderminster	26 Jan 06	SRD	17 Oct 06	44	G, BC	42,752
Kidderminster?	30 Nov 06	SWks	3 Apr 07	73	G, BC	50,562
Goodwick?	15 Jun 07					
At Goodwick	25 Apr 08	SWks	11 May 08	99	G, BC	72,122
Swindon Stock	18 Aug 08					
Croes Newydd	25 Aug 08	SRD	9 Jul 09	5	L, BC	100,903
Croes Newydd	14 Jul 09	SWks	29 Jan 10	54	G, BC	116,282
Swindon Stock	24 Mar 10					
Evesham	4 Apr 10					
Worcester	May 10					
Kidderminster	Jun 10					
Worcester	Oct 10					
Kidderminster	Dec 10					
Worcester	Jan 11	SWks	6 Mar 11	43	G, BC	149,207
Swindon Stock	18 Apr 11					
Didcot	28 Apr 11	SWks	13 Aug 12	65	G, BC	191,885
Didcot	17 Oct 12	SWks	15 Nov 12	8		
Didcot	23 Nov 12	SWks	28 Feb 14	77	H, BC	244,115
Swindon Stock	16 May 14					
Weymouth	25 May 14	SWks	18 Jan 15	88	H, BC	268,932
Swindon Stock	16 Apr 15					
Worcester	26 Apr 15					
Kidderminster	Jun 15					
Worcester	Feb 16					
Kidderminster	May 16					
Worcester	Jun 16					
Kidderminster	Aug 16					
Worcester	Sep 16	SWks	3 Apr 19	205	H, BC	318,205
Swindon Stock	25 Oct 19					
Bristol	28 Oct 19					
Yatton	Mar 20					
Bristol	May 20					
Bath	Jun 20					
Yatton	Aug 20					
Bath	Sep 20	BTL	2 Nov 20	44		
		SWks	11 Nov 20		H, BC	341,737
Swindon Stock	16 Dec 20					
Aberdare	21 Jan 21	SWks	15 Oct 21	136	H, BC	349,055

Allocation	*Date*	*Stop'd*	*Date*	*Days Stop'd*	*Catgy. Repair*	*Miles Run*
Swindon Stock	28 Feb 22					
Neath	7 Mar 22	SWks	19 Mar 23	185	H, BC	366,633
Stourbridge	20 Sep 23	SRD	2 Jul 24	32	H	382,673
Stourbridge	3 Aug 24	SRD	13 Dec 24	47		
		SRD	13 Dec 24		H, BC	391,852
Stourbridge	29 Jan 25	STB	29 Oct 25	18	R	
Stourbridge	16 Nov 25	SWks	16 Dec 25	471	L, BC	411,940
Swindon Stock	1 Apr 27					
Birkenhead	23 May 27	BHD	3 Mar 28	20	R	
Birkenhead	23 Mar 28	BHD	5 Jul 28	16	R	
Birkenhead	21 Jul 28	SRD	24 Jul 28	38	R	
Birkenhead	31 Aug 28	BHD	23 Nov 28	216		
		SWks	10 Dec 28		H, BC	454,371
Swindon Stock	27 Jun 29					
Neath	2 Jul 29	NEA	4 Oct 30	49	R	
Neath	22 Nov 30	NEA	29 Dec 30	44	R	
Neath	11 Feb 31	NEA	4 Jun 31	6	L	
Neath	10 Jun 31	NEA	21 Sep 31	107		
		SFPl	22 Sep 31			
		SWks	3 Dec 31		G, BC	481,888
Swindon Stock	6 Jan 32					
Reading	1 Sep 32	RDG	3 Dec 33	44	R	
Reading	16 Jan 34					
Exeter	13 Dec 34	EXE	13 Dec 34	30	R	
Exeter	12 Jan 35	SFPl	28 May 35			512,257
		SWks	4 Jun 35			
Condemned	19 Oct 35					513,052
Broken up.						

No.38 (Diagrams K1, K)

Allocation	*Date*	*Stop'd*	*Date*	*Days Stop'd*	*Catgy. Repair*	*Miles Run*
New	Mar 05					
Swindon Stock	1 Apr 05					
Weymouth	28 Apr 05					
Trowbridge	May 05	SWks	30 Oct 05	42	G, BC	28,720
Frome	11 Dec 05	SWks #	21 Mar 06	16	L	
		SWks #	27 Mar 06	90	G	42,371
?	6 Apr 06					
?	25 Jun 06	NA	23 Jul 06	50	G, BC	50,940
?	11 Sep 06	NA	8 Apr 07	51	L, BC	67,758
?	29 May 07	SWks	20 Jul 07	11	G, BC	72,605
?	31 Jul 07	NA	30 Nov 07	4	L, BC	82,591
Penzance?	4 Dec 07					
At Penzance	25 Apr 08					
Exeter	Jul 08					
Newton Abbot	Aug 08					
Exeter	Sep 08					
Newton Abbot	Oct 08	NA	16 Nov 08	10	L, BC	119,199
Newton Abbot	26 Nov 08					
Newquay	Dec 08					
Truro	Jan 09					
Newquay	Jan 09					
Truro	Feb 09	NA by	15 Feb 09		BC	127,633
Truro	Feb 09	NA	26 May 09	9	L, BC	135,464
Laira	4 Jun 09	SWks	9 Oct 09	74	G, BC	149,929
Southall	22 Dec 09	SWks	11 Jan 11	30	G, BC	176,358
Swindon Stock	10 Feb 11					
Southall	2 Mar 11	OOC	16 Aug 11	8		
Southall	24 Aug 11	OOC	18 Oct 11	15		
Southall	2 Nov 11	SHL	10 Apr 12	69		
		SWks	29 Apr 12		G, BC	215,882
Weymouth	18 Jun 12	WEY	1 Nov 12	64		
		SWks			L, BC	228,831
Swindon Stock	4 Jan 13					
Weymouth	24 Jan 13	Bgwtr	9 Mar 14	98		
		SWks	23 Mar 14		H, BC	274,564
Swindon Stock	15 Jun 14					
Whitland	7 Jul 14					
Pontypool Road	15 Sep 14	PPRD	12 Feb 15	259		
		SWks	22 Feb 15		H, BC	291,766
Swindon Stock	29 Oct 15					
Cheltenham	30 Nov 15					
Chalford	Jan 16					
Cheltenham	Feb 16					
Chalford	Apr 16					
Gloucester	Jul 16					
Chalford	Aug 16					
Gloucester	Sep 16					
Chalford	Oct 16					
Gloucester	Dec 16					
Cheltenham	Jan 17					
Gloucester	Feb 17	GLO	9 Jun 17	868		
		BTL	Nov 18			
		SDN	Jan 19			
		SWks	26 Mar 19		H, BC	349,564
Swindon Stock	25 Oct 19					
Truro	8 Nov 19	TR	18 May 20	<14	R, BC	363,523
Truro	by 1 Jun 20	SWks	6 Jan 21	95	H, BC	378,469
Swindon Stock	11 Apr 21					
Penzance	25 Apr 21					
Helston	Jul 21					
Newton Abbot	Aug 21					
Helston	Sep 21					
Penzance	Oct 21					
Aberdare	15 Oct 21	SWks	18 Dec 23	466	H, BC	410,695
Swindon Stock	28 Mar 25					
Gloucester	30 Mar 25	SWks	29 Apr 25	6	L	
Stourbridge	5 May 25	SWks	28 Sep 25	23	L	
St Philip's Marsh	21 Oct 25					
Yatton	Jul 26					
St Philip's Marsh	Aug 26					
Bath	Sep 26					
Yatton	Oct 26					
Bath	Oct 26					
St Philip's Marsh	Nov 26					
Bath	Feb 27					
St Philip's Marsh	Mar 27					
Bath	Apr 27					
St Philip's Marsh	May 27	SPM	9 Jul 27			
		SWks	26 Jul 27			453,689

Converted to Trailer No.146 (Dia. A23)

NOTE

 # Conflicting dates and information given

No.39 (Diagrams K1, K)

Allocation	*Date*	*Stop'd*	*Date*	*Days Stop'd*	*Catgy. Repair*	*Miles Run*
New	Apr 05					
Swindon Stock	Apr 05					
Laira	19 Apr 05	NA?	29 Jul 05		BC	11,595
Laira	?	NA	Nov 05		BC	25,328
Laira	Dec 05	NA	26 Jan 06	48	G	34,486
Laira?	15 Mar 06	NA	16 Jun 06	11	G, BC	48,123
?	27 Jun 06	NA	8 Jan 07	4	G, BC	62,406
?	12 Jan 07	SWks	30 May 07	34	G, BC	76,119
?	3 Jul 07	NA	17 Oct 07	0	BC	83,070
Exeter?	17 Oct 07					
At Exeter	25 Apr 08	NA	11 May 08	9	L, BC	115,447
Laira	20 May 08	NA	20 Jul 08	68	G, BC	115,858
Laira	26 Sep 08	NA	26 Sep 08		BC	133,998
Laira	by 1 Jan 09	NA	22 Jul 09	79	G, BC	152,922
Laira	9 Oct 09	NA	Jun 10		†	184,276
Laira	Jul 10	NA	13 Sep 10	15		
Laira	28 Sep 10	NA	21 Sep 11	8	G, BC	228,086
Laira	29 Sep 11	NA	23 Jan 12	3	BC	238,272
Exeter	26 Jan 12	SWks	8 May 12	86	G, BC	244,737
Swindon Stock	2 Aug 12	SWks	6 Aug 12	7		244,737
Kidderminster	13 Aug 12					
Worcester	Jan 13	SWks	22 Feb 13	12	BC	
Swindon Stock	6 Mar 13					
Kidderminster	11 Mar 13					
Worcester	May 13					
Kidderminster	Jun 13	SWks	26 Jun 13	37	H, BC	274,124
Monmouth	2 Aug 13					
Pontypool Road	Sep 13					
Trowbridge	1 Oct 13	Trwbg	15 Apr 14	90		
		SWks	23 Apr 14		H, BC	296,802
Swindon Stock	14 Jul 14					
Southall	27 Jul 14	SWks	5 Apr 15	61	H, BC	321,476

Allocation	*Date*	*Stop'd*	*Date*	*Days Stop'd*	*Catgy. Repair*	*Miles Run*
Swindon Stock	5 Jun 15					
Pontypool Road	30 Jul 15					
Aberdare	Jan 17	SWks	5 Feb 20	329	H, BC	362,544
Swindon Stock	30 Dec 20					
Southall	14 Jan 21	SHL	8 Aug 21	11		
Southall	19 Aug 21	SHL	12 Feb 22	74		
		SWks	10 Mar 22		H, BC	375,776
Swindon Stock	27 Apr 22					
Cambrian lines	3 Jul 22					
Machynlleth	Aug 22					
Oswestry	Sep 22					
Moat Lane	Jul 23					
Oswestry	Aug 23	OSW *	10 Jan 24	152		
		SWks	21 Feb 24		H, BC	419,297
Swindon Stock	10 Jun 24					
Gloucester	17 Jun 24	SWks	3 Apr 25	35	H, BC	441,772
Gloucester	8 May 25	SWks	5 Feb 26	236	H, BC	463,159
Swindon Stock	29 Sep 26					
St Philips Marsh	6 Oct 26					
Westbury	Nov 26	WES	14 Nov 26	20	R	
St Philip's Marsh	4 Dec 26	SPM	13 May 27	26	R	
St Philip's Marsh	8 Jun 27	SPM	12 Aug 27	22		
St Philip's Marsh	3 Sep 27					
Yatton	Mar 28					
St Philip's Marsh	Apr 28	SWks	27 May 28	172	H, BC	495,388
St Philips Marsh	15 Nov 28	SPM	24 Jan 29	98	R	
St Philips Marsh	2 May 29	SPM	6 May 30	224		
		SWks	17 Jun 30		H, BC	512,348
Reading	16 Dec 30	RDG	26 Jun 31	15		
Reading	11 Jul 31					
Swindon Stock	Jun 32	Cnstr	2 Dec 32			
		SWks	Jun 33			537,101

Converted to Trailer No.197 (Dia A23)

NOTES

† Wheels & boiler change

** Stoppages Register gives NA*

No.40 (Diagrams K1, K)

Allocation	*Date*	*Stop'd*	*Date*	*Days Stop'd*	*Catgy. Repair*	*Miles Run*
New	Mar 05					
Swindon Stock	Apr 05					
Croes Newydd	28 Apr 05	SRD	8 Jan 06	29	G	
Croes Newydd	6 Feb 06	SRD	5 Jun 06	24	G	34,016
Croes Newydd	29 Jun 06	SWks	15 Dec 06	49	G, BC	46,721
Gloucester?	2 Feb 07					
At Gloucester	25 Apr 08	SWks	30 Jun 08	72	G, BC	101,978
Swindon Stock	10 Sep 08					
Laira	25 Sep 08					
Newquay	Oct 08					
Penzance	Nov 08	NA	18 Feb 09		BC	118,831
Newquay	Feb 09					
Truro	Mar 09					
Newquay	May 09	NA	19 Jun 09	79	BC	125,477
		SWks	19 Jun 09		G, BC	125,477
Swindon Stock	6 Sep 09					
Bath	18 Sep 09					
Swindon Stock	Nov 09					
Evesham	19 Nov 09	SWks	3 Sep 10	14	G, BC	150,949
Weymouth	17 Sep 10	SWks	1 Jul 12	33	G, BC	214,960
Swindon Stock	3 Aug 12	SWks	6 Aug 12	7		
Stourbridge	13 Aug 12					
Tyseley	Nov 12	SWks	10 Apr 13	75	H, BC	233,611
Worcester	24 Jun 13					
Kidderminster	Aug 13					
Worcester	Nov 13					
Kidderminster	Nov 13	SWks	21 Mar 14	18	H, BC	257,273
Swindon Stock	8 Apr 14					
Croes Newydd	12 Apr 14					
Corwen	May 14					
Croes Newydd	Jun 14					
Corwen	Jul 14					
Croes Newydd	Aug 14					
Corwen	Sep 14	CNYD	22 Jan 15	4		
Corwen	26 Jan 15	CNYD	11 Feb 15	20		
Chester	3 Mar 15					
Croes Newydd	Jul 15	CNYD	9 Aug 15	39	L	
Croes Newydd	17 Sep 15					
Chester	Oct 15					
Croes Newydd	Jan 16					
Chester	Mar 16	SWks	4 Apr 16	487	H, BC	304,270
Swindon Stock	4 Aug 17					
Cheltenham	6 Aug 17					
Gloucester	Dec 17					
Cheltenham	Jan 18					
Gloucester	Feb 18	SWks	25 Feb 18	137	H, BC	321,537
Swindon Stock	12 Jul 18					
Chester	22 Jul 18	CHR	5 Feb 19	29	L	
Chester	6 Mar 19	CHR	17 May 19	109	L	
Chester	3 Sep 19	OXY	15 Dec 19	497		
		SWks	14 Jan 20		H, BC	352,452
Swindon Stock	25 Apr 21					
Neath	6 Jul 21	NEA	25 Feb 22	108		
		SWks	7 Mar 22		H, BC	363,938
Swindon Stock	13 Jun 22					
Cambrian Lines	3 Jul 22					
Machynlleth	Aug 22					
Dolgelly	Sep 22					
Machynlleth	Oct 22					
Dolgelly	Nov 22					
Machynlleth	Dec 22					
Oswestry	Dec 22	SWks	1 Mar 23	37	H, BC	373,804
Swindon Stock	7 Apr 23					
Bath	2 May 23					
Yatton	Jul 23					
Bristol	Aug 23	BTL	4 Oct 23	1		
Bath	5 Oct 23	SWks	15 Jan 24	73	H, BC	393,325
Swindon Stock	28 Mar 24					
Bristol	1 Apr 24					
Bath	Jun 24	BTL	3 Aug 24	101		
		SWks	15 Aug 24		H, BC	402,117
St Philip's Marsh	12 Nov 24	SWks	4 Apr 25	31	L	
Bath	Jan 25					
St Philip's Marsh	Feb 25					
Bath	Mar 25					
Stafford Road	5 May 25	Clhm	6 Sep 25			
Stafford Road	Oct 25	SRD	29 Apr 26	22	H, BC	437,407
Stourbridge	21 May 26	STB	15 Oct 26	69	R	
Stourbridge	23 Dec 26	OXY	14 May 27	46		
		SRD	10 Jun 27		L	
Stourbridge	29 Jun 27	STB	4 Nov 27	31	R	
Stourbridge	5 Dec 27	SWks	14 Feb 28	202	H, BC	464,149
Stourbridge	3 Sep 28	SWks	13 Apr 30	159	H, BC	500,614
Stourbridge	19 Sep 30	SRD	14 Mar 31	48	G, BC	515,035
Stourbridge	1 May 31	TYS	5 Dec 31	67	L	
Stourbridge	10 Feb 32	STB	29 Feb 32	33		
		SWks	4 Mar 32		L	
Stourbridge	2 Apr 32	STB	9 Dec 32			
		SStk	Dec 32			
		Cnstr	Mar 33			
		SWks	4 Mar 33			539,980

Converted to Trailer No.198 (Dia. A23)

No.41 (Diagrams L1, L)

Allocation	*Date*	*Stop'd*	*Date*	*Days Stop'd*	*Catgy. Repair*	*Miles Run*
New	Jan 05					
Evesham	31 Jan 05					
Southall	10 Jun 05	SWks	15 May 06	73	G, BC	35,088
?	27 Jul 06	SWks	8 May 07	36	BC	52,316
Croes Newydd?	13 Jun 07	SRD	29 Jan 08	7	L, BC	65,760
Croes Newydd?	5 Feb 08					
At Croes Newydd	25 Apr 08	SRD	7 May 08	5	L, BC	70,454
Croes Newydd	12 May 08	SRD	21 Aug 08	6	L, BC	74,993
Croes Newydd	27 Aug 08	SWks	23 Sep 08	71	L, BC	76,828
Swindon Stock	3 Dec 08					
Bath	21 Aug 09					
Swindon Stock	4 Oct 09					
Bath	11 Oct 09					
Bristol	10 Dec 09					

Allocation	*Date*	*Stop'd*	*Date*	*Days Stop'd*	*Catgy. Repair*	*Miles Run*
Bath	Jan 10	SWks	16 Feb 10	59	BC	97,087
Swindon Stock	16 Apr 10					
Merthyr	6 May 10					
Swindon Stock	Jun 10					
Gwaun-Cae-Gurwen	29 Jun 10					
Neath	Aug 10					
Whitland	Sep 10					
Gloucester	6 Oct 10					
Oxford	1 Nov 10	SWks	25 Oct 11	76	G, BC	129,063
Swindon Stock	9 Jan 12					
Aberdare	2 Feb 12					
Monmouth	Jul 12					
Neath	16 Aug 12	NEA	10 May 13	16	L, BC	156,437
Neath	26 May 13	SWks	11 Aug 13	59	H, BC	160,938
Swindon Stock	9 Oct 13					
Bath	13 Nov 13					
Yatton	Dec 13					
Bath	Jan 14					
Bristol	Feb 14					
Bath	Apr 14					
Bristol	Jun 14					
Bath	Aug 14					
Bristol	Sep 14					
Bath	Oct 14					
Yatton	Nov 14					
Bath	Dec 14					
Bristol	Jan 15					
Yatton	Feb 15					
Bristol	Apr 15	SWks	10 May 15	21	H, BC	208,213
Swindon Stock	31 May 15					
Bristol	10 Sep 15					
Yatton	Oct 15					
Bristol	Nov 15					
Bath	Jul 16					
Bristol	Aug 16					
Bath	Sep 16					
Bristol	Oct 16	BTL	7 Nov 16	1094		
		SWks	9 Dec 18		H, BC	235,322
Swindon Stock	6 Nov 19					
Croes Newydd	25 Nov 19	SWks	1 Feb 21	293	H, BC	252,235
Swindon Stock	21 Nov 21					
Gloucester	11 Mar 22					
Chalford	May 22	SWks	5 Jul 22	160	H, BC	261,261
Swindon Stock	12 Dec 22					
Southall	7 Jul 22	SHL	21 Feb 24	22	R	
Southall	14 Mar 24	SHL	27 Mar 24	21	R	
Southall	17 Apr 24	OOC	17 May 24	132		
		SWks	26 May 24		H, BC	287,764
Swindon Stock	26 Sep 24					
Southall	15 Nov 24	SWks	20 Feb 26	185	H, BC	310,010
Swindon Stock	24 Aug 26					
Reading	6 Oct 26	SWks	5 Jan 28			320,261

Converted to Trailer No.147 (Dia. A24)

No.42 (Diagrams L1, L)

Allocation	*Date*	*Stop'd*	*Date*	*Days Stop'd*	*Catgy. Repair*	*Miles Run*
New	Jan 05					
Chippenham	2 Feb 05	SWks	8 Feb 05	15		
Brynamman	23 Feb 05					
Garnant	Apr 05					
Neath	May 05					
Whitland	Jun 05					
Tenby	Jul 05					
Whitland	Aug 05					
Trowbridge	30 Sep 05	SWks	8 Nov 05	37	G, BC	22,178
Swindon Stock	15 Dec 05					
Southall	22 Dec 05					
Neath	26 Feb 06	NEA	29 Mar 06	43	LG, BC	28,332
Neath	11 May 06	SWks	18 May 06	39	G	28,674
Neath?	26 Jun 06	SWks	5 Oct 06	28	G, BC	35,999
?	2 Nov 06	SWks	23 Oct 07	96	G	60,349
Swindon Stock?	27 Jan 08					
In Swindon Stock	25 Apr 08					
Southall	25 May 08	SWks	15 Apr 09	60	G, BC	85,072
Swindon Stock	14 Jun 09					
Aberystwyth	29 Jun 09					
Neath	Oct 09	SWks	8 Apr 10	31	G, BC	103,327
Swindon Stock	9 May 10					
Aberystwyth	29 Jun 10					
Carmarthen	Oct 10					
Swindon Stock	Nov 10					
Yatton	9 Nov 10					
Bristol	Dec 10	SWks	6 Jan 11	33	G, BC	115,064
Swindon Stock	8 Feb 11					
Bristol	23 Feb 11					
Bath	Mar 11					
Bristol	May 11					
Bath	Jul 11					
Bristol	Aug 11					
Yatton	Nov 11					
Radstock	Dec 11					
Bath	Dec 11					
Bristol	Jan 12					
Bath	Mar 12					
Bristol	May 12	BTL	6 Jun 12	118		
		SWks	8 Jul 12		G, BC	162,889
Bristol	2 Oct 12					
Radstock	Nov 12					
Bristol	Nov 12					
Bath	May 13					
Bristol	Jul 13					
Yatton	Aug 13	SWks	3 Sep 13	16	H, BC	196,911
Swindon Stock	19 Sep 13					
Bath	5 Dec 13					
Bristol	Mar 14					
Radstock	Apr 14	SWks	11 May 14	54	H, BC	211,383
Whitland	4 Jul 14					
Gloucester	19 Sep 14					
Swindon Stock	Nov 14					
Neath	1 Dec 14	SWks	28 Oct 15	502	H, BC	242,199
Swindon Stock	13 Mar 17					
Trowbridge	5 Jun 17	SWks	22 Nov 17	(No repairs)		
Swindon Stock	22 Nov 17					
Bath	26 Dec 17					
Bristol	Feb 18					
Bath	Mar 18					
Bristol	Apr 18					
Bath	May 18					
Swindon Stock	Jun 18					
Yatton	Jun 18	SPM	22 Jun 18	26	R	
Bath	18 Jul 18					
Bristol	Aug 18					
Bath	Sep 18					
Bristol	Oct 18					
Bath	Nov 18					
Bristol	Dec 18					
Stopped work	4 Jun 19	SDst	4 Jun 19	406		
		SWks	12 Dec 19		H, BC	282,859
Swindon Stock	14 Jul 20					

Sold to Mr Graham for Port of London Authority, 10 Sep 20

No.43 (Diagrams M1, M)

Allocation	*Date*	*Stop'd*	*Date*	*Days Stop'd*	*Catgy. Repair*	*Miles Run*
New	Feb 05					
Laira	17 Feb 05					
Newton Abbot	Dec 05					
Laira	Jan 06					
Truro	Feb 06	NA	6 Jun 06	9	G, BC	47,522
Laira?	15 Jun 06	NA			BC	67,501
?		SWks	28 Feb 07	40	G, BC	67,501
?	9 Apr 07	SWks	14 Nov 07	62	G, BC	89,382
Swindon Stock?	15 Jan 08					
At Southall	13 Apr 08	SWks	19 Feb 09	92	G, BC	110,536
Swindon Stock	22 May 09					
Aberwystywth	29 Jun 09					
Neath	Oct 09					
Swindon Stock	1 Nov 09					
Neath	19 Nov 09	SWks	27 Jul 10	71	G, BC	145,526

Allocation	Date	Stop'd	Date	Days Stop'd	Catgy. Repair	Miles Run
Swindon Stock	6 Oct 10					
Gloucester	12 Oct 10					
Chalford	Dec 10					
Swindon Stock	Jun 11					
Southall	14 Jul 11					
Radstock	25 Jul 11					
Bath	Sep 11					
Bristol	Oct 11					
Bath	Nov 11					
Yatton	Dec 11					
Bristol	Jan 12					
Yatton	Feb 12					
Bristol	Mar 12	BTL	8 Jun 12	32		
		SWks	22 Jun 12		G, BC	192,823
Oxford	10 Jul 12					
Bristol	5 Oct 12					
Bath	Dec 12					
Bristol	Jan 13					
Bath	Feb 13					
Bristol	Mar 13					
Bath	Apr 13					
Bristol	May 13	BTL	29 May 13	20	L	
Bath	18 Jun 13					
Bristol	Sep 13	BTL	16 Sep 13	17	L	
Bath	3 Oct 13					
Bristol	Dec 13	SWks	12 Jan 14	84	H, BC	237,467
Bristol	6 Apr 14					
Bath	May 14					
Bristol	Aug 14					
Yatton	Sep 14					
Bath	Oct 14					
Bristol	Nov 14	BTL	24 Feb 15	19	L	
Bath	15 Mar 15					
Yatton	Apr 15					
Bristol	May 15					
Yatton	Jul 15					
Bath	Sep 15					
Bristol	Oct 15					
Yatton	Nov 15					
Bristol	Dec 15					
Bath	Feb 16					
Bristol	Apr 16	SWks	26 Jun 16	56	H, BC	293,929
Swindon Stock	21 Aug 16					
Newport	25 Sep 16	SWks	29 Mar 20	452	H, BC	310,842
Swindon Stock	24 Jun 21					
Gloucester	5 Jul 21					
Chalford	Aug 21					
Gloucester	Jan 22					
Chalford	Jan 22					
Swindon Stock	Feb 22					
Gloucester	1 Mar 22					
Chalford	Apr 22					
Gloucester	May 22	SWks	11 Oct 22			346,888

Converted to Trailer No.134 (Dia. A17)

No.44 (Diagrams M1, M)

Allocation	Date	Stop'd	Date	Days Stop'd	Catgy. Repair	Miles Run
New	Feb 05					
Laira	17 Feb 05					
Exeter	Jul 05	NA	10 Aug 05		BC	22,644
Exeter	1 Sep 05	NA	25 Jan 06	9	G, BC	44,056
Exeter	3 Feb 06	NA	2 Jul 06	19	G, BC	66,987
Exeter?	21 Jul 06	NA	27 Aug 06	0	L, BC	70,395
Exeter?	27 Aug 06	NA	8 Mar 07	20	L	
Exeter?	28 Mar 07	SWks	7 Mar 08	87	G, BC	97,897
Neath	2 Jun 08	SWks	3 Sep 08	29	G, BC	108,089
Swindon Stock	2 Oct 08					
Neath	6 Jan 09	SWks	20 Apr 09	21	L, BC	120,813
Swindon Stock	11 May 09					
Weymouth	28 May 09	SWks	20 Sep 10	64	G, BC	168,194
Swindon Stock	23 Nov 10					
Southall	2 Feb 11					
Bath	29 May 11					
Bristol	Jun 11	BTL	20 Jun 11	20	L	
Bath	10 Jul 11					
Bristol	Aug 11	BTL	18 Sep 11	21	L	
Bristol	9 Oct 11					
Bath	Nov 11	SWks	9 Dec 11	143	G	198,500
Swindon Stock	30 Apr 12					
Bath	28 May 12					
Bristol	Jul 12					
Yatton	Aug 12					
Bath	Sep 12					
Bristol	Nov 12					
Radstock	Dec 12					
Bath	Jan 13	BTL	7 Feb 13	18	L	
Bristol	25 Feb 13					
Bath	May 13					
Yatton	Nov 13					
Bristol	Nov 13	SWks	8 Dec 13	100	H, BC	247,166
Chalford	18 Mar 14					
Gloucester	Nov 14					
Chalford	Dec 14					
Gloucester	Feb 15	SWks	20 Mar 15	30	H, BC	283,677
Gloucester	19 Apr 15					
Chalford	Jul 15					
Gloucester	Oct 15	SWks	7 Oct 15	204	H, BC	300,669
Gloucester	28 Apr 16					
Chalford	Jul 16					
Gloucester	Aug 16					
Chalford	Sep 16					
Gloucester	Oct 16					
Chalford	Dec 16					
Gloucester	Jan 17	GLO	17 Feb 17	49		
		SWks	19 Feb 17		H, BC	325,225
Swindon Stock	7 Apr 17					
Gloucester	10 May 17					
Cheltenham	Aug 17					
Swindon Stock	Sep 17					
Newport	8 Oct 17	NPT	26 Aug 19	626		
		SWks	29 Mar 20		H, BC	345,281
Swindon Stock	13 May 21					
Chalford	5 Jul 21					
Gloucester	Aug 21	GLO	12 Mar 22	75		
		SWks	9 May 22		L	
Swindon Stock	26 May 22					
Worcester	5 Jul 22	SWks	1 Nov 22			373,664

Converted to Trailer No.135 (Dia. A18)

No.45 (Diagrams M1, M)

Allocation	Date	Stop'd	Date	Days Stop'd	Catgy. Repair	Miles Run
New	Feb 05					
Southall	28 Feb 05	SHL	3 May 05	8	L	
Southall	11 May 05	SWks	14 Oct 05	39	G, BC	28,912
Penzance	22 Nov 05	NA	12 May 06	4	LG	
Laira?	16 May 06	SWks	27 Nov 06	94	G, BC	68,692
Laira?	1 Mar 07	NA	20 Jul 07	34	L, BC	84,469
Laira?	23 Aug 07	NA	22 Feb 08	0	BC	128,332
Laira /	22 Feb 08					
At Laira	25 Apr 08					
Newton Abbot	Jan 09					
Laira	Feb 09	SWks	16 Jul 09	78	G, BC	143,586
Swindon Stock	2 Oct 09					
Chippenham	16 Nov 09	SWks	22 Feb 10	10		
Chippenham	4 Mar 10	SDst	31 May 10	14		
Chippenham	14 Jun 10					
Bath	1 Oct 10	BTL	27 Oct 10	40		
Bath	6 Dec 10	SWks	8 Feb 11	94	G, BC	191,690
Swindon Stock	13 May 11					
Chester	29 May 11	CHR	23 Jan 12	23	BC	205,858
Chester	15 Feb 12	Sltny	21 Nov 12	14		
Chester	5 Dec 12					
Stourbridge	18 Dec 12					
Worcester	24 Jan 13					
Swindon Stock	1 Mar 13	SWks	18 Apr 13	22	L, BC	225,408
Swindon Stock	10 May 13					
Oxford	2 Jun 13					
Swindon Stock	Aug 13					
Neath	11 Aug 13	SWks	24 Jun 14	73	H, BC	261,193

Allocation	Date	Stop'd	Date	Days Stop'd	Catgy. Repair	Miles Run
Swindon Stock	5 Sep 14					
Bristol	10 Sep 14					
Bath	Nov 14					
Bristol.	Dec 14					
Bath	Nov 15	BTL	11 Jan 16	16	L	
Bristol	27 Jan 16	BTL	18 Apr 16	32		
Bristol	20 May 16	SWks	24 May 16	491	H, BC	313,664
Swindon Stock	27 Sep 17					
Southall	26 Oct 17					
Swindon Stock	Dec 17					
Invergordon (HR)	1 Jan 18	SWks	4 Aug 20	117	H, BC	332,667
Swindon Stock	29 Nov 20					
Trowbridge	22 Dec 20					
Swindon Stock	Jan 21					
Gloucester	5 Jul 21	SWks	29 Sep 21	27	H, BC	340,987
Swindon Stock	26 Oct 21					
Gloucester	1 Nov 21					
Chalford	Jan 22					
Gloucester	Apr 22	SWks	30 Oct 22	140	H, BC	368,947
Swindon Stock	19 Mar 23					
Croes Newydd	9 Jul 23					
Birkenhead	Jul 23	BHD	13 Dec 24	47	R	
Birkenhead	29 Jan 25					
Croes Newydd	Apr 25	SWks	29 Jun 25	236	H, BC	404,691
Swindon Stock	20 Feb 26					
Birkenhead	3 Feb 27					
Oxley	Jun 27					
Stourbridge	Aug 27	SRD	30 Sep 27			
		STB	9 Oct 26			
		SWks	5 Jan 28			414,820

Converted to Trailer No.148 (Dia. A25)

No.46 (Diagrams M1, M)

Allocation	Date	Stop'd	Date	Days Stop'd	Catgy. Repair	Miles Run
New	Feb 05					
Evesham	6 Mar 05	WOS	23 Oct 05	35	LG&T	
Evesham	27 Nov 05	WOS	11 Jun 06	51	LG	46,146
Evesham?	1 Aug 06	SWks	11 Oct 06	43	G, BC	47,343
?	23 Nov 06	NA	20 Jul 07	11	LG, BC	81,406
?	31 Jul 07	NA	1 Feb 08	63	BC	
		SWks	11 Feb 08		G, BC	97,478
Southall	4 Apr 08					
Weymouth	18 May 08	SWks	29 May 09	82	G, BC	141,336
Swindon Stock	19 Aug 09					
Bath	22 Feb 10					
Bristol	Mar 10					
Bath	Apr 10	SWks	12 Jul 10	86	BC	158,960
Swindon Stock	6 Oct 10					
Gloucester	25 Nov 10					
Swindon Stock	Jun 11					
Bristol	19 Jun 11					
Radstock	6 Oct 10					
Bristol	Nov 11					
Bath	Dec 11					
Bristol	Dec 11					
Bath	May 12					
Yatton	Jun 12					
Bath	Jul 12	SWks	3 Oct 12	74	BC	220,727
Chalford	16 Dec 12					
Gloucester	Feb 13	SWks	19 Apr 13	13	H, BC	232,332
Swindon Stock	2 May 13					
Gloucester	15 May 13					
Swindon Stock	Jun 13					
Neath	25 Jun 13	SWks	11 Aug 13	72	H, BC	239,056
Swindon Stock	22 Oct 13					
Chalford	17 Nov 13					
Swindon Stock	Mar 14	SWks	14 Apr 14	36	L, BC	252,422
Swindon Stock	20 May 14					
Yatton	26 May 14					
Bath	Aug 14					
Bristol	Nov 14					
Bath	Jan 15					
Bristol	Feb 15					
Bath	Apr 15					
Bristol	May 15	SWks	24 Sep 15	113	H, BC	287,885
Chalford	15 Jan 16	SWks	20 Mar 16	274	H, BC	294,010
Swindon Stock	19 Dec 16					
Chalford	13 Feb 17					
Gloucester	Apr 17					
Chalford	May 17					
Gloucester	Jun 17					
Chalford	Aug 17					
Gloucester	Feb 18					
Chalford	Mar 18	Chlfd	1 Apr 18	488		
		SDst	Dec 18			
		SWks	25 Mar 19		H, BC	331,611
Swindon Stock	2 Aug 19					
Croes Newydd	4 Aug 19					
Chester	Jan 20					
Stourbridge	Feb 20	STB	18 Oct 21	22	R	
Stourbridge	9 Nov 21					
Worcester	Feb 22	SWks	28 Apr 22			352,209

Converted to Trailer No.136 (Dia. A15)

No.47 (Diagrams M1, M)

Allocation	Date	Stop'd	Date	Days Stop'd	Catgy. Repair	Miles Run
New	Feb 05					
		SWks	24 Mar 05	1	L	
Swindon Stock	25 Mar 05					
Neath	27 Mar 05	SWks	1 May 06	56	G, BC	32,456
?	26 Jun 06	SWks	10 Nov 06	23	G, BC	41,986
?	3 Dec 06	SWks	16 Apr 07	23	G	50,589
Laira?	9 May 07	NA	16 Sep 07	7	G	59,468
Laira?	23 Sep 07	NA	6 Feb 08	46	G, BC	73,647
Laira	23 Mar 08	NA	4 May 08	3	L, BC	75,615
Laira	7 May 08	SWks	20 Nov 08	92	G, BC	90,380
Swindon Stock	20 Feb 09					
Oxford	12 May 09					
Chalford	Jun 09					
Neath	Jul 09	SWks	6 Nov 09	70	G, BC	110,044
Southall	15 Jan 10					
Swindon Stock	Feb 10					
Southall	22 Mar 10					
Swindon Stock	Apr 10					
Paddington	13 May 10					
Southall	Jun 10					
Laira	25 Oct 10	NA	16 Nov 10	19	BC	115,964
Laira	5 Dec 10	NA	31 Mar 11	4	BC	123,419
Laira	4 Apr 11	NA	1 Dec 11	17	BC	149,645
Truro	18 Dec 11					
Laira	Jan 12	NA	7 Sep 12	83		
Laira	29 Nov 12	SWks	6 Aug 13	23	H, BC	184,586
Swindon Stock	29 Aug 13					
Pontypool Road	9 Oct 13					
Swindon Stock	Dec 13					
Yatton	20 Jan 14					
Bristol	Mar 14					
Bath	Jun 14					
Bristol	Jul 14					
Yatton	Aug 14					
Bristol	Sep 14					
Yatton	Oct 14					
Bristol	Nov 14					
Bath	Feb 15					
Bristol	Apr 15	SWks	30 Apr 15	417	H, BC	220,560
Swindon Stock	20 Jun 16					
Bristol	26 Jun 16					
Bath	Aug 16					
Bristol	Sep 16					
Bath	Oct 16					
Bristol	Jan 17					
Yatton	Mar 17					
Bristol	May 17					
Bath	Jul 17					
Yatton	Aug 17					
Bristol	Sep 17	BTL	16 Nov 17	22	L	
Yatton	8 Dec 17					
Bristol	Jan 18					

Allocation	*Date*	*Stop'd*	*Date*	*Days Stop'd*	*Catgy. Repair*	*Miles Run*
Bath	Feb 18					
Bristol	Mar 18					
Bath	Jul 18	SWks	26 Jul 18	6	L	
Bristol	1 Aug 18					
Bath	Dec 18					
Bristol	Feb 19	BTL	7 Apr 19	445		
		SWks	29 Dec 19		H, BC	267,502
Swindon Stock	25 Jun 20	SWks	11 Aug 20	1	In & out	
Swindon Stock	12 Aug 20					
Southall	25 Apr 21	SWks	20 Jan 22			281,677

Converted to Trailer No.137 (Dia. A15)

No.48 (Diagrams M1, M)

New	Mar 05					
Neath	24 Mar 05	SWks	16 Jan 06	52	G, BC	23,493
?	9 Mar 06	SWks	11 Aug 06	27	G, BC	37,502
?	7 Sep 06	SWks	19 Feb 07	86	G, BC	52,767
Gloucester?	16 May 07					
At Gloucester	25 Apr 08	SWks	31 Jul 08	49	G, BC	90,175
Chalford	18 Sep 08					
Gloucester	Feb 09					
Chalford	Apr 09					
Gloucester	May 09	GLO	17 May 09	26	L	
Gloucester	12 Jun 09	SWks	25 Aug 09	57	G, BC	121,543
Swindon Stock	21 Oct 09					
Gloucester	9 Dec 09					
Chalford	Mar 10					
Gloucester	Jun 10					
Chalford	Aug 10	SWks	6 Oct 10	70	BC	152,014
Swindon Stock	15 Dec 10					
Trowbridge	25 Jan 11					
Frome	Feb 11					
Neath	7 Mar 11	SWks	15 May 11	17	G, BC	160,281
Bath	1 Jun 11					
Yatton	Jul 11					
Bath	Aug 11					
Yatton	Sep 11					
Bath	Oct 11					
Bristol	Nov 11					
Radstock	Dec 11					
Bath	Jan 12					
Bristol	Mar 12	BTL	12 Apr 12	18		
Radstock	30 Apr 12	SWks	10 Jun 12	74	G, BC	191,465
Swindon Stock	23 Aug 12					
Neath	29 Aug 12	SWks	7 Mar 13	70	H, BC	210,552
Swindon Stock	16 May 13	SWks	30 May 13	5	H, BC	211,440
Swindon Stock	4 Jun 13					
Southall	29 Jul 13	OOC	14 Mar 14	25	L	
Southall	8 Apr 14	SWks	10 Oct 14	68	H, BC	263,377
Swindon Stock	17 Dec 14					
Neath	20 Feb 15	SWks	9 Jun 15	43	L	
Swindon Stock	22 Jul 15					
Gloucester	4 Sep 15					
Chalford	Oct 15	GLO	23 Dec 15			
Chalford	N/R					
Destroyed by fire	8 Jan 16					285,634
Condemned w.e.f.	8 Jan 16	SWks	17 Jan 16			

NOTES

The engine and boiler survived the 1916 fire.

The Allocations Registers show the car at Swindon until Apr 1918.

No.49 (Diagrams (N1, N)

New	Feb 05					
Ashburton	28 Feb 05	NA	Apr 05			
Ashburton	May 05	NA	Jun 05		BC	28,508
Penzance	Jul 05					
Laira	Dec 05	NA	26 Oct 06	27	G	51,733
Laira?	22 Nov 06	SWks	24 Apr 07	52	BC	66,403
Neath?	15 Jun 07					
At Neath	25 Apr 08	SWks	4 Jun 08	99	G	99,724
Swindon Stock	11 Sep 08					
Worcester	9 Oct 08					
Evesham	Nov 08					

Allocation	*Date*	*Stop'd*	*Date*	*Days Stop'd*	*Catgy. Repair*	*Miles Run*
Swindon Stock	Jan 09					
Neath	19 Apr 09	SWks	6 Jul 09	25	L	117,097
Swindon Stock	31 Jul 09					
Gloucester	25 Aug 09					
Chalford	Dec 09	SWks	29 Apr 10	38	G	140,093
Swindon Stock	6 Jun 10					
Whitland	4 Jul 10					
Neath	Sep 10	SWks	7 Mar 11	49	G	164,560
Swindon Stock	25 Apr 11					
Laira	26 May 11	NA	23 Dec 11	27	S	190,098
Laira	19 Jan 12	NA	15 Jul 12	26	G	208,619
Newton Abbot	10 Aug 12					
Laira	Nov 12	NA	17 Jan 13	11	H	224,275
Laira	28 Jan 13	SWks	3 Oct 13	78	H	249,903
Trowbridge	20 Dec 13					
Frome	Feb 14	SWks	6 Apr 14	52	H	254,539
Bristol	28 May 14					
Bath	Jul 14					
Bristol	Aug 14					
Bath	Sep 14					
Bristol	Oct 14					
Bath	Nov 14					
Bristol	Dec 14					
Bath	Dec 14					
Yatton	Jan 15					
Bristol	Feb 15					
Yatton	Mar 15					
Bristol	Apr 15					
Bath	May 15					
Yatton	Sep 15					
Bath	Oct 15	SPM	9 Nov 15	941		
		SWks	9 Dec 15		H	294,492
Swindon Stock	7 Jun 18					
Bristol	26 Jun 18	BTL	26 Jun 18	31	R	
Bristol	27 Jul 18					
Bath	Aug 18					
Bristol	Sep 18	BTL	28 Dec 18	440		
		SWks	3 Jan 20	69	H, BC	303,966
Swindon Stock	12 Mar 20					

Sold to Mr Graham for Port of London Authority, 10 Aug 20, with boiler change made

No.50 (Diagram N)

New	Mar 05					
Chalford	16 Mar 05	SWks	19 Dec 05	60	G, BC	27,773
Chalford	17 Feb 06	SWks	19 May 06	24	L, BC	39,398
?	12 Jun 06	SWks	13 Oct 06	12	G, BC	50,625
?	25 Oct 06	SWks	23 Oct 07	61	G, BC	86,151
Gloucester?	23 Dec 07					
At Gloucester	25 Apr 08	SWks	7 Aug 08	42	G, BC	92,644
Gloucester	18 Sep 08					
Chalford	Mar 09					
Gloucester	Apr 09					
Chalford	May 09					
Gloucester	Jun 09					
Chalford	Jul 09					
Gloucester	Dec 09	SWks	9 Dec 09	90	G, BC	130,548
Swindon Stock	9 Mar 10					
Laira	17 Mar 10	LA	14 Apr 10	62		
Laira	15 Jun 10					
Newton Abbot	Jun 10					
Laira	Jul 10	NA	10 Sep 10	58		
		SWks	15 Sep 10		G, BC	147,559
Swindon Stock	7 Nov 10					
Southall	20 Jan 11	OOC	1 May 11	11		
Southall	12 May 11					
Neath	19 May 11	SWks	10 Aug 12	84	BC	203,991
Swindon Stock	2 Nov 12					
Chester	19 Nov 12	SRD	13 Jan 14	21		
Chester	3 Feb 14	SRD	1 Jul 14	18	H, BC	256,832
Chester	19 Jul 14	SRD	16 Dec 14	6	BC	274,118
Chester	22 Dec 14	SRD	4 Jun 15	13	H, BC	287,989
Chester	17 Jun 15	SWks	3 Aug 15	13		
Swindon Stock	16 Aug 15	SWks	9 Sep 15	99	Nil	

Allocation	Date	Stop'd	Date	Days Stop'd	Catgy. Repair	Miles Run
Swindon Stock	17 Dec 15					
Chalford	24 Dec 15	SWks	13 Jan 16	89	H, BC	292,027
Swindon Stock	11 Apr 16					
Newport	15 Apr 16	NPT	27 Aug 16	988		
		SWks	16 Dec 18		H	294,864
Swindon Stock	12 May 19					
Aberdare	24 Jun 19	SWks	3 Nov 22			329,420

Converted to Trailer No.138 (Dia. A19)

No.51 (Diagram N)

Allocation	Date	Stop'd	Date	Days Stop'd	Catgy. Repair	Miles Run
New	Apr 05					
Weymouth	26 Apr 05	SWks	27 Mar 06	42	L, BC	30,413
?	8 May 06	SWks	29 May 06	27	G, BC	32,408
?	25 Jun 06	SWks	22 May 07	56	G, BC	64,301
Weymouth?	17 Jul 07					
At Weymouth	25 Apr 08	SWks	17 May 08	39	G, BC	91,613
Swindon Stock	25 Jun 08					
Bath	17 Jul 08					
Neath	3 Sep 08	SWks	7 Jan 09	91	G, BC	115,017
Swindon Stock	8 Apr 09					
Oxford	12 May 09					
Swindon Stock	Jun 09					
Tyseley	29 Jun 09					
Southall	23 Jul 09	SWks	13 Jan 10	42	G, BC	127,406
Swindon Stock	24 Feb 10					
Southall	22 Mar 10					
Swindon Stock	Apr 10					
Gloucester	29 Apr 10					
Oxford	Jun 10					
Gloucester	Jul 10	GLO	5 Oct 10	20		
Chalford	25 Oct 10	SWks	25 Nov 10		G, BC	146,247
Swindon Stock	15 Dec 10					
Trowbridge	24 Jan 11					
Bristol	16 Feb 11					
Yatton	Mar 11					
Bristol	Apr 11					
Chalford	2 Jun 11					
Gloucester	Jul 11	SWks	17 Jul 11	36	BC	161,919
Swindon Stock	22 Aug 11					
Chalford	30 Aug 11	SWks	7 Nov 11	70	G, BC	167,506
Swindon Stock	16 Jan 12					
Chalford	29 Jan 12					
Gloucester	Apr 12					
Chalford	May 12					
Gloucester	Jun 12					
Chalford	Jul 12					
Gloucester	Nov 12	SWks	20 Jan 13	88	H, BC	201,876
Chalford	18 Apr 13	SWks	10 May 13	12	L, BC	
Swindon Stock	22 May 13					
Gloucester	28 May 13					
Chalford	Nov 13					
Gloucester	Nov 13					
Chalford	Apr 14	SWks	8 Jun 14	43	H, BC	239,450
Swindon Stock	21 Jul 14					
Kidderminster	27 Jul 14					
Neath	31 Aug 14	SWks	19 Feb 15	101	H, BC	260,812
Neath	31 May 15	NEA	29 Nov 15	16		
Neath	15 Dec 15					
Chalford	5 Feb 16	SWks	10 Apr 16	514	H, BC	284,631
Swindon Stock	6 Sep 17					
Gloucester	31 Oct 17					
Chalford	Jan 18					
Gloucester	Mar 18					
Cheltenham	Apr 18					
Gloucester	May 18					
Cheltenham	Jul 18					
Gloucester	Aug 18	SWks	31 Mar 19	92	H	310,743
Swindon Stock	1 Jul 19					
Aberdare	9 Jul 19	ABDR	21 Jan 21	348		
		SWks	19 Feb 21		H, BC	328,323
Swindon Stock	4 Jan 22	SWks	12 Jun 22			328,550

Converted to Trailer No.139 (Dia. A19)

No.52 (Diagram N)

Allocation	Date	Stop'd	Date	Days Stop'd	Catgy. Repair	Miles Run
New	Feb 05					
Swindon Stock	Feb 05	SWks	20 Mar 05	26		
Swindon Stock	15 Apr 05					
Chalford ‡	22 Apr 05	SWks	10 Nov 05	21	G, BC	23,049
Swindon Stock	1 Dec 05					
Chalford	15 Dec 05	SWks	28 Sep 06	21	G, BC	50,301
Chalford?	19 Oct 06	SWks	6 Jun 07	23	BC	71,992
Chalford?	29 Jun 07	SWks	24 Sep 07	13	L, BC	80,480
Chalford?	7 Oct 07					
At Chalford	25 Apr 08					
Gloucester	Aug 08	SWks	17 Sep 08	111	G, BC	111,137
Swindon Stock	6 Jan 09					
Southall	19 Feb 09	SWks	15 Jun 09	15	G, BC	123,854
Swindon Stock	30 Jun 09					
Laira	19 Jul 09	NA	16 Mar 10	30	G, BC	144,802
Laira	15 Apr 10	NA	6 Sep 10	7	BC	157,845
Laira	13 Sep 10	NA	17 Oct 10	0	BC	160,666
Laira	17 Oct 10					
Truro	Nov 10					
Laira	Dec 10					
Gloucester	30 May 11					
Chalford	Jul 11					
Gloucester	Aug 11					
Chalford	Dec 11					
Gloucester	Jan 12	SWks	30 Jan 12	125	G, BC	200,788
Chalford	3 Jun 12					
Gloucester	Aug 12	SWks	23 Dec 12	53	H	219,436
Swindon Stock	14 Feb 13					
Chalford	18 Feb 13					
Gloucester	Nov 13	SWks	26 Nov 13	61	H, BC	249,058
Swindon Stock	26 Jan 14					
Bristol	5 Feb 14					
Bath	Mar 14	SWks	31 Mar 14	8	L	
Swindon Stock	8 Apr 14					
Basingstoke	30 Apr 14					
Chalford	30 May 14	SWks	23 Sep 14	40	H, BC	264,174
Swindon Stock	2 Nov 14					
Chalford	20 Nov 14	SWks	4 Sep 15	408	H, BC	294,876
Swindon Stock	16 Oct 16					
Chalford	29 Dec 16					
Gloucester	Feb 17					
Chalford	Apr 17					
Gloucester	May 17					
Chalford	Jun 17					
Gloucester	Aug 17	GLO	31 Oct 17	584		
		SDN	Dec 18			
		SWks	25 Mar 19		H, BC	324,412
Swindon Stock	7 Jun 19					
Truro	26 Jun 19					
Bristol	Nov 19					
Swindon (Shed)	14 Nov 21	GLO	12 Mar 22	99		
		SWks	9 May 22		H, BC	343,857
Swindon Stock	19 Jun 22					
Chalford	5 Jul 22	SWks	11 Sep 22			350,567

Converted to Trailer No.139 (Dia. A19)

NOTE

‡ Allocation Register gives Chalford 22 Mar 05.

No.53 (Diagram O)

Allocation	Date	Stop'd	Date	Days Stop'd	Catgy. Repair	Miles Run
New	Sep 05					
Stourbridge	30 Sep 05	SRD	9 Apr 06	3	L, BC	13,567
Stourbridge?	12 Apr 06	SRD	25 Oct 06	35	G, BC	25,252
Stourbridge?	29 Nov 06	SRD	21 Jan 07	39	L	
Stourbridge?	1 Mar 07	SRD	8 Aug 07	27	G, BC	36,143
Stourbridge?	4 Sep 07	STB	13 Apr 08	25	LB	
Stourbridge	8 May 08	SWks	7 Aug 08	76	BC	51,966
Trowbridge	22 Oct 08	SWks	23 Apr 09	6		
Trowbridge	29 Apr 09	SWks	24 Jun 09	36	G, BC	74,949
Kidderminster	30 Jul 09	SWks	4 Apr 10	64	G, BC	96,916
Swindon Stock	7 Jun 10					
Aberystwyth	29 Jun 10					

Allocation	*Date*	*Stop'd*	*Date*	*Days Stop'd*	*Catgy. Repair*	*Miles Run*
Cheltenham	Oct 10					
Evesham	Oct 10					
Kidderminster	Jan 11					
Worcester	Mar 11	WOS	18 Mar 11	10	Boiler	
Evesham	28 Mar 11	SWks	14 Jul 11	48	G, BC	121,739
Swindon Stock	31 Aug 11					
Cheltenham	10 Sep 11					
Gloucester	Dec 11					
Cheltenham	Dec 11	GLO	24 Jan 12	30		
Gloucester	23 Feb 12					
Cheltenham	Apr 12	SWks	2 Jul 12	32	G, BC	151,679
Cheltenham	3 Aug 12	SWks	29 Aug 12	2	L, BC	152,558
Cheltenham	31 Aug 12	SWks	16 Apr 13	71	H, BC	179,906
Swindon Stock	26 Jun 13					
Aberwystwyth	7 Jul 13					
Neath	Oct 13					
Swindon Stock	Nov 13					
Pontypool Road	13 Nov 13	SWks	6 Aug 15	347	H, BC	234,366
Swindon Stock	18 Jul 16					
Pontypool Road	4 Sep 16					
Aberdare	Jan 17					
Newport	Jun 18	SWks	25 Mar 20	221	H, BC	254,906
Swindon Stock	1 Nov 20					
Bristol	5 Nov 20	SPM	20 May 21	87		
		SWks	7 Jul 21		H, BC	274,112
Swindon Stock	15 Aug 21					
Bristol	24 Aug 21					
Yatton	Sep 21					
Bristol	Nov 21					
Yatton	Dec 21					
Bristol	Jan 22					
Bath	Feb 22					
Bristol	Mar 22					
Yatton	May 22					
Bristol	Jul 22	SWks	25 Aug 22	88	H, BC	303,445
Westbury	21 Nov 22	WES	3 Aug 23	293		
		SWks	22 Aug 23		H, BC	323,129
Swindon Stock	22 May 24					
Garnant (Neath)	Sep 24	NEA	11 Nov 24	36	R	
Garnant (Neath)	17 Dec 24	NEA	16 May 25	177		
		SWks	29 May 25		H, BC	337,344
Swindon Stock	9 Nov 25					
Pontypool Road	7 Dec 25					
St Philips Marsh	16 Feb 26					
Bath	Jun 26					
St Philip's Marsh	Aug 26	SWks	5 Mar 28	206	H, BC	382,297
Stourbridge	27 Sep 28	STB	23 Oct 28	18	R	
Stourbridge	10 Nov 28	SRD	6 Aug 29	20	H, BC	404,787
Stourbridge	26 Aug 29	SRD	3 Apr 30	47	H, BC	425,086
Stourbridge	20 May 30	SWks	3 Oct 30	157	H	435,281
Exeter	9 Mar 31	SWks	4 May 31	1	R	
Exeter	5 May 31	EXE	23 Aug 31	50		
		SWks	8 Sep 31		L	
Exeter	12 Oct 31					
Swindon Stock	24 May 32					
Cirencester Stock	6 Dec 32	SWks by	end Jun 33			462,884
Condemned	1 Jul 33					

Recovered parts used for Trailer No.199 (Dia. A26)

No.54 (Diagram O)

Allocation	*Date*	*Stop'd*	*Date*	*Days Stop'd*	*Catgy. Repair*	*Miles Run*
New						
Kidderminster	20 Sep 05	SRD	23 Feb 06	20	L, BC	13,170
Kidderminster?	15 Mar 06	SRD	17 Sep 06	25	G, BC	30,475
Kidderminster?	12 Oct 06	SWks	3 Apr 07	64	BC	48,788
?	6 Jun 07	SWks	4 Nov 07	26		
?	30 Nov 07	SWks	11 Apr 08	20	BC	60,263
Swindon Stock	1 May 08					
Oxford	11 May 08	SWks	5 Dec 08	18	G, BC	76,532
Swindon Stock	23 Dec 08					
Stratford on Avon	1 Jan 09	SWks	29 Jul 09	77	G	88,368
Kidderminster	14 Oct 09					
Worcester	Feb 10					
Kidderminster	Mar 10					
Worcester	Jun 10					
Evesham	Jul 10					
Worcester	Aug 10					
Kidderminster	Sep 10	SWks	10 Dec 10	31	BC	128,844
Swindon Stock	10 Jan 11					
Merthyr	16 Jan 11	SWks	15 May 12	56	G, BC	170,690
Pontypool Road	10 Jul 12	SWks	1 Nov 12	78	H, BC	181,422
Swindon Stock	18 Jan 13					
Stratford on Avon	21 Jan 13	SWks	14 Jan 14	114	H, BC	215,417
Swindon Stock	8 May 14					
Oxford	13 May 14					
Didcot	Jan 15					
Oxford	Feb 15					
Swindon Stock	May 15					
Pontypool Road	27 Sep 15	NPT	28 Aug 16	212		
		SWks	4 Sep 16		H, BC	255,938
Swindon	28 Mar 17					
Chester	23 Apr 17	OXY	18 Jul 18	709	H, BC	297,740
		SRD	Aug 18			
		SWks	8 Jan 20			
Swindon Stock	26 Jun 20	SWks	11 Aug 20	1	In & out	
Swindon Stock	12 Aug 20					
Neath	8 Sep 20					
Bristol	Oct 20					
Yatton	Nov 20					
Bristol	Dec 20					
Bath	Jan 21					
Yatton	Feb 21					
Bristol	Mar 21	SPM	13 Jul 21	21	R	
Bristol	3 Aug 21					
Bath	Nov 21					
Bristol	Dec 21	SPM	14 Jun 22	51	R	
Yatton	4 Aug 22	BTL	6 Dec 22	14	R	
Bristol	20 Dec 22					
Yatton	Mar 23	SWks	4 May 23	213	H, BC	359,607
Swindon Stock	3 Dec 23					
Aberdare	8 Dec 23	SWks	20 Jun 24	13	H, BC	366,201
Aberdare	3 Jul 24					
Pontypool Road	Nov 24	PPRD	28 Nov 25	60		
		NPT	30 Nov 25		L	
Pontypool Road	27 Jan 26	SWks	26 Oct 26	265	H, BC	394,112
Southall	18 Jul 27	SHL	10 Jan 28	39	R	
Southall	18 Feb 28	SHL	14 Mar 28	41	R	
Southall	24 Apr 28	SHL	11 Sep 28	30	R	
Southall	11 Oct 28	SHL	20 Oct 28	20	R	
Southall	9 Nov 28	SHL	3 Jun 29			
		SWks	23 Jul 29			415,980

Converted to Trailer No.181 (Dia. A26)

No.55 (Diagram O)

Allocation	*Date*	*Stop'd*	*Date*	*Days Stop'd*	*Catgy. Repair*	*Miles Run*
New	Oct 1905					
Chippenham	11 Oct 05	SWks	5 Mar 06	19	G, BC	18,891
?	24 Mar 06	SWks	25 Jun 06	4	LG, BC	30,818
?	29 Jun 06	SWks	12 Sep 06	12		
?	24 Sep 06	SWks	27 Nov 06	8	L, BC	44,795
?	5 Dec 06	SWks	28 Aug 07	30	G, BC	67,143
?	27 Sep 07	SWks	2 Mar 08	31	G, BC	83,545
?	2 Apr 08	SWks	20 Apr 08	10	L, BC	85,439
Swindon Stock	30 Apr 08					
Tenby	24 Jun 08					
Neath	Oct 08	SWks	21 Oct 08	30	BC	94,906
Swindon Stock	20 Nov 08					
Oxford	2 Dec 08	SWks	21 Jan 10	75	G, BC	121,644
Tyseley	6 Apr 10	SRD	28 Jan 11	16	BC	146,482
Tyseley	13 Feb 11	TYS	12 Aug 11	9		
Tyseley	21 Aug 11	SRD	27 Sep 11	36	G, BC	165,515
Tyseley	2 Nov 11	TYS	29 Dec 11	26		
Tyseley	24 Jan 12	SRD	9 May 12	28	G, BC	173,534
Tyseley	6 Jun 12	TYS	4 Sep 12	29		
Tyseley	3 Oct 12	TYS	3 Oct 12	25	BC	186,542
Tyseley	28 Oct 12	SRD	9 Apr 13	22	H, BC	201,264
Tyseley	1 May 13	SWks	6 Jun 13	50	H, BC	203,902
Swindon Stock	26 Jul 13					

Allocation	Date	Stop'd	Date	Days Stop'd	Catgy. Repair	Miles Run
Stourbridge	4 Aug 13	SWks	4 Sep 13	9	L	
Stourbridge	13 Sep 13	SRD	28 Aug 14	11	H, BC	234,412
Stourbridge	8 Sep 14	SWks	11 Nov 14	77	H, BC	258,883
Swindon Stock	27 Jan 15					
Stratford on Avon	1 Feb 15					
Malvern Wells	Jun 17					
Stratford on Avon	Aug 17					
Stourbridge	8 Sep 17					
Wolverhampton	Jun 18					
Croes Newydd	Jul 19	SWks	14 Jan 20	210	H, BC	265,863
Swindon Stock	11 Aug 20					
Bristol	15 Oct 20					
Yatton	Mar 21					
Weymouth	May 21					
Bristol	Sep 21					
Bath	Dec 21					
Yatton	Jan 22					
Bristol	Feb 22					
Yatton	Mar 22					
Bristol	Apr 22					
Yatton	Jul 22	SPM	26 Jul 22	128		
		SWks	25 Aug 22		H, BC	319,033
Swindon Stock	1 Dec 22					
Gloucester	6 Dec 22					
Chalford	Feb 23					
Gloucester	Jul 23					
Chalford	Aug 23	GLO	6 Sep 23	182		
		SWks	12 Sep 23		H, BC	347,356
Swindon Stock	6 Mar 24					
Garnant	1 Apr 24					
Llanelly	Feb 25					
Garnant	May 25					
Llanelly	Jan 26	SWks	28 Jan 26	187	L	
Swindon Stock	3 Aug 26					
Gloucester	Oct 26	SWks	22 Feb 27	38	H, BC	363,254
Swindon Stock	1 Apr 27					
Neath	27 May 27	NEA	30 Oct 28	65	R	
Neath	3 Jan 29	NEA	15 Jan 29	287		
		SWks	8 Mar 29		H, BC	399,265
Slough	29 Oct 29	SLO	2 May 30	29	R	
Slough	31 May 30	SHL	4 Aug 30	24	L	
Southall	28 Aug 30	RDG	2 Oct 30	56	R	
Reading	27 Nov 30	SHL	22 Jan 31	55	R	
Southall	18 Mar 31	SHL	20 Apr 31	113		
		SWks	13 May 31		G, BC	426,771
Swindon Stock	11 Aug 31					
Stourbridge	1 Feb 32	TYS	20 Aug 32	82	L	
Stourbridge	10 Nov 32	STB	17 Sep 33	292		
		MtSdg	27 Sep 33			
		SWks	14 May 34		G, BC	448,523
Swindon Stock	6 Jul 34					
Stourbridge	23 Jul 34	STB	1 Apr 35			
		SFPl	16 Apr 35			
		SWks	23 Apr 35			463,101
Condemned	19 Oct 35					
Broken up.						

No.56 (Diagram O)

Allocation	Date	Stop'd	Date	Days Stop'd	Catgy. Repair	Miles Run
New	Sep 05					
Frome	10 Oct 05	SWks	15 Nov 05	30	G, BC	4,617
Swindon Stock	15 Dec 05					
Newport	27 Dec 05					
Neath	16 Jan 06					
Merthyr	28 Jan 06	SWks	25 Aug 06	25	G, BC	19,122
?	19 Sep 06	Trwbg	2 Mar 07	28	L	
?	30 Mar 07	SWks	19 Nov 07	91	G, BC	52,457
Swindon Stock	18 Feb 08					
Merthyr	23 Feb 08					
Aberdare	Feb 09					
Merthyr	Mar 09	SWks	27 Sep 09	56	BC	104,824
Swindon Stock	22 Nov 09					
Southall	26 Nov 09	OOC	17 May 10	11		
Southall	28 May 10	SHL	19 Sep 10	7		143,073
Southall	26 Sep 10	SWks	2 Feb 11	32	G, BC	162,645
Swindon Stock	6 Mar 11					
Southall	23 May 11	OOC	6 Jan 12	13		
Southall	19 Jan 12	OOC	8 Feb 12	98		
		SWks	24 Feb 12		G, BC	195,407
Swindon Stock	16 May 12					
Corwen	23 May 12					
Croes Newydd	Jul 12					
Corwen	18 Jul 12	CNYD	20 Nov 12	18		
Corwen	8 Dec 12					
Croes Newydd	Mar 13					
Corwen	Apr 13	SRD	2 Sep 13	25	BC	229,402
Croes Newydd	27 Sep 13	CNYD	3 Oct 13	12	L	
Croes Newydd	15 Oct 13	CNYD	12 Dec 13	6	L	
Croes Newydd	18 Dec 13					
Corwen	Nov 13	SWks	13 Jun 14	100	H, BC	245,015
Swindon Stock	21 Sep 14					
Pontypool Road	28 Sep 14					
Newport	Oct 15	NPT	16 Oct 17	931		
		SWks	19 Sep 19		H, BC	286,061
Frome	4 May 20					
Westbury	Jul 22	SWks	27 Feb 23	217	H, BC	357,369
Chalford	2 Oct 23					
Gloucester	Nov 23					
Chalford	Jan 24					
Gloucester	Apr 24	SWks	1 May 24	21	H, BC	378,190
Swindon Stock	22 May 24					
Gloucester	28 May 24					
Stratford on Avon	Jul 24					
Chalford	Aug 24					
Gloucester	Oct 24					
Chalford	Dec 24	GLO	17 Mar 25	21		
		SWks	24 Mar 25		H, BC	407,050
Taunton	7 Apr 25	SWks	8 Feb 26	234	H, BC	436,150
Swindon Stock	30 Sep 26	GLO	24 Oct 27	15	R	
Gloucester	15 Oct 26					
Chalford	Sep 27					
Gloucester	8 Nov 27	SWks	5 Mar 28	103	H, BC	473,953
Birkenhead	16 Jun 28	SWks	15 Jul 29			504,781

Converted to Trailer No.182 (Dia. A26)

No.57 (Diagram O)

Allocation	Date	Stop'd	Date	Days Stop'd	Catgy. Repair	Miles Run
New	Sep 05					
Weymouth	30 Sep 05	SWks	30 Jul 06	21	G, BC	18,020
?	20 Aug 06	SWks	31 Jan 08	103	G, BC	70,970
Swindon Stock	13 May 08					
Tenby	24 Jun 08					
Neath	Oct 08					
Swindon Stock	Nov 08					
Worcester	1 Jan 09					
Kidderminster	Mar 09					
Worcester	Apr 09	SWks	6 Aug 09	74	G, BC	97,849
Swindon Stock	19 Oct 09	SWks	22 Nov 09	75	G, BC	98,757
Swindon Stock	5 Feb 10					
Merthyr	15 Mar 10	SWks	30 Jan 11	32	G, BC	132,042
Evesham	3 Mar 11					
Stratford on Avon	Jul 11					
Worcester	Oct 11					
Stratford on Avon	Nov 11					
Worcester	Mar 12					
Kidderminster	Apr 12	SWks	6 May 12	72	G, BC	163,356
Swindon Stock	17 Jul 12					
Monmouth	18 Jul 12	PPRD	2 Jul 13	14	L	
Monmouth	16 Jul 13					
Pontypool Road	Sep 12	SWks	8 Oct 13	57	H, BC	199,862
Worcester	4 Dec 13					
Kidderminster	Mar 14	SWks	27 Jul 14	4	H, BC	221,388
Swindon Stock	31 Jul 14					
Kidderminster	14 Sep 14	WOS	16 Feb 15	8	L	
Worcester	24 Feb 15					
Kidderminster	Apr 15					
Worcester	Jun 15	SWks	7 Oct 15	755	H, BC	262,938
Swindon Stock	31 Oct 17					
Taunton	22 Nov 17	TN	29 Jan 18	804		
		BTL	Apr 18			

Allocation	Date	Stop'd	Date	Days Stop'd	Catgy. Repair	Miles Run
		TN	May 18			
		SWks	26 Sep 18		H, BC	267,690
Swindon Stock	12 Apr 20					
Frome	26 May 20	SWks	24 Jul 20	16	L	
Swindon Stock	9 Aug 20					
Frome	27 Aug 20					
Westbury	Jul 22	BTL	25 Sep 22	101		
		SWks	Dec 22		H, BC	321,119
Swindon Stock	4 Jan 23					
Reading	1 Feb 23	OOC	24 Aug 23	15	R	
Reading	8 Sep 23	OOC	26 Nov 23	590		
		SWks	3 Dec 23		H, BC	349,249
Neath	8 Jul 25	NEA	3 May 26	65	R	
Neath	7 Jul 26	NEA	13 Aug 27	39		
Neath	21 Sep 27	SWks	1 Nov 27			384,115

Converted to Trailer No.149 (Dia. A26)

No.58 (Diagram O)

Allocation	Date	Stop'd	Date	Days Stop'd	Catgy. Repair	Miles Run
New	Sep 05					
Chippenham	5 Oct 05	SWks	23 Dec 05	25	G, BC	10,869
Swindon Stock	17 Jan 06					
Laira	23 Jan 06					
Newport	27 Feb 06	SWks	14 Mar 07	57	G, BC	47,628
?	10 May 07	SWks	6 Apr 08	10	L, BC	67,212
Evesham	16 Apr 08	SWks	7 Jul 08	51	L, BC	77,165
Swindon Stock	27 Aug 08					
Oxford	5 Oct 08	SDst	11 Apr 10	67		
Oxford	17 Jun 10	SWks	12 Oct 10	19	G, BC	120,672
Newton Abbot	31 Oct 10	NA	29 Aug 11	10		
Newton Abbot	8 Sep 11	NA	21 Oct 11	12	BC	148,538
Newton Abbot	2 Nov 11	NA	22 Oct 12	3	G	
Newton Abbot	25 Oct 12	NA	11 Jan 13	4	BC	172,230
Newton Abbot	15 Jan 13	NA	19 Dec 13	5	L, BC	207,717
Newton Abbot	24 Dec 13	NA	17 Mar 14	77		
Newton Abbot	2 Jun 14	NA	17 Mar 15	2	H, BC	250,091
Newton Abbot	19 Mar 15					
Penzance	May 15					
Exeter	Apr 16	SWks	10 Nov 19	705	H, BC	282,637
Swindon Stock	15 Oct 21					
Cambrian Lines	3 Jul 22					
Machynlleth	Aug 22					
Llandiloes	Sep 22	SWks	20 Dec 22	50	L	
Swindon Stock	8 Feb 23					
Frome	Feb 23					
Westbury	8 May 23	WES	13 May 24	10	R	
Westbury	23 May 24					
Frome	Jul 24					
Westbury	Aug 24					
Frome	Oct 24	BTL	26 Nov 24	205		
		SWks	8 Dec 24		H, BC	326,917
Croes Newydd	19 Jun 25	SRD	16 Aug 26	45	H, BC	345,098
Stourbridge	30 Sep 26	STB	11 Mar 27	43	R	
Stourbridge	23 Apr 27	STB	30 Aug 27	15	R	
Stourbridge	14 Sep 27	STB	4 May 28	18	R	
Stourbridge	22 May 28	STB	21 Aug 28	269		
		SWks	5 Sep 28		H, BC	378,854
Swindon Stock	17 May 29					
Exeter	27 May 29	SWks	19 Nov 29	162	H, BC	400,984
Stourbridge	30 Apr 30	STB	17 Jul 31	125		
		SWks	11 Aug 31		G, BC	430,983
Swindon Stock	19 Nov 31					
Exeter	21 May 32					
Swindon Stock	Jan 33					
Cirencester stock	Mar 33	SWks	Jun 33			452,138
Condemned	1 Jul 33					

Recovered parts used in Trailer No.200 (Dia. A26)

No.59 (Diagrams P, T)

Allocation	Date	Stop'd	Date	Days Stop'd	Catgy. Repair	Miles Run
New	Sep 05					
Swindon Stock		SWks	25 Nov 05	26		
Laira	21 Dec 05	NA	13 Aug 06	4	LG	24,654
Laira	17 Aug 06	SWks	9 Mar 07	18	G, BC	52,995
Laira?	27 Mar 07	NA	23 Sep 07	107	LG, BC	56,076
Laira?	8 Jan 08	NA	5 Mar 08	8	L, BC	91,112
Laira?	13 Mar 08	SWks	7 Apr 08	14		
Swindon Stock	16 Apr 08					
Laira	21 Apr 08	NA	2 Sep 08	44	G, BC	106,825
Laira	16 Oct 08	NA	Dec 08		BC	114,082
Laira	Dec 08	NA	1 May 09	25	L, BC	128,188
Laira	26 May 09	SWks	20 Jul 09	59	G, BC	134,273
Swindon Stock	17 Sep 09					
Laira	19 Nov 09	NA	28 Sep 10	104	G, BC	196,561
Laira	10 Jan 11	SWks	5 Aug 11	86	G, BC	220,402
Laira	30 Oct 11	NA ¶	19 Jan 12	139	G, BC	244,438
Laira	6 Jun 12	NA	13 Dec 12	91	BC	271,581
Laira	14 Mar 13	SWks	15 Sep 13	80	H, BC	295,071
Swindon Stock	4 Dec 13					
Pontypool Road	10 Dec 13	SWks	15 Sep 14	93	H	316,493
Swindon Stock	17 Dec 14					
Weymouth	21 Dec 14					
Bristol	May 15	SWks	18 Jun 15	301	H, BC	324,718
Swindon Stock	14 Apr 16					
Yatton	17 Apr 16					
Bristol	May 16					
Yatton	Jul 16					
Bath	Aug 16					
Bristol	Sep 16					
Yatton	Sep 16					
Bath	Oct 16					
Bristol	Nov 16					
Yatton	Dec 16					
Bath	Jan 17					
Bristol	Feb 17					
Yatton	May 17					
Bristol	Jul 17					
Yatton	Sep 17					
Bristol	Sep 17					
Yatton	Oct 17					
Bristol	Nov 17					
Bath	Dec 17					
Bristol	Jan 18					
Yatton	Feb 18					
Bristol	Mar 18					
Yatton	Apr 18					
Bristol	May 18					
Yatton	Jul 18					
Bristol	Aug 18					
Yatton	Oct 18					
Bristol	Dec 18	BTL	30 Dec 18			
		SWks	11 Nov 19			394,817

Converted to Trailer No126 (Dia. A13)

NOTE

¶ *Visit to NA in Jan 12 not shown in Allocations Register*

No.60 (Diagrams P, T)

Allocation	Date	Stop'd	Date	Days Stop'd	Catgy. Repair	Miles Run
New	Oct 05	SWks	25 Nov 05	9		
Laira	4 Dec 05	SWks	5 Jun 06	52	G, BC	19,181
Laira?	27 Jul 06	NA	15 Feb 07	20	LG, BC	39,786
Laira?	7 Mar 07	SWks	1 Mar 07 §	20	G	
Laira?	28 Mar 07	NA	1 May 07	2	LG, BC	45,179
Laira?	3 May 07	NA	10 Jan 08	48	L	
Laira?	27 Feb 08					
At Laira	25 Apr 08	NA	22 Aug 08	3	L, BC	93,024
Laira	25 Aug 08	SWks	19 Jun 09	75	G, BC	124,965
Swindon Stock	2 Sep 09					
Tyseley	10 Sep 09					
Laira	12 Oct 09	NA	23 Apr 10	9	LG	
Laira	2 May 10	NA	19 Aug 10	28		
Laira	16 Sep 10	NA	10 Jan 11	22	BC	187,885
Laira	1 Feb 11	NA	N/R		BC	190,824
Laira	15 Mar 11	SWks	12 Oct 11	60	G, BC	215,233
Laira	11 Dec 11	NA	16 Feb 12	13	BC	228,739
Truro	29 Feb 12					
Laira	Jun 12	NA	6 Sep 13	27	BC	228,739
Swindon Stock	3 Oct 13	SWks	6 Oct 13	NR		290,323
Swindon Stock	Dec 13					

Allocation	*Date*	*Stop'd*	*Date*	*Days Stop'd*	*Catgy. Repair*	*Miles Run*
Stratford on Avon	14 Jan 14	SWks	1 Feb 15	59	H, BC	323,234
Gloucester	1 Apr 15	SWks	25 May 15	0		
Gloucester	25 May 15					
Chester	9 Jun 15	CHR	26 Oct 15	25		
Chester	20 Nov 15	SRD	26 May 16	41	H, BC	366,982
Croes Newydd	6 Jul 16					
Chester	Aug 16	SRD	14 Aug 16	44	H, BC	371,276
Chester	27 Sep 16	CHR	May 17			
		CNYD	May 18			
		SWks	22 Jul 19			387,653

Converted to Trailer No.127 (Dia. A14)

NOTE

§ *Conflict of dates here. Car sent to Swindon while still apparently at NA Shops.*

No.61 (Diagram O)

Allocation	*Date*	*Stop'd*	*Date*	*Days Stop'd*	*Catgy. Repair*	*Miles Run*
New	Mar 06					
?		SWks	5 Oct 06	71	G, BC	10,800
?	15 Dec 06	SWks	6 Aug 07	64	BC	43,823
Southall?	9 Oct 07	SWks	21 Apr 08	18	BC	58,926
Swindon Stock	9 May 08					
Southall	14 May 08	OOC	5 Sep 08	17	L	
Southall	22 Sep 08	SWks	1 Apr 09	43	G, BC	85,572
Swindon Stock	14 May 09	SWks	15 Jun 09	22	L	
Swindon Stock	7 Jul 09					
Truro	19 Jul 09	NA	19 Nov 09	4	L, BC	95,566
Truro	23 Nov 09					
Penzance	Dec 09					
Laira	Jun 10	NA	4 Jun 10	6	BC	117,559
Truro	10 Jun 10					
Newquay	Nov 10					
Truro	Dec 10					
Newquay	Dec 10	NA	19 Jan 11	13	BC	130,409
Truro	1 Feb 11	NA	8 Feb 11	63	BC	130,956
Newquay	12 Apr 11					
Truro	May 11					
Helston	Aug 11					
Penzance	Oct 11	NA	30 Dec 11	0		
Penzance	30 Dec 11	NA	3 Jan 12	7	BC	151,255
Penzance	10 Jan 12					
Truro	Feb 12	NA	20 Aug 12	71		
Newton Abbot	30 Oct 12	NA	30 Nov 12	6	BC	165,402
Newton Abbot	6 Dec 12	NA	27 May 14	62	H	194,487
Newton Abbot	28 Jul 14	SWks	26 Nov 14	72	H, BC	199,696
Swindon Stock	6 Feb 15					
Newton Abbot	11 Feb 15					
Penzance	Apr 15					
Truro	Mar 16					
Yatton	25 Mar 16					
Bath	May 16					
Yatton	Aug 16					
Bristol	Sep 16					
Yatton	Oct 16					
Bristol	Nov 16					
Yatton	Jan 17					
Bath	Feb 17					
Bristol	Apr 17					
Bath	May 17					
Yatton	Jul 17					
Bristol	Aug 17					
Yatton	Sep17					
Bristol	Oct 17					
Yatton	Dec 17					
Bristol	Jan 18	BTL	21 Jan 18	404		
		SWks	25 Feb 18		H, BC	274,720
Stourbridge	1 Mar 19	STB	11 Feb 21	19	R	
Stourbridge	2 Mar 21	SWks	30 Mar 21	288	H, BC	300,639
Swindon Stock	12 Jan 22					
Gloucester	Feb 22					
Penzance	5 Jul 22					
Bristol	10 Oct 22					
Yatton	Jan 23					
Bristol	Mar 23					
Bath	Apr 23					
Yatton	May 23	SPM	24 May 23	114		
		SWks	3 Jul 23		H, BC	327,557
Yatton	15 Sep 23					
Bath	Oct 23					
Yatton	Nov 23					
Bristol	Jan 24	BTL	13 Mar 24	65		
		SWks	23 Apr 24		H, BC	339,444
Swindon Stock	17 May 24					
Southall	26 May 24	SHL	30 Sep 24	23	R	
Southall	23 Oct 24	OOC	18 Apr 25			
		SWks	27 Apr 25	231	H, BC	354,266
Swindon Stock	14 Dec 25					
Neath	22 Jan 26					
Llanelly	Feb 26					
Garnant	Oct 26					
Llanelly	Nov 26					
Garnant	Dec 26					
Neath	Jan 27	SWks	19 Apr 27			367,909

Converted to Trailer No.150 (Dia. A29)

No.62 (Diagram O)

Allocation	*Date*	*Stop'd*	*Date*	*Days Stop'd*	*Catgy. Repair*	*Miles Run*
New	Apr 06					
?		SWks	28 Jul 06	51	G	11,257
?	17 Sep 06	SWks	7 Mar 07	28		38,676
?	4 Apr 07	SWks	23 May 07	14	L	
?	6 Jun 07	SWks	17 Sep 07	27	G, BC	50,645
Southall?	14 Oct 07					
At Southall	25 Apr 08	SHL	13 Jul 08	5	L	
Southall	18 Jul 08	SHL	25 Nov 08	14	L	
Southall	9 Dec 08	SWks	19 Feb 09	73	G, BC	104,390
Swindon Stock	3 May 09					
Southall	29 May 09					
Tyseley	22 Jul 09					
Croes Newydd	Oct 09	SRD	5 Nov 09	8	G, BC	119,362
Croes Newydd	13 Nov 09	SRD	31 May 10	30	G, BC	131,961
Stourbridge	30 Jun 10	STB	22 Nov 10	164		
		SWks	8 Feb 11		G, BC	138,733
Swindon Stock	5 May 11					
Southall	19 May 11	SHL	11 Mar 12	19		
Southall	30 Mar 12	SHL	20 May 12	5		
Southall	25 May 12	SWks	5 Sep 12	102	G, BC	195,336
Yatton	16 Dec 12					
Bristol	Jan 13					
Radstock	Apr 13					
Bristol	Jun 13					
Yatton	Nov 13					
Radstock	Dec 13					
Yatton	Jan 14					
Bristol	Feb 14					
Radstock	Mar 14					
Bristol	Apr 14					
Yatton	May 14					
Bristol	Jun 14	BTL	3 Jul 14	69		
		SWks	12 Aug 14		BC	239,982
Bristol	10 Sep 14	SPM	28 Sep 14	15	L	
Radstock	13 Oct 14	SWks	16 Nov 14	70	H, BC	243,268
Bristol	25 Jan 15					
Radstock	Feb 15					
Bath	Mar 15					
Yatton	Aug 15					
Bristol	Oct 15	SPM	12 Nov 15	33		
Yatton	15 Dec 15	SWks	17 Jan 16	21	L	
Bath	7 Feb 16					
Bridgewater	Sep 16					
Taunton	Sep 16	TN	9 Mar 17	21	L	
Taunton	30 Mar 17	TN	24 Oct 17	562		
		SWks	10 Dec 18		H, BC	310,812
Swindon Stock	9 May 19					
Bath	15 May 19					
Yatton	Aug 19					
Bristol	Aug 19	SPM	25 Oct 19	487		
		SWks	22 Dec 19		H, BC	323,695
Swindon Stock	23 Feb 21					

Allocation	Date	Stop'd	Date	Days Stop'd	Catgy. Repair	Miles Run
Reading	25 Apr 21	RDG	10 Jun 22	21	R	
Reading	1 Jul 22	RDG	6 Sep 22	15	R	
Reading	21 Sep 22	SWks	22 Feb 23	848	H, BC	366,071
Southall	19 Jun 25	SWks	16 Sep 25	16	L	
Southall	2 Oct 25	OOC	3 Dec 25	21	R	
Southall	24 Dec 25	SHL	2 Jul 26	12	R	
Southall	14 Jul 26	OOC	12 Nov 26	193		
		SWks	13 Dec 26		H, BC	384,340
Swindon Stock	24 May 27					
Taunton	2 Jun 27	SWks	7 Mar 28	237	H	406,614
Swindon Stock	30 Oct 28					
Exeter	17 Nov 28	SWks	24 Oct 29			440,019

Converted to Trailer No.186 (Dia. A29)

No.63 (Diagram O)

Allocation	Date	Stop'd	Date	Days Stop'd	Catgy. Repair	Miles Run
New	Apr 06					
?		SWks	9 Jan 07	36	LG	
?	14 Feb 07	SWks	15 Jun 07	61	G, BC	32,087
Goodwick?	15 Aug 07					
At Goodwick	25 Apr 08					
Fishguard	Jul 08					
Goodwick	Aug 08	SWks	18 Jan 09	93	G, BC	63,852
Swindon Stock	21 Apr 09					
Stratford on Avon	8 May 09	SWks	25 Nov 09	28	G, BC	76,355
Swindon Stock	23 Dec 09					
Oxford	17 Jan 10	SDst	30 Dec 10	13		
Swindon Stock	12 Jan 11					
Oxford	2 Feb 11	SWks	13 Jun 11	115	G	110,853
Swindon Stock	6 Oct 11					
Worcester	22 Nov 11					
Stratford on Avon	Dec 11	SWks	3 Oct 12	43	BC	137,993
Swindon Stock	15 Nov 12					
Trowbridge	20 Nov 12	Trwbg	9 Jan 13	49	L	
Trowbridge	27 Feb 13					
Frome	Apr 13					
Trowbridge	May 13	Trwbg	10 Sep 13	16	L	
Trowbridge	26 Sep 13	SWks	22 Dec 13	96	H, BC	168,072
Swindon Stock	28 Mar 14					
Penzance	3 Apr 14					
Helston	Sep 14					
Penzance	Oct 14	SWks	3 Apr 15	187	H, BC	200,091
Swindon Stock	7 Oct 15					
Southall	27 Nov 15	SWks	12 Apr 16	153	H, BC	214,680
Swindon Stock	12 Sep 16					
Worcester	23 Oct 16					
Kidderminster	Jun 18					
Worcester	Jul 18	SWks	19 May 19	238	H, BC	258,924
Swindon Stock	12 Jan 20					
Chippenham	19 Jan 20	SWks	3 Jan 21 †	561	H	304,388
Penzance	18 Jul 22 †					
Gloucester	11 Oct 22	WOS	3 Nov 23	18	R	
Chalford	21 Nov 23	SWks	17 Jan 24	537	H, BC	339,938
Stafford Road	7 Jul 25					
Birkenhead	Sep 25					
Croes Newydd	Oct 25					
Birkenhead	Nov 25	SWks	10 Sep 27			385,029

Converted to Trailer No.151 (Dia. A29)

NOTE

† Stoppages Register indicates at SWks until 18 Jul 22, but Allocations Register gives:

Chippenham	19 Jan 20
Trowbridge	Aug 21
Chippenham	Nov 21
Swindon Works	Jan 22
Penzance	18 Jul 22

No.64 (Diagram O)

Allocation	Date	Stop'd	Date	Days Stop'd	Catgy. Repair	Miles Run
New	Apr 06					
?		SWks	18 Aug 06	18	L	
?	5 Sep 06	SWks	16 Feb 07	69	G, BC	24,286
?	26 Apr 07	SWks	14 Nov 07	33	G, BC	47,659
Kidderminster?	17 Dec 07	SWks	10 Jun 08	52	G, BC	65,394
At Kidderminster	25 Apr 08					
Swindon Stock	1 Aug 08					
Stourbridge	6 Aug 08	SRD	13 Feb 09	25	L, BC	76,341
Stourbridge	10 Mar 09	SRD	24 Sep 09	22	L	
Stourbridge	16 Oct 09	SRD	10 Jan 10	33	L, BC	94,024
Stourbridge	12 Feb 10	SRD	13 May 10	26	L&B, BC	98,955
Stourbridge	8 Jun 10	SWks	18 Oct 10	111	G, BC	110,199
Stourbridge	6 Feb 11	SRD	10 Aug 11	11	BC	125,657
Stourbridge	21 Aug 11	SRD	2 May 12	20	G, BC	144,213
Stourbridge	22 May 12	STB	11 Oct 12	40		
Stourbridge	20 Nov 12	STB	25 Jan 13	27	L, BC	161,302
Stourbridge	21 Feb 13	SWks	4 Mar 13	69	H, BC	164,519
Stourbridge	12 May 13	SRD	16 Aug 13	6	L	
Stourbridge	22 Aug 13	SWks	17 Apr 14	105	H, BC	192,937
Southall	31 Jul 14	SHL	27 Oct 14	20		
		SWks	2 Nov 14		H, BC	203,730
Southall	16 Nov 14	OOC	13 Jun 15	20		
Southall	3 Jul 15	SWks	27 Nov 15	357	H, BC	242,223
Yatton	18 Nov 16					
Bath	Dec 16					
Yatton	Feb 17					
Bristol	Mar 17					
Yatton	Apr 17					
Bristol	May 17					
Yatton	Jun 17					
Bath	Aug 17					
Yatton	Sep 17	SPM	28 Sep 17	42	R	
Bristol	9 Nov 17					
Yatton	Jan 18					
Bristol	Feb 18	SPM	7 Mar 18	56	R	
Bristol	2 May 18	SPM	22 Jul 18	35	R	
Yatton	26 Aug 18	SWks	3 Jan 19	88	H, BC	290,404
Swindon Stock	1 Apr 19					
Bristol	22 Apr 19	SPM	16 May 19	84	R	
Bristol	8 Aug 19	SPM	24 Sep 19	511	H, BC	294,712
		SWks	10 Oct 19			
Swindon Stock	16 Feb 21					
Reading	25 Apr 21	SWks	2 Feb 23	844	H, BC	344,666
Neath	26 May 25	NEA	5 Jun 25	35	R	
Neath	10 Jul 25	SWks	28 Aug 25	33	L	
Neath	30 Sep 25	SWks	10 Jan 27	154	H, BC	366,518
Swindon Stock	13 Jun 27					
Gloucester	20 Jul 27					
Southall	17 May 28	RDG	19 Nov 28	14	R	
Southall	3 Dec 28	RDG	1 Feb 29	40	R	
Southall	13 Mar 29					
Slough	Jul 29	SLO	12 Aug 29	18	L	
Slough	30 Aug 29	SLO	31 Oct 29	51	L	
Slough	21 Dec 29	SWks	15 Jan 30	180	H, BC	419,820
Southall	14 Jul 30	SHL	13 Oct 30	24	R	
Southall	6 Nov 30	SHL	9 Dec 30	35	R	
Southall	13 Jan 31	SHL	18 Mar 31	45	R	
Southall	2 May 31	SHL	25 Jul 31	149		
		SWks	4 Aug 31		G, BC	438,880
Southall	21 Dec 31					
Reading	23 Jun 32	SWks	8 Sep 32	8	L	
Reading	16 Sep 32					
Cirencester Stock	Dec 32					
Swindon Stock	Apr 33					
Stourbridge	Oct 33	STB	4 Jun 34			
		SFPl	28 Nov 34			
		SWks	30 Nov 34			452,124
Condemned	9 Feb 35					

Converted to Trailer No.216 (Dia. A29)

No.65 (Diagram O)

Allocation	Date	Stop'd	Date	Days Stop'd	Catgy. Repair	Miles Run
New	Apr 06					
?		SWks	18 Aug 06	18	L	
Worcester?	5 Sep 06	WOS	8 Nov 06	139		
		SWks	26 Jan 07		G, BC	18,694
?	27 Mar 07	SWks	18 Feb 08	83	BC	52,490
Swindon Stock	11 May 08					
Kidderminster	11 Jun 08					
Worcester	Jul 08					

Allocation	*Date*	*Stop'd*	*Date*	*Days Stop'd*	*Catgy. Repair*	*Miles Run*
Kidderminster	Aug 08					
Worcester	Dec 08	SWks	1 Jan 09	83	G, BC	72,174
Swindon Stock	25 Mar 09					
Southall	1 Apr 09	SWks	25 Nov 09	73	G, BC	101,386
Swindon Stock	6 Feb 10					
Chippenham	22 Feb 10					
Southall	22 Mar 10					
Cheltenham	4 Apr 10					
Gloucester	May 10					
Cheltenham	Jun 10	SWks	5 Aug 10	8	BC	111,943
Cheltenham	13 Aug 10					
Gloucester	Sep 10					
Cheltenham	Oct 10					
Gloucester	Dec 10	GLO	30 Dec 10	19	Tubes	
Gloucester	18 Jan 11					
Cheltenham	Jan 11	GLO	8 Sep 11	77		
		SWks	12 Sep 11		G, BC	157,069
Swindon Stock	24 Nov 11					
Weymouth	4 Dec 11	SWks	25 May 14	99	H, BC	207,965
Swindon Stock	1 Sep 14					
Weymouth	7 Sep 14	SWks	21 Dec 14	26	L, BC	214,375
Weymouth	16 Jan 15	SWks	27 Mar 16	319	H, BC	236,059
Cheltenham	9 Feb 17					
Gloucester	Mar 17					
Cheltenham	May 17	GLO	28 Jul 17	9	L	
Gloucester	6 Aug 17	GLO	20 Nov 17	6	R	
Gloucester	26 Nov 17	GLO	29 Dec 17	31	R	
Cheltenham	29 Jan 18					
Gloucester	Mar 18	SDst	8 Apr 18	547		
		SWks	26 Mar 19		H, BC	276,720
Chippenham	7 Oct 19	SWks	9 Dec 19	0		
Chippenham	9 Dec 19	SDst	19 Jan 20	60		
		SWks	5 Mar 20		L	
Swindon Stock	19 Mar 20					
Frome	22 Apr 20					
Gloucester	Nov 20					
Frome	Dec 20					
Gloucester	Dec 21	SWks	3 Jan 22	233	H, BC	327,807
Gloucester	24 Aug 22	SWks	4 Sep 22	17	L	
Gloucester	21 Sep 22					
Chalford	Nov 22	SWks	6 Jan 23	13	H, BC	337,838
Swindon Stock	19 Jan 23					
Bristol	3 Feb 23	BTL	6 Sep 23	15	R	
Bristol	21 Sep 23	BTL	5 Oct 23	21	R	
Yatton	26 Oct 23					
Bristol	Dec 23					
Bath	Mar 24					
Bristol	Apr 24	BTL	26 Aug 24	133		
		SWks	18 Sep 24		R, BC	380,630
Gloucester	6 Jan 25	SWks	12 Jun 26	315	H, BC	427,134
Neath	23 Apr 27	NEA	21 Dec 27	268		
		SWks	31 Jan 28		H, BC	440,971
St.Philip's Marsh	14 Sep 28					
Yatton	Nov 28	SPM	17 Dec 28	22	R	
St.Philip's Marsh	8 Jan 29					
Yatton	Mar 29					
St.Philip's Marsh	Apr 29					
Yatton	May 29					
St.Philip's Marsh	Jun 29					
Yatton	Jul 29					
St.Philip's Marsh	Sep 29	WES	7 Feb 30	131		
		SWks	18 Feb 30		H, BC	476,840
Yatton	18 Jun 30					
St.Philip's Marsh	Aug 30	SFPl	5 Nov 31	95		
		SWks	31 Dec 31		G, BC	509,038
Swindon Stock	8 Feb 32					
Southall	29 Aug 32	SHL	6 Jan 33	14	R	
Southall	20 Jan 33	SHL	12 Jun 33	26	L	
Southall	8 Jul 33	SHL	20 Nov 33	343		
		SFPl	7 Dec 33			
		SWks	4 Jun 33		G, BC	525,160
Neath	29 Oct 34	SFPl	16 Oct 35			538,908
Condemned	19 Oct 35					

Broken up. One of five cars replaced by three diesel cars.

Allocation	*Date*	*Stop'd*	*Date*	*Days Stop'd*	*Catgy. Repair*	*Miles Run*
No.66 (Diagram O)						
New	May 06					
?		SWks	26 Jun 06	13	L	
?	9 Jul 06	SWks	25 Oct 06	37	G, BC	16,904
Croes Newydd?	1 Dec 06					
At Croes Newydd	1 Apr 08	SWks	22 Jun 08	71	G, BC	57,960
Swindon Stock	1 Sep 08					
Truro	25 Sep 08	NA	Nov 08	NR	BC	62,422
Truro	Nov 08					
Newquay	Jan 09					
Truro	Jan 09	NA	14 Feb 09	20	G, BC	69,297
Truro	6 Mar 09					
Newquay	Apr 09					
Truro	May 09					
Newquay	Jul 09	NA	12 Aug 09	5	L, BC	80,084
Truro	17 Aug 09					
Laira	Sep 09	SWks	18 Mar 10	95	G, BC	97,680
Swindon Stock	21 Jun 10					
Stratford on Avon	6 Jul 10	WOS	28 Oct 10	14		
Stratford on Avon	11 Nov 10					
Kidderminster	Dec 10					
Worcester	Jan 11					
Kidderminster	Jan 11	WOS	11 Feb 11	12	Boiler	
Kidderminster	23 Feb 11					
Worcester	Jun 11	WOS	10 Jul 11	14		
Kidderminster	24 Jul 11	SWks	9 Dec 11	115	G, BC	144,942
Swindon Stock	2 Apr 12					
Kidderminster	6 May 12					
Worcester	Aug 12					
Kidderminster	Nov 12	SWks	3 Dec 12	107	H	164,005
Swindon Stock	20 Mar 13					
Stourbridge	4 Apr 13					
Stafford Road	May 13	SRD	21 Oct 13	16	BC	178,573
Stafford Road	6 Nov 13	OXY	20 Feb 14	22	L	
Stafford Road	14 Mar 14	SRD	16 Jul 14	12	BC	191,300
Stafford Road	28 Jul 14	SRD	23 Sep 14	28	H	193,972
Stafford Road	21 Oct 14	SRD	13 Mar 15	16	R, BC	202,375
Stafford Road	29 Mar 15	SRD	17 Jun 15	37	H, BC	207,075
Stafford Road	24 Jul 15	SRD	19 Sep 15	46	L	
Stourbridge	4 Nov 15	STB	1 Feb 16	21		
Stourbridge	22 Feb 16	SWks	13 Jun 16	241	H, BC	216,490
Swindon Stock	9 Feb 17					
Stourbridge	13 Feb 17	SRD	30 Nov 17	406		
		SWks	30 Apr 18		BC	
Swindon Stock	10 Jan 19					
Chester	27 Jan 19	CHR	26 Apr 19	27	R	
Chester	23 May 19	OXY	15 Oct 19	434		
		SWks	13 Jan 20		H	242,644
Swindon Stock	22 Dec 20					
Southall	14 Jan 21	SHL	10 Aug 21	15	R	
Southall	25 Aug 21	OOC	3 Oct 21	17		
Southall	20 Oct 21	SHL	28 Jan 22	62	R	
Southall	31 Mar 22	SHL	10 Apr 22	18	R	
Southall	28 Apr 22	SHL	15 Jun 22	189		
		SWks	23 Jun 22		H, BC	266,019
Swindon Stock	21 Dec 22					
Chalford	6 Jan 23	SWks	9 May 23	24	H, BC	278,051
Swindon Stock	2 Jun 23	SWks	28 Jul 23	19	H, BC	283,079
Chalford	8 Jun 23					
Chalford	16 Aug 23	SWks	2 Oct 23	9	H, BC	287,128
Swindon Stock	11 Oct 23					
Chalford	17 Oct 23					
Gloucester	Dec 23					
Chalford	Apr 24					
Gloucester	May 24	SWks	17 Jun 24	13	H, BC	310,740
Swindon Stock	30 Jun 24					
Moat Lane	8 Jul 24					
Oswestry	Aug 24	SWks	19 Oct 25	210	H, BC	347,352
Swindon Stock	17 May 26	GLO	31 Aug 26	26	R	
Gloucester	12 Jun 26					
Gloucester	26 Sep 26	GLO	1 Nov 26	33	R	
Chalford	4 Dec 26					
Gloucester	May 27	WOS	8 Jul 27	109		
		SWks	15 Jul 27		H, BC	371,146

Allocation	*Date*	*Stop'd*	*Date*	*Days Stop'd*	*Catgy. Repair*	*Miles Run*
St Philip's Marsh	25 Oct 27					
Frome	Oct 27	SWks	4 Aug 28	90	L	
Stourbridge	2 Nov 28	SRD	15 Apr 29	33	H, BC	405,809
Stourbridge	18 May 29	STB	6 Jan 30	19	R	
Stourbridge	25 Jan 30	STB	24 Aug 30	221		
		SWks	16 Sep 30		G, BC	435,398
Swindon Stock	2 Apr 31					
Stourbridge	28 Jul 31	TYS	11 Dec 31	53	L	
Stourbridge	2 Feb 32	TYS	13 Sep 32	86	L	
Stourbridge	8 Dec 32	STB	12 Nov 33	40	L	
		SRD	30 Nov 33			
		SRD	14 Dec 33			
Stourbridge	22 Dec 33	STB	16 Jul 34			
		SFPl	28 Nov 34			
		SWks	5 Dec 34			481,498
Condemned	9 Feb 35					

Converted to Trailer No 217 (Dia. A29)

No.67 (Diagram O)

Allocation	*Date*	*Stop'd*	*Date*	*Days Stop'd*	*Catgy. Repair*	*Miles Run*
New	Jun 06					
?		SWks	29 Dec 06	60	G, BC	15,400
	27 Feb 07	SWks	27 Apr 08	96	BC	42,337
Swindon Stock	1 Aug 08					
Cheltenham	6 Aug 08					
Chalford	Sep 08					
Swindon Stock	Oct 08					
Evesham	11 Nov 08	SWks	9 Jan 09	65	L, BC	53,706
Swindon Stock	15 Mar 09					
Chippenham	20 Mar 09					
Frome	Apr 09					
Bristol	30 May 09	SWks	5 Jun 09	40	G, BC	61,839
Taunton	15 Jul 09	SWks	15 Apr 10	77	G, BC	81,092
Swindon Stock	1 Jul 10					
Bristol	9 Jul 10					
Bath	Sep 10					
Bristol	Dec 10					
Bath	Mar 11					
Bristol	Apr 11					
Bath	May 11					
Bristol	Jun 11	SWks	19 Jun 11	45	G, BC	119,036
Swindon Stock	3 Aug 11					
Chalford	11 Aug 11					
Stourbridge	2 Sep 11	STB	13 May 12	40		
		SRD	+		G, BC	138,093
Stourbridge	22 Jun 12	SRD	17 Feb 13	31	H, BC	156,626
Stourbridge	20 Mar 13	SWks	26 Jun 13	121	H, BC	163,174
Swindon Stock	25 Oct 13					
Stourbridge	4 Nov 13	SRD	8 Jun 14	44	H, BC	180,360
Stourbridge	22 Jul 14	SRD	17 Oct 14	21	H, BC	189,562
Stafford Road	7 Nov 14	SWks	18 Dec 14	21		
Stourbridge	8 Jan 15	STB	18 Mar 15	32		199,286
Stourbridge	19 Apr 15	SRD	14 Jul 15	28	H, BC	203,497
Stourbridge	11 Aug 15	STB	3 Nov 15	213	BC	
		SWks	28 Dec 15		H, BC	207,902
Southall	3 Jun 16	SHL	5 Feb 17	33	R	
Southall	10 Mar 17	OOC	4 Jul 17	17	R	
Southall	21 Jul 17	OOC	3 Dec 17	16	R	
Southall	19 Dec 17	SLO	20 Dec 17	39	R	
Southall	28 Jan 18	OOC	9 Mar 18	51	R	
Bristol	29 Apr 18	SPM	22 May 18	1225		
		SWks	22 Dec 19		H, BC	244,480
Chippenham	28 Sep 21					
Swindon Stock	Nov 21					
Bristol	16 Nov 21	SPM	6 Jun 22	32	R	
Bristol	8 Jul 22	BTL	3 Sep 22	58		
		SWks	15 Sep 22		H, BC	266,492
Aberdare	31 Oct 22	SWks	11 Feb 25	194	H, BC	292,281
St Philip's Marsh	24 Aug 25					
Yatton	Nov 25					
St Philip's Marsh	Nov 25					
Yatton	Dec 25					
St Philip's Marsh	Jan 26					
Bath	Mar 26					
St Philip's Marsh	Apr 26					
Bath	Oct 26					
Yatton	Dec 26					
St Philip's Marsh	Jan 27	BTL	16 Feb 27			
		SWks	26 Feb 27			317,575

Converted to Trailer No.152 (Dia. A29)

No.68 (Diagram O)

Allocation	*Date*	*Stop'd*	*Date*	*Days Stop'd*	*Catgy. Repair*	*Miles Run*
New	May 06					
?		SWks	18 Aug 06	12	L	
?	30 Aug 06	SWks	5 Oct 06	18	L	
?	23 Oct 06	SWks	8 Feb 07	91	G, BC	24,918
?	10 May 07	SWks	4 Nov 07	31	BC	32,909
?	5 Dec 07					
Oxford	27 Jan 08					
Swindon Stock	Aug 08					
Oxford	20 Aug 08	SWks	15 Jan 09	96	G, BC	57,631
Swindon Stock	21 Apr 09					
Oxford	12 May 09					
Cheltenham	Jun 09					
Whitland	Jul 09					
Neath	Oct 09					
Stafford Road	6 Nov 09					
Croes Newydd	18 Nov 09	SRD	12 Jan 10	20	G, BC	71,959
Croes Newydd	1 Feb 10	SRD	3 May 10	11	L&B, BC	79,221
Croes Newydd	14 May 10	SRD	14 Jul 10	25	BC	83,331
Stourbridge	8 Aug 10	SRD	30 Jan 11	31	G&Blr, BC	96,255
Stourbridge	2 Mar 11	SRD	15 Sep 11	13	BC	108,590
Stourbridge	28 Sep 11	STB	17 Feb 12	20		
Stourbridge	8 Mar 12	SWks	22 May 12	121	G, BC	121,543
Swindon Stock	20 Sep 12					
Stourbridge	27 Sep 12	STB	30 Oct 12	87		
		SWks	5 Nov 12		H, BC	124,879
Swindon Stock	25 Jan 13					
Stourbridge	29 Jan 13	SRD ‡	9 Mar 13	4	L	
Stourbridge	13 Mar 13	SRD	2 Aug 13	20	H, BC	142,164
Stourbridge	22 Aug 13	SRD	23 Sep 13	10	L	
Stourbridge	3 Oct 13	SRD	12 Feb 14	7	BC	152,578
Stourbridge	19 Feb 14	SRD	26 Aug 14	27	H, BC	162,873
Stourbridge	22 Sep 14	SRD	4 Feb 15	8	L	
Stourbridge	12 Feb 15	SWks	27 Sep 15	768	H, BC	183,260
Swindon Stock	3 Nov 17					
Frome	22 Jan 18					
Swindon Stock	Mar 18					
Gloucester	22 Mar 18					
Cheltenham	May 18	GLO	3 Jul 18	30		
		SWks	23 Jul 18		H, BC	195,791
Swindon Stock	2 Aug 18					
Southall	29 Aug 18	SHL	21 Nov 18	126	R	
Southall	27 Mar 19	SWks	15 Jan 21	238	H, BC	215,429
Swindon Stock	10 Sep 21					
Yeovil	Oct 21					
Bristol	May 22	BTL	10 Jun 22	132		
		SWks	4 Jul 22		H, BC	234,827
Swindon Stock	20 Oct 22					
Worcester	1 Nov 22	WOS	1 May 24	5	H, BC	273,502
Worcester	6 May 24	SWks	9 Jan 25	238	H, BC	294,895
Swindon Stock	4 Sep 25					
Stourbridge	Dec 25	STB	19 Jun 26	21	R	
Stourbridge	10 Jul 26	STB	31 Dec 26	56	R	
Stourbridge	25 Feb 27	SWks	7 Jun 27			327,882

Converted to Trailer No.153 (Dia. A29)

NOTE

‡ *This stoppage shown as in 1913, but not entered in the Register until 26 Apr 15, so it may have taken place 9-13 Mar 15.*

No.69 (Diagram O)

Allocation	*Date*	*Stop'd*	*Date*	*Days Stop'd*	*Catgy. Repair*	*Miles Run*
New	Jun 06					
?		SWks	20 Aug 06	44	G	9,460
?	3 Oct 06	SWks	20 Mar 07	22	L	
?	11 Apr 07	SWks	27 Aug 07	70	G, BC	36,589
?	5 Nov 07	SWks	27 Jan 08	3	BC	43,564
Oxford	30 Jan 08	SWks	5 Oct 08	71	BC	63,125

Allocation	*Date*	*Stop'd*	*Date*	*Days Stop'd*	*Catgy. Repair*	*Miles Run*
Swindon Stock	15 Dec 08					
Goodwick	13 Jan 09	SWks	7 Aug 09	73	G, BC	77,775
Swindon Stock	19 Oct 09					
Stourbridge	13 Nov 09	SRD	18 Apr 10	12		87,126
Stourbridge	30 Apr 10	SRD	7 Aug 10	15	G&B	94,561
Stourbridge	22 Aug 10	SRD	19 Jan 11	19	G&B, BC	105,668
Stourbridge	7 Feb 11	SWks	2 Oct 11	138	G, BC	117,374
Swindon Stock	17 Feb 12					
Taunton	26 Feb 12	TN	17 Sep 13	26	L	
Taunton	13 Oct 13	TN	21 Oct 13	15	L	
Taunton	5 Nov 13	SWks	12 Oct 14	110	H, BC	180,249
Swindon Stock	30 Jan 15					
Radstock	6 Feb 15					
Bath	Mar 15					
Yatton	Apr 15					
Bristol	May 15					
Yatton	Jun 15					
Bristol	Jul 15					
Bath	Aug 15					
Bristol	Sep 15	SWks	24 Sep 15	780	H, BC	199,711
Swindon Stock	12 Nov 17					
Frome	19 Nov 17	WES	2 Jan 18	35	L	
Westbury	6 Feb 18					
Frome	Mar 18	SDst	1 Jul 18	64		
		SWks	25 Jul 18		H, BC	210,535
Swindon Stock	3 Sep 18					
Trowbridge	22 Sep 18					
Frome	Oct 18	SWks	27 Apr 20	331	H, BC	205,723
Swindon Stock	24 Mar 21					
Bristol	4 Jul 21					
Yatton	Aug 21					
Bristol	Oct 21					
Yatton	Nov 21					
Bristol	Dec 21	SPM	19 May 22	7		
Bath	26 May 22					
Bristol	Jul 22	BTL	2 Nov 22	14	R	
Bristol	16 Nov 22	SWks	6 Feb 23	149	H, BC	295,274
Weymouth	5 Jul 23					
Westbury	Dec 23					
Frome	Feb 24					
Westbury	Oct 24	BTL	8 Oct 24	84	H, BC	329,474
		SWks	19 Nov 24			
Swindon Stock	31 Dec 24					
Worcester	3 Jan 25					
Gloucester	Feb 25					
Chalford	Apr 25					
Gloucester	Jun 25					
Chalford	Aug 25	SWks	11 Aug 25	189	H, BC	351,365
Southall	16 Feb 26	SWks	22 Jul 27	87	L	
Swindon Stock	17 Oct 27					
Birkenhead	25 Oct 27	SRD	8 Feb 28	177		
		SWks	20 Feb 28		H, BC	378,080
Pontypool Road	3 Aug 28	SWks	26 Mar 29	262	H, BC	390,926
Croes Newydd	13 Dec 29	SRD	6 Jun 30	15	R	
Croes Newydd	21 Jun 30	SWks	2 Sep 30	232	G, BC	401,385
Southall	22 Apr 31	SHL	21 Mar 32	18	R	
Southall	8 Apr 32	SHL	10 Oct 32			
		Cnstr	Dec 32			
		SWks	Jun 33			419,343

Condemned 1 Jul 33

Converted to Trailer No.201 (Dia. A26)

No.70 (Diagram O)

Allocation	*Date*	*Stop'd*	*Date*	*Days Stop'd*	*Catgy. Repair*	*Miles Run*
New	Jun 06					
Penzance		SWks	19 Dec 06	85	G	17,910
?	14 Mar 07	SWks	22 Feb 08	101		50,899
Swindon Stock	2 Jun 08					
Croes Newydd	18 Jun 08	SRD	18 Nov 08	19	L	
Croes Newydd	7 Dec 08	SRD	18 Jun 09	28	G	78,972
Croes Newydd	16 Jul 09	SWks	19 Nov 09	92	G, BC	89,202
Croes Newydd	19 Feb 10	SRD	18 Oct 10	22	BC	108,188
Croes Newydd	9 Nov 10	SRD	17 Dec 10		BC	112,636
Croes Newydd	N/R	CNYD	16 May 11	6		
Croes Newydd	22 May 11	SRD	28 Sep 11	27	G, BC	132,395
Croes Newydd	25 Oct 11	SWks	16 Apr 12	56	G, BC	146,056
Swindon Stock	11 Jun 12					
Whitland	5 Jul 12					
Swindon Stock	Oct 12					
Stratford on Avon	8 Oct 12					
Worcester	Nov 12					
Stratford on Avon	Dec 12	SWks	21 Jan 13	58	H, BC	157,240
Swindon Stock	20 Mar 13					
Tyseley	9 Apr 13	TYS	9 Aug 13	5	L	
Tyseley	14 Aug 13	SRD	7 Nov 13	22	H	186,188
Tyseley	29 Nov 13	SWks	9 Feb 14	59	H, BC	190,960
Swindon Stock	9 Apr 14					
Stourbridge	17 Apr 14	SWks	30 Nov 14	11	#	
Stourbridge	11 Dec 14	SRD	10 Jun 15	26	H, BC	223,659
Stourbridge	6 Jul 15	SRD	3 Mar 16	39	H?, BC	239,900
Stourbridge	11 Apr 16	STB	31 Jan 17	1051		
		SWks	28 Mar 19		H, BC	248,708
Gloucester	18 Dec 19					
Bristol	Feb 20	SPM	9 Mar 20	25	R	
Bristol	3 Apr 20	SWks	27 Oct 20	91	H, BC	275,537
Swindon Stock	26 Jan 21					
Stourbridge	30 Mar 21	SRD	25 Apr 22	42	H	290,748
Stourbridge	6 Jun 22	STB	24 Oct 22	16	R	
Stourbridge	9 Nov 22	SWks	7 May 23	343	H, BC	309,431
Bristol	14 Apr 24					
Bath	Jul 24					
Bristol	Aug 24	BTL	6 Oct 24	23	R	
Bath	29 Oct 24					
Bristol	Dec 24					
Yatton	Mar 25					
St Philip's Marsh	May 25	SPM	5 Jun 25	32	R	
Bath	7 Jul 25					
St Philip's Marsh	Aug 25					
Yatton	Sep 25					
St Philip's Marsh	Oct 25	SPM	29 Oct 25	356		
		SWks	17 Dec 25		H, BC	346,869
Pontypool Road	20 Oct 26	SWks	5 Oct 27	62	H, BC	364,436
Gloucester	6 Dec 27					
Chalford	Apr 28					
Gloucester	May 28					
Neath	4 Jan 29	SWks	18 Mar 29	336	H, BC	387,799
Swindon Stock	17 Feb 30					
St Philips Marsh	Mar 30	SPM	7 Oct 30	78		
		SWks	29 Oct 30		H, BC	404,890
Southall	24 Dec 30	SHL	17 Sep 31	279		
		SWks	2 Dec 31		G, BC	422,027
Swindon Stock	22 Jun 32					
Neath	Jul 33	NEA	25 Apr 34	31	R	
Neath	26 May 34	NEA	22 Sep 34			456,495
		SFPI	23 Jan 35			
		SWks	25 Jan 35			456,633

Condemned 19 Oct 35

Broken up. One of five cars replaced by three diesel cars.

NOTE

 # Carriage work only

No.71 (Diagram O)

Allocation	*Date*	*Stop'd*	*Date*	*Days Stop'd*	*Catgy. Repair*	*Miles Run*
New	Jun 06					
Taunton?		SWks	24 Dec 06	93	G, BC	11,513
?	27 Mar 07	SWks	17 Dec 07	91	G, BC	40,185
Taunton	17 Mar 08	SWks	17 Jul 09	52	G, BC	75,694
Swindon Stock	7 Sep 09					
Merthyr	21 Sep 09	SWks	9 May 10	17	G, BC	96,906
Merthyr	26 May 10	SWks	17 Jan 11	11	BC	117,609
Merthyr	28 Jan 11	SWks	20 Jun 11	16	L, BC	129,235
Whitland	6 Jul 11					
Neath	Oct 11					
Swindon Stock	Nov 11					
Chalford	7 Nov 11	SWks	12 Dec 11	122	G, BC	137,601
Swindon Stock	12 Apr 12					
Merthyr	14 Apr 12	SWks	26 Mar 14	70	H, BC	196,652
Basingstoke	4 Jun 14					

Allocation	*Date*	*Stop'd*	*Date*	*Days Stop'd*	*Catgy. Repair*	*Miles Run*
Reading	Jul 14					
Basingstoke	Aug 14					
Southall	Oct 14	SWks	5 Apr 15	89	H, BC	219,979
Swindon Stock	3 Jul 15					
Worcester	7 Oct 15					
Kidderminster	Feb 16					
Worcester	May 16					
Kidderminster	Jun 16					
Worcester	Aug 16					
Kidderminster	Sep 16					
Malvern Wells	Aug 17	SWks	21 Dec 19	618	H, BC	271,956
Swindon Stock	30 Aug 21					
Bristol	30 Sep 21	SWks	16 Nov 21	22	H, BC	277,054
Swindon Stock	8 Dec 21					
Taunton	26 Dec 21	TN	15 Jan 23	56	R	
Taunton	12 Mar 23	NA	9 Jul 23	8	H, BC	323,997
Taunton	17 Jul 23	NA	20 Nov 23	16	H	338,382
Taunton	6 Dec 23	SWks	13 Jan 25	185	H, BC	367,722
Carmarthen	17 Jul 25					
Chalford	10 Aug 25					
Gloucester	Nov 25					
Chalford	Nov 25	GLO	6 Feb 26	18	R	
Gloucester	24 Feb 26	GLO	14 Apr 26	313		
		SWks	21 Apr 26		H, BC	391,962
Swindon Stock	21 Feb 27					
Gloucester	2 Apr 27					
Chalford	May 27					
Gloucester	Sep 27					
Chalford	Oct 27	SWks	7 Feb 28	143	H, BC	419,622
Swindon Stock	29 Jun 28					
St Philips Marsh	2 Jul 28	SWks	13 Aug 30	224	L, BC	467,653
Swindon Stock	25 Mar 31					
Southall	11 May 31	SHL	10 Jun 31	16		
		SWks	20 Jun 31		L	
Southall	26 Jun 31	SHL	17 Sep 31	57		
		SWks	12 Oct 31		L, BC	477,298
Southall	13 Nov 31	SHL	17 Feb 32	68	R	
Southall	25 Apr 32	SHL	16 Sep 32	29	R	
Southall	15 Oct 32	SHL	22 Jul 33	226		
		SFPI	6 Sep 33			
		SWks	2 Jan 34		G, BC	499,021
Exeter	5 Mar 34	SFPI	1 May 34	36		
		SWks	9 May 34		L	503,435
Swindon Stock	6 Jun 34					
Exeter	27 Jun 34	EXE	13 Sep 34	28	R	
Exeter	11 Oct 34	EXE	7 Nov 34	121		
		NA	8 Feb 35		L	
Exeter	8 Mar 35	EXE	28 May 35			
		SFPI	12 Jun 35			
		SWks	19 Jun 35			520,169
Condemned	19 Oct 35					

Broken up. One of five cars replaced by three diesel cars.

No.72 (Diagram O)

New	Jul 06					
?		SWks	5 Mar 07	67	G, BC	13,293
?	11 May 07	NA	22 Oct 07	4	L	43,369
?	26 Oct 07					
At Newton Abbot	25 Apr 08	NA	4 May 08	5	G	58,614
Exeter	9 May 08					
Newton Abbot	Jul 08	NA	20 Jul 08	4		
Truro	24 Jul 08	SWks	26 Sep 08	45	G, BC	73,706
Swindon Stock	10 Nov 08					
Laira	6 Jan 09					
Newton Abbot	Mar 09					
Laira	Apr 09					
Newton Abbot	May 09					
Truro	Jun 09					
Newquay	Oct 09	NA	8 Dec 09	37	G, BC	99,018
Truro	14 Jan 10	NA	5 Jul 10	42	BC	116,252
Laira	16 Aug 10					
Truro	Nov 10	NA	26 May 11	69	G, BC	143,005
Truro	3 Aug 11	SWks	6 Sep 11	65	G, BC	146,302

Allocation	*Date*	*Stop'd*	*Date*	*Days Stop'd*	*Catgy. Repair*	*Miles Run*
Swindon Stock	10 Nov 11					
Truro	16 Nov 11					
Newquay	Feb 12					
Truro	Mar 12	NA	4 Jun 12	38	G, BC	156,606
Truro	12 Jul 12					
Newquay	Nov 12					
Truro	Dec 12					
Newquay	Jan 13					
Truro	Feb 13					
Newquay	Apr 13					
Penzance	May 13					
Helston	Aug 13					
Penzance	Oct 13	NA	15 Jan 14	48	H, BC	197,066
Newton Abbot	4 Mar 14					
Penzance	Jun 14	SWks	10 Feb 15	126	H, BC	221,836
Swindon Stock	16 Jun 15					
Stourbridge	28 Sep 15	SRD	29 May 16	50	H, BC	241,371
Stourbridge	18 Jul 16	SRD	17 Jul 17	78	H, BC	260,072
Stourbridge	3 Oct 17					
Chester	Apr 18					
Croes Newydd	Jun 19	SWks	22 Jul 19	287	H, BC	279,553
Swindon Stock	4 May 20					
Exeter	27 May 20	NA	5 May 21	29	H, BC	295,711
Exeter	3 Jun 21	SWks	4 Nov 22	115	H, BC	322,763
Swindon Stock	27 Feb 23					
Neath	10 Mar 23	NEA	19 Nov 23	25	R	
Neath	14 Dec 23	SWks	31 Dec 23	107	H, BC	341,563
Swindon Stock	16 Apr 24					
Reading	3 May 24	RDG ‡	23 Dec 24	37	L	
Reading	29 Jan 25	SWks	30 Apr 25	216	H, BC	364,618
Swindon Stock	2 Dec 25					
Stourbridge	10 Dec 25	SRD	5 Apr 27	30	H, BC	387,030
Stourbridge	5 May 27	STB	8 Jul 27	32		
		SRD	26 Jul 27		L	
Stafford Road	9 Aug 27					
Stourbridge	Nov 27	STB	10 Feb 28	17	R	
Stourbridge	27 Feb 28	STB	25 Jul 28	173		
		SWks	7 Aug 28		H, BC	407,907
Laira	14 Jan 29	SWks	2 Feb 29	34	L	
Laira	8 Mar 29	NA	18 Jun 29	4	BC	415,359
Laira	22 Jun 29					
Exeter	Oct 29	EXE	15 Feb 30	52		
		NA	3 Mar 30		L	
Exeter	8 Apr 30	EXE	7 Oct 30	175		
		SWks	7 Oct 30		G, BC	444,402
Swindon Stock	31 Mar 31					
Reading	Jun 31					
Southall	Aug 31	SHL	19 Oct 31	45		
		SWks	4 Nov 31		L	
Southall	3 Dec 31	SHL	19 May 32	41	L	
Southall	29 Jun 32	SHL	31 Dec 32	27	R	
Southall	27 Jan 33					
Swindon Stock	Jun 33	SFPI	8 Dec 34			
		SWks	13 Dec 34			471,286
Condemned	9 Feb 35					

Converted to Trailer No.218 (Dia. A29)

NOTE

‡ Allocation Register gives at OOC Jan 25.

No.73 (Diagram O)

Delivered?	Feb 06					
Swindon Works	Mar 06					
To Stock	Apr 06					
?		SLP	19 Jul 06	43	G	7,502
Much Wenlock?	31 Aug 06	SWks	20 Nov 06	84	G, BC	13,203
?	12 Feb 07	SWks	21 Jan 08	86	G, BC	46,959
Swindon Stock	16 Apr 08					
Frome	27 Apr 08					
Trowbridge	Apr 09	SWks	18 May 09	73	G, BC	81,039
Southall	30 Jul 09	SWks	8 Apr 10	26	G, BC	115,150
Southall	4 May 10	OOC	10 Oct 10	12		
Southall	22 Oct 10	SHL	23 Jan 11	12	L	
Southall	4 Feb 11	SWks	3 Mar 11	60	G, BC	145,586

Allocation	*Date*	*Stop'd*	*Date*	*Days Stop'd*	*Catgy. Repair*	*Miles Run*
Swindon Stock	2 May 11					
Kidderminster	13 May 11					
Stratford on Avon	Jul 11					
Worcester	Dec 11					
Kidderminster	Jan 12	SWks	7 Feb 12	136	G, BC	169,725
Swindon Stock	22 Jun 12					
Aberystwyth	5 Jul 12					
Neath	Oct 12					
Goodwick	Nov 12					
Neath	Sep 14	SWks	8 Sep 14	87	H, BC	223,875
Southall	4 Dec 14	SWks	11 May 15	945	H, BC	241,564
Swindon Stock	11 Dec 17					
Croes Newydd	26 Dec 17	SWks	10 Oct 19	1,012	H, BC	275,279
Swindon Stock	18 Jul 22					
Gloucester	3 Aug 22	GLO	1 Nov 22	16	R	
Gloucester	17 Nov 22	SWks	8 Nov 23	46	H, BC	307,849
Swindon Stock	24 Dec 23					
Oswestry	19 Jan 24	OSW	17 Mar 24	36	L	
Oswestry	22 Apr 24	SRD	9 Oct 24	25	H	330,140
Oswestry	3 Nov 24					
Bristol	19 Dec 24	SPM	19 Dec 24	20	R, BC	
Yatton	8 Jan 25					
St Philip's Marsh	Mar 25	BTL	14 Apr 25	407		
		SWks	25 Apr 26		H, BC	336,479
Swindon Stock	26 May 26					
Pontypool Road	7 Mar 27	SWks	1 Jun 28	312	H, BC	364,422
Neath	9 Apr 29	NEA	8 Jun 31	191		
		SWks	3 Jul 31		G, BC	395,789
Exeter	16 Dec 31	EXE	4 Oct 32	22	R	
Exeter	26 Oct 32					
Swindon Stock	Dec 32					
Cirencester Stock	Mar 33	SWks	16 Jun 33			425,868
Condemned	1 Jul 33					

Recovered parts used for Trailer No.202 (Dia.A31)

No.74 (Diagram O)

Allocation	*Date*	*Stop'd*	*Date*	*Days Stop'd*	*Catgy. Repair*	*Miles Run*
Delivered	Feb 06	SWks	12 Feb 06	22		
Swindon Works	6 Mar 06					
To Stock	Apr 06					
?		SRD	18 Jul 06	14	G	6,750
Much Wenlock?	1 Aug 06	SWks	12 Jan 07	33	G, BC	16,768
?	14 Feb 07	NA	6 Jun 07	29	L, BC	24,344
?	5 Jul 07	SWks	31 Oct 07	21	G, BC	33,292
Trowbridge?	21 Nov 07					
At Trowbridge	25 Apr 08					
Frome	Oct 08	SWks	27 Oct 08	129	G, BC	58,469
Swindon Stock	5 Mar 09	SWks	5 Apr 09	18		
Swindon Stock	23 Apr 09					
Frome	18 May 09	SWks	25 Jan 10	36	G, BC	78,652
Swindon Stock	2 Mar 10					
Frome	8 Apr 10					
Trowbridge	Oct 10					
Frome	Dec 10	SWks	3 Mar 11	78	G, BC	102,116
Swindon Stock	20 May 11					
Bristol	9 Jun 11	SWks	22 Jun 11	15	G, BC	103,548
Aberystwyth	7 Jul 11					
Carmarthen	Oct 11					
Oxford	25 Oct 11	SWks	2 Jul 12	74	G, BC	122,020
Oxford	14 Sep 12	SWks	22 Sep 14	80	H, BC	178,948
Swindon Stock	11 Dec 14					
Didcot	28 Jan 15					
Reading	8 Mar 15	SWks	31 Mar 15	9		
Swindon Stock	9 Apr 15					
Southall	10 May 15	SWks	3 Dec 15	967	L, BC	210,708
Swindon Stock	27 Jul 18					
Bristol	7 Aug 18					
Yatton	Sep 18					
Bristol	Oct 18	BTL	14 Feb 19	1,127		
		SWks	29 Dec 19		H, BC	225,782
Swindon Stock	17 Mar 22					
Cambrian lines	4 Jul 22					
Oswestry	Aug 22					
Machynlleth	Sep 22					
Dolgelly	Oct 22					
Machynlleth	Nov 22					
Dolgelly	Dec 22					
Penmaenpool	Dec 22					
Machynlleth	Apr 23					
Penmaenpool	Jun 23					
Machynlleth	Jul 23					
Penmaenpool	Aug 23					
Machynlleth	Sep 23					
Penmaenpool	Dec 23					
Chester	Jun 24	SWks	22 Aug 24	133	H, BC	263,866
Exeter	2 Jan 25	NA	29 Dec 25	3	H	292,526
Exeter	1 Jan 26	SWks	24 Jan 27	632	H, BC	316,623
Southall	17 Oct 28	SHL	9 Jan 30	22	L	
Southall	31 Jan 30	OOC	30 Jun 30	16	R	
Southall	16 Jul 30	SHL	2 Aug 30	229		
		SWks	20 Aug 30		G	337,111
St Philips Marsh	19 Mar 31					
Swindon Stock	3 Oct 32		Dec 32			
Cirencester Stock	6 Dec 32					
Condemned	1 Jul 33	SWks				364,555

Recovered parts used in Trailer No.203 (Dia. A31)

No.75 (Diagram O)

Allocation	*Date*	*Stop'd*	*Date*	*Days Stop'd*	*Catgy. Repair*	*Miles Run*
Delivered	7 Mar 06					
To stock	Apr 06					
?		SWks	30 Jul 06	85	G	14,362
?	23 Oct 06	SWks	22 May 07	82	G, BC	39,151
?	12 Aug 07	SWks	27 Apr 08	31	L, BC	64,097
Swindon Stock	28 May 08					
Stourbridge	6 Jun 08	SRD	14 Apr 09	21	G, BC	73,571
Stourbridge	5 May 09	SWks	8 Nov 09	44	G, BC	79,746
Swindon Stock	22 Dec 09					
Frome	13 Jan 10	SWks	15 Aug 10	28	BC	96,219
Swindon Stock	12 Sep 10					
Bath	29 Sep 10					
Weymouth	Nov 10	SWks	4 Dec 12	85	BC	124,433
Swindon Stock	27 Feb 13					
Gwaun-Cae-Gurwen	13 Mar 13					
Garnant	Jan 15					
Gwaun-Cae-Gurwen	Apr 15	LLY	27 Dec 15	19		
Gwaun-Cae-Gurwen	15 Jan 16	SWks	8 May 16	1,408	H, BC	138,306
Swindon Stock	16 Mar 20					
Llanelly	10 May 20					
Garnant	Apr 21					
Neath	May 21					
Garnant	Nov 21	SWks	11 Nov 21	257	H, BC	141,912
Swindon Stock	26 Jul 22					
Bristol	24 Aug 22					
Yatton	Oct 22	SWks	1 Nov 22	35	H	148,587
Machynlleth	6 Dec 22					
Penmaenpool	Apr 23					
Machynlleth	Jun 23					
Penmaenpool	Jul 23					
Machynlleth	Aug 23					
Penmaenpool	Sep 23					
Machynlleth	Dec 23					
Croes Newydd	13 Jun 24	SWks	27 Jun 24	341	H, BC	179,868
Swindon Stock	3 Jun 25					
Yatton	8 Jun 25					
Bath	Aug 25					
St Philip's Marsh	Sep 25	SWks	22 Feb 26	261	H, BC	194,225
Swindon Stock	10 Nov 26					
Frome	1 Apr 27					
St Philip's Marsh	Jul 27	SWks	29 Jul 27	211	L	
St Philip's Marsh	25 Feb 28					
Pontypool Road	25 Aug 28					
St Philip's Marsh	7 Sep 28					
St Blazey	18 Jan 29					
Laira	Aug 29	SWks	25 Oct 29	288	H, BC	230,266
Swindon Stock	9 Aug 30					
Southall	19 Aug 30	SHL	30 Apr 31	18	R	
Southall	18 May 31	SHL	21 Aug 31	70	L	

Allocation	*Date*	*Stop'd*	*Date*	*Days Stop'd*	*Catgy. Repair*	*Miles Run*
Southall	30 Oct 31					
Swindon Stock	23 Nov 32					
Cirencester Stock	6 Dec 32					
Swindon Stock by	Jan 34	SFPl	27 Apr 34			
		SWks	3 May 34			250,365

Converted to Trailer No.207 (Dia. A31)

No.76 (Diagram Q)

Allocation	*Date*	*Stop'd*	*Date*	*Days Stop'd*	*Catgy. Repair*	*Miles Run*
New	Apr 06					
Shrewsbury	21 Jul 06					
Much Wenlock?	?	SWks	1 Nov 06	48	G, BC	13,280
?	19 Dec 06	SWks	7 Mar 07	7	BC	28,058
Laira?	14 Mar 07	NA	27 Aug 07	3	L, BC	30,076
Laira?	30 Aug 07	NA	6 Feb 08	68	G, BC	44,437
Laira	14 Apr 08					
Penzance	Oct 08					
Truro	Dec 08					
Newton Abbot	Jan 09	SWks	2 Feb 09	112	G, BC	74,000
Swindon Stock	25 May 09					
Bristol	3 Jun 09	SWks	21 Sep 09	9	G, BC	86,097
Swindon Stock	30 Sep 09					
Yatton	11 Oct 09					
Bristol	Jan 10					
Yatton	Feb 10					
Bristol	May 10	SWks	17 Jun 10	36	G, BC	110,242
Swindon Stock	23 Jul 10					
Frome	10 Aug 10					
Trowbridge	Dec 10	SWks	2 Oct 11	52	G, BC	145,850
Swindon Stock	23 Nov 11					
Gloucester	20 Dec 11					
Cheltenham	Jan 12					
Taunton	12 Feb 12	SWks	18 Jun 13	107	H, BC	176,920
Swindon Stock	3 Oct 13					
Southall	1 Jan 14	SWks	19 Feb 14	20	H	183,357
Swindon Stock	11 Mar 14					
Southall	20 Mar 14	SWks	30 Apr 14	54	H, BC	188,791
Neath	23 Jun 14					
Goodwick	Dec 14	SWks	18 Jan 15	536	H, BC	206,574
Swindon Stock	7 Jul 16					
Southall	12 Jul 16	OOC	14 Mar 18	8	R	
Southall	22 Mar 18	SHL	3 May 18	1,056		
		RDG	Jul 18			
		SWks	15 Dec 19		H, BC	248,682
Swindon Stock	24 Mar 21					
Bristol	31 Jul 21	SPM	31 Oct 21	42		
		SWks	16 Nov 21		H, BC	260,759
Swindon Stock	12 Dec 21					
Llanelly	9 Mar 22					
Garnant	Apr 22					
Llanelly	Jan 23					
Garnant	Mar 23	NEA	18 Feb 24	210		
		SWks	11 Apr 24		H, BC	275,949
Machynlleth	15 Sep 24					
Penmaenpool	May 25					
Machynlleth	Jun 25					
Penmaenpool	Jul 25					
Machynlleth	Aug 25					
Penmaenpool	Sep 25					
Machynlleth	Oct 25					
Penmaenpool	Nov 25					
Machynlleth	Nov 25	MCH	26 Feb 26	105		
		OSW	+		R	
Machynlleth	11 Jun 26	SWks	23 Sep 26	144	H, BC	317,052
Swindon Stock	14 Feb 27					
Neath	14 Jun 27	NEA	10 Mar 28	25		
		SWks	21 Mar 28		H, BC	326,441
Swindon Stock	4 Apr 28					
Exeter	May 28	SWks	30 Jul 28	4	H, BC	335,906
Exeter	3 Aug 28	SWks	24 Nov 28	109	L	
Swindon Stock	13 Mar 29					
Pontypool Road	18 Mar 29	PPRD	1 Jul 30	167		
		SWks	11 Jul 30		H, BC	363,676
St Philips Marsh	15 Dec 30	SPM	9 Feb 31	136		
		SWks	18 Mar 31		L	
St Philips Marsh	25 Jun 31	SPM	10 Mar 33	34		
		SWks	13 Mar 33		L	
St Philips Marsh	13 Apr 33	SPM	10 Oct 33	16		
St Philips Marsh	26 Oct 33	SPM	17 Sep 34	19		
St Philips Marsh	6 Oct 34	SPM	12 Oct 34			
		SFPl	9 Jan 35			
		SWks	11 Jan 35			409,636
Condemned	9 Feb 35					

Converted to Trailer No.219 (Dia. A31)

No.77 (Diagram Q)

Allocation	*Date*	*Stop'd*	*Date*	*Days Stop'd*	*Catgy. Repair*	*Miles Run*
New	Apr 06					
?		SRD	30 Jun 06	26	LG	
Much Wenlock?	26 Jul 06	SWks	5 Dec 06	34	G, BC	12,721
?	8 Jan 07	SWks	7 Mar 07	7	L, BC	16,072
?	14 Mar 07	SWks	23 Oct 07	152	G, BC	27,684
Goodwick?	23 Mar 08					
At Goodwick	25 Apr 08					
Fishguard	Jul 08					
Goodwick	Aug 08					
Whitland	22 Feb 09	SWks	22 Mar 09	77	G, BC	52,476
Swindon Stock	7 Jun 09					
Laira	19 Jun 09					
Helston	Jul 09					
Truro	Aug 09					
Newquay	Sep 09					
Penzance	Oct 09	SWks	30 Oct 09	54	LG, BC	61,878
Swindon Stock	23 Dec 09					
Frome	24 Jan 10	SWks	6 Jun 10	49	G, BC	71,226
Swindon Stock	25 Jul 10					
Evesham	4 Sep 10					
Kidderminster	Dec 10					
Evesham	Jan 11					
Kidderminster	Mar 11	SWks	13 May 11	20	G, BC	98,023
Swindon Stock	2 Jun 11					
Whitland	4 Jul 11					
Neath	Oct 11					
Swindon Stock	Nov 11					
Bristol	10 Nov 11	SWks	3 Feb 12	158	G, BC	113,782
Oxford	10 Jul 12	SWks	13 May 14	49	H, BC	162,535
Swindon Stock	1 Jul 14					
Aberystwyth	7 Jul 14					
Goodwick	Oct 14	SWks	29 May 15	391	H, BC	181,508
Swindon Stock	23 Jun 16					
Bristol	10 Jul 16	SPM	27 Jul 16	263	No repairs done	
Yatton	16 Apr 17					
Bristol	Jun 17					
Bath	Jul 17					
Bristol	Sep 17					
Yatton	Sep 17					
Bath	Oct 17	SPM	24 Nov 17	49	R	
Bath	12 Jan 18					
Yatton	Mar 18	SPM	28 Mar 18	1,602		
		SWks	27 Oct 19		H, BC	209,387
Swindon Stock	16 Aug 22					
Taunton	27 Aug 22	TN	3 Aug 23	15	R	
Taunton	18 Aug 23	NA	12 Sep 23	64	R	
Taunton	15 Nov 23	NA	2 Sep 24	2	H, BC	262,375
Taunton	4 Sep 24	SWks	1 Oct 25	266	H, BC	290,830
Swindon Stock	24 Jun 26					
Exeter	21 Jan 27	EXE	10 Feb 28	118	R	
Exeter	7 Jun 28	SWks	17 Oct 28	231	H, BC	331,988
Pontypool Road	5 Jun 29	PPRD	16 Sep 30	228	G, BC	350,763
		SWks	6 Oct 30			
Swindon Stock	2 May 31					
St Philips Marsh	16 Aug 32					
Yatton	Apr 34					
St Philips Marsh	May 34	SPM	8 Oct 34			364,555
		SFPl	3 Dec 35			
		SWks	2 Jan 35			399,403
Condemned	19 Oct 35					

Broken up. One of five cars replaced by three diesel cars.

No.78 (Diagram O)

Allocation	Date	Stop'd	Date	Days Stop'd	Catgy. Repair	Miles Run
New	Jun 06					
?		SWks	22 Aug 06	64	G	6,773
?	25 Oct 06	SWks	15 Aug 07	35	BC	17,368
?	19 Sep 07	SWks	20 Nov 07	5		
?	25 Nov 07	SWks	25 Jan 08	12	BC	29,409
Bath?	6 Feb 08	SWks	21 Jul 08	28	L, BC	52,373
At Bath	25 Apr 08					
Swindon Stock	18 Aug 08					
Bath	3 Sep 08	SWks	9 Nov 08	40	BC	62,430
Swindon Stock	19 Dec 08					
Bath	7 May 09	SWks	23 Jun 09	64	G, BC	72,323
Trowbridge	26 Aug 09					
Frome	Jun 10					
Trowbridge	Jul 10	SDst	23 Jul 10	14		
Trowbridge	6 Aug 10	SDst	27 Jan 11	20	L&T	
Trowbridge	16 Feb 11					
Frome	Apr 11	SWks	7 Oct 11	94	G, BC	131,299
Swindon Stock	9 Jan 12					
Croes Newydd	5 Feb 12					
Corwen	Sep 13					
Croes Newydd	Nov 13	CNYD	27 Dec 13	6	L	
Chester	2 Jan 14					
Corwen	Feb 14					
Croes Newydd	Apr 14	CNYD	27 Jul 14	89		
		SWks	18 Aug 14		H, BC	176,817
Swindon Stock	24 Oct 14					
Southall	29 Oct 14	SWks	14 Dec 14	42	L	
Swindon Stock	25 Jan 15					
Stourbridge	1 Feb 15	SWks	27 Apr 15	13	L	
Swindon Stock	10 May 15					
Neath	3 Nov 15					
Southall	8 Apr 16	SHL	22 Jul 16	1,152		
		RDG	Jul 18			
		SWks	5 Dec 18		H, BC	198,478
Swindon Stock	17 Sep 19					
Wolverhampton	25 Sep 19					
Croes Newydd	Oct 19	CNYD	2 Feb 20	51	R	
Croes Newydd	24 Mar 20	CNYD	3 Aug 20	14	R	
Croes Newydd	17 Aug 20	SRD	29 Dec 21	28	H, BC	220,172
Croes Newydd	26 Jan 22	SWks	12 Sep 22	153	H, BC	230,131
Swindon Stock	12 Feb 23					
Oswestry	26 Feb 23					
Llanidloes	Apr 23					
Oswestry	Jul 23					
Machynlleth	Aug 23					
Oswestry	Oct 23					
Machynlleth	Jun 24	SRD	9 Sep 24	11	H, BC	269,868
Birkenhead	20 Sep 24	SWks	27 May 25	393	H, BC	282,129
Swindon Stock	24 Jun 26					
Pontypool Road	7 Mar 27	PPRD	29 Jul 27	40	R	
Pontypool Road	7 Sep 27	PPRD	19 Dec 27	128		
		SWks	7 Jan 28		H, BC	295,635
St Philip's Marsh	25 Apr 28					
Yatton	Jun 28					
St Philip's Marsh	Aug 28	SWks	18 Dec 29	335	H, BC	336,344
Pontypool Road	18 Nov 30					
Swindon Stock	13 Sep 32					
Cirencester Stock	2 Dec 32					
Croes Newydd	Apr 33	OXY	28 Dec 33			
		SFPI	27 Apr 34			
		SWks	2 May 34	(see notes)		354,245

Converted to Trailer No.208 (Dia. A31)

NOTES

Engine 0840 ex-car No.71 condemned with car No.78

Engine 0846 from car No.78 put on car No.71.

No.79 (Diagram O)

Allocation	Date	Stop'd	Date	Days Stop'd	Catgy. Repair	Miles Run
New	Jun 06					
?		NA	15 Nov 06	30	G, BC	12,596
?	15 Dec 06	NA	8 Apr 07	18	L, BC	22,607
?	26 Apr 07	SWks	17 Jul 07	35	G, BC	27,991
Trowbridge?	21 Aug 07					
At Trowbridge	25 Apr 08	SWks	30 Oct 08	83	G, BC	53,493
Swindon Stock	21 Jan 09					
Goodwick	Feb 09	SWks	8 Feb 10	77	BC	78,477
Yatton	26 Apr 10					
Bristol	Jun 10					
Bath	Jul 10					
Yatton	Sep 10	BTL	4 Oct 10	21		
Yatton	25 Oct 10	BTL	5 Nov 10	40		
		SWks	5 Nov 10		BC	96,695
Swindon Stock	15 Dec 10					
Port Talbot	20 Jan 11					
Bristol	1 Apr 11					
Yatton	May 11					
Bristol	Jun 11					
Trowbridge	22 Jun 11	SDst	23 Jun 11	15		
Trowbridge	8 Jul 11					
Bristol	6 Sep 11	Trwbg	4 Oct 11	8		
Trowbridge	12 Oct 11					
Bristol	Nov 11	WEY	3 Nov 11	106		
		SWks	9 Nov 11		G, BC	118,593
Swindon Stock	17 Feb 12					
Stourbridge	26 Feb 12					
Tyesley	Oct 12					
Stourbridge	Nov 12	SRD	12 Dec 12	8	BC	135,217
Stourbridge	20 Dec 12	SRD	2 Jun 13	12	BC	146,127
Stourbridge	14 Jun 13	SRD	19 Dec 13	35	H, BC	154,996
Stourbridge	23 Jan 14	SRD	1 May 14	11	L, BC	158,376
Stourbridge	12 May 14	SRD	29 Jun 14	38	H, BC	161,139
Stourbridge	6 Aug 14	STB	3 Sep 14	29		
Stourbridge	2 Oct 14	SWks	8 Jan 15	118	H, BC	169,186
Swindon Stock	6 May 15					
Yatton	4 Oct 15					
Bristol	Nov 15	SPM	15 Mar 16	34		
Bristol	18 Apr 16	BTL	10 Apr 17	1,823		
		SWks	23 Oct 19		H, BC	218,380
Swindon Stock	7 Apr 22					
Worcester	5 Jul 22	WOS	7 Feb 24	37	H, BC	242,684
Worcester	15 Mar 24	SWks	7 Feb 25	251	H, BC	266,163
Taunton	16 Oct 25	NA	13 Aug 26	71	R	
Taunton	23 Oct 26	SWks	22 Jan 27	220	H, BC	288,706
Pontypool Road	30 Aug 27	PPRD	10 Jan 28	22	R	
Pontypool Road	1 Feb 28	PPRD	1 Jun 28	60	R	
Pontypool Road	31 Jul 28	SWks	6 Jun 29	284	H, BC	319,932
Croes Newydd	17 Mar 30	SRD	22 Sep 30	114		
		SWks	2 Oct 30		H, BC	330,084
Croes Newydd	14 Jan 31					
Swindon Stock	Apr 33	SFPI	27 Apr 34			
		SWks	7 May 34			370,148

Converted to Trailer No.209 (Dia. A31)

No.80 (Diagram O)

Allocation	Date	Stop'd	Date	Days Stop'd	Catgy. Repair	Miles Run
New	Jun 06					
?		SWks	17 Sep 06	63	G	13,239
Much Wenlock?	19 Nov 06	SRD	27 Sep 07	22	L, BC	29,873
?	19 Oct 07	SWks	9 Nov 07	82	G, BC	30,828
Swindon Stock	30 Jan 08					
Oxford	8 Apr 08					
Swindon Stock	May 08					
Bath	13 Jun 08					
Chippenham	7 Jul 08					
Swindon Stock	Aug 08					
Trowbridge	14 Oct 08					
Frome	Dec 08	SDst	5 Jul 09	22	L	
Frome	27 Jul 09					
Trowbridge	Sep 09					
Frome	Oct 09					
Taunton	26 Mar 10	SWks	8 Apr 10	63	G	82,785
Swindon Stock	10 Jun 10					
Bristol	25 Jun 10					
Radstock	Sep 10	BTL	2 Nov 10	19		
		SWks	7 Nov 10	14	BC	92,069
Swindon Stock	21 Nov 10					
Yatton	8 Jan 11	SWks	23 Feb 11	6		

Allocation	*Date*	*Stop'd*	*Date*	*Days Stop'd*	*Catgy. Repair*	*Miles Run*
Frome	1 Mar 11					
Trowbridge	Apr 11					
Bristol	23 Jun 11	SWks	28 Aug 11	26	G, BC	115,396
Swindon Stock	23 Sep 11					
Trowbridge	2 Oct 11					
Bristol	24 Feb 12					
Trowbridge	28 Feb 12	SWks	28 Oct 12	14	L	153,218
Stratford on Avon	11 Nov 12	SWks	19 Jul 13	73	H, BC	173,489
Swindon Stock	30 Sep 13					
Southall	16 Dec 13	SWks	16 Apr 14	39	H, BC	190,552
Monmouth	25 May 14					
Pontypool Road	Sep 14	SWks	27 Sep 15	1997	H, BC	221,850
Swindon Stock	16 Mar 21					
Croes Newydd	6 Jul 21	SRD	8 Aug 22	32	H, BC	237,946
Croes Newydd	9 Sep 22	Sltny	13 Mar 23	58	L	
Croes Newydd	10 May 23	Sltny	5 Jun 23	31	R	
Birkenhead	6 Jul 23					
Croes Newydd	Aug 23					
Birkenhead	Nov 23					
Croes Newydd	Dec 23					
Birkenhead	Jan 24					
Croes Newydd	Mar 24					
Birkenhead	Apr 24	SWks	16 Jul 24	255	H, BC	255,981
Westbury	28 Mar 25					
St Philip's Marsh	Jul 25					
Yatton	Aug 25					
St Philip's Marsh	5 Sep 25					
Yatton	Nov 25					
St Philip's Marsh	Dec 25					
Yatton	Feb 26					
St Philip's Marsh	Mar 26					
Yatton	Jun 26					
St Philip's Marsh	Jul 26					
Yatton	Aug 26					
St Philip's Marsh	Oct 26					
Yatton	Oct 26					
St Philip's Marsh	Dec 26					
Yatton	Jan 27					
St Philip's Marsh	Feb 27					
Yatton	Mar 27					
St Philip's Marsh	Apr 27	SPM	16 Apr 27	26	R	
Westbury	12 May 27	SPM	27 May 27	329		
		SWks	16 Jun 27		H, BC	295,085
Frome	20 Apr 28					
Neath	18 Oct 28	NEA	25 Feb 29	533		
		SWks	2 Sep 29		G, BC	319,209
Swindon Stock	12 Aug 30					
Pontypool Road	21 Aug 30	PPRD	11 Dec 30	48	R	
Pontypool Road	28 Jan 31	PPRD	13 Feb 31	28	R	
Pontypool Road	13 Mar 31					
Swindon Stock	14 Sep 32					
Cirencester stock	2 Dec 32					
Exeter	May 33	EXE	27 Jun 33	22	R	
Exeter	19 Jul 33	EXE	29 Jan 34			
		SStk	8 Mar 34			
		SFPI	15 Dec 34			
		SWks	21 Dec 34			346,667
Condemned	19 Oct 35					
Broken up						

No.81 (Diagram Q1)

New	May 07					
		NA	4 Dec 07	10	L, BC	17,145
?	14 Dec 07	NA	24 Feb 08	5	L, BC	22,425
Newquay ?	29 Feb 08					
At Newquay	25 Apr 08	NA	7 Jul 08	3	G, BC	25,219
Truro	10 Jul 08	SWks	26 Sep 08	47	L, BC	41,986
Trowbridge	12 Nov 08					
Bath	18 Mar 09					
Trowbridge	31 Mar 09	SWks	7 May 09	81	G, BC	58,026
Swindon Stock	27 Jul 09					
Goodwick	6 Aug 09	SWks	25 Oct 10	98	G, BC	93,326
Swindon Stock	31 Jan 11					

Allocation	*Date*	*Stop'd*	*Date*	*Days Stop'd*	*Catgy. Repair*	*Miles Run*
Radstock	3 Feb 11					
Bristol	Mar 11					
Bath	Apr 11					
Radstock	Jun 11					
Bristol	Aug 11					
Bath	Sep 11					
Yatton	Oct 11					
Bristol	Nov 11					
Radstock	Jan 12					
Bristol	Feb 12					
Yatton	Mar 12					
Bath	May 12					
Bristol	Jul 12					
Bath	Nov 12	SWks	18 Dec 12	61	H,BC	158,286
Swindon Stock	17 Feb 13					
Bristol	20 Feb 13					
Radstock	Jul 13	BTL	21 Aug 13	16	L	
Bristol	6 Sep 13					
Yatton	Apr 14					
Bristol	May 14					
Radstock	Jun 14	BTL	1 Sep 14	92		
		SWks	12 Sep 14		H,BC	219,055
Swindon Stock	2 Dec 14					
Trowbridge	9 Dec 14					
Frome	Dec 15	TN	20 Jun 17	967		
		BTL	Apr 18			
		TN	May 18			
		SWks	10 Dec 18		H,BC	275,193
Bristol	12 Feb 20					
Bath	Apr 20					
Bristol	Jun 20	SPM	22 Aug 20	318		
		SWks	27 Sep 20		H,BC	289,010
Swindon Stock	6 Jul 21					
Southall	30 Jul 21	SHL	15 Feb 22	229		
		SWks	12 Jun 22		H,BC	302,511
Swindon Stock	2 Oct 22					
Exeter	13 Nov 22	NA	31 Dec 24	1	H,BC	358,456
Exeter	1 Jan 25	SWks	15 Apr 25	187	H,BC	367,182
Swindon Stock	19 Oct 25					
Oswestry	31 Oct 25					
Penmaenpool	Dec 25					
Machynlleth	Oct 26					
Penmaenpool	Oct 26					
Machynlleth	Dec 26	MCH	17 Jan 27	35	R	
Machynlleth	21 Feb 27	MCH	23 May 27	22	R	
Machynlleth	14 Jun 27	SWks	13 Aug 27	193	H,BC	395,025
Croes Newydd	22 Feb 28	SRD	6 Aug 28	30	L	
Croes Newydd	5 Sep 28	SRD	31 Oct 28	20	H,BC	411,080
Croes Newydd	20 Nov 28	SWks	11 Nov 29	301	H,BC	426,287
Croes Newydd	8 Sep 30	CNYD	24 Oct 30	57		
		SRD	15 Dec 30		H,BC	428,701
Stourbridge	20 Dec 30	STB	18 Feb 32	35		
		SWks	25 Feb 32		G, BC	453,450
Swindon Stock	24 Mar 32					
St Philip's Marsh	Mar 33	SPM	17 Jul 33	54	R	
St Philip's Marsh	9 Sep 33	SPM	2 Mar 34	14	R	
St Philip's Marsh	16 Mar 34	SPM	8 Oct 34			
		SFPI	20 Nov 34			
		SWks	23 Nov 34			483,549
Condemned	17 Nov 34					

Converted to Trailer No.211 (Dia. A34)

No.82 (Diagram Q1)

New	May 07					
		SWks	16 Dec 07	19	L	
Trowbridge?	4 Jan 08					
At Trowbridge	25 Apr 08	SWks	12 Oct 08	39	L, BC	47,490
Bath	20 Nov 08	SWks	20 Mar 09	24	LG	
Swindon Stock	13 Apr 09	SWks	27 Apr 09	52	L, BC	69,335
Swindon Stock	18 Jun 09					
Bath	24 Jun 09	SWks	21 Aug 09	45	G, BC	80,955
Swindon Stock	5 Oct 09					
Bristol	22 Oct 09					

Allocation	Date	Stop'd	Date	Days Stop'd	Catgy. Repair	Miles Run
Bath	Dec 09					
Bristol	Jan 10					
Yatton	Feb 10					
Bath	Mar 10					
Bristol	Apr 10	SWks	28 Apr 10	49	G, BC	96,721
Swindon Stock	16 Jun 10					
Radstock	24 Jun 10					
Bristol	Aug 10	BTL	3 Dec 10	17		
Bristol	20 Dec 10	BTL	25 Jan 11	101	G, BC	113,312
		SWks	3 Feb 11			
Swindon Stock	6 May 11					
Oxford	9 May 11	SWks	21 May 13	71	H, BC	160,761
Oxford	31 Jul 13	SWks	17 Jun 14	5	H, BC	186,735
Oxford	22 Jun 14					
Swindon Stock	May 15					
Southall	4 Dec 15	SWks	7 Mar 16	289	H, BC	215,539
Swindon Stock	21 Dec 16					
Chippenham	29 Dec 16					
Trowbridge	Apr 17					
Frome	Aug 17					
Trowbridge	Sep 17	SWks	23 Sep 18	522	H, BC	260,396
Swindon Stock	27 Feb 20					
Pontypool Road	19 May 20					
Neath	Jun 20	SWks	10 Sep 20	0		
Swindon Stock	10 Sep 20					
Neath	19 Sep 20					
Garnant	Apr 21					
Neath	May 21					
Garnant	Nov 21	LLY	22 Feb 22	244		
		SWks	9 Mar 22		H, BC	266,551
Swindon Stock	24 Oct 22					
Bristol	1 Nov 22					
Yatton	Dec 22					
Bristol	Jan 23					
Yatton	Jul 23	SWks	11 Jul 23	23	H, BC	285,884
Westbury	3 Aug 23					
Swindon Stock	14 Aug 24	BTL	23 Sep 24	15	R	
Westbury	8 Oct 24					
Frome	Dec 24					
Westbury	Jan 25	BTL	17 Mar 25	48		
		SWks	24 Mar 25		H, BC	333,445
Exeter	4 May 25	NA	27 Nov 26	5	H, BC	372,663
Newton Abbot	2 Dec 26					
Exeter	Jan 27	SWks	22 Oct 27	422	H, BC	398,215
Croes Newydd	17 Dec 28	CNYD	2 Dec 29	202		
		SWks	7 Dec 29		H, BC	419,799
St. Philip's Marsh	27 Jun 30	SPM	31 Jan 31	16	R	
St. Philip's Marsh	16 Feb 31	SPM	9 Feb 32	29	R	
St. Philip's Marsh	9 Mar 32	SPM	10 Mar 33			
		SStk	Mar 33			
		SWks	Jun 33			464,795
Condemned	1 Jul 33					

Recovered parts used for Trailer No.204 (Dia. A31)

No.83 (Diagram Q1)

Allocation	Date	Stop'd	Date	Days Stop'd	Catgy. Repair	Miles Run
New	May 07					
?		SDst	23 Nov 07	20	L	
?	13 Dec 07	SDst	14 Feb 08	18	L	
Chippenham	3 Mar 08	SDst	7 Jul 08	37	LG	
Chippenham	13 Aug 08	SWks	21 Oct 08	52	G, BC	71,470
Swindon Stock	12 Dec 08					
Oxford	15 Jan 09	SDst	2 Feb 11	29		
Oxford	3 Mar 11	SWks	17 Apr 11	106	G, BC	118,931
Southall	1 Aug 11					
Neath	30 Aug 11					
Goodwick	Nov 11	FGD	24 Feb 12	6		
Goodwick	1 Mar 12	FGD	24 Nov 13	9		
Goodwick	3 Dec 13	SWks	1 Dec 14	77	H, BC	207,892
Swindon Stock	16 Feb 15					
Goodwick	30 May 15					
Neath	Jun 17					
Tenby	Dec 18	SWks	2 Feb 20	519	H, BC	253,144
Swindon Stock	5 Jul 21					
Garnant	14 Nov 21					
Llanelly	Jan 23					
Garnant	Feb 23					
Llanelly	Mar 23					
Garnant	Apr 23	LLY	7 Feb 24	30	R	
Llanelly	8 Mar 24					
Garnant	Apr 24					
Llanelly	May 24	SWks	30 May 24	147	H, BC	270,448
Swindon Stock	24 Oct 24					
Neath	30 Oct 24					
Garnant	Nov 24					
Llanelly	Feb 25					
Garnant	May 25					
Llanelly	Jan 26					
Garnant	Oct 26					
Llanelly	Nov 26					
Garnant	Dec 26					
Neath	Jan 27	SWks	16 Jun 27	275	H, BC	296,007
Swindon Stock	17 Mar 28					
Neath	20 Apr 28	NEA	2 Aug 28	4	R	
Neath	6 Aug 28	SWks	19 Oct 28	159	H, BC	304,715
Pontypool Road	27 Mar 29					
Neath	21 Oct 29	NEA	26 May 30	161	H, BC	315,491
		SWks	9 Jul 30			
St Philip's Marsh	3 Nov 30	SPM	23 Feb 32	16	R	
St Philip's Marsh	10 Mar 32					
Swindon Stock	Sep 32					
Cirencester Stock	Dec 32	SWks				339,463
Condemned	1 Jul 33					

Recovered parts used for Trailer No.205 (Dia. A31)

No.84 (Diagram R)

Allocation	Date	Stop'd	Date	Days Stop'd	Catgy. Repair	Miles Run
New	Dec 07					
At Kidderminster	25 Apr 08					
Worcester	Jun 08					
Kidderminster	Jul 08					
Worcester	Nov 08					
Kidderminster	Dec 08	SWks	20 Jan 09	41	L	
Swindon Stock	2 Mar 09					
Southall	1 Apr 09	SWks	23 Dec 09	54	G, BC	61,840
Swindon Stock	15 Feb 10					
Tyseley	9 Mar 10	SRD	9 Aug 10	18	BC	77,130
Tyseley	27 Aug 10					
Stourbridge	Jan 11					
Tyseley	Feb 11	SRD	10 Mar 11	29	BC	90,449
Tyseley	8 Apr 11	SRD	22 Jun 11	22	G	96,339
Tyseley	14 Jul 11	TYS	29 Dec 11	13		
Tyseley	11 Jan 12	SRD	8 Feb 12	44	G	110,975
Tyseley	23 Mar 12	TYS	21 Jul 12	69		
Tyseley	28 Sep 12	SWks	20 Nov 12	87	H, BC	118,439
Swindon Stock	15 Feb 13					
Merthyr	20 Feb 13	SWks	7 Apr 15	261	H, BC	187,661
Swindon Stock	24 Dec 15					
Croes Newydd	5 Jan 16					
Chester	May 16	CHR	13 Jul 16	43	L	
Chester	25 Aug 16	SRD	13 Dec 16	29	H, BC	212,535
Stourbridge	11 Jan 17	SRD	22 Feb 17	25	H	214,412
Stafford Road	19 Mar 17	CNYD	6 Apr 17	15	R	
Stafford Road	21 Apr 17	CNYD	8 May 17	17	R	
Croes Newydd	25 May 17					
Swindon Stock	Jan 18					
Taunton	18 Feb 18	BTL	12 Apr 18	780		
		TN	May 18			
		SWks	22 Dec 19		H, BC	227,547
Swindon Stock	31 May 20					
Taunton	1 Jul 20	TN	17 Oct 21	53	R	
Taunton	9 Dec 21	SWks	15 Dec 21	75	H, BC	261,171
Swindon Stock	28 Feb 22					
Cambrian lines	4 Jul 22					
Stourbridge	26 Jul 22	SWks	4 Jun 23	266	H, BC	281,759
Gloucester	25 Feb 24					
Chalford	May 24					
Gloucester	Jun 24					

Allocation	*Date*	*Stop'd*	*Date*	*Days Stop'd*	*Catgy. Repair*	*Miles Run*
Chalford	Oct 24					
Gloucester	Dec 24	SWks	4 Feb 25	26	H, BC	313,102
Reading	2 Mar 25	OOC	6 Nov 25	15	R	
Reading	21 Nov 25	RDG	2 Mar 26	30	R	
Reading	1 Apr 26	SWks	12 Aug 26	91	L	
Swindon Stock	11 Nov 26					
Southall	9 Dec 26	OOC	31 Jan 27	294		
		SWks	25 Feb 27		H, BC	333,613
Southall	21 Nov 27	SWks	30 Apr 28	31	H, BC	343,738
Southall	31 May 28	SHL	19 Nov 28	18	R	
Southall	7 Dec 28	SHL	4 Apr 29	41	R	
Southall	15 May 29	SWks	2 Sep 29			365,949

Converted to Trailer No.183 (Dia. A26)

No.85 (Diagram R)

New	Dec 07					
In Swindon Stock	25 Apr 08					
Tyseley	28 May 08	SRD	3 Dec 08	13	BC	14,272
Tyseley	16 Dec 08	SRD	15 Sep 09	20	G	36,562
Tyseley	5 Oct 09	SRD	11 Apr 10	12	BC	54,370
Tyseley	23 Apr 10	SRD	30 Aug 10	20	BC	65,033
Tyseley	19 Sep 10					
Stourbridge	Dec 10	SRD	17 Mar 11	24	BC	77,754
Stourbridge	10 Apr 11					
Kidderminster	30 Jun 11					
Stourbridge	18 Jul 11	SWks	4 Sep 11	109	G, BC	86,822
Swindon Stock	22 Dec 11					
Stratford on Avon	30 Dec 11					
Worcester	Jan 12					
Kidderminster	Feb 12					
Worcester	Apr 12					
Kidderminster	May 12					
Worcester	Jun 12					
Kidderminster	Aug 12					
Worcester	Sep 12					
Kidderminster	Oct 12					
Worcester	Nov 12					
Kidderminster	Dec 12					
Merthyr	20 Feb 13	SWks	6 May 13	56	BC	131,908
Aberystwyth	1 Jul 13					
Neath	Oct 13					
Swindon Stock	Nov 13					
Southall	26 Nov 13	OOC	23 Feb 14	25	L	
Southall	20 Mar 14	SWks	30 Apr 14	65	H, BC	154,010
Aberystwyth	4 Jul 14	SWks	28 Sep 14	9	L	
Swindon Stock	7 Oct 14					
Taunton	12 Oct 14	BTL	22 Jan 15	14		
Taunton	5 Feb 15	SWks	1 Mar 15	1		
Taunton	2 Mar 15	TN	17 Mar 16	528		
		SWks	27 Mar 16		H, BC	189,954
Frome	27 Aug 17					
Trowbridge	Sep 17					
Frome	Nov 17	WES	11 May 20	745		
		SWks	5 Jul 20		H, BC	258,494
Swindon Stock	26 May 22					
Cambrian lines	14 Jun 22					
Oswestry	Aug 22					
Llanidloes	Dec 22					
Oswestry	Apr 23	SWks	12 Oct 23	60	H, BC	290,078
Reading	11 Dec 23	RDG	23 Apr 25	28	R	
Reading	21 May 25	SWks	31 Jul 25	195	H, BC	337,019
Swindon Stock	11 Feb 26					
Gloucester	10 Mar 26	GLO	17 Aug 26	20	R	
Gloucester	6 Sep 26					
Chalford	Oct 26					
Gloucester	Dec 26	SWks	5 Apr 27			369,060

Converted to Trailer No.154 (Dia. A26)

No.86 (Diagram R)

New	Dec 07					
In Swindon Stock	25 Apr 08					
Tyseley	22 Jun 08	SRD	24 Nov 08	3	BC	12,748
Tyseley	27 Nov 08	SRD	6 Aug 09	36	G, BC	36,078

Allocation	*Date*	*Stop'd*	*Date*	*Days Stop'd*	*Catgy. Repair*	*Miles Run*
Tyseley	11 Sep 09	SRD	5 Jan 10	15	L, BC	46,720
Tyseley	20 Jan 10	SWks	16 Jul 10	66	G, BC	58,477
Swindon Stock	20 Sep 10					
Weymouth	29 Sep 10	WEY	1 Dec 11	88		
		SWks	4 Dec 11		G, BC	87,982
Swindon Stock	27 Feb 12					
Stourbridge	20 May 12	SWks	23 Aug 12	48	G, BC	96,385
Swindon Stock	10 Oct 12					
Bristol	15 Oct 12					
Yatton	Nov 12					
Bristol	Dec 12					
Radstock	Feb 13					
Bristol	Apr 13					
Yatton	Jul 13					
Radstock	Oct 13					
Bristol	Nov 13					
Radstock	Nov 13					
Bristol	Dec 13	SWks	5 Feb 14	81	H, BC	138,880
Swindon Stock	27 Apr 14					
Merthyr	6 May 14	SWks	7 Apr 15	14		
Swindon Stock	21 Apr 15					
Ebbw Junction	Aug 15	SWks	1 Dec 15	715	H, BC	173,278
Swindon Stock	15 Nov 17					
Southall	16 Dec 17	SWks	11 Sep 18	97	H	189,927
Swindon Stock	17 Dec 18					
Bristol	22 Dec 18					
Yatton	May 19					
Bristol	Jun 19					
Yatton	Jul 19					
Bath	Aug 19					
Bristol	Aug 19					
Bath	Nov 19	BTL	25 Nov 19	23	R	
Bath	18 Dec 19					
Yatton	Apr 20					
Bristol	May 20	SWks	11 Nov 20	110	H, BC	230,150
Swindon Stock	1 Mar 21					
Exeter	25 Apr 21	NA	11 Apr 22	35	H	260,750
Exeter	16 May 22	NA	20 Jun 23	19	R	
Exeter	9 Jul 23	NA	5 Feb 24	21	H, BC	299,101
Exeter	26 Feb 24	SWks	5 Jan 25	266	H, BC	316,271
Yatton	28 Sep 25					
St Philip's Marsh	Nov 25					
Yatton	Jan 26					
St Philip's Marsh	Feb 26					
Yatton	Apr 26					
St Philip's Marsh	May 26					
Bath	Nov 26					
St Philip's Marsh	Jan 27					
Yatton	Feb 27					
Bath	Mar 27					
St Philip's Marsh	Apr 27	SWks	30 Aug 27	48	H, BC	348,907
Yatton	17 Oct 27					
St Philip's Marsh	Nov 27					
Yatton	Dec 27					
St Philip's Marsh	Jan 28					
Yatton	Aug 28					
St Philip's Marsh	Sep 28	SWks	14 Mar 29	188	H, BC	381,640
St. Philips Marsh	18 Sep 29					
Yatton	Dec 29	SWks	24 Dec 29	113	H, BC	389,579
Slough	16 Apr 30					
Southall	Jun 30	SWks	9 Aug 30	12	R	
Southall	21 Aug 30	SHL	26 Nov 30	140		
		SWks	11 Dec 30		G, BC	398,722
Swindon Stock	15 Apr 31					
Neath	Oct 31	NEA	23 Apr 32	33	L	407,694
Neath	26 May 32	NEA	20 Jun '32	25	L	
Neath	15 Jul 32	NEA	11 Jan 33			
		SWks				417,181
Condemned	1 Jul 33					

Converted to Trailer No.206 (Dia. A16)

Allocation	Date	Stop'd	Date	Days Stop'd	Catgy. Repair	Miles Run
No.87 (Diagram R)						
New	Dec 07					
In Swindon Stock	25 Apr 08					
Tyseley	22 Jun 08	SRD	31 Dec 08	9	L BC	13,780
Tyseley	9 Jan 09	TYS	7 May 09	30	L	
Tyseley	6 Jun 09	SRD	19 Nov 09	7	G, BC	35,157
Tyseley	26 Nov 09	SRD	16 Jun 10	29	BC	50,867
Tyseley	15 Jul 10	SRD	30 Sep 10	25	BC	55,902
Tyseley	25 Oct 10	TYS	6 Feb 11	4	L	
Tyseley	10 Feb 11	TYS	24 Feb 12	8		
		SRD	+		G, BC	91,509
Tyseley	3 Mar 12	SWks	14 Jun 12	98	G, BC	96,298
Swindon Stock	20 Sep 12					
Yatton	30 Sep 12					
Bristol	Jul 13					
Radstock	Jan 14					
Yatton	Feb 14					
Bristol	Apr 14					
Yatton	Jun 14					
Bristol	Aug 14					
Yatton	Sep 14					
Radstock	Oct 14					
Yatton	Oct 14					
Radstock	Nov 14					
Yatton	Dec 14					
Bath	Jan 15	SWks	4 Feb 15	64	H, BC	167,263
Swindon Stock	9 Apr 15					
Cheltenham	21 May 15	SWks	9 Dec 15	208	H, BC	197,956
Swindon Stock	4 Jul 16					
Croes Newydd	13 Jul 16	SRD	27 Sep 16	27	H, BC	205,665
Stafford Road	24 Oct 16					
Croes Newydd	29 Oct 16					
Chester	Jan 17	CHR	10 Apr 17	1,675		
		CNYD	Jan 18			
		SWks	22 Jul 19		H, BC	219,744
Swindon Stock	10 Nov 21					
Chippenham	22 Dec 21					
Trowbridge	Jan 22					
Chippenham	Jan 22					
Gloucester	May 22	SWks	5 Aug 22	34	H, BC	232,055
Swindon Works	8 Sep 22	SWks	30 Sep 22	20	BC #	232,069
Swindon Stock	20 Oct 22					
Gloucester	27 Oct 22	GLO	28 Nov 22	38		
		SWks	7 Dec 22		L	
Swindon Stock	5 Jan 23	OOC	19 Jun 23	15	R	
Reading	1 Feb 23					
Reading	4 Jul 23	OOC	19 Sep 23	54	L	
Reading	12 Nov 23	RDG	24 Dec 23	44	R	
Reading	6 Feb 24	OOC	4 Mar 24	14	R	
Reading	18 Mar 24	OOC	11 Aug 24	14	R	
Reading	25 Aug 24	OOC	23 Feb 25	274		
		SWks	10 Mar 25		H, BC	280,832
Swindon Stock	24 Nov 25					
Bath	10 Dec 25					
St Philip's Marsh	Jan 26	SPM	15 Mar 26	33	R	
St Philip's Marsh	17 Apr 26	SPM	11 Apr 27	14	R	
St Philip's Marsh	25 Apr 27					
Bath	May 27					
St Philip's Marsh	Jun 27	SPM	25 Jul 27	32	R	
St Philip's Marsh	26 Aug 27	SWks	5 Jan 28			313,946

Converted to Trailer No.155 (Dia. A26)
NOTE
† *Car failed on a trial run following its repairs from 5 Aug - 8 Sep 22.*
The 14 miles run were on the trial trip.

Allocation	Date	Stop'd	Date	Days Stop'd	Catgy. Repair	Miles Run
No.88 (Diagram R)						
New	Jan 08					
At Swindon Stock	25 Apr 08					
Tyseley	22 Jan 09	SRD	6 Jul 09	22	L, BC	29,917
Tyseley	28 Jul 09	SRD	15 Oct 09	8	L, BC	38,727
Tyseley	23 Oct 09	SWks	10 Mar 10	106	G, BC	51,241
Swindon Stock	24 Jun 10					
Croes Newydd	17 Jul 10					
Corwen	Aug 10					
Croes Newydd	Oct 10					
Corwen	Aug 11					
Croes Newydd	Oct 11	SRD	1 Jan 12	33	G, BC	97,739
Swindon Stock	3 Feb 12					
Croes Newydd	Feb 12					
Corwen	Jul 12					
Croes Newydd	Aug 12					
Corwen	Nov 12					
Croes Newydd	Dec 12	BHD	22 Jan 13	24	L	
Croes Newydd	15 Feb 13	SRD	29 Apr 13	8	BC	125,509
Croes Newydd	7 May 13	CNYD	18 Nov 13	8	L	
Croes Newydd	26 Nov 13	CNYD	18 Dec 13	5	L	
Croes Newydd	23 Dec 13	CNYD	3 Jan 14	6	L	
Croes Newydd	9 Jan 14					
Wrexham	Feb 14	SWks	27 Feb 14	92	H, BC	143,367
Swindon Stock	30 May 14					
Croes Newydd	12 Jun 14					
Corwen	Nov 14					
Croes Newydd	Dec 14					
Corwen	Feb 15					
Chester	Mar 15					
Croes Newydd	Apr 15					
Corwen	May 15					
Croes Newydd	Jul 15	OXY	30 Oct 15	39	H, BC	183,091
Croes Newydd	8 Dec 15	SWks	11 Jul 16	319	H, BC	194,035
Taunton	26 May 17	SDst	9 May 18	14	L	
Taunton	23 May 18	TN	10 Dec 18	20		
		BTL			R	
Taunton	30 Dec 18	TN	5 Sep 19	98	L	
Taunton	12 Dec 19	SWks	12 Jul 20	611	H, BC	257,392
Swindon Stock	15 Mar 22					
Southall	Jun 22	OOC	19 Oct 22	16	R	
Southall	4 Nov 22	OOC	22 May 23	17	R	
Southall	8 Jun 23	SWks	16 Jul 23	45	H, BC	283,788
Bristol	30 Aug 23					
Yatton	Sep 24					
Bristol	Oct 24					
Yatton	Nov 24					
St Philip's Marsh	Nov 24	SWks	15 Apr 25	131	H, BC	333,992
St Philip's Marsh	24 Aug 25					
Frome	Oct 25	WES	6 Dec 26	16	R	
Frome	22 Dec 26					
Westbury	Feb 27					
Frome	Mar 27					
Westbury	Apr 27	SPM	20 Apr 27	15	R	
Frome	5 May 27	WES	25 May 27	23	R	
Frome	17 Jun 27	SWks	4 Nov 27	98	H, BC	376,238
Neath	10 Feb 28	NEA	11 May 28	6	R	
Neath	17 May 28	NEA	9 Jun 28	53		
		SWks	11 Jun 28		H, BC	383,808
Swindon Stock	3 Aug 28	NEA	3 Jan 29	55	L	
Neath	27 Feb 29	SWks	8 Apr 29	273	H, BC	401,927
Reading	6 Jan 30	SWks	14 Jul 30	210	H, BC	410,076
St. Philip's Marsh	9 Feb 31	SWks	31 Mar 31	37	G	413,113
Swindon Stock	7 May 31					
Southall	9 Jan 32	SHL	8 Apr 32	27	R	
Southall	5 May 32	SHL	29 Oct 32	18	R	
Southall	16 Nov 32	SHL	6 Dec 32	25	R	
Southall	31 Dec 32	SHL	18 Feb 33	20	R	
Southall	10 Mar 33	SHL	17 Jul 33	282		
		SFPI	15 Aug 33			
		SWks	31 Jan 34		G,	433,415
Swindon Stock	25 Apr 34					
Stourbridge	15 Jun 34	STB	27 Aug 34	49		
		SFPI	7 Sep 34			
		SWks	12 Sep 34		L	
Stourbridge	15 Oct 34	STB	2 May 35	28		
		SRD	14 May 35		L	
Stourbridge	30 May 35	SFPI	16 Oct 35			456,375
Condemned	19 Oct 35					
Broken up.						

No.89 (Diagram R)

Allocation	*Date*	*Stop'd*	*Date*	*Days Stop'd*	*Catgy. Repair*	*Miles Run*
New	Dec 07					
In Swindon Stock	25 Apr 08					
Cheltenham	26 Jun 08					
Chalford	Jul 08					
Cheltenham	Sep 08					
Gloucester	Jun 09					
Chalford	Jul 09					
Cheltenham	Dec 09					
Gloucester	Jan 10	SWks	4 Apr 10	24	BC	60,464
Southall	28 Apr 10	OOC	14 Nov 10	12		
Southall	26 Nov 10	SHL	22 Feb 11	3	L	
Southall	25 Feb 11	SHL	1 Mar 11	16		
Southall	17 Mar 11	SWks	23 May 11	87	G, BC	106,232
Swindon Stock	18 Aug 11					
Kidderminster	22 Nov 11					
Stratford on Avon	Mar 12					
Worcester	May 12					
Kidderminster	Jun 12					
Stratford on Avon	Jul 12	SWks	9 Oct 12	35	H, BC	130,616
Pontypool Road	13 Nov 12	NPT	25 Oct 13			
		PPRD		20		
Pontypool Road	14 Nov 13	SWks	16 Sep 14	67	H, BC	177,799
Yatton	22 Nov 14					
Radstock	Dec 14					
Yatton	Jan 15					
Bristol	Apr 15					
Yatton	May 15					
Bristol	Jun 15					
Yatton	Jul 15					
Bristol	Aug 15					
Bath	Sep 15					
Yatton	Oct 15					
Bristol	Nov 15	SWks	22 Jan 16	270	H, BC	209,357
Swindon Stock	18 Oct 16					
Bath	20 Nov 16					
Bristol	Dec 16					
Bath	Feb 17					
Bristol	May 17	BTL	25 Jul 17	22	R	
Bristol	16 Aug 17					
Bath	Oct 17					
Yatton	Nov 17					
Bath	Dec 17					
Bristol	Jan 18					
Yatton	Feb 18					
Bath	Mar 18					
Bristol	May 18					
Yatton	Jul 18					
Bristol	Aug 18					
Yatton	Sep 18					
Bristol	Oct 18					
Yatton	Dec 18					
Bristol	Feb 19					
Yatton	Mar 19	BTL	2 Apr 19	968		
		SWks	29 Dec 19		H, BC	275,019
Swindon Stock	25 Nov 21					
Yeovil	17 Jun 22	SWks	17 Apr 23	22	H, BC	312,105
Swindon Stock	9 May 23					
Stourbridge	21 May 23	STB	28 Mar 24	21	R	
Stourbridge	18 Apr 24	SRD	20 Sep 24	23	H, BC	344,426
Stourbridge	13 Oct 24	SWks	20 Apr 25	253	H, BC	354,134
Swindon Stock	29 Dec 25					
Taunton	6 Feb 26	NA	20 Jan 27	37	R	
Taunton	26 Feb 27	TN	28 Mar 27	16	R	
Taunton	13 Apr 27	NA	2 Jun 27			
		SWks	2 Jun 27			376,400

Converted to Trailer No.156 (Dia. A29)

No.90 (Diagram R)

Allocation	*Date*	*Stop'd*	*Date*	*Days Stop'd*	*Catgy. Repair*	*Miles Run*
New	Dec 07					
At Truro	25 Apr 08	NA	1 Jul 08	3	BC	
Helston	4 Jul 08	NA	3 Oct 08	6	L, BC	19,404
Exeter	9 Oct 08	EXE	26 Nov 08	77	L, BC	28,946
		NA	Jan 09			
Penzance	11 Feb 09					
Truro	Apr 09					
Newquay	Jun 09	NA	5 Jul 09	4	L, BC	47,740
Truro	9 Jul 09					
Newquay	Aug 09					
Truro	Sep 09					
Penzance	Nov 09	NA	3 Dec 09	5	L, BC	57,698
Newquay	8 Dec 09	NA	19 Feb 10	10	L, BC	64,348
Newquay	1 Mar 10					
Truro	Apr 10					
Laira	May 10					
Penzance	Jun 10					
Helston	Jul 10					
Penzance	Oct 10	NA	3 Nov 10	8	L, BC	83,226
Penzance	11 Nov 10					
Truro	Mar 11	NA	4 May 11	51	G&B, BC	99,349
Truro	24 Jun 11	NA	3 Oct 11	2	BC	102,480
Truro	5 Oct 11	NA	7 Mar 12	60	BC	113,417
Laira	6 May 12					
Truro	Jun 12	NA	17 Jul 12	52	G&B, BC	115,319
Newton Abbot	7 Sep 12					
Truro	Nov 12	SWks	2 May 13	46	H, BC	137,813
Taunton	17 Jun 13	SWks	2 Nov 14	114	H, BC	175,675
Swindon Stock	24 Feb 15					
Pontypool Road	5 Mar 15					
Newport	Oct 15					
Aberdare	Nov 15					
Weymouth	7 Feb 16					
Bath	Sep 16					
Bristol	Sep 16	BTL	18 Nov 16	966		
		SWks	9 Dec 18		H, BC	216,277
Cheltenham	12 Jul 19					
Taunton	14 Aug 19	BTL	26 Sep 19	14	R	
Taunton	10 Oct 19	TN	2 Jan 20	21	R	
Taunton	23 Jan 20	TN	29 Nov 20	28	R	
Taunton	27 Dec 20	SWks	12 May 21	292	H, BC	265,494
Swindon Stock	28 Feb 22					
Bristol	26 May 22	SWks	30 Nov 22	209	H, BC	285,851
Pontypool Road	27 Jun 23	PPRD	24 Oct 24	55		
		SWks	3 Nov 24		H, BC	322,119
Bath	18 Dec 24					
St Philip's Marsh	Jan 25					
Yatton	May 25					
St Philip's Marsh	Jun 25	SWks	28 Sep 25	77	H, BC	347,603
Swindon Stock	14 Dec 25					
Southall	27 Jan 26	SHL	8 Dec 26	63	R	
Southall	9 Feb 27	SHL	20 Feb 27	46	R	
Southall	7 Apr 27	OOC	12 Nov 27			
		SWks	28 Nov 27			361,864

Converted to Trailer No.192 (Dia. A26)

No.91 (Diagram R)

Allocation	*Date*	*Stop'd*	*Date*	*Days Stop'd*	*Catgy. Repair*	*Miles Run*
New	Dec 07					
At Merthyr	25 Apr 08	SWks	17 Mar 10	72	G, BC	74,991
Swindon Stock	28 May 10					
Taunton	20 Jun 10	SWks	25 Jan 12	133	G, BC	118,920
Swindon Stock	6 Jun 12					
Whitland	5 Jul 12					
Southall	26 Sep 12	SWks	11 Aug 13	29	H, BC	161,001
Swindon Stock	9 Sep 13					
Southall	12 Sep 13	SWks	26 Nov 13	66	H, BC	171,708
Swindon Stock	31 Jan 14					
Didcot	26 Feb 14	SWks	28 Jan 15	146	H, BC	212,930
Swindon Stock	23 Jun 15					
Yatton	24 Sep 15					
Bath	Oct 15	SWks	8 Jan 16	100	H	222,569
Swindon Stock	17 Apr 16					
Stourbridge	15 May 16	SRD	5 Jun 17	36	H, BC	245,041
Stourbridge	11 Jul 17					
Kidderminster	12 Feb 18					
Worcester	May 18	SWks	19 May 19	176	H, BC	259,644
Swindon Stock	11 Nov 19					
Chippenham	20 Nov 19	SWks	9 Dec 19	0	In & out	
Swindon Stock	9 Dec 19					

Allocation	Date	Stop'd	Date	Days Stop'd	Catgy. Repair	Miles Run
Chester	11 Dec 19					
Croes Newydd	Jan 20	SWks	22 Feb 21	193	H, BC	284,393
Swindon Stock	3 Sep 21					
Bristol	21 Nov 21					
Bath	Jan 22					
Bristol	Jan 22					
Yatton	Feb 22					
Bath	Mar 22	BTL	14 Apr 23	26	R	
Bath	10 May 23					
Bristol	Jun 22					
Bath	Sep 22					
Bristol	Nov 22					
Bath	Dec 22					
Bristol	Dec 22					
Bath	Jan 23					
Bristol	Jan 23					
Yatton	Sep 23	BTL	17 Sep 23	223		
		SWks	31 Oct 23		H, BC	338,944
Bristol	27 Apr 24					
Yatton	May 24					
Bristol	Jun 24	SWks	3 Jul 24	29	H, BC	347,614
Swindon Stock	1 Aug 24					
Yatton	9 Aug 24					
St Philip's Marsh	Sep 24	SWks	14 Feb 25	28	H, BC	368,722
St Philip's Marsh	14 Mar 25	SWks	22 Jun 25	25	L	
St Philip's Marsh	17 Jul 25					
Bath	Nov 25					
St Philip's Marsh	Dec 25					
Yatton	Mar 26					
St Philip's Marsh	Apr 26	SWks	5 Oct 26	209	H, BC	402,071
Swindon Stock	2 May 27					
Yatton	1 Jun 27					
St Philip's Marsh	Aug 27	SPM	20 Oct 27	22	R	
Yatton	11 Nov 27					
St Philip's Marsh	Dec 27					
Yatton	Feb 28					
St Philip's Marsh	Mar 28					
Yatton	Apr 28					
St Philip's Marsh	Jun 28					
Yatton	Sep 28					
St Philip's Marsh	Oct 28	SWks	30 Jan 29	188	H, BC	444,876
Neath	6 Aug 29	NEA	30 Oct 29	30	R	
Neath	29 Nov 29	NEA	31 May 30	31	R	
Neath	1 Jul 30	NEA	4 Jun 31	46	L	
Neath	20 Jul 31	NEA	12 Nov 31	19	L	
Neath	1 Dec 31	NEA	14 Dec 31	14	R	
Neath	28 Dec 31	NEA	13 Jan 32	287		
		SWks	12 Feb 32		G, BC	488,297
Swindon Stock	26 Oct 32					
Southall	Aug 33	SHL	2 Feb 34	53		
		SFPI	27 Feb 34			
		SWks	6 Mar 34		L	
Southall	27 Mar 34	SHL	3 Jan 35			
		SWks	21 Jan 35			512,641
Condemned	9 Feb 35					

Converted to Trailer No.210 (Dia. A26)

No.92 (Diagram R)

Allocation	Date	Stop'd	Date	Days Stop'd	Catgy. Repair	Miles Run
New	Jan 08					
Southall	16 Apr 08	SWks	15 Dec 09	27	G, BC	66,423
Southall	11 Jan 10	SHL	11 Jul 10	12	L	
Southall	23 Jul 10	SWks	20 Jan 11	78	G, BC	112,588
Swindon Stock	8 Apr 11					
Merthyr	20 Jun 11	SWks	4 Jan 13	58	H, BC	156,350
Swindon Stock	3 Mar 13					
Cheltenham	16 Apr 13	GLO	27 Dec 13	2		
Cheltenham	29 Dec 13	SWks	27 Feb 14	22	H, BC	191,562
Swindon Stock	21 Mar 14					
Kidderminster	31 Mar 14					
Worcester	Sep 14					
Kidderminster	Feb 15					
Worcester	Apr 15	SWks	26 Apr 15	283	H, BC	230,985
Swindon Stock	3 Feb 16					
Bristol	7 Feb 16					
Yatton	Mar 16					
Weymouth	Apr 16					
Yatton	Sep 16					
Bath	Sep 16	BTL	26 Oct 16	1,372		
		SWks	28 Oct 19		H, BC	247,608
Gloucester	29 Jul 20					
Swindon Stock	Dec 20					
Trowbridge	17 Jan 21					
Swindon Stock	Feb 21					
Stourbridge	4 Mar 21	SWks	31 Jul 22	389	H, BC	293,441
Southall	24 Aug 23	SHL	24 Nov 23	17	R	
Southall	11 Dec 23	OOC	5 Feb 24	16	R	
Southall	21 Feb 24	SHL	26 Jul 24	35	R	
Southall	30 Aug 24	OOC	8 Sep 24	22	R	
Southall	30 Sep 24	SWks	17 Nov 24	35	H, BC	316,704
Swindon Stock	22 Dec 24					
Frome	29 Dec 24	SWks	9 Sep 25	203	H, BC	336,446
Frome	31 Mar 26	SWks	20 Oct 26	215	H, BC	345,618
Frome	23 May 27	WES	9 Nov 27	21	R	
Frome	30 Nov 27					
Pontypool Road	14 Jan 28	PPRD	14 Feb 28	226		
		SWks	28 Feb 28		H, BC	361,706
Swindon Stock	27 Sep 28					
St. Philip's Marsh	29 Sep 28					
Yatton	Oct 28					
St Philip's Marsh	Nov 28					
Yatton	Jan 29					
St Philip's Marsh	Mar 29					
Yatton	Jun 29					
Bath	Jul 29					
St Philip's Marsh	Sep 29	SPM	4 Jun 30	141		
		SWks	17 Jun 30		H, BC	412,825
Exeter	23 Oct 30	EXE	15 Oct 31	131		
		SWks	10 Nov 31		L, BC	446,261
Swindon Stock	23 Feb 32					
Southall	Jun 33	SHL	7 Feb 34	279		
		SFPI	8 May 34			
		SWks	27 Jul 34		G, BC	457,301
St. Philip's Marsh	13 Nov 34	SPM	31 Jul 35			
		SFPI	15 Oct 35			
		SWks	19 Oct 35			483,696
Condemned	19 Oct 35					

Broken up.

No.93 (Diagram R)

Allocation	Date	Stop'd	Date	Days Stop'd	Catgy. Repair	Miles Run
New	Feb 08					
Southall	5 Mar 08	SHL	29 Mar 09	12	L	
Southall	10 Apr 09	SWks	30 Aug 09	84	G, BC	54,806
Swindon Stock	15 Nov 09					
Stourbridge	22 Nov 09	SRD	5 May 10	8	L&B, BC	66,349
Stourbridge	13 May 10	SRD	25 Nov 10	24	G, BC	82,107
Stourbridge	19 Dec 10	STB	23 Mar 11	22		
		SRD	+		BC	89,620
Stourbridge	14 Apr 11	SRD	23 Nov 11	194		
		SWks	6 Dec 11		G, BC	105,882
Swindon Stock	4 Jun 12					
Whitland	5 Jul 12					
Stratford on Avon	3 Oct 12	SWks	11 Nov 12	23		
Swindon Stock	4 Dec 12	SWks	10 Dec 12	4		
Swindon Stock	14 Dec 12					
Pontypool Road	27 Dec 12	SWks	3 Mar 13	9	L, BC	118,398
Swindon Stock	12 Mar 13					
Pontypool Road	7 Apr 13	SWks	2 Sep 14	79	H, BC	157,840
Swindon Stock	20 Nov 14					
Stourbridge	1 Dec 14	SRD	12 Aug 15	49	H, BC	178,281
Stourbridge	30 Sep 15	SRD	14 Oct 15	22	H, BC	178,541
Stourbridge	5 Nov 15	STB	5 May 16	30		
Stourbridge	4 Jun 16	SWks	8 Aug 16	374	H, BC	188,029
Swindon Stock	13 Aug 17					
Bath	17 Aug 17					
Bristol	Sep 17					
Bath	Nov 17					

Allocation	*Date*	*Stop'd*	*Date*	*Days Stop'd*	*Catgy. Repair*	*Miles Run*
Bristol	Dec 17					
Yatton	Jan 18					
Bristol	Feb 18					
Yatton	Apr 18	SPM	7 May 18	17	R	
Yatton	24 May 18					
Bristol	Jul 18					
Yatton	Aug 18					
Bristol	Sep 18					
Yatton	Oct 18					
Bristol	Nov 18					
Yatton	Jan 19					
Bath	Feb 19					
Trowbridge	9 Feb 19					
Yatton	Mar 19					
Bristol	Apr 19	SPM	6 May 19	17	R	
Yatton	23 May 19					
Bristol	Jul 19					
Yatton	Aug 19					
Bristol	Nov 19					
Yatton	Dec 19					
Bristol	Feb 20	SPM	22 Mar 20	301		
		SWks	7 Apr 20		H, BC	245,594
Swindon Stock	17 Jan 21					
Croes Newydd	22 Feb 21	CNYD	14 Feb 22	15	R	
Croes Newydd	1 Mar 22	CNYD	26 Apr 22	94	R	
Croes Newydd	29 Jul 22	SWks	12 Sep 22	70	H, BC	261,681
Bristol	21 Nov 22	SPM	19 Apr 23	197		
		SWks	7 May 23		H, BC	278,024
Swindon Stock	2 Nov 23					
Gloucester	7 Nov 23	SWks	9 Jan 25	83	H, BC	319,522
Gloucester	2 Apr 25					
Chalford	Jun 25					
Gloucester	Aug 25					
Chalford	Nov 25					
Gloucester	Nov 25	SWks	8 Jan 26	140	L	
Swindon Stock	28 May 26					
Reading	19 Aug 26	SWks	8 Oct 26	83	H, BC	347,005
Swindon Stock	30 Dec 26					
Taunton	22 Jan 27	NA	9 Aug 27	3	H, BC	364,658
Taunton	12 Aug 27	TN	12 Oct 27	21	R	
Taunton	2 Nov 27	TN	11 Nov 27	19	R	
Taunton	30 Nov 27	TN	22 Feb 28	28	R	
Taunton	21 Mar 28	SWks	21 Aug 28	185	H, BC	385,649
St Philip's Marsh	22 Feb 29					
Yatton	Mar 29					
St Philip's Marsh	Apr 29					
Yatton	Jan 30					
St Philip's Marsh	Apr 30	SPM	19 Feb 31	158		
		SWks	31 Mar 31		G, BC	433,261
Swindon Stock	27 Jul 31					
Stourbridge	23 Jan 32	TYS	6 Aug 32	54	L	
Stourbridge	29 Sep 32	STB	28 Jun 33	84		
		SFPI	11 Jul 33			
		SWks	11 Aug 33		L	
Stourbridge	20 Sep 33	BAN	20 May 34			
		SFPI	5 Jun 34			
		SWks	17 Nov 34			479,006
Condemned	19 Nov 34					

Converted to Trailer No.212 (Dia. A26)

No.94 (Diagram R)

New	Feb 08					
Truro	25 Apr 08	NA	25 Jul 08	4	L, BC	15,608
Newquay	29 Jul 08					
Truro	Sep 08	NA	1 Oct 08	4	L, BC	17,486
Truro	5 Oct 08	NA	21 Jan 09	5	L, BC	25,547
Exeter	26 Jan 09	NA	24 Feb 09	66	G, BC	39,911
Exeter	1 May 09	NA	26 Jul 09	0	BC	54,760
Exeter	26 Jul 09	NA	12 Nov 09	7	L, BC	74,155
Exeter	19 Nov 09					
Truro	Dec 09					
Exeter	Jan 10	NA	2 Mar 10	10	L, BC	91,129
Exeter	12 Mar 10	NA	13 Jul 10	16	BC	

Allocation	*Date*	*Stop'd*	*Date*	*Days Stop'd*	*Catgy. Repair*	*Miles Run*
Exeter	29 Jul 10					
Newton Abbot	Oct 10					
Exeter	Nov 10	NA	10 Oct 11	2	BC	
Exeter	12 Oct 11	NA	19 Jan 11	2	BC	137,700
Exeter	21 Jan 11	NA	17 May 11	3	BC	156,848
Exeter	20 May 11	NA	9 Aug 11	36	BC	
Exeter	14 Sep 11	NA	31 Oct 11	28	G, BC	185,675
Newton Abbot	28 Nov 11	NA	19 Jan 12	99		
Penzance	27 Apr 12	NA	7 Sep 12	34	BC	210,155
Penzance	11 Oct 12	SWks	15 May 13	61	H, BC	232,299
Stratford on Avon	15 Jul 13	SWks	30 Jun 14	95	H, BC	262,780
Yatton	3 Oct 14					
Bristol	Oct 14					
Yatton	Dec 14					
Weymouth	Jan 15	SWks	7 Feb 16	157	H, BC	302,999
Swindon Stock	13 Jul 16					
Stratford on Avon	29 Jul 16					
Malvern Wells	Apr 17					
Stratford on Avon	Jun 17					
Kidderminster	Aug 17					
Worcester	Mar 18	SWks	19 May 19	260	H, BC	322,405
Bristol	3 Feb 20	BTL	22 Jun 20	21	R	
Yatton	13 Jul 20	SWks	27 Oct 20	49	H, BC	349,958
Swindon Stock	15 Dec 20					
Trowbridge	21 Jan 21					
Chippenham	Aug 21					
Trowbridge	Oct 21	WES	10 Jul 22	346		
		SWks	15 Aug 22		H, BC	375,966
Swindon Stock	21 Jun 23					
Neyland	29 Jun 23	NEY	21 Sep 23	25	R	
Neath	16 Oct 23	SWks	5 May 25	225	H, BC	426,209
Swindon Stock	16 Dec 25					
Chalford	4 Feb 26					
Gloucester	Jun 26	GLO	26 Sep 26	25	R	
Gloucester	21 Oct 26	SWks	19 Jan 27	334	H, BC	455,802
Reading	19 Dec 27	RDG	14 Dec 28	20	R	
Reading	3 Jan 29	RDG	5 Aug 29	10	L	
Reading	15 Aug 29	SWks	17 Oct 29			492,799

Converted to Trailer No.185 (Dia. A26)

No.95 (Diagram R)

New	Feb 08					
In Swindon Stock	25 Apr 08					
Stratford on Avon	23 Jul 08					
Worcester	Jan 09					
Stratford on Avon	Feb 09	SWks	8 May 09	51	G, BC	17,642
Swindon Stock	28 Jun 09					
Tenby	5 Jul 09					
Tyseley	11 Oct 09	SWks	31 Mar 10	61	G, BC	38,248
		SWks	[May 10]		BC	38,318
Swindon Stock	31 May 10					
Tyseley	8 Jul 10	SRD	30 Aug 11	25	G, BC	80,780
Tyseley	24 Sep 11	TYS	28 Nov 11	10		
Tyseley	8 Dec 11	SRD	5 Jan 12	22	BC	90,769
Tyseley	27 Jan 12	TYS	22 Feb 12	11		
Tyseley	4 Mar 12	TYS	13 Jun 12	30	BC	96,811
Tyseley	13 Jul 12	TYS	3 Sep 12	88		
		SWks	11 Sep 12		G, BC	102,327
Swindon Stock	30 Nov 12					
Tyseley	3 Dec 12	SRD	19 Apr 13	18	H	112,993
Wolverhampton	7 May 13					
Stourbridge	Jun 13					
Tyseley	Jul 13	SRD	28 Sep 13	17	L, BC	122,596
Stourbridge	15 Oct 13					
Tyseley	Nov 13	SRD	9 Dec 13	10	L	
Tyseley	19 Dec 13	CNYD	9 Jan 14	4	L	
Tyseley	13 Jan 14					
Stourbridge	Feb 14	STB	7 Jul 14	23	L	
Stourbridge	30 Jul 14	SRD	16 Oct 14	22	H, BC	143,857
Stourbridge	7 Nov 14	SRD	4 Nov 15	55	H, BC	161,163
Stourbridge	29 Dec 15	STB	1 Jan 17	1,346		
		SRD	Jun 18			
		CNYD	Jul 19			
		SWks	28 Dec 19		H, BC	172,749

Allocation	*Date*	*Stop'd*	*Date*	*Days Stop'd*	*Catgy. Repair*	*Miles Run*
Swindon Stock	8 Sep 20					
Bristol	15 Oct 20					
Bath	Dec 20					
Yatton	Jun 21					
Bath	Oct 21					
Bristol	Nov 21					
Bath	Jan 22					
Bristol	Feb 22					
Yatton	Apr 22	SWks	26 May 22	106	H, BC	213,992
Swindon Stock	9 Sep 22					
Bath	12 Sep 22					
Bristol	Nov 22					
Bath	Dec 22					
Bristol	May 23					
Bath	Jul 23					
Yatton	Sep 23					
Bristol	Oct 23					
Bath	Dec 23					
Bristol	Jan 24					
Yatton	Mar 24					
Bristol	May 24					
Yatton	Jul 24					
Bristol	Aug 24					
Bath	Sep 24					
Yatton	Oct 24	SWks	13 Oct 24	290	H, BC	274,427
Stourbridge	30 Jul 25					
Stafford Road	Nov 25	SRD	14 Apr 26	31	H	294,666
Stafford Road	15 May 26					
Stourbridge	Jun 26	STB	24 Sep 26	48		
		SRD	9 Oct 26		H	302,516
Croes Newydd	11 Nov 26	CNYD	16 Feb 27	8	R	
Croes Newydd	24 Feb 27	SRD	18 Oct 27	9	H, BC	315,228
Shrewsbury	27 Oct 27					
Croes Newydd	Dec 27	SRD	7 Jun 28	173		
		SWks	4 Oct 28		H, BC	331,935
Birkenhead	27 Nov 28	SWks	10 Sep 29			354,024

Converted to Trailer No.184 (Dia. A26)

No.96 (Diagram R)

Allocation	*Date*	*Stop'd*	*Date*	*Days Stop'd*	*Catgy. Repair*	*Miles Run*
New	Feb 08					
Swindon Stock	25 Apr 08					
Stratford on Avon	23 Jul 08	SWks	1 Jan 09	8	L, BC	10,710
Swindon Stock	9 Jan 09					
Truro	2 Feb 09					
Newquay	Mar 09					
Penzance	Apr 09	NA	20 Jul 09	9	L, BC	26,918
Laira	29 Jul 09					
Helston	Aug 09	NA	27 Sep 09	10	L, BC	32,178
Laira	7 Oct 09					
Truro	Nov 09	NA	14 Dec 09	4	L, BC	35,818
Truro	18 Dec 09	NA	21 Jan 10	7	L, BC	39,083
Newquay	28 Jan 10					
Truro	Mar 10					
Newquay	Apr 10					
Trour	May 10	TR	1 Jul 10	17	BC	48,864
Truro	18 Jul 10					
Newquay	Aug 10					
Truro	Sep 10	NA	4 Nov 10	6	BC	52,980
Truro	10 Nov 10	NA?			BC	60,055
Penzance	Mar 11					
Helston	Jul 11	NA	12 Aug 11	82	G, BC	73,509
Truro	2 Nov 11					
Penzance	Dec 11					
Helston	Jul 12					
Penzance	Oct 12	NA	19 Oct 12	20	BC	100,087
Truro	8 Nov 12	TR	2 Dec 12	46		
Truro	17 Jan 13	NA	19 Mar 13	47		
		SWks	2 May 13		BC	105,823
Kidderminster	5 May 13					
Worcester	Jun 13					
Kidderminster	Jul 13					
Worcester	Aug 13					
Kidderminster	Nov 13	SWks	22 Nov 13	65	BC	122,065
Swindon Stock	26 Jan 14					
Cheltenham	27 Feb 14	SWks	20 Apr 15	289	H, BC	175,902
Swindon Stock	3 Feb 16					
Chalford	17 Mar 16					
Cheltenham	Apr 16					
Gloucester	1 Feb 17	GLO	19 Feb 17	123		
		SWks	19 Feb 17		H, BC	223,851
Swindon Stock	22 Jun 17					
Croes Newydd	25 Jun 17					
Chester	Sep 17	OXY	28 Mar 18	335		
		SWks	30 Apr 18		H, BC	242,122
Stourbridge	26 Feb 19	TYS	27 Feb 20	17	H, BC	263,314
Stourbridge	15 Mar 20	SWks	4 Mar 21	175	H, BC	281,008
Swindon Stock	26 Aug 21					
Gloucester	31 Aug 21	SWks	25 Nov 21	45	H, BC	292,387
Swindon Stock	9 Jan 22					
Southall	7 Mar 22	SLO	25 Aug 22	22	R	
Southall	16 Sep 22	OOC	6 Mar 23	14	R	
Southall	20 Mar 23	SWks	7 Jun 23	138	H, BC	320,807
Bristol	23 Oct 23					
Bath	Apr 24					
Yatton	Jun 24					
Bristol	Jul 24	SPM	1 Aug 24	61	R	
Bath	1 Oct 24					
Bristol	Nov 24					
Yatton	Nov 24					
St Philip's Marsh	Jan 25					
Bath	Apr 25					
St. Philips Marsh	Jul 25	SWks	10 Aug 25	233	H, BC	362,175
Swindon Stock	31 Mar 26					
Gloucester	May 26	SWks	22 Oct 26	196	H, BC	377,799
Swindon Stock	6 May 27					
Stourbridge	2 Jun 27	STB	6 Feb 28	30		
		SRD	23 Feb 28		H, BC	401,675
Stourbridge	7 Mar 28	SWks	18 Nov 28	221	H, BC	421,719
Swindon Stock	27 Jun 29					
Southall	3 Jul 29	SHL	17 Apr 30	48		
		SWks	2 May 30		H, BC	435,828
Yatton	4 Jun 30					
St. Philips Marsh	Jul 30	SWks	5 Nov 31	224	G, BC	454,164
Swindon Stock	16 Jun 32					
Exeter	Jan 33	EXE	19 Jun 33	106		
		SFPl	1 Aug 33			
		SWks	31 Aug 33		L, BC	468,728
Exeter	3 Oct 33	EXE	10 May 34			
		SFPl	30 May 34			
		SWks	19 Nov 34			490,590
Condemned	17 Nov 34					

Converted to Trailer No.213 (Dia. A26)

No.97 (Diagram R)

Allocation	*Date*	*Stop'd*	*Date*	*Days Stop'd*	*Catgy. Repair*	*Miles Run*
New	Feb 08					
Swindon Stock at	25 Apr 08					
Aberystwyth	23 Jul 08					
Neath	Oct 08					
Chippenham	21 Oct 08	SDst	19 Mar 09	26	L	
Chippenham	14 Apr 09	SDst	27 Aug 09	13	L	
Chippenham	9 Sep 09					
Trowbridge	Dec 09					
Frome	Jun 10	SDst	6 Jun 10	45		
Trowbridge	21 Jul 10	SWks	25 Jan 11	54	G, BC	88,155
Swindon Stock	20 Mar 11					
Oxford	13 Jul 11	SWks	30 Oct 11	19	BC	95,951
Swindon Stock	18 Nov 11					
Stourbridge	6 Dec 11	STB	11 Mar 12	15		
Stourbridge	26 Mar 12	SWks	16 Jul 12	78	G, BC	112,351
Tyseley	2 Oct 12					
Stourbridge	Nov 12	SRD	30 Jun 13	22	L, BC	135,657
Stourbridge	22 Jul 13	SRD	26 Aug 13	9	L	
Stourbridge	4 Sep 13	SRD	21 Mar 14	10	L	
Croes Newydd	31 Mar 14					
Corwen	Jun 14					
Chester	Jul 14	SRD	3 Sep 14	16	H, BC	150,417

Allocation	*Date*	*Stop'd*	*Date*	*Days Stop'd*	*Catgy. Repair*	*Miles Run*
Croes Newydd	19 Sep 14	CNYD	19 Nov 14	18		
Croes Newydd	7 Dec 14	CNYD	30 Sep 15	15	L	
Croes Newydd	15 Oct 15	SWks	6 Jan 16	225	H, BC	180,037
Swindon Stock	18 Aug 16					
Stourbridge	16 Oct 16	SRD	7 Sep 17	77	H, BC	197,131
Stourbridge	23 Nov 17					
Wolverhampton	Jun 18					
Croes Newydd	Jul 19	SWks	14 Jan 20	274	H, BC	200,812
Bristol	14 Oct 20					
Weymouth	29 Oct 20	BTL	9 Dec 21	14	R	
Bristol	23 Dec 21					
Taunton	Jun 21					
Bristol	Jan-22	TN	12 Jan 22	18	R	
Taunton	30 Jan 22	TN	2 Mar 22	65	R	
Taunton	6 May 22	TN	17 Jun 22	23	R	
Taunton	10 Jul 22	SWks	16 Oct 22	138	H, BC	240,539
Swindon Stock	3 Mar 23					
Yeovil	16 Apr 23	SWks	24 Sep 23	158	H, BC	261,144
Swindon Stock	29 Feb 24					
Croes Newydd	17 Mar 24	SWks	27 Mar 25		BC	
Shrewsbury	8 May 25					
Birkenhead	Jun 25	BHD	20 Jan 27	408		
		SWks	4 Feb 27		H, BC	316,313
Taunton	3 Mar 28	EXE	15 Oct 28	32	R	
Exeter	16 Nov 28	SWks	18 Apr 29	336	H, BC	347,283
Exeter	20 Mar 30	EXE	20 Oct 30	60	R	
Exeter	19 Dec 30	NA	6 Jan 31	27	L	
Exeter	2 Feb 31	EXE	9 Jun 31	139		
		SWks	17 Aug 31		G, BC	380,551
Swindon Stock	26 Oct 31					
Neath	Feb 32	NEA	4 Nov 33	154		
		SFPI	22 Nov 33			
		SWks	15 Jan 34		G, BC	407,394
Southall	7 Apr 34	SHL	13 Oct 34	30	R	
Southall	12 Nov 34	SHL	19 Nov 34	53	R	
Southall	11 Jan 35	SHL	27 Mar 35			
		SWks	16 Apr 35			424,247

Condemned 4 May 35

Converted to Trailer No.214 (Dia. A26)

No.98 (Diagram R)

Allocation	*Date*	*Stop'd*	*Date*	*Days Stop'd*	*Catgy. Repair*	*Miles Run*
New	Feb 08					
Swindon Stock at	25 Apr 08					
Aberystwyth	25 Jun 08					
Neath	Oct 08					
Swindon Stock	Nov 08					
Kidderminster	11 Nov 08					
Worcester	Jul 09	SWks	24 Jul 09	16	G, BC	31,464
Swindon Stock	9 Aug 09					
Evesham	17 Aug 09					
Worcester	Oct 09	SWks	19 Oct 09	34	G, BC	37,406
Stratford on Avon	22 Nov 09					
Worcester	Jul 10					
Stratford on Avon	Aug 10					
Evesham	Dec 10	WOS	2 Jan 11	12	L	
Evesham	14 Jan 11					
Worcester	Apr 11					
Kidderminster	Jun 11					
Worcester	Nov 11	SWks	22 Nov 11	154	BC	88,505
Southall	24 Apr 12	OOC	30 Sep 12	5		
Southall	5 Oct 12	SWks	19 Apr 13	16	H, BC	134,604
Southall	5 May 13					
Swindon Stock	14 May 13					
Southall	20 May 13	OOC	6 Sep 13	18	L	
Southall	24 Sep 13	SWks	16 Apr 14	60	H, BC	175,265
Swindon Stock	15 Jun 14					
Stratford on Avon	30 Jun 14					
Worcester	May 16					
Stratford on Avon	Jun 16	SWks	29 Jul 16	605	H, BC	224,376
Swindon Stock	26 Mar 18					
Taunton	12 Apr 18	TN	19 Aug 19	630		
		SWks	14 Oct 19		H, BC	259,377
Swindon Stock	10 May 21					

Allocation	*Date*	*Stop'd*	*Date*	*Days Stop'd*	*Catgy. Repair*	*Miles Run*
Reading	6 Jul 21	OOC	8 Mar 22	15	R	
Reading	23 Mar 22	OOC	21 Aug 22	19	R	
Reading	9 Sep 22	OOC	26 Mar 23	17	R	
Reading	12 Apr 23	SWks	24 Nov 23	354	H, BC	323,667
Westbury	12 Nov 24	WES	9 Jan 26	21	R	
Frome	30 Jan 26	SWks	13 Apr 26	293	H, BC	351,054
Swindon Stock	31 Jan 27					
Southall	4 Feb 27	OOC	9 Jul 27	52		
		SWks	16 Jul 27		H, BC	359,717
Southall	30 Aug 27					
Neath	Mar 28	SWks	8 May 28	31	H, BC	371,605
Neath	8 Jun 28	NEA	21 Dec 28	188		
		SWks	10 Jan 29		H, BC	381,762
Swindon Stock	27 Jun 29					
Stafford Road	13 Jul 29					
Birkenhead	Oct 29					
Croes Newydd	Dec 29					
Birkenhead	Jan 30	SWks	14 Sep 31	31	L	
Birkenhead	15 Oct 31	SFPI	18 Apr 33	108		
		SWks	24 Apr 33		G, BC	430,266
Swindon Stock	4 Aug 33					
Southall	16 Feb 34	SHL	2 Mar 34	14	R	
Southall	16 Mar 34	SHL	3 May 34	40	R	
Southall	12 Jun 34	SHL	25 Oct 34	42	R	
Southall	6 Dec 34	SHL	18 Apr 35			
		SFPI	8 May 35			
		SWks				446,801

Condemned 1 Jun 35

Converted to Trailer No.215 (Dia. A26)

No.99 (Diagram R)

Allocation	*Date*	*Stop'd*	*Date*	*Days Stop'd*	*Catgy. Repair*	*Miles Run*
New	Feb 08	SWks	25 Mar 08	5		
Swindon Stock	30 Mar 08					
Swindon Stock at	25 Apr 08					
Evesham	7 Jul 08	SWks	13 Nov 08	18	BC	10,853
Swindon Stock	1 Dec 08					
Evesham	9 Jan 09	SWks	17 Aug 09	39	G, BC	35,724
Evesham	25 Sep 09					
Worcester	Apr 10					
Evesham	May 10					
Worcester	Jul 10					
Evesham	Aug 10	SWks	8 Sep 10	11	G, BC	68,375
Bristol	19 Sep 10					
Bath	Feb 11					
Bristol	Mar 11	SWks	7 Jun 11	26	G, BC	97,403
Aberystwyth	3 Jul 11					
Oxford	30 Oct 11	STB	11 Mar 12	14		
Oxford	25 Mar 12					
Pontypool Road	12 Jul 12	SWks	29 Aug 12	90	G	121,769
Swindon Stock	27 Nov 12					
Weymouth	3 Dec 12	SWks	24 Jan 13	28	L	
Swindon Stock	21 Feb 13					
Weymouth	27 Feb 13	SWks	7 Sep 14	61	H, BC	165,475
Swindon Stock	7 Nov 14					
Taunton	13 Nov 14	TN	26 Dec 16	29	R	
Taunton	24 Jan 17	TN	31 Mar 17	23	L	
Taunton	23 Apr 17	TN	28 May 17	1,099		
		SPM	29 May 17			
		SWks	28 Oct 19		H,	229,550
Swindon Stock	31 May 20					
Weymouth	5 Jul 20	SWks	5 May 21	18	H,	249,486
Swindon Stock	23 May 21					
Neath	13 Jul 21	NEA	24 Jul 23	136	H	286,616
Neath	7 Dec 23	NEA	7 Jun 24	45	R	
Garnant	Feb 24					
Neath	Apr 24					
Neath	22 Jul 24	SWks	16 Sep 24	325	H,	298,244
Bath	7 Aug 25					
St Philip's Marsh	Nov 25					
Bath	Jan 26					
St Philip's Marsh	Mar 26					
Bath	Apr 26					
St Philip's Marsh	May 26					

Allocation	Date	Stop'd	Date	Days Stop'd	Catgy. Repair	Miles Run
Bath	Aug 26					
St Philip's Marsh	Sep 26					
Frome	Oct 26	WES	15 Nov 26	23	R	
Frome	8 Dec 26	WES	5 Feb 27	27	R	
Frome	4 Mar 27					
St Philip's Marsh	Jun 27					
Bath	Jul 27					
Yatton	Aug 27					
St Philip's Marsh	Oct 27	SPM	22 Dec 27			
		SWks	5 Jan 28			340,474

Converted to Trailer No.158 (Dia. A26)

No.100 Petrol-Electric Railcar (Diagram U)

Allocation	Date	Stop'd	Date
To GWR Stock	May 13		
Slough	May 13	SWks	Sep 14
Slough	Mar 15		
Wormwood Scrubbs	Jan 17		
Slough	Sep 17		
Wormwood Scrubbs	Sep 17		
Swindon	Oct 17	SWks	Nov 17
Swindon Stock	Aug 19		
Stafford Road	21 Aug 19		

Sold to Messrs Lever, Port Sunlight, Oct 19
NOTE
The stoppages to this car were not recorded in RAIL254 210

Allocation	Date	Stop'd	Date	Days Stop'd	Catgy. Repair	Miles Run
Port Talbot No.1 (GWR Diagram S)						
New	1907					
PT taken over by	1 Jan 08					
Duffryn?		SWks	24 Jun 08	160		
Duffryn	1 Dec 08	SWks	Feb 09			
Duffryn	22 Mar 09	DYD	2 Sep 10	20		
Duffryn	22 Sep 10	SWks	23 Dec 10			
Swindon Stock	Mar 11					
Duffryn	1 Apr 11	SWks	24 Nov 11	148	G	67,440
Swindon Stock	20 Apr 12					
Duffryn	3 Jun 12	SWks	10 Feb 13	141	H	79,143
Duffryn	1 Jul 13	SWks	7 Aug 15	76	L	
Duffryn	22 Oct 15	SWks	7 Aug 16	84	L	
Swindon Stock	30 Oct 16					

Sold to Mr Graham for Port of London Authority, Jul 20

APPENDIX E
GWR AUTO TRAILERS – ADDENDA

The Great Western Railway were, of course, constructing auto trailers during the same period in which the Steam Railmotors were being built – and indeed well beyond. And as we have seen, many SRMs were converted into trailers at the end of their useful lives. These vehicles have been covered in some detail by the two volumes of *Great Western Auto Trailers*, written by the author of this work, and also published by Wild Swan. It is often the case that additional material comes to hand after publication, and *Auto Trailers* was no exception.

BRITISH RAILWAYS COACHING STOCK COLOURS

In Part One of *Auto Trailers* (page 44 onwards) and in Part Two (pages 159–162) there are discussions of BR coaching stock liveries. It is now evident that, in 1949, the colour scheme for multiple units was to be green; 'main line coaches' were to be carmine and cream with black and gold lining; and other (i.e. non-corridor) coaches were to be painted in a red, a shade which I called 'maroon', and lined in black and gold. This lined livery was applied to some compartment trailers (saloon trailers were being painted carmine and cream at this time). In April 1951, the Railway Executive issued instructions that the body sides of non-corridor stock were no longer to be lined; this instruction remained in effect until 1959, by which time the base colour had officially changed to maroon.

The shade of the 'red' colour of coaches painted between 1949 and 1957 continues to be a matter of debate, but in the *Model Railway Journal* No.138, page 273, there are colour pictures of trailer No.179 in pre-1956 plain red, and on the previous page a colour photograph of the interior of this trailer.

WHITE LINES

In Part One, page 17, the practice of painting white lines on the end windows of trailers is mentioned. Although this had become common by the 1930s, the practice seems to have started much earlier – about 1910 or so. The picture of trailer No.51 at Lampeter on page 90 of Part 1 is a case in point.

SMALL DESTINATION BOARDS

The colour of small destination (label) boards is covered in Chapter 4 of this work, in the liveries section. These were also fitted to trailers, and there are examples of the earliest style on page 54 of *Auto Trailers* Part 1; the shaded gold lettering on a white background in the picture of trailer No.51 on page 90 of Part 1; and the later style of black lettering on a white ground on page 33. In BR days, the boards reverted to white letters on a red background – see page 289, Part 2, the top picture.

Some Corrections and Additions to *Auto Trailers* Part Two.

The upper photograph on page 236 shows a Coryton – Bute auto train formed of ex-TVR trailers W2508 and W2521 leaving Cardiff Queen Street station on 6th October 1953. Photograph by S. Rickard.

Note that the official diagrams for the modern trailers of Dias. A38-A40 and A43 (page 287 onwards) show the driver's door finishing flush with the solebar, whereas in fact this door opened inwards, and finished a little above the solebar – the photographs will clarify this point.

The train in the snow on page 310 is approaching Heath Halt (Low Level).

ACKNOWLEDGEMENTS

I would like to thank all those who have helped and encouraged me with this book, including: Gerry Beale, Graham Bone, R. M. Casserley, Graham Carpenter, David Castle, Colin Chapman, John Copsey, Ken Davies, Keith Ettle, Ian Forsythe, Alan Hall, Mike Lewis, Harold Morgan, Jack Slinn, Robin Simmonds, Ralph Tutton, Chris Turner, Eric Youldon, and again, Pendon Museum.

A special thanks to Dick Riley for the loan of so many photographs. The National Railway Museum, York, holds some of the records and drawings of the GWR's steam rail motors, and I would particularly like to thank Philip Atkins and Lynne Thurston of the NRM. Other records are held in the Public Record Office, Kew, now part of the National Archives, and I would also like to acknowledge the help of their staff. Thanks are also due to the Historical Model Railway Society and the Welsh Railways Research Circle.

I would also again like to thank Paul Karau and June Judge for all their help.